The **ORBIT**
Magazine Anthology

The

RBIT

Magazine Anthology

RE-ENTRY

ROB ST. MARY

with a Foreword by Jerry Vile
and Afterword by Ben Blackwell

 A PAINTED TURTLE BOOK
Detroit, Michigan

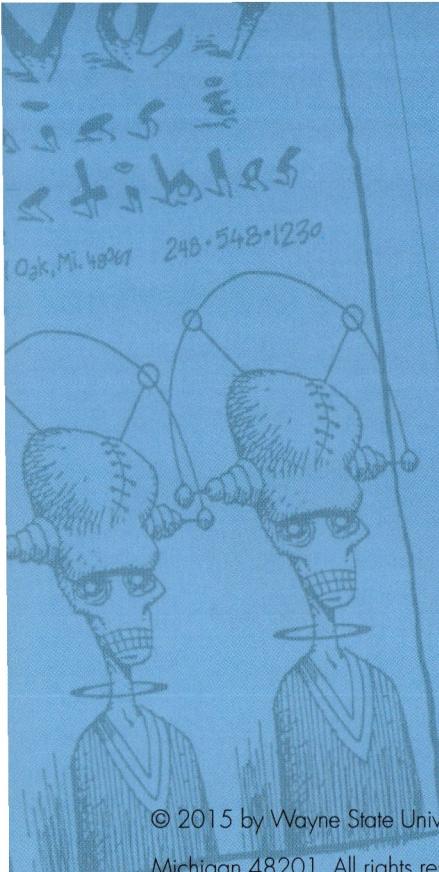

Curses, Foiled Again

Kelvin Floyd was convicted of car theft in Aiken, S.C., after he removed the vehicle's identification number and replaced it with his Social Security number, thereby arousing the suspicions of authorities.

The Honeymoon Is Over

After a year of marriage, Marius and Roxana Dumitrescu filed for divorce in southern Romania, citing "irreconcilable differences." According to court records, Marius wanted Roxana to wear mauve clothing, as his mother always did, but she preferred dressing in white, red and green.

Curses, Foiled Again

Police in Peru, Vt., arrested Hazen Campbell, 42, as a suspect in the abduction and assault of a 26-year-old Barnard woman after the victim said her attacker told her he had a "strange" first name and called his dog "Obie," short for Obidya. His dog's name was on record with the town clerk.

Chicken Little Was Right

The sky has fallen more than five miles in the past 40 years, according to researchers from the British Antarctic Survey, who checked records of radio waves bouncing off the ionosphere. Head scientist Martin Jarvis emphasized that the collapse of the upper atmosphere from 190 to 185 miles "is not in itself harmful to people," but,

blaming global warming, he added it is just "another warning signal about what damage to the atmosphere can be caused by human impact."

A 17-year-old Kmart employee in Prince Frederick, Md., was injured while working in a storage area when, according to Bo McKenny of the Calvert County Sheriff's Department, he went to grab something off one of the shelves and 21 toilet seats fell down on him.

Forgotten But Not Gone

Diane Thomas, 33, sought acupuncture treatment in Merthyr Tydfil, Wales, from Dr. Kevin Thomas. After inserting needles in her neck, back, ankles and wrists, he told her to lie face down for 40 minutes. Meanwhile, he was called away on an emergency and forgot about her. So did the other doctors, nurses and clerical staff, who did not hear her cries for help inside the soundproof treatment room when they locked up the medical offices for the day. That night, the cleaning staff found the woman in her underwear and called a senior physician to remove the needles. To prevent further mishaps, the practice began issuing hand bells for patients to ring if they are ever overlooked.

Poor Reflection

After capturing just 17 percent of the November vote in

Lost and Found

When Los Angeles police officer Kelly Benitez, 29, stopped a beat-up Ford Thunderbird with expired license plates, he noticed the driver's last name and his were the same. After a few questions, the son realized the driver was his father, Paul Benitez, 49, whom he hadn't seen since he was 4 months old. As the two men embraced in the street, the father noted afterward, "cars pulled over because they thought I was wrestling with a police officer."

Fur Fights Back

Elephants in Uganda are thwarting ivory poachers by being born without tusks. Researchers at Queen Elizabeth National Park reported that 15.5 percent of the female elephants and 9.5 percent of the males are now tuskless, up from 1 percent in 1930. Scientists credit the genetic adaptation for the recovery of the elephant population in the park from 200 in 1992 to 1,200 today and in Africa overall from 500,000 in 1989 to 600,000 now.

One Pill Makes You Larger

After withdrawing his savings, pawning his wedding ring and taking out a loan, Romanian Georgio Barrsan, 56, spent the money on black-market Viagra and two prostitutes. He took six of the anti-impotence pills, but then fell asleep. He awoke 12 hours later to find the women and his wallet gone. Investigators discovered that instead of Viagra, Barrsan had been sold

sion reported that a minister panel cut through the red tape, even though birth- control pills and the anti-depressant Prozac have awaited approval for many years. Since Viagra's introduction last year, the $10 pills have sold for between $30 and $30 on Japan's black market. Travel agencies there have even organized tours to the United States that include appointments with doctors who write prescriptions for Viagra.

Things That Go Boom

Friza Borokhova, 74, Borokhova, 44, Sophia S kova, 23, and two children and 2, suffered minor inj their New York City apa while honoring the mem dead relative when they they thought was a vo dle. It turned out to be fireworks explosive.

Vlad Cazacu, 43, a f eater in Romania ex ing a performance when he burped af tally swallowing so ble liquid, triggering

Bird Brains

Investigators look computer softwar Mountain Ash, couldn't find th until the o announced, " tress! Under They lifted it cases conta games. "The us an earach Jones of Eur ware Public told reporte on us wh squawking

Police in 10 days t tim of near B divers, search site. Fi iff dec that n peop roost rowe few sta sp

Pin-Up Collection
1970s

Orby Says:

"Those who fail to forget are doomed to remember."

CONTENTS

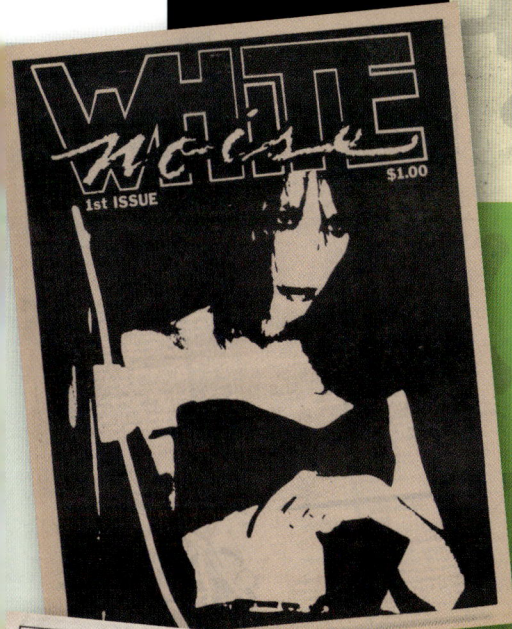

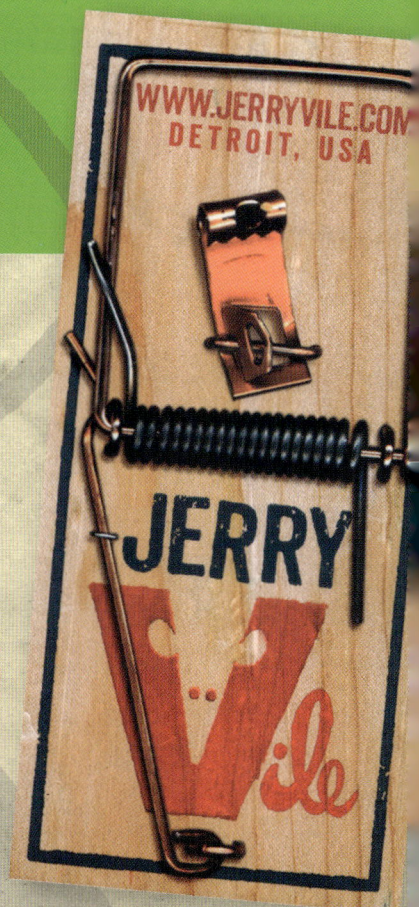

WWW.JERRYVILE.COM
DETROIT, USA

JERRY Vile

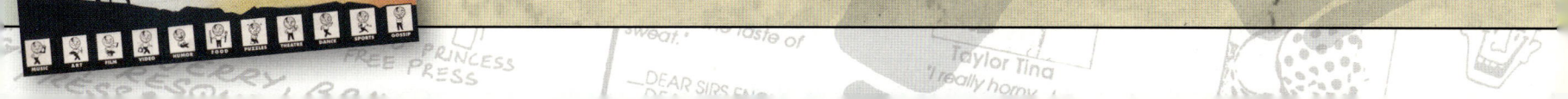

Signs in illustration: URBAN DETROIT FOODS — DOUBLE COUPONS — CRACK — 5$

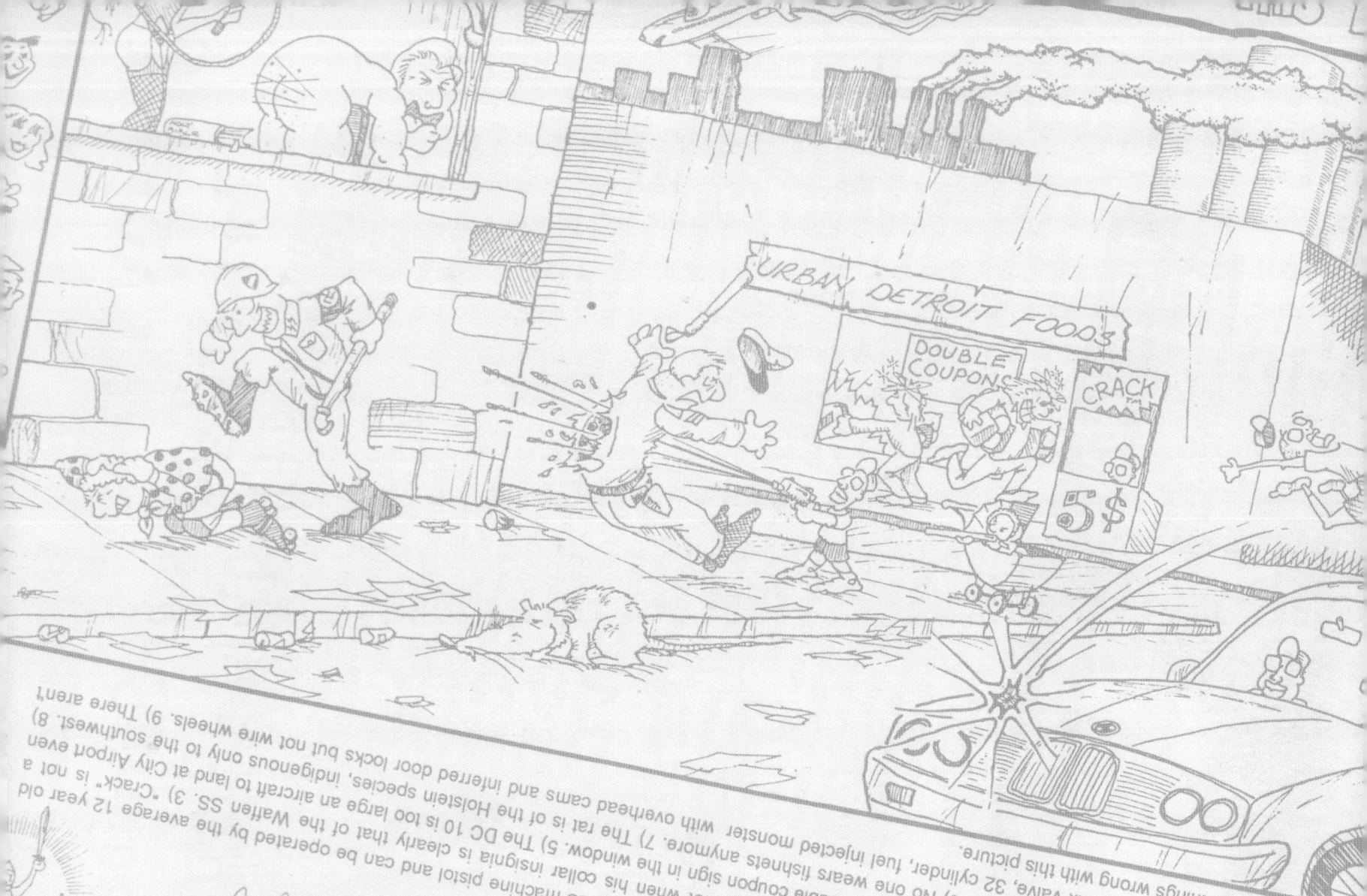

Labels: DETROIT NEWS GNOMES — RUPERT MURDOCH — GREASY STINGY ADVERTISERS — THE KINGS TAXMAN — GOOD PRINCESS FREE PRESS

ANT SIR JERRY
GHTS, RESOLU, BAN
E PRESSO

DEAR SIRS

PREFACE

The ringleader personality of Jerry Peterson, aka Jerry Vile, attracted a cadre of punk-infected personalities who between 1978 and 1999 created innovative new forms of media. Taking ideas from New York's *Punk* or L.A.'s *Slash* and blending them with *National Lampoon*–style satire, *White Noise* was quick, snarky, dirty, and dumb in the best way possible; it also held the DNA for every Vile publication that followed. As young punks grew up and found the yuppie 1980s staring them in the face, Vile's ragtag garage band of writers, cartoonists, and satirists created a completely new form of media—the free humor paper. Pre-dating *The Onion* by several years, *Fun: The Magazine for Swinging Intelectuals* [sic] conveyed more of Vile's earlier attitude, combined with the idea that humor mattered as much as real reporting. At the dawn of the 1990s, Jerry Vile became less punk and more professional. Reverting to his given name, Jerry Peterson decided it was time to mount a full-scale battle for free alt weekly supremacy in Detroit. While other papers copied the tried and true alt weekly format of lefty politics and arts and culture, Peterson found that pop culture, satire, and sharp design were what grabbed readers. Predating *Vice*'s approach of taking serious stories and giving them a humorous presentation, *Orbit* also beat all other Detroit publications, and most papers worldwide, by blazing a trail on the new digital playground of the Internet. Even though Peterson's battle for print supremacy is long over, a victim of bad business and the digital revolution, many of the innovative ideas and great stories created by the *White Noise*, *Fun*, and *Orbit* staffs still resonate. What's more, the stories, storytellers, and their spinoffs, including *Real Detroit Weekly* and the annual international erotic art exhibition the Dirty Show, prove once again that Detroit innovation is far from dead.

he Metro Times knowingly selling ads to prostitut...

...ro Times sprang out of the era
...ial revolution and free love.
...ver, a recent Orbit investigation
...he type of love offered in their
...on is not revolutionary and cer-
...e free.

...an when a friend of a friend
...he Orbit offices. His buddy had
...ed to an ad in the Metro Times, a
...l for a "Chocolate Fantasy." When
...ocolate Fantasy asked for money, he
...it might make a good exposé. We
...think so. Our opinion was: Who
...t know the Metro Times has hookers
...tising in it? It turns out a lot of peo-
...didn't know there was a sleazy side to
...oit's weekly. People who work at
...t, people who read it religiously, and
...n people who have worked for the
...ro Times are unaware of this dirty little
...eline.

...You may be surprised that Orbit, of all
...ublications, should take this moral high
...round. (We aren't.) But, then again, we
...on't consistently portray ourselves as the
...ity's socially conscious, politically correct
...alternative newspaper.

Conversely, the Metro Times professes
...to be a protector of women's rights, yet in
...practice it appears they may be participat-
...ing in the exploitation of women—we
...decided to prove it.

THE STING

Orbit would place our own prostitution ad
in the Metro Times. We had an intern call,

posing as a prostitute. Over the telephone,
she got the prices for regular classifieds.
Then she told them she was a prostitute
and tried to place an ad. She was shuffled
to Jennifer in the P.S. (Personal Services)
section, a seedy patch of paper chock full
of sleaze merchants.

Jennifer recommended the escort section. Our plant told her she was a prostitute, not an escort. That was OK, but she
would still have to go in the escort column if she wanted an ad in the Metro
Times. The smallest ad available would

cost $150, way more than any other clas-
sified in the paper.

The crowd listening in around our
intern was stupefied. Even the most jaded
Orbiteer could not believe the Metro Times
could be so blatant about it. Even if Orbit
had any moral qualms about accepting
this type of advertising, we certainly
wouldn't be stupid enough to admit it
over the phone.

Wasn't the Metro Times concerned
about legalities? Are there any legalities?
There are those who would consider this

pandering—the publication
much like a pimp. And, as
prostitution isn't legal in D

But, above all, the Metr
always reeked with that h
liberal agenda. Politically
be blatantly feminist. In
owner Laura Markham a
nist? Didn't she once wr
humiliation she endured
her legs for an underco
some type of male chau
the Metro Times once
to accept advertising f
Penthouse? Yet this sa
would allow sex for s
We had our intern ca
time we took notes

We were amazed
Metro Times respond
even more so that
make suggestions
price of a blow jo

It was confirm
phone call wasn't
ad in print in the
sure.

There was st
in our sex-for-s
would not take
appeared in pe
had problems
customers' cre
more victims
weekly has h
measures so
out of their

Exhibit A: Actual Call with Metro Times

MT: Good Afternoon,
Metro Times Classified.
How may I help you?
O: Hi, I just called about
the prostitution ad. I'm not
sure if I talked to you.
...you must have

O: But $150 for 18 words
for a personal ad—that's
ridiculous.
MT: Well, Jennifer, she's
the one that handles that
and...uh...she's who you'd
have to speak with. But
those are the rates though.

doesn't matter what trade?
MT: Yeah, you'd get a fre-
quency discount.
O: O.K., that works out
really good. Do prostitutes
usually get results with
your magazine?
MT: Uh. Yeah, they do.
(Laughs)
...How often does

I'd talk to about my fre-
quency rate?
MT: Yeah, she'd be the one
to talk to about
that...about...any adult
ad.
O: About how much business do prostitutes get? Do
you know?
MT: I don't know.
O: More than one girl

they're satisfied, I can tell
you that.
O: 'Cause I work alone.
I'm putting myself throug
school, I have two kids,
you know how it goes.
MT: Maybe more than you
can handle.
O: Girl!!! O.K. I have th
fax number...attention
Jennifer.
MT: Correct.
...I have to co

I will cringe when I read this book.

I won't be happy with whatever I write. I'm a sloppy perfectionist. I set my sights on great and hope to come out "GEFO."

That Terry Colon–coined acronym stands for "Good Enough for *Orbit*." It means it could have been better, but it will do.

I don't think there is a single issue of *Orbit* I was ever completely happy with. Always having to rush and do things on the cheap. Having to cut and cram. Having to shrink down graphics. Never having enough ads or pages or time. I spent a lot of hours bemoaning what might have been. What we were capable of. Saddest thing of all—we never even had an office monkey. Unlike you, I know what

we could have done—if only. But don't let me fool you—I'm proud of what we did.

"We" refers to most of the other people who should be in this book. I'd like to thank them for their time, effort, friendship—where applicable, and for the incredible impact they made. I stood on a lot of shoulders, and I have been pretty fat at times. I know it wasn't easy to carry my weight.

But rather than thank them all here and make this an even more boring foreword, I will hope the book thanks them for me. I'm sure St. Mary forgot some of them (or maybe they were too dull for publication), or maybe they were cut out by his overseers or the overseers' overseers. Plus, I'm not getting paid

by the word to write this—heck on a monkey stick, I'm not even getting paid. Just like working for *Fun*.

I guess I'm supposed to thank Rob St. Mary here. Big wet thanks. It doesn't seem real. It couldn't come soon enough—my memory continues to rot (probably some kind of dementia) and time moves in a blur. But of everyone I've met, just two have been life changers: Rick Metcalf, who demanded a new magazine—*Fun*—and then jumped ship for a life at sea (though that was the seed of *Orbit*). And Jeremy Harvey, who came aboard *Orbit* during the we-don't-give-a-fuck period and was responsible for the Dirty Show continuing after the first exhibition and the second. It was too much fun for him—I couldn't kill it. And it allowed me to become an artist.

Thanks, bros.

Confession: I have not read this book, but by the time you read this, I will have. I have a pretty good idea of what it's about, but I don't know what is in or out or how it will look. Hopefully, they've used *Orbit*-brand designers to lay it out.

I was hoping the typos on our old pages would be fixed. But this was not to be. No issue of *Orbit* is without them. There are two reasons for this: I get my best ideas under pressure, and I rewrite when I proofread. When I fix one typo, I usually add two more. We used to tell people ALL publications are full of typos. The only reason you see them in *Orbit* is because you actually read it. But we would have done a better job catching typos if we knew there was going to be a book. And of course, we didn't have proofreading robots like you future people have.

(This book will take a year to print. Everyone who is reading this is reading this in the future.)

When I started publishing—and I don't even know if you can call it publishing, because I don't know if I was ever a publisher or just an actor playing the part of a publisher—I had no training. I knew there were good publishers, like in Superman, and bad publishers, like in Spiderman. Other than that, publishers were businessmen, the kind that my idols, like Hunter S. Thompson, took advantage of. So I guess you could say I was more of a writer-editor than a publisher. I had to publish because who the fuck would hire me.

Anyhow, the copy machine was our go-to for graphics. We copied images over and over. We'd shrink them down and blow them up. This led to the images degrading until they just fell apart. But this also created something new. The degraded images looked cool to us, even if they looked horrible to the rest of the world.

Anytime you try to copy something—copy anything—your ineptness will show. If you're lucky, this process will create something different. A lot of what might be considered radical, avant-garde, or new is just result of inept thievery. (Even this concept is a copy of a theory that's already out there.)

When I was young, I grew up on a steady diet of television. Reading wise, there were the usual assigned books in school, but my lit of choice was underground comics and *National Lampoon*. And I loved movies, especially the crap they showed at drive-ins, so much that whenever I see breasts, I hear the sound of honking horns.

Music was as vital to me as it is to any teenager. My tastes were pretty mainstream: Hendrix, Pink Floyd, Alice Cooper. Until glitter—David Bowie, Lou Reed, and the New York Dolls—came along. The music was superior to radio hits, but the artists themselves actually alienated and angered most listeners. This delighted me, for the same reason John Waters movies and *Creem* magazine delighted me.

So when punk rock copied glitter, the result was everything I needed in life. I became a publisher. A musician. An artist.

So, if I was writing this book, it would start like this.

It was the early nineties. Sushi wasn't available in gas stations. Beer wasn't microbrewed. Only old men behind closed doors smoked cigars. Grunge had not yet been invented, and techno was underground. Martinis came in only two flavors. Publications were pretty boring. This is where I would say something about how spectacular *Orbit* was when it came along—if I wasn't the star of the book.

This just in: John Waters has agreed to do the Dirty Show, the international erotic art exhibition I've held annually, in 2015. Not only his art but his lecture, show, talk—whatever it's called. He's been one of the greatest influences on my art and publishing. Hopefully, two more of my influences will be in the exhibition as well. After sixteen years, this is the apex for the Dirty Show. After this, it becomes more of a formula, but you already know that. A month of Dirty Show in February pays better and is easier than publishing. Let's hope climate change doesn't force us to move to warmer climes than Detroit. One day, I hope to have Quentin Tarantino in the Dirty Show, perhaps in a giant shrimping photo. That way we can milk him for Dirty Show just like we did with the T-shirt in *Orbit*, twenty years ago.

What ever became of me? You know—but I don't. Was I an important six-figure artist? Did I ever make my movies? I'm sure my life was tragically over too soon. But I'll give a shout-out to my kid: Your dad is the star of a book! Now do you think I'm with it? (Is that right? Can you be a star of a

book?) I'd like to apologize to you, honey, for not taking better care of my health. I hope it wasn't a lot of drooling and you pushing my wheelchair. Anyhow, I love you more than anything and everything.

When I go—and I will go one day—I hope there won't be sobbing at my funeral. That's not for me. I want wailing and screaming. I want girls cutting their foreheads with seashells. I want people clinging to the casket as it is lowered into the ground.

Hopefully, I will be rich. 'Cause I want to do my last will and testament on film. I want to say cruel things to people. Like, you've waited for me to die so you can get your hands on my money. Like so-and-so who was an unfaithful lover and two-bit whore, I leave you the paltry sum of two bits.

JERRY VILE

◄ Jerry Vile with his "Joyride," a self-portrait moving sculpture at the Dirty Show, 2012. (Photo by Bruce Giffin)

...seemingly insatiable a...
opportunity to see how far we could push
this, we supplied Brandy with a disgusting wad of "dirty money." **[See Exhibit
C]** to pay for the ad. The filthy, crumpled
bills were snatched up for the company
coffers and Brandy was ready for business.

You're probably saying, "So what? Our
President got blow jobs from an intern,
any celebrity can get away with murder,
they're even playing rock music in church.
What's the harm in a little 'mommy
crushin' for Benjamins?" It's a victimless
crime. Nobody gets hurt, right?

And when you get right down to it,
the MT isn't supporting prostitutes, (even
though the prostitutes are supporting the
newspaper.) In fact, obviously they consider prostitutes potential criminals. Why
else would they demand money up front
and deny credit cards? Still, by charging
excessive advertising fees exclusively to
hookers, you could make the argument
they are getting a 'cut of the action.'
Look up pandering in the dictionary, and
you'll see a pimp by any other name is
still a pimp. **[See Exhibit D]**

After calculating what Brandy paid
($165) and multiplying it by the number
of other escorts on the same page (50),
it comes to over $8,000. Most ads were
larger than Brandy's, so our figure is
probably low. Our calculation also doesn't
include the cross dressing, domination,
job opportunities or the multitude of display ads for phone sex, also in the P.S.
section. A very conservative guesstimate
is the Metro Times pulls in over $20,000
every week on the flesh trade. That's over
a million dollars a year (still a conservative figure) made off of by what many
would consider the exploitation of
women. That could add up to some
mighty high-style living for Metro Times
owners Ron Williams (whose residence is
in the Virgin Islands) and Laura Markham
(the avowed feminist)

THE LAST LAUGH

The following Wednesday, our advertisement was getting response before we
had even picked up our own copy of the
Metro Times. To make the gag work, we
needed a phone number for Brandy's ad.
As the icing on the cake, we used publisher Jerry Peterson's cell phone.

By mid-day Wednesday, Peterson's
phone was ringing off-the-hook. Brandy
was a hit! About a dozen, mostly creepy-
sounding, older men were looking to
party with our Southern Belle.

Throughout the day, various people...
pretended to be Brandy. This quickly
became boring.

Returning to the office the next day,
we were amazed to discover 48 calls.
After checking caller ID, they turned out
to be from 11 lonely guys all desperately
...to do something...

...and threat...
creep who would call a 14-year-...
school night.

* We even told the truth, that they had
reached investigative journalists at
Orbit—would they mind if we printed
their name and phone number in our
prostitution story?

* Finally we came up with our best
scam. We convinced the would-be John
that Brandy was just murdered; we were
the police and the caller was now a prime
suspect. We confirmed their number from
our caller ID, in case they would be needed for further questioning.

EPILOGUE

While the calls are slowing down,
this story is just beginning. Calling back
to confirm the classified prices, we ended
up talking to Jennifer again. She asked
what business our caller was in, and we
just had to say escorts. She perked up and
inquired how many girls our caller had.
"Uh…six," he said. She made her pitch,
suggesting if he had 10 girls or less, he
could book up a whole weeks schedule
with an ad in the P.S. section. She surmised that, since most places charge $75
for a half hour, he would make his ad
money back in the first hour. And just in
case he was still thinking about a free ad,
he was warned that the paper carefully
screened them

Essentially, what we have here is
an "alternative weekly" that desperately
wants to be politically correct, but can't
say no to the green. They're running ads
for services that you couldn't get away
with in Hustler. Sure, many publications
have personal ads (just look at the back
of this one), but how many magazines
are as pious as the Metro Times? What
others would be blatant enough to have a
prostitute policy in place? Free love ain't
what it used to be, Detroit's hookers are
getting screwed. ☙

PROLOGUE

> "I really, really enjoy making people upset.
> I think that is my art."
>
> Jerry Peterson a.k.a. "Jerry Vile" (2011)

Jerry Peterson—"Jerry Vile," as he's known—has been described in many ways during his almost four decades in Metro Detroit's media and arts. Some have called him a genius or big brother, while others have said he's just an asshole. But no matter what has been said about Peterson, he is not someone who is easily forgotten, nor has his impact on Detroit's arts and culture scene diminished with time.

Those hip to the arts in Detroit know Jerry Vile for many things: as a singer in Detroit's punk scene in the late 1970s; as the publisher of influential, semi-successful free humor magazines in the 1980s and 1990s; and as the creator of a long-running annual international erotic art event. But broad interest in Peterson didn't peak until his hometown was headed for financial ruin.

Throughout 2013, talk was swirling about what Detroit's bankruptcy filing—the largest in US history—would mean. Would employee pensions be slashed? Would the water department be sold? Would the Detroit Institute of Art's world-renowned collection be auctioned off? It was a time of anxiety for the Motor City, which was saddled with an estimated $18–20 billion debt due to decades of deindustrialization, abandonment, disinvestment, financial mismanagement, and corruption.

On the morning of July 30, 2013, the city woke up to find an iconic piece of public art transformed. Right below the huge Joe Louis fist at the base of Woodward and Jefferson Avenues, within sight of the City-County Building, was a five-foot-tall replica can of Crisco shortening, described by a nearby sign as a "vessel of hope" to help ease the pain of bankruptcy on Detroit's citizens. This Warholesque sculpture was the work of Jerry Vile.

While not everyone got the sexual reference right away, images of Vile's work quickly went viral. One image was shared almost two thousand times from a local TV station's Facebook page.

Before the day was out, someone had created a fan page for the can on social media. For many, the art piece perfectly captured their feelings about the city's impending bankruptcy. However, the concept for this piece of street art did not originate with the city's precarious finances. It was something Vile had thought of years earlier, sometime during the run of *Fun* or *Orbit* magazines. "Thank god for my procrastinating nature," Peterson said, "Because I can just see how fucking pissed off people would have been had I done the Crisco can when I thought of it. That's Joe Louis. People would have seen it as a slight to Joe Louis. Which it is not at all. You know, I don't see it as the Joe Louis Fist, I see it as the big fist. I just see it as an oversized object."

"At a certain point in my life, a fist was no longer balled-up anger, it became a sexual act. All of a sudden this stupid, puerile joke meant something. A sophomoric joke became a huge statement," said Peterson.

By lunchtime, the city of Detroit had removed the can and the sign. But the images and stories were enough. Within two days, the website BuzzFeed listed "Crisco Fist" as number 14 on its "Best Street Art in the World 2013" list. A few days later, Vile was able to retrieve his art object from the city.

On August 8, 2013, Vile decided a better way to help ease the pain of financial hardship would be to auction off the can and donate the money to the city or a charity of the city's

▼ Vile and Vessel of Hope. (Photo by Bill McGraw)

▲ Liquidation sale ad, *Metro Times*, August 14–20, 2013. (Designed by Jerry Vile and Gary Arnett)

choosing. The object was pulled from the eBay auction site the next day due to a complaint over the wording, but it went back up the following day, and the value started climbing. The end of the giant Crisco can auction was carried in live reports from the Music Hall by some local TV stations as the final bids came in. The auction ended with a local collector paying thirteen hundred dollars.

But this was not the last time that Detroit's bankruptcy would become a target of Vile's artistic impulse. The morning of August 14, 2013, Vile and his co-conspirators struck again, not only on the streets but also in print. Detroiters awoke that Wednesday morning to find large price tags hanging from objects all over the downtown area and an ad for a liquidation sale in the local alt weekly the *Metro Times*.

"Once the bankruptcy came into play, it was like oh, my God, they are taking pensions away. I have to do this. It consumed me. The price tags in some ways are better than the fist. In some ways, it's not. It is two different things. To do them both at the same time would have diluted both ideas," said Peterson.

Those two weeks in August were a wild ride for Peterson. The street art statements attracted more attention than he had ever received for anything he had created up to that point. Print, radio, local TV talk shows, and the Internet were buzzing with stories related to him and his work. Peterson joked, "You know, before the Crisco can I had never 'gone viral' . . . except for herpes."

Much like Peterson's earlier work, the street art pieces spoke to his love of satire—a biting sarcasm aimed at a beloved place, a target dear to him. "I've always loved Detroit," said Peterson. "Fuck, we satire our friends. We are hard on our friends. And it's hard having the people who are my friends being friends because you have to have a pretty thick skin and someone always goes too far. Yeah, I have hope for Detroit. You know, I never expected it to completely crumble. There's a lot I hate about this town. Like, how there is a lot of the really nice, beautiful stuff . . . and people don't give a shit about it."

But to get a real understanding of where the attitude and ideas came from, one needs to understand Peterson's youthful passions in mid-seventies Detroit.

The **ORBIT** Magazine Anthology

WHITE *noise*

1978–1980

WHITE *noise*

1st ISSUE

$1.00

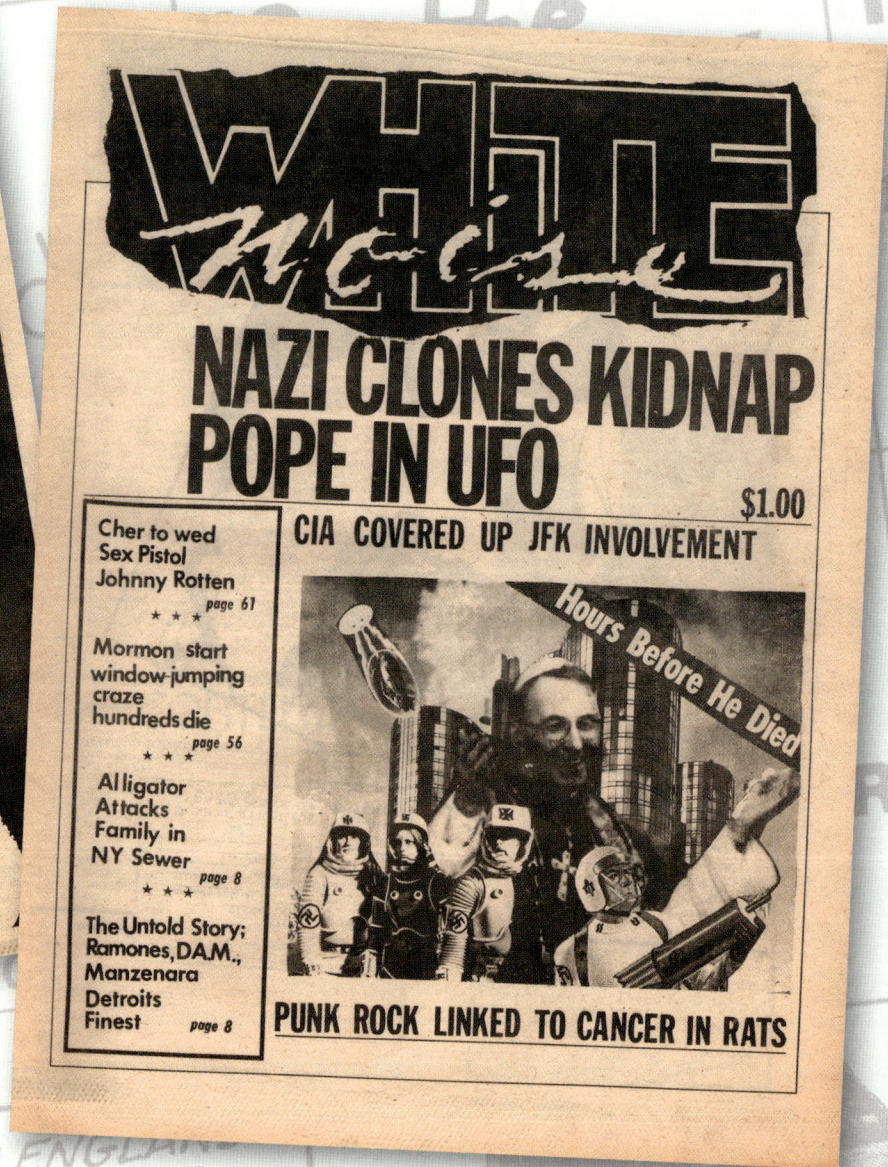

WHITE *noise*

NAZI CLONES KIDNAP POPE IN UFO

$1.00

CIA COVERED UP JFK INVOLVEMENT

Cher to wed
Sex Pistol
Johnny Rotten
page 61

★ ★ ★

Mormon start
window-jumping
craze
hundreds die
page 56

★ ★ ★

Alligator
Attacks
Family in
NY Sewer
page 8

★ ★ ★

The Untold Story;
Ramones, D.A.M.,
Manzenara
Detroits
Finest   *page 8*

Hours Before He Died

PUNK ROCK LINKED TO CANCER IN RATS

WHITE noise

NO.3 $1

OH NO! ITS...

DEVO!

WHITE noise

NO.4 $1.00

COMPULSORY ROMANTICS COVER

WHITE noise

real live blood

ow

guess who??

flash! w.n.'s circus ends with freak limbo accident

WHITE noise

NO.6 $1.00

—80's ROCK: THE 27—
ALSO: 2 MAGS FOR PRICE OF 1!!
IN THIS ISSUE: 'STREET LIFE' no.1

$1

WHITE Noise

Chasing Punk

Before the premiere issue of Jerry Peterson's first publication, *White Noise*, was ever pasted up on a Ping-Pong table in the basement of a house on Detroit's west side, the magazine's eventual co-creators saw the project as a great ruse for infiltrating the Los Angeles punk rock scene. In the summer of 1977, the scene was gaining traction in L.A., with the Masque, a club in central Hollywood, as its epicenter. At that same time, Peterson and his friend, Paul Zimmerman, were heading west to California, where Peterson had been admitted into USC's School of Cinematic Arts and was expected to start in the fall.

By the time Peterson and Zimmerman arrived in L.A., they had already visited most of the now legendary punk rock clubs in the country, including Chicago's La Mere Vipere and San Francisco's Mabuhay Gardens. During their travels, they'd discovered that anyone covering the punk rock scene was treated like royalty because the bands were starved for attention. It was the perfect cover for two broke guys from Michigan. The pair grabbed a camera and attended shows at the Masque and other Los Angeles area clubs posing as writers for New York's *Punk* magazine. Free admission, free drinks, and other perks came their way since they

were perceived as having the power of the pen. "That's what attracted me to journalism—just getting in free, getting drinks bought for you. And I was the photographer. I was so poor and cheap that I didn't take many pictures at all. I was so conservative with what I would take photos of. I would go to see the Ramones and take like three pictures of the band. Well, I got them! I wouldn't use a whole roll of film on the Ramones . . . or DEVO. They were pretty young then. [DEVO] had T-shirts and HAZMAT suits. I just had a lot of fun in L.A.," said Peterson.

But they were not writers. They were not even with a magazine.

5

Jerry Peterson was born on February 7, 1956, at Beaumont Hospital in Royal Oak, Michigan. The second of three boys, he grew up in the western suburbs of Wayne County. Peterson said his childhood consisted of "getting beat up and protected by my older brother while beating up and protecting my younger brother." Such is the life of many middle children. For many years, Peterson's father, Robert, owned a tool and die shop. In his youth, the elder Peterson trained and raced horses. That's where he met his wife, Miriam. The couple married and started a family in the early 1950s. Their first son was Thomas Peterson in 1950, followed by Jerry in 1956, and Robert two years later. By 1968, however, the Peterson family was headed toward a split. The Petersons divorced, and soon after twelve-year-old Jerry moved to Florida with his mother. By the early 1970s, he returned to Michigan, living in a house his father built in a then-wooded area near Seven Mile and Haggerty Roads. Peterson graduated from Northville High School in 1974.

They were just two punks from Detroit. At some point, and neither seems to remember when, they changed their cover story. Instead of reporting for *Punk*, they were covering bands for *White Noise* magazine. Zimmerman said the name was, for him, the next extension of the Velvet Underground album title *White Light, White Heat*. White noise is also the scientific name for the sound of static.

As the summer of 1977 ended, Zimmerman headed back to Detroit, leaving Peterson to start school, but Peterson didn't attend classes. Instead, he lived out of his van in the driveway of someone he'd met in the L.A. punk scene because the house was infested with cockroaches. He would go into the house only once a day to shower and use the bathroom. Peterson went to shows, took photos, and met people in the scene like Darby Crash of the Germs (then known as Bobby Pyn) and punk musician/producer Geza X. Many of the meetings were scheduled under the pretext that Peterson was with a publication. At the same time, he was also reading other punk papers. *Slash* and *Search and Destroy*, the magazines covering the L.A. and San Francisco scenes, were part of a network of local papers covering punk's development as a music and philosophy. By late 1977, Peterson's Los Angeles adventure came to an end. Figuring it would be easier to be broke back in Detroit than try to scrape by in L.A., he packed up whatever stuff wasn't already in the van and headed home. Upon his return, Peterson felt the birth pangs of Detroit's in-utero punk rock scene.

"Bookie"

The sign above the door may have said Frank Gagan's, but the matchbooks on the bar said Bookie's Club 870. Samuel "Bookie" Stewart, so called because he had been an illegal bookmaker during Prohibition, bought Gagan's in 1970 and began catering to Palmer Park's gay population.

Before buying the worn, art deco supper club at 870 West McNichols, Stewart worked with his brother-in-law at a bar called the Silver Dollar on Farmer Street after World

Bookie's Club 870, circa 1978. (Photo by Joseph Sposita) ▲
Samuel "Bookie" Stewart, circa 1978. (Photo by Joseph Sposita) ▶

War Two, just northeast of Detroit's Campus Martius Park. Much like Bookie's Club 870, thirty years later, the Silver Dollar became a meeting place for Detroit's gay community. By the late 1950s, Stewart was offering drag shows at the Silver Dollar, featuring elegant performances by dolled-up men brought in from New York City. These would be considered some of the earliest drag shows in Detroit. In 1962, Stewart opened the Diplomat, located on Second Avenue near the Fisher Building in the New Center. The Diplomat would also cater to the gay community.

Upon his retirement from the bar business in 1982, Stewart was called "The Godfather of Detroit's Gay Community" in *Cruise*, a local gay magazine. Stewart was acknowledged as

someone who welcomed the gay community's business, offered entertainment, and acted as an intermediary between the community and the police. During Stewart's time as a businessman, it was not uncommon for gays to be arrested, beaten, and mistreated by the police. Gary Mamrot, a fifteen-year employee of Stewart's, told *Cruise*, "There are a lot of people in this town who owe him a lot, in more ways than one. He respects each customer, sits and talks with them. He honestly doesn't consider himself above them like some bar people can sometimes. You really can't name names, but he has bailed a lot of people out with advice, and, when they needed it, cash."

Stewart was also credited with training the next era of club owners to cater to the gay community in Palmer Park and

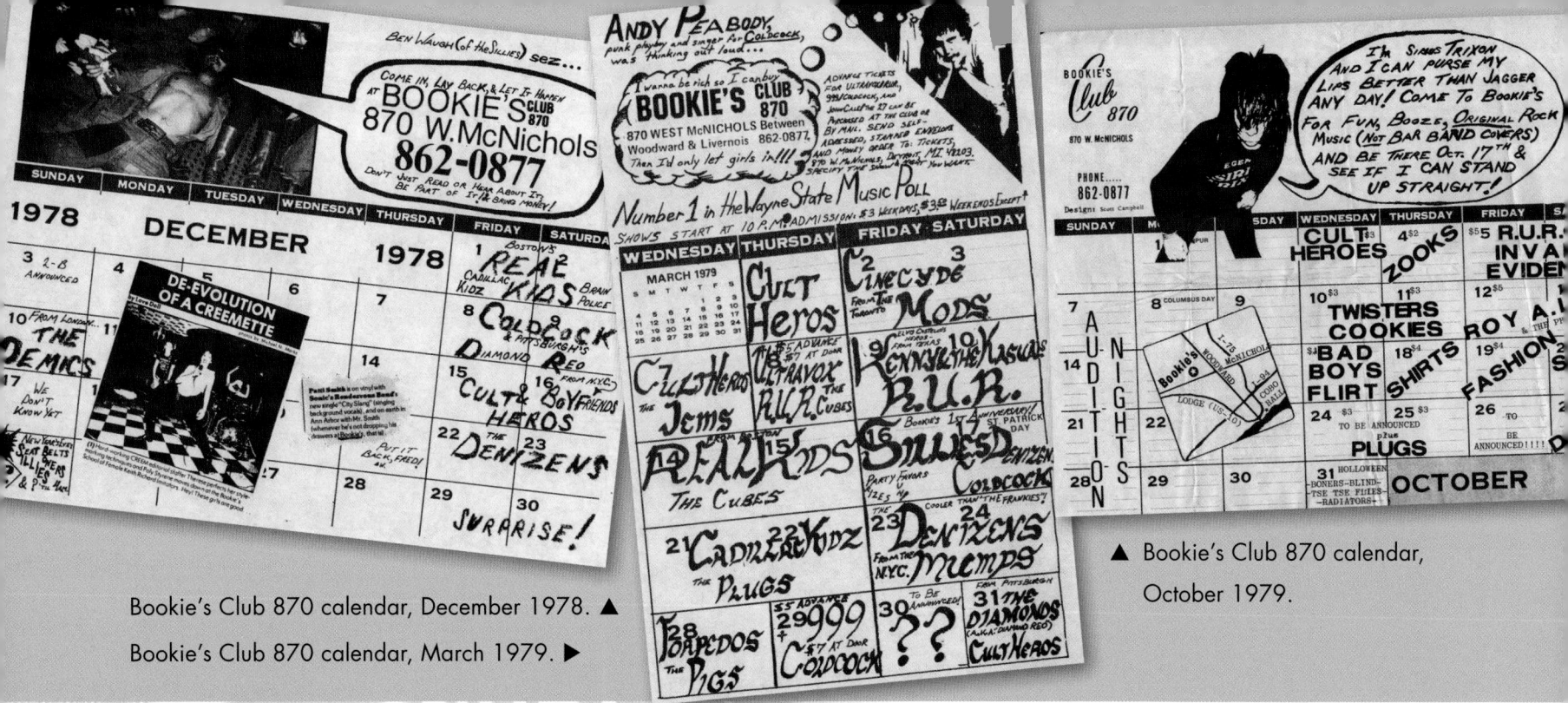

Bookie's Club 870 calendar, December 1978. ▲

Bookie's Club 870 calendar, March 1979. ▶

▲ Bookie's Club 870 calendar, October 1979.

beyond. Stewart told *Cruise* that he decided to retire from the bar business at the age of seventy-two at the urging of his wife of fifty years, Betty, because the pair planned to travel and enjoy their retirement together. A few years prior to retirement, however, throat cancer had claimed Stewart's larynx, led to a tracheotomy, and caused him to speak in a gruff Donald Duck-like voice. After leaving the bar business, health issues continued to plague him. Samuel "Bookie" Stewart died in March 1984 at the age of seventy-four.

Detroit Punk Thrives at Bookie's

Due to a confluence of youthful energy, new ideas, and a lack of interest by other club owners, Bookie's Club 870 became the epicenter of Detroit punk. Punk had developed out of a sense of contempt for popular rock and radio, which was favoring musically intricate progressive rock and subdued singer-song-writers during the early to mid-1970s. That Detroit would have an interest in punk is really not that out of the ordinary. While it caught on first in New York, L.A., and London, the

DNA of punk sprang from the sound of two Detroit groups from the late 1960s Grande Ballroom scene—the MC5 and the Stooges, featuring Iggy Pop. Not only would albums like the MC5's *Kick Out the Jams* and the Stooges' *Raw Power* help to inspire bands like the Ramones, and other key punks, but members of both bands would play a part in the Bookies scene born in early 1978. According to Scott Campbell, founder of Detroit punk band the Sillies, in late 1977 there were very few bars in Detroit where bands could play original music: "You had to play five sets at least forty-five minutes long and they all had to be covers. In some cases, if you were an agency act, you could do one original set in a night of five sets. The bar would often give you a list of songs you had to do. I didn't feel like doing that. I was already working in a factory. I wasn't going to go and make fifty dollars a night and try to be a human jukebox. I had no interest in that."

Campbell said that if he wanted to play original music. . . he could sometimes get a one-night-only gig at shady bars that often didn't have signage, regular business hours, or front doors.

▲ Bookie's Club 870 calendar, May 1980.

Bookie's Club 870 calendar, June 1980. ▲

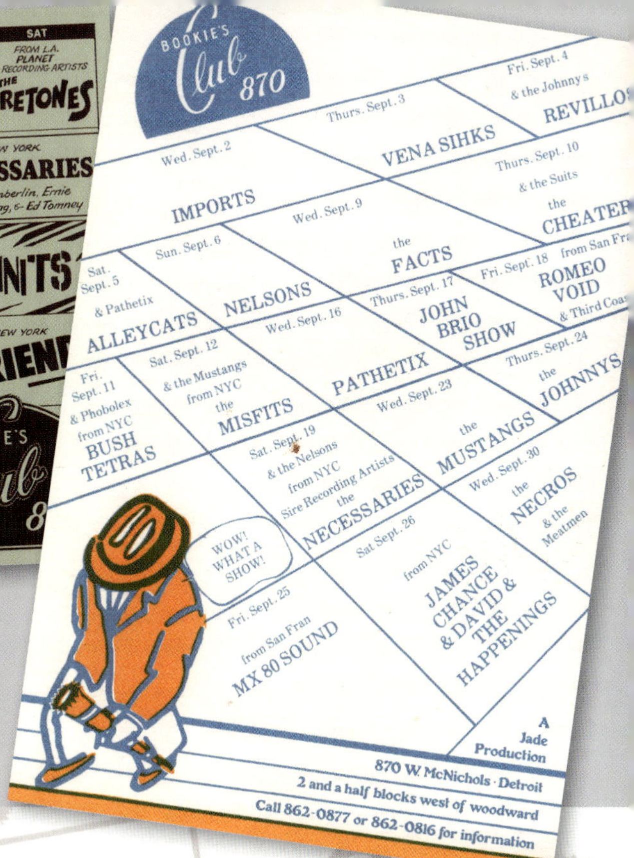

Bookie's Club 870 calendar, September 1981. ▶

At the time, there were legitimate places like the Red Carpet on Detroit's east side and the Second Chance in Ann Arbor that offered a stage for young bands to play their own music. But opportunities were limited. The situation was frustrating.

In February 1978, Campbell was able to get his band into Bookie's Club 870 for a one-night show. He would soon book shows there for other bands, but he said he was not really interested in taking over booking at Bookie's:

[The Sillies] had actually been offered two other bars that we could have taken over and run, but instead we were going to do Bookie's. Just before we got there, Don Fagenson—you know Don Was—he and his business partner had done a show at Bookie's with the new MC5—Rob Tyner and four other guys—and then the next weekend they did the Traitors, which was Don's punk band . . . or fake punk band as we said because nobody knew him from the scene. He didn't go

to any of the shows. The third weekend was a production company called Sure Shot, and then the fourth weekend was us—myself and Vince [Bannon]. They offered us the room after the first night. I didn't want the room. But Vince begged me. They took half the door; it's not worth my time. So, we did the second night and the owner, Bookie, offered the room to us to book exclusively and run from then on in.

Bookie's concert flyer, ▶ circa 1979.

BOOKIES CLUB 870 870 W. McNichols
PRESENTS A SPECIAL
BENEFIT CONCERT
FOR THE POVERTY STRICKEN
ALGEBRA MOTHERS
WITH...
COLDCOCK
R.U.R.
THE PIGS
Retro & Zooks
THURS. JULY 5
ADMSN: $3.
ONE NIGHT ONLY
THE A-MOMS AFTER THEIR EQUIPTMENT WAS STOLEN

Bookie's
R.U.R. / CINE CYDE / THE BOYDOGS
Fri. Jan. 12
Sat. Jan. 13

THE SILLIES
Detroit's Lowest Form of Entertainment
SPECIAL GUESTS
WEDNESDAY THE IVORIES
THURSDAY RETRO PLUS THE SLIDERS
HEAR THE SILLIES INTERVIEWED LIVE
FRIDAY MORNING 12 a.m. to 3 a.m. on
WDET – 101.9 FM
ADMISSION $3
Bookies Club 870
W. McNichols 862-0877

862-0877

estroy all monsters

DESTROY ALL MONSTERS
Frl. & Sat. Sept. 14 & 15 BOOKIEIS Club 870

FRIDAY ONLY JUNE 6 BOOKIE'S

Bookies club

DEC. 15-16
LIVE! IN PERSON
BOYFRIENDS
CULT HEROES
The New Source
BE THERE...
OR BE SQUARE!
"It's All Perfectly Natural..."

SEPT 1980				
SUN	MON	TUES	WED	
	1 Closed	2	3 FBI	4 HEAVEN SEVENTEEN
7 The Man Who Fell To Earth / Clockwork Orange	8 Closed	9	10 HOI POI	11 SEAT BELTS
14 MO-DETTES	15 Closed	16	17 MUSCULAR DYSTROPHY BENEFIT	18 LIPS ARE BACK
21 Quadrophenia Sextet	22-27 6 NIGHTS IGGY POP			Mon-RE Fri-
28 C**ksucker Blues	29 Closed	30		A JADE PRODUCTION 862-0877 862-0816

BOOKIE'S CLUB 870
70 W. McNichols ••••
WED, THURS FEB 14, 15
COLDCOCK
COLDCOCK
COLDCOCK
COLDCOCK
COLDCOCK
COLDCOCK
VALENTINE'S DAY MASSACRE!

870 W. McNichols • DETROIT
2½ blocks west of Woodward
862-0877
862-0816
JADE PRODUCTION
YOU MUST BE 18 WITH VALID I.D.

SUN	MON	TUES	WED	THURS	FRI	SAT
			1 CLOSED	2 R.U.R.	3-4 THE MUTANTS	
5 FILM: C**ksucker Blues	6 CLOSED	7 THE PSYCHEDELIC FURS	8 CLOSED	9 THE STINGRAYS KICKS	10 THE ROCKATS ROCKABILLY CATS	11 THE TREMBLERS
12 The ENGLISH BEAT	13 CLOSED	14	15 VIA SATELLITE VICTIM EYES	16 SEAT BELTS	17 CULT HEROES	18 COLDCOCK COLDCOCK COLDCOCK
19 Freaks THE JOHNNIES	20	21	22 SECRETS	23 SHAKE!	24 RAY-BEATS	25 DESTROY ALL MONSTERS
26 Animal House HEAVEN SEVENTEEN	27 CLOSED	28	29 SLANT SIX	30 RETRO	31 Halloween Party BONERS RUBBER CITY REBELS	

OCT 1980

ONE NIGHT ONL

R.U.R.

At first, Bookie allowed Campbell and Bannon to book music for Friday and Saturday night. Within a year, business was booming, and the booking calendar had expanded to Wednesday through Sunday. By 1980, Bookie's Club 870 would have a band on its stage seven nights a week, showcasing local groups and rising international acts.

The local band roster included the Sillies, the Denizens, the Pigs, the Mutants, RUR, Nikki and the Corvettes, Cinecyde, the Ramrods, Coldcock, the 27, Sirrus Trixton and the Motor City Bad Boys, Destroy All Monsters, Sonic's Rendezvous Band, the Algebra Mothers, the Seatbelts, the Cult Heroes, the Boners, and the Romantics. National and international acts included Iggy Pop, Pere Ubu, Ultravox, the Police, John Cale, the Dead Boys, the Cramps, 999, the Damned, Johnny Thunders and the Heartbreakers, J. Geils, and more. As the scene was building through 1978 and 1979, Bookie's Club 870 became the place for young people looking for new music, fun, and adventure to hang out. Robert Mulrooney, later known by his stage name

▼ Assorted Bookie's Club 870 flyers from 1978 to 1981.

▲ Flyer for Iggy Pop at Bookie's Club 870, September 1980. (Designed by Gary Grimshaw)

Flyers for Jerry Vile's band the Boners at Bookie's Club 870, 1978–80. ▶

Bootsey X, was a drummer and singer for several bands including the Ramrods and Coldcock. He described it as "a totally cool scene. People used to go there every weekend night and they didn't care who was playing because it was such a small scene. You just see all your new friends. I read this article in the book *Desert Island Discs* and it was about the CBGBs scene—every single person you met was into doing something creative that they always wanted to do all their life. It was exactly the same thing [at Bookie's Club 870]. You know, writers, poets, musicians, artists, you were always meeting people. Interesting people. It was easy to meet girls. Everyone was into the same things. Bookie's was wild. People were having sex in the bathrooms all the time . . . in the parking lots."

The Detroit punk scene was also much more egalitarian among the sexes than other scenes in the past. Katy McNerney, a fixture at Bookie's and a member of the Sillies for a time, said, "punk did kind of turn into something that was kind of darker and 'kill me now' kind of music, later. But when it was first starting for all the Detroit people, it was just a celebration of the outcast and the odd, and people were just having a blast. I had friends from a little older generation who were hanging out with the MC5 and the Stooges, and the attitude was the chicks are over there and do with them as you wish. This was different. It was kind of like people were empowered, if that sounds a little corny."

A regular presence at Bookie's Club 870 was Jerry Peterson's comic punk band the Boners. The Boners' stage shows were legendary. Peterson's penchant for the theatrical made them memorable—in the beginning more for the antics than the music. Among the historic live shows was "The Honey-Boners"—a musical version of the 1950s classic sitcom *The Honeymooners*, with Peterson playing the part of Jackie Gleason's Ralph Kramden. A more notorious, and darkly funny, per-

▲ Jerry Vile as the Flying Nun, Halloween 1979.
(Photo by Sue Rynski)

formance featured Peterson emerging from under a bride's dress on stage wearing a 1970s wedding tuxedo with various forms of used feminine hygiene products in his mouth and attached to his face while the band played. After working himself into frenzy, Peterson stripped naked while singing, and by the end, he was wearing only a tiny leather G-string. But Peterson's most iconic and well-remembered performance with the Boners was as the Flying Nun. Dressed like Sally Field from the 1960s TV show, Peterson belted out tunes while being suspended by aircraft cable from the ceiling of the club.

Campbell and Bannon continued booking the shows at Bookie's Club 870 together until they had a falling out in late 1979. Bannon took over until early 1982, when he started a new club, Clutch Cargo's, at the Women's City Club near Grand Circus Park. Then in the fall of 1982, Bannon moved his booking operations again, this time setting up shows at Saint Andrew's Hall, near Detroit's Greektown.

Many of the changes in booking at Bookie's Club 870 coincided with evolutions in music, culture, and even the law. By 1980–81, punk was mutating into two different forms. The first incorporated more pop and electronic sounds under the term "new wave." The second form was called "hardcore"—a faster, stripped down, and more distilled version of punk. Hardcore bands often wrote songs that were not melodically centered but rhythmically intense and short. It was not uncommon for a hardcore song to be under two minutes; some were less than a minute. By 1981 hardcore acts started to appear at Bookie's Club 870 as the scene's original bands started to move to Clutch Cargo's, Todd's, and other clubs around Detroit.

Some Bookie's Club 870 regulars also point to the change in drug use in the late 1970s and early 1980s as responsible for a shift in the scene. As marijuana and alcohol gave way to cocaine and heroin, some said the focus seemed to shift from having a good time to maintaining a serious addiction.

After Sam "Bookie" Stuart retired in 1982, the club continued to limp along booking mostly hardcore and other rock acts. In 1989, the club burned in a fire. Today, like many well-known and historic places in Detroit, Bookie's Club 870 is a parking lot.

From Punk Kids to Punk Editors

What was originally a ruse to get free admission to shows, free drinks, and face time with bands became what could be

White Noise #1, early 1978. ▶

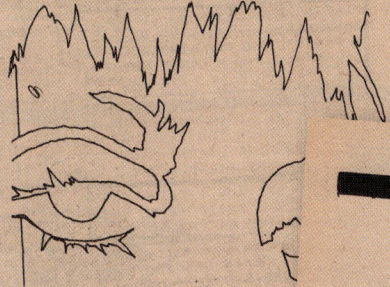

considered Detroit's version of New York's *Punk* magazine, Los Angeles's *Slash*, or San Francisco's *Search and Destroy*. Inspired by what Jerry Peterson saw in the L.A. punk scene, and by his friend Paul Zimmerman's interest in writing, cartooning, and graphic design, the pair decided to start *White Noise*. The co-editors used the "noms de punk" Jerry Vile and Paul Stillborn for the first two issues. Afterward, Zimmerman switched to other pseudonyms like Paul Ginsuknife and Paul X. "I changed my punk name with every issue, and my dad couldn't keep

The Ramrods, *White Noise* #1. ▲

The Pigs & the Sillies, *White Noise* #1. ▶

DENIZENS:

MIKE

DEAN

TIMMY

BOB RYNSKI

ROB

JOHN

SHOCKING TRUTH

The Denizens are a young quintet from Livonia that happen to play great rock music in New Wave bars such as the cosmic Bookie's Club 870. I'd like to tell you why they're great but in order to condense from the original 15,000 manuscript and to delete obviously incriminating sections like the one about the horling of seven home-made bombs into a near by 7-11 store,

I'll have to break their exciting story into little categories. Only crucial info remains: Names: Mike Murphy plays drums and sings back-up vocals. Rob Sullivan plays

lead guitar. John Sullivan-rythm guitar, and rock bus boy Dean Bonarek plays bass extraordanaire. Tim Butler is lead singer and is a macho guy. ROOTS: Flamin' Groovies, Rolling Stones, 60's punk bands like the Standells and Count Fove. Any good rock and roll.

HISTORICAL EARLY DAYS STORY: Typical bored teenagers form rock band after school. School happens to be a Catholic institution which makes them perverted enough to like Iggy And The Stooges. Band gets a set together but their tastes run akimbo with school dance committee who want Uriah Heep-Pat Boone death music. Band retreats in disgust to basement and practices loud enough to shatter nearby ping pong table. Cartoons wail above the noise upstairs. Next door neighbor has nervous collapse. Next thing you know, New Wave comes along to save the day. Original are written, Twisted Brain, Abba Cadabra, I Know You Hate Me. One million matchbooks are printed up bearing slogans like "The Denizens-at least they say hello". Match books are shoved into the hands of key booking agents. Gigs, popularity, interviews, hysteria follows. Everyone is cheerful.

MUSIC: Along with Peter James of the Nikki Corvette group, Rob and Mike write the best mainstream rock and roll songs in the city. Each does his teenage thing. Danger In Disneyland one is built around one murderous guitar riff, tough rythm section, great vocal arranging and they all seem to be about this "quiet kid" who shows up and features the kid and many 14 year old girls and their moms, one of which has success to the neutron bomb, hence the title.

But Twisted Brain is probably the best representation of their originals. Here, the quiet little geek gets together a potion of deadly chemicals from the high school lab and drinks it down and it makes him goofy. He gets home and naturally he's fucked up, can't maintain, starts singing I Got My Mojo Workin'at the dinner table. Dad drops fork in disbelief: "My-My son you've really changed, you've become a twisted brain".

The troubled parent flings the guy into a mental institution. Things look grim but all ends well: "I work really hard, I crayon Christmas cards, When I get out I'll be the same, I'll still be a twisted brain." So it's cool. He's not worried. He's got his crayons. Meanwhile the music sounds quite violent, great bass line, the vocals flying over' the top of everything. O.K., so they got the music down but in the big bad turbulent world of rock and roll, you need more. The Denizens got it. IMAGE: Irish Catholic. of course! John F. Kennedy was Irish Catholic and just recently we foung out what a rockin' guy he was. In fact this image is very accessible. Punks like them sad they don't wear ripped up clothing or bags. Power pop patrons can relate even tho they're not Beatles-clones. Hippies don't try and slap the shit out of them because they play. They're family entertainment. SEX APPEAL: They fuck with their boots on. DANCE APPEAL: Hey, you can shimmy you can pogo, you can hump the dance floor, you can prance around like an insect, you can do the swim

like Mr. M. Fifty of Ferndale, Mich., you can whip out your wazoo and lurch back and forth, you can just be as fucking idiotic as possible, and you won't feel out of place. The Denizens inspire zany antics and senseless behavior of all the kids and really it should be one of the true goals of any rock band: people going wild to your own music, them not worrying about looking like a bunch of laffing hyenas instead of the latest solmn gang at CBGB's. Because when that craziness happens, and the bands really wailing and maybe even Rob's size 20 feet will start shuffling back and forth on stage, it's just beautiful. It's cool. "It's rock and roll, man." And that's what the Denizens are. A bunch of cool guys who love rock and roll. They look like it. They sound like it. See them.
-Bob Mulrooney

cinecydes gutter punch

If your a small band around Detroit you probably bitch in general safe terms about how awful the state of music is (radio and record), but the enemy you refer to is always an unseen force (or farce) too big to fight etc.,etc. Not so with Cinecyde. Their new single Black Vinyle Threat goes right to source and attacks the horse-China Jones program director for WABX. Not because of any public help or sense of marterdom, but just pure vengence. "China Jones you're next-Your actions mean your death..". Still gutless like the rest." Lead singer Gary Reichel, slashes with an icy whine of detience. Strong stuff and if this came out elsewhere you would have heard by now in exaggeratted tales of; as Travis Bickel would say "A man who stood up." Cinecydes first single 'Gutless Radio' was OK but never so bold, articulate or demanding in it's presentation. A basically good song. it was overshadowed by length, a sense of urgency and a trite neo-Nazi cover. With this single Cinecyde becomes Detroits most outspoken, honest and undera ted band. If I was writing this from London, 'Chinas gotta Die" would be covering T-shirts, alley walls and buttons. A cry to arms would be called in a abused over hyped way. These guys would instantly become spokesmen for a variety of political and social issues. Over there. HA-HA Not here. Instant martyr. Technically the e.p. is amazing. It proports a wall of sound even if that wall comes from a basement and not some expensive studio. Let local bands blame their singles ineptness on paid technitions theres no weaseling out here. All four songs are exellant with "Rock Meat (and the Hard-ons)'" and a cover of "Secret Agent"Man" being the stand outs. "Rock Meat" for it's urgency and drive and "Secret Agent" for it's bass. The mix is incredable as new bassist Clay dominates the old Johnny Rivers tune, which is admittedly overplayed, offering a new thump-twist. People don't expect this kind of awareness, guts and power from a midwestern state. Suprize and tough shit; wake up to the potential any city can produce.

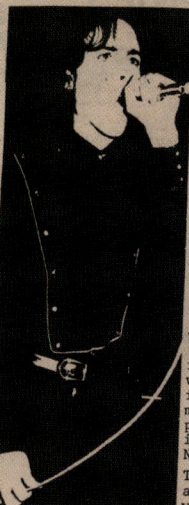

PAUL STILLBORN

COLDCOCK

LIVE AND IN CONCERT
AT BOOKIE'S CLUB 870
SEPTEMBER 24
SPECIAL GUEST

Photo by Sue Rynski

▲ Cinecyde, *White Noise* #2.

track of them and referred to us as Paul Puke and Jerry Jerk. I always liked that," said Zimmerman.

Compared to the ease of blogs and desktop publishing, producing *White Noise* in early 1978 would be seen today as a primitive chore. The magazine was created around hand-made graphics, paste-ups, and other now archaic technologies that were somewhat expensive. But favors and friends, and even a little low-rent thievery, helped to make it happen. "I remember in my parents' house, in the basement, on a Ping-Pong table, doing the old cut-and-paste layout, you know, when you use a waxer and a razor blade and every bit had to be typed up on a composer. It was a nightmare," said Zimmerman.

According to Peterson, the design of the first issue was influenced, in its own makeshift way, by the larger New York and L.A. punk magazines: "I had no idea that people could do something like that. It was only when we saw these newspapers, and Paul had experience, horrible experience but experience nonetheless, and the idea of *Punk* magazine. *Punk* was handwritten. But these other magazines [*Slash* and *Search and Destroy*] were typeset, and typesetting was expensive. So, we would type it on a typewriter and then shrink it down on a Xerox." In the late 1970s, the reduce function on a copy machine was a rare and expensive thing—costing a few dollars per page.

The first issue of *White Noise* cost about two hundred dollars to print and was sold by hand at Bookie's Club 870 for a dollar an issue. For perspective, cigarettes at the time were about forty cents a pack, a gallon of gas was about sixty cents, and first-class postage was fifteen cents. The exact date of the first issue is lost to history, but March or April 1978 seems about right given that a benefit was held in early May to fund the second issue.

white noise

DESTROY All MONSTERS

PLAYBOY INTERVIEW: ~~MEL BROOKS~~

a candid conversation with the emperor of off-the-wall comedy

White Noise: Are you guys ever going to get your hair cut?
Larry: I'm aim'n to get it trimmed pretty soon.
WN: Niagra, we want to talk about addiction to lifesavers.
Niagra: What are you talking about?
WN: I notice you are always eating lifesavers.
Niagra: Your so perceptive buy me some wine and I will talk about it in depth.
WN: They don't have any Boones Farm or Maddog.
Niagra: M.D. 20/20 (giggle).
WN: Well if they have any good wine.
Niagra: How about Silver Satin anything.
WN: If we put food coloring in beer it would taste just the same, and put it in a nice glass too. Do you take drugs?
Larry: Yeah, I take

drugs in fact, I stopped doing LSD in regular doses four years ago. How about that. Since then 6/10ths of a degree which happens to be the best way to take it, and I read .that's the way it should have been originally. And a, You know I've gone thru all those things.
Ron: He plugs himself in and out every day. Sometime plugs him in, he's gotta be up at a certain time, unplugs him at night. Hi bed is actually a big guitar case, especially molded to his body, when we travel we slip him in the equipment truck.
Larry: It's true.
Ron: Put in the power pack and he's gotta play, reherse or party. His brother takes care of unplugs the pack, then he knows it's time for him

to rest and recharge.
WN: Does the rest of the band do drugs.
Ron: Just beer and (cat scream sound effects by Scott Ashton)
WN: How do you like Devo?
Ron: I dont care for them well enough. I can appreciate the bands that are hated, but want to be professional and go thru the stage thing-it seems they worked a long time and well with each other, but as far as the music is concerned- I don't really care for it. They've got what they do down to a professional level.
WN: I saw a Destroy All Monsters magizine- what was that?
Ron: Something that Kerry and Niagra put together. It was part of their side trade, art work

"ight as well be honest. I'm crowd-x, one. Got a mass of blond hair, mal eyes, bluer than Newman's - but whippy, like Redford. Only 't I have no ass. It fell off."

"One day I was making $5000 a week, the next day zilch. All I had was a limited edition of 'War and Peace' and an iron skate key. I kissed the key four times a day just to have something to do."

"In real life, people fart, right? But before 'Blazing Saddles,' America had not come to terms with the fart. Wind was never broken across the prairie in a Ken Maynard picture."

Destroy All Monsters, *White Noise* #2. ▲ ▶

besides the band, various xeroxes, collages, and pix they've taken. Just sort of a cultural border.
WN: I heard Cale's version, he left the Velvet Undergroung and just mosied along and came to Detroit and really loved you, he had'nt heard anything he just saw you and loved you and said he wanted to produce you.
Ron: Well it was, he'd never seen us and was afraid of Danny Fields, and Danny and he talked and they were pretty tight, and uh, Cale was somewhat of a staff producer and Danny was kind of lost there for a while, uh, they thought he would-be the most obvious person being that he was in the Velvets trying to get everything worked out, he was kind of a long shot thing. There was a real small contract. There were real small somebodies, and they wanted to see what would happen on their album. He thought we were liked crazed nobodies. That was the first time we'd ever met him. That was actually-we've been to his house a couple times in New York. We recorded that album in New York. Getting to know him actually came when doing the album. First

he tried to be like a pretty nice doctor, but he tried to get to pushy, cause he wanted to direct everything. We would revolt and go on ministrikes, and I thought fuck-if it ain't doing it fuck-you. So after not really any really big hassle, half the medium would work together and he suggested, Oh fuck you guys do what you want to do, I'll do the best I can do on my side. Other than that I didn't see him after that for awhile, then he sort of hoped up again in L.A. that was uh, 2 years later. We got to know him a little bit better-here and there and just things like party scenes-MainMan parties at houses by his west office in L.A., when he gets drunk he gets weird. There was a girl there as big, strange and ugly as she was he comes up and slaps her and bitched at her. She's just a lucky, I don't know what she did , I couldn't believe it,'so I just yelled at her. I wanted to get her thrown out of the party, and Lee Childers was taking me aside, and goes it's Cale again,up to his old games, he was hassling the shit out of her. I went to his apartment where there must have been some kind of

mutual admiration society, cuz she wore boys clothes and he had all these drag things. 'These are my clothes.' All this weird drag stuff, make-up and stuff, and get really high. The first time I noticed him was when he was in the Velvets, and Warhol had the Factory, and he went there once and that was really freaky seeing all of getting really high. We were like kids. They were shooting and snorting up speed, basically I just sort of stayed away.
WN: Did you mean Lou Reed was snorting too?
Ron: Sure, he didn't care much about any of the other guys in the band. He wasn't into rapping. The only things I remember was when Bowie did his first concert at the Rainbow in London. Reed was there, and he comes up to me and he says'Got these really good fucking pills called Mandrils. I've been up for 3 days tripping.' He kept trying to get me to take them, and I said , sorry I don't want that. Clue me out of this mind-that's wandering around. It's so funny' like all the Stooges were at the bar-they have bars in theaters and clubs in London- so we got all these great seats, so he plays 2 songs

and I stood up and walked to the bar. I spent the rest of the time hanging around the bar.
WN: You have a majic touch where you're in a band, and it's really popular after it's broken up and you can't profit.
Ron: It's so weird, I don't know it's the devils touch.
WN: Your in the wrong place at the wrong time;
Ron: It's always been like that for me pretty much, that's why this time it isn't gonna happen to me . This is all in the right place at the right time, I've stuck out a number of other times and this time it's gonna be it.
WN: Can you see in 3 years from now people saying "Destroy All Monsters" was the best group ever.
Ron: No, well stick-we're diffrent from other people-there is no weird personal problems-like in New Order Dave Gilbert was a fuck-up-he was drugged out and care more about other things besides the band. And there was Ray Gunn with his huge ego and peanut brain which screwed everything up. Finally Thompson and I said fuck-it we're splitting-fuck this shit
WN: Are you going to talk Niagra?
Niagra: Get me some wine you have time.

WN: What do you think we are elaborates from Life magazine?
Do any of you work?
Ron: 3 of the guys work, Ben and Larry work a Rob works a bit, Mike is sort of subsidized with an inheritance and his girl-friend and I sort of sell things to make piddily money. but it dose'nt last very long.
WN: Niagra-how did you get into the group?
Niagra: I made the group-Yes I was the originator-about 2 years ago 73 or 74.
WN: Was that magizine thing a one shot deal?
Niagra: It was one issue.
WN: Was it sucessful?
Niagra: Wildly sucessful.
WN: Niagra-How did you get started with the Monsters? Are you from art school?
Niagra: No I'm from heaven.

more
poop
next
issue

Five more issues were published between September 1978 and December 1979. Music reviews, interviews with bands, photos of shows and humor were all part of the *White Noise* mixture. The contributing writers included not only the co-founders but local writers and musicians.

One such contributor was Walter Wasacz, who had already been published in *The South End, Creem, New Music Express,* and *Sounds* by the time he started writing for *White Noise.* After *White Noise,* he wrote for *Trouser Press,* the *Metro Times,* and *Orbit.* "[*White Noise*] was more hit-and-run style, kind of gonzo, real trashy, as stupid as can be. You know, writing drunk. Stories about drunk people doing stupid things on a Friday night when you are nineteen, twenty years old. They captured that very well," said Wasacz.

The music profiles in *White Noise* covered the local scene, mostly shows at Bookie's Club 870 in Detroit and the Second Chance in Ann Arbor, but it also featured interviews and reviews of larger out-of-town acts. Local scene favorites covered or reviewed included the Sillies, the Pigs, the Ramrods, the Denizens, Cinecyde, the 27, Coldcock, Nikki Corvette, Destroy All Monsters, the Boners, the Romantics, Cult Heroes, Sonic's Rendezvous Band, Cadillac Kids, the Mutants, RUR, and more. National acts covered or reviewed in the pages of *White Noise* included the Ramones, Iggy Pop, DEVO, Patti Smith, Blondie, Pere Ubu, Dead Boys, the Clash, John Cale, the Mumps, 999, Lou Reed, Johnny Thunders, Public Image Limited, Siouxsie and the Banshees, and Ultravox.

The coverage in *White Noise* included photos of the bands in action, many in Detroit, in tasteful black and white. Although Jerry Peterson had an interest in photography, he admitted his drinking habits made him less than the ideal person for the job of photo editor at his own paper. His secret weapon was someone who had honed her craft at the feet of the Paris ballet. Her name was Sue Rynski. "Jerry and I were monkeying around a little with photography, but I don't think either of us had the patience for it, and Sue would sit off to the side of the stage, and she would wait and wait and wait—this is all pre-digital. She would wait to get the perfect shot, and she would wait like an hour and shoot three frames," said Zimmerman.

Sue Rynski recalled Peterson's proposal to join *White Noise*: "I don't remember exactly where I met Jerry, but I do remember that he contacted me. He said, 'There's this gig and I know you are a photographer. Why don't we go . . .' Whatever, it wasn't a date. I went along with him. He showed up in a white truck or van, and he had his dog collar on and he had this punky smirk, and it was OK but I knew it wasn't him. [Laughs] We went to this gig, and I think even before we got out of the car he told me he was going to start a magazine and asked me to contribute, and if I was kind enough to contribute. 'We'll call you the photo editor, but don't worry, you won't have to do any work. [Laughs] Just take the pictures.'"

Peterson's sarcastic attitude carried over from his everyday life to the magazine and his work with his staff. Beyond arts, culture, and music, trying to make people laugh was always paramount, and the humor in his later magazines, *Fun* and *Orbit*, is deeply rooted in the early days of *White Noise*. The punks satirized the death of Sex Pistols bassist Sid Vicious, created an advertisement for a children's play set based on the mass suicide in Jonestown, posted an offer of ten dollars to Patti Smith or

Sue Rynski self-portrait, circa 1978. ▶

Dee WHIte noiSE BOyz HAve It ouT-faCE Ta faCE Wit' Da-

RAMONES

BY MIKE MUPHEY

THE FOLLOWING STORY IS SUPOSEDLY AN INTER- VIEW WE DID WITH THE RAMONES.BEING THE AL- RITE GUYS WE ARE WE DECIDED TO GIVE ROOKIE WRITER MIKEY(KEYWORDS) MIRFEE WITH DISASTER- OUS RESULTS.CERTAIN JOUNALIISTIC LIBERTIES WERE TAKEN WITH THE INTERVIEW.WE ARE NOT RESPONSABLE FOR ANY EXATERATION,IN THE FOLLOWING ESSAY OF WHIM AND FANTASY,THIS SIMPLY MEANS WE CANT BE SUED FOR LYING..... The Ramones have finally arrived. No more bootlicking for them, no more just a face in the crowd, it's the bigtime now. The White Noise staff plus one(me) travelled all the way from the suburbs of Detroit to be present at the recent Ramones con- cert in Lansing. For a few dollars more we could've had a few days of the old R&R in Toledo, a fact which Jerry kept bring- ing up all night. That wasn't such a bad idea now that I think about it, but as you know bus- iness comes before pleasure, and the old Ramones were pre- tty damn good. We had come in the hopes of getting a great interview from a great band, for this great magazine, and I have to admit we didn't succeed to that great of a degree.

We did get in free though and as I was saying before the band was pretty good and I liked 'em so it was worth goin for me. Anyways, after the show we badgered their road manager Monty who was eating pizza(I notice these things because I'm a stickler for details-really I am) into letting us have an interview. He asked us to wait and didn't offer us any Pizza, but that was O.K. with me,because I wasn't hungry any- ways, and Jerry was too drunk to even know old Monty was eating pozza, and to tell you the truth, I think Paul was a little too worried about trying to look in- telligent to notice anything else. I was kinda kaboozled myself. After awhile of wait- ing around we saw Dee-Dee just stand- ing by some people and getting his hand shook alot, so we decided to ask him if he'd like to fill out one of the McDonalds applications Jerry had brought along. Wait, I better explain about these forms. See, what it was was this Whenever you go on an interview, you should always remember to

bring along what'cha call an Ace In The Hole, and old Jerry-co-editor decided on using these McDonalds applicat- ions as our ace in the hole in case we didn't get a real good interview. He had his heart set on those applications. He really did. Needless to say, al- though I'll say it anyway,we failed with the Ace In The Hole. If we didn't you'd be reading it right now but as it hap- pened we asked Dee- Dee, and he said to ask Monty, and Montee gave it the once over, and just said no. I think Monty was just thinking about people being trapped into buying swamp-land in Florida by signing their names to things they don't know much about. He was prob- ably just trying to protect his wards against a shady deal. In other words, he probably smelled a rat. That's the only explanation I can think of. So we finally got in and started the inter- view. I was assigned to write down the cir- cumstances, we had neithe tape recorder, nor steno- grapher. That last point given is the only reason I am involved in this. And since neither Dee- Dee or Montie were in the room, Paul asked Johnny if he'd like to

fill out one of our Aces in the Hole. John just said he'd sign it and we could fill it out later. That kind of makes you wonder though. I mean John might have some guy writ all his letters home for him, you know what I mean, and then he probably signs 'em and sends 'em away. Joey didn't want to fill one out either, he didn't say anything, but you could tell because as soon as Paul brought it up, old Joey started having a staredown with himself. There was a mirror on the wall(like I said before, I'm a stickler for detail). (Anyway the interview starts like this): Paul: Stiv Bators says PUNK magazine sucks your cocks. Is this true? Johnny: Aw that old Stiv. What a card. D'ya hear that Joey? Joey: Mirror, Mirror... what d'ya say? Johnny: Nothin Joey. Forget it. Anyways Stiv was probably just drunk. You gotta watch him on that. Paul: Oh. Jerry: Do you guys like playin big places or small places? Johnny:Well both really. The thing is we've come to the point where someplaces are just too small. For in- stance we can't play CBGB's anymore. Paul: I thought you said you could right

fast. Me: I'm getting it. Paul: you only have two words written down. Me: Those are the key words. Paul: Oh. Jerry: Are someplaces better than others? Johnny:(amazed that Jerry asked a stupider question than his first one) Well, yeah but... Joey: They went crazy in Toledo! Jerry: Oh yeah? That's where we vacationed! At this point Johnny realized Jerry was in no condition for an interview, and turned towards Paul. Paul: What are your favorite comic books? Johnny: I don't read comic books. You should ask Dee-Dee

about comic books. Joey: Yeah, he collects em'. Paul:He's not here. Hohnny: I know. Jerry: Hey! You only have five words writ- ten down! Me: Those are the key words Jerry. Jerry: Oh. Hey if you Ramones are all brothers how come you've got different moms? Johnny: Uh, we've gotta get going now, Nice meeting you guys. Jerry: Thanx alot! Joey: Yeah. Bye. Jerry: Bye Joey! Bye Johnny! Say goodnite to Dee-Dee and Tommy for me! Paul: Hey, don't get in any trouble on the way home. Drive Safely!

ALL LIES

▲ The Ramones, *White Noise* #2.

markie

SUE RYNSKI

WN- Were you popular in high school?
J- NO! We were outcasts. We were our only friends.

WN- What was the last fight you remember?
J- (leering) With my girlfriend.

WN- What bugs you?
J- Nothing!!

WN- How do you like being the new Ramone brother?
    M- Love it.
WN- How did they convince you to join up and leave the Voidoids?

    M- They asked me. (all laff)

WN- Do you agree about New York stiff state? M- Yeah, all the talent is out.

WN- Any new ones you like?
M- Yeah, Sik Fuks, the Fast, Transister and Schrapnel.

(Poor Markie being the new kid was less available for majority of questions, thus the briefness.)

johnny

SUE RYNSKI

WN- Do you get lots of girls?
J- Everybody thinks we get all these girls, but they get rushed out and the roadies get all those who waited...it took two years after the band started to get girls, Dee Dee couldn't get girls at all before.

WN- What's your favorite drink?

J- BUD!

WN- Was there a big audition for the new drummer?
J- Oh, yeah we did with him and Mark. Our new album was supposed to be a double live album recorded in Europe but when the bosses heard ("Road to Ruin") they said 'release the studio first'. We even have the live one cover artwork and a title.

WN- What's the story behind Tommy leaving?
J- He just couldn't take road life anymore. You should have seen him at the hotel just laying there. We couldn't get him to come out so we had to cancel. I caught him once in a hotel room squatting down, walking around the floor talking to himself and clucking like a chicken. (All laff and nod in agreement). Now that Tommy's gone the show is better any-   WN- Any hard feelings?
way.   J- Naw. It was a mutual agreement, he just wants to spend more time producing.   WN- Making lotsa dough now that you're starz?
J- (sitting up official-like) Yeah, paying the bills, keeping our heads above water, in the black...you know, I didn't ever expect to make it (pause and really evil smile) I'm gonna go to hell for this!!!

J- No.

jenny lens

deedee

joey

WN- Does the fact that the press and the industry never seem to take your musicianship seriously ever bother you?

DD- Yes! We've been playing a long time and I get pissed when I hear how Sid is voted best bass player of the year. You see that? They got to be kidding! Who can take that seriously?

WN- How was touring the South? Any redneck troubles?

DD- (in drawl) Naw. Da South was jus' fine. Jus' a few rebel yells like (yelling) YAHOO and it all goes swell.

WN- What's some of the song titles that were scrapped?

DD- Oh, let's see (perks up) ah... "Crippled", "Don't Wanna Bath", "Stinkie"...

WN- Do you prefer these small places?

DD- No they're MURDER. I would love to (headline) play at Cobo Hall!

ramones remake

WN- What's your favorite album to date?

DD- "Road to Ruin".

WN- Do you agree New York is washed up for new talent?

DD- Yeah, plus its pretty hard to watch amateur bands after you've been a pro for a while. You know what most reporters ask us? What we know about the Pistols break-up (laffs). Really, still. That's what bugs me!

WN- Did you ever think you would make a career out of being a musician?

DD- NO! I thought I was gonna get a real job. (after a pause, smiling) THIS IS WRONG!!

WN- What's your favorite drink?

J- (deadpans) Mineral water.

WN- Do you have something going with Edith (Massey)?

J- Yes, I love her.

SUE RYNSKI

WN- What's YOUR favorite album?

J- (mumbles in agreement to rest) "Road to Ruin" (then turns and whispers to Paul with child-like smile) Yeah, but I really liked "Rocket to Russia".

WN- What's the shortest song you ever recorded?

J- Oh, about 50 seconds, but the new album will have songs well over three minutes!! (Paul and Jerry mimic heart attacks).

WN- Was there ever any previous band names?

J- Ummm...no there never was.

WN- How did you ever come up with "The Ramones"?

J- I drew it out of a hat! (proud expression) Have you seen the Punk magazine with me in it?

WN- No, its not here yet. I'd sure like one 'tho (hint, hint)

J- (later) Here's a copy. It's real funny.

(WN (Paul)- Thanks.

J- (even later) I'll trade the mag for that shirt. (Points to only black on yellow White Noise t-shirt ON EARTH!!)

WN (Paul)- Deal! (P.S. If anyone out there ever sees this shirt in a famous magazine send it in for free sub! Come on! I didn't give the shirt off my back just for fun!

Debbie Harry to be the first to pose nude in the magazine, and even featured a dubious sexual health advice column. Beyond deliberate humor pieces, the magazine's editorial tone—from the interviews, to reviews, to other music news features—was always biting. To keep *White Noise* in production after the first issue, the creators looked to their friends in the Detroit punk scene for fi-

DEVO, *White Noise #1.* ▼ ▶

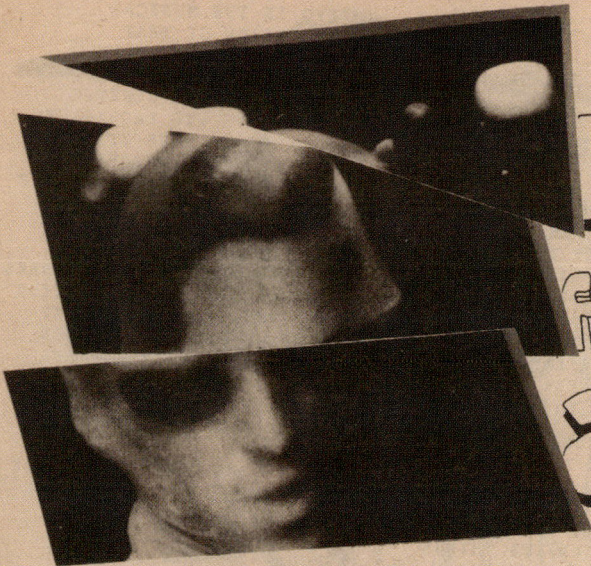

noizkids from acton

DEVO INTERVIEW AND PHOTO BY JERRY VILE

WN- WHEN YOU JUMP DO YOU PUPOSELY AIM FOR SOMEONE IN THE CROWD?
BOB-YEA...YEA USUALLY I WATCH WHEN MARK GOES OUT IN THE AUDIENCE && SOMEBODY GIVES HIM A HARD TIME.
WN-DO YOU JUMP EVERY T TIME YOU PLAY?
B-ONLY WHEN WE DO THAT SONG.
WN- WHAT SONG?
BOB-MR. DNA.
BOB 2-ITS MORE OR LESS AN ODE TO D.N.A.
B1-MR. KAMAKAZI,MR DNA
B2-HE'S AN ALTRUISTIC ASSHOLE.
WN-DO YOU CONSIDER YOUR GROUP FUTURISTIC?
B1-OH NO. ARE WE FUTUR-ISTIC?
GIRL-DO YOU BELIEVE IN CLONING?
B1-CLONES
B2-WE ARE CLONES
WN-IS JERRY A ROBOT?
B1-JERRY...MENTALY
B2- HE APPROACHES EVERY THING LIKE A ROBOT.
B1-HEY YOU SAW A SPRING BOUNCE OFF HIS HEAD .
WN-YEA.HOW LONG HAS THIS BAND BEEN TOGETHER?
B1-PLAYING WHITH EACH OTHER?
B2-NOW CUT THAT OUT.. SOME YEARS 3 OR 4.
WN-BUT THERES BEEN A DEVO FOR ABOUT 6 YEARS?
B2-YEA BUT IT WASNT PUB-LICALLY ACTIVE,IT WAS JUST A REAL ACTIVE IN-DULGENCE.
WN-WAS THERE ANY NAME BEFORE DEVO?
B2-NO.ITS JUST SHORT FOR DEVOLUTION.DEVO IS JUST A CONCEPTUAL THING.

WN-YOU ALL TAKE DEVOLU-TION VERY SERIOUSLY HUH?
B2-YOU HAVE TO. ITS NOT A THING THAT WE MADE UP ITS WHAT WE SAW OCCURING WE TERMED IT DEVOLUTION THE PROCESS SEEMS TO BE BASED ON ENTROPY.
WN-DO YOU THINK YOU THREATEN THE AUDIENCE?
B1-HOW,PHSICALLY?
WN-PHSICALLY OR MENTALY.
B1-OF COURSE WERE THROW-ING NEW IDEAS ON THEM. ALOT OF PEOPLE ARE A--FRAID OF CHANGE.
WN-PHSICALLY?
B1-USUALLY THEY THREAT-EN US MORE.
WN-DO YOU FEEL THREATEND ON STAGE?
B1-NO,THE LAST TIME WE WERE THREATEND WAS IN CLEVELAND.
WN-TONIGHT?
B2-NO,IN THE STREETS A-LONE IT WAS AN UNFOUND-ED OR AN OBSCURE KIND OF THING,PEOPLE ACTUALLY THREATENED US,THEY WAIT-ED FOR US THEY WANTED TO KILL US.
WN-WHO WRITES YOUR SONGS?
B1-WE HAVE THIS COMPUTER AT HOME,JUST TYPE INFOR-MATION AS YOU PLAY.
WN-WHAT ARE SOME GOOD QUESTIONS TO ASK MARK?
B1-MARK?..ASK HIM WHAT KINDA EYESIGHT HES GOT.
WN-ARE THOSE REAL GLASS-ES HE WEARS?
B1-YAP.
WN- HAS HE CHANGED THEM SINCE JUNIOR HIGH?
B1-YAP...HE USE TA WEAR REALLY UGLY BLACK..SORTA HORNRIMS.

B2-THEY'RE NOT WIDE ENUFF FOR HIS HEAD EITHER.
WN-HOWS THE FOOD HERE?
B1-YAP.
B2-ITS ALL RIGHT.FOR 3:00 IN THE MORNING...
WN-HAVE YOU FINISHED YOUR CHRISTMAS SHOPPING YET?
B!-YAP.HAD IT ALL DONE LAST YEAR.
B2-YEA, GOT ALL THE KIDS NEW STRETCH ARMSTONGS
WN-DID YOU DRIVE BACK FROM L.A.?
B2-NO, WE FLEW BACK. (SUE-"COM'N WE GOTTA GO")
WN-OK,OK,OK...
B1-SHE FROM DETROIT?
WN-YEAH, SHE WANTS TO GO TO A PARTY WITH THE MONSTERS.
B1 HOW DO YOU LIKE THE MONSTERS?
WN-THEY'RE ALRIGHT, I LIKE THEM. HOW DO YOU LIKE THEM?
B1-THEY'RE KINDA HIPPIE. OLD WAVE.
WN-HOW ABOUT NIAGRA?
B1-WHO'S HE?
WN-HTATS THE LEAD GUITAR-IST.
B1-LEAD GUITARIST,YEAH, LES PAULS HTATS THE ONE I HAVE, THAT LITTLE SKIN-NY ONE THATS A LES PAUL.
B2-PUT A DIFFERENT PICK-UP ON IT.I hAINTED IT DIFFERENT.
WN-WHT DID YOU GUYS DO DRIVING BACK...?
B!-(SNAPS)WE FLEW BACK. DAVID BOWIE SAID MUSICANS AS GOOD AS YOU BOYS YOU FLY BACK,YOU HIRE PEOPLE TO DRIVE YOUR EQUITMENT BACK. WE SAID OK.
WN-IS IT TRUE ABOUT BOWIE

nancial support through benefit shows. At Bookie's Club 870, on Friday and Saturday, May 5 and 6, 1978, fourteen bands played a benefit for the second issue. The cash raised was more than enough to help publish the magazine. "The amount was a ton for us at the time, I think around the $1,200-$1,400 range. Of course that didn't just pay for the printing bill, but also for rent at

PRODUCING YOUR ALBUM?
B2-YEAH,THATS WHY WERE
GOING TO FLY TO TOKYO.
WN-WHEN ARE YOU GOING?
B1-IN FEBUARY,WERE GONNA
RECORD AN ALBUM THERE.
WN-GONNA PUT ALL YOUR
SONGS ON IT?
B1- YEAH!ABOUT 30SECONDS
OF EACH SONG...
B2-NO SEE WE HAVE ABOUT
50 OR 60 SONGS AT LEAST.
WN-YOU DO?? I'VE HEARD
A BUNCH OF THEM BUT ITS
MOSTLY THE SAME ONES.
B1-YEAH BUT WITHOUT OUR
EQUIPMENT.
B2-WHERES JUST CETAIN
THINGS THAT ARE MORE
POSSIBLE LIVE.
WN-DO YOU THINK HE MAY
SABATAGE YOUR ALBUM AS
OTHERS HAVE ACCESED HIM
IN THE PAST?
B1-I'D LIKE TO SEE HIM
TRY. HAHAHAHA.WELL BEAT
HIM UP IF WE DON'T LIKE
WHAT IT SOUNDS LIKE.
YOU MEAN STEAL OUR MAT-
ERIAL?
WN-NO.YOU'VE HEARD THE
RAW POWERE MIX?
B1-HE DIDN'T MIX RAW PO-
WER, I THOUGHT IT WAS
JUST LUST FOR LIFE AND
THE IDIOT.
WN-HE ALSO DID RAW POWER.

WN-THENTRANSFORMER
B1-YEA BUT HE SAID IGGY
THATS THE MIX IGGY WANTED,
HE TOOK ORDERS FROM IGGY,
IGGY LIKES IT.
WN-DO YOU LIKE IGGY?
B1-YEA I DO.I LIKE HIS NEW
STUFF, IT HAS PRETTY BIZZARE
MIXES ON IT, LOTTA SUSUTILTI
MIXES ON IT,LOTTA SUBTLETIES
LOTTA STUFF IS RIPPED OFF
GERMAN BANDS LIKE NUE.HES
GOT A GOOD BACK UP BAND.
WN-WHATS YER FAVE TV SHOWS
B1-DIVORCE COURT.
B2-WE HAVENT SEEN ANY FOR
A LONG TIME.
B1-DRAGNET.
WN-DID YOU MAKE LOTS OF
MONEY WHILE YOU WERE OUT
IN LA?
B2-MORE THAN HERE.WE PLAY-
ED A LOT MORE PLACES
B1-ABOUT ---HUNDRED A NITE

B2-WHICH ISNT VERY MUCH
WHEN YOU SPIT BETWEEN 5 OR
6 PEOPLE, CAUSE YOU CANT
PLAY 5 NITES A WEEK.
WN-IM DEVO?
B2-AND YOU MAY NOT EVEN
KNOW IT.
B1-YOU BET.
WN-EVERYONE IS, NO EX-
CEPTIONS?
B2-EVERYBODY IS,JUST IN A
DIFFERENT CONTEXT.THERE IS

GOOD DEVO AND THERE IS BAD
DEVO.
WN-HOW BAD IS BAD DEVO?
B2-J.EDGAR HOOVER WAS REAL
BAD DEVO. IF YOUR DEVO A
AND YOU KNOW IT AND UN-
DERSTAND IT AND CAPITAL-
IZE ON IT,ITS NOT(BAD)
ITS WORKING WITHIN YOUR
LIMITATIONS THEN.
WN-YOU MUST BE THE PERFECT
PERSON TO EXPLAIN THE
PHENOMENA OF DEVEVOLUTION
JERRY-THATS TRUE!..PLEDGE
OF SOLIDARITY AMONG THE
HAVE NOTS,ALL THE MUTANTS
ALL THE DISENFRANCHISED
AND DISPOSSESSED.THE DIS-

EASED,SICK,EXCEPTIONAL
AND RETARTED. ALL THESE
WHO DONT FORM THE SO CALL-
ED NORMAL CENTER,THE WAD
THAT IS REALLY THE SCOPE
OF DEVEVOLUTION.ITS THINGS
FALLING APART,DEVOLVING,
GOING FORWARD TO GO BACK-
STRIPPING DOWN REDUCTIVE
SYNTHESIS.
WN-I SAW YOU GET HIT WITH
A SPRING AND IT DIDNT FAZE
YOU.SO I KNOW YOU NOT HUMAN
J-YEA THERES NOTHING IN MY
HEADTHAT COULD BE HURT,ES-
PECIALY ME. WERE NOT HUMAN
THIS IS NOT A RAP WERE NOT
HUMAN.WE APPEAR TO BE HU_
MAN.WE HAD THERANDOM MIS-
FORTUNE OF BEING BORN TO
TO HUMAN PARENTS.HETROSEX-
UAL PARENTS OF THIS COM-
MON GENETIC PULL SAUD PAR-
ENTS,WORKING CLASS PEOPLE
WHO HOSTED OUR ENTRY AND
WERE JUST DOING OUR DUTY
WERE ACTUALLY PREFORMING
A SERVICE AND FOLLOWING
OUR GENETIC IMPAIRATIVE,
IF YOU KNOW WHAT I MEAN.
WN-DO YOU HAVE ARTIFICIAL
ORAFICES?
J-NO UNFORTUNATLY WE STILL
SHIT,PISS,PUKE,GET SICK
AND HAVE SEXUAL DESIRE
WERE WORKING ON ALL OF THAT.
THAT.
WN-ANY TITLES FOR YOUR ALBUM
ALBUM.
J-IT WILL MOST LIKLY BE
THE MOST IMPORTANT QUESTION
AND ANSWER ARE WE NOT MEN IS
THE QUESTION AND OF COURSE
THE ANSWER IS WE ARE DEVO.
SO IT WILL BE A QUESTION
AND ANSWER ALBUM IN THE
DIDACTIC MODE.
WN- WHO IS MR.DNA

J-MR. DNA IS A PERSON-
IFICATION OF THE MAJOR
FORCE THAT BECAUSE
IN SOME PEOPLE THERE
IS AN ALTRUISTIC GENE
THAT MAKES THEM SAC-
RIFICE THEMSELVES FOR
THE GOOD OF THE RACE

DEVO IS THE MUSICAL
EXPRESSION OF THAT
FACTOR AS A GROUP WE
PRESENT A COLLECTIVE UNIT
PREFORMING ITS GENETIC
INPARITIVE ITS SACRAFICED
IN ORDER TO MOVE IT AHEAD
WE'RE THE ONLY PEOPLE
NOT GIVING PEOPLE THE SAME
OLD SHIT IS WHAT IT COMES
DOWN TO. THE ONLY PEOPLE
WHO REALLY ARE PUNK WE
DON'T HAVE TO WEAR LEATHERS
AND SWASTIKAS FOR POSITIVE
MUTATION RATHER THAN OUT-
MODED OLD WAVE REBELLION
WHICH IS AS AN IMAGE AND
AS AN ASTETIC AN STUPID.
THATS THE DIFFERENCE BE-
TWEEN US AND PUNK.PUNK
IS STUPID. NO PUNK SHOULD
GET MAD ABOUT THAT BECAUSE
THATS THE ESSENCE OF PUNK-
STUPIDITY AND IF THEY
CANT TAKE ITS LIKE IF
SPUD FITS WEAR IT WHICH
I TELL PEOPLE OFTEN.
WN-SHOULD PEOPLE TAKE
DWVO SERIOSLY?
J- ABSOLUTELY! WE'RE ALL
DEVO!

WN-THE BAND I MEAN.
J-WELL THE BAND IS A MAN-
IFESTATION OF THE WORK-
ING REALITY OF DEVOLUTION
AND IN THAT SENSE SHOULD
BE TAKEN SERIOSLY AS SE-

RIOSLY AS ANYTHIG SHOULD
BE TAKEN WHICH IS THAT
EVERYTHING IS A JOKE SO
YOU CAN TAKE IT FROM THERE.
WN-MARK WHERE DID YOU GET
THAT BUFFALO SKIN ROBE:
REAL SEXY.
M-I GOT IT FROM JOE WALSH.
WN-REALLY OUT OF PLACE IN
YOUR ACT.
M-ABSOLUTELY!WE DID IT
CAUSE WE'RE FROM OHIO.
J.-IT DENEGRATES THE MTYH-
OLOGY OF WESTERN MAN WITH
ONE SWIFT STROKE OF THE
PONCHO.
WN-HOW COME YOU DIDN'T DO
BOOJIE BOY TONIGHT?
M-NOBODY WANTED IT.
J-NOBODY DESERVED IT.
M-NOBODY WANTED IT. HE HAD
A FRESH PLAYPEN THAT WAS
JUST PAINTED BRITE PINK IN
THE WINGS.
WN- WERE PEOPLE SUPPOSED TO
TO SCREAM OUT FOR HIM?
M-WHY NOT. IT HAPPENS
EVERYWHERE ELSE. OHIOS
THE ONLY PLACE THAT DOES-
N'T KNOW WHATS HAPPENING!
J-IS THAT WHAT I GOT HIT
WITH A SPRING?
WN-YEAH,OUT OF A SEAT.
J-WHO THREW IT.DIDYOU SEE?
WN-NO, I JUST SAW IT BOUNCE
OFF YOUR HEAD.
J-HE'LL BE PUNISHED BY GOD.
WN- IS GOD DEVO?
J-ABSOLUTELY.

Q.are they nòt devo?
A.thëy are pëe-pol!

PAUL GINSUKNIFE

If 'NEVER MIND THE BOLLOCKS' was indeed the shot heard around the world, then the premier DEVO album is the answer. You can call it art-rock, parody, next wave, machine music, clone music, sci-fi, or even the music of the 80's. No matter, its at least the most original, vital, freshest, and most listenable album of the year. EXTERIOR PUNCH & JUDY THEATER Paul: Hi you guys, going in or coming out?

Gary Richel: Coming out. We just ran the first show. Know anyone who needs a ticket. We decided not to see the second show.

PAUL: Maybe. Wasn't the first that good?

GARY: Yeah, but we gotta go.

PAUL: How many encores?

GARY: Two. Good show.

CUT TO VINYL: Some complain, i.e. 4 songs already released on singles, too many good songs left out (Mr. DNA 'Smart Patrol') etc,. Perhaps with some validity, but I have no complaints with the exception of 'Shrivel VP' which is impossible to get out of your head. (Which is not a compliment) DEVO delivers the combination TALKING HEADS are supposed to Urban mores exposed for their inherent humor plus rolling rock laced with a twist of repitition as seen thru the sound board of Brian Eno; or the supposed ultimate colaberation of producer and group. After all, which two enities have a better sense of humor and total dissrespect for sytherisers and any electronic advance? INTERIOR PUNCH & JUDY DEVO opens with two songs not even on the album which none the less cuts thru the shit and captures the audience.

S. Kay Young

S. Kay Young

S. Kay Young

Mark dives into the fray latter courtesy of a radio mike. The first enco re ends signaling the traditional yell for the appearance of 'Boo-ji Boy' in his crib. Of course, no one (almost) in Detroit knows of the tradition, but he appears anway. A hilarious falsetto version of 'THE WORDS GET STUCK IN MY THROAT' is presented san the usual complex back-up. Mark seizes the audience anc creaks 'We're like from Akron where the rubber tires are made and we just wanted to see Detroit and find out just what you do with them.' Many laugh, many just look at each other. Mark then closes with 'Good Night Detroit' I really dig where you're Heads are at (pause). We are all DEVO!! CUT TO VINYL The album is selling well, but from the breaks they've had, you'd expect another pound of MEATLOAF su (ex)cess. E., stories both in Time & Newsweek, Saturday Night Live, Midnight Special, all major & minor American rock rags plus the creme of ENGLISH PRESS

Too much too soon? They also earned the prestigious gushes from I. POP, David Bowie, B. Eno, M. Jagger, & N. Young. So why hasn't the album rocketed? How should I know? If I did I probably wouldn't be writing this, but I will guess this is thier speak. With their odd fussions of swell noise and sure shrieking vocals, their appeal can only spread so far. Still though the image in print, on vinyl and in person is an easy to remember slogan.

CUT TO: CLOSED OFF BALCONY OF THE PUNCH & JUDY AFTER THE SHOW. While no general interview was planned, we were told to get a drink, eat, and enjoy the party while the boys unwinded. What bits we could get from them individually was encouraged. Myself, I was a bit hesitant, the

DEVO, *White Noise* #3. ▲ ▶

combo of how sticky their past interviews had got, plus their new found fame, ga pause. However, May I now submit 'The Boys R-All Rite' by me. Their egos ranged from on guard (Jerry)entertaining (Mark) to out and out humble (Ian). Alan to the point of awe, shucking the fact that he can't really be seen in the albums group shot. 'We were given the choice of two pictures & I couldn't be seen in either.' I don't recall seeing any two members together after the show   I offer some isolated tidbits stuck together for my convenience.

ALAN: (On Saturday Nite Live) It was real good, we hung around with them all week. They were all real nice. (On Eno) Kinda quiet& real nice.

MARK: (Who has a full garage of many decades of kitch) Yeah we pulled into Birmingham and I thought we were in Grosse Pointe, they both look the same to me .....weird.

PAUL: Yeah, Like even the Kroger Store is middle of the road in its tasteful appearance-wierd on a different line.

MARK. Yeah, I heard Creem was from around here.

PAUL: Yeah, Birmingham.

MARK: Yeah, well I guess that fitting.

S. Kay Young

S. Kay Young

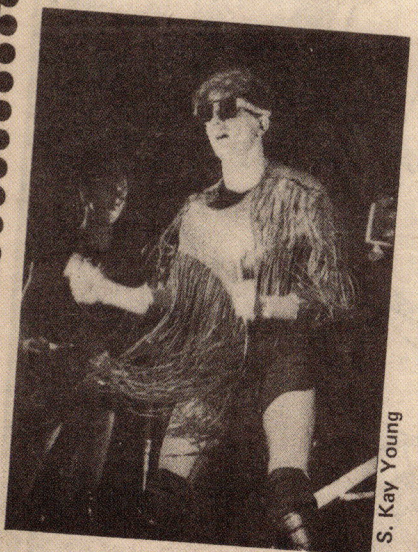

S. Kay Young

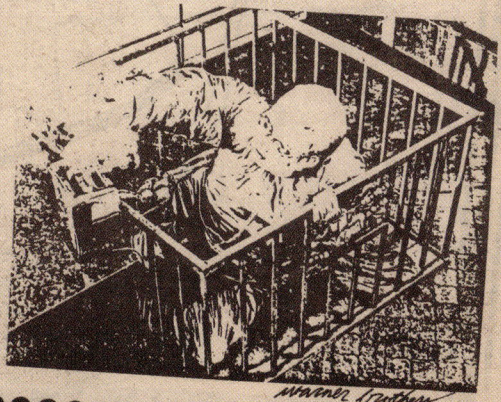

Sue Rynski

PAUL: How was Europe?

MARK: Oh they loved us and in Yugoslovia Satisfaction was No. 1 until it was knocked out by Andy Gibb.

PAUL: I saw your artwork in CLE No. 2, isn't there a book....

MARK: Yaw (with chicken bone stuck sideways in cheeks) My Travels by Booji Boy. (followed by child-like self-contented smile).

PAUL: What's the deal with the Booji Boy appearance?

MARK: They (the audience) have to want it.

PAUL: Yeah, but the way they were frenzied it could have been the usher they were screaming cause you had them.... what's the story I heard about how Jagger was shouted down by you at the Mabuhay in San Francisco.

MARK: Oh, no that wasn't really me I just yelled somption but someone from the audience was supposed to have called him an old fart. I didn't hear abuot it till after the show.

PAUL: You ought to get an inflatable plastic Mr. Potato Head for the spud song...(Mark laffs)

MARKS FEMALE COMPANION: Oh, I design the stuff and I have worked with alot of plastic and oh Mark! (pointing to giant tarp being moved across the stage by the crew) that would be real nice I bet you would like some clothes made out of that.

MARK: Yeah!

UNIDENTIFIED CREWMAN: Who are the clowns in the mock-devo suits?

PAUL: Oh, those are W4 djs and whatever. Don't you LIKE them, they're in YOUR honor! (to Mark)

MARK: (Odd smile) Hmmm.

BREAKTIME Around the end of the party Todd Rungren showed up (in a shirt with a 3 foot picture of his face on it) yelling 'Where's the hermaphradite, Where's the hermaphradite' (Skafish was at Bookies that night.) Most ignored him but when he finally got in the way of traffic with his plaroid, Mr. Vile leaped in front and bellowed in mock embarassment, "DON'T TAKE MY PICTURE". Runt stopped dead and stared, "Don't worry, I won't!!"

EPILOUGECUT TO LONG SHOT FROM BALCONY Of in the darkness a few gold spots on stage reveal two crewman chatting with Mark. Suddenly, an unidentified face from the balcony yells in perfect fan glee, "Hey Mark, We All Devo" Mark looked up a little bewildered and paused. He looked down a moment and then directly up and paused. Finally he stared back up and merely shrugged.

The show was over but alas the image had caught up with the man. Still here was a comical figure of a man who knew damn well what he was doing and laughing all the way (to the bank?)   His smile was near animated but not really insincere. More like the guy who always gets the joke or like the way the puppeter looked on the old Thunder-bird show.

I was reminded of F. Scott Fitzgerald's, "The Last Tycoon's" hero Monroe Starr at theend of the film; Alone, entering a dark abyss of a studio. I looked back to see Mark slowy adjust his polyester hounds tooth Kojak hat, turn and half skip out the darkened exit to the waiting bus.

Sonico Rendezvous Band

City Slang

Sonic's Rendezvous Band
City Slang Orchide Records
I remember seeing Sonic's Rendezvous
back when they started out in Ann
Arbor. Nothing else was going on in
Detroit musically (except bar bands),
so it was alot of fun to see something
starting again. And who better to do
it than people who started Detroit
music in the 60's, Fred"Sonic"Smith-
ex MC5, Scott Morgan-ex Rationals,
Gary Rasmussen-ex Up, and Scott
Asheton-ex Stooge. I was getting
really bored with them when good
bands started showing up everywhere,
but they kept playing unrelentislly

till they built up an avid audience.
Now after playing together over two
years, they've finally come out with
a single, City Slang. I couldn't
figure out most of the words, but I
did catch "outside of society" a line
from a Patti Smith song (it's rumored
Patti sings some backup vocals. A
gimick to get people to buy it?) However I do like this song, true Detroit
rock&roll. I guess Scott Asheton was
right when he said "It's gonna kick
ass, man." But I didn't expect a band
with as much potential as them to gyp
you by putting the same song on both
sides. It's better than their true
fans could expect, much better than
I would.   Katy Hait

what in the hell
DO YOU HAVE TO
DO TO GET IN
WHITE LIES?

BEATS THE SHIT
OUTTA ME. I LIVE
HERE TOO!

NEW DETROIT CLASS
COUPLE !!!

the *White Noise* mansion [the house Peterson and Zimmerman rented on Detroit's west side]. Seriously, I think it paid for two or three whole issues," said Zimmerman.

Sales of *White Noise* were not particularly lucrative. The co-creators learned that the best way to sell the magazine was to bring a stack to Bookie's and other local bars, and to get their "cute girl-friends to go sell 'em," as Zimmerman put it. "Guys would give them a dollar just to talk to them." Trying to distribute and sell them beyond the bars was almost pointless.

"There was no good way to do it," Zimmerman said. "We would go to record stores and say, 'Would you carry the magazine on consignment?' So, that meant with the cover charge of a dollar, we could check back in a few weeks or few months, and we might get like forty cents per issue or something. So, you couldn't say we were doing it for the money." Though it didn't sell well and lacked editorial polish, *White Noise* was the only publication writing about the Detroit punk rock scene at the time. "Mainstream press wasn't covering this stuff and there wasn't really any alternative press—so we were it," Zimmerman said. "The bands were super nice to us. We got into all the shows for free. When Bookie's came about, I was like the resident artist—I designed most of the flyers, like the first fifty flyers—and the first T-shirts and stuff. We were on something at Bookie's called 'the guest list for life'—so we never paid for shows. The arrangement for shows was, 'I can't pay you, but you can have as much beer as you want when you come for shows.' And then we had free run of the place. Upstairs is where we did the interviews."

White Noise also went to great lengths to meet international punk legends when they came to town. In late 1979, the Clash released their landmark album *London Calling*. In early 1980, the band was touring the United States with a stop in Detroit. The *White Noise* crew hatched a plan to meet their idols. According to Zimmerman, when the Clash played at the Motor City Roller Rink in Warren, they "played like a

rock & roll swindle pt. 2

PATTY SMITH/DSO BENEFIT/
MAY 17/ROC/UMD

PORTAIT OF THE ARTIST AS A POSEUR

BEFORE

Patti, constantly holding Fred Smith's hand and carressing him, insisted on silence regarding her new LP, and on her recording career entirely. "We know why we're here.", she remarked eying me suspiciously. What could she mean, I wondered. To talk about her confessions of being an old MC5 groupie? (Remember her "Free Wayne Kramer!" yelps?) Was she going to confess to writing her so-called poetry while on the can after a long night at Taco Bell? Nope. All Ms. Smith wanted to do was play huggy-bear with

Fred, and give contrived answers about her deep, deep devotions to the Detroit Symphony Orchestra. Contrived answers? Patti? Just check this out and I defy you to keep a straight face or refrain from coughing your cookies— "The symphony is like a really nice drug man...like if you're out of dope go to the symphony." Wow Patti, that is so-o-o-o heavy. Cosmic man... One must admit though, when Patti was asked why she decided to make Detroit her home, she was cute in a school-girlish way, batting her eyes — "Well, let's just say that all the things a girl could ever dream about, I found in Detroit." Awww...

Fred, on the other hand, actually seemed a little embarressed by all Patti's " Wow, it's so cosmic" replies. One believed him when he said he enjoys the orchestra.

About a year and a

half ago, I saw a considerable change going on in Detroit and also in myself. I enjoy the Symphony and think it deserves so much, but they seem to have so little knowledge of public relations." Although Patti never directly answered the questions as to whether she has seen Detroit, she says "I love Dorati, he's a great guy." And just to show her love for this type of music runs deep in her soul, Patti told us about her intimate relationship with classical- "I've seen other symphonies on television." Hey, that's great But I must admit that Ms. Smith must truly love and support the Detroit Symphony Orchestra. Why else would she do two benefit concerts for that cause? Surely not for the good press she was bound to get from her Time and Newsweek interviews regarding it. Naw...

DURING

OK, brief and to the point-RUR and Flirt were good, the classical group and the jazz band were a decent change of pace(you know, to go walk aroung outside, make a liquor run,etc.), Sonic's sucked, and the only thing which made Patti's set interesting were the oldies the band performed (Jailhouse Rock, Secret Agent Man,.......)

AFTER

Well, I'm really glad I didn't have to pay the $10.00 to get in like you suckers did! But then again, I had to help clean up the mess you slobbish assholes made, (I never knew that MD 20-20 came in that many flavors..) but it was worth it anyway-who-ever lost the bottle of Placidyl 750's, thanx.

by Steve O'Leary

HEARTBREAKERS

HEARTBREAKERS/BOOKIES/
JUNE 8&9

Johnny Thunders. The first time I saw him was onstage at the Michigan Palace in '73, when the Dolls were in the midst of there first tour. It was the first concert I had ever been to where the band actually seemed to care about it's audience, and Thunder with his maniacal riffing (not to mention his cub scout shirt...) became my no.1 hero, replacing Dick McAullife of the Tigers who had attained that position in '68 by rushing the pitchers mound and beating the absolute shit out of pitcher Tommy John (OK, I think we're getting a little off track here).

OK, point taken. Anyway, when J.T. and the Heartbreakers hit Detroit in early June for 2 nights, I didn't know exactly what to expect. After all, the group had been in existance for a couple of years, had officialy broken up last summer, and here they were making there Motor City debut a year later. (Motivation? I won't even mention lack of money and four guys with very well published hard-core habits. Hey, ya think it's free?)

The Heartbreakers- Walter Lure, Billy Rath, Jerry Nolan and Thunders- are known for both very hot performances and also for extremely erratic ones. Bookies saw both the former Friday and the later Saturday.

(let's just say that the first night all four could walk onstage without help. How ya doin' Jerry?)

Opening with 'Leave Me Alone' (aka 'Chatterbox' on the Dolls 2nd LP) and following with his dig at Johnny Lydon cum Rotten, 'London Boys' which containes the best cut down lines since Dylan's 'Postively 4th Street', 'You need an escort to take a piss/He holds your hand and he shakes your dick' -those two

were the only two songs performed off Thunders solo album, 'So Alone'. (The unreleased title cut of which was performed, with this formidable intro: 'This is dedicated to Jimmy Osterberg, before he became a David Bowie puppet. I understand Jimmy used to have a pair of balls.')

The only new song Thunders played was a rocker entitled 'M.I.A.', which wasn't bad but not special either. 'You don't need no junk just LSD...' Maybe Thunders sang that song to the Pistols but it don't work that way with these guys, as they re-titled Chuck Berry's 'Too Much Monkey Business' to the more appropriate 'Too Much Junkie Business'. Other love songs to the drug (Hey, why do ya think they call it drugs...) included 'Chinese Rocks', (which sounded miles better than the studio version) 'All By Myself', the classic 'Born To Loose', and my personal fave 'One Track Mind' ('I got tracks on my arms and tracks on my face/there's tracks on the walls all over the place'). None of that Moon/June mushy shit from these guys...

The encore Friday had an added 'attraction' -Wayne Kramer, who sat in an the Heartbreaker version of the Dave Clark 5s 'Do You Love Me'. I thought Kramer was just in the way, and from the bored expression on Johnny's face I'd say he thought so too.

The show was extremely energetic, but the best (and most amazing) thing about it was that Thunders was coherent and didn't even fall down once, even though he came pretty close to it. It's really too bad these were probably the last- ever Heartbreakers shows, but Thunders and the rest of the guys 'just can't bear it no more', too many egos, not enough luck. As Johnny himself said in late '72- 'I used to be lucky. What happened?' I guess it's just a case of going from 'Too Much Too Soon' to 'Too Little Too Late'.

—steve o'leary

Photos: Steve O'Leary

▲ The Heartbreakers, *White Noise* #5.

PAUL - What's your favorite movie?
WALTER - Um....favorite movie... gsgarble mshk....
P - What's the ugliest person you ever met?

W - Ah...ummm...ok...ahhh
JERRY - That movie we saw earlier it was not Johnny's mother and a doberman.
W - (opening eyes) What movie?
J - Somethin about a guy's mother, a doberman pincher and it was really sick.
P - What's the dumbest band you have ever seen?
W - Schrapnel...they suck, they all suck.

J - Do you like the B-52's?
W - They're funny, the girls inna the ban' are cool, the guys are real wimpy.
J - Who gives the best blow jobs in N'.Y.?
W - I couldn't devulge the secret
J&P - OH COME ON!! Give us a hint.
P - Ok-ok, lets not be silly.... who gives the second best blow job in the city?
HEIDI - What do you think of Legs McNeil?
W - E's obsolete.
J - Who's shorter than Legs McNeil?
H - Johnny Thunders (moronic squeal)
W - Yeah, Johnny gives the best blow jobs you've ever seen.
CHRIS - Is that why you came back in his band?
W - HIS band? OUR band.
P - AHAAAA (scoop rivalry)
J - Who's the fattest girl in Detroit...and don't say (she asked us not to say her name)
P - What's the thing with Heartbreakers : here just for tonight and last night?

W - Well it was supposed to be a Johnny Blunder's gig but he couldn't get a fuckin' band ta back 'em up so he called us.
J - Do you know what chunders means? (Austrailian slang meaning puke for all you uneducated curs)
W - See can't get a fuckin' band to back 'em up so he just asks the Heartbreakers and that's that.
P - Do ya think it was worthwhile?

W - Yeah... I suppose.
J - You are like buddies aren't 'cha always chummin' around?
W - We never got along - we never hang out...
J - Do you know what chunders means....
C - I thought you guys were fighting all the time.
W - Yeah its fightin' it's minor really. Anyone got a butt? (Looks at shocked Chris and Heidi) A cigarette ya know...
P - What do you think of interviews?
W - Usually they ask...dumb questions...
P - (insulted) Can you tell me any good ones? So I can be better in the future?
W - Uhhh...um..no..ahhh
P - Any closing remarks?
W - Ah...you haven't heard the last of da Heartbreakers...
P - Really? You mean even as a feature group?
W - Well there's an album out now a new live album...its out in N.Y. now it'll be out...
BILL - ALRIGHT GIRLS OUT! WHY DO YOU STAND THERE LOOKIN' SO FUCKING DUMB? THE MAN'S GOING TO GIVE A TICKET.I DON'T GIVE A SHIT! OUT THE DOOR!!!
W - The world thinks we're all drug fiends but it's not true...
J - Who pushed Billy Doll in the pool? (Dolls first drummer who died of an overdose)
W - (Unintelligible answer)

mr. ed and mr. lure

photos by sue ryaski

▲ Walter Lure of the Heartbreakers, *White Noise* #5.

gurls page...

cubes

PENATRATION/THE CUBES/ BOOKIES CLUB 870/ IS IT LOVE OR IS IT ...CONFUSION ? WHEN THE GIRLS MEET THE GIRLS...

What stuck me about Pauline Murray of Penetrtion as I watched her was that she was in a position of devastating romance-in part of a burgeoning global scene (isn't it?); what struck me was that she was dark-eyed, stooped over when she skipped around the stage, elfin-like, a black bandana on darker hair, dwarfed next to her fellow Penetration players, a tiny pretty girl committed, it appeared, to MAKING THE SHOW WORK: a zoom girl from side to side, microphone in hand, she utilized her limited space to high effect bouncing in front of a band that prefered to bang it out without glamor, professionally. The Steve Jones method of HM, make the guitars ring out HEAVY without losing the speed attack andyou've got a suitable music for headbanging.

A cool beat and a girl of action. "Life's a Gamble" was ten times better than the single ,much more drama,booming, guitar drive, "Stone Heroes" was the heaviest number: a near Black Sabbath chord gloom frenzy introduced the song, and "Lovers of Outrage", which simmers at the berage, which simmers at the beginning and breaks loose at the chorus,was the pretiest. Penetration encored with 'Nostalgia", the first Peter Schelly-algia (possizbly the best romantics song writer in England) (WHO?- tune to Mr. all for america Ed.)-tune to ever be performed in Detroit. Penetration are aband for the Great Lakes, a sure winner in this part of the world-young, loud,neat,heavy,clena,no ostentation or flacid glamor power trips, or wimpy gimmickry. A true band for the heartland. As for the Cubes, who opened for Penetration, I would like to digress a bit, put it into real perspective.

Recently, at the New Miami, my friend asked:"Isn't that the girl from the Cubes?" I turned around, and she was there, at a table near the pinball machines. "Yes," I said. Later that night, at home, I thought "i would like to kiss her entire body."The LENGTH of her.(Really Walter,does your mother know you write for this paper? -outraged Ed.) During the Cubes gig at Penetration I thought similarly, only, as I support the cause of music in its pertant the exhileration in its performance, I watched and listened to as MUCH as I could. I told another friend, along the waym to watch her eyes,very expressive, I warned. To my horror,with no concern whatever for my anticipation, she appeared initially with dark sunglasses, a huge mistake for my moneym covering up an essential performance asset-eyes that LOOK out and RESPOND. "Love those eyes", the friend said.

The set-up is really quite good, Laurie plays the organ on occasion, dances with lovely clumsy enthysiaam earnestly, and moves naturally very well super-good real horrorshow rock'n'roll style not like a girl at all except maybe Tina Turner who has not been a girl for some time now. I'm all for girls in show business. What I lile about the band is that they really don't sound like anybody: not to say,sorry all, that they have a sound of their own. Most times I could not distinguish ANYTHING,but........ a raunchy blast,itchingly brittle and metally,scratchy,icyunbalanced. A horrible musical show. Punk-stop-ndings and those went out when Mark Perry changed the stsvle of Alternative TV. (warning watch All trends)-and that was near a year ago. Still, htere is something to this band. And eventually I want a TASTE of it.

-WALTER STOOGE

The Cubes, *White Noise* #5. ▲

"White Noise End of the World Circus," *White Noise* #5. ▶

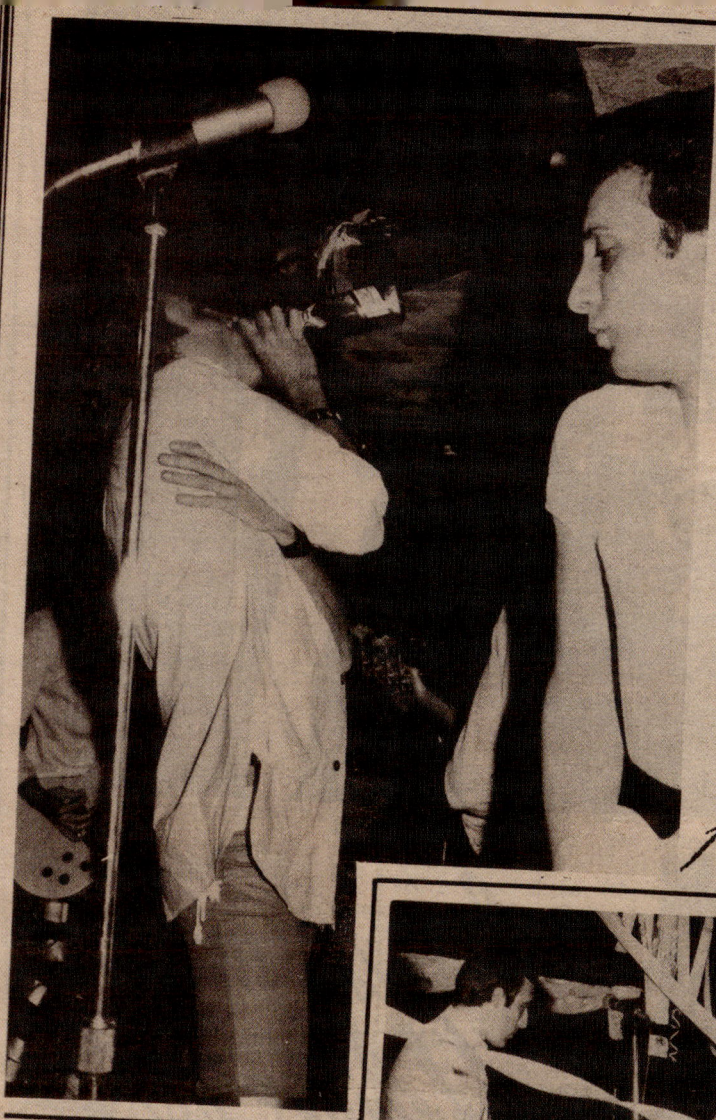

photos: randy rauf

— coldcock —

*you i had real fun.
WE WOULD LIKE TO
THANK ALL THE SWELL
BANDS. THANK RUR,
RETRO, CINECIDE, BLIND
BONERS, DENIZENS,
COLDCOCK, CAPITAL
PUNISHMENT, PIGS &
EVERYONE ELSE!!!
I CAN'T WAIT TILL
THE NEXT W.N. SHOW.
I HOPE IT HAS
SAFER GAMES THAN
THAT BLOODY LIMBO!*

— Retro —

THE WHITE NOISE END OF THE WORLD CIRCUS/WEDNESDAY/MAY 23rd/BOOKIES CLUB 870/

NIGHT OF TERROR

I had a baseball game that night and prayed for rain so I could attend the 'White Noise End of the World Circus' without missing the ballgame losing my chance for playing time, which has been so limited anyway, and the rain, although it threatened to fall, never did and I ended up missing and now, as I write this trendy little piece find myself benched and unhappy-a good ball player like myself needs steady work, essential to his game.

Not only that, but the fucking newspaper I write (and write) for wouldn't allow me a guest on that night- do I see any of that money you greedy mother-fuckers ?!(Yes, we are buying you the book 'How to Express Ones Self Without the Use of Four-letter words-Ed.)

I should mention, before I begin the actual story, that none of this effected my time at the club Bookie that night, a real trouper that I am, when it comes to watching THINGS IN THE WORLD,like rock'n'roll shows. Firstly, I forced my eyes and ears on the Blind, who feature that tall green haired punk with all the un-hip badges and earings and ripped leather and shit which is just SO UNCOOL. The band was real loose and stunk and despite this the bartenders all had a good time dressed up with white faces and costumes as they frequennly looked at the brightly decorative streamers criss crossing the bar or served drinks as is their job.

As for the decorations, Mark Norton said, commandingly,"Tear 'em down, right now!"(some guys ya just can't trust even at your own party-P.O.ed ED.)

And they did. And Mark, slicked hair sun glasses Dawn of the Dead T-shirt,smiled in triumph. The Twenty Seven were really good (which they should have been after disappearing for an hour when it was their cue-time-Mr. Kept waitng Ed.) their first show without a keyboard in some time,tight,hard,funny,Mark mentioning Roger Corman and George Romero,the new single "Don't Go to Extremes, rendered expertly,an encore featuring the flip-side "Catastrophe and "Life-blood.

Then came the Romantics (really local gals Chris ,Heidi,Connie and Sue) who were as cute as I've ever seen them and "Little White Lies" sounded just like the record. (Their miming to the record was the kind of thing you had to be their to believe,but take my word for it ,it was AWFUL.I almost busted a gut-meddlesome Ed.) Oh,and I should hate to forget those great posters downstairs (the foto and kissing boothes-Mr. tellin' the truth for the unfortunates not there Ed.)and the people responsible for them who I would hate to forget to mention in this story.

I will mention, at this point, htat I intend to be fair, that none of the White Noise fortune will tempt mw into the inferno of deceit,lying,pre-judjement,slanted reporting and all other propaganda.This all in preface to a report on the Boners,whom I watched in all seriounes(reflected by this writing , no?).

The Boners are simultaneously funny,angry,frightful,anti-artful, hate-ful,juvenile,pre-nuptial,over-dressed,non musical,compulsively ly orchestral,image hounds,dogs of alcoholic fury,a group that should LEAVE this century to model the Savage State for the next one.

Jerry Vile is better than Stiv Bators and Mike Rushlow cannot be compared to any other guitarist.

Which left Cinecide, who are a good group. This writer, who believes that now is not the time to discuss the Cinecide group the way he would like (he would like to say 'good group,professional,abitious,serious'-but the tone is inappropriate here and it has to be another magazine,where the band can be appreciated for what they ARE),(hurumph-Ed.) merely reports that he liked the beat, was dancing to the group, liked 'Gutless Radio,' was infinitely more tired than when he walked in, and left at about the middle of the set, an unflattering remark but true.
(But better than Trouser Press,eh guys?)

-WALTER A. BRAT

Art in any media has always had to be able to come up and slap me in the face. Whether it's on canvas, film or in music, if it doesn't have this quality, then it becomes just a part of the background. Something that can be ignored as easily as not. I respect nothing more than an artist with the guts to say, "Here's my work - take it or leave it." No compromise. This isn't always a popular view. In fact, this can cause quite a bit of friction between an artist and the observer. One of my first experiences of this "friction" in a live performance was an Iggy and the Stooges concert right before "Funhouse" came out in 1970. In his pre-Bowie days, Iggy Pop was an artist, using his body as his media. The Stooges music wasn't presented to the audience, but rammed down their throats. People loved it or hated it. I remember three guys pulling Iggy off the stage and punching him in the middle of a song. But art created under pressure is often art at it's best. It was a long time until I say this kind of energy again...

One winter night in January 1978, I wandered into the red carpet lounge and sw a band called the Ramrods perform. The place was packed to capacity and it was no surprise. The Ramrods, wearing black pants and white shirts drenched in sweat, gave one of the most energetic performances I've seen. And Mark Norton's vocals made sure no one was going to hang out in the bathroom during this set.

The Ramrods broke up shortly after this and went separate ways. But it wasn't long until another band with Mark Norton - the 27 - began appearing around town generating this same kind of energy. I saw this band for the first time in March 1978 at a bar called the Red Grape, which was experimenting with new music at that time. Backed by Craig Peters on guitar and Steve McGuire on bass, the 27 soon became one of the most forceful groups in Detroit, taking a firm no-nonsense approach to music.

During the summer of 1978, the 27 added Russel Sumner on electronic keyboards. I remember one night in particular at Bookie's when Russel, wearing a white lab coat, opened up the 27's set with a short electronic solo. People literally stopped in the middle of conversations to listen in amazement. This solo evolved into "Short and Sweet" which Russel also sang, followed by Mark coming on stage to do "Pablo Picasso." This set reached out and slapped everyone in the face, showing just how creative Detroit bands can be if they want to.

The 27 have gone thru various personnel changes and currently has Steve McGuire taking over vocals as well as playing bass. The 27 sound as powerful as ever as they recently demonstrated at the Tremor Record Revue at Bookie's. Mark Norton hasn't lost any energy either as he also demonstrated at the Tremor revue, being backed by a new band. But I don't need to wish Mark any luck in this new venture. Mark Norton has proven himself to be a survivor.

By Kirk Widdis

w.n. history no.1

ramrods '77

©'77 S

mark norton

NO.6

WHITE noise

—80's ROCK·THE '27—
ALSO:2 MAGS FOR PRICE OF 1!!
IN THIS ISSUE:'STREET LIFE'no

band possessed, because the show before that one, their first in Detroit, they'd been blown off stage by the opening act [former New York Dolls front man] David Johansen. I think they played close to three hours, and it was brutally hot inside."

Zimmerman remembered the plan to meet the band:

I was hanging with [Mark] Norton [of the Ramrods] that night, and he got word the band was going to Lili's [a bar in Hamtramck] afterward. So we scrambled over to Hamtramck. We found Joe Strummer, Paul Simonon, and filmmaker/Big Audio Dynamite co-founder Don Letts at the end of the bar. I went up to Strummer and asked if he wanted to buy a copy of *White Noise*. Letts, indignant, stepped forward and said, "Do you know who you are asking for money?" "Yeah," I said, "and I know he can spare a buck." Joe mumbled something about supporting the local scene and bought a copy. We started talking about the show, how important it was for them to conquer Detroit, and someone to my right offered them some coke. "Oh, no thanks," Joe said politely, "We have our own."

The sixth and final issue of *White Noise* was created in late 1979. By then, Zimmerman was running the magazine solo without the benefit, or liability, of Peterson, who ended his hands-on role after the fourth issue. Looking back on it, Zimmerman said he hadn't planned for issue six to be the final one, but the money just wasn't there. Advertising was scarce. The magazine mostly took ads for Bookie's and a few clothing resale and record shops around town. The magazine's sporadic print schedule didn't help build confidence in advertisers, which made it hard to bring in the money.

The idea behind the sixth issue was that customers would get two magazines for the price of one. The split magazine was based

After a while, *White Noise* started getting attention outside of Detroit and beyond the punk scene. According to Zimmerman: "David Keeps [former manager of Destroy All Monsters] became buddies with [future *Silence of the Lambs* director] Jonathan Demme. Keeps and I went to Chicago because [Demme] was doing a premiere [of *Melvin and Howard*]. And we got to go to like a big, ritzy hotel. . . . Demme just kept asking us about music. . . . He was going to do this movie called *Urgh! A Music War*, and his idea was to do like two or three songs from each band, but the key would be that all bands had to be unsigned. . . . And we of course told him about Jerry Vile and Boners, and there was some Super 8 footage of it. We sent that to Demme."

Demme never made *Urgh! A Music War*, but a director named Derek Burbridge did. In 1982, that version featured performances by many punk and new wave favorites including DEVO, the Cramps, Oingo Boingo, Dead Kennedys, Pere Ubu, Echo and the Bunnymen, the Go-Go's, Gary Numan, and the Police. However, Demme tapped Vile to act in his film *Who Am I This Time?*

on a strategy some punk and independent music labels had used: offering a split single as a way to broaden the appeal of their bands and share the cost. The final offering featured an issue of *White Noise* on one side and a new publication, *Street Life*, on the other.

Street Life writer Mark Kliem said the magazine was an off-shoot of another short-lived Detroit punk rock magazine called *Spooee!*, which was created by Detroit writer Johnny Chamberlain and published three times between December 1978 and April 1979.

In terms of design, the first issue of *Spooee!* was much more professional looking than the first few issues of *White Noise*. Both were tabloid size, but Chamberlain's magazine was professionally typeset. With a cover price of twenty-five cents, Kliem said, he didn't believe Chamberlain sold many issues of *Spooee!*, but that really didn't seem to matter. "It was really just a vanity project of Johnny's. He had aspirations of being a writer," Kliem said.

WHAT KIND OF ANIMAL READS

WHITE NOISE MAIL FRAUD DEPT.

SEND $5 TO: WHITE NOISE, p.o. box 5301
(6 ISSUES) NORTHVILLE, MICHIGAN
48167
name
address
City   state
zip   age
sex   fathers' salary
favorite color   favorite position
CHECK INTERESTS
BELOW
like to walk the dog
like to push around handicaps
like to have sex while watching t.v.

▲ Subscription ad, *White Noise* #2.

◀ Patti Smith/Debbie Harry contest, *White Noise* #2.

HEY GALS! OUR AMAZING OFFER STILL STANDS! ALL YOU HAVE TO DO IS POSE NEWD FOR THE WHITE NOISE CENTERFOLD! IT'S FUN! IT'S EASY!

$10.00

REMEMBER — IN A FEW YEARS YOU'LL BE PLAYING SOCCER WITH THOSE BAZOOMS ANYWAY!

In an editorial for the first twelve-page issue of *Spooee!*, Chamberlain wrote, "This magazine is the culmination of hard work, a fantasy, and a vendetta against people who've censored and sneered at what I do best—write. . . . I don't care what anybody thinks about this project; it's mine. It's my best shot. I don't even care of [sic] the publication folds after this inaugural issue. All I want to do is give a good, honest try. Thirty years from now, I won't be wondering why I didn't. I've made one of my dreams reality. Everybody who ever tried to thwart me from realizing my fantasy, can, to paraphrase Richard Pryor, kiss my fat, happy, ass." Next to the editorial was a photo of Chamberlain looking like writer Hunter S. Thompson—sporting a fishing hat, aviator-style sunglasses and a cigarette in a holder hanging out of his mouth. The first issue included features on Detroit bands Cinecyde, RUR, and the Romantics, as well as interviews with David Johansen and former David Bowie guitarist Mick Ronson.

White Noise co-creator Paul Zimmerman remembered seeing an issue of *Spooee!* at Bookie's Club 870 and knew Chamberlain from the scene. "Johnny was kind of a nerdy-looking nice guy and one of the very first black guys to make the scene," said Zimmerman.

▼ *SPOOEE!* #1, December 1978.

Spooee! contributor Linda Roy published three issues of *Street Life* before it ceased in 1981.

After Mark Kliem moved from Detroit to San Francisco in the early 1980s, he said Roy would contact him from time to time with plans to restart the magazine. But he never got involved. Roy was a little like Jerry Peterson in his early *White Noise* days. "[Linda Roy] would get away with murder with just saying that she was putting out a magazine. Which prompted the old joke: 'How many punk rockers does it take a change a light bulb?' 'One to change the light bulb and thirty to be on the guest list,'" said Kliem.

After publication ceased in 1981, the magazine's creators tried a few times to restart it in the early 1980s. It's not known exactly how many issues were created before *Street Life* ended for good, but issues dated as late as 1983 have been found.

Kliem and several other staffers from *Spooee!* brought *Street Life: The Magazine of Detroit Street Culture* together with the sixth, and final, issue of *White Noise* in late 1979/ early 1980. Roy was the chief architect of the magazine. In her first-issue editorial, she wrote, "You and I both know this city needs a vehicle for advant-garde [sic] music, politics and entertainment. Surprisingly enough, music/politics/ entertainment and truth are the fundamentals of *Street Life* Magazine." Little did Roy know that a new vehicle for such things would take shape less than a year later and on a larger scale. The new free paper would hit the streets of Detroit twice a month starting in October 1980. It was called the *Detroit Metro Times*.

◄ *Street Life* #1, late 1979.

SPOOEE!
November, 1978
ONLY 25 CENTS!

SKY DANIELS on chits & chats
TRAITORS
COMPUTE
ANALYSIS
NEW WAY
PATT and SON VISIT

Fred "Sonic" Smith

MUTANTS   FLIRT   NIKKI COR

PREMIER ISSUE!
$1.00
STREETLIFE
The Magazine Of Detroit Street Culture

INSIDE: ROMANTICS/DAVID JOHANSEN/MICK RONSON
Fashion, film...FUN!!
ALSO INSIDE: WHITE NOISE no.6!
2 mags for price of 1!

▼ Crab Monkeys ad, *White Noise* #3.

The Jonestown Play Set ad, *White Noise* #3. ▲

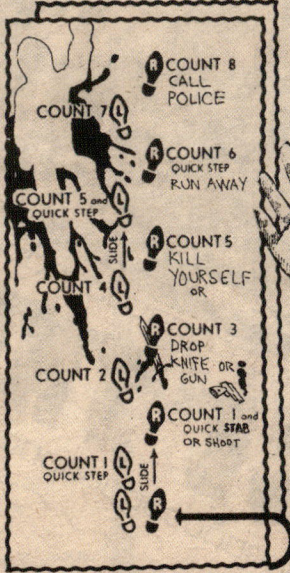

Sid Vicious murder, *White Noise* #3. ▲

WHITE NOISE BENEFIT no.1

GALLERY OF WHITE NOISE BENEFIT STARS (CLOCKWISE)
TIMMY DENIZEN SNEAKING A FEEL—NIKKI OF CONVERTABLES BEG PETER NOT TO FIRE
TIMMY BREAKS DOWN EMBARASSING OTHER DENIZENS—GEATINO UPSTAGES NIKKI
CORVETTE—RON ASHTON BEHIND THOSE FOSTER GRANTS—MIKE PIG YODELS—VINCE
SILLY IN KATY HAIT'S SUIT—27'S BEFORE DRASTIC CHANGES—MITCH RYDER SPOTS EX-CLEBS
ROB TYNER AND LESTER BANGS—TED LUCAS SPLITS QUICK—M-50 FORGETS HOW TO
STAND UP, AGAIN—SEATBELTS—NORTRON ACCIDENTLY HEARS HIS VOICE THROUGH
P.A.—BEN WAUGH SHOWING OFF HIS CHAINS—KATY HAIT GROWS A THIRD LEG WHILE
GLORIA LOOKS ON UNIMPRESSED—MARK AND STEVE.

PHOTOS BY SUE RYNSKI AND S.KAY YOUNG .

m-50

sillies

nikki

fans   all ph

▲ *White Noise* benefit report, *White Noise* #2.

thanks to

denizens

cinecyde

27's

coldcock

WHITE NOISE BENEFIT

pigs

chas

seat belts

capital punishment

plus
destoy all monsters
subdafuge
and
all who helped

s by sue rynski except fans by s. kay young design by paul

▲ *White Noise* benefit and centerspread, *White Noise #2.*

Punk's Not Dead

By the early 1980s, the original Bookie's punk scene was dying out. New wave and other styles of new music were becoming popular, and Jerry Peterson was diversifying his portfolio. He formed new bands like the Big Time Country Orchestra, Jerry Vile and the Martini Set, and 52 Devil Babies Born with Tails to work on new music and performance ideas. By 1982, Peterson was gaining recognition for his performances outside of Detroit and was cast by director Jonathan Demme in his PBS film *Who Am I This Time?*, based on a short story by novelist Kurt Vonnegut Jr. and starring Susan Sarandon and Christopher Walken.

Boners flyer also promoting Jerry Vile's PBS debut, circa 1982. ▶

GAME OF DETROIT

The FUN Magazine Game Of Detroit is a action packed ex[...] and fun filled game for the entire family. It can be played by a[...] the ages of eight to eighty who enjoys non-stop thrills [...] shenanagins. You'll spend hour after exciting [...] troit, where anything can happen, and us[...]

You can throw out all your ot[...] The Game of Detroit is not unlik[...] does not skirt the real iss[...] which violence, pain, and misf[...] it's not. It's the Game [...]

ZONE [...]

WEST SIDE, ZO[...]

2) Forgot to hide your money [...]
3) Flat tire, stop at Amirs Mobil [...]
4) No turning back, free turn.
5) Hitchhiker, call Americas Most Wanted, ear[...] bucks.
6) You are in a high speed chase, 2 free turns.
7) Watch crackhouse burn down , lose 1 turn.
8) Need money for crack, sell child for sex, earn $35.
9) Car forced off road and you are shot. Roll die for injuries.
10) Bum asks for money, tell him to get a job, he shoots you, roll die for injuries.
11) Stop to pee in alley, rat bites gonads, lose 2 turns.
12) Jet crashes on freeway, pretend you are a priest, earn $2000.

DOWNTOWN, ZONE [...]

2) Leg [...]
3) 911 [...]
4) Sport [...]
and 1 a[...]
5) Select [...]
6) Childre[...]
7) Accide[...]
8) Meet p[...]
9) Drafted [...]
10) Bowling [...]
11) Bum as[...]
die for injur[...]
12) Rap sho[...]

EAST SI[...]

2) Meet the mayor, bodyguards beat you up, earn $75 hush money.
3) Suspected of shoplifting, no [...] arn $200.00.
4) Sto[...] in [...] take THE BUS!
5) Car [...]
6) Gun [...]
7) Eat a[...]
8) Eat G[...]
1 turn.
9) Caug[...]
10) Mee[...]
11) Stop[...]
12) Pull a[...]

PEOP[...]

2) Get arr[...]
3) Pass G[...]
4) Tram ru[...]
5) Local tu[...] lose [...]
6) Cut down in gun battle on train, roll die for injuries.
7) Meet pimp, gain one child.
8) Sit on transvestite prostitutes works, lose 1 pt. blood
9) Stop to look at beautiful Station Art, lose one turn.

START

$

WEST SIDE

1986–1990

3-357 Magnum. Spend 3 turns in [...] Receiving.
4-44 Magnum. Spend 4 turns in Detroit Receiving.
5- 5 sticks of Chaldean dynamite. Spend 5 turns in Detroit Receiving.
[...] AK47 YOU ARE DEAD. GO HOME GAME'S OVER

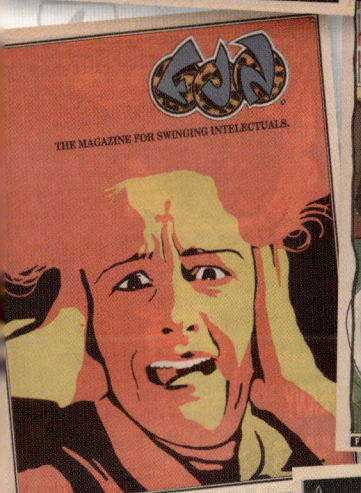

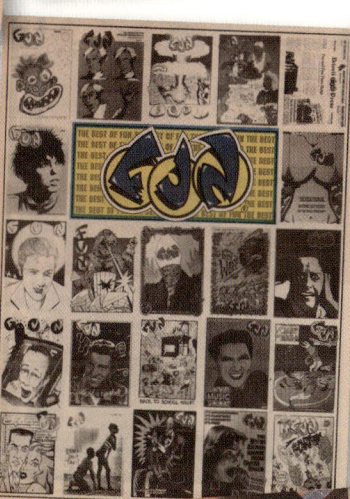

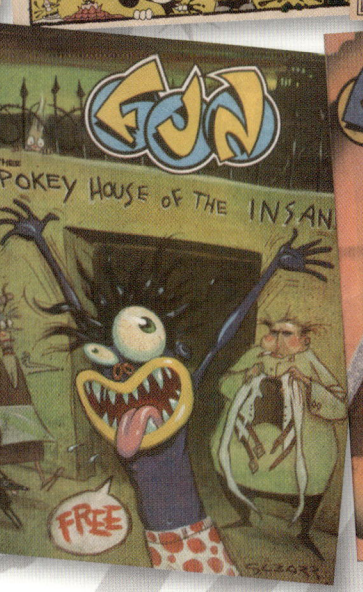

"Are We Having *FUN*, Yet?"

By the time *Fun* premiered in September 1986, Jerry Peterson was considered a respected businessman. By day, he was the president of the Detroit-area company PMX for CADCAM, selling computer-aided drafting and manufacturing software to businesses; by night, he continued his punk rock persona, playing in various bands around Detroit. In 1985, Peterson said his old friend "Sailor Rick" Metcalf asked him about doing another magazine. It had been about six years since *White Noise* disappeared, and some of Peterson's creative friends were looking to do something new. Metcalf envisioned a free, satirical humor magazine for Metro Detroit. With Peterson making plenty of money from his day job, he decided to develop Metcalf's idea.

Peterson's plan was to create a more polished version of what had been done with *White Noise*. With an understanding of what was available in the computer market, Peterson invested about twenty thousand dollars in new Macintosh computers, equipment, and software. The key program was PageMaker, which used Apple's graphic interface to lay out, paste up, and create publications. *Fun* magazine became an experimental training ground for what

was possible in the early days of desktop publishing.

The first issue of *Fun* was a fourteen-page black-and-white tabloid that dubbed itself "The Magazine for Swinging Intelectuals" [sic] and featured a demented, comput

▼ *Fun* #1, September 1986.

"THE MAGAZINE FOR SWINGING INTELECTUALS"

47

"Big Fun Page," *Fun*, September 1986. ▲

er-designed monkey on the front. With his wide grin, maniacal eyes, and frizzed-out hair, "Winky" visually embodied the crazed ideas and aesthetic of the new free monthly.

Despite his "respectable" day job, Peterson was still living the "rock-and-roll lifestyle" (which included having a bed and a shower in his office), and this attitude permeated *Fun*. Retaining the "Jerry Vile" moniker, he listed himself as publisher on the masthead. In the first editorial, Peterson wrote, "The only reason why we started Fun is because we are bored, bored, bored!!! We are sick to death of living

"Big Fun Page," *Fun*, April 1988. ▲

in a city that celebrates mediocrity. . . . We will not ignore local art, music, events, etc. (provided it meets our stringent requirements for being *Fun*; different, senseless, stupid, dangerous, or providing of payola)." Vile emphasized that there was something readers needed to understand: "All we ask of you is that you don't take us seriously. We promise to never take you seriously. If you can't live with that, then throw this paper away now! We didn't ask you to pick up our paper. We don't want you to read our paper. Go start your own paper."

MERRY CHRISTMAS FROM US AND OURS TO YOU AND YOURS!

X-MAS is a time for caring and sharing, for living and giving, and more than anything else, it's a time for GETTING! We are going to make this the best X-mas you ever had! Here's your present : A brand new sparkling; almost OFFICIAL FUN PRESS PASS! The FUN Magazine Press Pass is your gravy train. You will never have to pay for anything again. Eat at the finest restaurants "on the house". Travel in first class luxury, "complementary". Hob-nob with the "beautiful people", snooping in on their private conversations and swilling their expensive wines, that you can't even pronounce. Go anywhere you want and do anything you want, without ever having to pay so much as a dime.

But remember with this pass comes an awesome responsibility. The responsibility of acting like a professional newsman, just like us. So if you don't get your way SCREAM! Make a stink! A BIG Stink. Kick, scratch, dig, jab, cry, cajole, and beg. Say you're going to write a bad review, a real bad review, until you get your way. These are the reactions of a true journalist. Now, go out there and get 'em tiger!

DIRECTIONS:
1. SIGN YOUR NAME AND GLUE ON YOUR PHOTO.
2. FOLD IN HALF AND MAKE SURE TO LAMINATE IT, SO WE DON'T LOOK LIKE A CHEAP OUTFIT.
3. START LIVING FOR ONCE IN YOUR LIFE.

TO WHOM IT MAY CONCERN:

The Constitution of the United States GUARANTEES freedom of the press. It is imperative the bearer of this card be allowed to express said freedoms. Upon demand, the bearer of this card shall get in free. This includes but is not limited to: nightclubs, concerts, movies, bars, sporting events, amusement parks, plays and musicals, weddings, wakes, tractor pulls, taffy pulls, religious events, limousines (moving or parked), art openings, and to cross all police lines and view dead bodies, act like a big deal, and get good seats at lurid murder trials. Now if you value your job, if you don't want your business to suffer the wrath of the Press, tthan you better treat me right. And while you're down there...

PRESS PASS
LET ME IN

ACE REPORTER

PUT PHOTO HERE

OFFICIAL SIGNATURE

WARNING: THIS IS NOT A TOY, IT'S AN ALMOST OFFICIAL FUNPRESS PASS. LET US KNOW IF IT WORKS FOR YOU. AND IF IT DOES, TELL US WHERE IT WORKED FOR YOU.

▲ Press pass, *Fun*, Winter 1989/1990.

When *Fun* went into production, friends and collaborators from Vile's punk days signed up. *White Noise* co-creator Paul Zimmerman took part but was not as involved as he'd been with the previous magazine; though, due to Zimmerman's interest in comics, Peterson gave him the editor's mantle for two special annual issues focusing on cartoons. Peterson's longtime girlfriend and fellow traveler in the Bookie's Club 870 scene Katy McNerney came on board to help with the business end, and former *White Noise* photographer S. Kay Young also got involved. But the new magazine also opened the door to younger, newer talents who hadn't been around during the punk rock days. Some, like film reviewer Chris Gore, would stay a short time, but others, like designer Mark Niemenski, would have a lasting impact.

Making *Fun*

As the *Fun* team was preparing the first issue, it was also going head-to-head with the more serious-minded *Metro Times*. Peterson said his mouth got him in trouble even before the launch of his new magazine: "The only mistake we made was telling people that this was going to be a *Metro Times* kind of thing, but with cartoons. And at the time, the *Metro Times* had almost no visuals in it and *Fun* was going to be super visual, and someone squealed to them."

FUN EXCLUSIVE!

BY DOUGLAS BLAIR

Hostile Suburbs' Plot to Invade Peaceful Detroit is Exposed!
Probable Attack Routes, Targets:

While other papers scoffed, FUN Magazines award winning investigative journalists exposed the truth.

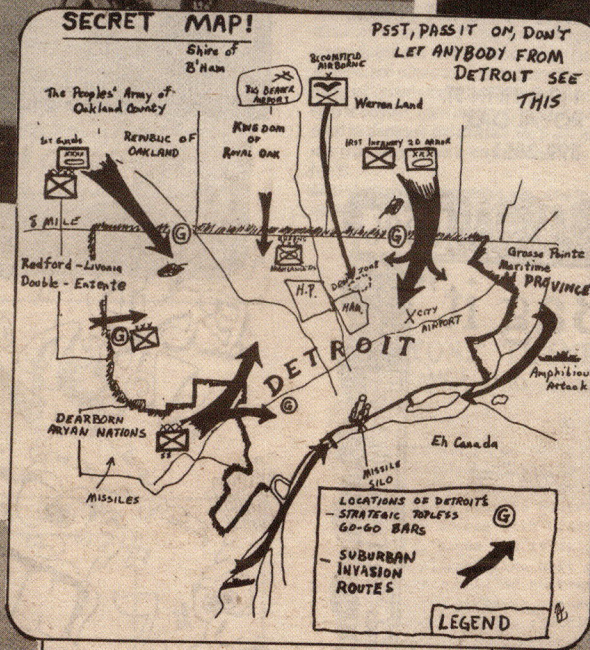

missile launcher.

nuclear device

SECRET MAP!

PSST, PASS IT ON, DON'T LET ANYBODY FROM DETROIT SEE THIS

Shire of B'ham

The Peoples' Army of Oakland County

Republic of OAKLAND

KINGDOM OF ROYAL OAK

Warren Land

Redford-Livonia Double-Entente

Grosse Pointe Maritime PROVINCE

DETROIT

DEARBORN ARYAN NATIONS

Eh Canada

MISSILE SILO

MISSILES

Amphibious Assault

LOCATIONS OF DETROIT'S STRATEGIC TOPLESS GO-GO BARS

SUBURBAN INVASION ROUTES

LEGEND

"Northwest Detroit (is) good tank country," according to Oakland County People's Army Commander, General George S. Patterson, "Coleman may talk big but, the flat ground and wide streets across Eight Mile Road should allow us to punch past the topless go-go bars on Eight, assault and exploit right down the old John C. Lodge!"

Sources in the US Department of Energy and the Defense Department have confirmed that City of Detroit scientists now possess the ability to produce weapons grade nuclear devices. Rumor has held that Tower #4 of the Ren Cen is actually a missile launcher. Will the mayor of the fair city resort to his secret nuclear arsenal in the Ren Cen if the suburban axis stormtroopers do "Hit Eight Mile Road"?

The maritime communities of Grosse Pointe and Grosse Isle will certainly conduct naval forays on Detroit's peaceful coastline. Both the Ambassador Bridge and the Belle Isle Bridge are sure to be prime targets—and the prelude to the assault on downtown and the Mangoonian Mansion itself.

Now that the ban on foreigners entering Deaborn Parks has been lifted, the truth can be known. Secret weapons of awsome power have been secretly developed by Aryan scientists and stored in park-like settings within the Dearborn suburb.

"Suburbs to Attack Detroit," *Fun*, October 1986. ▲

▲ "Annual Bunch of Lists," *Fun*, January 1988.

A review of the *Metro Times* archives bears out some of Peterson's claims. At the time, the *Metro Times* had editorial cartoon boxes placed throughout the magazine but no organized comics page. That changed in 1986 with the April 2–8 issue. The cover highlighted the introduction of a new cartoon feature called "Life in Hell." It would be another five months until *Fun* hit the streets in September 1986. This stung Peterson, who said he discovered the work of cartoonist Matt Groening in an out-of-town alt weekly about a year earlier and had been in contact with the artist to land "Life in Hell" for his magazine. The problem was that Groening, who would later create *The Simpsons*, wanted to syndicate to alt weeklies, and *Fun*, at the time, was planned as a monthly. The deal fell through. Peterson believed that his discussions around town about "Life in Hell" and featuring more cartoons in his upcoming magazine helped to motivate the *Metro Times* to pick

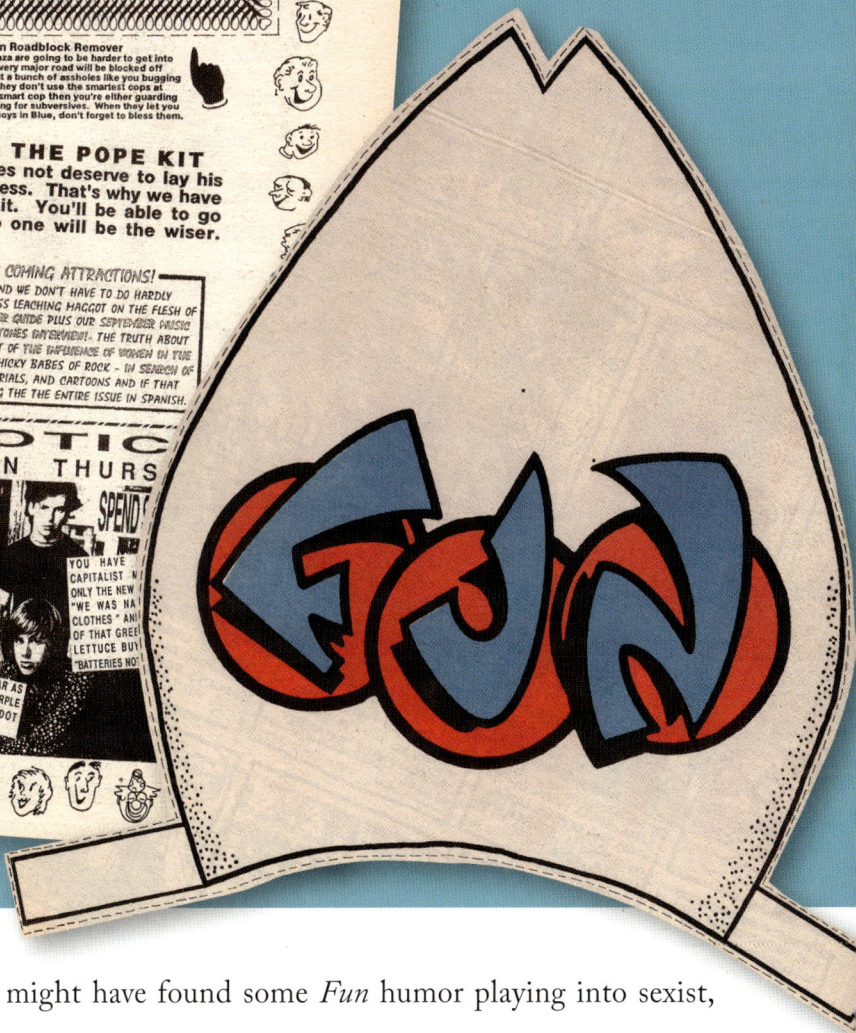

PHONY PRIEST COLLAR
Mingle with the Monsignors, cavort with the Cardinals, badger the Bishops and nudge the Nuns! Tell 'em your from some parish in Toledo. That way, they won't catch on as Michigan and Ohio Catholics are not on speaking terms. Remember, save a little of their wine for the ceremony.

FAKE POPE BUTTON
Wear this free button rather than sporting one of the shoddy unofficial tourist rip-off trinkets. We just saved you five bucks.

Kiss me
I Saw
The Pope

HOLY WATER

OFFICIAL HAMTRAMCK ✝ PRIEST PASS #278437

THIS PASS ALLOWS THE AUTOMOBILE AND ITS OCCUPANTS UNLIMITED ACCESS TO ANYWHERE THE POPE MAY BE APPEARING. IF YOU GIVE THE BEARER OF THIS PASS A HARD TIME YOU CAN PRETTY MUCH COUNT ON GOING TO HELL WHEN YOU DIE. AMEN.

Right-On Roadblock Remover
Hamtramck and Hart plaza are going to be harder to get into than a Nun's panties. Every major road will be blocked off because they don't want a bunch of assholes like you bugging the Pope. Fortunately, they don't use the smartest cops as roadblocks. If you're a smart cop then you're either guarding his holiness or out looking for subversives. When they let you wizz by the Befuddled Boys in Blue, don't forget to bless them.

SNEAK A PEEK AT THE POPE KIT
A sniveling sinner like you does not deserve to lay his blasphemous eyes on his holiness. That's why we have included this priest disguise kit. You'll be able to go anywhere the pope is and no one will be the wiser.

HOLY WATER HIDE A BREW
Your excessive drinking will always give you away. With the Holy Water Hide A Brew you can booze it up all the live long day. Remember- Don't get caught peein' in front of His Most Holy One or you'll be Hailing Mary till you're old and grey!

OH BOY! NEXT ISSUES COMING ATTRACTIONS!
IT'S BACK TO SCHOOL FOR YOU AND WE DON'T HAVE TO DO HARDLY ANYTHING! NOW YOU CAN BE A USELESS LEACHING MAGGOT ON THE FLESH OF HUMANITY LIKE US WITH FUN'S CAREER GUIDE PLUS OUR SEPTEMBER MUSIC SPECTACULAR! WITH AN EXCLUSIVE STONES INTERVIEW! THE TRUTH ABOUT DETROIT MUSIC! - AND SPECIAL REPORT OF THE INFLUENCE OF WOMEN IN THE CURRENT MUSICAL TRENDS-THE HOT CHICKY BABES OF ROCK - IN SEARCH OF BILL KENNEDY. AND LETTERS, EDITORIALS, AND CARTOONS AND IF THAT WASN'T ENOUGH, WE WILL BE PRINTING THE THE ENTIRE ISSUE IN SPANISH.

HYSTERIC NARCOTIC
HAMTRAMCK PUB SAT. 8
TOKEN THURS

SEE SEE SEE
HEAR HEAR HEAR
FEEL FEEL FEEL
SPEND

THE SONIC REVERBERATIONS OF THE LOVE GENERATION. THE WAY OUT GUITARS, THE THUMPING BEAT OF A THRILL-CRAZY GANG, HELL-BENT ON SELF-DESTRUCTION.

THE MIND BLOWING PSYCLOTRONIC SHOW. GUARANTEED TO MELT IN YOUR MIND, NOT IN YOUR HANDS!!!

YOUR INHIBITIONS DISAPPEAR AS YOUR LIBIDO EXPLODES IN PURPLE TIE-DIE PAISLEY POLKA-DOT ECSTASY.

YOU HAVE CAPITALIST ONLY THE NEW "WE WAS MA CLOTHES" AN OF THAT GREE LETTUCE BUY "BATTERIES NOT

"Big Fun Page" and Pope's hat, *Fun*, August 1987. ▲ ▶

up the syndicated feature and cobble together a comics page before the launch of *Fun*.

The first issue of *Fun* set the tone for what was to come— cartoons, a gossip column titled "Slander," movie and music reviews, features on local bands and artists, and a puzzle page called the "Big Fun Page" in the back. The core of *Fun*'s editorial philosophy was that everything, and everyone, was fair game for ridicule, satire, or outright derision. Casual read-ers might have found some *Fun* humor playing into sexist, racist, or ethnic stereotypes, much like comedians who use shock to provoke and make points. Nursed on a heady cock-tail of *National Lampoon* and *Mad* magazines, underground comics, and punk rock, the staff couldn't help but aspire to high standards of snark. The magazine focused on what was hip and making headlines nationally, but it also zeroed in on Metro Detroit, its celebrities, and the "8 Mile divide"—the

GAME OF DETROIT

The FUN Magazine Game Of Detroit is a action packed exciting and fun filled game for the entire family. It can be played by anyone between the ages of eight to eighty who enjoys non-stop thrills, adventure, and shenanigins. You'll spend hour after exciting hour In the Game O' Detroit, where anything can happen, and usually does.

You can throw out all your other games, for they are now obsolete. The Game of Detroit is not unlike Art Linkletters, The Game of Life, except it does not skirt the real issues. In fact, the game is filled with so much violence, pain, and misfortune It could be dubbed the Game of Death. But it's not. It's the Game of Detroit.

ZONE ACTION TABLES

WEST SIDE, ZONE 1
2) Forgot to hide your money in your sock go back-1.
3) Flat tire, stop at Amirs Mobil, pay 50 for patch.
4) No turning back, free turn.
5) Hitchhiker, call Americas Most Wanted, earn 25 bucks.
6) You are in a high speed chase, 2 free turns.
7) Watch crackhouse burn down , lose 1 turn.
8) Need money for crack, sell child for sex, earn $35.
9) Car forced off road and you are shot. Roll die for injuries.
10) Bum asks for money, tell him to get a job, he shoots you, roll die for injuries.
11) Stop to pee in alley, rat bites gonads, lose 2 turns.
12) Jet crashes on freeway, pretend you are a priest, earn $2000.

DOWNTOWN, ZONE 2
2) Leg Cramp! Drive car into Detroit river, lose all children.
3) 911 no answer. Wait 1 turn for operator.
4) Sports riot, You are severely burned under an overturned cop car lose 1 leg and 1 arm.
5) Selected for jury duty on murder trial lose five turns.
6) Children Kidnapped. Wait 3 turns for cop to show.
7) Accident. Lose one turn gawking.
8) Meet pimp gain one spouse.
9) Drafted by Lions lose 1 arm and 1 shred of human dignity.
10) Bowling-ball thrown from overpass, lose 1 spouse.
11) Bum asks you for money, hand over twenty dollars, he shoots you, roll die for injuries.
12) Rap show riot, break dance on your face, lose 1 pt. blood.

EAST SIDE, ZONE 3
2) Meet the mayor, bodyguards beat you up, earn $75 hush money.
3) Suspected of shoplifting, no convictions, earn $200.00.
4) Stop for gas in Chaldean Drug war, lose car in explosion take THE BUS!
5) Car Stolen, take THE BUS! Back to START
6) Gun jams, breakdown weapon and reload, lose one turn.
7) Eat at coney island, contract diarrhea, squat on chair next three turns.
8) Eat Chicken from Half barrel Barbecue Toxic waste go to Detroit Receiving, 1 turn.
9) Caught throwing Rocks at little Rock Baptist Church, pay $100.00 bale.
10) Meet pimp, lose 1 child.
11) Stop for "not so fast food" at McDonalds, lose 2 turns.
12) Pull along side mini-truck with bed of speakers. Lose hearing and one turn.

PEOPLE MOVER
2) Get arm caught in door, lose 1 arm
3) Pass Greek Town, lose 1 turn.
4) Tram runs down skate board punks and derails, lose 1 turn.
5) Local tuffs hold you up with screwdriver, lose $50.00.
6) Cut down in gun battle on train, roll die for injuries.
7) Meet pimp, gain one child.
8) Sit on transvestite prostitutes works, lose 1 pt. blood
9) Stop to look at beautiful Station Art, lose one turn.
10) Concrete tracks crumble, tram crashes to earth, go to Detroit Receiving.
11) Bum asks you for money, you shoot him, earn $1.00
12) Accused by DPM security, pay $50.00 or go to Detroit Receiving.

START

WEST SIDE

SHORTCUT

96

12

DO

"BULLETS ARE FLYING" ACTION TABLE
1- Bullet Misses You live
2- 22 Caliber. Spend 2 turns in Detroit Receiving.
3- 357 Magnum. Spend 3 turns in Detroit Receiving.
4- 44 Magnum. Spend 4 turns in Detroit Receiving.
5- 5 sticks of Chaldean dynamite. Spend 5 turns in Detroit Receiving.
6- AK47 YOU ARE DEAD. GO HOME GAME'S OVER
If someone else is shot while you are in hospital, you get bumped from bed, and out of the hospital, via exit.

▲ "Game of Detroit," *Fun*, Fall 1989.

FINISH

EAST SIDE

OTTO

1

DETROIT RECEIVING HOSPITAL

PEOPLE MOVER

TOWN

94

$

$

$

$

$

$

N
W ··· E
S

DETROIT RIVER

N
W ··· E
S

The Game Of

DETROIT

MORE DETAILS
AND GAME
INSTRUCTIONS
ON FOLLOWING PAGE

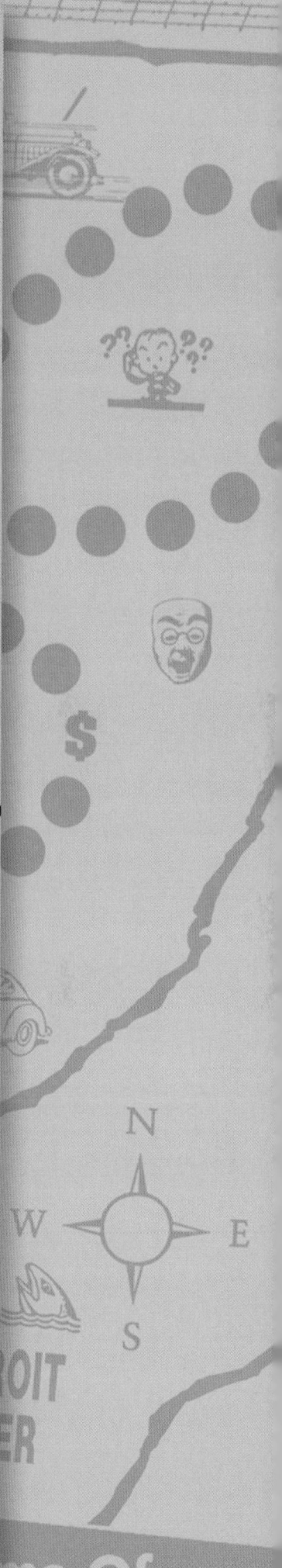

OFFICIAL RULES

OBJECT OF GAME

The object of the game is to win. To do that, drive your car and it's occupants through Detroit without dying. The person who makes it out alive with the most money, WINS! But beware, there are pitfalls and ethnic types at every U-turn.

You Start With:
1 car
6 pts. blood
1 spouse, 2 kids
1 life, 2 arms, 2 legs and 1 shred of human dignity.
12,000 dollars cash (Since we do not supply you with any money we suggest using spare change, i.e. penny = one dollar, dime = 10 dollars. REMEMBER Fun does not condone the use of US coinage for gambling purpose but if you do use coinage, anti-up $15,000 into a kitty for the bank.

Status Card

Each player starts with a Status card. This card lets the whole world know where you stand. Your financial worth, if your spouse has left you flat, or if you are turning the knob on deaths very door. Check off one box for each article you lose. i.e. lose 2 pts. blood, cross off two blood boxes, gain 2 pts. blood, erase two crossed off boxes or draw new ones. We also recommend photocopying status sheets on extra heavy card stock and not swiping four magazines to play one stupid game with your four stupid friends!

STATUS CARD

NAME _____ are you alive ☐ dead ☐
CHILDREN ☐☐
SPOUSE ☐
BLOOD pts. ☐☐☐☐☐☐
BLOOD PRESSURE, ____over____
LEGS ☐☐   ARMS ☐☐☐   DIGNITY ☐
WEAPONS GUN ☐ KNIFE ☐ LEAD PIPE ☐
WRENCH ☐
ROPE ☐ CANDLESTICK ☐
CREDIT
VISA ☐ AMERICAN EXPRESS ☐ DISCOVER CARD ☐
☐ PLAYERS CLUB ☐
WIGS
AFRO ☐ PROCESS ☐ AVA ☐ FRENCH CURL ☐
TOYS
VCR ☐ CAR PHONE ☐ WATCH MAN ☐ ALLIGATOR ☐
BRIEFCASE ☐ FUN T-SHRIT ☐

Use push or straight pins to secure your car to the gameboard. **DO NOT PLAY ON COFFEE TABLE!** For added action, tape your car to the back of a live cockroach!

Ready To Play?

Roll dice (dice not included) for turn. Move your car the appropriate amount of spaces. Next look up the number of your roll and match to the corresponding number in the "Zone Action Table" then pay the consequences. i.e. if you are in the West Side Zone and roll a seven, move 7 spaces and look under 7 in the West Side Zone Action Table, for prize or penalty.

LOTTO CARDS

If you land on a spot marked $ (LOTTO) draw a card and follow its directions.

PEOPLE MOVER

Landing directly on either P.M. station you must enter the P.M. circle, to exit you must also land directly on either station, unless you are shot and sent to hospital. People Mover travels only in a clockwise direction.

THE BUS

If you lose your car you must take THE BUS! Go back to START, Pay one dollar (to the bank) for each member of your family in order to ride.

BANG BANG

If you land on a Bang Bang spot you are shot. you must see the "BULLETS ARE FLYING TABLE". Roll a single die to asses your injuries and follow instructions.

DETROIT RECEIVING

You must stay in the hospital for as long as directed by the game. If someone else is shot or injured while you are in hospital you get bumped from bed and can continue game via exit.

WIG SHOPS

Wig Shops are free spaces and nothing can happen to you.

WINNING

After every player has crossed the finish line, or one hour has elapsed since the first player has crossed the finish line, count your money and total up your points. Because this is America all points are assessed in dollar value:
your life $500.00
each arm $100.00
each leg $200.00

your dignity $50.00
your car $99.00 down
your spouse -$200.00
each kid -$100.00
The player with the must money WINS!

IF YOU...

Run out off blood you die and lose.
Run out of arms and legs you die and lose unless accompanied by spouse to act as chauffeur.

FOLD HERE

PROFESSIONAL GAME RULES AND TECHNICAL INFORMATION

PROFESSIONAL GAME BOARD

The professional game board is distinguished from the amateur gameboard by having more than four Bang Bang, Lotto, Or Wig shop squares

BULLET PROOF VEST

The bulletproof vest renders you immune to all gunfire. Any player Wearing the bullet proof vest is safe from harm. Only the player with the most wigs may wear the bullet proof vest.

WIGS

Players may purchase wigs from Wigshops if they know the secret word. There are 30 additional 'unmarked Wig Shops. Space 1-20 28-48 &.%2-72. There Is no need to slow down the game by telling the other players you've purchased any wigs until you have four.

POWER PILLS

The super power pellet allows you to roll continuously for 30 seconds, and gobble up any opponents who cross your path. Simply be the first to yell out 'Methamphetamine!' and roll away.

SECRET WORD

The secret word is "Sucker"

NOT TELLING OTHER PLAYERS ALL THE RULES

If you tell the other players all of rules you are disqualified, even if you really want to and think it isn't fair. However, not telling all the rules makes the game more fun and exciting, so it is not. we repeat NOT Cheating.

CHEATING

The GAME OF DETROIT is impossible to cheat at. If you have accused one of your fellow players of cheating please apologies to them and give them some

THE GAME O DETROIT CHEATING KIT GIVES YOU EVERYTHING YOU NEED TO CHEAT YOUR FRIENDS, FAMILY, ACQUAINTANCES, ROOMATES, AND CHURCH GROUPS.

"Certain Victory" Game Cards
Since wagering can make The Game of Detroit a whole lot more interesting, use the 'Certain Victory' game cards to insure huge winnings. Do not put them in the deck with the other cards. That way none of your opponents will be able get their hands on them. These cards are for your use only. They will be your winners insurance. When you land on a square don't hesitate to take the card. Read it aloud. The other players will most likely accuse you of lying, and ask what your card really says. Since the Game of Detroit cards are so small, they can easily be palmed. When your opponents demand to see the card, simply substitute one of the 'Certain Victory' cards. Remember,

nobody likes a cheat, but we know that cheaters never cheat.

SPURIOUS GAME SQUARES

Because this is a game of chance, the dice might not be rolling the way you want them to. Cut out the extra squares (Bang Bang, Lottos, and Wig Shops) and apply a non-drying sticky substance such as Spray-Mount to the back. Using a lightly tacky substance (dried ball of rubber cement) fasten the face of a card to your index finger. Count the dots using your middle finger, but when you get to the last dot use your index finger. Your opponents will never catch you. You'll be amazed how stupid people really are.

INSTANT VICTORY

In the highly unlikely event you find yourself losing or if you get bored and want to end the game quick, the instant victory rules are for you.

SPECIAL CHEAT YOUR FRIENDS SECTION, CUT OUT AND HIDE BEFORE THEY SEE IT.

Cheaters RULES The only time your opponents should read these rules is when they need them to figure out your instant victory.

Unlimited wigs, a bulletproof vest, and 1 super power pellet. If someone's about to win, pull out your wig tokens and declare yourself the automatic victor. The other players might wonder what these items are for. Of course only you know the special extended rules.

EXTENDED RULES

They will call you Liar, Cheater, Charlatan. Let them. These extra rules give you everything you need to back up your cheating. We even go as far as giving you an excuse for not to tell the rules. We further claim that the Game is impossible to cheat people with and try to make your opponent feel guilty.

LOTTO CARDS (row 1)

$ LOTTO	$ LOTTO	$ LOTTO	$ LOTTO	$ LOTTO
Subscribe to Lotto. Pay $104.00	You hit five numbers! So did 745,638 people. earn $25.00	Instant Lotto. Win 10 measly bucks.	Lotto Club! Retain this card and receive half of next lotto players winnings.	Whoop it up after big win. Pay $5000 for five weeks stay in the Betty Ford Clinic.
$ LOTTO	$ LOTTO	$ LOTTO	$ LOTTO	$ LOTTO
Too vocal about winnings. Get your ass robbed. Lose 10,000 big ones	Win 8,000,000 in Lotto club! After court dispute receive $250.00	Daly Three Game. Win $100.00	Fame & Fortune, forth place. Win 200.00	Win $25,000,000 but lose ticket on way to Lansing. Shoot self and die
$ LOTTO	$ LOTTO	$ LOTTO	$ LOTTO	$ LOTTO
Instant Lotto Winner Free ticket! Draw another card	E-Z Pick! Collect one booger from each player	Win 10,000 dollars! Buy brunch at the Whitney. Retain $80	Back taxes! IRS cramps your style, mooch $10 from all.	Spouse gives Lotto winnings to P.T.L. Shoot spouse.

LOTTO CARD DIRECTIONS: WITH A PAIR OF VERY SHARP SCISSORS CUT OUT LOTTO CARDS, APPLY GLUE OR STICKY STUFF TO THE BACK SIDE AND FOLD OVER AT DOTTED LINE. CARDS ARE NOW READY TO BE STACKED ON 'LOTTO' SPACE ON GAME BOARD.

Cheater LOTTO CARDS

$ LOTTO	$ LOTTO	$ LOTTO	$ LOTTO	$ LOTTO
MAYOR'S PAL Cheat all you want. If caught, present this card & get off scott free	Invent Bullet Proof Vest Retain card., you are safe from bullets for rest of the game	You get to drive in The Grand Prix Move ahead 30 spaces.	JACKPOT! Collect 30 Million	Find $25,000,000 ticket on way to Lansing
$ LOTTO	$ LOTTO	$ LOTTO	$ LOTTO	$ LOTTO
Serial Murderer kills opponent with most points	E-Z Pick! Collect one thousand from each player	Miracle Cure Get out of hospital free	Garage Sale! Purchase any opponents Car for $1	Whiplash! Send any opponent back to start!

$$$$$$

▲ "Game of Detroit," rules and pieces, *Fun*, Fall 1989.

"BULLETS ARE FLYING" ACTION TABLE
1-Bullet Misses You live
2-.22 Caliber. Spend 2 turns in Detroit Receiving.
3-.357 Magnum. Spend 3 turns in Detroit Receiving.

MELVINDALE COMMUNITY COLLEGE

URNUM WAGUS VIA MENIAL LABORUM

A message from our president.

Welcome future leaders of america

As future stundets to Melvindale Community College and our Continual Education Program you are already on your way to learning top dollar. It's a proven fact college graduates make more money. A heck of a lot more money. So whether you are stuck in a dead end job or simply going no where fast, there is bound to be a course of higher learning that will lead to higher earnings.

Where industry looks for labor.

Don't settle for a job when you can have a career. At Melvindale College, whether you are 18 or 99 there is sure to be a class that will fill your thirst for higher education. We offer classes and more classes, in the subjects that will prepare you for a life of hard labor. As wise man once said "Work makes you free". At Melvindale we still believe in that ethic.

Every bit as good as a two year college.

Why waste money on a two or a four year college. Unlike hoity toity institutions we offer degrees in as little as five months. Many of our students are already earning top-dollar in the fields of study and thinking.

Start planning for your tomorrow today at Melvindale.

If you read the want ads you will see they need smart brains now more than ever. A school is only as good as is students, if all you want to do is watch TV then go to some other college. We develop bright minds for tomorrow's tough marketplace.

Even those thought untrainable can have a bright outlook on the future. Thanks to recent changes in the Minimum Wage Laws, Melvindale graduates are earning more than ever.

Some myths about college.

FALSE: I can't afford to go to college.

FACT: If you thought college was only for the rich and smart, think again. By Michigan State Law you are guaranteed a college education. Although we prefer cash, money orders, and "certified" checks, we also offer financial aid and our cafeteria accepts food stamps.

FALSE: You have to go away to college if you want to have fun and party.

FACT: Melvindale campus life is fun too. Our annual Sadie Hawkins Day dance is only one of the many social activities that await our student body.

FALSE: College is hard work and exams

FACT: A lot of you think college means years of hard work. Our one year program will get you a diploma pronto. Best of all the State only pays us for successful retraining, so we guarantee you won't flunk. You don't even have to show up.

FALSE: Inbreeding produces inferior genes

FACT: While many of our students share a common genetic heritage, they also share a quest for smarter knowledge. Melvindale college gives them the edge they need in today's dog eat dog job market.

THE TRUTH IS MELVINDALE COMMUNITY COLLEGE is the best investment you can make. Instead of investing in a bank, you invest in your self, and your brain is the bank vault. Then you make more money because you are smarter. So go ahead, make a deposit at the Bank of you and start being a somebody today.

Melvindale Community College 1.

▲ "Melvindale Community College," *Fun*, Summer 1990.

COURSE DESCRIPTIONS SPRING 1990

COLLEGE OF ENGINEERING

Applied Petroleum Sciences 101
You will learn the skills needed to supply internal combustion engines with hi-octane petroleum and lubricants.

Applied Petroleum Sciences 201
Advanced techniques cover the latest New-matic inflation dynamics including radial technology, compression techniques, and tube flow dynamics.
Pre Rec Ap Pet Sci 101 or Two years experience and tire gauge

I was once cold pumping gas, now I'm inside where it's warm.

Applied Petroleum Computer Science 330
You will develop the skills necessary to operate in a supervised atmosphere, the petroleum control computers used in today's most advanced service stations.
Pre Rec Ap Pet Sci 201

Genetic Engineering 101
As a test subject at the Toxico Industrial Clinic, you'll learn first hand, all about genetic engineering. You will learn the legalities of a release form and get to participate in experiments, many using your own DNA.

Applied Dust Management 101
Learn the fundamentals of pushbroom dynamics, and advanced theories including the bi-polarity of debris in regard to partial reclamation and disposal. *Materials Needed: Dustpan, brooms.*

Applied Sanitation Chemistry 102
In addition to the latest mopping physics, you will learn the complicated compositions of elemental make-up solutions, cleansers, and stain removers.

Principals of Urinal Chemistry 151
Learn the latest laser technology for the eradication of pubis follicles and skid mark termination. You'll assimilate theoretical techniques for placement of modern urinal cakes and splash guards.

SCHOOL OF BUSINESS

Dress For Success 220
Clothes are an essential part of an executive wardrobe. Materials Fee $2.00 for hair-net

Advanced Office Automation 372
Upon graduating this class student will be capable of unsupervised operation of a time clock using punch card technology.

Business Computers 423
You will acquire vital skills and the knowledge required for cleaning high tech computer cases and monitors without disturbing or destroying the data of your superiors. Windex and rag provided.

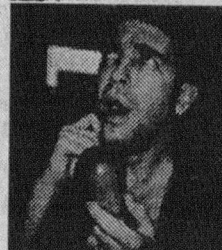

I couldn't spell employee, and now I are one.

Time Management 166
You will learn to set alarm clock, from basic windup models to advanced timepieces with snooze.
Pre Rec.. AM & PM Differentiation

Principles of Accounting 777
Upon completion student will have developed necessary skills for counting, making change, breaking a ten.
Pre Rec: One year of Melvindale high school mathematics or finger counting 101.

Modern Retailing Methods
This course will instruct you in ways of retailing your shoddy possessions and using your garage as a marketing tool into a positive cash flow empire.

Marketing 616
Emphasis on placement of consumer products in plastic and paper bags. This course familiarizes the student with marketing procedures, and culminates with a shopping cart roundup.

Business Communication 976
You'll learn when to say "Yes sir" and when to say Yessss siiiir! When they say jump you will know how high.

Labor Relations 101
In this ever changing field you will learn how to build cars, mine coal, drive busses, while avoiding picket lines and dodging bullets.
(Formerly Goonology 101)

Labor Relations 102
A cash paying career in the field of strikebreaking, designed primarily for the student over six feet, and two hundred & twenty-five lbs.

HOTEL & RESTAURANT SCIENCES

Basic Frying Technology 101
Learn valuable industry skills such as oil temperature control, beep verification, crispness identification, and methods of sodium application.

Advanced Frying Technology 202
You'll be trusted with higher ticket items such as hot apple pies, fish sandwiches, and chicken pieces.
Pre Rec Fries 101

Contamination Control 133
Course teaches principals of hydro-pressure systems as used in the food industry. Student will solve problems involving edible waste contaminants and properties of porcelain.

Refuse Systems 234
Students learn modern management techniques for loading, unloading, and, fumigating dumpsters and greasepits.

Thanks to MCC I may earn over $100,000 in my life

Hostelry Time Coordination 199
Student acquires skills useful for nocturnal motel administration including intercourse interlude time management and emission control systems.

Lavatory Sanitation Sciences 313
Student will master the art of hotel commode inspection, and learn the decision making for efficient purification.

Hotel Entertainment Matron 548
Class indoctrinates students in reproduction arts and sciences. Graduate thesis includes pupil administering poly prophylactic techniques and hydro-vaginal cleaning systems.

Introductory Speech 9797
"Would you like fries with that"... "Would you like fries with that"... "Would you like fries with that"...

Campus life is Groovy

THANKS TO A GENEROUS DONATION FROM THE MELVINDALE CHEMICAL MUNITIONS PLANT, "OLD MELVY C" BOASTS A HANGOUT, THE LARGEST OPEN AIR STUDENT LOUNGE IN THE COUNTY. PICTURED ABOVE: *SPRINGTIME AT THE HANGOUT, STUDENTS ARE AGLOW.*

2. Melvindale Community College

▲ "Melvindale Community College," *Fun,* Summer 1990.

CIVIL ENGINEERING

Know Your Potholes 100
Our civil engineering course prepares your career in bituminous surface pavement shoveling and hernia management.

Strategic Planning-Automotive
Ever wonder how they fit so many cars in so little space. You will utilize your analytical qualities to accomplish this .

Physical Mechanics 101
Students are taught techniques of soil displacement, positive drainage, and hydraulic gradients for corrugated metal culverts. *(Dirt provided, student must supply shovel.)*

Advanced Physical Mechanics 102
Students dig deeper into the science of soil displacement. Additional academia includes cadaver distention and displacement, and jewelry and gold filling reclamation.
PRE REC APM 101

Only two years on the job and I might even get a raise

TRANSPORTATION SCIENCES

BUS COURTESY 101 (Mandatory)
Learn how to use public transportation politely. *Exact Change required.*

Applied Transportation Theory 666
The country depends on the men and yes, even women to brings goods and services from one point to another. Training includes, route efficiency, and thermal dynamics of product delivery in thirty minutes or less. *(Student must have license and auto, uniform provided.)*

Applied Chemical Transportation 198
You will study the sewer systems, lakes and rivers of the Tri-county area. Meets midnights at the Toxico Chemical Plant site.
Materials needed: Rubber gloves and clothespin.

LAW ENFORCEMENT

Transportation Security 714
If you like to work outside in the fresh air this is the class for you. In a short time you'll acquire the skills needed to signal automobiles using flashlights, flags, even your own hands.

Advanced Transportation Security 715
If you like to interact with people and can be trusted with small amounts of cash, the opportunities afforded by this advanced class should not be missed.

Principals of K-9 Security 724
Employment is picking up in this field. Scoop and Bag provided.

Aviation Security 103
Learn your way to minimum wage in just four short hours. Our students are given high prestige low pay jobs with major airports throughout the country.
(Class shared with X-Ray Techniques)

MELVINDALE HAS PLENTY OF ON CAMPUS HOUSING. OUR OWN ARCHITECTURE STUDENTS CONVERTED EACH ONE OF THESE OLD PIGEON COOPS TO EIGHT PERSON DORMITORIES. PICTURED ABOVE: *STUDENTS ENJOYING A GAME OF CRATEBALL OUTSIDE "THE COOPS".*

Swing into Campus living

LIBERAL ARTS AND CRAFTS

Psychology 200
You'll tear your opponent to mental shreds when you master the the deadly art of psychology.

Career Planning 000
Discover your potential. (Meets at MESC office)

Music Appreciation 1234
You will hear and identify the musical masterpieces from Foghat to BTO, absolutely nothing after 79'.

Art Appreciation 265
If you need easy credits, this is the class you want. All you have to do is sit around and compare your van murals and tattoos.

Home Rendering For Fun & Profit 221
Save thousands on lard, grease, soap, candles, fertilizer, and gum.

I like to work with my hands without getting my fingernails dirty

Intro to Journalism 222
The field of journalism offers opportunities in distribution networks. In addition you will learn the mathematics of folding and basic trajectories for throwing *(Auto or bike required)*

Modern Dance 121
Learn to communicate using the graceful swan like movements of dance. You will learn to gracefully accept the gifts of art patrons in your costume or orifices without falling off the table.

Cinema 101
A dream come true for students with Hollywood in their blood. You will learn all aspects of cinema from the ground up, from ticket taking to cleaning the "sticky" from peep shows booths.

Living With Industrial Accidents
Study group teaches one how to cope and relate with those tragically injured in industrial accidents. If you live with someone who is horribly disfigured, by chemical burns, or perhaps some one who had all of the skin on their face scrapped off by a sanding machine, or maybe had their limbs crushed by a twenty ton press then you will enjoy our depressing "rap-type" group discussions.

SCHOOL OF MEDICINE AND CARPET CLEANING

Institutional Pustlogy 900
Identify abscesses of the mouth and rectum. Learn boil and carbuncle lancing. *Straws & Mouthwash Provided*

Advanced Excretions 999
Hospital excretions require trained professionals. Students are offered immediate positions at the Zug Island Leper Placement Center.

Fundamentals of Contagious Waste 987
You'll get "hands in experience" in a field that always has job openings
Pre Rec. Pustules 101

Hemotology 101
Course teaches student to identify donor centers who pay or give donuts for blood.

Institutional Restraints 564
This special education course teaches methods and practices in dealing with the mentally deficient, in an institutional environment.
Cattle Prod Provided, *(batteries not included)*

Intro to Proctotecniques 784
As a proctological apprentice the course may be complex but you will get it in the end.

Nursing Home Hygeinics 983
There are always plenty of openings in Nursing homes. Our students are knowledgeable in enema hydraulics and organic discharge identification, and basic bedsore and malignancy sampling for both medicaid and medicare frauds .

Only here a month and they just gave me a brush.

Basic Carpet Cleaning 972
Course provides you for the rigors and demands of a career in professional carpet cleaning.
SPECIAL EXCHANGE STUDENT PROGRAM
Earn A Medical Degree In Pakistan
In just 8 short months you can earn a real doctors degree at our sister college in Pakistan. You don't even need a high school diploma or have to buy a white uniform.

Melvindale Community College 3.

Melvindale Community College

Dixie Hwy. Campus of Engineering

Buzy Bee School of Business

Toxico College Of Industrial Sewage

Institute of Medicine & Carpet Cleaning

PETROLEUM SCIENCES

ENVIRONMENTAL RECLAMATION

BIOLOGICAL SCIENCES

APPLIED ENGINEERING

CULINARY ARTS

ADVERTISING ARTS

ENTREPRENEURIAL ENTERPRISE

LANDSCAPE MANAGEMENT

See You In the Fall

4. Melvindale Community College

▲ "Melvindale Community College," *Fun*, Summer 1990.

long-standing line between the majority-black city and its mostly white suburbs. With his incendiary humor and attitude, Peterson acknowledged he often bit the hand that fed him—upsetting some advertisers.

Fun's satire of Detroit developed from the staff's mixed feelings about the place. There is a great love and affection for the town, its people, the creative output, and the genuine trendsetting history of the Motor City. On the other hand, because of that love, *Fun* writers and artists were willing to take southeast Michigan to the woodshed for its faults hoping, maybe, that the place could improve. Much like Jonathan Swift advocating the sale of Irish children to the British as food in his *A Modest Proposal*, the staff of *Fun* used the publication to hold up a funhouse mirror to the town. So, was there a political motivation involved? Possibly. But, at its core, it was all about not being boring and making people laugh—pure and simple.

One of the memorable humor features was "Melvindale Community College." Published in the last issue of the magazine, in the spring of 1990, the feature, a staff favorite, satirized most of southeast Michigan's downriver community. Writer Rick Metcalf said, "It offended the white working class. That was fun to put together. A great project where just about everybody had a hand in it. The whole crew contributed copy or photography or design." The four-page mock catalog offered such courses as "Applied Petroleum Sciences 101 and 201," aimed at giving people the skills for a rewarding career working at a gas station. "Dress for Success 220" informed students how to make sure their wardrobe is executive-ready, with a two-dollar materials fee for a "hair-net." A mandatory class in "Bus Courtesy 101" taught "how to use public transportation politely."

Former Detroit mayor Coleman Young came up several times for ridicule in *Fun*, mostly for his management of the city, his scandals, and his "love child." Young symbolized many things to Detroiters during his tenure, from 1974 to 1994. To some, he was a hero, showing the promise of African Americans taking control of the levers of power; to others, he was a heel who exacerbated the city/suburb divide.

For *Fun*, Coleman Young was simply excellent fodder. The August 1987 issue proclaimed, "Fun Exclusive: Coleman Young's Ultra-Secret, Ultra-Posh Bachelor-Style Fairy Castle Retirement Villa." It featured a diagram of a secret plan by the mayor to tear down the Brewster Projects and construct his own castle, outfitted with such amenities as a cellar stocked with only the finest fortified wine, a trapdoor on the draw-

▼ Coleman Young's retirement villa, *Fun*, August 1987.

FUN EXCLUSIVE: COLEMAN YOUNG'S ULTRA-SECRET, ULTRA-POSH BACHELOR-STYLE FAIRY CASTLE RETIREMENT VILLA.

Gazing across the sagging Brewster Projects, one man has a dream. He hires a wrecking crew, misappropriates a little change, tosses a few deadbeats to the Dobermans. A month later, maybe two, he wanders thoughtfully through the rubble. Something to salvage here, something there. A bottle of wine, maybe a couple jaguar lampshades, Motown mementos. For a politician (he reminds himself) retirement is as near as Donna Rice's douchebag. He wanders further, his pace quickening. The dream solidifies. All that's needed is a warehouse of Quick-crete and a couple dozen delinquents itching for a shot at the Summer-release program.

Labels:
- ARMED GUARD AND FISHING TROPHIES
- MASTURBATORIUM WITH VELVET-SEATED TOILET AND MAGNIFYING MIRROR
- WHITE SHOE ROOM
- POOR SIGN PAINTER LOOKING FOR PLACES WITHOUT COLEMAN YOUNG'S SIGNATURE
- 130 mm. M-46 FIELD GUN AIMED AT HOSTILE DEARBORN
- PRETEND OVAL OFFICE
- BACK END OF LIMO
- CHIMBLY
- PETTY CASH
- TIKI IDOL
- SMOKE HOUSE
- LANDMARKS SLATED TO BECOME CASINOS
- GOOFY HAT ROOM
- CARP HATCHERY
- LIBRARY
- LIMOUSINE PORT
- DUNGEON CONVERTED TO MD 22 CELLAR
- TABASCO PROCESSING MINI-PLANT WITH PIPELINE DIRECTLY TO BANQUET HALL
- BASEMENT SUITE RESERVED FOR YOUNG GIRLS, INC. WITH PIPELINE DIRECTLY TO MASTER BEDROOM
- SPARE HUBCAPS
- GATOR
- FREE PRESS BOX (WITH FALSE BOTTOM) OVER FIREPLACE
- EMILY GAIL COMMEMORATIVE TOILET
- MEDIA RECEPTION CLOSET
- JIMMY HOFFA
- BOB TALBERT HITCHIN' POST
- WADING POOL FILLED WITH PEPSI
- OLYMPIC SWIMMING POOL FILLED WITH COURVOSIER.
- FUNKY BUT GENUINE LEOPARD-SKIN LAMPPOST
- TRAP DOOR FOR MINICAM CREWS
- CHRIS K.

IMPORTANT INFORMATION IMPORTANT INFORMATION IMPORTANT INFORMATION IMPORTANT

ATTENTION FUN READERS
DUE TO LACK OF ADVERTISING FUN MAGAZINE IS NOT IT'S USUAL TWENTY FOUR PAGES. INSTEAD OF CUTTING OUT EVERYTHING WE HAD TO CONDENSE A BUNCH OF STUFF AND DO A TON OF ADDITIONAL LAYOUT. ELIMINATED ARTICLES INCLUDED THE NEW FALL LINE-UP BY CHRIS KASSEL, A BIG BACK TO SCHOOL EXTRAVAGANZA COLOR CENTERFOLD, FUNS CAREER GUIDE, SLANDER, COOL GUY BOOK COVERS AND A BUNCH OF OTHER REALLY GREAT STORIES AND ADS. SOME OF IT WILL BE PRINTED IN LATER ISSUES OR IN OUR EXCITING NEW VENTURE FUNGALORE

OUR NEW HOURS ARE:
SPACE RESERVATION & DEPOSIT- 2nd WEEK OF MONTH
AD ARTWORK & BALANCE DUE- 3rd WEEK OF MONTH
SINCE FUN IS NOW A YEAR OLD IT WILL NOW COME OUT BEFORE THE FIRST WEEKEND OF EACH MONTH, TYPICALLY WEDNESDAY, BUT NOT ALWAYS, WEDNESDAY

ATTENTION ADVERTISERS
SORRY IF WE HAD TO CUT OUT YOUR AD. THE MOST PROBABLE REASON IS YOU WERE LATE FOR ONE THING OR ANOTHER. DUE TO EXCESSIVE UNTIMELINESS BY A FEW OF YOU WE HAD TO CUT DOWN THE NUMBER OF PAGES. THIS AD SPACE COULD HAVE BEEN SOLD TO OTHER ESTABLISHMENTS. SORRY BUT WE CAN NO LONGER BE THE FRIENDLY FUN MR. NICE GUY ATTITUDE IN BUSINESS. SINCE WE ARE STARTING A NEW YEAR WE ARE GOING TO BE REAL PRICKS! WE'RE PLAYING HARDBALL NOW. BUT NOT TO YOU NICE ADVERTISERS

IMPORTANT INFORMATION IMPORTANT INFORMATION IMPORTANT INFORMATION IMPORTANT

▲ "Big Fun Page," *Fun*, March 1987.

Hair'em, Scare'em

Help Bill find his rug before the big broadcast!

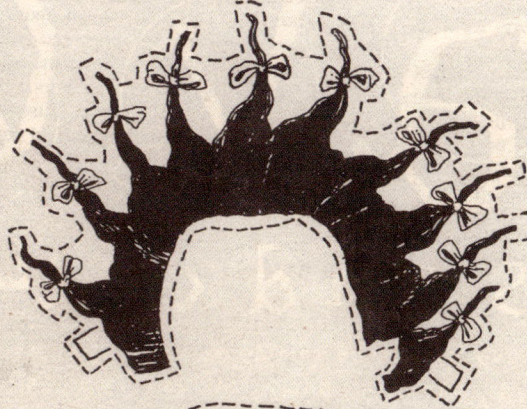

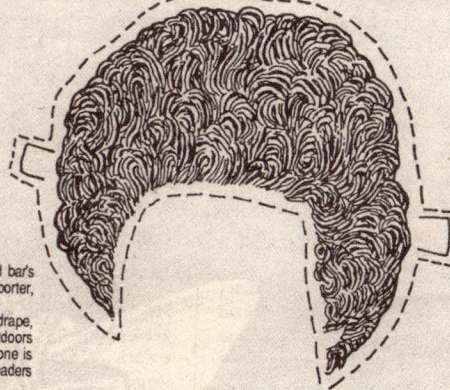

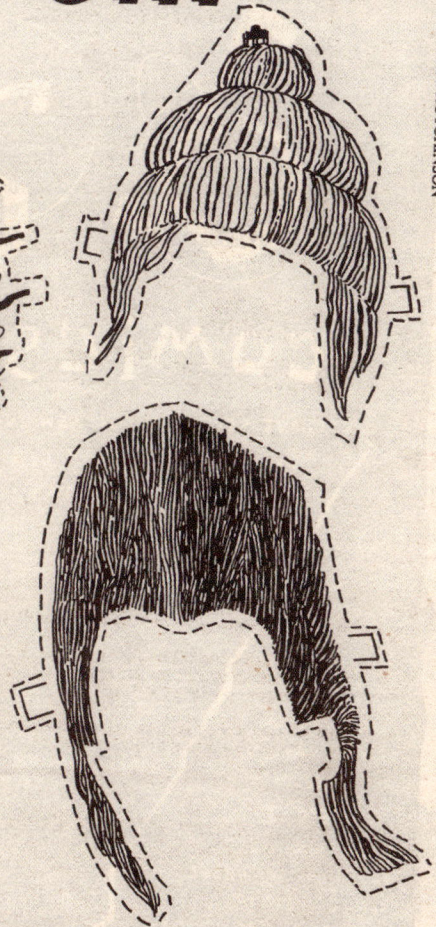

While on a super-duper secret, in-depth, nine-part undercover investigation of the Southfield bar's and disco's despicable "Happy Hour" practices, ace TV anchor, commentator and, urp, all-around party animal Bill Bombed lost his toupee!

During the ensuing super-duper, in-depth, nine-county undercover search for Billy's dome drape, hundreds of rugs were turned into the police. Saxony's, piles, plushes, sculptures, indoor-outdoors (with free pad included). It was enough to turn Irving Nussbaum goyem with envy. Which one is Bill's? Lt. Beaufford "Bull" Buttbuddy, Southfield's police chief, is asking FUN®'s astute readers to help identify the missing coconut cover.

Simply cut out each potential cube cape and place over Bill's stubbled sphere. Or, draw your own. Send your best guess to FUN® magazine (the magazine for swinging intellectuals). The best entry gets to actually meet Bill, drink with him, be introduced to his family and vacation with him in the sunny Bahamas! Second best will get a FUN® t-shirt (this one is legit). We'll print the most interesting entries. As usual, all entries become property of FUN® magazine and we reserve the right to publish them, use them in other issues and make smart-ass comments about them on these pages.

LAMP OF THE MONTH

Hey readers! How would you like to see your lamp on the pages of FUN®? Here's all you gotta do:

1) Take picture of lamp (B&W or color).
2) Put picture of lamp in envelope.
3) Mail envelope to FUN®.

Hints- All lamps are not created equal. We prefer lamps that scream "Look at me, I'm ugly." The more unusual your lamp, the better your chances are. Use a white background if possible. Be sure to take the lens cap off your camera. If you do not have a museum quality lamp, make one.

This Months Lamp - "Eye of the Beholder"
Owner - Mr & Mrs. C. Arbunkle, Inkster.

BAZOOKA WINKY and his GANG®

SAY, WAITER! WHAT'S HARDER THAN FINDING THE G-SPOT?

WINKY WHEN IT COMES TIME TO PAY THIS TAB.

THE WIND BLOWS FREE—WHY DON'T YOU !!

469 FALSE TEETH! SHOW OFF TO YOUR FRIENDS! SEND $3.00 PLUS 9,999 COMICS & DENTAL CHART

one size fits all

VALUE 10 COMICS
ALLOW 4 TO 6 WEEKS FOR SHIPMENT. VOID WHERE PROHIBITED. REGULATED OR TAXED

MR KNOW IT ALL

How many Fun Magazines would you have to stack up to reach the moon?
More than all the grains in a thirty two ounce carton of salt.
Who invented corn?
Corn was invented on a Tuesday by an American Indian named Hachichawa.
What's the deal with Albanians anyway?
They breast fed from hairy nipples.
How come vanilla only comes in one flavor?
Supply and demand.
DID YOU KNOW?
That people from Taylor can actually be taught how to read.
In 1978 a doctor taught a 13 year old native the alphabet. Skeptics claimed he was given physical cues by the doctor and did not actually understand the concept.

SPUDS MacKENZIE

EVERYONE'S TALKIN' ABOUT THAT "PARTY ANIMAL"...

AND GUESS WHAT "PARTY" GIVES ME THE BIGGEST WELCOME?

THE REPUBLICAN PARTY!

YUP!

YO!

YEW BETCHA!!

YEAH, THEY'RE THE ONES WHO HOPE YOU'RE DRUNK AND STUPID ALL THE TIME SO YOU WON'T NOTICE ALL THE SNEAKY THINGS THEY'RE DOING IN THE GOVERNMENT!

THEY'VE UPDATED AN OLD SAYING FROM THE SIXTIES. NOW THEY SAY DRINK UP! THROW UP! PASS OUT! THAT WAY, YOU WON'T KNOW WHAT THEY'RE UP TO—'TILL IT'S TOO LATE!

WHA'?! HOW DID THIS HAPPEN?

CONGRESS PASSES DRAFT LAW!!

PARTY GUY

©1987 CAROLE SOBOCINSKI

▲ Bill Bond's hair contest, *Fun*, March 1987.

Hair'em, Scare'em

Help Bill find his rug before the big broadcast!

Winner: Tom Jones afro

Grand Prize Winner
No one! That's Right nobody was smart enough to guess the Tom Jones afro. Sorry kids. Guess that means no trip to the Bahamas. Better Luck next time.

• A romantic evening
Honorable Mention
Gail Uchalik
You don't get doodly-squat.

Last Place
Hillbilly

Second Place Winner
Any Sayler
You get a FUN® T-shirt.

...and the weiners are:

Bill sports his new "Moe Howard" by BoRics after a trip to the Stooges Film-Fest

ZIPPY

▲ Bill Bonds hair contest winners, *Fun*, April 1987.

Peanuts parody, *Fun*, Fall 1989. ▲

bridge for visiting TV crews, and even a military field gun "aimed at hostile Dearborn."

Fun also found good material in Bill Bonds, the combative news anchor for Detroit's ABC affiliate, WXYZ. Bonds was legendary not only for his aggressive attitude during interviews, but for his prominent hairpiece and struggles with alcoholism. In the March 1987 issue, readers were invited to give the hard-drinking hairpiece-wearing Detroit native a new hairdo. The winners were printed in the next issue.

Despite the irreverent treatment of locals, it was actually *Fun*'s lampoon of fictional characters that drew legal fire. Inside the fall 1989 issue of *Fun* was a one-page comic created by illustrator Doug Dearth and publisher Jerry Vile—*"It's the Great Pumpkin Part VI Charlies [sic] Revenge."* The piece parodied the annual television cartoon special featuring the Peanuts gang and 1980s slasher films. The comic made the clean-cut, fun-loving gang into foul-mouthed, sexually depraved, murderous drug fiends. For the attorneys representing the work of Peanuts creator Charles M. Schulz, that was a problem. The *Fun* team said a cease-and-desist letter arrived a few months after the issue hit newsstands.

"There was a quote [from Schultz]: 'No one does this to my children.' We were supposed to destroy all the remaining copies. We thought it was awesome, I'm sure. Nobody was frightened by it. It was a badge of honor," said Dearth. A search by the archivist at the Charles M. Schulz Museum in California did not turn up a copy of the letter, and sadly, Peterson and Dearth said their copies have long since vanished into the dustbin of history.

Laughing Hyenas, *Fun*, April 1987. ▶

Laughing Hyenas

What is a laughing hyena?

A hyena can make a remarkably wide range of sounds. Its usual cry begins on a low mournful note and rises to a shrill climax. It barks and growls and can imitate the roar of a lion. When a hyena finds a carcass, it gives out a weird cry that sounds like an insane human laugh. This cry has earned it the nickname of laughing hyena.

Hyenas look something like ugly dogs. But they are not members of the dog family. They form a separate family of their own.

While I was working on this article, I came across an old official British Government report on the damage done by

hy·e'na, hy·ae'na (hī-ē'nà), n. [L. hyaena, fr. Gr. hyaina. fr. hys hog.] Any of a family (Hyaenidae) of large and strong, but cowardly, carnivorous mammals of Asia and Africa.

The closest I have ever come to seeing a hyena birth was when, one afternoon, I met Bloody Mary carrying a new-born cub in her mouth. It cannot have been more than half an hour old, for it was still wet and the afterbirth was attached by the umbilical cord.

Hyenas, like wild dogs, kill by disembowelling ther prey and it is just as horrible to watch.

wild beasts in India during the year 1878. An especially interesting part of it was about these same striped laughing hyenas. It showed that in this particular year they had killed thirty-three people. Their record of 1877 was twenty-four people killed. So it looks as though they are even more ferocious than most of us think.

Almost the first animal, says Mr. Andersson, I saw at this place was a gigantic "tiger-wolf," or spotted hyena, which to my surprise, instead of seeking safety in flight, remained stationary, grinning in the most ghastly manner. Having approached within twenty paces, I perceived, to my horror, that his fore paws and the skin and flesh of his front legs had been gnawed away, and that he could scarcely move from the spot. To shorten the sufferings of the poor beast I seized my opportunity and knocked him on the head with a stone; and catching him by the tail, drove my hunting knife deep into his side. But I had to repeat the operation more than once before I could put an end to his existence. I am at a loss how to account for his mangled condition. It certainly could not have been from age, for his teeth were good. Could it be possible that from want of food he had become too weak for further exertions, and that, as a last resource, he had attacked his own body? Or was he an example of that extraordinary species of cruelty said to be practised by the lion on the hyena, when the latter has the insolence to interfere with the monarch's prey.

The spotted hyena lives in a burrow or cave. It sleeps by day. At night it comes out to eat. Like all hyenas, it is a meat-eater with big, strong jaws. It hunts as part of a pack.

Hyenas are frequently sick, and always they roll in it. It was not for some while that I realised that, for the most part, they hyena is not being sick in the normal sense of the word, but it actually regurgitating a mass of undigestible hair. Often, before or after rolling on this hair mass, a hyena picks out fragments of partially dissolved bone-when the hyena chews on them it seems that they are soft for there is no sound.

Exactly why hyenas, along with so many other carnivores, like to roll on strong-smelling substances we do not know. But after all, humans (expecially women) are fond of anointing their bodies with strong-smelling substances too. And considering that the foundation for so many expensive perfumes comes from the anal glands of civets, perhaps we should not be too surprised at or critical of the hyena's taste in suitable odours.

Soon the squabbling was fierce, and the sounds became loud and, louder, the whoops and the growls, the sudden spine-chilling roars, the nervous chuckles and giggles. And, mingling with these calls, was the slurping, chewing, tearing, crunching sould of some thirty mouths feeding on flesh, skin and bone. Small wonder that, during such scrums, unintentional cannibalism occasionally takes place as ears and noses and paws get bitten, for after a while it must be difficult to differentiate between the flesh of the prey and the bloodsoaked, meaty hide of another hyena. That night Nelson acquired yet another notch out of one ear. I suspect that Mrs. Brown lost the end of her nose during one of these hyena feasts.

"Man is more cruel than the tiger and has less of pity than the hyena"....Schopenhauer

"One day an older nun stopped me in the corridor. She asked me whether I knew what I was doing, and when I said I didn't understand, she said the staff had a name for people like myself: hyuaenidae. As I still failed to understand, she said: hyenas. Men of my kind, she said, lurked around bodies that were dying; each time I fed upon the woman, I hastened her death"....Jerzy Kosinski

'To keep in practice, Hemingway shot guinea fowl for the table and hyenas, because of his hatred for the "Hermaphroditic, self-eating devourer of the dead, the trailer of calving cows, hamstringer, potential biter-off of your face at night when you slept, sad yowler, camp-follower, stinking, foul....Ernest Hemingway

"Like a laughing hyena run out of breath—I've shot my rocks off till there's nothing left."...Iggy Pop

The underlying horror may be that we all inhabit the swollen tissues of a body politic that is drenched in bad conscience, so bad indeed that the laugh of the hyena reverberates from every TV set, and is in danger of becoming our true national anthem. ...Norman Mailer

T. Caldwell

(Tim- This article was supposed to be about The Laughing Hyenas Rock/Blues from Ann Arbor. You should have mentioned thier EP Merry-Go-Round which is due out this month. -ED)

In 1979, keyboarder Luis Resto was an original and integral component in Detroit's cult combo, Was (Not Was), playing on the bands critically-acclaimed first LP and accompanying the group on a small U.S. tour. Resto performed on this year's "What Up Dog?" as well and went along when the Was gang did Europe this past summer.

In between, Resto came to be regarded as one of the Motor City's most sought-after session players. He served as conductor-slash-pianist for a couple of musicals at he Birmingham Theatre; did studio or live appearances with Gladys Knight and the Pips and Michael Henderson; and performed on scores of 12" R&B singles.

In short, Luis has never been at a loss for work.

Although there was little time left over to create his own compositions, Luis made an exception when New York City choreographer Susan Marshall asked him to create a score for a 1984 modern dance piece. The work was so successful that Marshall has choreographed works around Resto's scores in each year since, staging performances at the Dallas Ballet and Boston City Ballet as well as in New York.

Resto's haunting musical scores captured the attention of New York City's Dance Theater Workshop which commissioned an evening of performance art -- "Could You Make It More Red, Yet Slightly Blue?". The work -- a bizarre mosaic which combines music, lyrics and motion -- premiered last February at the Bessie Schonberg Theater in New York City. In April, the show, re-titled: "Louie Restaurant's World" and streamlined somewhat for a more artistically-sophisticated Detroit audience, played for two standing-room-only performances in a Woodward Avenue bar.

It's appropriate that Luis Resto has chosen a venue halfway between Detroit's Medical and Cultural Centers to unveil the next embodiment of his unique performance art, "Luis Resto and Balls-Out Entertainment". Is it art or is it anarchy....? Friday, October 28, 1988, at the Majestic Theatre, 4140 Woodward Ave., Detroit.

▲ Luis Resto, *Fun*, October 1988.

Fun with Music

Each installment of *Fun* was also infused with music, film, and art. While the early issues included very little feature writing, each edition did include album and concert reviews. As the magazine's design and concept evolved, *Fun* started to spotlight Detroit musicians and groups, including some that would make an impact internationally.

The October 1988 issue of *Fun* included a short feature on Luis Resto. A well-regarded keyboard player since his early days as part of funk-rock group known as Was (Not Was),

Resto also collaborated with choreographers and other artists. Resto went on to pick up an Oscar in 2003 for Best Original Song, having helped compose Eminem's anthem "Lose Yourself," created for the Detroit-shot film *8 Mile*. It was the first hip-hop song to win the honor.

Garage rock favorites the Gories, forebears of the blues-influenced, lo-fi roots rock sound, were featured in the June 1987 issue of *Fun*. Formed in 1986 by Mick Collins, Dan Kroha, and Peggy O'Neill, the trio's stripped-down sound would put Detroit on the map about a decade

Winky's New Band Spotlight

Thunderbird E. S. Q. I love it more than I love you. That's an excerpt from the Gories songbook soon to be published nationwide. Included will be pictures, fun facts, artifacts, and three thumbtacks so you can nail the Gories on your wall.

Dan Kroha, (guitar, vocals), Peg O'Neil (drums) and Mick (guitar, vocals)...(yeah, that's right, Mick) gorified themselves about a year ago today with just intentions (i.e.we don't wanna be white-boy blues guys) and in doing so have become the best example of wild teen trash, gut-bucket R&B that Detroits been faced with in quite some time. Bonded toegether by Silvertone guitars, Vox amplifiers and half c starlight drum set with goals consisting of LP's on Crypt records (ask your local record dealer) which would be continually bubbling under the Top-40 and number 2--- the Fame of REM (they'd like to fill the Fox) The Gories are already planning their vinyl debut which will be two originals on the next Wanghead compilation album, "It Came from the Garage Too" namely "You Little Nothing" and "Gimme Love." Hopefully they'll get their now classic "Thunderbird E.S.Q.," out somehow (send money) in the near future.

Live shows have been few and far between as the band claims to have been kicked out of more clubs than actually exist but they'll be appearing June 13th at the Vanity Ballroom.

▲ The Gories, *Fun*, June 1987.

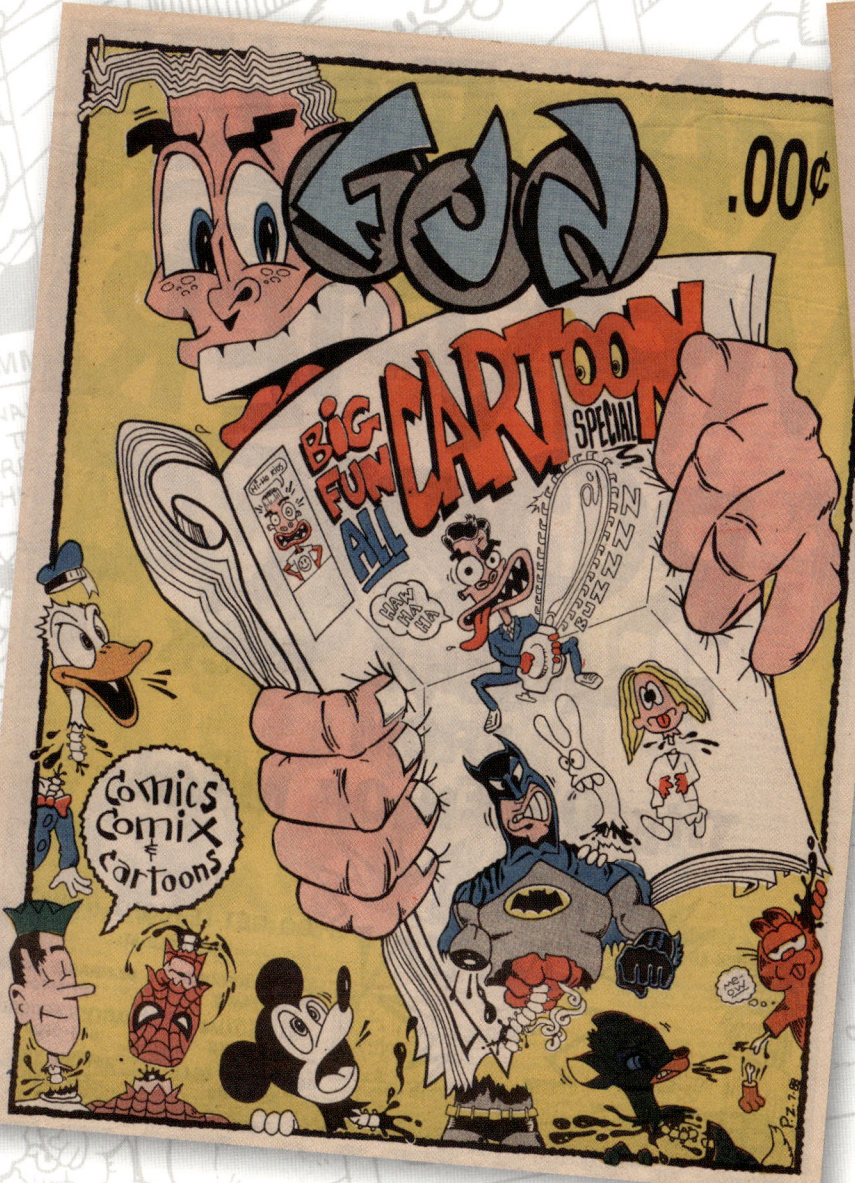

▲ Comics Issue, *Fun*, July 1987.

▲ Comics Issue, *Fun*, August 1988.

later. The Gories released their first album in 1989, but after three full-length LPs, the band broke up in 1992. Out of the ashes of the Gories, several bands formed and built sizable followings. Kroha created the Demolition Doll Rods, and Collins formed the Dirtbombs. The Gories would influence the late 1990s/early 2000s garage rock scene that helped catapult the White Stripes to international recog-

nition, and both Kroha and Collins found success in the scene with their new groups as well.

Fun was also one of the first magazines to cover the burgeoning techno movement in Detroit. The April 1988 issue ran a feature on Derrick May, techno innovator and founder of the Detroit Electronic Music Festival (now known as Movement). May's music career launched in 1987 with the release of his first record, *Nude Photo*, which many see as the

MAYDAY

MAYDAY

The first encounter with Derrick (MAYDAY) May was a few years ago at a short-lived club called Liedernacht in downtown Detroit. On this particular night the place was packed. It was a fairly new club only a few months old. It had the reputation of being a "new wave" dance club and doing pretty well for itself. The music on this night was a mix of dancey new wave and hi-energy dance music. And by the sound of it the D.J. was well versed in the art of mixing the records together. I was so intrigued that I had to talk to this person. As it turns out Derrick and I had mutual acquaintances but had never met until now. He said he had been spinning here for a short while and that Fridays were getting hotter every week (he only spun on Friday nights). But they wouldn't move him to Saturday nights, the better of the two-which wasn't doing as well as Fridays. The management apparently didn't want to move Derrick to Saturdays because he was attracting a large "black" crowd to a primarily white new wave club and didn't want it to get out of hand.

It wasn't too long after that that he was gone, and was replaced by a D.J. who couldn't mix at all. He said they kinda gave him the run-around and eventually let him go. Well two years later discussing a halloween party and weather or not to have bands or D.J.s play at it, and if so, who? The mention of Derrick was made, but we had no idea what he was up to, or if he was still around. So we sent out a few messages and got in touch with him.

As it turns out, Derrick had purposely kept a low profile over the past 2 years. He had been working in the studio, running his own record label (TRANSMAT) and putting out his own records which brings us to the current.

He records under the name **Rhythm Is Rhythm** and *HIGH PERFORMANCE DANCE MUSIC* is the moniker he uses to describe the music. Most of his compositions are instrumentals aside from some sampling, mainly because he doesn't sing well. He has no problem with using outside vocalists but its not a critical need at this point. In April a double compilation LP is due out on "Virgin" Records featuring himself and two others- Kevin Saunderson and Blake Baxter. At the time of this interview Reps from both Virgin & Chrysalis Records were vying for Derrick's wares. Derrick, who already been in the British Press was on the verge again, as both *New Musical Express* and the *Face* magazines were in town (Detroit) to see him exclusively.

As for Mayday, he likes the attention but would rather sign a label deal and get back to the studio. He also wants to try his hand in some new age music. He claims he's had several works in the can for some time. He also aspires to do some soundtrack work. And as for his own label Transmat, he wants to expand it with more artists and give it a little more credibility. Derrick gives alot of his credit to his friends and colleagues. One in particular is Juan Atkins of Metroplex Records. "Juan taught me how to spin (be a D.J.) and introduced to me a studio."

"This town ain't shit"

He claims most of his success is from other cities: Chicago, Washington D.C., New York, and especially Europe. And as for Detroit "This city ain't shit, and there's very little support here (sound familiar). Detroit "urban black" radio gives us very little support, never having added any thing to their formats." WGPR virtually none and WJLB only plays it on its mix-masters programs, usually 30 seconds of the song with no recognition as to who the artists are. The only big plug he gets is a 20 minute radio show called the MAYDAY MIX on Friday nights at 10:30 on WJLB, which is actually an example of his mixing abilities.

Well the jokes on them because rumor is that Derrick is so *hot* right now record labels are tossing offers at him right and left. Could 1988 be the year of MAYDAY?, wait and see.

In a recent Detroit News article about "Detroit Rockers on the move" no mention of Mayday was made at all, and he along with a small collective of colleagues probably have more going for themselves than anyone in the entire city.

BY GARY ARNETT

EVIL GUYS

INTERVIEW WITH DIRECTOR SAM RAIMI AND PRODUCER ROB TAPERT

I proceeded to the offices of Renaissance Pictures (right next to Sams Jams in Ferndale), in this real cheap rent hole-in-the-wall office building that must be set for demolition vbecause the creaky floors are scarier that Sam Raimi's Evil Dead) hoping to get an interview with the Ferndale Boys for my magazine, Film Threat. Of course, Jerry Vile weaseled me into asking a few questions for his rag.

First of all, Sam Raimi is a Keith Moon Look-a-like who has made films all his life and probably got to his state of sucess from rich parents, (his mom owns Lu Lu's Lingerie). Rob Tapert is a portly (ie:fat) fellow who produces Sam's movies which means he is on the phone all day begging for money. (Most likely from Dad).

We talked in this dingy back room and kept being interrupted by phone calls but here are the Fun questions that I got in:

Chris Gore: What is the scariest thing that ever happened to you?

Sam Raimi: The scariest thing? I was living in New York and I heard this horrifying noise next to my apartment. I went to the apartment next door to see what happened in the middle of the night. I found a woman who had fallen off the top of her bunk bed. It was gross because she was eating chocolate ice cream, and she was bleeding and the blood was mixed in the ice cream. It was gross.

Chris Gore: What are some of your favorite pranks?

Sam Raimi: Well the old shaving cream on the telephone reciever.... go in the other room and call the number and they get an earful of shaving cream. Or my favorite pranks are ones that are long term.

Rob Tapert (butting in)- Some he may not want to devulge at this time because they are still -

Sam Raimi: - in the works. But some gags it all depends on how you eat them up. Like a good tip can be gotten from a friend. A friend may call you and tell you about his car is in a shop at Leo's Auto Shop. Then when he goes home, you have just been planted with a very particular piece of information. You can call him and pretend to be from Leo's Auto Shop an pretend his car was destroyed! Or that you found a dead body in the trunk, or some crap that he would believe, because it is coming so far out of left field. So in planning a prank, look for the secret tip that make it uniquely powerful.

Chris Gore: What is the best prank that was ever pulled on Rob?

Rob Tapert: Scott Spiegel (writer for Evil Dead 2), and Sam have pulled pranks but each of them would deny it. I know Scott actually pulled the worst stunt on me. He put a load in my cigarrette and it scared the shit out of me, and I veered up into the median, and then the cops came and arrested me for drunk driving although I was'nt drunk and they finally released me when the story got cleared, but for a little while they assumed the sulphur smell in the car was dope, and I was saying " No! No! It was a cigarette load's I am going to torture Scott to his grave for that one.

Sam's gags are always different than Scott's. Sam plants ones that you won't find for years. When we were living together in college, he was the one who put the honey under the plates so it would stick in the cabinet or put "stink" perfume in your bedroom.

LOGO-PAUL ZIMMERMAN

◄ Derrick May, *Fun*, April 1988.

FILM TREAT
by chris gore

Evil Dead 2- Dead By Dawn
This is not a horror movie but a comedy in the vein of the three Stooges. Everyone dies in the end except for Bruce Campbell who is transported back to 1300 A.D. just in time for Evil Dead 3. It's a BLAST!

Raising Arizona
Really cute movie about a couple who can't have a kid so they kidnap one. Nicholas Cage and wife end up returning the kid however and don't go to jail. It looks like DirectorJoel Cohen and Sam Rami (Evil Dead) exchanged notes for their films because there are quite a lot of similarities (chase through houses, motion sickness, moving camera, ect.). This movie is fun too!

Hollywood Shuffle
Elvis Mitchell gave it a ten so it must be good. Although as this movie does a hilarious job of satirizing the stereotyping of blacks it ends up making fun of Jews (the Jewish writer a gum smacking J.A.P. girl) and it is showing exclusively at the Americana in Southfield! Where are the protesters? C'mon all you Yiddish people! Get off you duffs! The Catholics did it for Hall Mary! Geta move on! Help this movie make more money!!

▲ "Film Treat," *Evil Dead 2* review, *Fun*, May 1987.

opening of attention on Detroit's then-underground techno scene. "Jerry [Vile] and Gary [Arnett, *Fun* and *Orbit* designer] are my bros," said May. "I did the interview because they asked me. I love the guys. Helpful? I think not; it was just fun to do. We were young and full of fire, dreams, and kick-ass attitude. You had to be there to know what I'm talking about. Basically, we all had the same quest, to change the world, and we did. Life changers, game breakers, dream makers. They scared the powers that be. We all did."

Another consistent feature in *Fun*, with its focus on comics and cartoons, was "So, You Think You're an Artist?" showcasing local cartoonists, illustrators, and painters. The title of the page is a spinoff from a feature in *White Noise*, "So, You Think You're a Poet?" which highlighted lyrics and poetry from readers. An

Chris Gore, a Royal Oak native, started working at Thomas Video after presenting a fake ID and lying about his age in 1982. Gore, who was about sixteen at the time, said the owners, Jim Olenski and Gary Reichel, wouldn't hire anyone under eighteen because the store carried adult videos. At his new job, Gore met Paul Zimmerman.

Gore said before long he was dubbed "Junior" because he was about ten years younger than the other staff members and their old friends from the Detroit punk scene, who treated him like a little brother.

"[Thomas Video] really did attract all the misfits. If you couldn't hang, if you were too normal, you wouldn't be working there," said Gore. Because of his interest in shooting Super 8 and video, Gore created music videos for local bands connected to the store and their friends, like Cinecyde and the 3-D Invisibles. His love of print developed while working on a Xeroxed zine at Royal Oak's Kimball High School called *The Truth*, which lasted for about six issues. In February 1985, while attending Wayne State University, Gore and his friend Andre Seewood started *Film Threat*, which would eventually capture the zeitgeist of the early 1990s independent film boom.

Because of his love of cult films and his combative attitude, Gore was often confined to the back room of the video store, where he had minimal interaction with customers. "I was, frankly, filled with pointless arrogance . . . I was a punk and angry for no reason. I was just a poor, lower-middle-class kid from divorced parents who was looking to do something of note," said Gore.

At work, Gore and Zimmerman said they would compete to be the biggest slacker. Gore would transfer Super 8 home movies to videotape while Zimmerman would create flyers and ads for the store. Around this time, Gore's film zine started to take off. Other hip video stores around the country started carrying it. By his twentieth birthday, Gore had dropped out of Wayne State University's film program to make *Film Threat* into a full-fledged magazine.

Gore said Peterson saw his energy and hired him at his computer software company. He said his new boss knew he would be terrible at the software company, but Peterson wanted him in the room to help with the launch of *Fun*.

Since his beginnings in Royal Oak, Gore has written books on film and filmmaking, become an awards show and television host for various cable channels, and made his own independent films, including the comedy *My Big Fat Independent Movie*.

"Film Treat," *Fun*, December 1986. ▲

annual comics issue edited by Paul Zimmerman was released in July 1987 and August 1988 and featured pieces submitted by *Fun* readers, including early works by respected Detroit artists Mark Dancey, Niagara, and Glenn Barr.

During the first year of *Fun*, the film reviewer was Chris Gore, whose own fanzine *Film Threat* gained popularity at the crest of the early 1990s independent film boom. At sixteen, Gore got his start in the scene at Thomas Video, the legendary Metro Detroit cult video store owned and operated by members of the punk band Cinecyde, working alongside *White Noise* co-conspirator Paul Zimmerman.

Gore's piece for *Fun* was called "Film Treat"—a reference to his own magazine. Beyond offering a few words on each film, the idea was to give the reviews a visual shorthand:

"I would write these sort of very simple synopsis reviews, just a couple of lines, and we would come up with these icons. So there was a legend at the top of the page, and it was like, the sex icon was just boobs, the violence icon was someone being punched in the face, and those just got ridiculous."

Even though Peterson brought Gore on because of his energy, their personalities often clashed, and the two eventually had a falling out. Gore said he worked well with Peterson at *Fun* due to their similar sensibilities, but he started to feel like the older punk was being a weasel. "If Jerry owed you money, you would never get the money, but he would even it out in the universe in his mind. For example, if he owed you twenty dollars, he would say, 'Well, I bought you a popcorn, so, I think I only owe you ten.' Or it would be like, 'Well, I paid for parking and I bought you a beer when we went to the City Club, so, I guess we're good.' This is not a unique experience. So, after a while it was like, 'What the fuck? This guy screws me at every turn.'" By May 1987, Gore was listed as the "Universally Hated Editor" on the *Fun* masthead because of his complaints. In the August 1987 issue, Gore's column was replaced by another film review called "Film-o-Movietron"

written by "Alfredo Garcia," a reference to director Sam Peckinpah's 1974 film, *Bring Me the Head of Alfredo Garcia.*

Fungus Rodeo and the Mutiny

Chris Gore felt disrespected and cheated after *Fun* started to become a small success, and he discovered he was not alone. Over the years, many of Peterson's friends and co-conspirators

▲ *Fungus Rodeo* cover by Glenn Barr, Fall 1987.

INTERVIEW

FR: How come you are so fat?

JV: What else have I got to do with all my money?

FR: What's this about a bet between you and Bob Talbert?

JV: We've got a bet, who can lose 1/2 a pound in a month, winner gets a box of Dove Bars!

FR: This question is for the oldsters out there, where did you get the name for your ancient band, Jerry Vile and the Boners?

JV: Well, before shows my band would always have hard-ons so I'd have to suck them off so we wouldn't be so embarrassed on stage.

FR: I see, you were quoted in FUN magazine as saying Halloween was one of your favorite times of the year, what have you dressed up as in past costume parties?

JV: I've been Fred Flintstone, Elvis, in his later period of course, Jabba the Hut, Jackie Gleason as Minnesota FATS, I can dress up as just about anyone fat, which means I have a lot of FUN charactors to choose from. This year I'm gonna shave my head bald and leave just a little patch of hair on the top of my head, guess who I'm gonna be?

FR: I don't know, who?

JV: Charlie Brown! And what's so great is my head is in proportional size to the real character!

CONTEST

Guess the number of double chins under Jerry's beard and win a FREE subscription to FUNGUS RODEO! Only one entry per person. Family, friends, and employees of Big Fun, Inc., are not eligible for prizes (and that includes you Jer!). HINT: When you see Jerry at a bar, on stage or at the Windsor Ballet just scream out, "Hey Jerry, how many double chins under that beard?" He'll be more than happy to give you the answer.

▲ "Jerry Vile: The *Fun* Emperor" comic by "Sailor Rick" Metcalf, *Fungus Rodeo*, Fall 1987

▲ Dave's Comics ad, *Fun* (Art by Glenn Barr).

were roped into the creation of the magazine but weren't happy with how his print plantation was run. Gore decided to use the collective animosity to strike back.

Those involved in the plot included many of Peterson's old friends dating back to the Bookie's scene along with *Fun* contributor Paul Zimmerman, cover artist Glenn Barr, salesperson Christy Burns, and writers Tim Caldwell and "Sailor Rick" Metcalf. "[On *Fun*] nobody was really making any money," said Metcalf. "But to me it was like, 'Jeeze, you know, he's getting the glory and maybe a little bit of the money, but what are we getting? Something's gotta happen here.' Gore was the impetus for this."

The end result was a twenty-four-page screed titled *Fungus Rodeo*. Peppered throughout were little jabs and big punches at Peterson. A fake ad for a non-existent back issue of *Fungus Rodeo* listed Peterson as a gay celebrity, and a cartoon created by Metcalf titled "Jerry Vile: The FUN Emperor" satirized what was perceived as the publisher's self-aggrandizing behavior. The page also includes a fake interview with the *Fun* publisher and a contest for a free one-year subscription to *Fungus Rodeo* for anyone who could guess the correct number of chins under Peterson's beard. "It was my way of saying, 'Hey Jerry, I do like you but you are kind of being an asshole,'" said Gore.

Beyond *Fun* staffers and Peterson's friends, Gore was also able to rope in a number of *Fun* advertisers for *Fungus Rodeo*. Noir Leather, Thomas Video, and Dave's Comics all took ads. The back-page ad for vintage clothing store Cinderella's Attic included another swing at Peterson. Featuring a caricature of the publisher with a cigarette hanging out of his mouth, holding a bottle and a greasy piece of pizza, the ad copy read,

"Clothes that will flatter anyone!" Peterson was rather notorious for wearing shabby, food-stained clothes.

Eventually, Detroit's alt weekly, the *Metro Times*, took notice of the dustup between Gore and Peterson. Over the previous year, *Fun* had dealt its share of jabs and jokes at its established rival's expense. In the second issue of *Fun*, *Metro Times* co-founder Ron Williams was listed as one of the "10 Most Unfun People in this City!" *Fun* went on to declare that "magazines like FUN can survive in the black hole of journalism created by this overly pompous weekly freebie rag." Three issues in, December 1986, *Fun* ran a page of ads for Noir Leather that the *Metro Times* refused to run. The subtext of the copy accompanying the ads was that the rival paper was too old, unhip, and concerned about offending the sensibilities of its readers and advertisers. A few months later, *Fun* said picking up a copy of the *Metro Times*, parodied as the "Metro Slimes," was one of the ways you could contract AIDS, satirizing the paranoia surrounding the disease in the mid-1980s. When *Fungus Rodeo* hit the streets, Fun's crosstown competitor finally decided to land a blow against the upstart rival's punk rock sensibilities when it published a feature on the feud.

In the October 14, 1987, edition of the *Metro Times*, writer Jerome Przybylski penned a feature headlined "The Only Magazine War That Matters: Forget *Detroit Monthly* and *Metropolitan Detroit*—this is where the real action is." It's obvious from the tone of the *Metro Times* piece that the writer enjoyed this little spat over at its scrappy, "not ready for prime time" competitor.

It's vile. It's gory. It's groovy. It's a war pregnant with sex, power and money. It's a piñata of lost

▲ *Fungus Rodeo* back cover, Fall 1987.

trust and bitterness. It's a trombone full of rat-bitten celebrities. It's Jerry Vile vs. Chris Gore.

Vile is editor and publisher of *Fun* magazine. A local monthly humor tabloid that's free and, unlike the *Metro Times,* isn't burdened by intellectual horsehair or an unfashionable social conscience. *Fun* gleefully exploits the computer age in which information overload has created a backlash of eager non-readers. I'm talking about Americans with an attention span of a hiccup.

Fun also exploits the pent-up angst of honky-chauvinist-racist-porkers who long to see minorities and women ridiculed with good, old-fashioned abandon.

Actually, inasmuch as *Fun* slams everyone, maybe it's not prejudiced. I don't know. Let Robert Bork be the judge.

After taking shots at *Fun*, Przybylski asked a salient question about Gore's intentions with *Fungus Rodeo:* "How do you defame a man whose willfully adopted name is Vile? Run an exposé that he's a vegetarian philanthropist? A closet gentleman? A subscriber to the *Effete Times* and *Smithsonian* magazine. No. Gore had other ideas." Przybylski writes that Gore's tactics were sophomoric, "yet it communicates and, because it's art, who am I to judge if it's good or bad?"

In the piece, Przybylski showed the stark philosophical division between the *Metro Times* and *Fun.* One paper espoused a social activist philosophy born out of the civil rights struggle and anti-war left of the mid- to late 1960s; while the other satirized contemporary America, its political cynicism a product of the Watergate Scandal and the depressed economy of the late 1970s.

The *Metro Times* piece also highlights a discussion in a *Detroit News* column that said Peterson was going to sue his former girlfriend Heidi Lichtenstein, the owner of Cinderella's Attic, over the ad featuring his unflattering likeness. Lichtenstein responds, "All I did was ask an artist to draw me a big, fat gross slob, and this is what he came up with. Any likeness to Jerry Vile is purely coincidental. Jerry's crying like a baby. If this looks like him, he must have flies around his head. Because the guy in the ad does."

Continuing, Przybylski added, "Vile said he's not upset for vanity reasons. He's miffed because Cinderella's Attic used his picture for commercial purposes without his authorization. That's why he had this lawyer send the letter threatening suit."

Przybylski asked Lichtenstein if the *Fungus Rodeo* ad had been borne out of romantic anger at Peterson over a possible infidelity she found out about during their relationship. She denied it. The article continued, "Lichtenstein and Gore's anti-Vile rhetoric was meant to be contagious. Like singing 'Deutschland Uber Alles,' it held the promise of warming the blood, quickening the pulse and stirring the libido if you joined in. Meanwhile, Vile seemed to not care what I thought of him or Gore. I've remained ambivalent about this struggle. Expect for one question. Doesn't either publisher pay more than the *Metro Time*s?"

Przybylski grudgingly respected Gore, having read copies of *Fungus Rodeo* and *Film Threat* dropped off at the *Metro Times* offices: "I read both magazines, was envious that a twenty-one-year-old punk/brat/nerd could put out such things." Then Przybylski asked Gore if his experience at *Fun*, working with Peterson, helped him to become a better humor writer. Gore responded, "If anything, Paul Zimmerman did."

Przybylski continued:

Well, I tried to get Vile credit for being the Uncle Russ/John Sinclair/Savage Grace of underground Detroit humor in the last decade. But Gore wouldn't budge. He told me that Vile's problem is that he doesn't pay. And that almost all the staff and freelancers are expected to work for the sheer moral goodness of labor. "Arbeit Macht Frei." Now we touch on the reason why Gore left *Fun*. Gore said he left because he was promised payment that he never received. Vile said Gore was ignored and fraternally held in contempt because he never turned in his material on time. Well, well, well. That's where the initial fissure is located. Which brings us to the following questions: Is money the root of all evil? And if it is, could you tell me where twins go fishing for genius on Tuesday?

When asked about his thoughts on the matter in the *Metro Times* piece, Peterson tried to downplay the feud: "Of course the rumors are now out that Vile is going to kill, maim or paddle the behind of Mr. Gore. These intentions he denied on the phone. Vile seemed fatigued by the feud. 'Chris is starting a fake war to get publicity for his new venture. I don't have any anger or animosity. In fact, I don't care.'"

Peterson may have played it cool in the press, but Gore said he knew his former friend and boss was gunning for him, and he knew it would only be a matter of time before he ran into Peterson. "So, I go to Gusoline Alley, and

Fungus Rodeo is out, and I know Jerry is looking for me. He's hurt by it. And Jerry is one of those guys, as much as he was trying to come off being tough, he's very sensitive. He would get worked up over things, little things, and he would hold grudges," said Gore.

Gore said he was feeling very pleased with his "go fuck yourself" and the *Metro Times* article when he ran into Peterson at the bar. "I had the biggest smile on my face. He came right up to me and punched me in the face. Just SLAM. Punched me in the face. Immediately after he punched me in the face, he said, 'Dude, I'm sorry. Let me buy you a drink,'" said Gore.

This is where their stories differ. Peterson said he didn't punch Gore in the face after grabbing him by the collar. He says Dave Huxley of Dave's Comics held him back from attacking the young publisher. But what upset Peterson was that Gore gave the name of his company and his secretary in the *Metro Times* piece. Peterson said he was concerned the negative press would affect his software company since he had multi-million dollar contacts with the Big Three auto companies and their suppliers.

But someone who did feel bad about his part in *Fungus Rodeo* was "Sailor Rick" Metcalf. He said the cartoon he'd drawn of Vile also made fun of Katy McNerney, and that meanness haunted him. At sea with the Merchant Marines, Metcalf wrote her an apology dripping with "blood." "I remember on the ship, I wrote her a sorry note, and I did it in this, like, pirate-type talk and I shook hot sauce on like it was pirate blood or something, and a couple of the cooks on the ship were going, 'What the hell are you doing that for? Ain't you got no hot sauce at home?' I was like, 'No, where we live, we are so poor we can only send it in a letter,'" said Metcalf.

Looking back on the *Fungus Rodeo* dustup, Gore said Gusoline Alley has immortalized him. "They named a drink after me there called 'Chris Gore Punch' because everyone wanted to punch me. I would describe myself as an irritant. I really loved to fuck with people. Like the way Bugs Bunny likes to fuck with Daffy Duck," said Gore.

Peterson tried to have the last laugh about the dustup about a year later, in the final regular issue of *Fun*. Using the same font as the *Metro Times* story about *Fungus Rodeo*, Peterson ran a humorous feature called *"The No-Big Deal Magazine War that Doesn't Matter: Forget the Jam Rag and Trading Times—This is Where the Real Boredom Is"* allegedly written by a "Geraldo Gore." In the piece, *Fun* satirizes the *Fungus Rodeo* incident in a story about the launch of a new Detroit magazine called *313 International* created by a former *Metro Times* advertising representative: "Many of you *Fun* readers may not be familiar with the *Metro Times*. The *Metro Times* is a humorless bar listings tabloid that pads itself with [what] we would consider pseudo-intellectual left-wing political drivel. Actually, most of the articles are too boring to read. Kind of a tenth-rate *Village Voice* but without the urban hipness."

So will the *Metro Times* be going out of business? We don't think just one issue of *313* will crumble the paper, or even force them to change. But who knows? Stranger things have happened. The crusader of extremist politics could not be reached for comment at the headquarters of Detroit's only magazine devoted to a guilty conscience. We don't know and we don't care. Is it true, guys who are politically correct, are lousy in bed? Can anyone believe a story this boring was allowed to run in *Fun*.

Peterson's strongest barbs were against *Metro Times* co-founder/editor Ron Williams, whose publication's philosophy was criticized in the *Fun* piece: "There are those who view the *Metro Times* as Ron Williams [*sic*] personal political soapbox. He prints only the stories he wants told, from the political slant he wants understood. Bush is bad, Dukakis is good, and Libertarians and others who are not in line with Williams [*sic*] correct political views are simply ignored. Well, it's a free country, it's a free magazine. I guess if you don't like it, you can have your parents give you the money to start up your own magazine."

Maybe Peterson was talking to himself in the piece, because before long he would reinvent *Fun* and seek to challenge Williams and the *Metro Times* for alternative media supremacy in southeast Michigan.

Following the *Fun* mutiny, Chris Gore left the magazine in October 1987 and later moved to Los Angeles to take *Film Threat* international. In the early 1990s, he sold the magazine to Larry Flynt Publications, best known for *Hustler* magazine, and continued to edit *Film Threat* and several other titles owned by Flynt over the next few years. In April 1994, Gore brought his old Thomas Video colleague Paul Zimmerman to L.A. to write and edit *Film Threat*. After Larry Flynt dumped the magazine in 1996, Gore bought it back and tried to re-launch it. But after two issues, the print version of *Film Threat* was retired in 1997, just as the magazine's online presence ramped up. Gore eventually sold the rights to *Film Threat* in 2010. In early 2015, Gore reacquired his old magazine and announced new plans for *Film Threat*.

In an interview, Gore agreed that maybe he and his *Fungus Rodeo* target, Jerry Peterson, are just too much alike. Maybe even like family:

We are both creative people, had aspirations, and we were both turned on by anything alt-culture. And in a way, we both had this kind of kinship. I never had an older brother. I would almost consider him an older brother because he was mentoring in a way. I was this kid doing this punk rock *Film Threat* thing. I didn't know what I was doing. But from Jerry, I learned about ad sales. And if a creative decision went this way, he would take it like nine degrees that way. [Peterson] was like an older brother who was an asshole to me. I mean, what older brother doesn't abuse, in some way—verbally, physically—a younger brother?

The Business of *Fun*

Beyond its humor features and art covers, *Fun's* advertisements became recognizable and popular in their own right. Business owners said they liked advertising in *Fun* because it was less restrictive than Detroit's dailies and alt weekly, and readers wanted to see what Peterson would print next. Besides Glenn Barr's ads for Dave's Comics, the "Brown Bag It" ads featured women dressed in lingerie, and enticed people to pick up the paper, similar to the well-known "Page 3" girls in the British tabloid *The Sun*. "Some of our ads, like the Dave's Comics ads, were as important as any feature we had in the magazine. And the 'Brown Bag It' girl, people would just pick us up for the 'Brown Bag It girls,'" said Peterson.

As with any free magazine, *Fun's* business model depended on having enough advertisers to pay the staff, the cost of printing, and delivery to the newsstands. To make that happen, *Fun* salespeople like Christy Burns drove all over

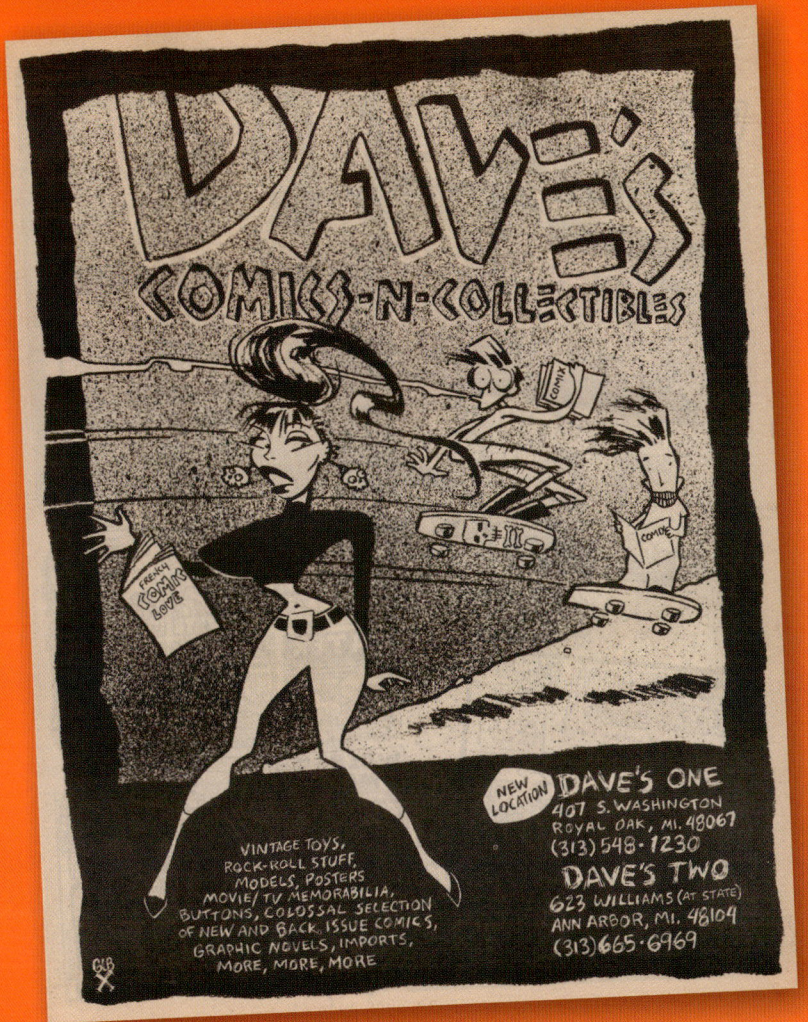

Dave's Comics ad, *Fun*. (Art by Glenn Barr) ▲

"Brown Bag It" ad, *Fun*. ▶

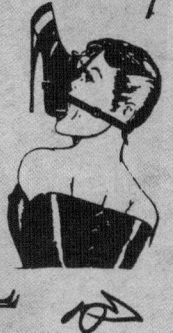

"Too Much *Fun*" party ad, *Fun*, January 1987. ▲

Metro Detroit and, at times, visited clubs at closing time to get ad money from the register. "Nightclubs were the core and it was a bit of a hard sell because *Fun* wasn't the *Detroit News*, it wasn't the *Metro Times*. Noir Leather was in from the very beginning because *Fun* would take their ads. The *Metro Times* rejected a lot of their ads. I had to cut a really wide swath, geographically. I went everywhere: Royal Oak, Ferndale, downtown, sometimes I went down to Southgate, even. I was in the car driving quite a lot," said Burns.

The magazine's "Too Much Fun" parties became a marketing tool and another source of revenue. Begin-

ning in February 1987, the magazine started to book Saint Andrew's Hall for special parties that were often dubbed "three floors of *Fun*." Burns said the parties were a huge hit because they brought the attitude of the magazine to life: "The first *Fun* party there was a liver toss with a warm liver. They had a big velvet painting of Elvis and Jesus and maybe *Dogs Playing Poker* with the faces cut out so you could put your face in there and have your picture taken. There was always a lingerie show with fashions supplied by secondhand stores. Noir Leather would get out there between bands."

FUN MAGAZINE,
& THE DREAM GROVE OF THE SACRED MOON, DOUG & MARY BLAIR, FRED SATLER, BARRY & IRENE PRESENT

HALLOWEEN

MASQUERADE BALL

AT THE LEGENDARY VANITY BALLROOM

14201 E. JEFFERSON AVE.

SATURDAY OCT. 31st at 8 PM

$500.00 CASH FIRST PRIZE PLUS MORE PRIZES

COSTUME CONTEST

HAUNTED HOUSE INSIDE

A FLOATING SPRING-LOADED DANCEFLOOR

FREE VALET PARKING

FOLLOW THE SEARCH LIGHTS

CASH BAR

LIVE DJ'S

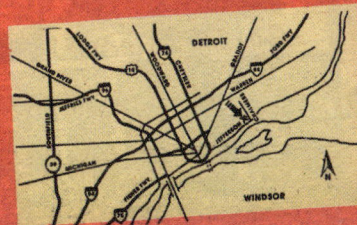

ADVANCE TICKETS AT ALL TICKETWORLD OUTLETS

▲ Halloween party ad, *Fun*, September 1987.

Burns recalled the second *Fun* party at Saint Andrew's Hall in July 1987 as a great time for those who attended and also a kind of sociological experiment to test what people would consume for free: "Jerry had this idea to have an hors d'oeuvres table that would consist of stale potato chips, stale Cheez-Its, crackers, and the worst spray cheese in a can, and then find the absolute worst wine possible. We got MD-20/20, Night Train, and poured it in a punch bowl . . . to see if people would actually eat it. They devoured it. It was gone in seconds. Just that in itself was hilarious." Saint Andrew's Hall liked the idea of "Three Floors of Fun" as a marketing tagline and used it for dance parties through the late 1990s.

In addition to the "Too Much Fun" parties, Peterson and company staged large Halloween costume parties at the Vanity Ballroom in 1987 and at the Majestic Theater a year later. Attendees with the best costumes received cash prizes. A costume maker named Hunter Jackson won one year with his creation, Techno Destructo. The creature was one of several he created for the humorous underground heavy metal band GWAR.

Beyond special events, the *Fun* crew created merchandise in keeping with the spirit of the magazine that also captured the zeitgeist of Detroit. During the 1980s, several locally produced T-shirts showed the bifurcated attitudes of those who lived in the area. The most popular slogans were "Say Nice Things about Detroit" and "Detroit: Where the Weak Are Killed and Eaten." As *Fun* was getting its footing, the creative team made its own T-shirt with a riff on a 1940s picture postcard featuring a drawing of the Detroit skyline, adding the words "Greetings from Detroit—The Murder Capital of the World." "The Snazzier Image" catalog page in *Fun* pitches it as "the T-shirt Detroiters have been dying for!" According to the fine print, "The old time postcard design is not intended to be derogatory of our fair city. It ridicules the unfair opinion of those who would debase our wonderful town. In fact it proves what a bang-up job the mayor's done cleaning up crime with such bold policies as No Crime Day and massive police lay-offs."

Keeping up with the home video boom at the time, *Fun* offered "The Best of *Fun* Video"—a VHS tape sold for $19.95. "They said it couldn't be done!" the ad read. "'A magazine on video?' They said it shouldn't be done! Well, here it is." Although the video sounds innovative, Peterson said he doesn't believe anyone besides his staff ever saw it. Not be-

◀ "Big Fun General Store" ad and *Fungalore* ad, *Fun*.

cause they didn't create it or receive orders, but because even he felt the joke was too mean: "Basically, that was just us videotaping turning the pages of the best-of issue and saying, 'Oh, isn't that great!' [Laughs] We put a really high price on it, and I know a few people sent in checks, but we never cashed them."

Merchandise aside, Peterson had another scheme to help expand the *Fun* brand, one that was more or less legitimate: a sister magazine. The September 1987 issue of *Fun* advertised a racier and more raucous version of the magazine called *Fungalore*. The new subscription-only magazine was to be "a brand new tri-annual minizine chock full of all the tasteless wicked nasty things that we can't print in *Fun*." For fifteen dollars, subscribers would get three issues a year of "the slimy and unsocially [*sic*] relevant FUNGALORE our new pornographic (well maybe not porno but if we say it in the ads nobody will be able to complain about the content) magazine." Announced in the concept stage, Peterson said lack of money and interest kept *Fungalore* from becoming a reality.

The *Fun* Stops Here

Fun ultimately ended due to lack of funds. The last regular monthly issue was December 1988.

After that, it would take almost eight months for another issue of *Fun* to arrive, and when it did, it was smaller, having moved from a tabloid size to a stapled magazine. *Fun* pushed on for two more quarterly issues before it was put to bed in the spring of 1990.

Peterson had wanted to make the magazine profitable by moving it to a weekly, but he was never able to raise enough advertising revenue. Compounding the problem was the tone. *Fun*'s irreverent humor had scared off and offended some advertisers. "The thing about *Fun* was that we insulted so many peo-

▲ *Fun*, December 1988. (Cover by Mark Niemenski)

GUN MAGAZINE

BIG FUN, INC.
919 S. MAIN #104
ROYAL OAK, MI 48067
313-456-9797

see ya suckers!

Gittin' while the gittin's good
Jerry "I'm not so dumb" Vile
Glad to be done with it
Gary "tasted it all" Arnett
We'll always have Paris
Doug "yo, later fo you" Dearth
Rambling Man
Mark "leavin' on a jet plane" Niemenski
Walked out before the credits rolled
the thrill of being Paul Zimmerman
Like a rat from a sinking ship
Rick "missed the boat" Metcalf
Valedictorian
Kevin "Up yours, wiseass!" King
Hit the road Jack
Chris "lone wolf" Kassel
Like a bat outta Hell
Suzanne Calamita
Ex. Supreme Court Justice
Judge I. Rankin
Long sense gone
Joe "Where to now?" Hutchinson
On the flip side
Todd Huskin
We'll all surely miss
Angela Maiuri
Always with us, in our hearts
Katy Hait

gone, daddy, gone

Tim "outta here" Caldwell - Daryl "never a trace" Hutchinson- Matt "pissed away" Beer - Debbi "defector" Findly - Rick "we hardly knew him" Ruby - you won't have Luis G. to kick around anymore - Slats "bye now" Myers -Gary "don't let the door hit you in the ass" Riechel - Paul "history" Corte -Scott "You'll see, I'll show them all!"Campbell- and Deb & Jeff are on the lamb

splitsville

·Genn Barr·Kevin Knapp·S. Kay Young·Joe Sposita·Steve Shaw·Blip Rimbo·Al Brantner·Rick Morris·B. Mitchell·Jeff Demick·Tina Suchy·N. Anselment· T. Wiloch·Dave Hanna·A Nice Girl Who Has Tremendously Large Breasts·Mr. Dave Higgins· Dumbo· A. Histler·Jean Lannon·Kieth Brown·Gary "Harv"Nowak·Ace Backwards·Baby Sue·Joe Sopkowitz·John Kelin·Diane "Too Busy" Schroder·Jim Gustafson·Tom Murphy·Kathy A Hoffman·Nark J. Norton·M. Fiscus

READ IT AND WEEP

THE LAST ISSUE OF FUN?

Due to continued rising costs in printing we can no longer provide a low quality inferior product to the public. To continue maintaining our substandard publications it is necessary we charge an exorbitant and prohibitive cover price. We are not sorry for any inconvenience this may cause you.

One does not need to be a mathematics professor to understand the simple implications of downside economics. However, knowing how stupid you are we have included this pictogram.

| DEMOGRAPHICS | CIRCULATION | COVER PRICE. | ADVERTISERS | RESULT |

THE BACKWARD YOKELS COMPROMISING OUR CURRENT AREA OF DISTRIBUTION ARE CERTAIN TO BE DEVASTATED BY THE INEVITABLE RECESSION

A LIMITED AND DWINDLING READERSHIP ALREADY TIRED OF OUR STALE JOKES AND VICIOUS ATTITUDE.

SHUCKS, WE CAN'T EVEN GIVE IT AWAY!

WE'RE SICK OF WHINY CHISELING DEADBEATS WHO WANT A FREE LISTING BUT ARE TOO CHEAP TO SHELL OUT A FEW MEASLY PENNIES FOR AN AD.

STARVATION

A COUNTRY LARGE ENOUGH TO SUPPORT OUR COLLOSAL EGOS, YET FRIENDLY ENOUGH TO FORGIVE OUR COLLOSAL SHORTCOMINGS

A CONSTANT SUPPLY OF "SUCKERS" WILL KEEP OUR WALLETS AND BELLIES FULL.

AN OUTRAGEOUS COVER PRICE ENSURES WE WILL BE ENJOYING THE BETTER THINGS IN LIFE; FAST CARS, PRETTY GALS, AND JUG-O-BEER.

OUR SPEEDWAY TO SUCCESS IS GUARANTEED. FAT CAT CORPORATE INVESTORS AND ADVERTISING CONGLOMERATES ALL VYING FOR THAT ELUSIVE "18-35" MARKET.

JACKPOT

Get the picture? Not a pretty one, is it. Wake up and smell the landfill.
Some of you may of wondered what happened to those starry eyed children who were going to change the world with word processor. The children who, long time ago, in one of those boring, pompous "we want to do something for the world" editorials, we wrote we would continue publishing FUN as long as it was FUN to publish. Those kids are dead. Working on FUN is about as much FUN as taking a shit after hemorrhoid surgery. We apologize for or naive stupidity. We are older and much more cynical now. We proved everything thing we had to prove. We don't owe you anything. We don't care about anything but money, we care for no one but ourselves.
So what are we going to do. Make money. Nobody ever said life was FUN. We are going to publish this magazine no matter how bored we are. The difference is people are going to pay for it.
FUN is going international, whether you like it or not. The sticky tentacles of our corporate octopus will span the landscape; reaching far and wide! Tee-shirts, record promotions, radio stations, television networks! WE WANT IT ALL! And what do you get when you cross an octopus and a publishing whore? I don't know but it sure can make money! Yes, we sold our souls to the Satan for a chance at the big time.

¹ Watch for Popular Amusement. BIG FUN Inc.'s new entry into the field of Freebie Tabuloids.
² If you are a rich investor (or know a rich investor) and would like the opportunity to speculate in the venture of a lifetime, send a letter (or money) to us.
³ BIG FUN GRAPHICS will continue to provide eye grabbing graphics at competitive prices, if your sick of your image, give one of our artistic consultants a call.
⁴ Subscribers, please be patient, you will be getting the new FUN, at our earliest convince, unlike the poor suckers who will have to pay

CONTENTS May have settled during shipping. Product sold by weight not by volume. Contains less than 1% of the US RDA of intellectual stimulation. Containing one or more of the following:sodium citrate, enriched wheat flower containing niacin, homophobia, reduced iron, thiamine bromonornitrate(vitamin x),, lysergic acid, penis envy, uric acid, sodium bicarbonate, sodium acid pyrophosphate, sue sue sodium, animal and/or vegetable shortening (lard and/or coconut oil and/or partially hydrogenated soybean oil and/or fully regurgitated hamster oil but not more than any two of the following, castor oil and/or baby oil and/or arab oil and/or crude oil, black gold, texas tea,monocalcium foozfeet rihnoflavin, ribocop, chrisgoreaslag,cheap jokesative, vicious slurssimine, juvinile humoraxicide, wuttza matter 4u, wuttza henway, twolbs., hot dog sex, poly vinyl chloride, caramel color, camel flavor, bicarbonate of aspercream, mescaline, clitoral slimulii, sorbil doxinfynalmite potash, grammatical errorcide, lead, arsenic, rodent excreta, hair, and insect pieces less than 1ppm.

LAST ISSUE EXTRAVAGANZA- All those regular features you have grown to love, we shit canned em'. And the writers too. And we ain't paying them neither.
THE TRUE MEANING OF XMAS- A fuckin heartwarmin story bout this son o' god guy who don't get to bang no chicks with gigantic monster jugs even though he has secret powers and knows magic tricks but then he gets killed and comes back but he does not become a real cool flesh eating zombie and kill the bad guys. **PHOTOS OF BEAUTIFUL NAKED GIRLS COVERED WITH HOT COME**-Maybe you have already seen this one, it was last months Penthouse. **BEYOND CRIME AND PUNISH-**

MENT-The typical parodys of newspaper, magazine, and comic book ads. **REVENGE ON PEOPLE WHO DIDN'T ADVERTISE**-FUN staffers explain their favorite recon tactics and recall search & destroy missions of those establishments who unwisely choose not to advertise. **LESBIAN CONTRAS SHARE THEIR FAVORITE JELLO DESERT RECIPES**-We scooped the Metro again **TINY TYPE DANGER OR EYESORE?**-We like to make you suffer. We enjoy your pain. We want to hear your corneas will scream. We never tire of you whiny assed pussys complaining about the teeny weeny type we use. We hate you . Don't like it? Too fucking bad. So Blow me, dickface Good Redence to bad rubbish. You wimps make us sick.

▲ Editorial from final monthly issue, *Fun*, December 1988.

ple. We were accused of everything. There were a lot of people who thought we went too far. That's why we had a problem [with advertisers]. We would write about our advertisers and make fun of them. That would piss people off because people who are supporting something didn't expect to be made fun of," said Peterson.

Infected by *Fun*

During its lifetime, *Fun*'s blend of anarchic humor and punk sensibilities appealed to certain young and creative Metro Detroiters. The magazine would leave a deep impression on two young men who, in their formative years, saw *Fun* as something wholly unique and inspiring.

Growing up in the western suburb of Plymouth, John Dunivant spent most of his time trying to find good music and lose himself in drawing. With long hair that covered his face and his black trench coat, Dunivant described himself as a quiet teenage loner. When he stumbled across *Fun*, the magazine seemed tailor-made for him. "Living in Plymouth, it was either we would go to Detroit and explore abandoned buildings or we would go to Ann Arbor. And in Ann Arbor was Dave's Comics, and that's where I saw *Fun* magazine. At the time, my world was opening up, and *Fun* felt like an extension of that. It was devious and funny and really cool," said Dunivant.

Fun was inspirational for Dunivant, for its attitude as much as its art. Dunivant said Jerry Vile and frequent cover artist Glenn Barr expanded his understanding of what art could be, how you could thumb your nose at the system and find an audience. *Fun* helped Dunivant persuade his parents that he wanted to be an artist and attend the Center for Creative Studies. He

Covers for the final three issues of *Fun*, ▶
Fall 1989, Winter 1989/1990, Spring 1990.

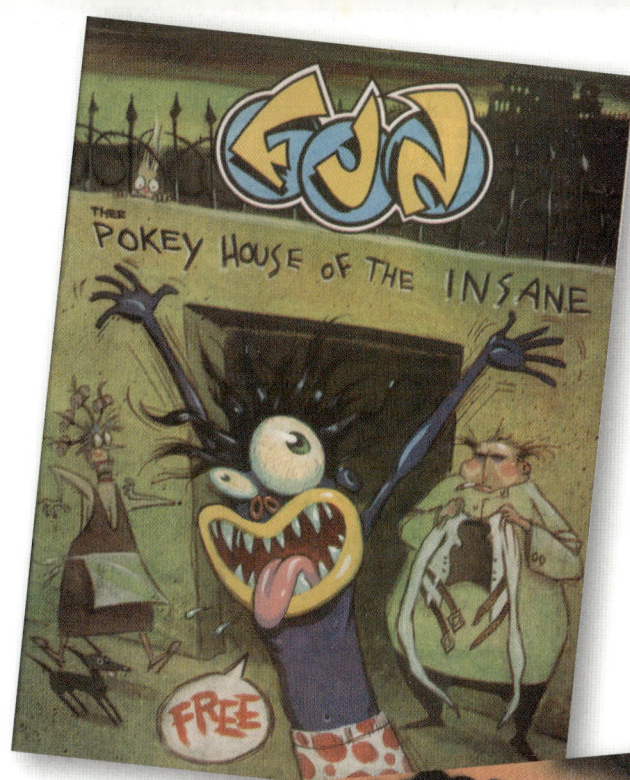

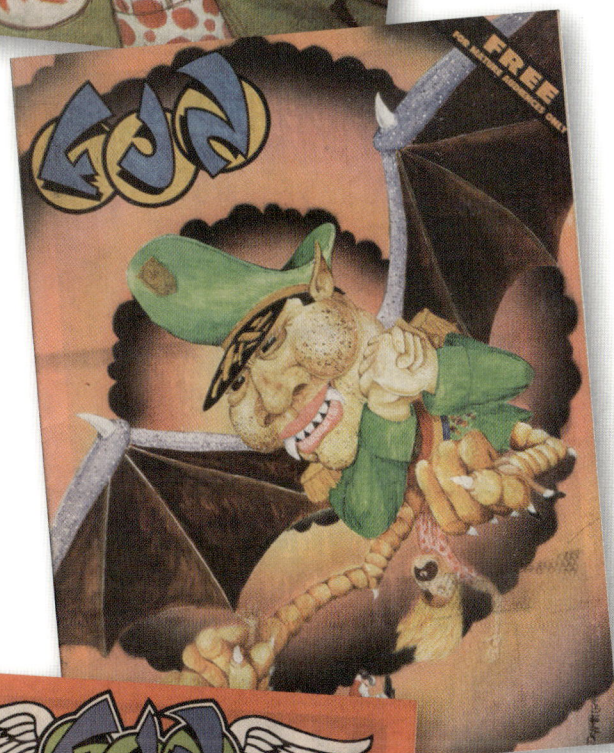

THE TELLTALE SIGNS OF

The war on drugs has to be fought on the front lines- your own home. If you are truly a loving, caring, parent, you should immediately suspect your teenage children of abusing mind-altering drugs.

You can't hide your child from the bad apples. A little pressure from this peer group will turn a good kid into a slobbering dope fiend overnight. Chances are your child has already experienced dangerous drugs and narcotics. Drugs make teenagers lazy, selfish, unfeeling, and generally difficult to manage.

The following list will act as your bible for determining if your child is a drug abuser.

Compulsion Towards Unnatural Independence

Has your teenager asked about choosing their own wardrobe? Perhaps they feel they are "mature" enough to go shopping without your help? Do they want to drive the car? Or in extreme cases think they could drive without a responsible adult accompanying them in the automobile? Some teenagers even demand trips to a barber or hairdresser for a fancy adult hairstyle, rather than a less expensive haircut at home. This symptom seems to be the rule of thumb in every tragic narcotic case. Illicit drugs wreak havoc on the portion of the brain that control responsible adult development and patience, and addicted teens may start "growing up a little too soon". So don't give in, do the "Big Shot" a real favor-keep them away from drugs. They'll soon be old enough to appreciate the responsibilities that go with the adult things in life.

Obsessive Compulsive Behaviour

Dope fiends will try to demand money under the guise of babysitting or payment for chores, to feed their insatiable appetites for narcotic habits. Some may sink a low as actually applying for a job at McDonalds to earn enough cash for a daily 'fix'.

Unusual Change In Appearance

Drug abuse often causes severe changes in physical appearance. Do your children look taller? Many drugs can promote excessive growth of bone proteins. A pronounced deepening of in vocal patterns in males, and menstruation in females is positive proof irreparable chromosome damage has already occurred. Check your child regularly for the appearance of facial hair and/or pubic hair, another blatant sign of the hormonal fury unleashed by unprescribed medications.

Overtly Stimulated Libido

Indicated by a developing interest in the opposite sex (All illicit drugs are severe libido stimulaters and dangerous aphrodisiacal properties) This drug induced aphrodisa can manifest itself in the use of salty language like "sexy", "A stone fox", or "excellent". Unchecked this bizarre behavior can lead to dating, prostitution, pregnancy, and death.

Unreasonable Rejection of Authority

Surliness and a bad attitude in general are proof positive of habitual narcotics abuse. An occasional lapse of "yes sir or mamn' or as serious offense such as sassing are usually signs of drug induced depravity. In know time at all, Mr or Ms Smartypants may start vocally expressing opinions which differ from yours. So your teen starts questioning your judgement, it is time for serious action. (Please realize that it is the drugs talking not the teen. Your child is suffering from an illusion of confidence brought about by narcotic euphoria.) Profound disrespect is cause for immediate action and may require the help of a third party such as the police, minister, or a USTA Drug Rehabilitation Center. You child must be forced to see that you are only are trying to help them.

Insomnia And Other Sensory Disorders

The Government recommended guideline for bed-times (9:00PM on week Days and 9:30 on weekends, one half hour later for youngsters over the age of eighteen). If teenager tries to get you to extend these bedtime

TEENAGE DRUG ADDICTION

hours, they may be hooked on mind altering drugs. Narcotics disorient time and space judgement. In the drug user's euphoric state they cannot make a reasonable judgement. Drugs also effect the sensory capacity. Your teenager may develop a inclination for sweets and junk food. If your teen is not a member of the "clean plate society" then chances are they are popping pills and playing spin the bottle at wild all-night drug induced sex orgies.

Bizarre Obsession With Secrecy

This extreme behavior often is exemplified by your teenager wanting privacy. You may notice they keep the bedroom door closed. (They may even refer to it as THEIR room.) You may notice that your youngling is starting to act as if they are embarrassed of you. Perhaps they don't want you to pick them up in front of the crowd at concerts. You may notice them not wanting you to accompany them at shopping malls. You are made to feel unwelcome at their parties. Don't fall into this common "parent trap". You child should be under constant adult supervision, except during predetermined bathroom hygiene breaks.

Unusual Paraphernalia and Typical Methods of Deception

Stridex pads, and other paraphernalia in the bath room. Teen agers use medicated pads for rolling "reefers" (powerful handmade cigarettes made from marihuana, PCP, and Crack Cocaine). Junkies wear shorts and bathing trunks which stop just below the knee, to hides "tracks" (needle marks).
Sunglasses are certainly an unnecessary luxury item for anyone under the age of twenty one. Or your teen may express an inexplable interest in contact lenses. The pupils of the drug user are typically dilated, contact lenses and sunglasses mask this obvious side effect.
Girls may start asking permission to wear makeup. This covers up the "Dope lines" on their faces, and the circles under their eyes.
Boys may start tucking in their shirts and use cologne to cover up the sickly sweet odor of marihuana fumes.

Rejection of Family Values

Suddenly being with Mom and Dad isn't cool anymore. It's quite common for the drug abuser to go through complete withdrawal of emotional interaction. Not wanting to go on vacation with the family should be your early warning sign. The refusal to play with younger siblings is not at all uncommon behaviour with addicts. Interests outside the family are additional clues to potential drug abuse: excuses include "sports", an "after school job", or supposed social activities. The most typical reason given by addicts is "Better things to do". So if they refuse to go to Grandmas because it's Homecoming Night", it may be time for you to call in the experts.

Pronounced Listlessness

As mentioned earlier, drug addiction makes people lazy, insensitive, stupid and selfish. Dope fiends would rather watch television than help with household chores. Drug abusers rarely do chores without having to be "asked" first.

Inexplicable Loss of Faith

Your teenager may express a to go to Church. (Not just Sundays but all of the extra curricular activities and Vacation Bible School). It is scientifically proven that Satan is responsible for most of the drug addiction and other problems in the world. Therefor, would he not expect your child to reject religion, is the best road to recovery for drug abusers. Here are some other signs of SIDA (Satan Influenced Drug Abuse)
A) Worship of false idols
They may prefer posters of Johnny Depp (Lucifer) and Tiffany (The Whore of Babylon) instead of the pretty pastel goose decorations you bought at Meijer Thrifty Acre.
B) Speaking In Tongues
Does your teenager come up with new expressions and slang terms? They may be possessed by a demon.
C) Tendency Towards Self Destruction
If you don't like the music that you are hearing from you kid's room, they are on drugs. Heavy Metal in particular is a sure sign of both drug addiction and Satanism. ∎

▲ The humor piece John Dunivant's father used to justify drug testing the artist as a teen, *Fun*, Fall 1989.

said that Peterson "sounded like a really interesting person and was about the things that I was into. [He was] like a juvenile delinquent that didn't want to grow up. . . . Then Glenn's work. Being at Dave's Comics and seeing the Dave's Comics ads and the kind of covers and art that he was doing. That was the kind of art I wanted to do."

A few years later, Dunivant would become a respected artist in his own right. In 2000, Dunivant, with friend Ken Poirier, merged two separate Halloween parties into a unique immersive experience. Poirier owned several rental properties across from the Michigan State Fairgrounds, and over several years they transformed the connected lots into "The World's Greatest Masquerade," an event known as Theatre Bizarre.

Theatre Bizarre was Dunivant's canvas. The grounds provided a place to design and build elaborate sets, stages, a carnival midway, and sideshow banners that felt as though they'd emerged from an alternate universe at the dawn of the twentieth century. Created with the help of more than a hundred volunteers, and without the permission of the City of Detroit, the dusk-till-dawn masquerade would eventually draw people from as far away as Australia and Dubai. "Theatre Bizarre is

Theatre Bizarre in action, circa 2008. ▼

▲ Theatre Bizarre in action, circa 2008.

a turn-of-the-century carnival, an abandoned carnival that all takes place in a man's mind. It's an idealization of another time. It's also my art installation piece. It's a culmination of my life, my history, my obsessions. It's also a big underground illegal party," said Dunivant.

By 2010, the annual one-night Halloween party would sell more than three thousand tickets, mostly through word of mouth. By then, Theatre Bizarre had added a roller coaster and a Ferris wheel to the grounds in a burned-out section of Detroit. That year, the illegal party caught the attention of the city's zoning division. The day before costumed revelers were scheduled to show up, the city closed Theatre Bizarre.

Moving fast, Dunivant and Poirier created a scaled-down version the next night at the Fillmore Theatre.

Since 2011, Theatre Bizarre has found a home at Detroit's historic Masonic Temple, which allows Dunivant to play off the mythologies and symbolism of secret societies like the Freemasons. Though they've continued to create and entertain "in exile," Dunivant and Poirier were forced in the spring of 2012 to dismantle the Theatre Bizarre grounds or face fines of up to ten thousand dollars a month. "It was a perfect little spot and we kind of used the concept that we were right across from the fairgrounds, that we were the original fairgrounds that [had been] aban-

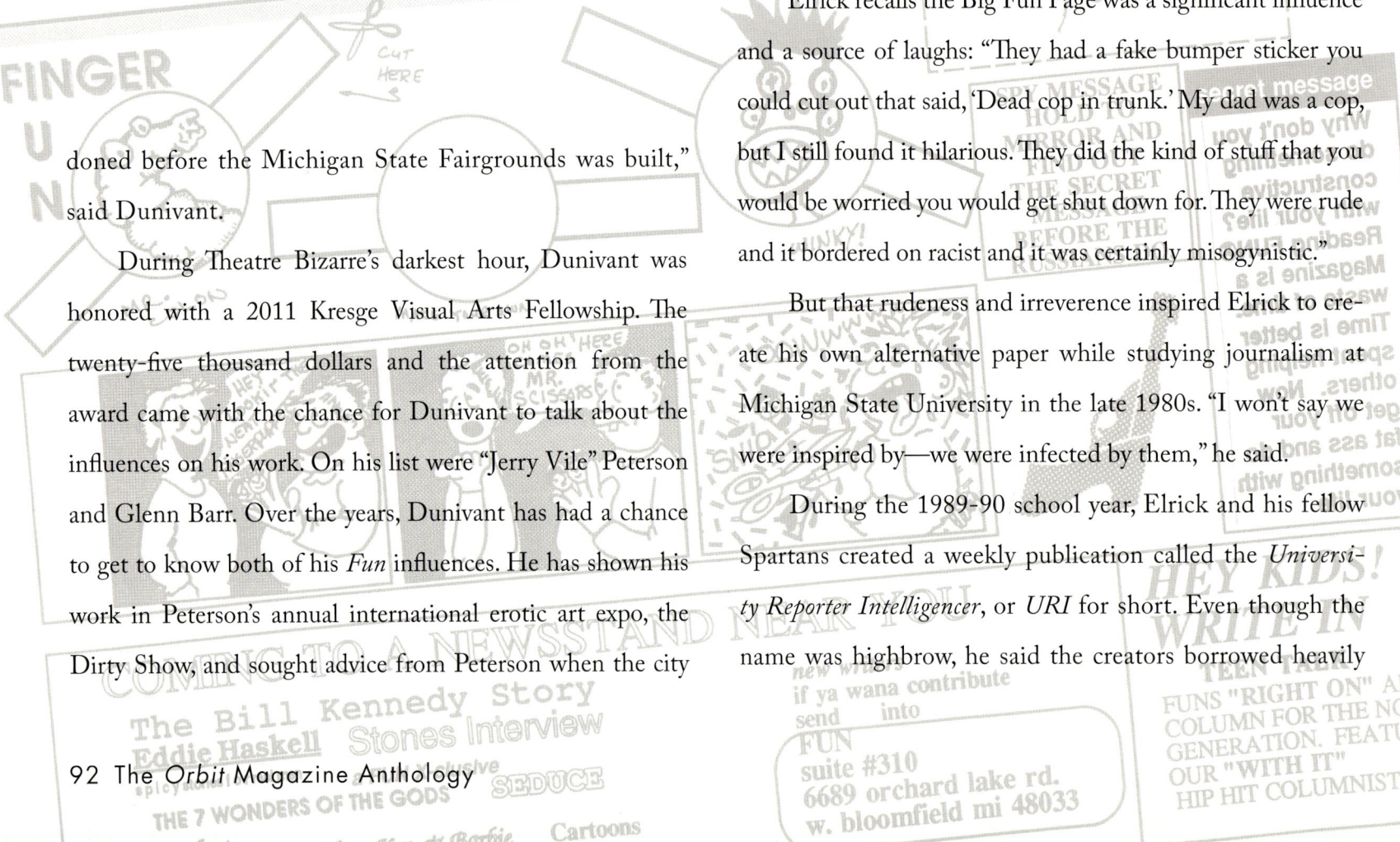

▲ John Dunivant, circa 2014.

doned before the Michigan State Fairgrounds was built," said Dunivant.

During Theatre Bizarre's darkest hour, Dunivant was honored with a 2011 Kresge Visual Arts Fellowship. The twenty-five thousand dollars and the attention from the award came with the chance for Dunivant to talk about the influences on his work. On his list were "Jerry Vile" Peterson and Glenn Barr. Over the years, Dunivant has had a chance to get to know both of his *Fun* influences. He has shown his work in Peterson's annual international erotic art expo, the Dirty Show, and sought advice from Peterson when the city

shut down Theatre Bizarre. Dunivant also gave Peterson a platform, inviting his band, 52 Devil Babies Born with Tails, to play at Theatre Bizarre.

Reflecting on *Fun*, Dunivant remembers how novel the magazine was in its heyday: "It's amazing things like *Fun* were being produced. Back then, it felt even more precious because you had to hunt for it. There was no Internet. You would get hand-me-down fanzines out of Boston through the mail. *Fun* was part of that. These treasures that have held up, they stand the test of time."

While John Dunivant was soaking up the *Fun* influence in a western Detroit suburb, M. L. Elrick heard the dog whistle of *Fun* on the eastside. Enamored by journalism since the fifth grade, when he created a neighborhood newspaper with some friends, Elrick said *Fun* had a huge impact on his late-teen and college years. He said *Fun* always amazed him—just that someone could, or would, have the guts to publish some of the things it did.

Elrick recalls the Big Fun Page was a significant influence and a source of laughs: "They had a fake bumper sticker you could cut out that said, 'Dead cop in trunk.' My dad was a cop, but I still found it hilarious. They did the kind of stuff that you would be worried you would get shut down for. They were rude and it bordered on racist and it was certainly misogynistic."

But that rudeness and irreverence inspired Elrick to create his own alternative paper while studying journalism at Michigan State University in the late 1980s. "I won't say we were inspired by—we were infected by them," he said.

During the 1989-90 school year, Elrick and his fellow Spartans created a weekly publication called the *University Reporter Intelligencer*, or *URI* for short. Even though the name was highbrow, he said the creators borrowed heavily from the lowbrow humor and attitude of *Fun*. "We didn't completely rip [Jerry Vile] off, but we did similar things. . . . We did a reader's poll. 'Got some spare time on the crapper?' We would do fun pages. We had a cut-out doll—'Dress the Poser.' You could cut [out] a beret, a clove cigarette, Doc Marten boots, and put it on your paper doll. We never would have done that if we never saw *Fun*," said Elrick.

The paper also picked a person or thing each week for a *Fun*-inspired special feature called "Geek of the Week." "One week it was Sammy Davis Jr.'s throat cancer. We took criticism because people didn't get it," said Elrick. Then, inspired by the *Fun* gossip column "Slander," Elrick's *URI* created a similar column called "The Provocateur."

URI was popular during the 1989-90 school year, with twenty-seven issues and ten thousand copies per week. A complete collection is now housed in the MSU library archives. As school was coming to an end in the summer of 1990, Elrick didn't know where he was going to go to use his new degree and talents. During an internship at the *Detroit Free Press*, Elrick decided that writing a story on Jerry Peterson's new paper, *Orbit*, would be a great opportunity to get to know the man whose magazine had been such

▼ "Dead Cop in Trunk," "Big Fun Page," *Fun*, January 1987.

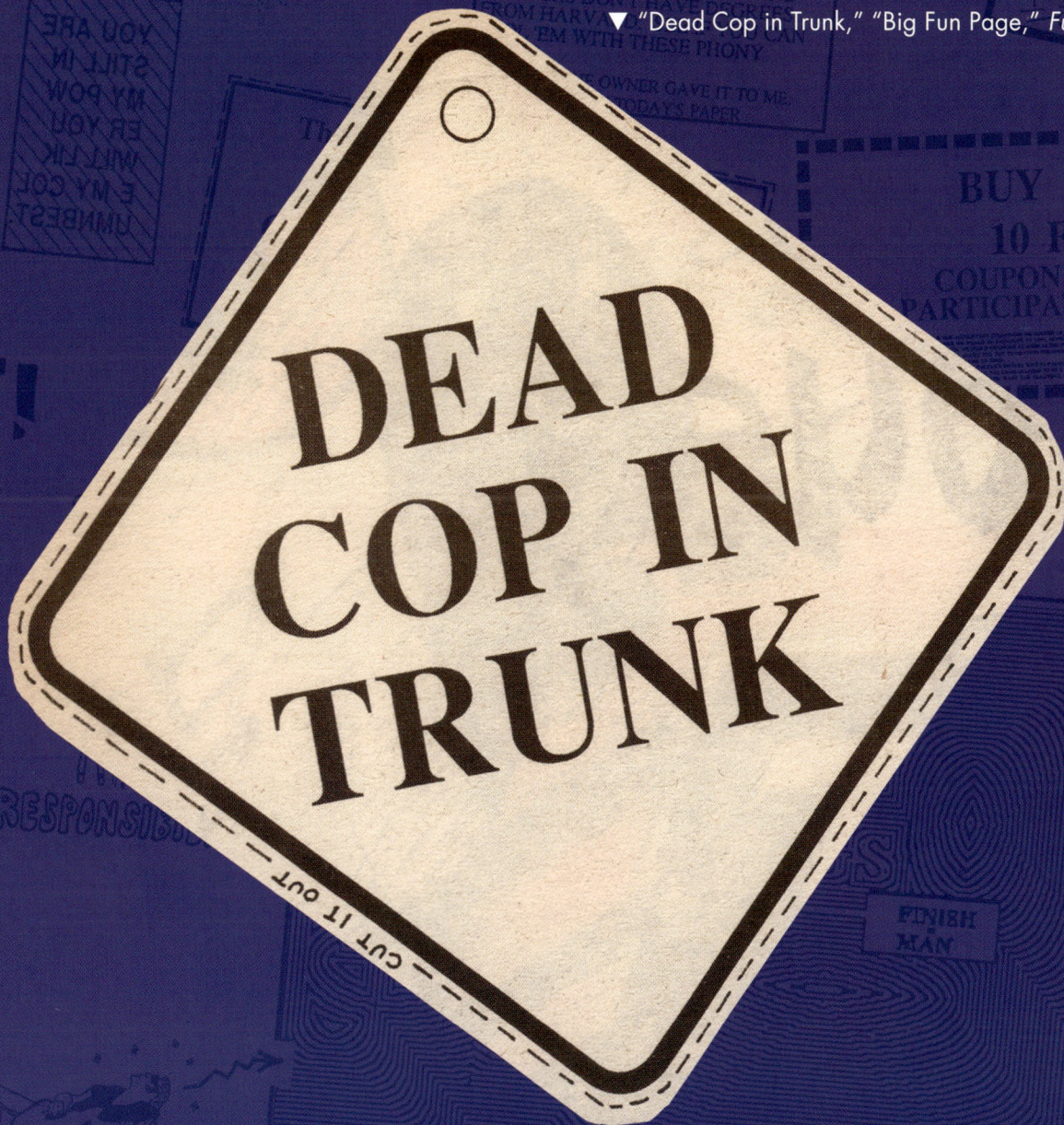

DEAD COP IN TRUNK

CUT IT OUT

▲ "Foreign Correspondent," *Orbit*, June 13–27, 1991.

an influence. "I was looking for an excuse to write about Jerry. I knew of him from *Fun*, which I just thought was the greatest magazine ever. So when *Orbit* came up, I did some research and I had no idea he had this colorful past—he was just this outsized guy who did the sort of outrageous stuff that I always wished I could do and he did it regularly. It was in his DNA," said Elrick.

When Elrick met him, Peterson wasn't all that vile. He was a thirty-something trying to move beyond his crazier days and go legit as a publisher. Still, Elrick said if you listened carefully, the echoes of the punk rock past could still be heard: "It wasn't what I expected. He was sort of an average-sized guy, maybe a little lumpy. I think he had a mustache, maybe a goatee. He wasn't wearing a nun outfit or horns, but it was a little off-putting. The guy I met was 'Jerry the software salesman,' but once you started talking to him, he had all that impishness and troublemaker inside of him. It was great."

The Peterson feature would be one of Elrick's first by-lines for the *Detroit Free Press* as an intern. After Elrick's internship, Peterson asked the young reporter if he was interested in writing for *Orbit*. Elrick was heading to Europe for a vacation and was keeping a journal. From time to time, during the trip, Elrick would send a dispatch noting the fashion and a little something about the cities he visited. Peterson and the *Orbit* editors stitched together a column from Elrick's dispatches for the June 13-27, 1991, issue titled "Foreign Correspondent." The byline is credited to Mike Elrick. It was the only piece he wrote for *Orbit*. "You know," he said, "I didn't get it at the time like they did. I thought in order to write that it had to be significant. Instead of just DO IT! And if it's great, great. If it's not, do it again next week."

▲ Elrick shaking hands with former Detroit mayor Kwame Kilpatrick. (Photo by Mandi Wright, courtesy of the *Detroit Free Press*)

Peterson asked Elrick about freelancing when he returned from his trip abroad, but Elrick declined.

Metro Detroiters would see Elrick's bylines seventeen years later at the *Detroit Free Press* when, along with reporting partner Jim Schaefer, his investigative work helped to remove Detroit mayor Kwame Kilpatrick and former chief of staff Christine Beatty from office and put them behind bars for perjury. Elrick and Schaefer's investigative work earned them a 2009 Pulitzer Prize for local reporting.

Reflecting on *Fun*, Elrick said, "There was nothing like it. There was *Metro Times*, but all the funny stuff they ran was syndicated comics and cartoons. I would describe them as the 'tragically hip.' But *Fun* was all the stuff that you never had the nerve to put out somewhere. It was so raw."

Fun's rawness and edge helped to create its legacy and impact, but while Jerry Vile, his co-creators, and hardcore fans enjoyed it, the magazine had its enemies in advertisers and others in the community. But if Jerry Vile couldn't create something that was both palatable and profitable, maybe Jerry Peterson could. Maybe a new idea could lead to the stratospheric success he'd always wanted. It was time to bring in the rocket scientists.

ORBIT

1990–1999

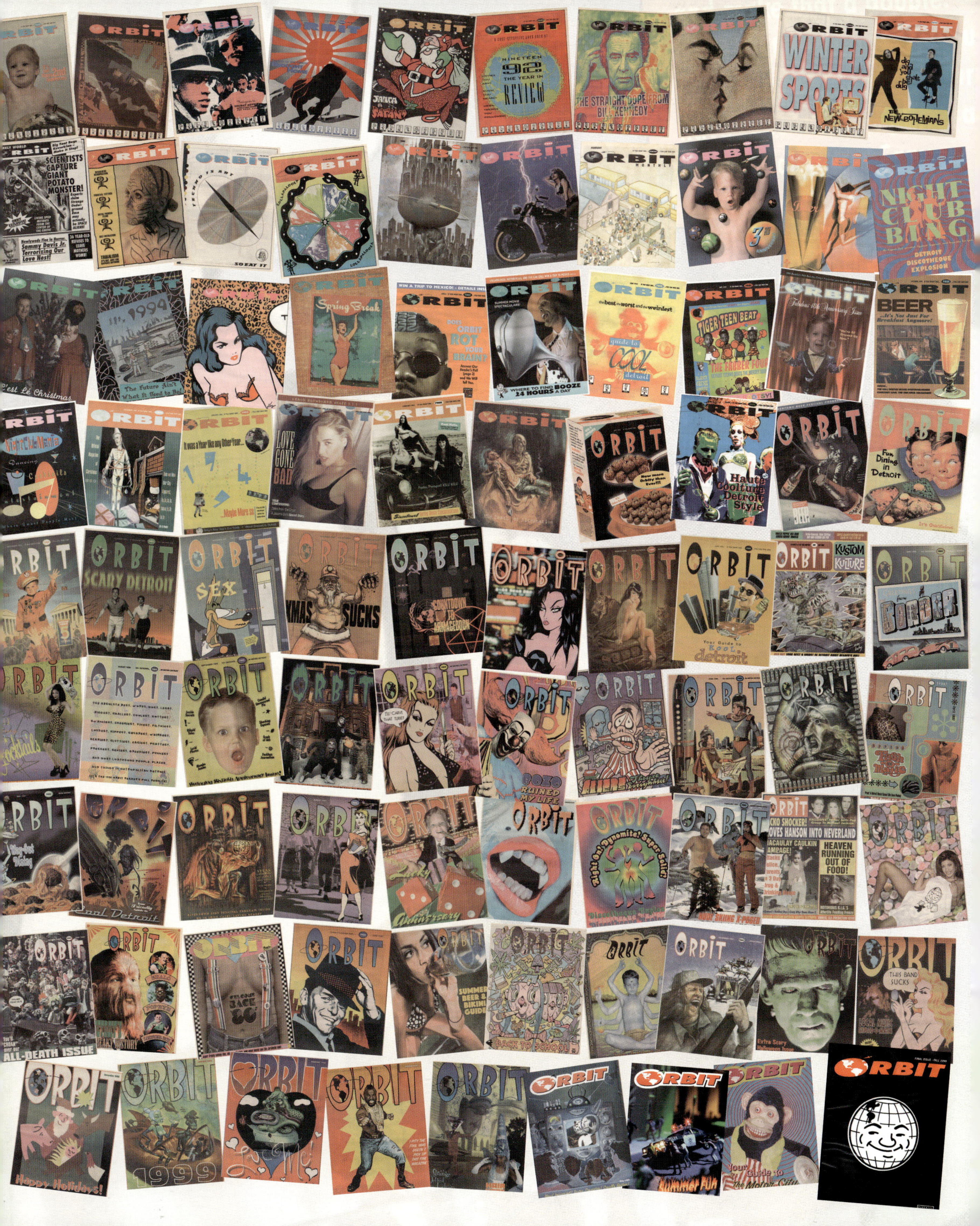
ORBIT
NINETEEN 92 THE YEAR IN REVIEW
THE STRAIGHT DOPE FROM BILL KENNEDY
WINTER SPORTS
THE NEW BOHEMIANS
SCIENTISTS CAPTURE GIANT POTATO MONSTER!
Sammy Davis Jr. Terrorizing Our Love Nest!
NIGHT CLUB BING
DETROIT DISCOTHEQUE EXPLOSION
C'est Le Christmas
The Future Ain't What It Used to Be
Spring Break
WIN A TRIP TO MEXICO! - DETAILS INSIDE
WHERE TO FIND BOOZE 24 HOURS A DAY
the best the worst and the weirdest
TIGER TEEN BEAT
BEER ...It's Not Just For Breakfast Anymore!
LOVE GONE BAD
Haute Coolture Detroit Style
Fun Dining in Detroit
SCARY DETROIT
SEX
XMAS SUCKS
COUNTDOWN TO ARMAGEDDON
KUSTOM KULTURE
BORDER
BOZO RUINED MY LIFE
Cool Detroit
JACKO SHOCKER! MOVES HANSON INTO NEVERLAND
MACAULAY CAULKIN RAMPAGE!
HEAVEN RUNNING OUT OF FOOD!
ALL-DEATH ISSUE
SUMMER BEER & BIKINI GUIDE
THIS BAND SUCKS
Extra Scary Halloween Issue
Happy Holidays!
1999
Summer Fun

ORBIT

Preparing for Launch

By 1989, Jerry Peterson had had enough of trying to balance the day-to-day work at his software company, PMX for CADCAM, and running *Fun*, an entertaining but money-losing magazine. When *Fun* started as a monthly in September 1986, the plan was to build the resources to take it weekly, but by early 1989, the monthly publication had become a quarterly one.

At the same time, Peterson's software business was hemorrhaging money due to what he said were problems with a business partner, his dabbling in questionable products that didn't work as

advertised, and his own personal 1980s Gordon Gekko-style greed. Peterson's new plan was to create a magazine that would be able to go head-to-head with the long-established Detroit alt weekly the *Metro Times*. Like *Metro Times*, *Orbit* would be free at newsstands throughout southeast Michigan. But unlike its progressive, left-leaning rival, Peterson's magazine would leave politics at the door, focusing instead on Detroit arts, culture, humor, and entertainment.

The new magazine would go out twice a month because Peterson knew he didn't have the money, staff, or training to publish weekly. The plan was to build the

audience and advertising revenue to eventually do so. By 1989 *Fun* had moved from the PMX boardroom in Livonia to a simple office space above B&B Collision on Main Street in downtown Royal Oak. In early 1990, just as *Fun* was winding down, a meeting was held to hatch the plans for the new, yet unnamed, magazine. About twenty people, mostly staffers, attended.

Designer Terry Colon discussed the idea-generation process. "You can't tailor this. You have to do what you like, what you love, and hopefully people will be entertained. Don't gear it for a specific demographic group," he

BLAST OFF

SCUTTLEBUTT & MINUTIAE

Orbitorial

Just when we were starting to feel safe, we learn Detroit is the Murder Capital of the US.

Now, before you start heading for the suburbs or staying home on Saturday nights, you must realize that once again, Detroit is being picked on by the national media.

Look close at these dubious statistics (based on antiquated 1997 data). You'll notice they don't play up the fact there were only 450 homicides—that's only about 21 *Orbit* readers per year, a figure which pales in comparison to the amount of murders it used to take to get to the top back in the day (try almost double those numbers).

They based this data on a *per capita* murder rate rather than the more scientifically correct *how many people got a cap in their ass* murder rate. So, sure, Detroit is going to look bad. What this nonsensical mumbo-jumbo doesn't take into account is Detroit's declining population. There's less than a million people here and not just because everybody is getting murdered. But, apparently the murderers are not leaving the city with a seemingly high-disproportionate number of murderers to murderers. But you won't see that in these surveys, surveys which are designed to make Detroit look bad in the eyes of the world.

Why? Well, it seems we have the most money for empowerment zones—and that has made a lot of other cities jealous. Cities that were already covetous of our automobile industry, musical heritage and big tire.

Obviously, Detroit has worked hard to clean up its image. These so-called experts, whomever they are (we haven't met one, have you?), possibly unfairly hired by other cities (no doubt, green with envy over our forthcoming casinos), are working hard to shatter that image.

Still there are those who may feel Detroit is dangerous. It certainly felt safer a few days before you knew we once again were the U.S.A. murder champs. Still, it's a proven fact, what you don't know can't hurt you. That you are reading this should be proof enough for you—you weren't murdered. Heck, you probably weren't even assaulted.

Ask Minnie

Dear Minnie,
Everything in my life was perfect—until my husband started taking Viagra. The problem is he was never much to look at, but now that he is older, fatter and uglier, I find the very idea of sex with him repugnant. If that wasn't bad enough, he refuses to let go of the ink pen. To make matters worse, he appeared in a TV commercial for the drug, which pretty much ended any chances I had running for public office.
Bummed Out Barbie

Dear BOB,
There are few things as hideous as a naked old person. However, our creator cleverly also diminished sexual interest at the same time—seemingly foolproof way of keeping down the orphan population. 'Tis a dangerous thing when man messes with nature—the abomination which struts nakedly before your eyes was simply not meant to be. So do what I and many others do: eat. Become as obese as possible. This should remedy the problem. As far as the commercials, all Tom cats howl.

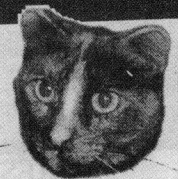

World Famous in Detroit

Megapolis of Cheap

Do you really need seven dollar burgers and a faux rain forest to get your shopping fix? Franchise-choked strip malls and snotty clerks got ya down? Drop your hard-earned shekels at the Motor City's palace of cheap—the Gibraltar Trade Center.

Every weekend these twin Goliaths (six football games could be played simultaneously beneath the roof) bulge with over 800 dealers ready to bargain and dicker. With a minimum of cash you'll outfit yourself, home, garage or aquarium.

There's name-brand cooking gear for 60 percent off or car stereos cheaper than in a parking lot. Plenty of leathers, musical instruments and an occasional blue grass jam to keep pace. Well-organized and clean enough, that even the antique baby toys don't smell "funny."

Each weekend a section is devoted to specialized merchandise such as computers, boats, guns and knives, and home improvement.

Where else can you get a tattoo, a pair of spatulas, and a case of ammo all under one roof?

The Gibraltar Trade Centers are located in the heart of lumpen-proletariatville, right off I-75 and I-94 in Gibraltar and Mt. Clemens.

New Urban Folklore

The Roach Who Lived in a Toaster

A Special Reality (To Be Read Aloud For Inner-City Munchkins)

Once upon a time–yesterday actually–there was a roach who lived in a toaster. It wasn't a deluxe, high rise, four-slice toaster, just an old beat up one of the two-slice variety. It didn't even have a setting for bagels.

The toaster rested on the shelf in someone's extremely oversized loft apartment down by the river. The toaster had not been used for ages, at least not since the Tim Horton's opened and toast, mere toast, became obsolete.

The tray on the bottom of the toaster was as cozy as could be. It was padded with plenty of delicious crumbs. The roach could not believe his luck when he found it. He settled down, snug as a bug in a rug. (But that was his grandfather.)

Every night, when the kitchen was dark and safe, the roach would join his friends, the silverfish, for fun and games: roll the raisin; potato chip Frisbee; sniff the tampon. Life was good.

Then one fateful morning, the roach woke up feeling strange. His toaster home was suddenly smaller, and hot, getting hotter! A giant crumb fell from above just missing the roach. One of those disgusting humans was making toast! The roach barely escaped with his antenna intact.

Today, the roach is being nursed back to health under the sink by a recently widowed silverfish. When recovery is complete, they plan to relocate. Forward all crumbs to the box in the bathroom marked: I.U.D.
—*Ellen Hildreth*

If you would like to tell us a New Urban Legend you've heard, please write us at NUL, c/o Orbit Magazine, 919 S. Main St., Royal Oak, MI 48067

▲ "Blast Off," *Orbit*, March 1999.

said. Paul Zimmerman echoed this sentiment: "As unorganized as *Fun* was, *Orbit* was going to be completely structured and organized."

The group included core designers Gary Arnett, Mark Niemenski, and brothers Terry and Craig Colon. The business staff included Katy McNerney, while the editors, writers, and photographers included *White Noise* co-creator Paul Zimmerman, former *Detroit News* columnist Matt Beer, Chris Kassel, Amy Yokin, S. Kay Young, Joseph Sposita, Tim Caldwell, and Walter Wasacz. The core of the staff had worked on one or both of the previous papers, and many were Peterson's longtime friends, dating back to the Bookie's Club 870 scene in the late 1970s.

Armed with the knowledge they'd gained from *White Noise* and *Fun*, the staff was ready to fight it out on the newsstand with fresh design, humor, and new ideas. One of the early ideas was to make the magazine as friendly as possible for all audiences while retaining a hip vibe. "*Orbit* was about having something on your coffee table that you wouldn't be embarrassed by if your grandmother or your kid

"Blast Off," *Orbit*, March 1999. ▶

TRUTHER THAN STRANGE

Curses, Foiled Again
Kelvin Floyd was convicted of car theft in Aiken, S.C., after he removed the vehicle's identification number and replaced it with his Social Security number, thereby arousing the suspicions of authorities.

The Honeymoon Is Over
After a year of marriage, Marius and Roxana Dumitrescu filed for divorce in southern Romania, citing "irreconcilable differences." According to court records, Marius wanted Roxana to wear mauve clothing, as his mother always did, but she preferred dressing in white, red and green.

Curses, Foiled Again
Police in Peru, Vt., arrested Hazard Campbell, 42, as a suspect in the abduction and assault of a 26-year-old Barnard woman after the victim said her attacker told her he had a "strange" first name and called his dog "Obie," short for Obidya. His dog's name was on record with the town clerk.

Chicken Little Was Right
The sky has fallen more than five miles in the past 40 years, according to researchers from the British Antarctic Survey, who checked records of radio waves bouncing off the ionosphere. Head scientist Martin Jarvis emphasized that the collapse of the upper atmosphere from 190 to 185 miles "is not in itself harmful to people," but, blaming global warming, he added it is just "another warning signal about what damage to the atmosphere can be caused by human impact."

A 17-year-old Kmart employee in Prince Frederick, Md., was injured while working in a storage area when, according to Bo McKenny of the Calvert County Sheriff's Department, he went to grab something off one of the shelves and 21 toilet seats fell down on him.

Forgotten But Not Gone
Diane Thomas, 33, sought acupuncture treatment in Merthyr Tydfil, Wales, from Dr. Kevin Thomas. After inserting needles in her neck, back, ankles and wrists, he told her to lie face down for 40 minutes. Meanwhile, he was called away on an emergency and forgot about her. So did the other doctors, nurses and clerical staff, who did not hear her cries for help inside the soundproof treatment room when they locked up the medical offices for the day. That night, the cleaning staff found the woman in her underwear and called a senior physician to remove the needles. To prevent further mishaps, the practice began issuing hand bells for patients to ring if they are ever overlooked.

Poor Reflection
After capturing just 17 percent of the November vote in Alaska's gubernatorial election, Republican John Lindauer blamed, among many others, the news media for contributing to his dismal showing, accusing one Anchorage television station of using a mysterious "radio-station mirror" to distort his words.

Lost and Found
When Los Angeles police officer Kelly Benitez, 29, stopped a beat-up Ford Thunderbird with expired license plates, he noticed the driver's last name and his were the same. After a few questions, the son realized the driver was his father, Paul Benitez, 49, whom he hadn't seen since he was 4 months old. As the two men embraced in the street, the father noted afterward, "cars pulled over because they thought I was wrestling with a police officer."

Fur Fights Back
Elephants in Uganda are thwarting ivory poachers by being born without tusks. Researchers at Queen Elizabeth National Park reported that 15.5 percent of the female elephants and 9.5 percent of the males are now tuskless, up from 1 percent in 1930. Scientists credit the genetic adaptation for the recovery of the elephant population in the park from 200 in 1992 to 1,200 today and in Africa overall from 500,000 in 1989 to 600,000 now.

One Pill Makes You Larger
After withdrawing his savings, pawning his wedding ring and taking out a loan, Romanian Georgio Barrsan, 56, spent the money on black-market Viagra and two prostitutes. He took six of the anti-impotence pills, but then fell asleep. He awoke 12 hours later to find the women and his wallet gone. Investigators discovered that instead of Viagra, Barrsan had been sold sleeping pills.

Despite the customary reluctance of Japan's Health Ministry to approve foreign-made drugs, usually taking years and sometimes decades, if ever, it needed just five months to approve Viagra. Japan's NHK public television reported that a ministry panel cut through the red tape, even though birth-control pills and the anti-depressant Prozac have awaited approval for many years. Since Viagra's introduction last year, the $10 pills have sold for between $30 and $300 on Japan's black market. Travel agencies there have even organized tours to the United States that include appointments with doctors who write prescriptions for Viagra.

Things That Go Boom
Friza Borokhova, 74, Voya Borokhova, 44, Sophia Shomekova, 23, and two children, 4 and 2, suffered minor injuries in their New York City apartment while honoring the memory of a dead relative when they lit what they thought was a votive candle. It turned out to be an M-100 fireworks explosive.

Vlad Cazacu, 43, a circus fire-eater in Romania exploded during a performance in Romania when he burped after accidentally swallowing some flammable liquid, triggering the blast.

Bird Brains
Investigators looking for pirated computer software at a house in Mountain Ash, South Wales, couldn't find the master discs until the owner's parrot announced, "Under the mattress! Under the mattress!" They lifted it and found two cases containing some 200 games. "The parrot was giving us an earache," investigator Phil Jones of European Leisure Software Publishers' Association told reporters, "when it dawned on us what it was actually squawking."

Police in Kvam, Norway, spent 10 days trying to locate the victim of a motorcycle accident near Bergen, Norway, using divers, cameras and dogs to search a lake next to the crash site. Finally, the desperate sheriff decided to test a folk saying that roosters can find drowned people. He and a deputy put a rooster in a cardboard box and rowed away from shore. After a few hundred feet, the rooster started crowing, and the sheriff spotted the body.

Pushing the Envelope
Britain's Family Planning Association, which receives $3.3 million a year from the government to dispense advice on sex and contraception, announced it

Product Watch

Someone sent us a pack of these babies all the way from Amsterdam. These "nicotine delivery devices" will cost you about three Eurobucks (15 if you want to stick 'em in your mouth). The retro Vargas girl–style make these the perfect decorative touch to any sleazy motel nightstand, the perfect gift for someone you love, or for someone who just loves to love themselves. We hear that they come in king size, lights, and special Amsterdam strength (impossible to sneak through customs, I bet). Our prediction: If this product makes it across the big drink, we'll smoke 'em until we stop getting 'em for free. Sex sells, baby, especially cigarettes. What could possibly be more sexy than hacking up a phlegm ball as big as your head? Chewing it up and swallowing it back down, of course.

Actual Size!

Pin-Up Collection
1970s

CLASS A CIGARETTES

Nicotine-Delivery Device for Persons 18 or Older

would begin selling vibrators and other sex aids by mail order. A spokesperson explained the move was prompted by "people wanting this kind of confidential service"—particularly the disabled and house-bound who had no other way of getting such aids.

The family planning body insisted that its intention was not to titillate or encourage sexual experimentation. "We want to de-stigmatize sex aids for people," the spokesperson said. "We would be very much at the boring end of the market. We're not talking about blow-up dolls or handcuffs."

Handicapable
Herbert Council, 39, was fined $513 for drunken driving after he smashed his friend's BMW into a tree in Murfreesboro, Tenn. Council, who is blind, said he thought he knew the roads well enough to find his way when, after having a few drinks, he and his friend Jeffrey Hamilton took Hamilton's car for a spin in the rain. Council missed a sharp curve, however, and slammed head first into a tree.

Reach Out and Touch Someone
Someone impersonating a police officer called a McDonald's in Milwaukee claiming that some money had been stolen from the restaurant. The caller convinced the female manager to strip-search a male employee to look for the money while holding the telephone to the man's genitals so the caller could "hear" the search.

Planned Obsolescence
Critics of compact discs say that far from being indestructible, CDs have a shelf life of only 10 to 15 years. Speaking on the National Public Radio show "Anthem," Chicago recording engineer Steve Albini noted that the aluminum used to make CDs deteriorates when it is exposed to oxidizing agents, leaving the discs susceptible to what he calls "CD rot."

Most recording industry experts disagree with Albini's charge. What's more, Mark Goorsky, an associate professor of material science and engineering at the University of California at Los Angeles, said the controversy is a moot point "because the next technology coming up will replace this one anyway." Albini, who favors vinyl, called the rapid progression from one recording technology to another

over 2 1/2 trillion dollars in Monopoly money has been printed. ...the first computer was invented in 1833. ...Robbie the Robot cost $125,000.00 to build. ...dogs have been domesticated for 14,000 years, cats for about 4000. ...the U.S. Secret Service was originally formed to track down counterfeiters. ...the FTC get 1100 complaints per month about fraudulent Internet sites. ...the average person eats eight spiders a year. ...some restaurants use the fluid from animals' eyeballs to make their milkshakes thicker. ...cats need only 1/6 the light we need to see. ...to be considered for a job with the FBI, you must not have smoked marijuana for the past three years and not more than 15 times ever, not taken any illegal drugs for the past 10 years and not more than five times ever.

a big part of the problem, noting, "With each incremental improvement in digital technologies, everyone wants to discard the old one."

Benefits Package
Germany's minister of women, Christine Bergmann, announced that she would submit a bill calling for health, retirement and unemployment benefits for prostitutes. The measure would also give the women a legal right to sue customers who refuse to pay for their services. Bergmann added that prostitutes should be able to retire, with full benefits, by age 60.

Curses, Foiled Again
Police in Victoria, British Columbia, found all the evidence they needed that the driver of a pickup truck was responsible for the death of a bicyclist in a hit-and-run accident. After striking the cyclist, witnesses said the truck crossed a busy six-lane highway and sped off. When police eventually located it in a driveway, they found the victim in the back, apparently having landed there after the collision without the driver's knowing.

Second Chances
Police in Davenport, Iowa, were notified of a man exposing himself on a busy city street by two women who spotted the 34-year-old suspect while driving by. The women explained that they felt it necessary to drive by again for a second look just to make sure.

After Kelly Lopez of Salem, Ore., hired a private detective to find out who was regularly making obscene phone calls to her, the detective traced the calls to a telephone in a Marion County jail cellblock and learned that an inmate there had been calling Lopez collect. Authorities advised the woman that she could stop the obscene calls simply by refusing to accept the charges.

Pre-Marital Anxiety
Town councilors in Hearst, Ontario, voted to end the tradition of locking prospective bridegrooms in cages in the center of town. While on public display, the men usually had eggs and tomatoes thrown at them by townspeople, who pay for the privilege in part to raise a nest egg for the couple, although in one recent incident a would-be groom was given an enema with a grease gun. The councilors acted after local clergy pointed out that some men were so fearful of the practice that they were forgoing marriage altogether.

Just Can't Get Enough
When police in St. Petersburg,

---

picked it up. It took more skill as a writer not to swear. That's really, really hard," said Peterson.

The Look

It was well known that Peterson's earlier publications had been influenced by *National Lampoon*, *Mad*, *Creem*, and late-1970s regional punk magazines such as *Punk*, *Slash*, and *Search and Destroy*. The layout of *Orbit* took its cue from a range of sources, including New York culture and humor publication *Spy* magazine and the defunct 1970s adult magazine *Oui*. "I liked old retro graphics and things like that. That might have been from *National Lampoon*; R. Crumb would parody old stuff like that. That was a real graphic influence. At the time, *Esquire* had 'the dubious

▲ Former Soviet president Mikhail Gorbachev a.k.a. "Gorby," the inspiration for Orby, circa 1991. (AP Photo/Alexander Zemlianichenko)

"Blast Off," *Orbit,* ▶
March 1999.

Kid Rock, Midori, Jason with members of Orgy.

Kid's Rocks

Kid Rock hopped on stage with **Sugar Ray** and pulled out something other than a few stale rhymes. Yes, Mr. Rock (as he is now known in the biz,) shocked the all-ages crowd at the recent Everlast/Sugar Ray gig at the State when he whipped out his wiener, showing everyone where he gets most of his lyrical inspiration. The little fella seems to be plenty for Rock's new girlfriend, the vivaciously yummy porn star **Midori**. The two met after Rock saw one of Midori's movies—*Show Me the Money*. Then his people got in touch with her people and they got together. It was love at first sight–or something like that. The two have been seen buzzing about town, even getting hot and heavy in the balcony of the aforementioned show. When we caught up with the cute couple, we asked Midori about the attraction. "To me he is Kid Cock," and then went on to say, "He makes my rump shake." If you want to see Kid Rock's girlfriend doing more than you've seen your own girlfriend do, just punch up www.xxxmidori.com.

In other trouble...

Kenny Olson; fresh off tour with Kid Rock, is allegedly suing **Fifth Avenue Billiards**, claiming that the bouncers bounced his ass right down the stairs. An informed source at Fifth Avenue responded by saying that Kenny was extremely drunk and very lucky to have even found the stairs, unlike Diablo guitar cohort **Jeff "Baby" Grand**, who simply decided to sleep it off on the bathroom floor.

Jeff "Baby" Grand

I C Oscar

Insane Clown Posse's movie, *Big Money Hustlas* is shooting in New York. No, it's not a Merchant Ivory–period melodrama as we reported earlier, but they have managed to land big name talent. Who? (Hint: He's mean as snakes and twice as bad, he uses an earthquake to make his milk shake and he has a dong as big as King Kong.) That's right, screen legend **Rudy Ray Moore**, better known as **Dolemite**, muthaf... Also there is rumored to be a part for pro wrestler **Mankind**, who should be no stranger to acting.

New Job

Ex-Ritual runner, the always darling **Melissa Metuzak**, has a new job. She'll be managing a little-known band called **Smashing Pumpkins**. Duties vary from day to day, but word is that the job pretty much entails being Billy's babysitter.

Metro Slime

We've been noticing former **Metro Times** head ed. **Desiree Cooper's** smiling mug on the **Free Press** boxes and

thought...weird. The *Times* was a huge strike supporter (even though the *Times* itself is non-union; once, going so far as to replace workers who dared walk out over pay issues). While the strike is technically over, there are still a few unsettled issues, one of the biggest involving Cooper's new postion. Even though most workers have been called back, Cooper snagged the seat of 30-year veteran **Susan Watson**. Columnist Watson was fired after a sit-down strike and the union is still suing for her job. If Cooper took another position, it would be O.K.; but, by filling the Watson void, she is viewed by many (including old friends) as a scab. As far as the column itself, Cooper seems to be, well, pretty less. She seemingly won't take sides when it comes to hot city issues. Could it be that her "tight with Archer" hubby **Butch Hollowell** is toning down her once alternative voice? While she may not have the idealism of her last job, we are sure her new salary is very liberal. (*Editor's Note:* Glass houses aside, *Orbit Magazine* is non-union as well. In fact, conditions are deplorable even by Third World standards. Then again, *Orbit Magazine* doesn't have a finger-pointing, sanctimonious, liberal agenda.)

When It Rains, it Pours

Detroit is on fire. There are more major label releases from local bands this spring than the area usually gets in three years. **Eminem's** debut CD, *Slim Shady*, shipped platinum—which is rare for a new artist and virtually unheard of for a white rapper. The **My Name Is** guy is charting on alternative and urban and looks like he will be knocking **Celine Dion** out of the coveted national number one slot. Thank **Dr. Dre** for the cred and MTV for the exposure. **Sponge** and **Verve Pipe's** latest will be in stores this month, as well as releases from **Atomic Fireballs.** In May, **ICP** will follow-up their almost platinum

Blab Point System

I know Sean Harrington	+2
I'm showing at C-Pop	+3
I know Amir	+1
I know Amir in the Biblical sense	-5
I'm a poet	-2
I had sex with _____ Gun	+5
I danced with Tinky Winky	+10
I was at the Music Institute when Depeche Mode showed up	+3
VEGAS	-2
Physically seen Kid Rock's penis	-3

debut with a second CD and **Dennis White** (ex-**Charm Farm**) gets a new shot at the world with his new band **Control Freq.** Slightly lower key is the four-figure **GO** deal with SubPop and **StunGun,** whose Warren Defever–produced CD should land them a major deal. Meanwhile, **Robert Bradley's Blackwater Surprise** just finished recording their new CD and we hear it's the bomb. You can see them trying out their new material Friday at the Detroit Institute of Arts.

Papers please...

When we heard rumors that the **Wild Bunch** had been banned from Canada, we immediately jumped on the phone to get the full skinny. Finally, **Disco** got back to us; here's the dope... (Get it?...Dope) When trying to make it to a gig with the **Go** over in Windsor, they were informed by the border patrol after a quick background check that they couldn't admit felons into their country and they would have to go home. Being the resourceful rock 'n' roll rebels that they are, 20 minutes later they snuck onto a tour bus full of nuns on its way to the Windsor Casino. Despite their disguises (**M** and **Joebot** were in full drag,) they were again caught and this time detained for the drug residue on a driver's license. After some extensive strip searching and the threat of being in jail until the acid wore off, they were finally allowed to go, but were asked never to return. When the Go finally showed up, spoutin' the same "wild bunch" of crap, they were also asked to "*Go* away." Other band members were unavailable for comment, as they were relocating after being evicted from their crib for the recent bash they threw after their last Magic Bag gig.

Hit's from the Chong

With all the recent pressure from The Man, the people are still going ahead with **Hash Bash '99.** This could prove to be the best bash yet, as we heard through the grapevine that **Tommy Chong** will be there hangin' out with his pals from **Harm's Way** and promoting his new stoner flick, *Best Buds.* The Ann Arbor band has a song on the soundtrack called "Chong Size Bong," and rumor has it that Chong's gonna sit in on their jam session planned for the event. Hopefully, Chong will also team up with those crazed puppeteers, the **The Gepetto Files** who will also be providing entertainment for a crowd too stoned to understand or care.

Designer Terry Colon helped create the look of the magazine. Colon had cut his teeth working with his father in a Detroit-area family business that created car catalogs for the Big Three in the 1970s and 1980s. Colon came to *Fun* in 1989 after returning to Detroit from Los Angeles, where he'd worked for several years. When he picked up an issue of *Fun*, he immediately fell in love with its sense of humor. After sending his portfolio to the *Fun* offices, Jerry Peterson asked him to do several cartoons for the final issue. He was then recruited to work on *Orbit*.

At that time, Colon was starting to establish himself as a cartoonist and designer with an interest in mid-century modern styling. Combining space age–era ideas and a globe-headed mascot, Orby, he developed a visual syntax. Colon said the goal was to create a cool, retro look.

Colon went on to illustrate for one of the first ad-supported blogs on the Internet. From 1995 to 2001, Suck.com offered a satirical look at politics and pop culture. The website was created by several staffers from *Wired* magazine, including former *Fun & Orbit* editor Matt Beer. Colon also illustrated for *Time, Entertainment Weekly,* and *Atlantic Monthly.*

Designer Terry Colon's Orby. ▶

achievement awards' and *Oui* had 'the openers' ["Starters," a page or two of short stories]. I knew that was a huge influence on *Orbit*," said Peterson.

The memory of exactly how the name *Orbit* was finally selected is lost to history, and to the large quantities of alcohol Peterson and other members of

"Blast Off," *Orbit*, March 1999. ▶

Fla., charged Wayne David Sorg, 29, with exposing himself in public, the suspect explained he used to be a male stripper and missed the attention he got on-stage.

Creative Impulse
Annette Pappas of Metairie, La., has invented three-legged pantyhose to deal with the problem of runs. Each of the legs has a pocket above it in the panty area. In her patent application, Pappas explained that the wearer tucks the third leg into its pocket until a run develops in one of the leg portions being worn. Then the leg with the run is rolled up into its pocket and the third leg unrolled to replace it.

Kathy Harris of Herndon, Va., has invented two machines that combine gambling and exercise. One is a combination exercise bike and slot machine, called Pedal 'N Play. The other, Money Mill, combines a slot machine and treadmill. A timer inside the machines shuts them down if the user fails to continue with both functions.

Can't Buy Happiness
As more Americans inherit wealth or make fortunes in the stock market, many find themselves burdened by the abundance of money and are flocking to self-help groups to learn how to cope with their newfound affluence. The Washington Times reported that the main problems confronting the rich are fear, anxiety, suspicion and the loss of ambition. "People who suddenly acquire wealth are nervous and apprehensive," Los Angeles psychotherapist James Gottfurcht said. "They're concerned it will all be taken away. Money is symbolic of power, influence and importance. Its importance, coupled with a person's inexperience dealing with large sums, makes fear of loss extremely high."

Compiled by Roland Sweet from the nation's press. Send clippings, citing source and date, to POB 8130, Alexandria VA 22306.

Seven Wonders of the Moment

1. Homicide
We're number one! We're number one! It took years to clean up the image, but now Detroit is once back on top—The Murder Capital of the U.S.A.

2. Natasha Gregson Wagner
Spawn of Natalie Wood and Robert Wagner is the sexy, yet awkward, nubile for '99. You may remember her as the brunette number two girl with guy Robert Downey Jr. She plays just as dumb on chat shows as she does in the just released *Another Day In Paradise.*

3. Tom Green Show
Remember when Letterman and O'Brien were funny? Apparently, neither does Green, the new funniest guy on television. Since he's on MTV, that means he may be on 10 times a day then you won't see him for weeks.

4. Iggy Come Lately
Don Was takes the world's forgotten boy on a trip to the other side of cool—jazz. The lounged-up Mr. Pop is teeming up with Medeski, Martin and Wood for some sounds that should have Charlie Parker either rocking or rolling in his grave.

5. St. Patrick's Day
Religion + drinking. Not the green peein' amateur night frathole jive, but the down-on-your-knees prayin' at the altar of your choice. If it works for the Kennedys…

6. Elephant Herpes
O.K., who screwed Jumbo? Asian elephants are dying from this African virus in zoos across the U.S.A. Things aren't much better in the wild. Natural habitats are becoming Third World strip malls.

7. Real Detroit
Word on the street is they're aping our style. Still, we don't care because finally Detroit has a weekly paper even we would read.

Ask Minnie

Dear Minnie:

I am currently going out with one half of a pair of Siamese twins. How do I get her alone?

Sincerely, Sleepless with Siam

Dear Sleepless:

Are you sure you want to get her alone? This may be a great opportunity to get two spoonfuls of lovin'. But if you find yourself unmanly enough to satisfy two, co-joined women at the same time (loser), try any of the following when amour strikes: keep the unwanted one occupied with an Etch-a-Sketch; hit her over the head with a mallet; or simply blindfold her for a game of hide-and-go-seek, and while she's "hiding," go at it with your (and her) better half! Thanks for writing.

If you have questions for our office cat, please write Minnie, c/o Orbit Magazine, 919 S. Main St., Royal Oak, MI 48067

ORBIT • 3.23.93

Meet Jingo, World's Smartest Baby!

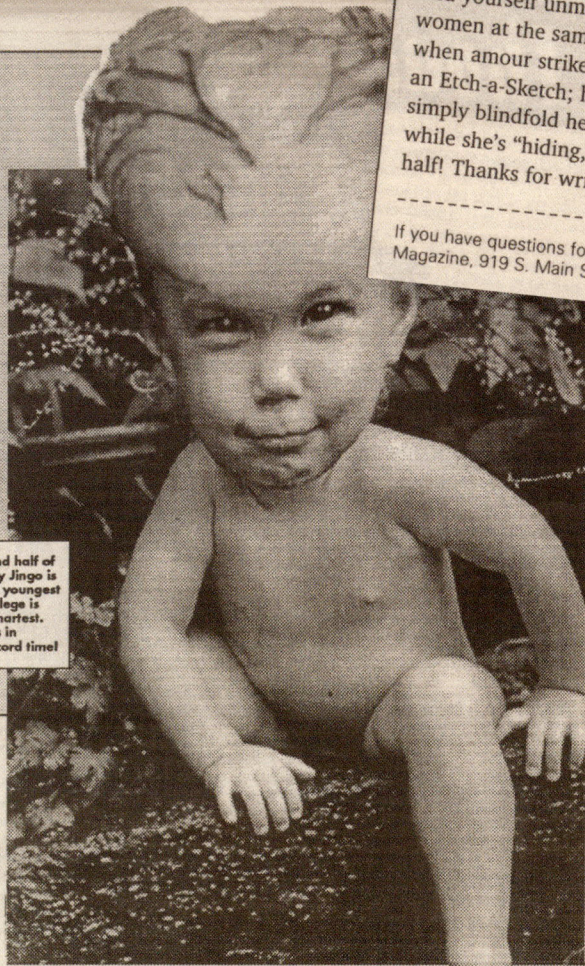

ONLY 2 1/2 FEET TALL! and half of that is his head! But Baby Jingo is Big Man On Campus! The youngest student ever to attend college is now recognized as the smartest. He got the highest grades in Harvard history, all in record time!

● He Speaks 10 Languages, Plays 12 Musical Instruments, and Even Does His Parent's Taxes!
● Jingo, World's Smartest Baby, Does it Again!
● Little Jingo Bodeen got a doctoral degree in Physics from prestigous Harvard University - before he grew a single tooth!
● Baby Jingo Graduates Harvard at 9 Months!

It's been three months since we first reported the story of Jingo, the smartest baby in the world! Since that time Baby Jingo has enrolled in the prestigious university, Harvard and will be graduating in four months - record time!

Jingo has a triple curriculum at the school; rocket science, neurology, and law! When he graduates next month he'll be better educated than his professors!

Professors at the snooty college were skeptical when parents Elmer and Lulu Bell enrolled their precocious infant, but changed their tune when the tiny genius proved that quantum mechanics was all wrong. "Though the former theory was quite elegant, it lacked fundamental cohesion with the lepton sized particles which underlie conceptual reality," explained the pint-sized mega-brain. "He's the smartest student I've ever had!" raved Professor Heinrich Katzenjammer. "The only distraction is when he fills his diaper during lectures!" Jingo reports that Dr. Katzenjammer is "a relatively harmless old man, content to ruminate endlessly over a subject matter whose sublime truth is light-centuries above him." Jingo's favorite subject is space time continuum statistics, because "a mathematical construct of the fabric of reality is quite stimulating." His proud parents have no immediate plans for Jingos postgraduate work, but dad Elmer assured *Biweekly World Orbit* that "a kid this brainy will make us millionaires!" Jingo says that although his parents "are barely sentient cretins, I have developed a begrudging affection out of our genetic similarities."

ASK BABY JINGO!

After Jingo first appeared in *Biweekly World Orbit*, we were flooded with questions for the world's smartest baby.

Baby Jingo,
My car won't start? Why?
I detected trace elements of H_2SO_4 on your letter, indicating a defective battery. Please have a trained service technician examine and replace the offending part.

Baby Jingo,
My life is miserable. Can you help me? Chemical analysis of a teardrop left on your manuscript revealed an imbalance of certain critical blood metals. I have forwarded an appropriate prescription and complete diet and excercise plan to your physician.

Baby Jingo,
How can I become rich?
After an exhaustive reconstruction of fingerprint fragments found on your letter's envelope, I have determined that you are the sole surviving heir of a Utah billionire. Please travel to Salt Lake City to claim your inheritance.

Baby Jingo,
This is the police. We have no clues. Can you help us catch the killer?
A thorough examination of the crime scene photo you provided revealed minute pipe tobbaco fragments in the carpet fibers - a serrated Morrocan leaf, obviously Dunhill's Limited Edition - Turkish Blend. Analysis of the impact and convex ash angle of said fragments indicates a left handed 200 pound Armenian Male.

Please conduct a systematic survey of local tobbaconists and your one -armed perpetrator will soon be safely behind bars.

Just How Smart is Baby Jingo?
● Scientists say that Jingo's I.Q. goes right off the Richter Scale! While an IQ test hasn't been designed that can measure his immense brain power, estimates put the tyke's IQ at over 16,000. In a nutshell:
● Jingo is smarter than one thousand Albert Einsteins!
● Baby Jingo thinks so quickly that he often has answers before the question has even been asked!
● Jingo is theoretically 100

SCIENTIFIC DISCOVERY WINNING IS EVERYTHING!
Researchers at the Palo Alto Cerebral Think Tank have discovered that winning is, indeed, everything, disproving earlier theories that winning isn't everything.

times smarter than Commander Data, from television's popular series *Star Trek, The Next Generation*!
● Baby Jingo's first words were E=MC²!
● There are enough electrons swirling around in Baby Jingo's brain to power the Hoover Dam!
● Baby Jingo beat World's Grand National Chess Master Boris Zgbronski in four moves - a universal record!
● Baby Jingo makes math calculations ten times faster than TRIDENT, NASA's new high-tech super computer!
● He also speaks ten languages fluently, including Russian, Hebrew, Chinese, Swahili, and Esparanto, all with his cute baby lisp.
● Jingo mastered classical piano in four hours, then wrote a new ending for Beethoven's unfinished symphony!

▲ "Orby Says" featured words of wisdom in each issue, *Orbit*, November 3–17, 1992.

▲ Jerry Peterson in Orby costume with Katy McNerney at an *Orbit* party. (Photo by S. Kay Young)

the staff admit to consuming during that era. All that is remembered is that hundreds of names were written down on notepads and white boards before "Orbit" was finally selected. "I know that one of the names it could have been would have been 'Xcite' with an X. 'Popular Amusements' didn't roll off the tongue and 'Pop' was another [idea], but would have people thinking it was about pop art," said Peterson.

The origin of *Orbit*'s globe-headed mascot, Orby, is also lost to history. Terry Colon said it probably took him only a few minutes to design the icon. "It just seemed like a natural fit. . . . [Mikhail] Gorbachev was popular at the time. So, Orby . . . Gorby . . . and instead of the wine stain [on his head], it was North and South America. It just seemed obvious." Colon said Orby was a throwback to when companies would use logos in their mascots—like Reddy Kilowatt or Speedy Alka-Seltzer.

Orby's role in the magazine was multi-faceted. In each issue, he would offer words of wisdom on the table of contents page. He'd chime in on everything from the environment ("Orby says: Please do your part. Recycle this paper") to junk food ("Orby says: The only bad doughnut is one left uneaten") to the status of the magazine as the final issue hit the stands ("Orby says: Fuck it!"). This *Orbit* feature was no doubt influenced by *Mad* magazine, which always featured words of wisdom from mascot Alfred E. Neuman on the table of contents page. Orby also served as a kind of visual shorthand, whether holding a knife and fork for the food section or sitting in a director's chair for the film section.

"*Orbit* Company Store" ad, *Orbit*, May 1997. ▶

At the time, Peterson wasn't big on the idea of *Orbit* having a mascot. He had created the crazed monkey mascot, Winky, for *Fun*, but it failed to help brand the magazine. But, Peterson said he liked Colon's design ideas, so he thought he should give it a chance.

Eventually, Orby's face would grace mugs, stickers, and T-shirts available through the magazine. Orby even went Hollywood with an appearance in the Oscar-winning 1994 film *Pulp Fiction*.

Beyond the art and interesting design that greeted readers in each issue, one young man became an annual fixture on the cover as readers watched him grow up. His name is Ryan Peterson, the Anniversary Boy.

Ryan, the son of Jerry's younger brother, Robert, was cast as the anniversary-edition cover model starting when he was just a year old. Appearing on issue number one, Ryan Peterson would grace the cover of *Orbit* every fall through the eighth anniversary of the magazine. He also appeared on the cover of the 1996 Halloween issue, along with his older sister and members of Insane Clown Posse.

Ryan Peterson never quite understood the point of his annual visits to his uncle's weird office: "I never really got it. I guess I never asked [why I was at the office]. Time to do another cover. We would walk up the ratty old staircase. Not sure I should be there. He always had some crazy outfit or thing for me to do."

"Orbowear" ad, *Orbit*, May 1997. ▶

◄ *Orbit* #1, September 27–October 11, 1990.

▼ 3rd anniversary issue, *Orbit*, September 1993.

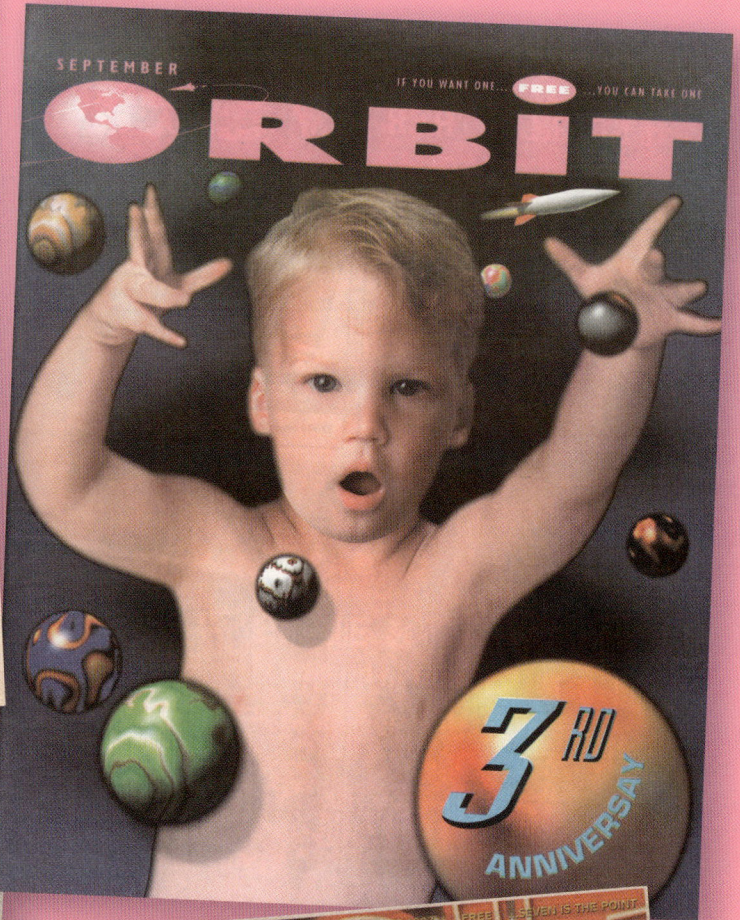

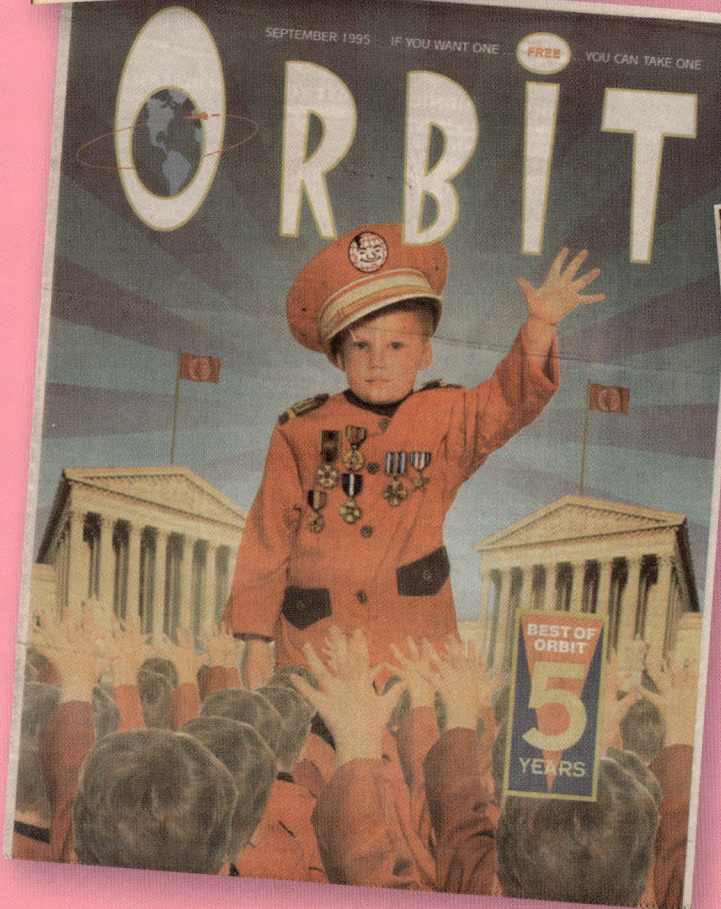

5th anniversary issue, *Orbit*, September 1995 ▲

7th anniversary issue, *Orbit*, September 1997. ▶

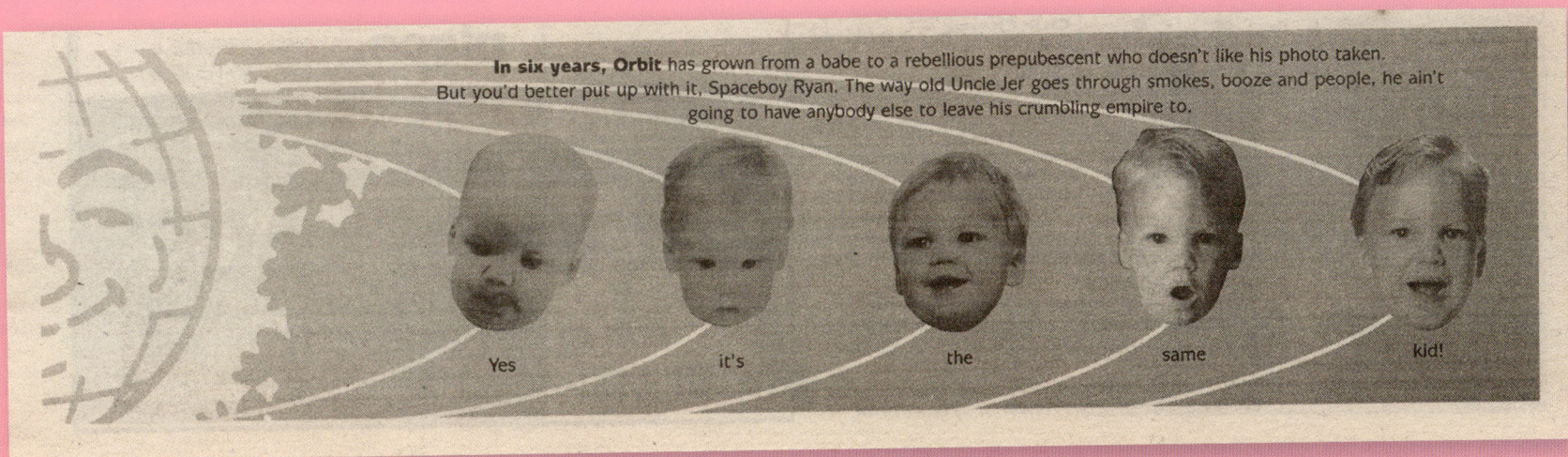

In six years, **Orbit** has grown from a babe to a rebellious prepubescent who doesn't like his photo taken. But you'd better put up with it, Spaceboy Ryan. The way old Uncle Jer goes through smokes, booze and people, he ain't going to have anybody else to leave his crumbling empire to.

Yes   it's   the   same   kid!

The evolution of Ryan Peterson, *Orbit*, September 1996. ▲
Ryan Peterson, Summer 2011. (Photo by Bruce Giffin) ▶

Peterson remembers some "interesting" times with his Uncle Jerry, despite never quite understanding the elder's eccentricities and punk rock reputation. "Never could really figure him out. Not in a negative way. I don't know. I have really bad anxiety and one of my therapists who helped me with that was a friend of Jerry's back in the day. The first thing he would say is 'How's Jerry doing? Man, we would get smashed back in the day!' This was my therapist! He's a very unique individual, but he was always good to us," said Peterson.

Looking back, Ryan Peterson said the covers were never really a big deal around his house: "We never really talked about it much. Apparently it's more special than I thought. Maybe my parents didn't want me to know? I don't know. I really enjoyed it. It would be cool if it would have continued."

▲ *Orbit* #0, August 1990. (Cover by Glenn Barr)

Blast Off!

A month before the official launch of *Orbit*, a zero-number test issue was released dated August 23–September 20, 1990. It featured an iconic retro-looking cover, showing a couple watching a rocket take flight, painted by artist Glenn Barr. "[Jerry] wanted you to look at it and think it was a school textbook from the 1950s," said Barr.

The first issue of *Orbit* featured news about local actress Sherilyn Fenn's role in *Twin Peaks*; a history of musician/producer Don Was; a tribute to Screamin' Jay Hawkins; a look at the Michigan Renaissance Festival; and reviews of David Lynch's new film *Wild at Heart*, the new issue of *Creem*, and local restaurant Kyla's, as well as a guide to the area's Thai restaurants. There was a spotlight on Detroit clothing designer Robert Stanzler, and the *Orbit* staff urged readers to take in the upcoming Michigan State Fair, the Montreux Detroit Jazz Fest, and a show by local band Big Chief. The issue also debuted a local gossip column called "Blab" as well as a back page of cartoons featuring the first *A Dog's Breakfast* strip by *Orbit* designer Terry Colon.

Office Culture

The *Orbit* offices were a mess, often filled with old issues, pasted-up pages, stacks of CDs, and boxes of T-shirts, with a haze of cigarette smoke hanging overhead. The office culture could be a little shocking for some. One self-described "square" was Brenna Sanchez. She was originally hired to sell ads.

Sanchez remembered her first day at *Orbit*:

I brought my lunch, and I had a little container of orange juice. And Jerry said, "You're not gonna drink that straight, are you?" And the next thing I know, this box comes down full of these little airplane bottles of vodka. And I was mortified . . . I was super square. I totally didn't fit in. I was there because it was a job. I think I had a briefcase. There were a couple of people like that. We were there for the work, and we found ourselves in this culture that probably we needed to be in, but it wasn't very comfortable and it was very frustrating. I'm here to work and you're all having fun. But you can't buck that for too long. Life teaches you how to deal with different people and different situations, and it was a pretty good environment for that.

Opportunity knocks at *Orbit*, January 1995. ▲

Orbit offices, September 19–October 3, 1991. ▶

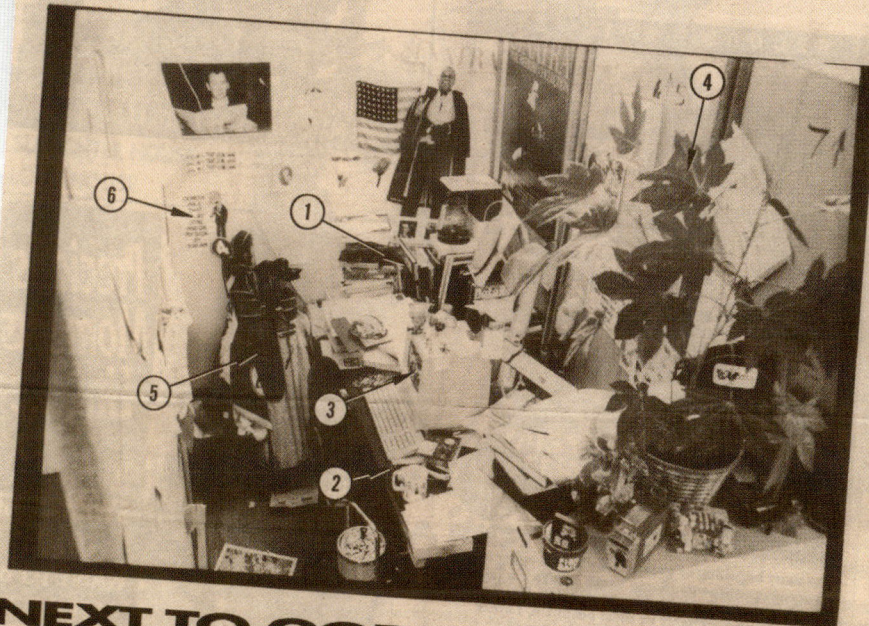

INTERIORS

NEXT TO GODLINESS

Order is conducive to creativity. A clean and tidy work place makes any task seem less tedious and more cheerful no matter how degrading. Such is the case with all Orbit work stations. All Orbit writers are afforded glorious working accommodations typical of the one represented here. The spacious 10' x 5' offices are tailor-made for easy access to anything from anywhere in the room. While many of our writers would gladly work out of cardboard boxes in the back hallway, management believes in treating its employees with the dignity and respect they deserve (besides it was ruled a fire hazard). Honest work for honest pay and a healthy environment in which to execute said work is the mandate of the people here at Orbit.

① Here we see volume after volume of reference material ranging from such works as; Kierkegaard's *The Concept of Dread*, Dickens' *Great Expectations* and *Li'l Lu Lu #34*. ② The luxurious linoleum appointed desk offers adequate filing space for many important papers and memorandums and is used in much the same way as your home's trash compactor. ③ The user-friendly Macintosh SE computer was once the backbone of the desk-top publishing industry. In the skilled hands of a trained professional, this little workhorse can turn out an average of three "puff pieces" an hour. ④ Fresh cut flowers brighten up the dingiest of work chambers and make a job seem more like a vacation. ⑤ All Orbit staffers are scratch golfers and many have played on the Ben Hogan mini tour. ⑥ Awards and certificates of achievement adorn the walls and attest to more than simple greatness but also to bleary-eyed sentimentality and gut-searing nostalgia.

Former editor Jayne Bowman Hallock remembers the staff's eccentricities but saw the creative value of the environment:

Most of the people who worked there were crazy people, a million times more creative than I was. Doug Dearth can write and draw circles around me. And Kevin King is brilliant. And Jerry. Jerry was, I don't want to say a dad, he's not that much older than me, but my goal in life was to make Jerry laugh. And it was so hard because he had so many funny people around him. When I'd write something and hand it to Jerry, I'd watch his face and he'd crack a smile and smooth his little moustache out. Then I knew I did it. But Jerry was crazy and so was everyone who worked there. Everyone there was absolutely nuts. I was normal. I was the most bor-

Behind the scenes of the printing of the September 5–19, 1991, ▶
issue. (Photographer unknown)

ing person there, but I think that's why I lasted there so long, because I wasn't the one going out to the big parties.

Designer Matt Feazell remembered what a shock to the system the *Orbit* offices were. "I was expecting it to be like another newspaper," he said. "This was the sixth one I had worked at. I was expecting it to be businesslike—strict deadlines, punching in, and keeping track. They were not too strict at *Orbit*; it was like going over to somebody's house and playing on their computers til two in the morning. I was kind of surprised that it was as casual as it was. Clients would bring in their own ads. They would talk directly to the designer instead of the ad rep. That surprised me. It was nice."

Feazell worked on ad design and layout for *Orbit* from 1994 until the magazine ended in 1999.

A single issue could have thousands of dollars' worth of advertising riding on meeting the print deadline. If *Orbit* was hitting the streets on a Thursday at the end of the month, the magazine was laid out the weekend before. This made the offices very chaotic in the days leading up to deadline.

It wasn't uncommon for the layout process to take all night and stretch on into the next day. Peterson's levelheaded managing editor—and longtime girlfriend—Katy McNerney remembered the long shifts leading up to the print cutoff: "Deadlines could be so horrible. There would be days when we were at it, even more than forty-eight hours straight, and people would stick with us—and we got that deadline met. It was hard. . . . Our faces would be frozen grimaces . . . but we always made it. We made our deadlines. We had to be at

the printer. This was old-school days, when you had to be at the printer with your pasted-up boards."

Long hours led to short tempers at times, and Peterson's was notorious. McNerney helped to keep spirits up, and on task, even under stress: "Jerry could get obsessed, and he would get really crazy, and then I would . . . kind of comfort them and say, 'It's ok, but we need it now. I know you can do it.' . . . I had already been kind of trained in that role because of being with Jerry, period. . . . He would yell. His blood would boil. You would see steam coming out of his ears. . . . Jerry would have more peaks and valleys, and I would keep things more level."

While long hours were the norm around deadlines, Peterson took care of his soldiers when they fought in the trenches beside him. Matt Feazell recalled, "Jerry would buy everyone deadline dinner, take out—tacos, pizza, or something—around 8:00 p.m. I think it helped with the creativity a lot. There were lots and lots of bad ideas out there, so that's how you get the good ideas—lots of humor and joking around. My favorite thing about him as a boss

was he always paid the invoice. He would pay me. That was great. He also knew how to do everybody's job. I could really respect that. He was good at writing and designing and taking pictures and would answer the phones—a real Jack-of-all-trades. If [my old bosses] could do all that stuff—they never did, they just answered the phone and told other people what to do."

Its lack of standardized professionalism and occasional typos notwithstanding, *Orbit* offered those who worked there the opportunity to learn about and express a part of themselves, just by virtue of showing up.

"When I quit, because I was a horrible ad salesman, they called me back and said, 'No, come back and be managing editor,'" said Brenna Sanchez. "Because I was already doing other things—I was writing, I was doing layout. Because there were all those holes that needed to be filled, and anyone, by just your sheer presence, could fill them. It wasn't like you had to wait your turn. Interns were, at certain points, running the thing because they showed up and did the work. It was a great place to just do."

INTERNS HAVE
UNLIMITED POTENTIAL AT

ORBiT

TRAVEL

NICE HOME

FINE CAR

You'll get ahead faster than you can say. "Yeah, right." We're looking for editorial and photo interns.

TELLER

GOOD SALARY

Call (810) 541-3900
to start your "Better Lifestyle."

Orbit Employee of the Month

Sara Yousuf

This month's Orbit Employee of the Month award goes to Sara Yousuf for work done above and beyond the call of duty. Her accomplishments include picking up Orbit editors from the bar when they were too drunk to drive, heroically putting out an office fire, fibbing in small claims court to ensure that her immediate supervisor would not have to pay back rent, and deducing that the window kept open to "let all the flies out" was the exact same one letting all the flies in. Good job, Sara! For all of the above, she will receive the complementary plaque and Orbit honey-glazed ham.

That kind of opportunity for expression was definitely exciting for Ron Wade. Working as a cytogenetic technologist in the Detroit Medical Center lab, Wade yearned for something more creative. As a fan of both *Fun* and *Orbit*, he found himself scratching his creative itch after a tryout with Peterson in 1995.

I had this creative side, and lab work is so monotonous and so boring, and it's very mechanical. I was dying to do anything creative. . . . *Orbit* said it was looking for writers. So, I thought I would go in. I would always drive by the offices late at night. Above this auto shop, kind of a smoke-filled loft is the only way I could describe it. Jerry was like, "Give me a sample of your writing." So, I wrote this fifty-word review of some album and came back the next day, and he was like, "OK, we're giving ten cents a word." So, I started writing music. . . . People didn't get paid much so there was a lot of turnover. No idea was discouraged. If you want to write a thousand words on how to make yourself a better stalker, go right ahead. . . . Jerry was like, "Do it and just get it in print before deadline."

By the end of *Orbit*, Wade was an editor.

The Competition

At the time of *Orbit*'s debut in 1990, there was only was one other free paper of note in Detroit: the *Metro Times*. Founded in 1980 with five thousand dollars of seed money by Ron Williams and Laura Markham, friends from Antioch College in

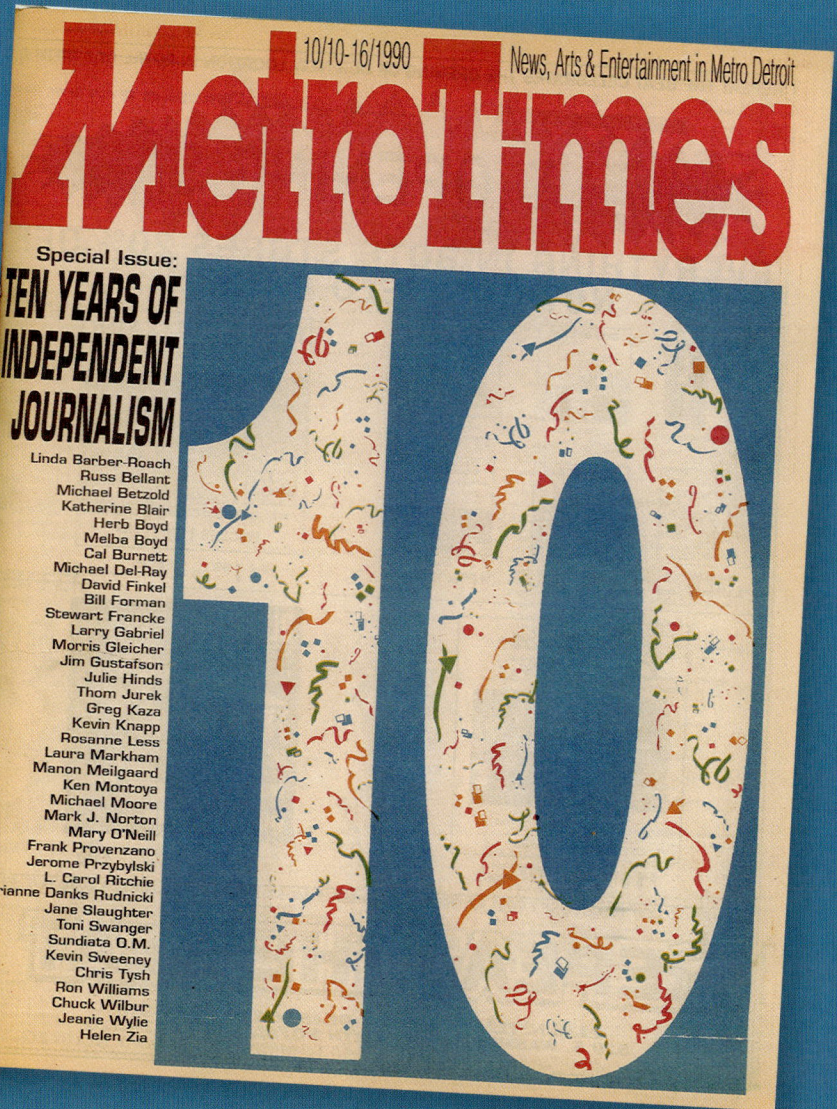

▲ *Metro Times* inaugural issue, October 16–30, 1980. (Cover image courtesy of the *Metro Times*)

▲ *Metro Times* tenth anniversary issue, October 10–16, 1990. (Cover image courtesy of the *Metro Times*)

Ohio, the *Metro Times* would, according to Williams, "establish a new journalistic voice to complement the existing media. We wanted to establish a publication that was respected on both sides of Eight Mile. We were committed to news reporting and advocacy, support for small entrepreneurial businesses, and the promotion of local artists, musicians, and writers."

What Williams and his partner were trying to accomplish was nothing new—the free alt weekly model was at least fifteen years old by the time the concept hit Detroit. "We were not exactly at the cutting edge of publishing," Williams acknowledged. "We merely borrowed the alternative newsweekly model already successful in dozens of other cities and adopted it to the

Detroit market. Saying that, few alt weeklies were as successful in publishing truly diverse journalistic voices, effective local arts advocacy and investigative reporting projects. We were consciously building an independent media institution that we hoped would continue long after we had left." Starting as a twice-monthly free paper in mid-October 1980, the *Metro Times* went weekly in mid-September 1983.

Detroit's longest-running alt weekly celebrates its thirty-fifth anniversary in 2015.

When *Orbit* started in 1990, the *Metro Times* watched the new upstart closely. "We did take *Orbit* seriously early on. Jerry and his team were talented and had a twisted, quirky

▲ *Metro Times* thirtieth anniversary issue, July 21–27, 2010. (Cover image courtesy of the *Metro Times*)

METRO TIMES

Fox initially hoped for a show that would win over the *Northern Exposure* audience, but instead ended up with *Metro Times*, an insipid combination of *WKRP in Cincinnati* and *Lou Grant*. This hour-long dramedy chronicled the travails of the staff of a struggling *Village Voice*-like alternative newsweekly in a depressed, culturally barren Midwestern city. Gary Sandy starred as publisher Don Wilson, a former '60s activist attempting to reconcile his old political beliefs with his upwardly mobile lifestyle and trying to live with the fact that he runs an "underground" publication where most of the articles are reprints from other newspapers and the overriding editorial policy is to not offend the advertisers.

In the opening moments of the unaired pilot, Wilson announces to his colorful, intern-screwing, drug-addled staff that the *Metro Times* needs to be made hipper in order to compete with a rival paper published by aging punk rocker Joey Puke (Andrew Dice Clay). News of the makeover adds an element of chaos to the paper's already volatile stew of interoffice romance and jealousy, as the weekly's hippie holdovers like music critic Stu Franklin (Glenn Frey) are forced to join with the new influx of well-intentioned but hopelessly misguided Volvo liberals like Liz Kavan (Rhea Pearlman).

The show's comic relief was provided by the paper's pompous, overbearing arts editor C.J. (Louie Anderson) and his ambitious young protégé Dinghy (Joey Lawrence), who balances his journalistic career with hilariously inept moonlighting gigs as a musician, stand-up comedian, and junkie. In the pilot episode, the duo attempts to woo a visiting rock star using the cash they received from surreptitiously selling promotional copies of her records, but are thwarted by the sudden appearance of several of Dinghy's hysterical ex-girlfriends.

Storylines were slated to deal with the left's perpetual battle against the usual demon "isms," plus the paper's unique blend of plagiarism, nepotism, and favoritism. Ironically, just as the fictional publication failed to attract a substantial readership, the series failed to win over test audiences and network execs, who found the show and all its characters "too pretentious" and "too insignificant," and ultimately decided that except for concert listings and personal ads, no one cares about alternative papers anyway. ■

sensibility. As the months went on, we came to the conclusion that, for a number of reasons—some journalistic, some related to business—that they would not present a real threat to anything that we were doing," said Williams. But staffers who worked at both *Orbit* and the *Metro Times* tell a different story of how the competition viewed Peterson's paper.

Cartoonist Matt Feazell had worked for the *Metro Times* as a designer for three years when *Orbit* launched: "Everyone in the production department loved *Orbit*. Everybody over in the publishing side, the suits, hated it. They thought *Orbit* was out to cut the *Metro Times*'s throat and they were going to steal our clients and bury us. I really get the impression that they were scared shit-

Satire of the *Metro Times* and *Orbit*, *Motorbooty* #8, Winter 1995. ▶

less of *Orbit*. I know we took their ideas. We would look at their ads. They were so much cooler than what we were doing."

Jim Dulzo, the *Metro Times* managing editor from 1992 to 1993, said that the paper understood what its main rival was trying to accomplish with its larger focus on entertainment, humor, and pop culture. However, Dulzo said, the *Metro Times* was trying to be a serious paper by competing with the *Detroit News* and the *Detroit Free Press* for hard news. "We wanted to be taken very seriously as an authoritative source for news and culture," he said. "I don't want to give the impression that we were contemptuous of *Orbit*, but we were more like, 'What's this?'"

Like Matt Feazell, Hobey Echlin worked at both the *Metro Times* and *Orbit*, but in reverse order. Echlin said that when he arrived at Williams' shop after his time with Peterson's publication, his bosses there didn't like to talk about the rivalry. Echlin believes the reason Detroit's more serious alt weekly had an attitude about Peterson was because of his ruthless ridiculing of Ron Williams and the *Metro Times* years earlier in *Fun*. He remembered one day when Williams got upset with him about a fashion choice:

Gary Arnett was working with Robert Stanzler at one point, [Arnett] was also designing *Orbit*, so *Orbit* became synonymous with the Made in Detroit [clothing design] camp. And I remember Ron Williams yelling at me once for wearing a Made in Detroit hat to the *Metro Times*. It got to that sort of level where it was sensitive. More than you might expect. The *Metro Times* always had a little bug up its butt about *Orbit*, because *Orbit* was fun. The *Metro Times* was having good kind of growing pains. They could

afford really outstanding investigative reporters, they were winning all these awards, but maybe *Orbit* reminded people what the good old days was all about because it had that startup energy back then.

The Detroit-based music magazine/underground comic *Motorbooty*, created by occasional *Orbit* cover artist Mark Dancey, found enough in the sensibilities of Williams and Peterson to lampoon both the *Metro Times* and *Orbit*. In issue #8 of *Motorbooty*, published in winter of 1995, the feature, "Not Ready for Prime Time: Ten T.V. Pilots That Didn't Make It" highlights a fictional Fox network show—*Metro Times*—that never made it to air, "an insipid combination of *WKPR in Cincinnati* and *Lou Grant*."

"Biggest Pimp in Detroit!"

After years of making digs and small jokes at the *Metro Times*, a publication Jerry Peterson saw as a stuffy left-wing political rag that didn't have a sense of humor, the publisher and his crew

▼ "The Biggest Pimp in Detroit," *Orbit*, November 1998.

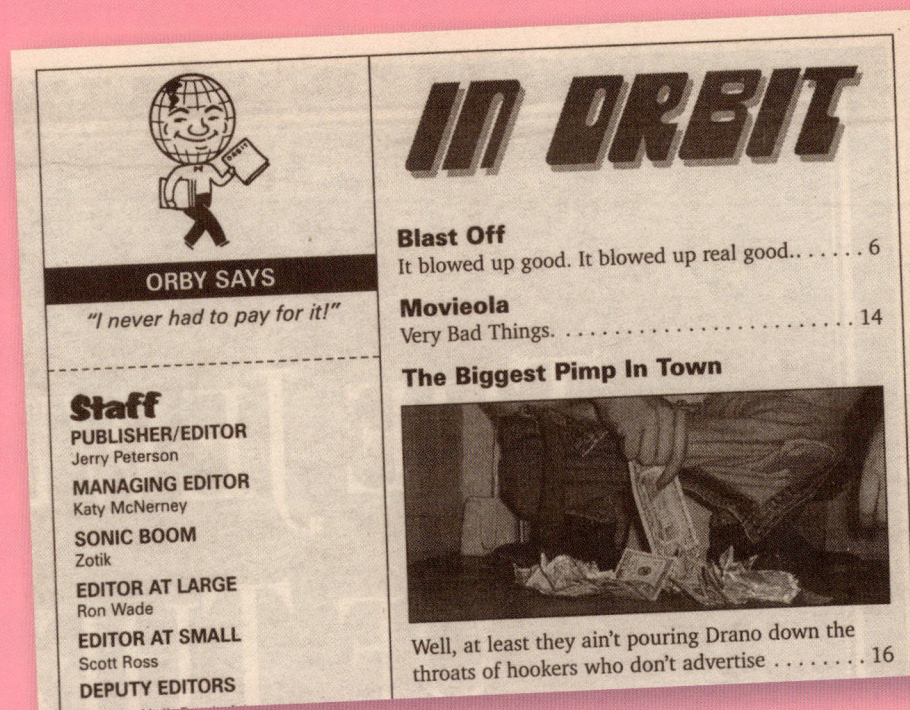

ORBY SAYS
"I never had to pay for it!"

Staff
PUBLISHER/EDITOR
Jerry Peterson
MANAGING EDITOR
Katy McNerney
SONIC BOOM
Zotik
EDITOR AT LARGE
Ron Wade
EDITOR AT SMALL
Scott Ross
DEPUTY EDITORS

IN ORBIT

Blast Off
It blowed up good. It blowed up real good....... 6

Movieola
Very Bad Things............................. 14

The Biggest Pimp In Town

Well, at least they ain't pouring Drano down the throats of hookers who don't advertise 16

The Biggest Pimp In Detroit

Is the Metro Times knowingly selling ads to prostitutes?

The *Metro Times* sprang out of the era of sexual revolution and free love. However, a recent Orbit investigation revealed the 'type of love offered in their publication is not revolutionary and certainly not free.

It began when a friend of a friend called the Orbit offices. His buddy had responded to an ad in the Metro Times, a personal for a "Chocolate Fantasy." When his Chocolate Fantasy asked for money, he thought it might make a good exposé. We didn't think so. Our opinion was: Who *doesn't* know the *Metro Times* has hookers advertising in it? It turns out a lot of people didn't know there was a sleazy side to Detroit's weekly. People who work at Orbit, people who read it religiously, and even people who have worked for the *Metro Times* are unaware of this dirty little sideline.

You may be surprised that Orbit, of all publications, should take this moral high ground. (We aren't.) But, then again, we don't consistently portray ourselves as the city's socially conscious, politically correct alternative newspaper.

Conversely, the *Metro Times* professes to be a protector of women's rights, yet in practice it appears they may be participating in the exploitation of women—we decided to prove it.

THE STING

Orbit would place our own prostitution ad in the *Metro Times*. We had an intern call,

Orbit's phoney prostitute, Brandy, leaving the *Metro Times*.

posing as a prostitute. Over the telephone, she got the prices for regular classifieds. Then she told them she was a prostitute and tried to place an ad. She was shuffled to Jennifer in the P.S. (Personal Services) section, a seedy patch of paper chock full of sleaze merchants.

Jennifer recommended the escort section. Our plant told her she was a prostitute, not an escort. That was OK, but she would still have to go in the escort column if she wanted an ad in the *Metro Times*. The smallest ad available would cost $150, way more than any other classified in the paper.

The crowd listening in around our intern was stupefied. Even the most jaded Orbiteer could not believe the *Metro Times* could be so blatant about it. Even if Orbit had any moral qualms about accepting this type of advertising, we certainly wouldn't be stupid enough to admit it over the phone.

Wasn't the *Metro Times* concerned about legalities? Are there any legalities? There are those who would consider this pandering—the publication becomes much like a pimp. And, as far as we know, prostitution isn't legal in Detroit.

But, above all, the *Metro Times* has always reeked with that holier-than-thou liberal agenda. Politically they appear to be blatantly feminist. In fact, isn't co-owner Laura Markham an avowed feminist? Didn't she once write about the humiliation she endured just by shaving her legs for an undercover story to exposé some type of male chauvinist plot? Didn't the *Metro Times* once brag how it refused to accept advertising from *Playboy* and *Penthouse*? Yet this same publication would allow sex for sale so indiscreetly. We had our intern call back—and this time we took notes. **[See Exhibit A]**

We were amazed at how casually the *Metro Times* responded to our "prostitute," even more so that their employee would make suggestions on the suggested list price of a blow job.

It was confirmed. Still, we decided a phone call wasn't enough. We had get an ad in print in the *Metro Times*, just to be sure.

There was still a hurdle to overcome in our sex-for-sale scam—the *Metro Times* would not take the ad, unless we appeared in person. They allegedly have had problems with "escorts" stealing their customers' credit cards and placing ads for more victims. It seems Detroit's political weekly has had to implement security measures so the whores won't cheat them out of their filthy lucre. We would have to

Exhibit A: Actual Call with *Metro Times*

MT: Good Afternoon. *Metro Times* Classified. How may I help you?
O: Hi, I just called about the prostitution ad. I'm not sure if I talked to you.
MT: No, you must have talked to Jennifer.
O: I just have a question. Why are the prices in your personal section so much higher than your Trades and Labor section?
MT: Now that is a Help Wanted. Trades and Labor is for business…uh…not for your field. It's strictly business for help wanted.

O: But $150 for 18 words for a personal ad–that's ridiculous.
MT: Well, Jennifer, she's the one that handles that and…uh…she's who you'd have to speak with. But those are the rates though.
O: They're non-negotiable? I mean if I place an ad for like, six months…do you guys work out a rate?
MT: Yeah, you would get what we call a frequency discount.
O: Oh, that sounds good. O.K., and that's the same for prostitution, too? It

doesn't matter what trade?
MT: Yeah, you'd get a frequency discount.
O: O.K., that works out really good. Do prostitutes usually get results with your magazine?
MT: Uh. Yeah, they do. (Laughs)
O: Great! How often does your magazine come out?
MT: We come out every Wednesday, and our readership is at 587,000.*
(*Figure is exaggerated.—Ed.)
O: Wow! So Jennifer would be the only one that

I'd talk to about my frequency rate?
MT: Yeah, she'd be the one to talk to about that…about…any adult ad.
O: About how much business do prostitutes get? Do you know?
MT: I don't know.
O: More than one girl could handle, if you know what I mean?
MT: Oh, you mean about how many responses?
O: Uh-huh.
MT: They do get a lot. I don't know exactly, but

they're satisfied, I can tell you that.
O: 'Cause I work alone. I'm putting myself through school, I have two kids, you know how it goes.
MT: Maybe more than you can handle.
O: Girl!!! O.K. I have the fax number…attention Jennifer.
MT: Correct.
O: And I have to come down there with cash?
MT: Right.
O: There's not much competition [among prostitutes], right? Because

$150 is a lot. I just want to make sure that I'm investing my money well.
MT: I can understand that. But she [Jennifer] is better familiar with that…
O: Because, you know, that's a lot of blow jobs.
MT: Is it? How many?
O: Like, five.
MT: Five? How much is that per?
O: Like, thirty.
MT: Why don't you go up on your rates?
O: That's a good idea!
MT: You should [charge] like fifty dollars.

Orbit investigates the *Metro Times*, November 1998. ▲ ▶

Exhibit C: Dirty Money

When it comes down to dollars, it seems the *Metro Times* has no shame. We wanted to see just how low they could go, so we collected the dirtiest, stickiest, most disgusting bills you have ever seen to pay "Brandy's" ad bill (So where have they been? You don't want to know). We really thought we might be pushing our masquerade and even supplied Brandy with normal money in the event they wouldn't touch it. But when Brandy forked the slimy simoleons, they didn't blink an eye, much less refuse to take it.

appear in person to sign an affidavit, which would give the *Metro Times* permission to charge our account. Or we could simply pay in greenbacks. Sure beats the typical, "Are you holding out on me, bitch?" employed by the competition.

THE TRAP

We hired an actress to pose as Brandy. We overdid her make-up, costumed her in fishnet stockings, halter-top, miniskirt, sunglasses and cheap wig. She adopted a low rent attitude, disguising her voice with a honey dripping Southern accent. Just to make sure the *Metro Times* knew what services Brandy was advertising, we wrote up a make-no-mistake-about-it-I'm-a-whore ad scrawled out for their perusal (or possible refusal). The ad read:

"Eager Beaver" I'll make you cum!
Hot Horny Pro Available for raunchy
'70s style fun. Oral, Anal, S&M's, GS, B&D.
I do it all! Phone (248) 225-3527 In&Out Calls.

Exhibit B: Actual Ad in *Metro Times*

Brandy's Ad as it appeared in the Oct. 28–Nov. 3 edition *Metro Times*

The *Metro Times* said, "No." They could not run that ad…as written. However, if Brandy reworked it, the ad (and the $150 floating amongst the condoms in her purse) would be eagerly accepted by Detroit's leading weekly. They even offered help in rewriting it. After a few suggested revisions, Brandy, the common street whore, became a Southern Belle promising real "Southern Hospitality" if you made an exotic, erotic, discreet

appointment. Basically, the *Metro Times* changed the entire ad so it would not be as obvious. **[Exhibit B]**

As a final measure of the *Metro Times'* seemingly insatiable greed, and a final opportunity to see how far we could push this, we supplied Brandy with a disgusting wad of "dirty money" **[See Exhibit C]** to pay for the ad. The filthy, crumpled bills were snatched up for the company coffers and Brandy was ready for business.

You're probably saying, "So what? Our President got blow jobs from an intern, any celebrity can get away with murder, they're even playing rock music in church. What's the harm in a little 'mommy crushin' for Benjamins?" It's a victimless crime. Nobody gets hurt, right?

And when you get right down to it, the *MT* isn't supporting prostitutes, (even though the prostitutes are supporting the newspaper.) In fact, obviously they consider prostitutes potential criminals. Why else would they demand money up front and deny credit cards? Still, by charging excessive advertising fees exclusively to hookers, you could make the argument they are getting a "cut of the action." Look up pandering in the dictionary, and you'll see a pimp by any other name is still a pimp. **[See Exhibit D]**

After calculating what Brandy paid ($165) and multiplying it by the number of other escorts on the same page (50), it comes to over $8,000. Most ads were larger than Brandy's, so our figure is probably low. Our calculation also doesn't include the cross dressing, domination, job opportunities or the multitude of display ads for phone sex, also in the P.S. section. A very conservative guesstimate is the *Metro Times* pulls in over $20,000 every week on the flesh trade. That's over a million dollars a year (still a conservative figure) made off of by what many would consider the exploitation of women. That could add up to some mighty high-style living for *Metro Times* owners Ron Williams (whose residence is in the Virgin Islands) and Laura Markham (the avowed feminist).

THE LAST LAUGH

The following Wednesday, our advertisement was getting response before we had even picked up our own copy of the *Metro Times*. To make the gag work, we needed a phone number for Brandy's ad. As the icing on the cake, we used publisher Jerry Peterson's cell phone.

By mid-day Wednesday, Peterson's phone was ringing off-the-hook. Brandy was a hit! About a dozen, mostly creepy-sounding, older men were looking to party with our Southern Belle.

Throughout the day, various people pretended to be Brandy. This quickly became boring.

Returning to the office the next day, we were amazed to discover 48 calls. After checking caller ID, they turned out to be from 11 lonely guys all desperately seeking Brandy. We had to do something to make sure these persistent bastards never called back.

• We told them Brandy was having sex with another man at the moment. They called back.

• We told them, teary voiced, "Brandy? Brandy was my nine-year-old daughter. She died of cancer last week." Some rang back, thinking they had misdi-

aled. Obviously we weren't brash enough.

• Eventually, we started answering the phone, "Operation Sting-A-John, Officer Johnson speaking." Most hung up, but two were too thick to get it.

• We pretended to be Brandy's father, and threatened to call the police on the creep who would call a 14-year-old on a school night.

• We even told the truth: that they had reached investigative journalists at Orbit—would they mind if we printed their name and phone number in our prostitution story?

• Finally we came up with our best scam. We convinced the would-be John that Brandy was just murdered; we were the police and the caller was now a prime suspect. We confirmed their number from our caller ID, in case they would be needed for further questioning.

EPILOGUE

While the calls are slowing down, this story is just beginning. Calling back to confirm the classified prices, we ended up talking to Jennifer again. She asked what business our caller was in, and we just *had* to say escorts. She perked up and inquired how many girls our caller had. "Uh…six," he said. She made her pitch, suggesting if he had 10 girls or less, he could book up a whole weeks schedule with an ad in the P.S. section. She surmised that, since most places charge $75 for a half hour, he would make his ad money back in the first hour. And just in case he was still thinking about a free ad, he was warned that the paper carefully screened them.

Essentially, what we have here is an "alternative weekly" that desperately wants to be politically correct, but can't say no to the green. They're running ads for services that you couldn't get away with in *Hustler*. Sure, many magazines have personal ads (just look at the back of this one), but how many magazines are as pious as the *Metro Times*? What others would be blatant enough to have a prostitution policy in place? Free love ain't what it used to be, Detroit's hookers are getting screwed. ◉

Exhibit B: Actual Ad in *Metro Times*

Is the Metro Times Gouging Whores?

Compare these classified prices:

Commercial (business): $1.48/word (18 word minimum).

Private Party (business): $1.01/word (18 word minimum).

Personal Ad (Lonelyhearts): First 30 words: Free.

Marquee Ad (on the back cover): $13.40 a line.

P.S. (adult): $150.00 (for 10 lines or less) if you're an "escort." (Prices vary depending on the adult service being offered.)

Clearly, we think the *MT* is ripping-off the hookers. Had Brandy been placing an ad to get on her hands an knees to scrub a floor, she would have had an extra $130 in her pocketbook. To add insult to injury, the P.S. section is buried in what most would consider to be the worst ad position, yet it is the most expensive.

Rocko's Story: I Found Sex for Sale in the Personal Ads

While most of the escort services are quickly ushered into the semen-encrusted ghetto that is the *Metro Times* P.S. section, the Free Personals section may be no safe haven either. Sex for profit may also be lurking among the lonely hearts. Just listen to the story of Rocko (name changed):

"Well, I was looking through the women seeking men ads, looking for potential date material, and I called a couple of ads. One ad I called stated: 'Your chocolate fantasy girl looking for a generous man.' I called and got a return call about a week later from a woman who said she could be my chocolate fantasy and asked how generous I was. I asked, 'Why do I have to be that generous? Can't we just go out sometime?' And she said, 'Well this is the way it works—either I come to your place and it's $200, or you come over here and it's $150.' I said, 'For what?' And she said, 'Whatever you want, baby!' I didn't engage her, but it did come as kind of a shock to me. I joked with her for a little while and asked her, 'What do I get? Can we get naked?' She said: 'You can do whatever you want, but you only get to cum once.' I've called about eight to ten other ads in the last 12 months, and that was the only one that ever called me back. I [think that they're] staging 'dummy ads' to get people thinking that a lot of people put ads in when they really don't. They're doing it just to make money."

Orbit could not confirm whether or not the Personal ads contain fakes. More likely, the girls didn't find Rocko worth the 35-cent callback.

But after investigating the special pricing MT charges hookers, it's no wonder Rocko's hooker took out a personal ad—it was a hell of a lot cheaper! That's a lot of extra money that could be spent on condoms, K-Y and mouthwash!

METROTIMES 733 St. Antoine, Detroit, MI 48226 (313) 961-4060

STATEMENT OF ACCOUNT
Date: 10/22/98

TO: Wagner, B

	CHARGES	CREDIT	BALANCE
Balance Last Statement			150
Charges This Month	10/28 P.S.		165—
Credits			
Please Pay			

This billing is current to the above date. Please contact us if balance shown does not agree with your records.

would finally print an attack on what they believed was the Achilles's heel of the rival's social agenda: hooker ads. The November 1998 *Orbit* exposé was titled "The Biggest Pimp in Detroit: Is the *Metro Times* Knowingly Selling ads to Prostitutes?"

The two-page spread addressed the sex ads in the back of the *Metro Times*. *Orbit* gleefully pointed to what the writers saw as hypocrisy: "Didn't the METRO TIMES once brag how it refused to accept advertising from PLAYBOY and PENTHOUSE? Yet this same publication would allow sex for sale so indiscreetly." To bolster its point, *Orbit* ran a transcript of a phone call between the intern and the *Metro Times* ad representative. In the conversation, the ad rep appears to be advising the "prostitute" how much she should charge for oral sex in order to recoup her costs on the ad.

Ron Williams, co-founder of the *Metro Times* and the publisher at the time, said he didn't remember the article but defended the paper's advertising business, which in his mind was in keeping with the industry standard. "Such ads appear in most alt weeklies around the country," said Williams.

New York University media professor Rodney Benson wrote about alternative weekly advertising in 2003. His findings were based on a 2001 survey by the Association of Alternative Newsmedia, a trade organization for alt weeklies: "Sex-related advertising, both display and classified, provided an estimated 10 percent of total alternative weekly revenues. Some publications, such as the owners of the *Chicago Reader* and *San Diego Reader*, refuse such ads, but they are the exceptions" (113). But Benson's article also

▼ "Biggest Pimps" ad, *Orbit*, Fall 1999.

GOOD LUCK JERRY! from the BIGGEST PIMPS in detroit! METROTIMES 313.961.4060 ✳ www.metrotimes.com

provides insight into the reasoning behind carrying such blatant sex-industry ads:

At one extreme, the *Bay Guardian's* Annalee Newitz sees sex advertising as "part of our political mission," that is, helping sex workers make it on their own "rather than rely on pimps," and in general, promoting a "sex-positive" attitude. For Sandra Hernandez of the *LA Weekly*, however, back-of-the-book quasi-pornography is an embarrassment or at best a necessary evil: "Look at the paper. I mean, it's kind of funny. We're supposed to be a left paper yet, if you look at the advertising in terms of women, it's completely demeaning to women. . . . I think there's a sense among the reporters and editors that we wish we had a different advertising base, sure" ("Commercialism and Critique" in *Contesting Media Power*, ed. Nick Couldry and James Curran [Rowman & Littlefield], 113).

Ben Burns is former executive editor of the *Detroit News* and head of Wayne State University's Department of Journalism. Burns said he thought the story worth running: "I think [alt weeklies] have value in the community. They appealed to a much younger audience than [the *Detroit News*] did. I think one of the interesting things that [*Orbit*] did . . . was [discuss] the fact that the *Metro Times* ran ads for whores. I think it was useful because the *Metro Times* was raking in the money and pretending to be more serious. The *Metro Times* the last couple of years has raked it in out of [medical] marijuana production and sales [advertising]. I guess that's limited a little bit, right now [because the law is under review]."

Orbit concluded their exposé with another jab at perceived hypocrisy: "Essentially, what we have here is an 'alternative weekly' that wants to be politically correct, but can't say no to the green. They're running ads for services that you couldn't get away with in *Hustler*. Sure, many publications have personal ads (just look at the back of this one), but how many magazines are as pious as the *Metro Times*? What others would be blatant enough to have a prostitute policy in place? Free love ain't what it use to be, Detroit hookers are getting screwed." Whether a sincere appeal or a declaration of superiority–moral or otherwise, the exposé didn't change a thing at the *Metro Times*. Ads for "erotic services" still appear in the alt weekly, but one could say the *Metro Times* had the last laugh when it said "Good Luck" to its rival with an ad in the final issue of *Orbit*.

Orbit Food

Long before the culinary culture of new millennium birthed the Food Network and thousands of websites dedicated to the finer points of tasty morsels, *Orbit* examined the offerings at Metro Detroit restaurants. As they wrote in the August 1995 "Fun Dining in Detroit" feature, it was hard work being an *Orbit* food critic:

Orby says "bon appetit."

Compared to manly occupations like lion-taming, porno acting, or any job that requires steel-toe boots or teeth guards, restaurant reviewing must seem like a piece of cake. Eating a bunch of sissy food and getting drunk in the middle of the afternoon, then billing a triple-digit check to the

Fine Food
EATING
IN ORBIT

SHORT ORDERS

TOULOUSE
248 Culver Street
Saugatuck, 857-1561

STABLE SEATING **FRENCH**

Totally '90s... Eighteen, that is, though gratefully, the horse pucky's gone, the stable sweat, the blowflies. Been replaced (in this restored livery) by starchy linens, floral carpets, matching burgundy-and-teal plateware, dazzling service (at least by Stephanie, ours was) and a thoroughbred menu reminiscent of a charming south-France *auberge*. Chef Curt Bass understands the rules well enough to bend them a little: his luminous Angeleno *bouillabaisse* is redolent of saffron; he naps impeccable, blood-red steaks in walnut/chartreuse butter; and especially, his signature *cassoulet* (originated in the Languedoc town of Toulouse) which is among the best interpretations of this classic inn-dish ever. -*C.K.*

HEATHER HOUSE
409 N. Main
Marine City, 765-3175

COMFY COZY

In and around suburban Detroit, B&B's are an oft overlooked R&R. Marine City's but a stone's throw away, pretty podunk, but touching it up with a smidgen of couth are Grosse Pointe Bill and Ireland Heather. Heather House is a destination rather than a pit stop. Faultlessly comfortable surroundings, great architectural restoration, major detail attention (Caswell/Massey soaps, antique silverware, carafes of wine on the porch) and breakfast by their pal Drew: mega-berries in cream, nutmeg-dusted eggs, fresh scones, blueberry muffins, homemade jams. -*C.K.*

WHITNEY'S THIRD FLOOR
4421 Woodward
Detroit, 832-5700

RITZY

In a world of gloppy soups, the Whitney offers a light, yet savory eggplant and onion chowder, just one of the lovely selections from the lighter menu. Their Caesar salad is one of the top two prepared in this area. It's still la-di-da upstairs but free (!?) live jazz is offered every Sunday evening. Skip the valet parking, don't opt for caviar and you can still afford to have a refined dining experience.
-*Maureen McCurdy*

RATTLESNAKE CLUB
300 River Place
Detroit, 567-4400

SCHMIDT EMPIRE

I found it hard – make that impossible – to believe Orbit has never reviewed this fine restaurant in town. Then Chris Kassel showed me his paycheck. Just kidding, Chris wouldn't show me his paycheck and the Snake never struck me as that expensive (go to NY, LA, or eat in a hotel –that's expensive). Lunches have always been reasonable and the grill side is always a steal. But now Mr. Schmidt is offering a downright deal, free appetizers, jazz and reduced drink prices. Enough of this value blab – The Snake is the coolest, my personal favorite. -*Herman Wiggley*

UNION STREET
4145 Woodward
Detroit, 831-3965

Mon-Fri: 11:00am - 2:00am
Sat-Sun: 5:00pm - 2:00am

Style: Progressive, seafood emphasis
Prices: Moderate
Standout Dish: Union Street Jambalaya
Alcohol: Thomas Hardy's Ale

A UNION DIVIDED CAN TOO STAND
by Chris Kassel

The shambling old **Whitney** casts a long shadow downtown. For their irreproachable service, they're an apotheosis (never mind the small stuff, like prices...*think the waitress gave you her phone number, hotshot? that's the bill...*) and to perfection-oriented establishments like **Union Street**'s John Lopez, service choreography is the paragon toward which even the most casual of cafes must strive.

When chef/co-owner Ron Stewart vamoosed, certain media grinches figured **Union Street** for a goner, rubbed a little salt in their wound, but evidentially (thanks mostly to the dedication/insight of Lopez) they never even missed a beat. In stepped Chef Dave Pillette (Midtown, Tom's Steamer) and the place metamorphosed, moved up a notch. As we read it, **Union Street** has emerged as a tri-entity, three entirely separate personalities:

THE BAR: Always a counter-culture magnet, especially under the watchful, semi-shy eye of nose-ringed Larry, a crucible of colorful Nirvanic characters, Doc Marten outlaws, the grunge-core mosh contingent chugging Bud alongside Bolshevik wide-eyed, politically bushy-tailed manifesto-sharers from nearby Wayne (State's) World; maybe a few banlon shirts and the odd crew cut from the friendly banks of, say, Madison Heights, seeping in around the edges. Sign reads *Life's Too Short For Cheap Beer* and we bite: a single 6 oz. seven-dollar Thomas Hardy Ale and we're out of drink money.

THE RESTAURANT: Exploits all the comfortable glories of dark toasty deco, carved wood, beveled glass, a gutsy menu heavy into fresh pastas and aquaculture. Love the fact that they refuse to cave in to middle-road tastes, even with dad and the kids tip-toeing in from Montreaux or Orchestra Hall: the Rasta Wings, for example, are not suburban tempered, they're blister-hot, and the entrees, while balanced, are ambitious, progressive: Tiger shrimp in fresh linguini was particularly noteworthy.

THE MICHIGAN ROOM: Far from the madding polyphonic droning crowd, this non-smoking annex is pricier, mellower, with up-scalier amenities: jazz, china, a long menu boasting promising all-regional possibilities: sauteed venison loin, buffalo burgers, paned trout in blueberry/feta compote, and without a doubt, a service ethic to compete with the big boys.

Despite the alternate alternate-press doomsayers (that confederacy of dunces) this **Union**'s a bar that's earned its stripes. ✂ CLIP AND SAVE RECIPE.

ORBIT SCORE DU JOUR
24 25   23 22
94 TOTAL
Service Ambience Food Value

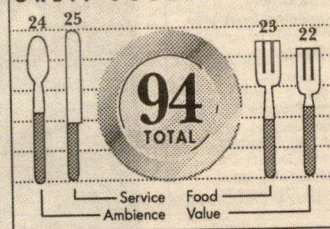

WORLD OF MOUTH...

FIELD REPORT: 14th Annual Michigan Championship Chili Cookoff (Hosted by The Lark) The Lark's lot was a trip by itself, an antithetical orgy; XK roadsters nuzzling Escorts, brawny 4X4's scamming on petite Carreras. If cars got busy, kids, there'd be your New World Order. Beneath the tent, it was more of a piece: denim and Dingos were *de rigueur* (except for the pepper-pants sported by Beer Guzzlin' champs). Judges, meanwhile (including **Dwayne X Riley** and **Earl Klugh** - *Earl Klugh?*), were sequestered behind Lark garden walls, sedately tasting flights of chili in Mary's magical herborium. Awaiting results, milling throngs of *con carne cognoscenti* sampled from forty triumphantly funky chili booths, making fart jokes and lip-reading names like No Respect Chili, Rodent Chili (booth sported a spasmodic plastic dying rat: I want one). *Causa del dia*, scholarshipping deserving kids through culinary school, may sound more chic than politically correct, but you could find a number of grateful parents who'd disagree. The chili? Well, chili's chili: it all tasted about the same; meat-clogged, gringo-style. The winner's secret (**Joe Janes** from Wyandotte, who now moves on to the National Championship in chili central; Scottsdale, Arizona) was marinating his meat first: thus confided Chief Judge **Bob Talbert** with his cosmic laugh and y'all drawl. Hard work paid off, **Orbit's** compliments to all concerned, especially co-ordinator **Pat Wilhite**. Bottom line, the day was a riot, wonderful, and the chili was a perfect foil to the stupendous hyper-gastronomy usually associated with the Lark's Portugese *cottage orné*. Rather than bringing Jim and Mary down to earth, the event elevates them to the coolest kind of elite: successful people who refuse to take it all too seriously.

▲ "Fine Food," Union Street restaurant review, *Orbit*, September 22–October 6, 1992.

FINE FOOD
EATING IN ORBIT

KEY LARGO
142 E Walled Lake Dr.
Walled Lake
669-1441

DECK

SEA MONSTERS

Life's a beach and then you order, hopefully from a perch on the deck sprawling o'er Walled Lake (a shimmering mirror which transforms this little suburban armpit into something like a way-up-north resort town). The feel of the place, however, is equally Bahamian as Houghtonesque, what with the raffia and the fleshview and the blast furnace heat, and a menu that covers such steamy tropicana victuals as swordfish ribs, Jamaican chicken, alligator sausage. You yourself may feel like gator bait as thrashing aquatic mystery-creatures in the waters below demand a baksheesh of table scraps, but don't let them dissuade you from an as-you-exit dip: the public access abuts the parking lot. -C.K.

PIZZAHUT
23050 Woodward,
Ferndale
548-4906

WORLD'S FATTEST MAN

This $4.00 all-you-can-eat lunch buffet has a catch—you'll have to fight for it. The fat-assed pork-bellied dregs instinctively migrate around the noon hour, and it's strictly survival of the fattest. They surround the buffet like hippos, snapping up food as quickly as it hits the danger zone. Towering above it all is The Behemoth! Close to seven feet tall with a butt as large as a razorback, he piles his plate hernia-high, with mounds of insipid pasta covering about two pizzas worth of slices. With nothing but but crumbs we scavengers found safe haven by the virtually ignored salad bar. Usually people complain about inattentive service, but here they thrive on it; scooping up what's left of all they couldn't eat, and stuffing the remains into pizza boxes. A great place for lunch and the best floor show in the city. -J.P.

UNO
6745 Orchard Lake,
West Bloomfield
737-7242

BURGERS

PIZZA

Like pasties are to Yoopers, pizza's ultimately a Chicago thing, and Texas-transplant Ike Sewell invented the deep-dish version (bringing Lone Star overkill to the Italian classic) for his Ohio Street UNO, which is still the town's best pizzeria. The franchise now extends to a hundred cities (including West Bloomfield) and turns out a killer variety all swollen with outrageous toppings. Actually, it's the best thing going from a menu that includes other regional cash-ins like buffalo wings and Philly burgers and trendapoid low-fat thin-crust plizetteas and ill-conceived ludicrosities like pizza skins. Big comfy room and cute, ditzy servers. -C.K.

FREE FOOF FROM A CORRIDOR CLASSIC

CASS CAFE
4620 CASS AVE. 831-1400

by Chris Kassel

We hit the Cass Cafe last winter on one of those eighty-below nights when the place couldn't help but be empty, and were disappointed with everything except the nicely weird staff. In fairness, however, it was the middle of the night and yucky weather and probably everybody in the kitchen had already gone home. Still, we were in the throes of a drink-induced famine and ordered across the board, one of everything, including the local legend, a six-fifty Delmonico steak that comes with potato and salad. Mid-meal, hand before heaven, some owner-type came bounding out to our table and with unsolicited fervor announced that the reason the steak was so cheap was that he bought it direct from the slaughterhouse. Pregnant pause, obviously. We grasp the no-middle-man concept, but first, that's illegal, and second, the nearest slaughterhouse is in Chicago. No matter, we didn't believe it anyhow; the reason the steak was cheap is because it was cheap steak. I believe the Spanish version is called 'huarache.'

TRENDY BOHEMIANS

CHEAP

LOCAL ART

Well, we tried 'em again, last week, a tepid summer eve, and this time, the place was filled to the chops, saucer-eyed X-ers, middle-aged mavens, bearded old zombie coots in Day-Glo caps... come to think of it, there seemed to have been an overabundance of these grizzly geezers for a gallery-type Wayne campus alternative cafe.

Centrally, a great slab of concrete divides two floors; downstairs, you feel like you're eating in a parking structure. Upstairs, you feel like a sniper. But none of those type jokes, by God, because for some surreal reason, Senator Carl Levin has just appeared off the port bow, peering over librarian specs, dressed in a sensible suit that Dick Nixon would have approved of, and Carl, good ol' overtiming palm-pressing public servant that he is, mounts a soapbox beneath a Dali/Star Wars-ish painting and begins spouting a grass-roots health-care FDR-tried-it-in-'36 speech. That would explain all the crunched-up old people, who evidently expected this, who came specifically, loaded with pertinent questions. You tend to forget about the amazing, dogged political conscience of these Corridorians.

Well, my diplomacy extends no further than the legalization of pot and repeal of that stupid no-running-stop-signs law, so we ignore the man and dive into the menu, and this time, the kitchen shows a pretty admirable side. A knockout lentil walnut burger is moist and packed with exotic flavors, there's an unusual chilled berry soup, (which could have used a scoop of vanilla or a shot of Bacardi), groovy gazpacho, and a hefty, hearty herby stew served over aromatic basmati. A range of fresh fish appears on a hand-scrawled specials list. Dawn, a frank, beautiful stranger plunked fortuitously on an adjacent barstool, fills in the gaps of our waning appetite, also adding helpful decor hints: ditch the foof and the lava lamps and paint the walls periwinkle... whatever that means. She's got the Lebanese vegetarian plate, hummus and babaghanosh and tabbouleh, and pronounces it all excellent. Mr. Peterson, of course, lured in by the nine-foot sign on the south side of the building which reads 'FREE FOOD', insists upon his blue-light Delmonico once again, and as of three-fifteen Sunday afternoon, was still chewing.

Steak aside, Cass Cafe seems to have found its stride, its temperature, its public.

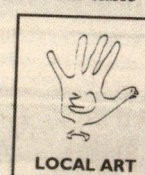

▲ "Fine Food," Cass Café restaurant review, *Orbit*, July 1994.

accounting department. Big misconception, pal. It's a testosterone-laden minefield, this "critic's life," between dealing with chef egos the size of Liberia, reading endless sycophantic drivel from desperate PR firms, and daily running the all-too-real ricks [sic] of dying from food poisoning, [having] to eat stinky cheeses or exotic nouvelle entrails from a species only *National Geographic* has heard of, or offending some dipshit maître d' who never heard of "honesty" and being blackballed out of the industry all together. And if you think for one second that *Orbit* subsidizes my penchant for Louis XIII cognac or my generous-to-the-point-of-irrationality tipping policy. Well, mister, I have some O. J. alibis to sell you.

Chris Kassel was the lead food writer for much of *Orbit*'s run. A holdover from *Fun*, Kassel, like many on staff, had known Peterson since his "Vile" days around the Detroit punk rock scene of the late 1970s. The pair reconnected shortly after *Fun* started. Kassel drew cartoons and covers and wrote articles for the free monthly humor magazine. When the new magazine started,

"Orby Profiles: Almighty Lumberjacks of Death," featuring food writer Jimmy Doom, *Orbit*, April 4–18, 1991. ▼

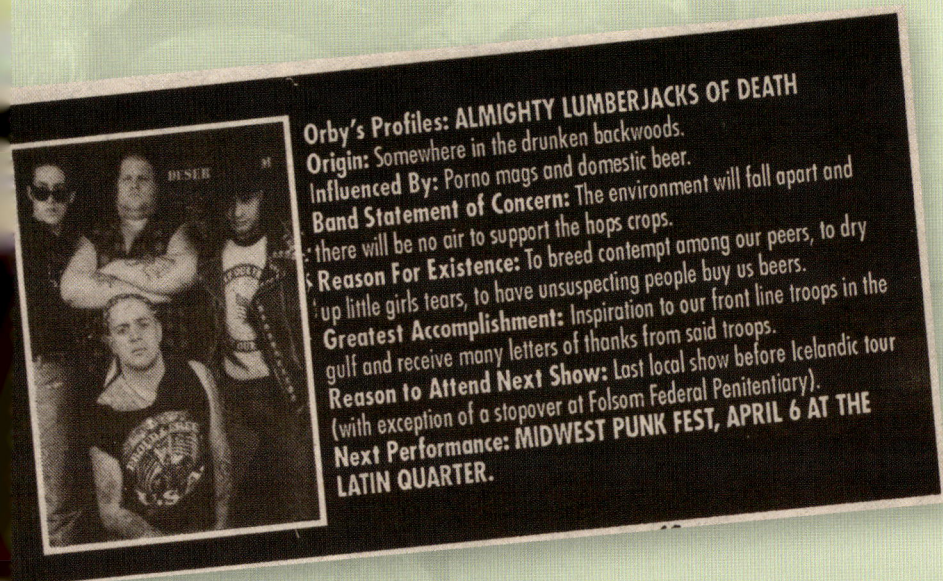

Orby's Profiles: ALMIGHTY LUMBERJACKS OF DEATH
Origin: Somewhere in the drunken backwoods.
Influenced By: Porno mags and domestic beer.
Band Statement of Concern: The environment will fall apart and there will be no air to support the hops crops.
Reason For Existence: To breed contempt among our peers, to dry up little girls tears, to have unsuspecting people buy us beers.
Greatest Accomplishment: Inspiration to our front line troops in the gulf and receive many letters of thanks from said troops.
Reason to Attend Next Show: Last local show before Icelandic tour (with exception of a stopover at Folsom Federal Penitentiary).
Next Performance: MIDWEST PUNK FEST, APRIL 6 AT THE LATIN QUARTER.

Peterson was originally hoping noted *Detroit News* columnist and future *Orbit* editor Matt Beer would write the food column. But when Beer wanted too much money, Peterson asked Kassel to go on gastronomic adventures around southeast Michigan.

The only guideline, Kassel said, was to be entertaining and honest: "It was simply a matter of telling the truth. If I want to say fuck, I'll say fuck. . . . That was the beauty of *Fun* and *Orbit*—you could always tell the truth. You were not beholden to anyone. You were not answerable to anyone or restaurants or distributors. That was an extremely intense experience to me. Previously, when I had written wine and restaurant reviews, you had to be very careful. You couldn't offend the wrong people, and all of a sudden Jerry allowed me to do anything I wanted to."

Beyond covering local dining spots, Kassel and a team of *Orbit* writers created special features on other consumable delights, including wine, champagne, booze—especially tequila and scotch—and cigars. Jimmy Doom took over most of the food writing during the final year and a half of the magazine. (Kassel was still on staff at *Orbit*, but had moved on to other writing.) At the time, Doom was best known as the singer for the Detroit punk rock band the Almighty Lumberjacks of Death, but he was also a writer, something that seemed to run in his DNA.

His uncle Bert Okuley, a friend of noted gonzo journalist Hunter S. Thompson, had covered Vietnam for UPI and was in country when Saigon fell in 1975. Doom's stepfather was a writer, and his mother, Molly Abraham, like her son, was a Detroit-area restaurant critic. "I had done freelance writing work, and Jerry knew me through my band . . . and I think was shocked, as some people are, to find that I could put together a complete sentence. And he knew that I worked in the restau-

fine food
EATING IN ORBIT

If you order the Road Kill Grill at Camp Ticonderoga, they bestow upon you a bumper sticker that says "I Eat My Road Kill." I think everyone who eats at Camp Ti should get one that says: "At The Top of The Food Chain And Damn Proud of It." Of the many places that have backlashed against quiche emporiums and heart-smart cottage cheeseburger menus this place does it the most unabashedly.

The Camp menu is a carnivorous three ring circus where the nightly specials are probably related to the stuffed hunting trophies that peer down from the walls.

Yeah, of course, it looks like an Upper Peninsula, Ted Nugent, whack 'em and stack 'em 12 gauge smokin' retreat. The center of the room has four pool tables but the high ceilings diffuse most of the noise and the perfectly lit dining room (with an open balcony) is somewhat serene, unless you're on the PETA board of trustees.

But then, if you were, you wouldn't have read this far, so pop in your *Free for All* 8-track, sharpen your Bowie knife and dig in.

For starters, don't miss the venison sausage appetizer with mustard dip, though it is inexplicably served only in combination with a small dollop of white-fish pate.

by Jimmy Doom

Unless you're on a first date you can amuse yourself by smiling at your wait staffer and saying, "I would like to have buffalo balls." No, they're not Rocky Mountain oysters but buffalo meatballs in Jack Daniels BBQ sauce.

The entrees range from your basic northern suburb grilled chicken breast to your basic marinated emu filet. Yep. Emu. I wish I could describe it as poor man's ostrich, but I have no idea what the market price for ostrich is. Before you get concerned that oppressed Maori tribesmen are being forced to go on non-union emu hunts, all the emu served at Camp Ti are farm raised in the good old U.S.of A. For the record, emu is less greasy than beef and is 97% fat free. Maybe Inn Season will put it on the menu.

Road Kill Grill is an appetite menacing trident of venison brochettes, wild boar sausage and broiled quail served with wild rice and corn in a "Michigan wild game sauce" that favors a light gravy. The boar and venison are excellent though the brittle bones of the quail(insert your outdated republican joke here) take some getting used to but if you're a duck fan, quail is right up your alley.

Freshwater fish, ribs and steaks round out the menu which is supplemented by daily specials (recently including Rabbit Tetrazini). Of course it's okay to puff a stogie at Ticonderogie.

And believe it or not, if vegetarians can deal with the taxidermy display, Camp Ti offers a few meatless salads in entree portions that a few Orbit herbivores raved to me about. I say stuff the salad in the rabbit before you Tetrazini it and throw another elk on the barbie. The camp and it's siblings (Beaver Creek and The Moose Preserve) are a whackin' and snackin' good time.

February 27th through March 1st Camp Ticonderoga hosts it's 3 day Beach Bash and Polar Open Golf Tournament featuring O.C. Roberts and the Samaritans and the Trinidad Tripoli Band. First Prize in the golf tournament (which, let me predict right here, will be won by Detroit's most beloved fine food czar and his well coifed partner, Jeff King, of Speedball fame) is a cruise to the Bahamas. Entry fee includes Polar Party packet , orange balls (BYO blue balls), one lei and a donation to the Michigan Humane Society.

▲ "Fine Food," Camp Ticonderoga restaurant review, *Orbit*, October 1996.

fine food
EATING IN ORBIT

Wayne's World

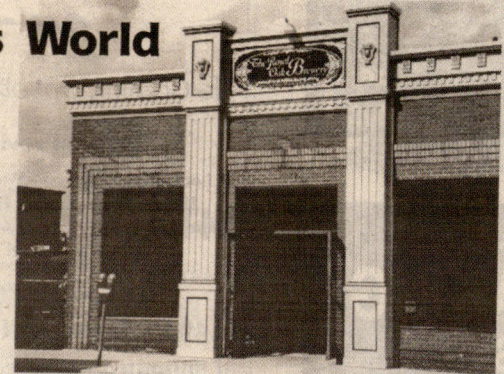

The Royal Oak Brewery, 215 E. 4th St., Royal Oak, MI, (810) 544-1141

Detroit shot and beer legend 'Diamond' Jim Brady once remarked, "I serve food for the convenience of my drinking customers." Convenient, yes but the burgers and chili were also legendary for their taste and their ability to soak up rot-gut vodka in the days before Absolut hit our shores.

But now we've become incredibly cultured (for a society that has allowed *Roseanne* to be on the air for eons), it's not enough for a tavern keeper to flip burgers and call the Bud distributor. Now it's handcrafted cream ale and creme brulee.

Ladies and gentlemen, welcome to the brew pub.

It is not a new concept. The brew pub has been flourishing on both coasts for decades. Just ask Drew Ciola. He helped open three west coast porter paradises before following his fiancee home to Michigan and unveiling The Royal Oak Brewery.

In my own humble opinion if a place is called a brewery you better make damn good beer, first and foremost, and if your food is sub-par I'm fairly certain I can find something to eat in downtown Royal Oak. But if you're glued to your barstool at. R.O. Brewery

by Jimmy Doom can suck down a couple of pints of Fourth Street Wheat and keep your happy ass planted on your stool until the Jambalaya shows up. Ciola and brother-in-law Mike have graced us with a brew eatery where both the kegs and the kitchen could survive on their own merits.

Local suds stud Wayne Burns mans the brew kettles, pumping out porters and ESB's at approximately 434 gallons per batch. The emphasis is on fresh, as the big sellers: Northern Light and Royal Oak Red, are gone in about two weeks. By comparison one would be lucky to find a mass market beer on the shelves less than three weeks after it is produced.

The unassuming Burns is on call 24/7 to start a new batch whenever one of his stainless steel kettles runs dry. All beers offered are subject to periodic "tweaking" in search of perfection but both owner and brewmaster have been pleased overall with the product since about a half dozen batches of each. "Now we never change a beer dramatically," says Burns. They do however rotate various styles in and out of the lineup depending on factors such as season and whimsy. There's been only one miscue since they opened labor day weekend of '95: a recent Mead that tastes similar to a large shot of Barenjager being dumped in a Bass Ale.

But this is no hit or miss proposition. Wayne Burns has a diploma in Malting and Brewing Science and Technology from the Siebel Institute of Technology in Chicago. It's the nation's most prestigious, if not only, college that teaches the art of brewing, according to Burns. His credentials are only truly impressive after having sampled (okay, guzzled) what flows from the taps. These beers are not Keystone derivatives hiding behind the guise of "Handcrafted Ales." Anyone with a pedestrian knowledge of malt beverages will find a friendly pint.

Not to be outdone by Wayne's World is Chef Sylvester Gordon's kitchen. Here again the emphasis is on fresh. The smoked corn highlights the otherwise traditional shepherd's pie (a damn good portion for $8.25). The brick oven pizza is another fave and for you true Alkies, it happens to be made with the grains they've already brewed the beer in. And for everyone who's ever choked down freezer burned bratwurst at Cedar Point's sorry excuse for a Biergarten, R.O.B.'s Chicken Beer Sausage will make you want to take Colonel Klink to a cheap motel. I hear the desserts are good, but I eschewed the dutch apple pie for an infusion; Stolichnaya and fruit (watermelon, raspberries, or lemons and limes soaked together for a minimum of 24 hours).

The brew pub. It's definitely trendy, and I usually abhor trends but I think I'm gonna enjoy this one for a while. And for all you basement brew makers who plan on opening your own little slice of honey porter heaven, go to Royal Oak Brewery and take notes.

▲ "Fine Food," Royal Oak Brewery restaurant review, *Orbit*, February 1997.

FINE FOOD
EATING IN ORBIT

O'LEARY'S TEA ROOM
1411 Brooklyn
Detroit 964-0936

NO BOOZE   **IRISH**

To most o' us, St. Paddy's Day is a fleeting semi-memory, but to the good folks at O'Leary's, corned beef and cabbage is a year-round deal. Genteel is not a word that usually pops up in our recommendographies, but this sweet little tea room, closed evenings and Saturdays, is quietly and discreetly serving up a sensational array of Celtic specialties. That the Irish are known more for poteen than cuisine (and for making starving-to-death politically correct) doesn't seem to have hurt the best-laid plans any. Shepherd's Pie and Mulligan Stew flesh out a sandwich-heavy lunch board that includes a killer Smoked Ham and Balarny Cheese and the Dublin Garden Sandwich, meant to satisfy the Gaelic macrobiotic in ya. Nothing's stronger than espresso, and the array of imported tea is impressive. -C.K.

BIG DADDY'S PARTHENON
6199 Orchard Lake Road
West Bloomfield
737-8600

GYROS   **FOOD FIRES**

What's not to like? Heaping plates of Monroe Street favorites in a user-friendly suburban cavern tavern, complete with oily-headed Beavis-waiters growling "Opa! Opa! Opa!" Service, incidentally, was perfect on our crisp Sunday afternoon jaunt: peppy, polite, properly parental when the kids burst into fright tears when the plate of cheese caught on fire. I should have warned 'em, huh? Requisite combo platters are suitably top-heavy, the gyros are superb. Likewise the cheap and copious flow of bright-flavored Aegean wines in a fun Ron Rea coliseum. So,why do local critics delight in slamming this place? S'Greek to us. -C.K.

INDO-PAK
27707 Dequindre
Madison Heights
541-3562

CHEAP   **INDIAN**

It's taken for granted that the Southeast Oakland area isn't well known for its South Asian cuisine. Ever since Moti Mahal took the high road and the Maharajah of Ferndale became the Maharajah of Sterling Heights, those looking for a good masala have been obliged to head out west to Farmington or down south to Windsor. The Indo-Pak, on Dequindre in Warren, seems to break all the rules when it comes to Indian joints. Not only is it located right across the street from Universal Mall, (just sounds unnatural, doesn't it?) it's *cheap*. Real cheap. Not just cheap for an Indian place—we're talking doggone, down and dirty *funky* cheap. All-you-can-eat buffet for $5. Three parathas for a dollar. Entrees beginning at $2.95. You'll be surprised at the range of the menu; everything from Indian basics, like vegetable curry to Pakistani specialities to western goodies like fish 'n' chips are offered. Once upon a time, the Indo-Pak was a grocery store; now it's a sort of diner/video shop with lots of...character. Although the service is slightly spartan, the food alone is enough to satisfy any hankering for South Asian fare. -I.M.S.

UPSCALE POSSUMBILITIES DOWNRIVER
by Chris Kassel

MUSKEY'S ON THE CHANNEL
3845 Biddle
(south of Eureka)
East Wyandotte

LARGE SMOKING SECTION   **EXOTIC LOCALE**   **SALT SHAKERS**

The dining room at Musky's On The Channel is a contrast of angles, textures: pine and blue sateen, wax fruit and flowers of human hair, staff-drawn cartouches and gravestone rubbings from historic Girod Cemetery. Perfect for this wild, magnificent downriver Creole roadhouse, which caters flawlessly to both snob and slob.

Contrast also noted: maitre d' Andre Moulin, who looks like he's climbed down from the front window at Barneys of New York and chef/owner Mick Muscovitz, who more nearly resembles that idiotic Barney of Kidvidia. Muscovitz, whose twelve years association with New Orleans' Commander's Palace has made him an inveterate connoisseur, is, in this small bedroom community, almost a pop culture icon. He's never far from his magnificently accoutered kitchen, which is decorated with ariel photos of himself and his mentor, Paul Prudhomme, to whom he jocularly refers as "Stringbean." Well, okay; Muscovitz is a big fella. So heavy that he requires a special standing wheelchair to move easily from Robotcoup to microwave, a hi-tech mobile gadget custom designed by prosthesis pioneer Saul Roth. He admits, like Brando, a passion for peppermint-stick snowballs.

Ironically, he proclaims loud disdain for muskrat, downriver's rodent of choice, as being "too greasy" (he pronounces it with a cute cajun burr, as if it rhymed with "breezy") for most of his Cordon Bleu-inspired sauces. Muscovitz prefers the delicate grains and textures of exotica like capybara and marmot, which are displayed in his stainless walk-in along with astronomical invoices from the importers. He's able to circumvent some of this cost by home-raising numerous species at his Northville mini-ranch, all of which are rigorously graded by an on-staff agent of the FDA. His mission is to provide well-prepared gastronomic rarities to an upscale clientele, particularly those (like him) with roots in the rural south, many of whom have wearied of elitist, overpriced Gaelic oddities like snails and fungi.

Musky's clientele is ninety-five percent regulars, and you need call only to say when you're not coming. The parlor is small, but jammed to the gills, the military-style coat check overflows with both flannel and cashmere. It's worth the wait. Our waiter calls himself "Eightball", and wheels out the restaurant's signature appetizer cart. Reflecting the chef's bayou heritage, the star of the cart is *sarigue gras*, the world's most exclusive pate, making foie gras seem like, well, chopped liver. Made from highly-prized bayou possums, sarigues are raised in cages and fed exclusive high-gluten diets, often blended with beer, for maximum liver growth. Also noted is *gumbo zhebe*, made only with eggs laid on Holy Thursday, which, according to Muscovitz, do not spoil. Entrees are frequently prepared tableside, and rarely without some theatrics; skewers, flaming hoops, dancing poodles. Ours includes rack of coon Daniel Boone, Tiger Mussels Rockefeller (Antoine's recipe, only napped in Warrendaise sauce), and a steaming bowl of *cavy curry* whose high-proof spices are cooled with poke-slaw and an imaginative, if excessively tart intermezzo, choke-cherry parfait.

Despite the obvious, jokes involving multimillionaire Jed Clampett's culinary habits, Fitzgerald said it best: "The rich are different." Musky's exudes its powerful musk, thematic integrity, and is custom-designed for the gourmet with an adventurous spirit. A little vodka helps, too.

WORLD OF MOUTH

LIFE IS A CABERNET: Purple gem of Madeline's Wine Bar this week was Beringer's newly-released Private Reserve Cab, '90. Deep, deep, deep (and cheap, considering: $5.75 the half-glass), simultaneously subtle and aggressive, sort of what you'd expect if they made ink out of blackberry juice...

GRANT'S TOMB? Best of luck to Jackie Grant and her courageous, if hard-to-grasp plans to re-reopen the ever hapless Money Tree. Money Pit, more like. Frankly, the Jackie this chilled-down hotspot needs is Kevorkian...

COCINA DEL SOLD: With rumor mills on the third shift, it seems that the Cuisine of the Sun has been entirely swallowed by native son Jimmy Schmidt who, freed from Ilitch shackles, will try an Italian theme in place of his upscale South-wex-Mex. At least that's what we read in the Free Press, and by golly, you can't print something if it isn't true. Can you?...

Had a great, ultra-cozy experience at **Malibu** one of those recent deep freeze nights. Coconut Chicken with fruit salsa, peachy Ca' Del Solo vino, Fred in his Buddy Holly specs, we outlasted everybody, stayed late, and nobody made us feel rushed. Great place... (Check out their $20 combo Main Art Theatre/ Malibu Dinner deal)...

WHAT A WAY TO GO DEPT: Along with fresh-ground coffees, Jeff Smith's six-seat 4th Street Bakery, filling in the former LA Express (opposite Durango Grill) is offering a signature Death By Chocolate cake that's devastatingly divine. A new breed of pastry shop to give dinosaurs like Hagelstein's a pause for reflection...

▲ "Fine Food," Musky's on the Channel restaurant review, *Orbit*, April 1994.

rant business, so I knew a little something about it. I was the cliché waiter who was also in a band," said Doom.

While Doom said humor was part of the style, *Orbit* didn't deliberately go out of its way to hammer restaurants:

> There were no parameters. It was gonzo from the word go, and obviously these restaurants might advertise and God knows we didn't want Jerry to starve. You wouldn't go someplace just to rip 'em so you could be funny. You would go someplace that *Orbit* readers would actually enjoy going to, but if there was a shortcoming here or there you could give them a hard time about it. I guess the editorial policy was so open and that made it a lot of fun. You know, if you didn't like something, you could bitch about it, and if you did like something you could give them a verbal blow job.

Beyond reviewing real places, *Orbit*'s food column was known for its April Fools' pranks. In the April 1994 issue, Chris Kassel wrote a review for a place called Musky's on the Channel. "I wrote about a non-existent restaurant downriver that served nothing but rodent," he said. "And I looked it all up and found all these exotic species of rodent and did this real, serious review of a restaurant from downriver and I had all the dishes listed, and it was hook, line, and sinker. I had the *Detroit News* writing me saying, 'We tried to find this restaurant. If it's that good,

Not saying that **Pronto 608** flames… only that if you drop your fork, better you should kick it under a table…

▲ Pronto comment, *Orbit*, April 20–May 4, 1993.

where is it? We looked at the address and we can't find it.' It's a joke. Every April Fools' Day we would do some off-the-wall shit. Paul [Zimmerman] and I would switch reviews. We thought it was funny."

If humor was one of the main pillars of the *Orbit* doctrine, it didn't take long for the magazine to get called out for its irreverence and for not being "politically correct." Chris Kassel wrote a one-sentence remark in the food column in the April 20, 1993, issue.

The reference was to the gay-owned restaurant that opened in 1991 on South Washington Avenue in Royal Oak.

Kassel said he wrote the comment after a suggestive conversation at Pronto: "I was on my way to work in the evening and I stopped into Pronto, and I knew the owners, we had written about them before. I knew everybody

Pronto apology, *Orbit*, May 4–June 1, 1993. ▶

"The only reason why I didn't get fired was [Jerry] had no one to put in my place, and he wasn't paying me anyway. And, yeah, it was too bad," said Kassel. In the next issue, on May 4–June 1, 1993, he made an apology in the food column.

But the damage was already done. That one-sentence comment ended up costing *Orbit* fifteen thousand dollars in advertising.

there was gay. Obviously, no issue with that. So, I went in to get a calzone. And they said, 'What do you want on your calzone?' I told them I didn't want any meat, just veggie because I was in hurry and I was looking at my watch. The guy behind him said, 'Oh, you don't want meat? We like meat. We're meat people here.' Then another guy came and said, 'We love meat here.' I was like 'Jesus Christ.'"

According to Peterson, Kassel had a tendency to pepper his copy with jokes to amuse the editors and proofreaders, but it was understood that these comments would never make it to print. "[The transition from *Fun* to *Orbit*] was hard for people like Chris Kassel. Every time [he] did his little food gossip column, he would put in really mean, horrible, racist jokes, and he knew that something was going to be cut, so he put in a sacrificial joke that was just fun like, 'John Wayne Gacy's out of jail and cooking at . . .' Horrible things, and we had just gotten a new editor who didn't know that he put in jokes for the proofreaders and editors. [The editor] didn't know what "flames" meant because he was so straight, or not part of that world, and he didn't get the joke." said Peterson.

Orbit Film

Film reviews had always been a part of Jerry Peterson's publications. From smaller capsule reviews in *White Noise* and *Fun* to full articles in *Orbit*, film always had a place. While Peterson was planning *Orbit*, Paul Zimmerman volunteered to do the film writing, and they came in with some very specific ideas on the

Orby says: "ACTION!"

reviews. "Jerry was so exact on what he wanted. For the film thing, we came up with an entire way to rate films with a combination of visuals, cartoons, icons, and all these other things, pie charts. So visually, *Orbit* was immediately a stylish, cool magazine," said Zimmerman.

The Movieola section usually included a center feature review and sometimes two smaller paragraph-length reviews. The ratings system was broken up into four key areas—acting, directing, script, and "x-factor." Each area could receive up to 25 points for a total of 100. Most of the reviews were middle of the road, but *Orbit* rated some, like David Lynch's *Twin Peaks: Fire Walk with Me* and the Robin Williams's family comedy *Flubber*, dismally, the movies receiving a 25 and 10 respectively.

During *Orbit*'s run, only twelve movies scored 95 out of 100, and only one film ever received a perfect score, *Island*—a fake film reviewed as an April Fools' Day joke in 1994.

Similarly, the only film to ever get lower than a 10 was *Harley Davison and the Marlboro Man* starring Mickey Rourke and Don Johnson.

"I gave it a zero," said Zimmerman. "And I had more people approach me, like, years later going, 'I remember that review! You said the only thing you can say positive about this film is that it's in focus.'" Zimmerman wouldn't last through the entire run of *Orbit* as the film reviewer. He accepted an offer from his former Thomas Video colleague Chris Gore to edit *Film Threat* and left Detroit for Los Angeles in April 1994. Before cutting loose from *Orbit*, Zimmerman would give the magazine's film cred a little boost. In 1992, Zimmerman was preparing to cover the Toronto International Film Festival. Before he left for Canada, he received a call from his old pal Chris Gore, who said he was going to send Zimmerman a VHS tape of a movie scheduled to play at the festival

MOVIEOLA

FILM • VIDEO

THE TEN SMOKIEST MOVIES IN HISTORY

CHINATOWN
BODY HEAT
TO HAVE AND HAVE NOT
WILD AT HEART
THE TOWERING INFERNO
THE KEEP
APOCALYPSE NOW
BAMBI
COLD TURKEY
REEFER MADNESS

NEW VIDEO RELEASES

LAST OF THE FINEST
Fair cops and robbers action pic starring Brian Dennehy. If you really want to see this bear of an actor in action (as in up close and *in your face*) check out his return to the Chicago stage at the Goodman Theater in October with the staggering 4 1/2 hour version of Eugene O'Neil's *The Iceman Cometh*. -P.Z. Street date: 10-4

THE GUARDIAN
William Friedkin's return to the horror genré left most patrons *laughing* in their boots. Just how frightening can one make a tree? (Ok, *The Evil Dead* and *Wizard of Oz* gave it a good try.) A better bet is go check out Friedkin's original, *The Exorcist*. A full 15 years later it's still the seminal scare classic all horror is judged against. - P.Z. Street date: 10-4

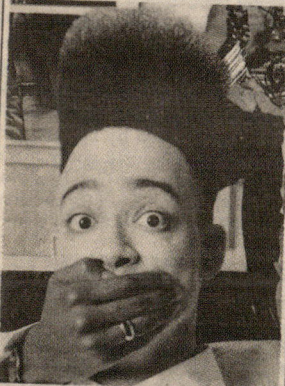

HOUSE PARTY
Hip-hopping good rude fun. How can one not like a film with characters like Kid'n'Play, Dragonbreath and Full Force? Basically it's a lame teen party story that's just a front for some great rap, dance and comedy around. Bold and refreshing debut from writer-director Reginald Hudlin. - P.Z. Now available.

ORBIT'S OUT OF THIS WORLD PICK

SORCERER
In a journey as arduous as the film itself, William Friedkin's neglected gem, *Sorcerer*, has finally reached home video. A south of the border truck driving epic about some out of luck losers and their explosive cargo is a gripping cliff hanger, literally. Roy Scheider stars and like most of his mid-70s films, he stands a good chance of dying and he usually obliges. (Now if they would only release the French original, *Wages Of Fear*.) -D.D.
Street date: 10-4

ORBIT FILM REVIEW

GOODFELLAS
by Paul Zimmerman

After only the first half hour I was certain—Martin Scorsese, arguably the world's best director, had returned to form. Ending a decade of erratic film making, Scorsese returns to where he's at his best, down deep in New York's underbelly. Scorsese virtually dominated the '70s, delivering great film after great film, and peaked in 1980 with *Raging Bull*. But while the rest of the '80s saw brilliant experimentation (*The King of Comedy*) and the fulfillment of a lifelong religious obsession (*The Last Temptation of Christ*), something seemed amiss. His new film, *GoodFellas*, remedies that with a vengeance. This is the street epic Scorsese only hinted at when he made *Mean Streets* in 1973. Now, 17 years later, he has created a bold mosaic on film; a big, beautiful, sprawling mess.

From the first scene, Scorsese is off and running with his patented mix of visceral violence and dark humor. This has to be the blackest mainstream comedy ever made in America. Working the audience over like a true pro, Scorsese can make you wince one moment and laugh the next.

Clocking in at around 2 1/2 hours and spanning three decades, the details come so quickly (names, faces, music, food, period details) it's like a hilariously violent history lesson set in a cuisinart. Taken from the nonfiction best seller, *Wiseguy*, by Nicholas Pileggi, this is the story of the rise and crash of organized crime figure Henry Hill. His life of crime begins in 1955 parking mobsters' Cadillacs and quickly moves on to the usual underworld functions: robbery, extortion, marriage, cookouts and murder. As played by Ray Liotta, Hill becomes a man obsessed with possessions. He wants it all: wife, home, kids, food, crime, coke, mistress *and* the respect of the neighborhood. Here doing the right thing means doing everything. And as Henry's life speeds up and swallows him, so does Scorsese's direction. That translates to quick cuts, slow motion, voice-overs, still frames and a virtual non-stop musical track. This all adds up to a film assault (and I mean that in the nicest way). By film's end you can practically hear Scorsese and crew groping for breath— and they're not alone. The audience is right there with them, on a film high that's not easy to shake off. Scorsese loves the medium and every scene bristles with his enthusiasm.

A lot of Scorsese film regulars are cast in *GoodFellas* including Robert DeNiro, Joe Pesci and even Scorsese's parents. But make no mistake: this is Ray Liotta's movie. Since he first shocked audiences in *Something Wild*, filmgoers have had their eye on Liotta. He plays Hill with no apologies, yet he makes this reprehensible character always fascinating. Liotta infuses every scene with his intense, stripped down, no frills acting style. He's ready to be one of the stars of the '90s.

Finely acted, densely layered, shockingly violent and hilariously dark, this is easily *the* film to beat for 1990.

ORBIT VIEWS REEL

ACTING · DIRECTING
25 · 25
25 · 20
95
SCRIPT · CAMERA

TOTAL
EACH CATEGORY 0-25 PTS.
100 PTS. POSSIBLE

REVIEW 'N THE PREVIEWS

TITLE	IMPRESSIONS PRO	IMPRESSIONS CON	ODDS YOU'LL GO
BOOK OF LOVE	Teen Sex	Bobby Soxer Fantasy	4 to 1
PREDATOR II	Predator I	No Arnie	4 to 5
PACIFIC HEIGHTS	Michael Keaton	Batman	3 to 5
THE TALL GUY	Boffing	Goldblum-boffing	13 to 112

CURRENTLY

AFTER DARK, MY SWEET

ORBIT VIEWS REEL **70**

At last! A hard-boiled story with a Hammett/Chandler title that delivers the gritty, malevolent film noir we've all been waiting for. Paradoxically shot in the brightest of sunshine, director James Foley (justifiably in hiding after 1987's *Who's That Girl?*) brings pulp author Jim Thompson's novel of evil and intrigue to the cinema. Forget about hunky, brooding star Jason Patric, consummate screen psycho Bruce Dern is back in his best role since he made The Duke a human colander in *The Cowboys*. Superlative characters and acting make *After Dark* a graceful, atmospheric thriller about misguided allegiances and love lost. -D.D.

HARDWARE

ORBIT VIEWS REEL **35**

In Richard Stanley's post-apocalyptic nightmare world we find the usual cast of comical mutants, mercenary scroungers and killer cyborgs one has come to expect in a world gone mad. Therein lies the problem. We've seen all the doomsday premonitions, heard all the radiation jokes and sat through countless film hours of a predestined future . If the earth doesn't explosively die to be reborn a sci-fi netherworld I'm afraid most of us will feel shortchanged. The film does sport a robot with a cool biblical name Mark 13 (*this is but the beginning of sufferings.* Mark 13.8), great lighting, camera and Iggy. But if formula, global anarchy gets you Mad to the Max, skip it. -D.D.

POSTCARDS FROM THE EDGE

ORBIT VIEWS REEL **75**

Call it the Carry Fisher Story, this tale has it all: drugs, booze, a tempestuous mother/daughter relationship and laughs. Shirley MacLaine can rattle off one-liners like a new aged Henny Youngman, and it's refreshing to see Meryl Streep use an American vernacular for a change. (Sorry, I missed *She Devil*. Darn.) -D.D.

PUMP UP THE VOLUME

ORBIT VIEWS REEL **70**

Above average script and fine star turn by Christian Slater makes for a solid teen drama. Nothing great here, but every generation can use an angry-youth anthem film. With a great, eclectic music score, this is *Talk Radio* for the teen-something crowd. -P.Z.

1 2 3 4 5 6 7 8 **9** 10 11 12 13 14 15 16 17 18 19 20 21 22 23 24 25 26 27 28
PAGE

▲ "Movieola," *Goodfellas* review, *Orbit*, September 27–October 11, 1990.

ORBIT 129

MOVIEOLA

CINEMA & FLICKS

Prevues

Sunset Boulevard
The Detroit run of the new musical has inspired a one-night-only screening of Billy Wilder's 1950 classic about a faded silent movie star whose relationship with a hungry screenwriter leads to murder. (Feb. 8 at the State Theatre)

Blast from the Past
Brendan Frasier, recently sprung from his parents' bomb shelter, quickly realizes that the modern-day L.A. isn't exactly Pleasantville. (Feb. 12)

Simply Irresistible
More romantic comedy, about an executive who falls in love with a woman with magical powers. (Feb. 12)

Message in a Bottle
Romantic comedy in which Robin Wright-Penn falls for sensitive Kevin Costner after she discovers the love note he set adrift. (Feb. 12)

The General
Deliverance director John Boorman reunites with actor Jon Voight in this Irish-made drama about a master criminal and the cop assigned to catch him. (Feb. 12–14 at the Detroit Film Theatre)

Office Space
An irreverent office comedy from Mike Judge, the man who brought you Beavis and Butt-head. (Feb. 19)

Just the Ticket
Andy Garcia and Andie MacDowell in (you guessed it) a romantic comedy about a small-time ticket scalper and the woman of his dreams. (Feb. 19)

Harold and Maude
Finally, a romantic comedy worth watching, screening one night only. (Feb. 25 at the Magic Bag)

Another Day in Paradise
Reviewed in last month's *Orbit* (we liked it), this dark, dark road picture with Melanie Griffith and James Woods keeps getting the release date pushed back. (Feb. 26)

The Corruptor
Hong Kong legend Chow Yun-Fat takes another crack at Hollywood, this time teamed with Mark Wahlberg, about an idealistic rookie cop battling big city corruption. (Feb. 26)

200 Cigarettes
No, not the average number smoked in the *Orbit* offices on a deadline weekend (it's way too few), but a (yep) romantic comedy with Courtney Love, Ben Affleck and Christina Ricci set on New Year's Eve in 1981. (Feb. 26)

Festival of Animation
The same folks who compile the Sick and Twisted Animation shows offer more family-friendly fare, highlighted by the latest from Wallace and Grommit creator Nick Park. (Feb. 26–28 at the Detroit Film Theatre)

Rushmore

Nerdlinger Comedy (R)

The Facts: Comedy about a poor nerd finding love in a rich prep school. Stars Jason Schwartzman, Bill Murray, Olivia Williams

ORBIT VIEWS REEL
ACTING 25 DIRECTING 15
SCORE 20 X-FACTOR 20
TOTAL 80

The Opinion: A quirky coming-of-age story set in a prep school, *Rushmore* has already been alternately hailed as the second coming and a complete bomb. As usual, the truth lies somewhere in between. The title refers to Rushmore, an East Coast prep school, a fine bastion of education, wealth and status. At the center of the tale is Max Fischer (Schwartzman), a jack of all trades and master of none, a nebbish go-getter who joins dozen of clubs, including the drama league, bee keepers institute and assorted science labs. The son of a barber, he's obviously at odds with the snazzy prep school he's trying so desperately to become part of. It seems Fischer's big dream is to just keep attending Rushmore. Yet, despite all his extracurricular activities, Fischer is on the verge of being expelled. Compounding his problems, he falls for one of his professors, Rosemary, a British widow (Williams) who's also the object of desire of the school's rich patron, Herman Blume (Murray). This sets up a three-way battle which takes up the bulk of the film, yielding surprising results.

Schwartzman, a first timer who is the son of actress Talia Shire and nephew of Francis Coppola, is a real find, and he wears his self-confidence and braces with a snotty bravado that has divided audiences: depending on your POV, he's either a loveable, misguided nebbish or something of a selfish prick. During his battle for Rosemary's heart, he's not above turning dirty tricks, ratting on a friend or even poisoning his opponent. Highlights include his theatrical version of *Serpico* and a climactic Vietnam piece ("Yeah, I was in the shit.").

by Paul Zimmerman

For the first 10 minutes or so, *Rushmore* appears to be a period piece set in the '70s. It's not until we glimpse a modern car that we realize it's a modern day tale. And thanks to a soundtrack that includes obscure hits from the British Invasion (circa early '60s) and the conservative clothes and hair cuts of the *uppa crust*, *Rushmore* is a film adrift in time. Director and co-writer Wes Anderson clearly identifies with his anti-hero and to shore up Max' stature, he surrounds his leading man with a variety of jerks, bores and a nice twist—the bully is a Scotsman(!) who later has a change of heart.

This is Anderson's second film and at times it resembles an art house version of *Revenge of the Nerds* and *Caddyshack*. His first, *Bottle Rocket* ('96), was something of a critic's darling and co-written by actor Owen Wilson (one of the quieter, enjoyable characters in the otherwise audience-pummeling *Armageddon*). Much like *Bottle Rocket*, *Rushmore* sets up an entirely believable self-contained universe in which quirky characters and quiet moments co-exist. Like other new Sons of Texas (Richard Linklater, Mike Judge et al.), quirky humor seems to be Anderson and Wilson's middle name. When it works, like the scene of Murray swimming away from his moronic sons, it's dead on and refreshing. When it doesn't, like choosing the song "Oh, Yoko" to augment a humorous montage, it's just forced goofy for the sake of being goofy.

All in all, *Rushmore* is a smart, refreshing take on the old outsider-goes-to-school genre, but thanks to this being a slow time for quality films, it's also been a victim of a critical rush to judgment. Anderson has already been compared to Buster Keaton, Woody Allen, Ernst Lubitsch and a host of others whose bags he's not yet worthy to carry. Expediting the critical overkill are the accolades for Murray's performance. While it's quite good, it's pound-for-pound less brilliant than his turn in *Ed Wood* and not as funny as his shyster lawyer bit in *Wild Things*. So why all the fuss? Take a look. What else is out right now?

Six-String Samurai
Post-Apocalyptic Comic Book (PG-13)

The Facts: Buddy Holly fights his way across post-apocalyptic America with an orphan in an attempt to ascend to the throne left vacant by the death of Elvis.

ORBIT VIEWS REEL
ACTING 15 DIRECTING 15
SCORE 15 X-FACTOR 30
TOTAL 75

The Opinion: A bizarre ride through a comic book netherworld with minimal dialogue, action sequences that range from Far East cool to pure camp, and villains that are part Hanna-Barbera, part Troma. If the image of Buddy Holly (Jeffery Falcon) as a sword-swinging, Fonzie-acting martial arts master who battles bowling thugs, Neanderthal hoodlums, and a cannibalistic Cleaver family doesn't make you at least chuckle, this is not the movie for you. If it does, you'll find at least a nugget of entertainment in Lance Mungia's film. *S-SS* is not without its slow points, most of which involve the whining of Buddy's orphan companion, but the music (a ska-surf blend provided by The Red Elvises) and sword-fighting scenes make up for any loss of momentum. (Playing Feb. 15 at the Detroit Film Theatre.) —*Ron Wade*

Payback
Two-fisted Action (R)

The Facts: "Gimme back my cash!" Stars Mel Gibson.

ORBIT VIEWS REEL
ACTING 20 DIRECTING 20
SCORE 20 X-FACTOR 20
TOTAL 80

The Opinion: Revenge is a great motive for anything, especially going to the movies. *Payback* has a plot like a '70s Italian drive-in movie, but this time with a big star, a decent budget and a good title. This is the Mel we love most—the anti-hero we remember, before Mad Max started saving children. Cool music (TV action jazz) sets the tone of this gritty noir crime drama. But it's Hollywood noir, so the grit is a little too perfect, and the violence isn't going to make you squirm. The filmmakers (the original director and, eventually, Mel at the helm) were too chicken to let the moral ambiguity of the hero wander too far (Hollywood just can't let sleeping dogs die). Still, it's the perfect Valentine's movie (at least guy guys will love it) and the best film of its type since the Armand Assante version of Spillane's classic, *I, the Jury* (rent it). —*JP*

My Favorite Martian
TV Rerun (PG)

Facts: Hilarity and hijinx happen when Martian lands on Earth and disrupts a man's life. Jeff Daniels, Daryl Hannah co-star.

ORBIT VIEWS REEL
ACTING 10 DIRECTING 10
SCORE 15 X-FACTOR 40
TOTAL 75

The Opinion: So the guy sitting next to me starts mumbling about how he's seen it all before. Of course he has. It's a remake of a TV show. You were expecting landmark cinema? It's exactly what it's supposed to be: the tried-and-true Disney formula. Meaning: state-of-the-art special effects, fumbling bad guys, innumerable cheap laughs, the sexy misguided love interest and the girl-next-door true love interest. If you've seen *The Absent-Minded Professor* or *The Love Bug*, you know how it's going to end. All this has a '90s twist, with computer-generated everything and vulgarity (apparently the fart has replaced the mud puddle). This shouldn't surprise you either. Primitive as they are, Herbie and Flubber were amazing special effects back in their day. —*JP*

Point adjustment scale: *I gave it a generous 75. If you are 10 years old (or easily amused), add 10 more points. If you are old enough to drive, subtract five; and subtract a point for each additional year—until you hit senility, which means you should then go back to the 10-year-old point adjustment system.*

▲ "Movieola," *Rushmore* review, *Orbit*, February 1999.

MOVIE FACTS

CUT THAT OUT!
The Censorship Hall of Shame

• Spitting was cut from all Australian movies through the 1940s.

• In South Korea, a teacher may not be ridiculed on screen.

• The Soviet Union allowed *The Grapes Of Wrath* to be shown, thinking it portrayed the U.S. in a poor light. The film was promptly banned when audiences were most impressed that the Joads, despite their abject poverty, owned their own automobile.

• When *Blazing Saddles* was released in Spain, censors cut the fart noises from the notorious "baked bean" scene.

• *Ben Hur* was banned in China because it spread "superstitious beliefs," namely Christianity."

• Brian de Palma's *Greetings* was the first film to receive an X-rating.

• Belgium is the only country never to have exercised censorship on any films.

• Because of his unique hold on the American psyche, no film depiction of John Dillinger was allowed until 1945.

• Communist China banned the educational film *Elementary Safety in Swimming in Rivers, Lakes and Seas*, calling it a bourgeois plot to undermine the daring of revolutionaries.

• Kansas banned all smoking on screen until 1930.

• An experimental French film was banned by English censors, who declared "if there is any meaning to this film, it is doubtless objectionable."

• The German film *The Riders of German East Africa* was banned by the Nazis in 1939 for being pacifistic, then by the Allies in 1945 for being militaristic.

Source:
Guinness Book of Movie Facts

ONE MAN IS AN ISLAND
by Kevin King

ISLAND (NC 17) Drama

The Facts: An excursion boat is shipwrecked, thrusting its disparate passengers and crew into a searing struggle for survival amidst personal discovery. Stars: Marlon Brando, Madonna, and Sharon Stone.

The Opinion: I was prepared to hate *Island*, certain that it would sink under the weight of its all-star cast and lush production values, not to mention the trade publication reports of ego battles between the director and stars. Imagine my surprise when the film lived up to its promise, delivering an exciting story filled with believable characters. *Island* is a three-hour *tour de force*, a cinematic experience that lingers long after the final shot of this tropical hell-hole.

Island opens on board the *Smelt*, a dilapidated fishing vessel skippered by Tub Guttman (Marlon Brando), a once-brave-and-sure sailor now ravaged by alcoholism. Guttman's dreams of independence have been shattered by corporate fishing trawlers and a nasty thyroid condition. His travails are compounded by the ineptitude of his first mate Gil Schmendrik (Crispin Glover), whose bungling provokes Guttman to beat him with the ship's anchor. Stuck in Atlantic City and desperate for money, Guttman is reduced to taking tourists on scenic tours of the Jersey coastline.

It is on one such tour that disaster strikes the *Smelt* when Gil accidentally throws the navigational equipment overboard with some contaminated medical waste. The ship soon finds itself in a hurricane, which drives it ashore a deserted island thousands of miles off course. Now it is a struggle for survival in which each character must conquer his or her demons or perish. Madonna portrays Gina Romantica, a glamorous movie star whose career has been hampered by a profound lack of talent. Her childhood friend Sally Muledeer (Sofia Coppola) had come to Atlantic City to stop Gina from ending her life, but now both must work out their personal problems in order to build a hut and ration their make-up. Oscar winner Tommy Lee Jones nearly steals the picture as Hank Spam, a Trump-like casino czar devastated by a situation his money cannot resolve. His feelings of impotence are aggravated by the constant carping of his European wife Kaplinka (Sharon Stone), whom he almost kills when she laughs at his attempts to catch fish with a money clip. Harvey Keitel rounds out this stellar cast as a math professor who schemed to break the bank of Spam's casino. Now he must use his practical knowledge to keep Spam and the others alive, building a crude radio from sea-shells and hammocks from the ship's store of dental floss.

Island is brilliant at several levels, most notably in the performance of Marlon Brando. Few actors can dominate the wide-screen like this living legend, whose brooding soliloquies on loneliness, failure and thigh chafing comprise his best work since *The Formula*. Brando displays comic ability in his scenes with Crispin Glover, delivering a hilarious slow burn on one hand, then performing a drunken rhumba that must be seen to be believed. Other stand-outs include Madonna, who comes into her own as a vulgar egomaniac whose ambition far outstrips her talent.

Much credit for *Island's* success should go to screenwriters Paul Schraeder and John Milius, who have fashioned a "Heart of Darkness" meets "Peyton Place" that transcends the absurdity of this concept. The direction of Francis Ford Coppola is flawless, building unbearable tension and suspense through the slow presentation of character development. This effect is enhanced by the brilliant camera work of Lazlo Kovacs, who shows us the unutterable beauty and terror of nature with endless close-ups of Madonna's naked body. Say what you want about the Material Girl's acting ability, for my money nobody does a better nude lesbian scene, except maybe Sharon Stone.

Orbit has never given a film a 100 rating, but I cannot in good conscience deny this film its due. Everything bad about Hollywood and its product has been reformulated into a picture that will take its place alongside such classics as *Cleopatra* and *The Greatest Story Ever Told* as an epic that will long be remembered.

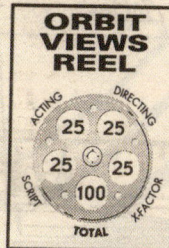

ORBIT VIEWS REEL
ACTING 25 DIRECTING 25
SCRIPT 25 R.FACTOR 25
TOTAL 100

MOVIEOLA
FILM & VIDEO

THE HUDSUCKER PROXY
(R) Comedy

The Facts: A naive young business graduate falls into the clutches of an evil tycoon, all the while investigated by a street-wise newspaperwoman. Stars Tim Robbins, Paul Newman and Jennifer Jason Leigh.

The Opinion: *The Hudsucker Proxy* is at heart a tribute to the comedies of Preston Sturges and Howard Hawks, with a little of Frank Capra's sentimentality thrown in for good measure. The dialogue is fast and witty, pushing its screwball plot along at a pace that's sometimes dizzying. Hudsucker is more than just a knock-off of the films it celebrates, however, thanks to the unique talents of its creators, Joel and Ethan Cohen. The elaborate set pieces and production values are presented with their stylized visual sense, creating a modernized version of an old-fashioned movie.

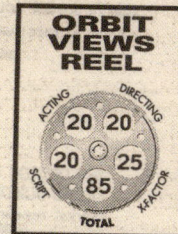

ORBIT VIEWS REEL
ACTING 20 DIRECTING 20
SCRIPT 20 R.FACTOR 25
TOTAL 85

Tim Robbins plays Norville Barnes, a good-natured, if somewhat dim, young man who comes to New York City to make his fortune. He finds himself in the mail-room of Hudsucker Industries, starting work the same day that founder Waring Hudsucker (Charles Durning) kills himself. The board of directors, led by evil chairman Sidney J. Mussberger (Paul Newman,) scheme to drive the company's stock price down in order to gain control of the company. They decide to install a fool as president, making Barnes the perfect selection. This move catches the interest of crack reporter Amy Archer (Jennifer Jason Leigh), who is determined to discover the real reason behind this mysterious appointment.

Film buffs will find many references to the films which *Hudsucker* pays homage, from *Meet John Doe* to *His Girl Friday*. The Cohen brothers know their stuff, framing shots in exact replicas of famous and obscure scenes from these movies. The artifice of this style is risky, because if the viewer's not willing to play along, the film may seem like a bizarre parody. Hudsucker is a high-concept movie that at times falls victim to its cleverness. Jennifer Jason Leigh does a Katherine Hepburn imitation that works about half the time, and the "wise old" narrator is too corny even for Capra. For the most part, however, the film hits the mark, from the excellent lead performances of Tim Robbins and Paul Newman to Peter Gallagher's hilarious cameo as a Dean Martin-like crooner.

The Cohens are sometimes criticized for emphasizing dazzling technique over a coherent storyline, a charge that even fans might admit could be leveled at their last film *Barton Fink*. The Hudsucker Proxy is really all technique, a live-action cartoon with a brain. This time it works because the format allows for a heart-warming, if lightweight, storyline. -K.R.K.

▲ "Movieola," *Island* review, *Orbit*, April 1994.

that he would really like. The film was called *Reservoir Dogs*, the first feature film from director Quentin Tarantino.

Zimmerman loved it and decided to write about the film in his coverage for *Orbit*. He interviewed Tarantino and four members of the cast in Toronto. When Zimmerman wrote up his coverage, he raved about *Reservoir Dogs* so much it became the cover story. "I wanted to put something in there, some hyperbole, something to grab their attention. Do you remember that old line somebody wrote about Bruce Springsteen: 'I've seen the future of rock and roll and it's Bruce Springsteen?' So, I took that line and I wrote, 'I've seen the future of action films and it has two heads: Quentin Tarantino and John Woo,'" said Zimmerman.

MOVIEOLA

ORBIT FILM REVIEW

HARLEY, MARLBORO & THE BIG GOOSE EGG
by Paul Zimmerman

THE FACTS: HARLEY DAVIDSON & THE MARLBORO MAN (R) Action-comedy. Adventures of two bikers set in 1996 Los Angeles. Stars: Mickey Rourke and Don Johnson.

THE OPINION: Somewhere Bruce Willis is smiling. Up until now his *Hudson Hawk* was destined to be remembered as *the* bomb of '91. That was before Mickey Rourke and Don Johnson set the new low in *Harley Davidson and the Marlboro Man*. So amazingly bad in every department that it has the dubious distinction of scoring the first-ever (!) zero on the Orbit Views Reel®.

Set five years in the future, *Harley* is the tale of two biker buddies who rob a bank to save the bar they call home. But instead of cash they steal drugs, sending a futuristic mob after them. Along the way we also meet a girlfriend (named Virginia Slim!), a lounge singer (Vanessa Williams!!) and a leather clad enforcer that's a cross between the Terminator and a pudgy GQ model (Baldwin brother No. 4, Dan!!!). While all these characters *are* annoying, they never detract from the true horror of the two over-acting leads. Least offensive is a bearded Don Johnson, who's suited up as a cowboy and is constantly spewing groan inducing homilies told him by his dear departed dad. The real man(nequin) of the hour is Mickey Rourke. Still sporting the fake-tan make-up from *Wild Orchid*, Rourke is beginning to most resemble Michael Jackson. His chin has been extended and his cheekbones raised, but what makes him really ghoulish is his (blindingly) white capped teeth and his ever-changing lipstick shades. (*These* are the bikers of the future?) In the final scenes Rourke's hair even sprouts from a 1/4 inch brushcut to a three inch shag.

Personal appearances aside, *Harley* sets new lows in several other areas. The real surprise is Aussie director, Simon Wincer. Past successes like TVs Lonesome Dove and last years sleeper western *Quigley Downunder*, hardly prepare one for how inept the storytelling is. *Harley* lacks character, momentum or even one well staged action scene. And on top of all the macho posturing is the endless parade of vapid and scantily clad women. (A movie hasn't been this surrealy sexually offensive since the Matt Helm series in the '60s.)

But the worst offender of all is screenwriter, Don Michael Paul. His prose can set your teeth on edge. Sample: "It's better to die and be cool than to live and be uncool." (Are Bill and Ted his ghostwriters?)

About the only positive thing I can say about the film is that it *is* in focus.

I suppose making a movie this bad is a feat in and of itself. (Kind of like, "you got to see it to believe it!") But from start to finish it's such a brain-numbing assault that you stagger punchdrunk from the theater, a cinematic mug victom.

ORBIT VIEWS REEL

EACH CATEGORY 0-25 PTS. 100 PTS. POSSIBLE

"Movieola," *Harley Davidson & the Marlboro Man* review, *Orbit*, August 23–September 7, 1991. ▶

Before the release of *Reservoir Dogs*, John Woo was best known for his 1992 Hong Kong shoot 'em up, *Hard Boiled*. "If you look at how much [Tarantino and Woo] have influenced movies, you would have to say that Paul was so right. . . . He's good at picking stars that are going to be big," said Peterson.

Zimmerman said he sent the *Reservoir Dogs* issue to the film's distributor, and they passed the issue on to Tarantino. "Apparently, when he saw it, he was jumping up and down saying, 'My first cover! My first cover,'" said Zimmerman. Tarantino got in touch with Zimmerman and asked for extra copies. When the writer mailed them, he threw in an *Orbit* T-shirt.

Zimmerman said Miramax, the distributor, was so impressed with *Orbit*'s coverage of *Reservoir Dogs* that they offered the magazine a special screening at the Maple Theatre in West Bloomfield. At the screening, some of the guests—elderly ladies—walked out during the notorious ear-cutting scene. Zimmerman said that after the movie was released, so many elderly ladies came to the theatre thinking the film was about "cute little doggies" that the theater had to put up a disclaimer.

About a year later, a call came into the *Orbit* offices. For Tarantino's next project, *Pulp Fiction*, he decided to pay homage to *Orbit*. Peterson had to sign a bunch of releases so Tarantino could put an Orby T-shirt in the film. "[I] filled out tons of paper work to get the shirt in the movie. I would send Quentin Tarantino T-shirts and I'd get reports back that he was wearing them out and about around L.A.," said Peterson.

"And we were like that's cool, maybe Bruce Willis will get shot in the film wearing the *Orbit* T-shirt or something. So, we didn't think that much of it," said Zimmerman.

▲ *Reservoir Dogs* cover, *Orbit*, September 22–October 6, 1992.

Orby appears front and center on the director's chest in *Pulp Fiction*. Quentin Tarantino cast himself as Jimmy, a friend of Jules (Samuel L. Jackson) who's trying to help out his hit-man friend. During a scene that features fellow hit man Vincent (John Travolta), Jimmy rants to Jules using his house to store a dead body while they wait for their fixer, the Wolf (Harvey Keitel), to arrive.

After a summer of hype, *Pulp Fiction* opened in October 1994 to critical praise and was a box-office success. The film became a pop culture milestone and won the Academy Award for Best Screenplay. The *Orbit* shirt may have played only a small part in the movie, but the appearance definitely made an impact.

As soon as Orby hit the silver screen, Peterson's phones started to ring. "Everybody wanted a free Orby shirt. All my friends who didn't wear them before that, every advertiser wanted a shirt. The cost went up for me. I don't think I sold many because you had to cut out a piece of paper, put in a

The BIG BANG Theory

TORONTO

FESTIVAL OF FESTIVALS '92 GOES TO THE DOGS

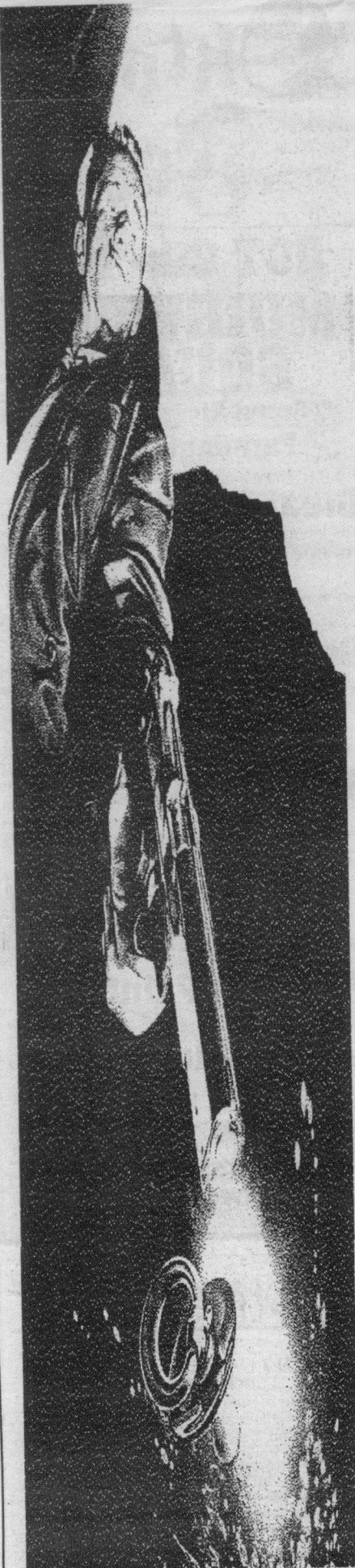

DATELINE TORONTO:

If you ever make a film, this is *the* Festival to get yourself stroked proper. While over 350 films compete over ten days at a dozen theaters, you'll never hear a discouraging word and you sure won't run the risk of geting booed like *Twin Peaks* did at that unruly Cannes. Yes, I'm back for the 17th Festival of Festivals in Toronto, the city of cosmopolitan utopia. Pricey perhaps, but if your film shows you'll get the best audience money can buy (and they'll even pay to get in). Indeed, sitting with a packed bunch of eager humanity you can almost hear them strain to laugh, sigh, cry or guffaw in all the correct places.

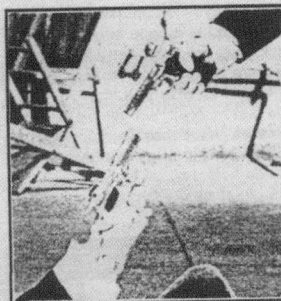

THE PLAYERS:

It was a fine time as the the old faithfuls and the new Turks mixed freely. Robert Redford and Billy Crystal were the big names in town. (I've tales of their woe but the person I saw the most was Ben Kingsley. Anywhere you went you couldn't swing a dead cat without fear of hitting 'ol Ghandi in his freshly shaved noggin'. Like Bogart and Eastwood he's one of those actors whose cranium is so enormous you're dumbstruck at close range- It's downright scary if you have knocked back a few and don't see him until he's right up in your face.) Billy Crystal was in town to promote his director debut, *Mr. Saturday Night* and most people I talked with couldn't get far enough away from the theater. (Like last year all sources of big time dirt come from our Canadian Deep Throat known only as The Shark.) Redford made an appearance for his heartfelt directed look at flyfishing and the meaning of life, *A River Runs Through It*, starring Brad Pitt. Redford was his earnest self, charming the old school journalist ladies and drawing scorn from the hip new breed (or for that matter anyone who had trudged through his last windy epic, *The Milagro Beanfield War*). No real good revelations here as he kept everything low key and all the Shark could mutter in amazement was "his hair, it's not blonde, it's yellow!" Pitt was spotted one night with a gaggle of party goers stumbling from a limo at the Four Seasons hotel. With long hair and a straggly beard he looked like Mickey Rourke's not so evil twin. Cult director Alex Cox brought his gritty new film *Highway Patrolman* to town and shocked everyone with his formal and somewhat shy demeanor.

THE FIND:

(Cue Trumpets) I have met the future of the action movie and it has two heads. Each year one film emerges from the festival. In past years it's been things like the Coen brothers' *Blood Simple*, Errol Morris' *The Thin Blue Line* and Michael Moore's *Roger & Me*. For 1992 it's two films, from two men from two countries. Sure they'd brought to town a full litany of genres, but the films on

This year's films were the usual perfect microcosm of the state of "the Art" (and make no mistake - we spell it here with a capital A), featuring the mega Duds, the little Surprises, the earnest Wellmeaners, the Midnight Madness and the big Breakthroughs. Instead of waiting for next year's Oscars and their ilk, lets just award them right now...

- MOST POLITICALLY CORRECT: *Bob Roberts*. Tim Robbins' mock documentary that's short on laughs and long on cameos and smugness.

- MOST EARNEST: *A River Runs Through It.* Oh Bob, you're so sincere!

- BIGGEST THING: *Indochina*: The story of Viet Nam back when the French were the ones having all the problems.

- BIGGEST CULT FILM: *Tokyo Decadence*. Featuring bondage, a dominatrix, something made of rubber and the kinkiest of them all, businessmen.

- BEST INTENTIONS: *ZebraHead.* Fresh cast, stale script. And what's with the burning grass motif?

- BEST POSTER: *Man Bites Dog.* (See inset)

- MOST EYEBROW-RAISING TITLES: *Rock Hudson's Home Movies* and *Thank God I'm a Lesbian.*

- MOST EAGER: *Passion Fish.* John Sayles hand delivered the work print of his new saga with Alfre Woodard.

- BEST PEDIGREE: **John Malkovich** in the remake of the classic *Of Mice and Men.* Complete with a happy ending. (Just kidding.)

- BIGGEST SCHTICK PER MINUTE: *Mr. Saturday Night*, Billy Crystal's ode du Uncles Miltie and the Nutty Telethoner.

- CLASSIEST ACT: *Blade Runner* at the enormous old Elgin theater. Director Ridley Scott even came in for the occasion.

- BEST FILM: TIE: *Reservoir Dogs/Hard Boiled*. Both films will change the future of the action genre. Why? Is this the only part you're going to read?

BRIAN DEPALMA:

One night at a party at a little joint called Maccheroni, whilst gulping down complimentary Carlsberg beer (the unsung hero of the fest), and inhaling steamed mussels we noticed a not so little director by the name of Brian DePalma. Yeah, that guy. Lord of style. Foe of critics and terror to Hitchcock nerds. Our troupe had this drunken rant going on about how '70s films hadn't received their due and betting each other who'd directed Hackman and Pacino's great ode to the road, *Scarecrow*. "He'd know!" my friend blurted, while pointing a wavering finger across the room at an unsuspecting DePalma resting against a rail. "Yeah," I piped in, "he owned the '70s." He knew alright and was so shocked we didn't assault him with a question about one of his films he joined us at a table we'd commandeered from unsuspecting party goers. I told him of John Woo's great single take in *Hard Boiled* in contrast to his opener in *Bonfire of the Vanities*. He said, "Everyone loves to do those kinds of shots. They're fun." Then he added that the *Bonfire* opener had required 37 takes. (Gee, I'd sure like to be on that crew.) Another round came and I decided to throw caution to the winds. "What do you *do* with all those bad reviews? Laugh? Yell? Stop when they say the H-word (Hitchcock)?" He shook his head laughing, "I stopped *caring* about that a long time ago." Suddenly he started bemoaning the state of things in Hollywood, "*No one will make any film unless it can be easily compared to another successful film. None.*" (Sorry readers, but the man *talks* in italics.) Next he was picking on the critics who review by reading other reviews. "Hey, wait a a minute pal," I interrupted in defense of fellow Word-Whores worldwide, "I gotta warn you, I agree *some* do slack off, but you're sitting with a writer right now!" He laughed and drained his Carlsberg. "Can we get more beer?" Later he let blurt that Bruce Willis was indeed "a jerk." When we asked why he didn't do the narration for the new Criterion laser disc release of *Carrie* he laughed and said, "They didn't *ask* me! I *bought* it in the store *like everyone else.*" Mostly we just laughed about the network versions of his films (a neutered *Scarface* being the funniest). By night's end I had to ask one deep question. "How come the shotgun blast in Pacino's back at the end of *Scarface* didn't cut him in two?!" He laughed again, "No, no, leave that to the hardcore horror films. I wanted to keep something to the imagination. I am working again soon with Al Pacino."

the most alert lips were John Woo's *Hard Boiled* and Quintin Tarantino's *Reservoir Dogs*. *Hard Boiled* boasted deliriously choreographed scenes of sustained mayhem. With earlier films like *The Killer* and *Bullet in the Head*, Woo has single-handedly elevated the action film to the next plane, crime drama that plays like a seamless meld of Peckinpah, Kubrick, Cameron, *Miami Vice*, Chinese ghost story and MTV. Simultaneously totally derivative and yet completely original. (During some shots audible gasps were actually heard in the darkened theater.) The highlight of *Hard Boiled* was a sustained three-minute tracking shot combining flying bodies, hundreds of blood squibs, breaking glass, surreal mayhem and dialogue in an elevator. Topping the long takes in *The Player*, *Raising Cain*, *Bonfire of the Vanities* and even *GoodFellas*, it sets the new standard.

Reservoir Dogs, on the other hand, was merely the most audacious directing debut in twenty years. In turns brutal, literary, profane, gripping, well acted, reverent, terse, disrespectful and, above all, hilarious, director-writer Quentin Tarantino is *the* hot property around town. Clearly these were the Big Two of the fest. And then the news broke of their collaboration.

QUENTIN AND WOO:

Meeting Quentin is a trip. He's a tall ball of energy and rapid-fire answers that reveal a film fanatic, a music buff and a hilarious raconteur. He's taller than average, has a jutting chin and his arms spin about as he speaks with great enthusiasm about *everything*. I talked to him the morning after the official announcement was made by the Wiliam Morris Agency-The two directors of the best films of the festival were teaming up. "The untitled film, an action thriller, will star an international Asian leading man and a prominent American actor." Quintin would script, ex-ecutive produce and John Woo would direct. Halfway through our talk a reporter from San Francisco named Judy-something barged in. Seeing Quentin she bleated "Aggghhh! It's that guy who never shuts up!" Ever the gent, he just laughed. Later he said, "I'm in a position now to write only for myself to direct. But I think Woo is the best action director since Sergio Leone. And they made it as easy as possible. Now, I had this treatment that I really didn't like. This silly story. So on the drive down to meet him I thought of a story I liked better. And he loved it. He's such a cool guy. Good stories are easy to write. Bad stories are hard because they don't have a life of their own. Just jerk motion. This will be after he does *Hard Target* and I do my new film I'm writing, *Cold Fiction*. Note: Orbit will feature even more on Quentin and the other Dog-Boys when the film opens October 16 nationwide.

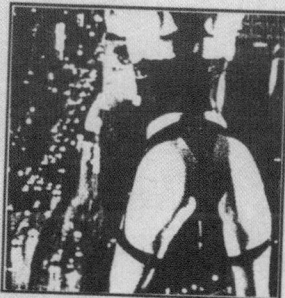

Meeting director John Woo (pronounced "Voo") is a lesson in politeness. He spoke fondly of American films and not so surprisingly his favorites include Sam Peckinpah, John Ford and Clint Eastwood. He is currently in New Orleans making *Hard Target*, the new Van Damme action fest. If anyone can make Van's breakthrough film, it's Woo. After many formalities, I asked him about the now legendary three-minute shot in *Hard Boiled*. In his soft broken English he explained. "We dressed the set one day and then did one take. Next we dressed again for a full day and did a second take. That's the one we used," (Don't tell DePalma.) After about twenty minutes of gushing, I asked him the question you all really want to know the answer to, "If Chow Yun-fat (his regular star) and Van Damme got into a fight, who would win?" For the first time he laughed out loud, "Van Damme, of course!" I was surprised by his quickness, "Really? But Chow's got more guns!" He shook his head, "No, no... Van Damme!"

FESTIVAL WRAP:

Many of the movies which played here have already hit our town. Woody Allen's latest documentary *Husband's and Wives* had to be ignored because by now it's in the Tel-X or other dollar theaters. The best movies like last year's cover story, *Johnny Suede* will take a long time to get here but thank god for video. (By the way *Johnny Suede* is due to open this October a mere year since Orbit highlighted it and it's the unknown star Brad Pitt.)

15

RESERVOIR DOGS

TOO ARTY FOR THE BLOOD CROWD AND TOO BLOODY FOR THE ART CROWD:

The Reservoir Dog Interviews by Paul Zimmerman

THE LOCAL COLOR

"THEY TOOK YOUR SKIN? MAN, that's personal tak'n a man's skin. *Worse than jus' robbin you.*" The grizzled street denizen shook his head. I was in New York's East Village. Boho central, Hipsville, USA. I'd only been there four hours and already I'd attended a Miramax cocktail party, visited old friends and had my black leather stolen from a bar across from the riotous Tompkin Square. My friends, the notorious outlaw comic filmmakers, the Murphy Brothers, were aghast. "Com'n we'll go buy it back," T. Murphy offered. "A few blocks from here they sell everything on the street that they just ripped off. You can get everything from clothes to kitchen appliances." I had to laugh. Here I was on a press junket courtesy of Miramax Films, and already I was getting sidetracked. Sure, I'd already met most of the Dog Boys a few weeks earlier in Toronto, but here was a chance to corner the ever elusive Harvey Keitel (prince of street movies). I had a job to do, but before the trip was over I needed some N.Y. street scenes to season the profiles. By trip's end, I had sucked oysters at Grand Central station, attended the Ave of Beer and a pub called Burp City: Temple of Beer (where the servers wore monk robes), been drooled on by a junkie and led a sing-along in a Country and Western dive, appropriately titled The Village Idiot.

THE INTERVIEWS

THE CAST AND DIRECTOR ASSEMBL ed at the Doral Hotel at 79th and Park Avenue. Not lavish by mega-studio junket standards but still bordering on plush. The gang had come in on the red eye, fresh from the LA premiere where the crowd had gone wild and Jack Nicholson had arrived late brandishing a cigarette and bellowing "*Where's my isle seat? I must have an isle seat.*" After some sap had been bumped so Jack could watch the show, the film proceeded with the usual gasps and occasional walk-out. Later, a big party was thrown in honoer of the conquering heros. LA native and writer-director, Quentin Tarantino, had become so overwhelmed by the "let's do lunch" attack and pressed so much flesh that he'd fled to save his sanity. This was hardly a surprise since when I'd last seen him in Toronto he was starting to show signs of "festival fever." This ailment comes from a lethal exposure to too-much-too-soon and vultures picking up on the smell of fresh meat. Tarantino was *the* hot fresh flesh of the fall season and the mob had begun it's fevered descent. The following is a tortuous blend of the Toronto and New York sessions. For optimum enjoyment, it is recommended that one first see the film and then read the story.

Writer/Director Tarantino barks direction to Producer/Star Keitel

Photo: Linda R. Chin

QUENTIN TARANTINO

Writer/director/player (Mr. Brown)

Tarantino, 29, was a video clerk in LA for five years before getting his big break with *Dogs.* He was willing to shoot it "guerilla style" in 16mm black and white, but his producer/friend Lawrence Bender said it was too good, to let him shop it around. His script found Harvey Keitel and he was so impressed that he agreed to produce as well as star. In all, I spent three sessions interviewing Tarantino, where in we got sidetracked one-upping the other in movie trivia. He's a tall, gregarious fella who speaks in staccato, rapid-fire bursts, is quick to laugh and whose enthusiasm is infectious. Reading the transcripts I was struck that what's spoken "aw-shucks" comes off in print as almost snooty. Don't believe it, Quentin's (humbly) relishing every adoring minute.

Orbit: I was surprised so many people have missed the humor in the film.

Tarantino: When I was in Cannes, the French journalists were getting it but the American journalists wouldn't bring up the humor, just "the violence, the violence." In the trailer, that I love, the humor is emphasized as well as the tough stuff. What I like is getting in a laugh and then (smashes fist into palm) knocking you down.

Orbit: Did you have the song "Stuck in the Middle With You" (from the notorious torture scene) in mind when you wrote the script?

Tarantino: It's actually *in* the script. See, I wanted to make films and the only thing I could get going was on the page. So I put it *all* in the script. The big shots. The chase is broken down shot for shot. It's cut in the script. "POV through windshield. Mr. Pink off screen." I was making the movie on page because it was the *only* way I could make movies. And then when I would show it to someone I could say "look, *this* is what I'm going to do. I'm not going to do *this.* Just *this.*"

Orbit: Your film has been compared to Kubrick's *The Killing* but I saw a lot of *Asphalt Jungle,* too.

Tarantino: Yes, but *Killing* is almost a paraphrase remake of *Jungle,* but I think it's a lot better.

Orbit: But Hayden's great when he does his "you're boning me" speech.

Tarantino: He's great in both, but what I love is when Hayden says to Marie Windsor, "I'll slap that pretty face into hamburger meat."

Orbit: Has Madonna seen the movie? (The film opens with a hilarious and profane theory on what "Like a Virgin" means.)

Tarantino: She's heard about it and wants to but they're making her wait until the N.Y. premiere. When she does, I know she's going to admit that's what *Like a Virgin* is about.

Orbit: Everybody in the film looks like they're having a good time.

Tarantino: They were all for the movie. The group first.

Orbit: You have one intense scene that ends with a great audience release. Have you had any audiences actually cheer?

Tarantino: I've had some cheering, it's cool.

Orbit: The closest I can equate it to is the Russian Roulette scene in *Deer Hunter.*

Tarantino: You've just paid me a hell of a compliment. Because I think that's one of best action scenes ever.

Orbit: Your cast mentioned your script stood out because they had all read such lousy scripts just prior. If you win any awards, you should thank all the hacks out there.

Tarantino: The problem with scripts now is people who have no business at all are writing scripts. And they're not writing what they have inside that they want out. They're writing what they think a movie should be, their version of *Romancing the Stone.* And they buy these Sid Field screenwriting books, and the only reason to buy it should be to burn it. They're their own worst oppressors. I didn't write to sell, I wrote it to direct it. And I didn't know if the dramatic structure would work. It was a theory I had. That if you were to take a novelistic structure and put it to film it would be very cinematic. Edit it like that. Tell a story like that. Chapter headings. And you know on the printed page the vulgarity is much stronger. People who read the script never mentioned the violence. Vulgarity stands out more on the page. They're most upset over the racial remarks.

Interviews with Quentin Tarantino and *Reservoir Dogs* cast, *Orbit*, November 3–17, 1992. ▲ ▶

HARVEY KEITEL
(Mr. White)

It's a good thing Harvey Keitel (*Mean Streets, Thelma and Louise*) is an actor. In person he's so alternately intense, distracted, confused, looney and hilarious, he needs a little direction. *Dogs* represented the first time he'd done the press route in years and years (even he couldn't remember when the last time was). With his bloodshot eyes, long, stringy hair and searing stare, I didn't know whether to push him (vague generalities are his forté) or get the hell away from him. Here's a sampler.

Orbit: What drew you to the material?

Keitel: (gesturing mildly) It was such a unique way of looking at universal themes. Mythological themes. The hero's journey... wanting to be a hero... a mentor at any cost. I feel in my life, once I was a boy, once a child, now a father. There are things... I wish people would have talked to me... about... when I was a child. (looking to ceiling) Which I intend to not talk to my daughter about. (fixing an intense stare) So maybe so we can give the people who come in back of us the perils we've survived so they won't have to go through the same perils. (pausing) And find their own. (picking up speed) Fear. Hell. Loneliness. How to survive. We have to discuss these things time and time again.

Orbit: (dumbstruck) You're so passionate, was it difficult that *Sister Act*...

Keitel: (lightly) No, no *Sister Act* is fun, just fun...to have a laugh. There's room... for that in the cinema...a little room... (suddenly darkening)...there's *too much* of it now...I'd like to see more serious stories discussed. (trancelike) The balance is not right...too much... lightweight stuff... for so bloodied, a world.

Orbit: Is that because of the high cost of films?

Keitel: No because it's the low vision of... people.

Orbit: If not for acting out these horrible things in film, would you have a hard time with daily life?

Keitel: I do have a hard time doing daily life. (laughs) My struggle is what I have to offer to my work... (long pause) You know we all run like hell... to get away from the fear of being abandoned. Scared to death of it... we have to discuss these ideas... so we're not dropping mortar shells ...on children ...in the name of ...God.

Orbit: You do a great primal yell from way down when you learn of a betrayal...

Keitel: I don't like to discuss things like that... because I like the audiences... to experience that. We rendered it as best we could, and now it's... up to... the... audience.

STEVE BUSCEMI
(Mr. Pink)

Steve Buscemi (*Barton Fink, Parting Glances*) is an ex-stand-up comic, ex-fireman, N.Y. stage actor and in the film biz, a stealer of scenes. As Mr. Pink in *Dogs*, he nearly steals the movie from all the others who nearly steal the movie. In person, he's a low-key, amiable guy, sipping on a beer and (unlike many actors) natural around the press corp.

ORBIT: Have you ever lost a role because they said "hey, you're too strong and you'll throw the whole movie out of whack"?

Buscemi: (laughing) Not to my face. Everyone (in *Reservoir Dogs*) is so respectful of each other and the script was so good there wasn't any of those petty jealousies. It's a real ensemble piece. Originally I was told to read for the part of Nice Guy Eddie (Chris Penn's role), but I liked Mr. Pink. They wanted me to send a tape of me reading, but I don't like those, and thank god, Harvey (Keitel) paid for Quentin and Lawrence Bender (the producer), to fly to N.Y. and see me. A lot of Pink's dialogue explains the plot so I thought it was important to deliver it double-time.

ORBIT: What's the title mean?

Buscemi: It's a great title and different people will say different things about it, so...

ORBIT: Did Quentin tell you?

Buscemi: He did. (big smile) But I'll take it to my grave.

TIM ROTH
(Mr. Orange)

CHRIS PENN
(Nice Guy Eddie)

STEVE BUSCEMI
(Mr. Pink)

CHRIS PENN
(Nice Guy Eddie)

After starring in some forgettable gems like *Wild Life*, Chris Penn began carving out a niche as a character actor. Glimmers of hope could be seen in films like *At Close Range*, with his older ex-acting brother Sean, but it wasn't until *Dogs* that his talent came to fruition. Now confident and somewhat serious, he's ready for much more...

Orbit: I heard you've done seven films since *Dogs*.

Penn: Yeah, not all starring parts, but good parts. I could have done more leads but the films weren't as good. It's what I'm calling my second career. The second phase. My first was in a bunch of OK entertainments, but in those days I was most interested in the booze and women. The fringes. Now it's the acting.

Orbit: What's Lawrence Tierney like? (He play's Penn's gangster dad.)

Penn: (broad smile) Everything you'd expect. He's mean, cranky, loving, a real pain and a great guy.

Orbit: How was working with Robert Altman in *LA Shortcuts*?

Penn: Great. My segment was with Jennifer Jason Leigh and we play husband and wife. I read the script and decided what I was gonna do and then I met with Bob and he said "never mind the script, I want you to bring whatever you want to the story." And I thought yeah, I know what I'm gonna do. But Bob works so subtly. After we'd done it, I realized he'd got just what *he* wanted. He's the best I've ever worked with. Not to take anything from Quentin. He's a great second.

Orbit: You have any insight on what Madonna will think of the speech on her in *Dogs*?

Penn: (with twisted smile) She'll love it.

TIM ROTH   MICHAEL MADSEN
(Mr. Orange) (Mr. Blonde)

Tim Roth (*Vincent and Theo*) and Michael Madsen (*Thelma and Louise*) preferred to be interviewed together. It is a living testament to the themes of how men talk around other men (see the *Reservoir Dogs* main review on the Movieola page), their comments in group a were less personal as they horsed around, cutting up and wrestling on the couch where they were interviewed.

Roth: I was blown away by the script. It was the best I'd read in years. When we were filming, I said to Quentin, you know you could make possibly one of the most controversial films ever made by just reversing the roles.

Madsen: (laughing) *Reservoir Bitches*.

Roth: Reservoir Bitches. Yeah. With exactly the same dialogue.

ORBIT: You'd have to change your (Madsen's) talk about sex in prison.

Roth: It'd be about fist f@#%ing or something.

ORBIT: Will you continue to make films in America?

Roth: I haven't worked in England in three years. They aren't making the kind of films I want to make. They're making costume dramas to sell to America. (looking totally disgusted) They don't make films about *my* country. My country is very poor and they make these very effete costume dramas where people get angry across two tables.

ORBIT: I liked when you chug-a-lugged paint thinner in *Vincent and Theo*. Was that in the script?

Roth: He (Van Gogh) drank turpentine and he ate paint. It was in the letters and at that point it seemed right. Most of the film was improvised. I drank turpentine with an alcohol free Pernod. And the paint that I ate was real paint.

Madsen: (exhaling smoke and shaking his head) I can't imagine playing someone like that and *not* doing something like that.

Roth: Steve Altman was the designer on that and he'd put a little toothpaste on the palate and I'd avoid it. (laughs) And he was like "fine, I put it there, but if you want to eat paint."

ORBIT: (to Madsen) Was the bit where you speak into the severed ear in the script?

Madsen: No. Spur of the moment. I had this ear in my hand and I wondered if it could hear. (long pause) I did it for myself and it was funny... which says something about me. And I didn't know if Quentin was going to leave it in.

ORBIT: You've said you were against the two-week rehearsal before *Dogs* began shooting and yet you have a Steppenwolf (Theater in Chicago) background, right?

Madsen: I did start out there. To be honest to god, I only went there for about two or three months. I'd seen John Malkovich play Lenny in a production of *Of Mice and Men*. I was an auto mechanic at the time. Afterwards, I stayed for the question and answer. And I told John "I've never seen anything like that in my life." And he said "why don't you come study." I did and I got a lot out of it... but it got to a certain point where... I felt like the teacher of an acting class becomes like a Svengali and they take away everyone's individuality. I didn't like that... and wanted to be on my own.

Roth: The diversity on this film was incredible. I was working with an ex-fireman (Buscemi), a guy who pumps gas (Madsen), Quentin worked in a video store for years and I went to an art college. All walks of life.

ORBIT: You guys all look like you were having a great time in the film.

Madsen: Every time you do a movie everybody says "here's my number, let's get together" and it never happens. This was different. Everybody got very close.

Roth: Yeah and that was Quentin. Quentin.

ORBIT: He's the glue?

Roth: Yeah, he's the glue and it's not like corny s%#t that most actors say when they're asked by journalists. But it's f*#@ing true. Never felt like this before.

THE CLOSE

So there you have it. Every breed and temperament to every principal dog. (Avoiding dog puns was the hardest part.) So, you ask, what *does* the title mean? I'd heard Quentin was keeping a journal of various theories and had to get my two cents worth in. Just before leaving I called his room.

Orbit: Hello, Quentin? I've got it. It's a variation on the term "rain dogs." Tom Waits named an album after this phenomenon. It's when after a big rainstorm you see all these lost dogs because it's washed away their urine trails left to get them home. Your title refers to how some lost dogs followed the urine trails down the gutter, or reservoir and walloh! Became lifeless dregs, lowlife gutter dogs. Reservoir Dogs. Ok? I got it, right?

Tarantino: (laughing) That's real good but that's not what I was thinking when I wrote it. I always had the title and when I wrote the story I said, "great, I can finally use it." I gotta write that one down though.

Orbit: Ah, I bet it's nonsensical. There is no right meaning. It just sounds cool.

Tarantino: (laughing more) I'm not saying. (pausing) I've been hiding up here in my room. I'm wiped out. They're trying to get me to go to a party at Ann Magnuson's. I need to relax. I think I'm going to go see a movie.

MOVIEOLA
FILM

ASK MR. MOVIE

Dear Mr. Movie:
Help settle a bet between me and my lazy, barefoot, scotch swillin', potato chip-stealing co-worker. What movie had the most stars?

—Doug Haite

Dear Haite-monger:
Your query is a hot potato that's been argued for many, many years. Obvious leaders come to mind like that grand acting battle between the U.S. and England, *A Bridge Too Far* (we lost), those overblown comic epics (and cult faves) *1941* and *It's a Mad, Mad, Mad, Mad World*. Many still believe *The Greatest Story Ever Told* holds the record for biggest and bestest cast. To these we would add *How the West Was Won* and most recently, *The Player*. In short, I have no real idea, so we consulted Mr. Thinks-he-knows-it-all Zimmerman. But we don't think he understood the question. He said it would have to be one of the Star Wars features.

Remember kids, if your letter is printed, we'll send you a unique badge inscribed with "No, I'm Not Orbit's Mr. Movie!"

HELD OVER

GLENGARRY GLEN ROSS - 90
Cutthroat, back-stabbing and unmerciful: how an office should be run.

LAST OF THE MOHICANS - 80
James Fenimore Cooper may have been the most boring writer in the annals of American history but not after he gets the Michael Mann treatment.

UNDER SIEGE - 45
A roller-coaster ride of non-stop action that you've seen a million times before, although Tommy Lee Jones is one great villain.

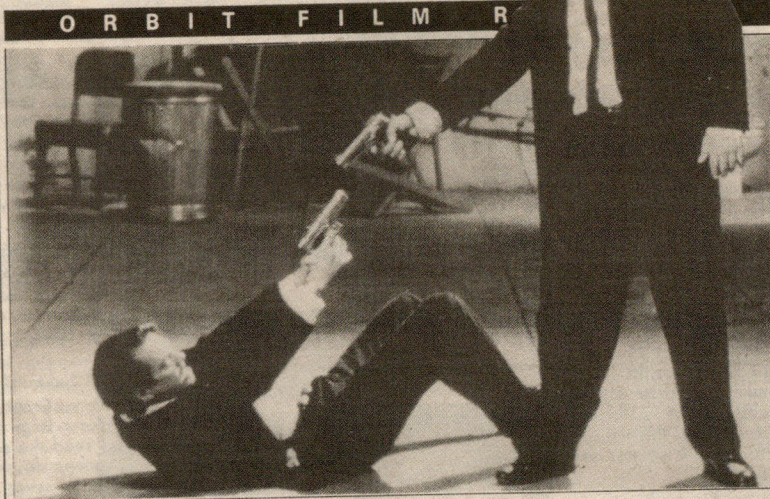

1492 - 55
The best Columbus movie this year is the winner by a nose.

CONSENTING ADULTS - 50
A movie this bad should be illegal even in the privacy of your own home.

CANDY MAN - 60
Satisfying and delicious.

A RIVER RUNS THROUGH IT - 65
Homespun and heartwarming and gosh darn it, that Robert Redford is such a sensitive guy.

DR. GIGGLES - 40
So scary, I forgot to laugh.

PUDDLE PUPPIES
by Paul Zimmerman

THE FACTS: Following a bungled jewelry heist the thieves regroup to discover what went wrong. Stars: Harvey Keitel, Tim Roth, Chris Penn, Steve Buscemi, Michael Madsen.

THE OPINION: I know what you're thinking. First Orbit puts *Reservoir Dogs* on the cover. Then three issues later it's the main review and virtually the entire cast is interviewed. What the hell is this, the second coming? Nope, it's just my way of making sure you know it's the find of the fall season. Or more to the point...

It is a common misconception about critics that the thing they most relish is gleefully ripping a film to shreds. While that can be fun, in fact, the best part is the heady rush you get discovering a fresh and rude new talent. And for 1992 you don't get any fresher, ruder or more talented than Quentin Tarantino. As writer and director of the new crime drama, *Reservoir Dogs*, he's balanced black humor, gut-wrenching violence and the best ensemble acting this side of *Glengarry Glen Ross* into 99 odd minutes of sheer audacity.

On the surface *Dogs* is a savvy updating of the classic noir B-movie classics of the '50s. It's about what happens when desperate men are pushed to their limits. But beneath all the sweat, blood and four letter torrents lurks something else. Listen closely and you'll hear the rhythms of how men relate to men. Not that this is a bunch of whining Iron John's banging on drums in a forest. It's society's dregs banging on a few heads in an abandoned LA warehouse. (With all of the physical and mental mayhem, it plays like the men's movement in a pressure cooker.) Boil all this bluster and machismo down to its basics and we find the real essence of the film – it's about how men *talk* around other men. When the situation is one on one, it's intimate and personal, but any added male results in an amalgamation of bravado and emotional closure. That said, let it be known that all of this metaphysicall mumbo jumbo is just the frosting on the cake. *Dog's* big bites come with suspense, hilarity and something missing from 90% of the current runs – originality and well earned surprises. That and the nearly palpable glee the entire cast seems to exude as they carefully chew on each wicked word. Indeed, several actors put in their best work to date including Buscemi, Penn and Madsen. So it's an actor's piece, a narrative lark, an art film, a sleazy potboiler and to tell more would be downright rude.

Note: While ostensibly a blistering black comedy, *Dogs* has gained notoriety from a brutal scene involving torture. While never gratuitous or graphic, audiences have been so repulsed that there have been walk-outs at many showings. This is merely a further testament to the power of the film, don't let it prevent you from seeing one of the best of the year.

ORBIT VIEWS REEL

ACTING 25 | DIRECTING 25
SCRIPT 20 | X-FACTOR 25
95 TOTAL

EACH CATEGORY 0-25 PTS.
100 PTS. POSSIBLE

REVIEW 'N THE PREVIEWS

TITLE	IMPRESSIONS PRO	IMPRESSIONS CON	ODDS YOU'LL GO
ALADDIN	Great Disney music	R. Williams: voice whore	3 to 2
CHILDREN OF THE CORN II	Scary grain	Corn I	15 to 1
DRACULA	Does B. Stoker proud	Where's Buffy when you need her?	Even
JENNIFER 8	Uma 10	Audience 0	8 to 1

ZEBRAHEAD
-(R) Drama

ACTING 20 | DIRECTING 5
SCRIPT 5 | X-FACTOR 10
40 TOTAL

THE FACTS: Interracial romance set in Detroit between two teens: one a white Jewish boy and an African-American girl.

THE OPINION: If good intentions were enough, *Zebrahead* the new interracial romance would rate a 100. Never mind the PC critics who are afraid to point out what a lackluster piece of filmmaking this truly is – it may look good and be well acted, but overall it's safe-city. In this age of holding budgets (2 mil.) and well meaning sentiments over insight and meat I suppose this kind of thing's inevitable. Credit writer-director Anthony Drazan for at least having the guts to go the white/guy, black/girl route. Even Spike Lee's (far better) *Jungle Fever* downplayed this societal tinderbox. Unfortunately, *Zebrahead* ain't got much to recommend it besides some snappy print ads. Blame the bland, derivative script (aping Shakespeare and *West Side Story*), some glaring miscasting (like the obtrusive Ray Sharkey) and a silly subplot with no follow-through (the burning grass is a metaphor, I guess). You're far better off renting *Mississippi Masala* for any real insight (or entertainment for that matter). -P.Z.

NIGHT AND THE CITY
-(R) Drama

ACTING 10 | DIRECTING 10
SCRIPT 10 | X-FACTOR 25
55 TOTAL

THE FACTS: New York lawyer with a sleazy exterior but a heart of gold schemes to build it as a big-time boxing promoter.

THE OPINION: From the beginning to the end of this disappointing picture, Robert De Niro as hack lawyer Harry Fabian is seen searching for intensity in all the wrong places. He finds it, to be sure, but then hurls it back at you like he's trying to douse a fire where there isn't even smoke. He's too much of a good thing, and yet he's probably the only thing worth watching inside of the wonderfully warm saloon interiors that give *Night and the City* its lower Manhattan authenticity. Jessica Lange is wasted as the woman on the periphery of Fabian's life. Eli Wallach, Jack Warden and Alan King are all nice to watch but their characters don't seem to inhabit real flesh. The soundtrack, featuring Sam the Sham, Smokey Robinson and a string of other hits from '65 & 66, is overripe and annoyingly familiar - quite like the De Niro performance, actually. -W.W.

OF MICE AND MEN
-(PG-13) Drama

ACTING 25 | DIRECTING 20
SCRIPT 25 | X-FACTOR 15
85 TOTAL

THE FACTS: Depression-era story based on John Steinbeck's classic novel.

THE OPINION: This baby has been around a few weeks so this is just a quick note to say "don't miss this one." Whether you favor the '39 Lon Chaney classic or the '81 TV movie this new (and reverently faithful) version from director/star keeper-of-the-Steinbeck-flame, Gary Sinise, is well worth your time. "You just can't beat the classics," an old guy said when I walked out, and he's right on the mark. More lyrical than the '39 model and less campy than the TV take (a streetwise Robert Blake was a hoot), this is the role that put Malkovich on the map ten years ago at Chicago's Steppenwolf theater. Controlled but never preachy, boasting an excellent supporting cast, *Of Mice and Men* is not required like it was in high school but if you're in the mood for one that's crafted "like they used to," it's just fine (and you could even bring your mom too). I'm shaving a few points because it borders on being too tasteful, it could use a little more movement and sweat. -P.Z.

1 2 3 4 5 6 7 8 9 10 11 12 13 **14** 15 16 17 18 19 20 21 22 23 24 25 26 27 28 29 30 31 32
PAGE

▲ *"Movieola," Reservoir Dogs* review, *Orbit*, November 3–17, 1992.

▲ Quentin Tarantino with *Orbit* writer Paul Zimmerman at the 1992 Toronto Film Festival. (Photo by Malcolm Ingram)

check, wait for us to cash it. It was a process. It wasn't easy to get one unless you were an advertiser, then you could wash your cars with it," said Peterson. But that didn't stop Peterson and company from capitalizing on their mascot's newfound fame. Ads after the release of *Pulp Fiction* play up the shirt's appearance in the film.

But that wouldn't be the last time Quentin Tarantino gave *Orbit* a nod. According to Peterson, "He also directed an episode of *E.R.* [in 1995], and there's an *Orbit* sticker on the side of the girl's boom box. I sent him something later with a note saying, 'I don't want you to be superstitious, but could Orby be your lucky talisman,' and 'you need him in every movie.'" Despite Peterson's entreaty, the lovable globe-headed scamp has never made another screen appearance in a Tarantino film.

Pulp Fiction coming soon, *Orbit*, May 1994. ▶

Pulp Fiction

Quentin "Consummate Director" Tarantino comes up with another stunning masterpiece when he dons an Orby shirt for his director's cameo. Orbit T-shirts are available for only 12.95 from 919 S. Main Royal Oak MI 48067. Expect this film to resurrect the careers of Bruce "Never Made a Bad Film" Willis, John "Up Your Nose With a Rubber Hose" Travolta and Harvey "Frontal Nudity, No Problem" Keitel. Word on the street is shirts are available in three sizes XL, XL and XL.

MOVIEOLA

FILM & VIDEO

Videos Out in October

Jurassic Park: The ultimate monster movie and monster hit, though you gotta wonder how scary it will be on the small screen.

Backbeat: Biography of Stu Sutcliffe, the so-called fifth Beatle and best friend of John Lennon. It's like a Yoko Ono record: better than it sounds.

Ink Well: Coming-of-age pictures with actors sporting the biggest afros since Link's in the Mod Squad.

The Paper: Ronnie Howard's take on the hectic world of a big city daily came and went at the theatre like yesterday's newspaper.

Crooklyn: Spike Lee's first mega flop takes an interminably long look at the funky days of his 70s childhood, assuming that any of us care.

Sirens: Elle MacPherson and other assorted beauties take it all off in the name of art and ticket sales.

Clifford: Yet another irritating Martin Short vehicle. At least he isn't doing that atrocious Katherine Hepburn imitation.

The Cowboy Way: How about a couple of rodeo cowboys, played by Woody Harrelson and Kiefer Sutherland, who come to New York City and get messed up with a beautiful girl and gangsters? How about we rent something else.

Guarding Tess: Nicholas Cage has his hands full trying to protect Shirley Maclaine from herself. I think in a past life she was a pain in the ass.

The Hudsucker Proxy: Under-rated tribute to screwball comedies from the Cohen brothers. Not for all tastes, but they're probably watching The Cowboy Way.

Jimmy Hollywood: Joe Pesci plays a loser who dreams of making it in pictures, while Christian Slater tags along as his brain-damaged best friend. Not as bad as you might expect.

ALL THIS AND TRAVOLTA TOO

PULP FICTION (R) Drama

The Facts: A pair of hitmen deal with the boss's wife, a prize-fighter on the lam and assorted denizens of the underworld. Stars John Travolta, Bruce Willis, Uma Thurman and Samuel L. Jackson.

The Opinion: Quentin Tarantino burst upon the film scene several years ago with the most audacious debut in recent memory. The cult hit *Reservoir Dogs*, which he wrote and directed, was a taut action classic filled with great dialogue and top-notch acting. Needless to say, expectations have been high for Tarantino's follow-up effort, a recipe for the "sophomore slump" which often plagues directors who score big their first time out. True to form, *Pulp Fiction* may disappoint the less discerning Tarantino fan with its slower pacing and quirky plot structure. Tarantino's gift with words almost sinks several scenes under the weight of sheer verbiage, while the final segment seems thrown in just to give Harvey Keitel and Quentin a chance to play a scene together. For all its failings, *Pulp Fiction* is still several cuts above most of the films released this year, owing largely to Tarantino's unique perspective, and repeated viewings reveal sly references to other films (including *Reservoir Dogs*) and a better appreciation for the film's inventive plotting.

Tarantino took some heat for the scripting of *Reservoir Dogs* when critics noticed its uncanny (some would say frame for frame) resemblance to Hong Kong director Ringo Lam's *City on Fire*. Tarantino responded that he steals from everybody, mainly the gritty film noir cliches of small time criminals and losers inhabiting the fringes of society. *Pulp Fiction* self-consciously parodies the B movie themes which its title calls forth: the boxer forced to take a dive, the henchman fending off the advances of the boss's wife and the pathetic logic of seedy criminals. Based upon early film ideas written by Tarantino and his partner Roger Avery during their days as clerks in a video store, the storyline gives evidence to the sheer number of gangster movies they rented.

Pre-release publicity made much of John Travolta's "comeback" performance in his portrayal of hit man Vincent Vega, but Samuel L. Jackson steals every scene as his partner Jules Winnfield. Spouting biblical passages before blowing away his victims and ruminating on divine intervention and the nature of foot massages, Jackson's character is far more

by Kevin R. King

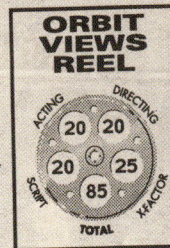

interesting than either Travolta or Uma Thurman, who plays a mobster's girlfriend that Travolta nervously takes on a date. Bruce Willis does a surprisingly good turn as a boxer trying to double-cross the mob, especially in scenes with his French girlfriend, played with charm by Maria de Medeiros. It's a role anyone could really play, but I guess the producers felt Willis would draw a whole lot of viewers, paying him three of the ten million bucks budgeted for the whole picture. That's Hollywood.

The real star of a Tarantino film is the script, and this one gets better as the film picks up steam. Quentin's best with the frantic dialogue of action, when characters are confronted with disaster and mayhem. When trouble breaks out in *Pulp Fiction*, whether it's the boss's wife having an overdose or a pair of freaks having their way with Willis, the audience is gripped by the tension that made *Reservoir Dogs* so compelling. Everything is colored by a wicked black humor, and the excellent soundtrack displays Tarantino's love affair with 60's music, and Dick Dale fans should listen close during the instrumental transitions.

For some there might not be enough action in *Pulp Fiction*: too much talk and gratuitous cameos by Tarantino pals Tim Roth and Christopher Walken. The jury's still out on whether Tarantino's comic-action shtick will become stale, but for me *Pulp Fiction* was like the T-shirt Quentin wears through out his scenes: sometimes good, sometimes bad, but always interesting.

ORBIT VIEWS REEL

ACTING	20	DIRECTING
	20	
SCRIPT	20	25
	85	X-FACTOR
	TOTAL	

QUIZ SHOW (PG-13) Drama

The Facts: True story of television's first scandal: the quiz show fixing of the late 50's. Stars: Ralph Fiennes, Rob Morrow and John Turturro.

The Opinion: Director Robert Redford has crafted a slick, highly entertaining film which also tries to say something about the corruptive power of TV. As entertainment it's a success, with first-rate performances and production values. As social commentary *Quiz Show* falls a little flat, because its "made-for-TV" plotting falls prey to the very ideas it attacks. The producers and corporate sponsors are suitably vulgar and crass, while the charm and priveildged background of quiz show co-conspirator Charles Van Doren lend him a sympathy he doesn't deserve. Redford makes it clear that this easy charm is Van Dorn's achilles heel, but the performance of Ralph Fiennes makes it almost impossible not to like him. John Turturro is equally effective as the working class nebbish who is sacrificed for the WASP appeal of Van Dorn, but he also plays to the very stereotypes the evil producers thought hurt ratings. I'll admit that such criticism is pretty nit-picky, but hey, it's always easier to find little faults than to shamelessly gush for 200 words. Go and see it and judge for yourself. -K.R.K.

ORBIT VIEWS REEL

ACTING	25	20
	20	15
SCORE	80	X-FACTOR
	TOTAL	

ED WOOD (R) Comedy/Drama

The Facts: Ambitious director struggles to make it in Hollywood, but ends up making the worst film of all time. Stars: Johnny Depp, Sarah Jessica Parker, Bill Murray, and Patricia Arquette.

The Opinion: Tim Burton (*Batman, Edward Scissorhands, Beetlejuice,* and *The Nightmare Before Christmas*) has pulled a fast one with his new film Ed Wood. It's funny offbeat and original but not in the usual Burton ways. Technically speaking this is Burton's simplest and best film. Decidedly low tech, all the flash and trash of the *Batman* films is jettisoned for his most lucid storytelling since *Edward Scissorhands*. (Indeed if not for the miniature tracking shots which open and close the film, you'd never know Burton helmed *Wood*.) Not that Ed is a traditional film. Far from it. Scenes repeat themselves, the drama sags in spots and the very subjects he so warmly illustrates, will surely scare great portions of the populace away. But as the story of an offbeat dreamer, *Ed Wood* succeeds brilliantly. Working on its own themes and at its own speed, Ed's the most original big-budgeted film of the year. But as a bio pic it stands alone. -Hiram Todd Norman

ORBIT VIEWS REEL

ACTING	25	25
	20	15
SCORE	85	X-FACTOR
	TOTAL	

▲ "Movieola," *Pulp Fiction* review, *Orbit*, October 1994.

1994

The year in movies was like most others: a few good pictures, a lot of bad ones. Here's our take on the winners and losers of 1994. While the list's not comprehensive (we can't see every movie) or very accurate (we make a lot of stuff up) you might discover a good film you missed this year.

BEST PICTURE

Pulp Fiction

With this film, Quentin Tarantino proved he's no fluke. Chock full of sharp dialogue, great acting and the brilliant casting of Orby, *Pulp Fiction* merges the aesthetics of film noir with the post-modern pop culture sensibility of the so-called X generation. Though certainly not perfect, *Fiction* is head and shoulders above anything else Hollywood offered this year.

▲ Ad for *Orbit* shirts, *Orbit*, January 1995.

◄ *Pulp Fiction*, best picture of 1994, *Orbit*, January 1995.

Orby says: "Boogie Down!"

Orbit Music

Scott Sterling, a fan of *Fun* and a University of Michigan grad, landed at *Orbit* in the early 1990s. "With Jerry, anything went," remembered Sterling. "You could never be too shocking, ever. It was very liberating in that sense to write the most insane shit and have it printed thousands of times and people would read it. Then the first time you get that public reaction, you know it's on."

Sterling spent several years as music editor of *Orbit* and eventually climbed the ladder to managing editor. When he left the magazine, WDET music host Liz Warner (née Copeland) took over as music editor. Writing and editing under the pen name Zxotic, Warner said working at *Orbit* forced her to think beyond the usual ways of writing: "My approach at the time was more serious because I was trying to find my voice, even as it applied to radio, but those who had experience helped me to find my voice. So, I'll always be thankful for that time."

Warner believed the reason the magazine resonated with readers, especially those in the music and arts scene, was that *Orbit* spent time on people who were not just the big names or the flavor of the month. She said, "It would get off the beaten track to highlight some things others weren't talking about."

SONIC BOOM

TRACKS & HOT WAX

LONG LIVE THE KING

ELVIS COSTELLO

In the peculiar world of mainstream Rock Journalism, history is generally written by those least qualified to write it. Take for instance, those infernal *Rolling Stone* infomercials, with former MTV veejay Alan Hunter waxing nostalgic about the whole history of Rock. Aside from the total omission of Punk Rock (only the single most important movement in music since the dawn of Rock 'n' Roll), *Rolling Stone* preposterously points to New Wave as the only significant movement in rock in the late '70s. And their prime example of New Wave? Why Elvis Costello, of course. Equally as ridiculous as the mere mention of New Wave as a legitimate movement, the misconception of Elvis as a New Wave artist is a prime example of the outrageous dunderheadedness of the mainstream Rock media.

One of the few true "songwriters" of the contemporary era, Elvis produced some of the most well-crafted *pop* records ever made. In the period from 1978 to 1982, Elvis put out an impressive body of work. From the Country-flavored Rock of *My Aim Is True*, to the all-out Punk-inspired assault of *This Year's Model* and *Armed Forces*, to the Soul/R & B masterwork, *Get Happy!!*, and the fully-matured self-confidence of *Imperial Bedroom*, it seemed Elvis could do no wrong (that is, if you don't count *Almost Blue*, a rather embarrassing collection of Gram Parsons-inspired Country cover songs).

Typically, Elvis' eventual mainstream success pretty much paralleled his artistic decline. Albums like *Punch the Clock*, *Goodbye Cruel World*, *King of America* (probably the best of his later work), and *Mighty Like a Rose* were decent, yet lacked the vibrancy of his earlier work. Still, Elvis has remained a uniquely gifted songwriter, although his penchant for puns and clever turns of phrase eventually grew tiresome, and musically, he took a turn for the saccharine. His frequent collaborations with schmaltzmeister Paul McCartney unequivocally signalled the end of Elvis' integrity, and his most recent projects, including writing an entire album for Wendy James and composing an uncharacteristically pretentious set of "classical" pieces (*The Juliet Letters*) leave little hope that Elvis will redeem himself in this lifetime.

Regardless, Elvis' initial body of work has stood the test of time, and is now being expertly reissued by Rykodisc. While the Columbia versions currently available are far inferior to their vinyl counterparts, the Ryko editions have been lovingly remastered, and the new editions contain many previously unreleased tracks. A limited edition box set of the first three LPs contains the legendary *Live at the El Macambo* album (previously available only as a bootleg) and will be out on October 12. -DPM

BLAH BLAH

MILES DAVIS
The late Jazz great not only pioneered uncharted musical territory, he also had some peculiar methods of communication. His vague, yet forceful manner of speech often proved confusing even to members of his own band. His explanation: "If you understood everything I said, you'd be me."

HISTORY OF MUSIC

105 Years Ago
The first patent for a gramophone is given to Emile Berliner. This paves the way for the mass-production of recorded music, a move that will forever diminish the cultural value of music, but will make a few people disgustingly rich.

61 Years Ago
RCA shows off the first 33-1/3 LPs and players. CBS completely reworks the process in order to make it functional. The success of the 33-1/3 RPM record leads to the development of "hi-fi" sound, and then, stereophonic sound, both of which are pooh-poohed by music enthusiasts of the day.

13 Years Ago
Philips introduces the Compact Disc which boasts "perfect digital sound." Naysayers and vinyl enthusiasts predict that CDs will go the way of the 8-track, but the near-total extinction of vinyl LPs within the next 7 years proves otherwise.

DANCE OF THE MONTH

—DROOGIE SHUFFLE—

A. Tap left toe behind right foot. **B.** Step forward quickly on left foot. **C.** Draw back right foot in graceful arc. **D.** Kick! **Helpful hints:** Rhythm is step-step-KICK-shuffle-pause-step-step-KICK! With emphasis on the kick. NOTE: Dance is ideally done to "Singing In The Rain."

SONICALLY SPEAKING...

Red Hot Chili Peppers have chosen former Jane's Addiction guitarist David Navarro to replace former Mother's Tongue guitarist Jesse Tobias, who was in the band for approximately three days.

From the Guaranteed Failure Dept: Geffen Records is releasing the fourth **Warrior Soul** album, *Chill Pill*, on October 12. Featuring former Detroit nobody/current national nobody Korey Clarke, Warrior Soul's first three albums are reported to have sold less than 1,000 copies combined, making them among the worst selling albums of all time.

From the Guaranteed Success Dept: November 23 is the scheduled release date for the long-awaited Beavis & Butt-Head album, *The Beavis & Butt-Head Experience Vol. One*. The album will feature tracks by Soundgarden and White Zombie, among others. A true testament to the outrageously low intelligence quotient of the average American, the success of Beavis & Butt-Head is said to be such that a video's inclusion on the show results in a 25% increase in album sales. There is no hope for the world.

Frank Sinatra's forthcoming album, *Duets*, which is slated for November 9 release features the vocal talents of such legendary voices as Luther Vandross, Aretha Franklin, Gloria Estefan, Julio Iglesias, and for some

The ever-accommodating Frank

strange reason, **Bono.** Even more curious than the appearance of U2's enigmatic frontman is the fact that none of the singers were in the studio with Ol' Blue Eyes when they cut the record. Apparently Frank recorded his vocals with the band, then sent the tapes off to the various singers, who added their vocal accompaniment. Frank has apparently also refused to do any press for the album, which has folks at Capitol (to which he recently resigned after a twentysomething-year absence) a bit bewitched, bothered, and bewildered.

New Releases for October: George Clinton (*Hey Man, Smell My Finger*), Julee Cruise (*The Voice of Love*), Pearl Jam (*Five Against One*), PJ Harvey (*The 4-Track Demos*), Boredoms (*Pop Tatari*), and Guns 'N' Roses (*The Spaghetti Incident*, an album of punk covers).

FOUND WAX

THE BEVERLY HILLBILLIES
-*Columbia/Legacy*
With the exception of *The Simpsons Sing the Blues*, Ren and Stimpy's *You Eediot*, and the forthcoming Beavis and Butt-Head CD, the fine tradition of TV show tie-in

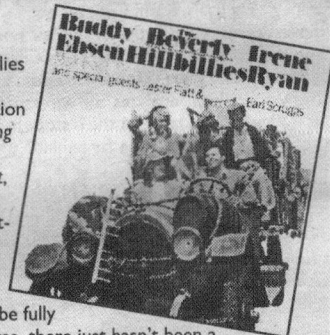

albums has yet to be fully exploited. Of course, there just hasn't been a show of the high artistic caliber of the Beverly Hillbillies in quite some time. This boot stompin' record features the show's unforgettable theme song (done here to perfection by Flatt and Scruggs), as well as many original numbers sung by the show's various characters. Beverly Hillbillies is a monument to an era in bad entertainment that is sorely missed (things now are much, much, worse). And the best thing about this rare, cultural gem is that it's just been issued on CD, so all of the subtle nuances of Jethro's plaintive warble are as crisp as a brand new thousand dollar bill.

▲ "Sonic Boom," Elvis Costello review, *Orbit*, October 1993.

RECORDING OF THE MONTH

PEARL JAM
Vs.
-Epic

What do you do when the solution becomes the problem? It's been nearly 20 years since Punk Rock exploded in the underground, setting out to destroy the dinosaurs of rock who were hogging the charts and making it impossible for anyone new and different to get any exposure. Sickened by the pretentious, self-important posturings of old-and-growing-older has-beens like Mick Jagger, Bob Seger, et al., bands like the Sex Pistols, the Damned, and countless others set out to tear down the walls of corporate rock and replace it with music that was raw, honest, and vital. Inevitably, this movement burned out, but its influence was felt by musicians and artists the world over. Unfortunately, the demon seed planted by the Punk movement has given birth to the bastard child that is "alternative," or "underground," or "college rock."

Complete with all the trappings of rebellious youth, Pearl Jam continue to produce retrograde, watered-down MOR rock, the pathetic likes of which haven't been heard since the glory days of REO Speedwagon and Styx, all the while selling it as "cutting-edge."

So what? Well, apart from the fact that the music is just plain bad ("Glorified G," for instance, is lame enough to be worthy of comparisons to Huey Lewis and the News), Pearl Jam (along with STP, Nirvana, and many others) are perpetrating an all-too-typical industry created fraud, by actually *being* the pretentious, corporate sell-outs that they pretend to be part of the movement to destroy. Even worse is the knowledge that most of this band (with the exception of the wildly overrated Eddie Vedder) used to be in Green River, one of the best hard rock bands of the last 10 years, and *the* best band of the entire Sub Pop/Seattle pre-grunge movement. This album has all the elements that any self-respecting patron of the Rock arts should hate. Predictable sounds (mid-to-late period Allman Brothers), predictable political stances (they're actually *against* police brutality!), and art-school pretensions (lyrics reproduced from the journal pages they were originally scrawled on). Pearl Jam is the enemy. Kill Rock Stars. -DPM

DISC-O-GRAPH

TEPID, STERILE AND DULL — TIRED '70s ROCK CLICHES

0

SIMPLY BAD — GRUNGE LITE

The DISC-O-GRAPH proportionally represents criteria (as indicated) by which recording was judged. Score represents the overall view on a scale of 1 to 10, 10 being the highest.

SOUND BITES

STEREOLAB
Transient Random-Noise Bursts With Announcements
-Elektra
Orbitron Rating 9

In these times, when the most vapid, tepid, sterile three-chord bar band rock is being re-made/re-modeled/re-packaged and thrust back into the airwaves bearing the clever, yet inaccurate tag "alternative," a band like Stereolab serves as a healthy reminder of what the term "new music" once-upon-a-time implied. Although they don't sell themselves as "dangerous" or "cutting edge," and although you sure as heck don't hear them on any "alternative" radio station 'round here, Stereolab are one of the most truly original, innovative, inspirational bands to come along in quite a while. To attempt to draw comparisons would be misleading; Stereolab has numerous combinations of Velvet Underground, Walter/Wendy Carlos, Sonic Youth, first album Modern Lovers, and Neu, but their tendency towards minimal/experimental sounds never renders them difficult or unlistenable. Stereolab is at once cacophonous and harmonious, with the rich, beautiful, Nico-esque vocals of Laetitia Sadier raising the throbbing, repetitious wall of noise-rock sound into the realm of pop. Musically naive, yet conceptually brilliant, songs like "Pack Yr Romantic Mind," "Golden Ball," "Jenny Ondioline," and "Analogue Rock" are ecstatic sojourns into seldom explored, yet highly pleasurable musical realms. Recommended for those who've just about given up hope. -DPM

SWERVEDRIVER
Mezcal Head
-A & M
Orbitron Rating 8

Guitars, glorious guitars, of countless shapes, sizes, textures and sonic dispositions gleefully run rampant all over this album. Proving that their excellent debut, *Raise*, was far from a fluke, *Mezcal Head* further explores the same thematic territory with most impressive results. Adam Franklin narrates the driving soundscapes with tales of finding freedom via speed and motion in his trademark gravelly-smooth croon. But *Mezcal Head*'s trump card is

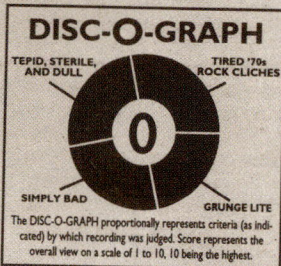

that in the midst of its dense storm lie hummable, sing-along songs. Even sprawling epics like the 11-minute-plus "Never Lose that Feeling/Never Learn" are built on insanely catchy hooks. And best of all, they never resort to the same tired cliches of so many post-Husker Du/Dinosaur Jr. noise-pop wannabes. This one's a keeper. -S.T.S.

COCTEAU TWINS
Four Calendar Cafe
-Capitol
Orbitron Rating 7

The release of a new Cocteau Twins LP just isn't anticipated with the same Pavlovian excitement that met albums like *Treasure* or *Echoes In a Shallow Bay*. Unlike the avant-garde author/director/poet/artist/playwrite from whom the group takes its name, the Cocteau Twins are essentially a one-trick pony. While still existing far outside the frayed edges of the mainstream, the Twins have instead created a mainstream all their own. Rather than exploring newer and more esoteric sounds, they've gotten locked into their own groove more and more with each record. Mind you, it's a damn fine groove, and songs like the album opener, "Know Who You Are At Every Age," and "Theft, The Wandering" are as good as anything they've done in years. No longer unusual, or even compelling, the Cocteau Twins are nonetheless still making some of the best mood music you'll ever hear. -DPM

PJ HARVEY
4-Track Demos
-Island
Orbitron Rating 9

If you have any doubt in your mind as to whether or not Steve Albini is one of the worst producers around (oh, that's right, he doesn't produce, he *records*), then listen to this album of home recordings, and you'll wonder how it's possible for one person with a guitar and a 4-track to create recordings with more intensity, and more primal power than those carefully engineered by a twerpy, obsessive creep with a 24-track studio. *4-Track Demos*, originally intended to be sold as part of the *Rid Of Me* package, sounds like what both PJ Harvey records should have sounded like; minimal, raw, and very intense. The album includes most of the songs from *Rid Of Me*, plus a number of never-before-released tracks. An essential addition to anyone's collection. -DPM

PLASTIK-MAN
Sheet One
-NovaMute
Orbitron Rating 9

Detroit/Windsor boy-genius and Plus 8 guru Richie "Rich" Hawtin's first full-length LP (under the moniker of Plastikman) raises the stakes in the techno arena to a whole new beautifully hypnotic dimension. This 11-track electronic dream machine simultaneously soothes and stimulates. In other words, you can dance if you want to, but unlike a lot of techno, this one sounds just as tasty when you're sitting down. Hawtin's sparsely constructed tracks create a stark, trippy vibe, but he never forgets the groove. Blending old-school acid with post-mod ambience, *Sheet One* comes off like the Orb (with some serious balls) meets mid-80's Detroit down-loaded to Warp Records-style tones & bleeps. It's a hallucinogenic trance thing that you'll love to understand. -S.T.S.

WILLIAM S. BURROUGHS
Spare Ass Annie and Other Tales
-Island
Orbitron Rating 8

Special thanks to the pinhead at SPIN who was fortunate enough to get an advance of this just to give it a bad review. Sometimes when someone pans a record, take Chuck Eddy or his journalism school classmate Gary Graff for example, you know you're just gonna love it. Said reviewer complained that the music didn't fit the words. Granted, Einsturzende Neubauten might be a better musical pairing, but something tells me that the nearly 80-year-old former junkie is a little too old to be doing the Teutonic angst-in-my-pants thing. Sure, Material's "Seven Souls" was the perfect match to Burrough's *The Western Lands*, but many of the Disposable Heroes of Hiphoprisy's backing tracks and producer Hal Wilner's soundscapes on *Spare Ass Annie* work very well. Instead of the anonymous, but strangely appropriate backing of the NBC Symphony Orchestra on Burrough's previous release, *Dead City Radio*, *Spare Ass Annie* has a much more concrete urban feel — kind of a cross between MC 900 Foot Jesus and Massive Attack. Uncle Bill fans should also check out the recently reissued *Break Through in Grey Room* (Sub Rosa), which contains vintage Burroughs tape experiments and cut-ups from the '60s and early '70s. It's as challenging and rewarding as anything you'll hear this year. -Doug Coombe

▲ "Sonic Boom," Pearl Jam review, *Orbit*, November 1993.

Sonic Boom
TRACKS & HOT WAX

DJ Top Pix

Munk's Mix (in no particular order): Funky and smooth, groovemaster Munk incorporates both old and new into his mix, which can currently be heard at Lush on Saturday nights.

Recloose *Welcome* (Planet e)

Bill Laswell *Rated X* (Giant Step)

Tito Puente *Take Five* (Concord Jazz)

Baby Buddah Heads *Latin Joint (Remix)* (ZXY)

Grover Washington Jr. *Inner City Blues* (Motown)

Moodymann *Sunday Morning* (Planet e)

James Mason *Sweet Power Your Embrace* (Chiaroscuro)

Shazz *New York City Vibes* (Yello)

Quincy Jones *Superstition* (A&M)

Three For Now *Kwazee* (White Label)

Sylk 130 *Uptown* (Ovum/Columbia)

Sonically Speaking

Shows not to miss... The Make-Up and **Rocket 455** open for **Dead Moon** at Magic Stick on the 7th for an evening of attitudinal garage rock. On the 15th at Magic Stick it's Quarterstick's **June of 44.** R.L. Burnside's guitarist, **Kenny Brown**, finds himself at Fifth Avenue on the 2nd. Locally, **Volcanos** bring the surf wave to Detroit at Magic Stick on the 22nd, and the rave around town is the funky-jazzy **Sugarfoot** at Music Menu each Sunday.

Releases of interest... Dirty, gritty blues man **R.L. Burnside**, with the help of Jon Spencer Blues Explosion, has gained a bit of notoriety amongst young hipsters. Now, to set it in stone, Bong Load Records has issued a remix EP, *Rollin' Tumblin'*, adding just the right amount of bass and drum overdubs to nearly make R.L. a dancefloor hit. **Money Mark**, known for his keyboard contributions to Beastie Boys, releases his new one, *Push The Button*. While his singing cuts could have been spared, instrumentally, he takes it home. Mixmaster **DJ Andy Smith**, normally spinning for the famous trip-hop group Portishead, has ventured out on his own with an engaging blend of the likes of The James Gang, Jungle Brothers, Tom Jones and even Grandmaster Flash on The Document. Dearborn's own Asha Vida releases Nature's Clumsy Hand on Burnt Hair Records, a combination of live, radio and home studio recordings displaying their many instrumental talents weaved together for a sweeping landscape of sound that ultimately leads to euphoria.

The Wildbunch live, with members Dick Valentine on vocals, Martin M. on drums, Surge Joebot and Rock & Roll Indian on guitars, and (not shown) Disco on bass and The Imposter on keys.

Photo by Doug Coombe

Wildbunch: This isn't your father's rock 'n' roll

by Liz Copeland

The Wildbunch are not your typical rock and roll. Not even for Detroit. Transcending music into communication, they're more about irony and parody, with high-voltage rock and roll as its translator. From live performances to their three vinyl-only releases, and one very limited 8-track recording, the Wildbunch challenge the aural and common senses.

First there's the song, "Gay Bar," an intriguing enough title, using the shock of it to pull the observer into a much deeper blackhole, the taunting of the start of a nuclear war. Then there's "The Ballade of MC Sucka DJ." In a city that boasts major-label act Insane Clown Posse, the song turns Detroit rap notions on end, bearing a pseudo-rap chorus, contrasted with a marked accent on crashing guitars and cymbal clutter—not your typical rap song.

Their sound could be attributed to the varying record-collecting habits of its band members. Valentine, weaned on '80s synthesizer pop-sensibility, finds his work augmented by the dirty-ass rock influences provided by the remaining band members, creating a collage that has been aptly described as "Kiss meets Devo."

The live experience carries yet another element of astonishment. Besides the self-confident, outrageous antics of one Dick Valentine, aspiring weatherman, singer and self-proclaimed "dictator" for the group, the sonic assault of their tailored version of "Rio" (yes, the same one by Duran Duran) is enough to leave one ultimately confounded, asking yourself who gave this group license to defy typical notions of rock music?

According to Martin M., drummer and co-founder of the band, "We're the Wildbunch. We can do anything we want. That's the whole point of the band."

Get a glimpse for yourself at The Blind Pig in Ann Arbor on Thursday, May 21.

Sonic Comics

by Tristan Eaton & Ron Wade

In 1989, Milli Vanilli had to return their Grammy Award after revealing that they didn't sing one note.

Last month, Rob Pilatus was found dead of an overdose of pills and vodka.

Knowing their past, how do we know he's not faking?

GIRL, YOU KNOW IT'S BULL$#!9

THERE'S NO VANILLI ON MY LIST!!

MILLI VANILLI

Consumed
Plastikman
Novamute

The latest recorded document by Richie Hawtin, a.k.a. Plastikman, continues to expand the mind and challenge the notions of the direction of electronica. Already showing evidence of greater things to come with 1994's *Musik*, yet not necessarily abandoning his signature style, Plastikman seems to have moved further outside of what's typically associated with Detroit acid-house and has placed himself on the international playing field of electronic sounds in general, bearing a close resemblance to the drugged-up, psychedelic Cabaret Voltaire soundtrack *Johnny YesNo*. The title cut is perhaps the most magnetic, a glorious combination of droning, industrial layerings (the factory, not the genre) and off-kilter beats worked precisely well enough to keep the listener entranced throughout. *Consumed*, with its dark, subdued beats, will rattle your mind to get to your body. —*Zotik*

Because of You
The Preservation Hall Jazz Band
Sony Classical

Every once in awhile, a CD comes along that can take you on a sonic journey that even Carmen Sandiego would envy. This is the case with *Because of You*, a collection of classic love songs by Earl Hines, and Dorothy Fields among others, that have been re-recorded by the Preservation Hall Jazz Band of New Orleans. With every plink of the piano and slide of the trombone, you are transported further down Bourbon Street on some humid night under dim gaslights with the sounds of the Mississippi River and your own humming ringing in your ears. —*Z. Lenn*

Accelerator
Royal Trux
Drag City

Everybody thought it was the end of RTX after their ultra-putrid "Sweet 16" boner last year on Virgin. Now they have crawled back to Drag City, and have given us a broken, evil gem to ponder. While still reminiscent of The Rolling Stones, their lack of drug intake has produced an album more focused than their previous efforts. Heck, this disc is so focused, it sometimes sounds like a broken record. Trux no longer boogie, but they still fall down the steps over and over again, and that makes for a cool 1998 winner. —*Partie*

The Crock Of Gold
Shane MacGowan and The Popes
ZZT Records

Upon first listen, I thought this was one of the biggest pieces of shit that I've ever heard. But then, getting past all the hype that has surrounded Mr. MacGowan from his days with The Pogues, and the general critical *disacclaim* of his solo debut, *The Snake*, I decided to give it a second listen, dropping my expectations by the wayside. What I discovered is that *The Crock Of Gold* is actually more traditional than his previous efforts—it's just a bunch of mates in some pub messin' around and railing against all them that "drink their trendy Irish beers," as it states in "Back In the County Hell." Most songs remind the listener of *Red Roses For Me* more than anything else, though "Skipping Rhymes" is vaguely Pogues-ish. Faves: "St. John of Gods" with its tale of an old man so morally impotent that the only thing he fires back at those who spite him is a chorus of "F'yez all," and "More Pricks Than Kicks," which sounds like a song that Tom Waits would've wrote but never did. All in all, a worthy record. —*Dick Richie*

continued on page 38

▲ "Sonic Boom," The Wildbunch (a.k.a. Electric Six) review, *Orbit*, May 1998.

THE NOW SOUND OF MOTORTOWN

No, this isn't yet another story about how Derrick May, Juan Atkins and Kevin Saunderson are superstars in Europe but virtually ignored at home. Truth be known, they are just as revered on the streets of Detroit and San Francisco as they are in dance clubs in Amsterdam or underground warehouses in Berlin. Everyone from Nine Inch Nails to Madonna to Curve has incorporated the Detroit Sound into their music. So shed no tears for these guys. Along with Eddie Fowlkes, Carl Craig and Terrence Parker, Detroit Techno thrives, and continues to make their imitators look quite foolish.

The Holy Trinity plus Eddie Fowlkes took time out of their globetrotting schedule to grant ORBIT this exclusive round table discussion.

THE GODFATHERS OF TECHNO

JUAN ATKINS, DERRICK MAY, KEVIN SAUNDERSON & EDDIE FOWLKES

IN THE BEGINNING...

DERRICK: Back in the early '70s, The Electrifying Mojo was a very important factor for the outlet of the music. That gave us a goal. Even though it was inspired from other forms of electronic music, techno was a black man's form of electronic music. I think WGPR was the only black FM station. This was like 1979. Juan would take his music down to Mojo's show and play it. Mojo gave us a reason to believe.

ATKINS   MAY   SAUNDERSON   FOWLKES

THE MIDNIGHT FUNK ASSOCIATION

DERRICK: Mojo always liked our stuff. The first time we went down to the station was a trip. We always imagined that Mojo was a big linebacker dude. Anyway, we get to the station and there's this little dude with dreadlocks. This was way before dreads were happening with everybody. He let us in and gave us cigars. He has Bob Marley playing on one radio and he's got something else playing on the other and he's sitting there and listening to this between the right ear and the left ear and we're just watching him like "damn." So we were like blew out. We knew he was deep. So he got the utmost respect from us from then on. That just made us go home and listen to music in a whole different way.

ONE STEP BEYOND

DERRICK: We had a sound company when we were kids called Deep Space, and the idea was to be DJ's and play parties. To play real music for the peo-ple, instead of this fabricated fake partying. That's where the whole Deep Space concept came from; Cybotron records and Deep Space Sound Works and the two of us (Derrick and Juan) doing parties.

DETROIT VS. THE WORLD

KEVIN: Through records like Inner City's "Big Fun," people got a real good look at Detroit, and it opened up a lot of doors for the music. At that point a lot of kids in England and Holland were influenced by what they read in the music magazines. They would read about how Derrick got into it and how Juan started out, and then I came into the picture, and these kids started to go out and make their own music.

THE WORLD LISTENS

KEVIN: We were young guys, we didn't know exactly what we were doing. We didn't realize the impact we were gonna have on the world. I was living in Chicago at the time and I saw what was happening there. And I was trying to tell Juan, "Look, there's something special going on here." Juan didn't really know what I was talking about. But I took the first Model 500 record to Chicago and it just exploded. But to us, we never realized how different it was. We sort of built our own society. Our own little clique. We didn't realize that our clique was cool. We just thought it was us. It was sort of lonely man's music.

DETROIT - TECHNO CITY?

DERRICK: Right now, it's not the greatest city in the world. But one day

➤ Continued on Page 24

it will be. Detroit has a certain standard of quality, a certain amount of excellence that comes through. Once you say you're from Detroit, your shit better be on, because people are expecting it to be on. The art of making music here is far superior to anything that comes from most places. I don't give a shit what anybody says, the party scene here is pretty messed up right now. Black people and white people are still not together in Detroit. That's a big problem. Hopefully, we can help inform people of things other than just music, but address the community as well.

EDDIE: Detroit is progressive. We see new car models on the street and it effects us subconsciously. LA is four hours behind; London is six hours ahead; Germany – they're perfectionists; Amsterdam – they're smokin'. So by us being a nine to five town you don't have anything else to do but make music.

DEEP SPACE RADIO

DERRICK: I think the radio show is a good thing because it will hopefully give people an outlet, something to look forward to. Alan Oldham used to be on the radio years ago on WDET, and his show ("Fast Forward") was very good. I think right now this radio show could be a very good thing. Because what it does in the long run is it inspires. And we need to inspire more people to get involved, to support the music. If we can somehow bring people in and inform people about what is happening, I think this could be a good thing for Detroit.

JUAN: One thing about this radio show is that it's like a worldwide musical explosion. America has no clue. America has totally either ignored it or they're just asleep and haven't woken up yet. So that's what we're trying to do with this radio show. We're going to try and pull it off in Detroit because we pulled everything else off in Detroit and to let people know that the music has progressed, that there is a whole explosion of music and we're going to try to spread it.

DERRICK: The four hours of Deep Space Soundworks is completely public radio. There will be about ten DJs all together. We rotate constantly. We like to keep variety in the show. We like to mix the guys up every week. There's four regulars and two platoons.

GLOBETROTTING AND NIGHTCLUBBING

JUAN: My favorite place to play in is Scotland. La Pier, because of the crowd. It's kind of small, a hole in the wall. Motherf@#kers are partiers.

EDDIE : I like to play in England, generally. I played in Holland recently, the IT. There's a club in Singapore.

KEVIN: Club Pod in Belfast. It's small and they've got a great sound system. They're just now being educated. They're

real open to whatever you're playing. They just don't want to hear one sound. That's always my favorite type of place to play. Where they like a good variety of music.

DERRICK: Amsterdam on Sunday nights. They have hell of a sound system. The best party is hard to say, because I'm thinking of how it used to be. The Music Institute right here in Detroit was my favorite place of all time. I've been all over the world and I've played a lot of places and I'd say the Music Institute tops any place that I've ever played. I don't know my favorite place at the moment, if that's what you want to know.

THE OTHER SIDE

JUAN: The next project is to start a 24 hour all-purpose radio format. Deep Space 24 hours. Hopefully some forward thinking program director would let me program their station. That's the priority.

EDDIE: Make an album with a funky ass black bass line. That's the current project. Not get funky, but stay funky, don't sell out, City Boy records all the way. Straight from the city— that's the program.

KEVIN: I'm working on a new Inner City album, which is almost done. Next I'm going to work on a solo album, a more experimental project for those who dare to believe from those who know. And just be a part of the music thing and do whatever I can to make the radio show work.

DERRICK: Yeah, that sounds cool.

▲ Techno feature: "The Now Sound of Motortown," *Orbit*, July 1994.

Esham, *Orbit*, July 1994. ▶

DETROIT ALWAYS GETS A BAD RAP

SATAN IS NATAS BACKWARDS

You may think of him as a lovable local satanic rapper. But Esham is perhaps the biggest underground rapper in the world. His records sell, his fans are legion and he has never had to play to an empty house at Paycheck's.

Getting Started
I started making records in '88. When I was in high school I met Mastamind he was flowing. His s@#t was dope. We hooked up after high school, and I always knew T, and that's where it came about. After that we made a record and the rest is history.

Detroit Rap
I think everybody has an identity crisis in Detroit. They don't know where they want to go as far as their music. They want to copy the L.A. sound, the New York sound. I think once everybody realized what kind of sound Detroit had that's when Detroit blew up.

Who are we?
I think Detroit does have it's own identity but it just has to come out. It'll happen when people realize that things happens here too and they don't necessarily have to blend in with what's going on across the coasts.

Local Versus National
Understand that you're only local when you let other people stereotype you like that. Our records sell just as good as everybody else's records. We move more units than anybody.

We're doing pretty good, considering that we do it all ourselves. So our s@#t ain't really local, it ain't local at all.

Popularity Contest
The most popular Detroit rap artist? I don't know. There's a lot of them that are popular. Well, I can't say that because there's only so many that are doing something. But I don't want to be the person to categorize that s@#t because there's a lot of people out there trying and that's good enough for me. If you're doing something, that's good as long as you keep your s@#t on.

A Sense of Community
No f@#kin' unity. It ain't s@#t here as far as unity. If you're cool with this person then they're cool with you and that's considered unity, but unity is when somebody gets to go in front of the recording industry or gets a chance to put the focus on Detroit and does it. But maybe that Detroit artist won't do that. He'll just get to where he's going and then say f@#k everybody else that's climbing up. That's why I say there ain't no unity. But then again, the right person hasn't got to that point to put the focus on Detroit.

The Future
We've got a new EP coming out called *Liquid Drano*. We got a new album coming out called *Closed Casket* and that will be out at the end of August. Then we'll be working on a new Natas album. That's what we're doing now and then we're going to L.A., motherf@#kin Tennessee, we're going everywhere.

NOW PLAYING IN DETROIT!

Thanks to the keen insight of our contributors, joined by the questionable motives of an Orbit advertising rep, we proudly present to you a portion of the area's talent. We took a random survey and asked each band, in their own words, to answer a few simple questions. No, this is not comprehensive; your band probably isn't even listed here. In fact, it's probably just a bad idea to begin with. But it's *our* idea, and we're somehow compelled to share it with you on the following pages. Love 'em or hate 'em, these bands are Detroit's, and we must contend with them. —*Editor*

by Colin Webcott, Liz Copeland and Orbit Staff

American Mars

The Articles

Bantam Rooster

American Mars

Members: Thomas Trimble – vision; Gary Watts – sound

Most Recent Release: *Late* CD (self-released)

Date Formed: 1995

Approach to Making Music: Modernist

Motto: "More Flower, Less Power"

Mascot: Talk Talk's *Spirit of Eden*

Most Surprising Live Performance Attendee: Dave Feeny

Communal Living or Separate Housing? Separate housing

The Articles

Members: Derek Phelps – trumpet, spiritual guidance; Dan Margulis – drums, fashion

risks; Mike Rehfus – alto sax, crowd control; Jim Hohner – double bass, groove enforcement; Jeff Cantwell – trombone, boyish charm

Most Recent Release: *Flip Freal* CD (Moon Ska NYC)

Date Formed: October 1995

Approach to Making Music: From behind, on tip toes, with an inflated paper sack.

Motto: "No, I'm Sorry. You Must Be Trying to Reach The Atomic Fireballs. No Problem. I Have Bunkley's Number Right Here. Got a Pen?"

Mascot: Jeff Postema

Most Surprising Live Performance Attendee: Tie: M. Doughty (the blond guy from Soul Coughing) and Dave Wakeling (the blond guy from English Beat)

Communal Living or Separate Housing? Before touring, semi-communal. After touring, separate area codes.

Bantam Rooster

Members: Mike Alonso – drums; T. Jackson Potter – guitar, vocals

Most Recent Release: *Deal Me In* LP/CD; coming in January 1999, *The Cross and the Switchblade* LP/CD

Date Formed: Like I could remember...

Approach to Making Music: We like to think of our instruments

as pallets, and music as our colors. Fuck that. We just approach and lay it on the line.

Motto: "We Can Kill a Brick or Drown a Drop of Water"

Mascot: Our Legal Council / Manager, Chris "Spanky" Fuller

Most Surprising Live Performance Attendee: Hell, it's surprising enough when *we're* sober enough to attend!

Communal Living or Separate Housing? Tom has been "in between" cribs for the last two months. So if crashing on Mike's couch once or twice a week counts as

Black Beauty — Sugarfoot

Caelum Bliss

communal, so be it.

Black Beauty

Members: George Friend – vocals, guitar; Jim Simonson – upright and slab bass; Alex Trajano – drums. From time to time, Todd Glass – drums; Tim Allen – steel; Chris Codish – organ; Thornetta Davis – vocals; Robert Gordon – vocals

Date Formed: January 1998

Approach to Making Music: We try to update old blues-derived material (such as country, rockabilly, R&B, and rock 'n' roll). You know, like the Stones did!!

Motto: "It Don't Mean a Thing if it Ain't Got that Swing!"

Mascot: George's Les Paul "Black Beauty"

Most Surprising Live Performance Attendee: Pistol Pete. He stood in the doorway of the Music Menu for 1 1/2 songs.

Communal Living or Separate Housing? We're all married, or almost. Separate.

Caelum Bliss

Members: Melissa – vocals, words, PR; Kurt – lead guitar, fx, words, music; Bill – drums, DAT; Tony – rhythm guitar, fx, music; Marv – the bass/fuzz; Caroline – b. vocals, keys, practice pad

Most Recent Release: *Death Girl*

Dragon Tears Descending

Destroy All Monsters

Demolition Doll Rods

Rod – rock asses off at all times

Most Recent Release: *Tasty* CD/LP (In the Red)

Date Formed: Fall 1993

Approach to Making Music: Just do it

Motto: "Shake Your Ass," "Founded on Love," "God Bless" and "Rock On"

Mascot: Girl Kitty and Girl Bunny

Most Surprising Live Performance Attendee: Traci Lords, Alan Vega and Daryl Hannah

Communal Living or Separate Housing? Live together like the Monkees

Destroy All Monsters

Members: Mike Kelley – percussion, vocals, samples, squeeze toys, electronic gizmos; Jim Shaw – samples, vocals, violin, treated guitar; Cary Loren – guitar, samples, vocals; Art Byington – guitar, samples; David Muller – bass, Moog

Most Recent Release: *Backyard Monster Tube* and *PIG* on CD (The End is Here!) 1998

Date Formed: 1974

Approach to Making Music: Exploit the audience for talent

Motto: 1. "Show No Shame"; 2. "Have No Fear"; 3. "Shake a Lizard Tail"

Mascot: 1. Baby Godzilla; 2. Sock Monkey; 3. Birds of Detroit

Most Surprising Live Performance Attendee: The Brain Police, the Boredoms, Harmony Korine, Timothy Leary and Ann Magnuson (all at one performance)

Communal Living or Separate Housing? Separate States

Dragon Tears Descending

Members: Calvin P. Simmons (Dragon) – lyrics, keyboards, vocals, drum programming,

Demo CD (Atlantic)

Date Formed: March 1993

Approach to Making Music: We lock ourselves in our rooms and don't come out until we have the hits.

Motto: "Live Life and Try Not to Fuck Up"

Mascot: Roscoe, Athena and Abbey

Most Surprising Live Performance Attendee: Dennis White

Communal Living or Separate Housing? A little of both

Demolition Doll Rods

Members: Danny Doll Rod, Christine R and Margaret Doll

"Now Playing in Detroit," band profiles, *Orbit*, November 1998. ▲ ▶

mixing, PR work; Patrick Hogan (Solice 7) – keyboards, guitar, bass, drum programming, mixing; Michael Schinke – guitar, vocals, graphic design; James Roussin – bass, mixing, editing; Heather Griswold – vocals, viola

Most Recent Release: *Edem* EP (Solice Records)

Date Formed: Original lineup formed December 1, 1992. Current lineup formed November of 1997

Approach to Making Music: Improvisational jamming, which is then carefully orchestrated and arranged into a rich, goth-infused, musical story.

Motto: "Never Forget Where You Came From" and "In for a Penny, In for a Pound"

Mascot: Nindoke, Maxwell and Morgan (cats)

Most Surprising Live Performance Attendee: Jennifer Jeffery

Communal Living or Separate Housing? Separate housing

ebeling hughes

Members: Charles Hughes – singing, pianos, organs, special treatments; Robert Ebeling – drums and love and special treatments

Most Recent Release: *Transfigured Night* CD (Zero Hour)

Date Formed: July 28, 1993

Approach to Making Music: From behind and with caution. Oh, and be sure to have plenty of 1.6 AMP fuses around for the monitors.

Motto: "Charlos and Roberto, Like Spicy Hot Peppers"

Mascot: A small, copper penny flute with a plastic tip in the key of F#, which keeps me company, calms the fidgets and requires no electricity or insurance or a flight case. It fits in my back pocket, is great for checking room acoustics, and could lullaby a baby to sleep or scare off a mugger.

Most Surprising Live Performance Attendee: The little sweetheart by the name of Kelly that Chuck had a crush on years ago and saw at the Tap Room show. She'll know who she is, and it's none of the rest of your's business what her precious little last name is. So naaaah.

Communal Living or Separate Housing? Mostly separate, but we'll camp out if need be.

Fathers of the Id

Members: Sean Ike – guitar, vox; Marko Smith – drums; Gustav Hoffman – bass, background vox

Most Recent Release: *Liberation By Hearing (on the After-Death Plane)* CD (Snatch Back Music)

Date Formed: Summer 1992

Approach to Making Music: Open up and step aside

Motto: "Let's Have a Cup of Tea!"

Mascot: The Unified Field

Most Surprising Live Performance Attendee: Kurtis Blow jammed with us

Communal Living or Separate Housing? Separate, after communal for seven years

FEZ

Members: Dean Olkowski – guitar, banjo, pump organ; Melinda Clynes – theremin, pump organ, glockenspiel, electric organ; Jim Morningstar – drums, hub cap, pan lids

Most Recent Release: *Elixir* CD (self-released)

Date Formed: 5/6/96

Approach to Making Music:
1 shotgun wedding
1 divorce
3 IOUsonofabitch
2 tsp. turpentine
1 cup Metamucil
2 wigs (greasy)
1 soiled love letter
Bake in greased bedpan for one hour.

Motto: "Ya Can't Take the Sting Out of the Hot Pants"

Mascot: Our Crippled St. Giles

Most Surprising Live Performance Attendee: Anthony Kiedis from

FEZ

Fathers of the Id

ebeling hughes

---

the Red Hot Chili Peppers.

Communal Living or Separate Housing? We all live in a beautiful trailer—but it's a double-wide.

Fortune & Maltese

Members: Freddy Fortune – vocals; Michael Maltese – vocals, bass, organ; Nat Cromlech – vocals, guitar; Karl Cromlech – organ; Dusty Sexton – drums; all members pitch in for recording and engineering duties

Most Recent Release: *Fortune & Maltese* CD (Get Hip Records)

Date Formed: Fall 1993

Approach to Making Music: Take one…take two…take three…THAT'S IT!!

Motto: "I Hate to Say It, But You're Wasting Time!"

Mascot: General Giggles & CLANKY the Syrup Robot

Most Surprising Live Performance Attendee: (In NYC) Ladies and gentlemen…Mr. Johnny Ramone!

Communal Living or Separate Housing? Separate during week, communal on weekends; cars in the day, houses in the evening.

Galicja

(pronounced 'ga-lee-see-uh')

Members: Eric McLand – drums; Megan Morrill – violoncello, accordion; Aaron Warshaw – guitar, vocals; Teri Williams – bass, occasional b. vocals

Most Recent Release: *Blocking Your View* 10" (Spectator Records), with a full-length album planned for Winter 1999

Date Formed: Summer 1997

Approach to Making Music: At their best, songs are certain feelings or emotions that, however stupid they may seem, deserve to be expressed honestly.

Motto: "The Ideal Thing for a Band is to Stay Unknown and Let Everybody Discover Them Years Later"

Mascot: Ché, the adorable black-and-white Havanese dog, currently residing in Toronto, Ontario, Canada.

Most Surprising Live Performance Attendee: An unknown late-night DJ

Communal Living or Separate Housing? Separate

The Go

Members: Bobby Harlowe – vocals; Johnny Krautner – guitar, vocals; Dave Buick – bass; Marc Fellis – drums; Jack White – red guitar, vocals

Most Recent Release: upcoming 45 RPM releases on Flying

Fortune & Maltese

Galicja

The Go

Godzuki

Bomb and Italy Records

Date Formed: Free-form improvisation

Approach to Making Music: On horses with diamond studded saddles

Motto: "Sex and Danger are our Various Breads and Various Butters"

Mascot: The Go-Nad

Most Surprising Live Performance Attendee: Ike Turner, slappin' us around

Communal Living or Separate Housing? Yes, please.

Godzuki

Members: Erika Hoffmann – nature; Dion Fischer – science; Scott Michalski – heart; Chris Fachini – love

Most Recent Release: >>*Your Future* CD/LP (March Records)

Date Formed: 1899–1999

Approach to Making Music: Broken Science / Nature Channel + Friendly Dance Beat = Sound of Your Future & Mine

Motto: "We Want You to Live 100 Years"

Mascot: Electric Bear

Most Surprising Live Performance Attendee: We're scientists. Nothing surprises us.

Communal Living or Separate Housing? We are a whole thing. We are a working model of the new paleo-cybernetic culture in action. There is no separation. We live together to work together, we eat together, fuck

---

together, get high together, walk down the street and through the world together. There is no separation.

The Hellbenders

Members: Arch Stanton – guitarist, singer, songwriter, storyteller, late night campfire song leader; Leo Marsh – guitarist, cook, barber; Billy Bones – skins, medicine man, rodeo clown; Jeth Rowe – bass guitarra, horse trainer, poker face

Most Recent Release: *Have a Good Funeral My Friend 7"* (Phonograph), with a full-length coming in early spring

Date Formed: Sometime in the late '80s as a pass-time when not rope-ing & rounding-up etc.

Approach to Making Music: Make music that is beautiful and at the same time rough-edged and obviously made by hand.

Motto: "Never Let Another Gringo Steal your Hat, Guitar, Gun, Horse or Girl"

Mascot: Coyote

Most Surprising Live Performance Attendee: The Ghost of Gabby Hayes

Communal Living or Separate Housing? Communal living is too dangerous. Arch & Leo lived on the same ranch & darn near killed each other. Now we all live an hour's ride apart.

The Hentchmen

Members: John – tickles the ivories (plastic); Mike – fondles the sticks; Tim – strokes the strings

Most Recent Release: *Motorvatin'* LP/CD (Norton Records) and Hentch fourth mini-LP (Italy Records)

Date Formed: October 31, 1992

Approach to Making Music: Ford Van

Motto: "Quality is Job 1"

Mascot: Ford Van

Most Surprising Live Performance Attendee: Mike Pitt (Brad's brother)

Communal Living or Separate Housing? Ford Van

His Name Is Alive

Members: Current and past members include Warren Defever, Karin Oliver, Trey Many, Chad Gilchrist, Scott Goldstein, Lovetta Pippen, Erika Hoffmann, Matt Smith, Jim Auge, Melissa Elliott, Denise James, Damian Lang, Scott MacKenzie, Ian Masters, Angie Carozzo, Deb Agolli and Dion Fischer

Most Recent Release: *Fort Lake* CD/LP (4AD)

Date Formed: Over ten years ago

Approach to Making Music: Our records are always a little bit faster.

Motto: "Michigan's Finest"

Mascot: Clouds

Most Surprising Live Performance Attendee:

Communal Living or Separate Housing? Why can't we all live together?

Howling Diablos

Members: Jerome Day – drums; A.J. – percussion; MO Hollis – bass; Jeff Grand – guitar, pharmacy; Johnny Evans – sax; Tino – vocals

Most Recent Release: *Green Bottle* CD (Overture)

Date Formed: Early '90s

Approach to Making Music: The Diablos' approach is simple, yet scientific. We start by kicking it live, get a groove goin on that touches people and makes the cop cars roll. We like to mix it all up. It's never the

The Hellbenders

The Hentchmen

His Name Is Alive

Howling Diablos

NOW PLAYING IN DETROIT!

same twice.

Motto: "I Wanna Be your Funky Daddy!"

Mascot: Fast Eddie (the Dance-master)

Most Surprising Live Performance Attendee: The Flying Wallendas

Communal Living or Separate Housing? Separate cribs because we're always hanging out together.

Immigrant Suns

Members: Djeto Juncaj – guitar, cello, qyteli, accordion, banjo; Ben Temkow – violin, accordion, mbira, pennywhistle, vocal; Doug Shimmin – ukulele, bouzouki, mandolin, guitar, percussion, strumstick, accordion, vocals; Joel Peterson – double bass, clarinet, cello, tenor sax, percussion, qyteli; Mark Sawasky – percussion, trap kit

Most Recent Release: *More Than Food* CD (Pho-Net-Ic Records)

Date Formed:

Approach to Making Music: Our songwriting is democratic; one member may introduce an idea or a complete song, or the ideas may come from group improvisation. We also try to promote a new repertoire of music made by people we know who deserve attention.

Motto: "Does Anyone Want the Last Piece?"

Mascot: Aunt Betty and Uncle Sweaty

Most Surprising Live Performance Attendee: We were playing Mac's Bar in Lansing, and John Engler walked in. He was out celebrating his cousin's birthday, and they were looking to quaff a few beers. They stayed for one.

Communal Living or Separate Housing? Our living is semi-communal. We've taken-up residence at our studio in downtown at one point or another. Ben was married this summer, so we only have a couple of members that actually live together, but we all spend more time there than home.

Insane Clown Posse

Members: Shaggy 2 Dope and Violent J

Most Recent Release: *The Great Milenko* CD (Island)

Date Formed: 1600s

Approach to Making Music: Before Mike E. Clark makes the beat, he likes to get naked and paint his body with monkey blood and berry juice. Then, he puts on his llama-skin slippers and dances about the studio sprinkling voodoo crystals and chanting the Brady Bunch theme backwards. After about two hours of this, he showers, gets dressed and gets funky. Before we cut our vocals, we like to sneak behind the rhinos in their den at the Detroit Zoo, flick them in the nuts and run. This gets our blood pumping, and we get hype. What better time to cut vocals? One time a rhino chased us all the way back to the studio, but Mike shooed it away with a broom.

Motto: "Death Only Comes Once in a Lifetime – Don't Miss Your Chance!"

Mascot: Our dead friend Tony. He died two years ago, but we never reported it. We still got him. He just lays around the studio dead. Mike's cats really like him.

Most Surprising Live Performance Attendee: Leif Garrett

Communal Living or Separate Housing? Separate mansions

Larval

Members: Mike Smith – violin; Toby Summerfield – guitar; Genevieve Badgett – cello; Josh Tillingast – bass; Marko Smith – drums; Matt Bauder –

Larval

Maschina

Medusa Cyclone

Saxophone; Bill Brovold – janitor

Most Recent Release: *Larval 2* CD (Knitting Factory)

Date Formed: Still forming

Approach to Making Music: Anything worth doing is worth over-doing

Motto: "The Loudest Band Wins"

Mascot: Chris Girard

Most Surprising Live Performance Attendee: Jerry Peterson (well, he didn't actually show up)

Communal Living or Separate Housing? Homeless

Maschina

Members: Seth "Queen Mas-chine" Hitsky – vocals; Mark "Bubbles" Kirschenmann – electric trumpet; John "Fifi" Maloney – percussion; Alana "Lady Anala" Rocklin – bass

Most Recent Release: *Purple Finger Syndrome* CD (self-released)

Date Formed: 10/96

Approach to Making Music: Arbitrary and unfocused

Motto: "Whipple"

Mascot: Purple boas and purple fingrrrrs

Most Surprising Live Performance Attendee: Froh

Communal Living or Separate Housing? Ardently communal

Medusa Cyclone

Members: Hmmmmmm. Well there's me, Keir. I play guitar, synths, and drums on the records. Sometimes I sing, but I'm not very good at it, as I tend to sound like I just woke up. Sometimes Jeff Oakes sings, but we have to bribe him with Classic Coke. John Nash, Mike Alonso and Chris Girard have also been part of the mix and well might continue at some point, time will tell. And lastly, there is/was Colin McDonald, who was gearing himself up to play on an upcoming LP (as drummer), but who passed on much too young and will be greatly missed.

Most Recent Release: *Mr. Devil* CD (Third Gear)

Date Formed: The first single came out in 1992 on the Manta Ray Fleet Label.

Approach to Making Music: I turn on The Practical Sportsman and count how many geese they kill and start writing, or sometimes I wonder: Will this get played on that late show on WDET? That sometimes works.

Motto: "We Are the Robots"

Mascot: A 4 ft. blue plastic alien doll my brother, Colin, bought at this year's Michigan State Fair.

Most Surprising Live Performance Attendee: El Santo sat in on Moog once.

Communal Living or Separate

Housing? We are all on work-release programs and wear tethers, so I really don't understand this question.

Morsel

Members: Miriam Cabrera – vocals, flute; Be Hussey – bass, grunt; Fat'hed – didjeri-doo, electronics; Jason Burbo – guitar; Chad Pratt – most recent drummer in an ever-spinning drummer carousel

Most Recent Release: *I'm a Wreck* CD 1998 (Small Stone); *Wrecked & Remixed* CD (Small Stone), to be released January 1999 featuring remixes and reworkings and other assorted fun

Date Formed: Morsel I formed in 11/91. Today, we are looking forward to Morsel VI.

Approach to Making Music: Build it from the bottom, and keep building it up until it falls down. Then we back up a step and play it.

Motto: "Pure Seth" (also known as "seth rock"). Somewhat derived from a St. Louis math rock weekend, this popular Morsel phrase seems to simultaneously describe and confuse the situation.

Mascot: As the dictionary

defines it, "a person, animal or object believed to bring good luck." In our case it is a person, John Rastafari. He has been our biggest supporter since day one, always on top of it. Thanks John.

Most Surprising Live Performance Attendee: Mike Watt was at our show in Long Beach a couple years ago. We were playing with his pal Greg Ginn. We don't think he liked Be's bass playing.

Communal Living or Separate Housing? Separate housing without a doubt. After living together for a few years and practicing in the basement, and watching bills and rent and money issues creep into our relationships, we have opted *never* to live with another bandmate again! The commune days are over for this crew.

Outrageous Cherry

Members: Deb Agolli – drums; Chad Gilchrist – bass; Larry Ray – lead guitar; Matthew Smith – vocals, guitar

Most Recent Release: *Nothing's Gonna Cheer You Up* CD (Third Gear) and *X-Rays in the Cloudmine* EP CD (Mind Expansion)

Date Formed: During indie rock heyday of 1992

Approach to Making Music: Not afraid of turning up the reverb

Motto: "Try Not to Think About It"

Mascot: Velvet painting of large dog

Most Surprising Live Performance Attendee: Jeff Oakes

Communal Living or Separate Housing? Separate housing

Perplexa

Members: Jonathan Wald – drums, percussion, soul; Schurgin – strings and wires, voice; Jenny Schmid – bass girl, traveling artist; John Howard – bass boy; Monty – electrons and sugary cups; Ephriam – sounds

Most Recent Release: *The Glorious Forward* EP CD (Small-stone Records) 1998, with a new full-length CD March of 1999

Date Formed: Idea spawned in Winter of 1993/Became Perplexa as we know it in the Summer of 1995

Approach to Making Music: To instill mystique and wonderment and hopefully provide a catalyst for expansion

Motto: "Where Has All the Mystery Gone?"

Mascot: The Rare and Elusive Goom

Most Surprising Live Performance

Insane Clown Posse

Immigrant Suns

Perplexa

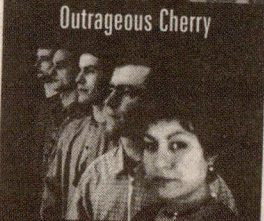
Outrageous Cherry

Morsel

"Now Playing in Detroit," band profiles, *Orbit*, November 1998. ▲ ▶

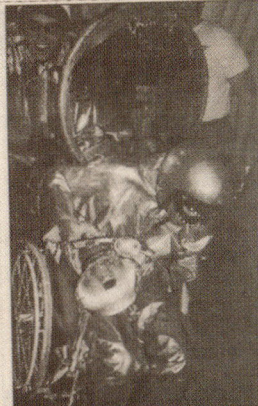

Princess Dragon-Mom

Queen Bee

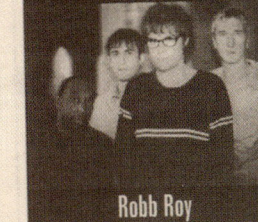

Robb Roy

---

ten 7" (Alternative Tentacles), due out this November. Also, *It's Alive* CD (Old Skool Records) out soon

Date Formed: February 1998

Approach to Making Music: We make *Bee*autiful music together.

Motto: Buzz – "We're Queen Bee and You're Not!"; Death Nectar – "Have Stinger, Will Travel"; Honey Suckle – "Bee-Shirts! Ten Bucks!"

Mascot: Not the Honey-Nut Cheerios Bee, 'cuz he's a pussy!

Most Surprising Live Performance Attendee: The Honey-Nut Cheerios Bee, 'cuz he's a pussy!

Communal Living or Separate Housing? Both. It feels good.

Robb Roy

Members: Graham Strachan – vocals; Michael Kudreiko – guitars; John Cuttos – bass; Duane Huff – drums

Most Recent Release: *Heroes and Cocktails* CD (Caos Music/U.K.), out January 1999

Date Formed: Re-formed in 1994

Approach to Making Music: Throw it up against the wall and see what sticks.

Motto: The Lord's shortest prayer, "F**k 'em."

Mascot: Angus McFearsom

Most Surprising Live Performance Attendee: Liam Gallagher

Communal Living or Separate Housing? Separate basements.

Rocket 455

Members: Jeff Meier – kazoo; Marco Delicato – comb/wax paper; Mark Walz – sliding whistle; Ken Tudrick – pot and pan; Steve Nawara – jug

Most Recent Release: *X-MAS Special Package Volume 2* 3-Song 7", featuring Rocket 455, the White Stripes, and the Blowtops (Flying Bomb Records)

Date Formed: Fall 1992

Approach to Making Music: Get Drunk, Play Loud, Repeat.

Motto: "Anytime You Deal with Rocket 455, You're Setting Yourself Up to be Fucked Over" [ed: yikes!]

Mascot: Fruit Pie the Magician

Most Surprising Live Performance Attendee: Boy Howdy

Communal Living or Separate Housing? Separate Housing. Partner swapping and the commune died in '93 with the hepatitis outbreak.

Scavenger Quartet

Members: Frank Pahl – automatic instruments, banjo, uke, farfisa, etc.; Ben, Joel and Doug from Immigrant Suns or

---

whomever I can scavenge other groups – toys, percussion, scavenged noisemakers, etc.; all member duties – making Frank smile

Most Recent Release: Frank Pahl's *Remove the Cork* CD (Demosaurus Records)

Date Formed: ongoing…

Approach to Making Music:

step 1: turn off the radio

step 2: collect antique, strange or broken instruments, motors & toys

step 3: reconfigure

step 4: don't let the left hand know what the right hand is doing

step 5: take off shoes, turn off lights

step 6: play, edit, smile

step 7: disregard steps when appropriate

Motto: "Convictions are for Convicts"

Mascot: Reddy Kilowatt

Most Surprising Live Performance Attendee: The band (namedropping is ugly)

Communal Living or Separate Housing? Both

60 Second Crush

The Silencers

Scavenger Quartet

Rocket 455

The Silencers

Members: Eric "Nate" Faas – drums, Dave Leeds – bass, Eric Toth – guitar

Most Recent Release: *Powered by Twang* CD (Bomp/Total Energy), and *The Souped Up–Go!!! Sound of: the Silencers 7" EP* (Bomp/Total Energy), out this spring

Date Formed: November 2, 1994, 8:15 PM

Approach to Making Music: Anything with fuzzy or raw twangy guitars is alright with us; a mixture of '60s biker-movie soundtracks, California surf, and Las Vegas grind trash.

Motto:

Mascot: Sigfried the Go-Go Cabbage

Most Surprising Live Performance Attendee: Johnny Winter stuck his head in the door once, but couldn't stay long. Some guys from Germany flew in to see the Silencers at our show at CBGB's in NYC, but they wanted to see a different band called the Silencers, so they left.

Communal Living or Separate Housing? Communal living, but not with each other.

60 Second Crush

Members: Brian "Super B" Smith – skin beater (drums); Jake "Big Daddy" Smith – lead guitar; Peder "Sex Machine" Seglund – rhythm guitar; Dana "Kinky Spice" Forrester – bass (with a capital B); Tom "Tommy Techno" Harman – vox

Most Recent Release: *Love For a Minute* CD (Aural Pleasure) September 1998

Date Formed: November 1997. It was a cold day in Ferndale…

Motto: We have two: 1) "Put Some Cheese on that Bitch!" It's not a sexist reference but a cheeseball expression to spice it up!, and 2) "Big Daddy's Gonna Put some Cream in Your Coffee!"

Mascot: Super B (our furry wild man drummer. He's like Wolverine from the X-Men)!

Most Surprising Live Performance Attendee: Marky Ramone's Hair Piece (we opened for him in Flint).

Communal Living or Separate Housing? Separate Housing, but Peder and Dana live on the same street!

Soul Clique

Members: Papa Joe Hayden – multi-instrumentalist and feeding the boys when they haven't eaten; The Blackman – beats, tables and to pledge the Booty;

NOW PLAYING IN DETROIT!

Duminie – guitar, subliminals, soul wrangler

Most Recent Release: *Only One Division* CD (Small Stone Records)

Date Formed: February 21, 1965

Approach to Making Music: Soberly and with reverence

Motto: "Wash your Ass, Vae Victus"

Mascot: Jerry Vile

Most Surprising Live Performance Attendee: Jerry Vile

Communal Living or Separate Housing? Communal living: Harbor Light

spyradio

Members: Dave Schroeder – guitar, bass, vox; Jon Moshier – drums, percussion; Don Button – bass, guitar, vox; Omar Hamza – alto/tenor sax (his last show will be 10/30 @ Alvin's; he's moving to CA); John Marshall – trumpet

Most Recent Release: *spyradio* CD (Flunk Company) Spring 1998

Date Formed: 1996

Approach to Making Music: It's definitely a group process. Sometimes it comes out of improv jamming in the loft and then gets ordered over a few rehearsals, or Don or Dave have the basic structure of a song, and we all warp and mold it into something that works for the band from the start to the end. I think that's the way any band that doesn't have a principal songwriter works. We tend to be less concerned about lyrics and hooks and attempting *anything* specific, and more concerned about how a piece feels or grooves and how fun it is to play.

Motto: "Motto? We Don't Need No Stinking Motto…"

Mascot: Don Button

Most Surprising Live Performance Attendee: Somebody named I.P. Freely once signed our mailing list.

Communal Living or Separate Housing? If we all lived together the band would've broken up long ago. Dave lives in the Wayne State Campus area, Jon lives over by Indian Village, Omar lives in Dearborn and Don and John both live in Royal Oak. We share a downtown rehearsal loft with the Immigrant Suns.

StunGun

Members: Danielle – vocals; Joell – guitar; Justine – keys; Tania – bass; Kelly – drums

Most Recent Release: *StunGun Live at the Gold Dollar* CD (Off Woodward Productions)

Date Formed: November 1997

Approach to Making Music: We do whatever we feel, but the key is simplicity…K.I.S.S.

Motto: "The Sparklier the Better!"

Mascot: Suzi Sparkle StunGun (the girl on the logo)

Most Surprising Live Performance Attendee: Ourselves. We're actually working on being more punctual.

Communal Living or Separate Housing? Separate housing

Sugarfoot

Members: George Friend – guitar; Chris Codish – organ; Keith Kaminski – tenor and soprano sax; Michael Graye – alto sax; Dwight Adams – trumpet; Jim Simonson – bass; Dave Taylor – drums

Most Recent Release:

Date Formed: February 1998

StunGun

spyradio

Soul Clique

Thee Lucky Stiffs

2 Star Tabernacle

TwitcH

Approach to Making Music: We kick it old school!! Lots of '60s and '70s soul/jazz, boogaloo, funk inspired dance grooves with improvisation.

Motto: "Shiiiit!"

Mascot: Pam Grier (who else??)

Most Surprising Live Performance Attendee: 1,000 dancing people at Montreux Detroit Jazz Festival

Communal Living or Separate Housing? We don't take the '60s to the extreme!! Separate.

Thee Lucky Stiffs

Members: Chuck Burns – drums; Ben Mancell – guitar, vocals; Ron Sakowski – bass, vocals; John Speck – guitar vocals

Most Recent Release: N/A

Date Formed: January 1998. Following the end of Hoarse, Chuck and John get together to jam in Chuck's basement. Chuck hears the songs, calls his buddy Ron, he likes 'em as well, the Stiffs are born. After two shows in 10 months, the Stiffs add Ben on guitar. Chuck still plays with Speedball, Ron is in Easy Action and formerly of the Necros and Laughing Hyenas, Ben comes from Pist-N-Broke and the Alchonauts, and John used to be in Hoarse and the Alchonauts.

Approach to Making Music: John writes the song, goes to practice, everybody gets their groove on, and suggestions may be made. Vocals are applied, bash it out a few more times for good measure. See, all that in 30 minutes or less! It's punk rock blues, not fucking rocket science.

Motto: "Go F**k Yourself"

Mascot: Bob Marley

Most Surprising Live Performance Attendee: Jennifer Bussiere

Communal Living or Separate Housing? All of us live far enough from each other so as to feel safe, yet close enough to walk over (drunk).

Trash Brats

Members: Brian O'Blivion; Ricky Rat; Toni Romeo; Craig Cashew

Date Formed: formed in summer of 1987

Approach to Making Music: Drunk and confused.

Motto: "Step Right Up And Win Some Crap"

Mascot: The WHOA-MAN

Most Surprising Live Performance Attendee: Cranford Nix

Communal Living or Separate Housing? A little of both…although we tried all of us together for awhile…but noone would take the garbage out.

The Twistin' Tarantulas

Members: Pistol Pete Midtgard – upright bass and lead vocals; Johnny Rebel – all guitars and lead vocals; Brad Bond – drums

Most Recent Release: *Attack of the Twistin' Tarantulas* CD (self-released) November 1996, with a new CD in the works

Date Formed: December 1994

Approach to Making Music: Never mind the smoke and mirrors, just get in there and do it.

Motto: "Oh Yeah?! Swing *This!*"

Mascot: A brick of dill Havarti cheese on the dashboard of the tour van. Apparently, this has become something of a TT tour tradition – i.e. the brick of cheese stays untouched (and unrefrigerated!) for the length of the tour. In this case, six weeks! Of course, so do the guys and all their laundry. At this point we're not sure which smells worse!

Most Surprising Live Performance Attendee: The Stanley Cup!

Communal Living or Separate Housing? Definitely Separate Housing! "The band that stays together, lives apart!"

TwitcH

Members: Rob – guitars, vocals and logistics; Scott – drums, vocals and angst; Tim – bass, horns, vocals and propaganda

Most Recent Release: *At Last* CD (Static Records)

Date Formed: Easter 1990

Approach to Making Music: We apply Chaos Theory and Heisenberg's Uncertainty Principle

Motto: "Weirdos are your Best Entertainment Value"

Mascot: Three-toed Sloth

Most Surprising Live Performance Attendee: Lately, any live performance attendee is a surprise

Communal Living or Separate Housing? Due to conditions of our parole agreement, TwitcH must maintain separate living arrangements.

2 Star Tabernacle

Members: T. Racee Mae Miller – bass; D. Buell Miller – vocal, guitar; Damian Lang – drums; Jack White – vocal, guitar

Most Recent Release: *Ramblin' Man 7"* (Bloodshot Records), recorded with Andre Williams

Date Formed: January 1, 1997

Approach to Making Music: Consistent failure of equipment to achieve just the right awkward silence at performances

Motto: "Negative Attitudes Yield Negative Results. Positive Attitudes Yield Negative Results"

Mascot: Ben Blackwell

Most Surprising Live Performance Attendee: Burl Ives in a blue limo

The Unfriendlys

Members: Jasper Unfriendly – lead vocals, guitar, songwriting; Inhospitable J – bass, backup vocals; Scott Unfriendly – drums

Most Recent Release: *Act I* Promotional Cassette

Date Formed: Late in 1997. First gig played in January 1998.

Approach to Making Music: We like to add the element of comic book fiction to our lyrics to appeal to those with a wild imagination. Musically, we try to stay true to the tradition of old-style punk/rock 'n' roll.

Motto: "RN'R MF'R (Rock N Roll Mutherf**ker)"

Mascot: Sarah Michelle Gellar as Buffy the Vampire Slayer

Most Surprising Live Performance Attendee: Tony Romeo of the Trash Brats and Jimmy Doom at a Paycheck's show.

Communal Living or Separate Housing? Separate housing

Velour100

Members: Trey Many – guitar, organ, etc.; Jeremy Dybash – drums & percussion; Roseanne Thomas – vocals, piano

Most Recent Release: *Of Color Bright* CD & LP (Tooth&Nail) 1997

Date Formed: Trey started recording with our first singer in early 1996, and we played our first show in February of

The Unfriendlys

Trash Brats

The Twistin' Tarantulas

"Now Playing in Detroit," band profiles, *Orbit*, November 1998. ▲ ▶

Velour100

The Volcanos

Volebeats

Walk on Water

could whistle. Don't waste anybody's time.

Motto: "Don't Surf Alone"

Mascot: Pet Shark

Most Surprising Live Performance Attendee: Lots of people from other bands, most of whom are not famous like us. Famous people generally hide cuz they know we'll ask for an autograph.

Communal Living or Separate Housing? No communes! We're saving that for when we quit making surf records and go into the folk/psychedelic phase of the Volcanos. It'll be beautiful man!

Volebeats

Members: Jeff Oakes – lead vocals; Matthew Smith – guitar, vocals; Russell Ledford – bass; Scott Michalski – drums; John Nash – guitar

Most Recent Release: *Sky and the Ocean* CD (Safe House) and *Maggot Brain 7"* (Bloodshot/Third Gear)

Date Formed: During the long, dreary Summer of 1987.

Approach to Making Music: Ruthlessly critical of each other's lyrics and other ideas, very attracted to certain sounds and instruments, paranoid/obsessive in the studio, afraid of one-dimensional categorization and other realities of today's music scene.

Motto: "Ain't No Joke"

Mascot: Plywood cut-out cactus and sundown (in cluttered rehearsal space)

Most Surprising Live Performance Attendee: Linda Evangelista/Kyle MacLachlan

Communal Living or Separate Housing? Communal living, only when on tour (two double-beds and one cot).

that year. Since then, we have worked with various singers, guitar players and drummers before settling on our current line-up.

Approach to Making Music: Hmmm… Find new tuning…4-track cut & paste…Rehearse with full band…Rework… Record & mix final… The end.

Motto: "I Have to Go Back to My Home Planet"

Mascot: Rainer Wolfcastle

Most Surprising Live Performance Attendee: Anyone other than our Significant Others

Communal Living or Separate Housing? Separate housing

The Volcanos

Members: Rick Mills – Fender guitar, main songwriter, occasionally sings; Chris Flanagan – Mosrite guitar, sometimes sings a line or two; Bill Bowen – plays drums, makes faces at people; Dave Fragale – Fender bass, introduces songs, chats with crowd, sings a little

Most Recent Release: *Finish Line Fever* CD/LP (Estrus), due out this November! Other recent recordings include *Pompeii 7"* (Estrus), and *Surfquake* CD/LP (Estrus). The guys are also featured on many compilations, including the upcoming Ventures tribute CD (Musick label)

Date Formed: Sometime in 1994, after the Zombie Surfers rode a wave to the grave

Approach to Making Music: Make it hot & sometimes melodic, maybe something you

Walk on Water

Members: Mark Kahaian – vocals, guitar, bong; Billy Reedy – guitars, vandal; Rock Action – bass, vitamin B, moving gear; Eric Miller – drums, viagra, Franklin planner

Most Recent Release: *Solvent Based Melodies* CD (self-release)

Date Formed: Still in formation (looking for a tambourine player; must collect a monthly government check).

Approach to Making Music: Openly admitting that we directly rip-off mustache-rock bands of the past

Motto: "Trust Everyone You Meet, Knowing Full-Well that A&R Reps from Major Labels are Full of Knowledge, Love and are Genuinely Interested in Your Band's Success (Eat on Their Credit Cards While You Can)"

Mascot: Our Pontiac Rocket Launchers Baby!

Most Surprising Live Performance Attendee: Joan Jett and her Not-So Blackhearts, who left after being informed by our manager that we didn't have any blow!

Communal Living or Separate Housing? Separate living. Unlike true artists, we have jobs and domestic responsibilities.

The White Stripes

Members: Jack White – vocals, guitar; Meg White – drums

Most Recent Release: *Lafayette Blues 7"* (Italy Records) on white vinyl!!

Date Formed: Bastille Day 1997

Approach to Making Music: Avoiding being in a box

Motto: "Stars and Stripes Forever"

Mascot: The Peppermint Candie

Most Surprising Live Performance Attendee: Mitch Mitchell

Communal Living or Separate Housing? Separate Housing

The Wildbunch

Members: Dick Valentine (DJ Lactose Intolerant) – lamination, vocalization; The Rock 'n' Roll Indian (DJ Me Gusta Your Daughter) – mid-range guitar support, sweatshop supervision, instigation, palpitation, Cherokee Nation; M. (DJ Water Buffalo) – propulsion systems support, dealing, exploitation,

The Witches

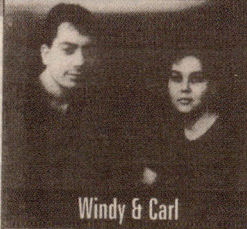

Windy & Carl

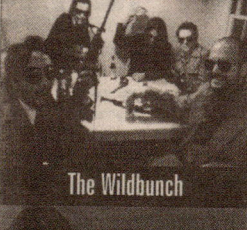

The Wildbunch

The White Stripes

computation, memorization; Surge Joebot (DJ Ethnic Cleansing) – high-frequency guitar support, regulation, computation, full-on degradation; Disco (DJ Exit Wound) – low-end guitar support, cleaning, violation, misrepresentation, heavy sedation

Most Recent Release: *The Wildbunch Live at the Gold Dollar* CD (Off Woodward Productions); Currently recording their first full-length, *Rock Empire*

Date Formed: August 6, 1996

Approach to Making Music: Valentine enters keywords into *The Machine. The Machine*, in turn, spits out a series of verses, choruses and on occasion, bridges.

Motto: "We Are an Empire…"

Mascot: Moesha, The Teenage Robot

Most Surprising Live Performance Attendee: Three-way tie: Suzy PlasterCaster, Jack Kevorkian, Stirling

Communal Living or Separate Housing? We Are an Empire….

Windy & Carl

Members: Windy Weber – bass guitar, vocal, occasional keyboard, guitar; Carl Hultgren – guitar, bass loops

Most Recent Release: *Depths* LP/CD (Kranky) April 1998

Date Formed: Summer 1993

Approach to Making Music: Waiting for the right moment

Motto: "Make the Most of Your Opportunities"

Mascot: Our dogs

Most Surprising Live Performance Attendee: Will Sargeant (of Echo & the Bunnymen)

Communal Living or Separate Housing? Communal

The Witches

Members: Troy Gregory – vocals; Deb Agolli – drums; Jim Diamond – electric twelve-string; John Nash – guitar; Matthew Smith – bass

Most Recent Release: *Let's Go to the No Go Zone* CD (Pushover Records)

Date Formed: Date Unknown

Approach to Making Music: Snake eats own self, disappears into electricity by sundown

Motto: "Everything Changes Reality"

Mascot: The Ghost of Joe Meek

Most Surprising Live Performance Attendee: The Ghost of Joe Meek

Communal Living or Separate Housing? Home in the hearts of good little children everywhere

Kid Rock

No one was talking about nineteen-year-old Bob Ritchie when he first caught the attention of the *Orbit* writers in late 1990.

"Talk about someone trying to get attention—running around with a flattop hair cut with too much Aqua Net screaming, 'I'm the pimp of the nation!' [Laughs] Yeah, I was definitely trying to get attention," said Ritchie.

By the end of the magazine's nine-year run, Ritchie's new musical style was just starting to catch fire and would soon make him a household name. Ritchie's first record as Kid Rock, *Grits Sandwiches for Breakfast*, was released by Jive in December 1990. A month later, his first appearance in issue #9 of *Orbit* would signal the start of *Orbit*'s relationship with one of the biggest names in music to come out of Detroit in decades.

During the 1990s, Ritchie was featured in the magazine as a recording artist and performer. He also advertised in the magazine and participated in *Orbit* events. Designer Craig Colon said Ritchie would come in from time to time with ads for shows or his records, often sitting down at the computers with the design team and working out how he wanted his ads to

"*Orbit* was always really supportive. They would always let people know if I was playing wherever—the Magic Bag, Alvin's, a VFW hall or anything, and they were always tongue in cheek about it . . . which is always fun. I'm sure I was a great subject—no shortage of fun jokes to be made about the crazy white kid making dirty rap music," said Ritchie.

Bob "Kid Rock" Ritchie, the son of a car dealer, grew up in the Macomb County village of Romeo. It's said Ritchie ran away from home at fifteen, lived in Mt. Clemens, worked odd jobs, performed in basement shows for little to no money, and sometimes sold drugs to make ends meet.

Still in his late teens, he developed the Kid Rock persona—a cocky, brash rapper with a penchant for four-letter words, sexual rhymes, and a great live show. After catching the notice of producers connected to Boogie Down Productions, the legendary 1980s hip-hop group that included KRS-One, Kid Rock was offered a demo deal and, finally, a contract with Jive Records. Jive was the home of several critically loved and successful rap acts in the mid-1980s through the early 1990s including Too $hort, KRS-One/Boogie Down Productions, A Tribe Called Quest, and DJ Jazzy Jeff and the Fresh Prince (Will Smith).

While the *Orbit* feature focused on Ritchie's major label release, the good times didn't last long. By mid-1991, Jive had released him from his contract, and Ritchie started working on the next phase of his career. In his 1993 release, *The Polyfuze Method,* Ritchie added a rock sound to his hip-hop songs. By 1995, the story goes, Ritchie was paying for recording time by working as a janitor at a Detroit-area studio. He continued down the rock path with the creation of his band, Twisted Brown Trucker.

MOVIEOLA
Absolutely no one under the age of five admitted without parent or guardian.

KID ROCK
When this hot, young rap artist recycles old songs he has the decency to hand out royalty checks.

▲ Kid Rock caricature from the table of contents, *Orbit*, January 24–February 7, 1991.

Home BOY MAKES Good

HOME SPUN HERO KID ROCK (PARENTAL ADVISORY, EXPLICIT LYRICS)

"The girls point in your face and say, 'You're so nasty,You're so nasty!' then I ask them, 'well, what's your favorite song,' and they say, 'Wax The Booty!"

STORY BY
Doug Dearth

ALRIGHT, SO MAYBE SOME OF ROBERT RICHIE'S (AKA KID ROCK) songs are written with a teenage mentality, but after all they were composed in high-school and 19 is still teenage.

Romeo's favorite son and self proclaimed best DJ in Mt. Clemens, Kid Rock has worked his way up through the ranks of the Detroit rap scene, as small as those ranks may be. From menial labor to local basement parties, all the contests, weddings, promotions, small clubs and everything else that could aid his career. Together with his "right-hand man," the Black Man, Kid has reached the big time.

They had recording offers from six major companies, including Atlantic and CBS. Finally, Kid chose Jive Records, the biggest rap label in the U.S., and just completed a 20-city, national tour with Ice Cube, D-Nice, Yo-Yos and Too Short, playing coliseum sized venues. "Out of·the eight or nine thousand people, maybe 50 know who I am but after the first or second song I get behind the turntables and start bustin' it up and they go, 'man this kid has got talent and sh-t!'.The people know, 'this kid's kinda cool, he's not some f—king put on,' like some other names we're not going to say."

But with a little gentle coaxing Kid did say, "Vanilla Ice started out on the wrong foot with me. He started talking sh-t in Atlanta about me." Apparently Mr. Ice wanted to get on the Jive label and told their representatives so. "He goes, 'why did you guys hire Kid Rock? You need a white rapper like me. I'm gonna be making all the money!'" Jive said no.

"I'm sure who ever turned him down at Jive got reamed!" Though Kid questions Vanilla's longevity, "He's got 13- and 14-year- old white girls buying all his music. They're gonna grow up and they're gonna go 'hey this kid is a big a—hole.' He goes to walk through the malls and people will be pointing and laughing and he'll probably commit suicide by the time he's 25." Kid further confided, "Yeah, me and Luther Campbell used to go to school together too and Chuck D. (Public Enemy) used to nurse me and tuck me in bed at night."

Then there's the parental advisory sticker. That little label that helps sell millions of otherwise unwanted merchandise. To date, Kid has made 40,000 sales in Michigan alone. But what do his parents think of all the graphic language? "She (Mother) made me sit down and play her the whole thing, God I was about beet red. She likes the *Abdul Jabar Cut* but she doesn't know why I have to swear so much at the end of it. My Pop likes *Yo-Da-Lin In The Valley*, him and his buddies get together and play that and kinda laugh, 'That's my boy!'"

Will success spoil Kid Rock? Hardly. He already has the attitude; a young, foul-mouthed, braggart with a strong work ethic and the talent to back it all up.

Kid Rock will be preforming, Feb. 8 at U of D's Callihan Hall with Too Short, 2 live Crew, The Afros and Hoes with Attitudes.

▲ "Homeboy Makes Good," Kid Rock feature, *Orbit*, January 24–February 7, 1991.

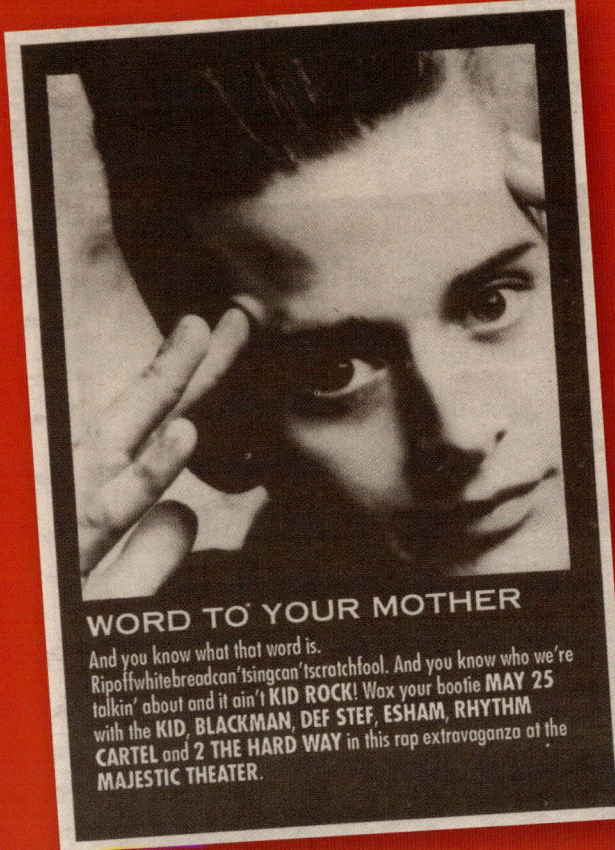

▲ Kid Rock calendar listing, *Orbit*, May 16–30, 1991.　　▲ Kid Rock calendar listing, *Orbit*, November 1993.

look. "He knew Jerry. He just came in. Typical chitchat you have with an advertiser. I didn't know who he was. No one did at the time. He was just a guy. And then he got pretty famous shortly thereafter. But he understood the value of promotion," said Colon. "He seemed to appear out of nowhere, but locally, people who knew him knew that there were lean times for him to get to where he's been able to get."

Ritchie remembers the *Orbit* offices as a messy place filled with cool, creative people: "They would help me design not only ads, but sometimes they would be nice enough to help me make some posters to advertise our show that we'd staple to telephone poles all up and down Gratiot, Woodward and Telegraph [Avenues]."

Food reviewer Jimmy Doom remembered a show in the early years when Kid Rock was trying to get attention.

Doom said that "Bobby," as he was known, showed up with a tape and wanted to do one song on an already overbooked bill:

There was a huge multiband gig at the Latin Quarter called Sonic Blur. Every band of that era was booked: Trash Brats, Crossed Wire, Second Self, Art Phag. Every band had a minimal time frame. I think the sets were like eleven minutes apiece. People with Bobby were asking every band if he could do one three-minute song. No one, understandably, was going to let him on and lose part of their set. The soundman was DJ Def Stef, who I grew up with on the west side and was very close to at one time. He made a deal with me. If I let Bobby go up for one song, he would make sure my band [the Almighty Lumberjacks of Death] kept our allotted minutes. We let Bobby go on before us, and when he was done, the stage manager ordered our minutes to be cut. Stef was not only very much respected in Detroit but was very physically imposing. I'll nev-

▲ Kid Rock ad, *Orbit*, April 1996.

▲ Kid Rock calendar listing, *Orbit*, April 1996.

▼ Kid Rock calendar listing, *Orbit*, May 1997.

er forget playing "Soul of the Storm" while one of the Sonic Blur production crew tried to "mute" us at the sound board, while Def Stef and legendary sound man Cool Chris stood in his way, laughing, but threatening physical violence. It's funny now because none of the artists actually booked on Sonic Blur have gone on to Bobby's level of success.

Kid Rock also shined at *Orbit* events. His time rocking the mic at the magazine's karaoke nights became legendary. Held at the Royal Kubo, a Filipino bar and restaurant, karaoke nights attracted Ritchie and a stable of local singers like Dan John Miller ("Goober" of Goober and the Peas), Jimmy Doom, and Meg White (of the White Stripes). Kid Rock also lent his time and talent to the magazine's legal defense fundraising concert in March 1997.

"They were just people I wanted to be around and hang out with; they were cool. If they had something going on, if I was lucky enough to be invited, back then . . . I was lucky enough to be invited anywhere at the time. [Laughs] They were a different type of cool; it seems like they

RAPPER ROCK HAS ALWAYS BEEN ABOUT SEX AND DRUGS—NOW HE'S WORKING ON THE ROCK 'N' ROLL.

SO CAN KID ROCK?

Prologue: Detroit, 1991. From the first moment we met Kid Rock, we were skeptical. We didn't think much of white rappers. America was, after all, still in crisis, suffering the embarrassment of Vanilla Ice. However, 19-year-old Romeo boy, Bob Ritchie, came highly recommended by local legend DJ Def Stef, and was backed up by the Black Man. Rock had some heavy cred: he had just finished a 20-city tour with Ice Cube, Too Short, and D-Nice. He was signed to Jive. From the second he opened his foul mouth, we liked him. You felt Rock was going to make it, but somehow shit always happened, and he remained underground, releasing a slow, but steady, stream of cult classics.

by Jerry Peterson

Cut to 1998. Fresh off the cover of Grand Royale, Kid Rock is signed to Atlantic Records. He's backed by Twisted Brown Trucker, a killer band of some of Detroit's best musicians and strangest characters; he's got the pedal to the metal. Fresh off the Warped Tour, playing alongside the likes of Rancid, Kid Rock was the most punk rock thing on the bill. He's getting some radio play for the first time in his life and should be scooping up new fans and scaring parents everywhere.

Gangsta Winnebagos

Kid Rock has just finished with the Warped Tour—"a lot of work for no money. They pay everyone shitty"—so there's still a little time left on the rented Winnebago. We're eating Tubby's in the sub shop parking lot with Rock's son, Junior, who is playing some noisey computer keyboard toy thing.

Kid Rock philosophizes, "Alone these [Warped Tour] bands couldn't draw this many people. Which is good for me—nobody knows who the fuck I am. [Except] in every city there's about three kids standing around going 'Yo-da-lin in the valley!' Other than that…"

Record company clout landed Rock on the bill and this may have caused him to step on a few toes. "At first, when we got on that tour, nobody liked us. We were like the outsiders, like Atlantic got us on the tour and everyone thought bla bla bla. But after about three or four shows, everyone was ridin' a dick. Everything came out cool, and we became friends with everybody. Spent a lot of time on the Def Tones bus. Stefanie, our drummer, was hanging out with the Specials; we got drunk with them plenty of times. The guys from Rancid were really cool, but the promoter, Kevin Lymon, was still treating us like shit."

The band had some main stage appearances worked out contractually, but Lymon stuck the band on the second stage in bad time slots whenever possible.

"We went up and rocked the same way wherever they put us. We were winning over crowds. [Lymon] was pissed that no one could shake me up. I was telling everybody to fuck off, let me play my show. They sent big fuckin' thug boy Fletcher (from Pennywise) to check me when I was going on stage. The fucker comes over, starts talkin' shit, all fucked up. So I drank his bottle of rum with him and we get all fucked up, and I'm supposed to be on stage at this point. I don't know who he is. I don't know anything about punk rock; I don't know shit. Sex Pistols, that's about it.

"So, to make a long story short, he snaps me up by this big silver chain around my neck. So I snatch him by his chain around his neck, and I'm just waiting for him to pound my fucking ass. He yanks my chain off, I yank his off, he throws 'em over the fucking fence and puts me in a fucking bear hug. I'm trying to get up on him, so he can't hit me hard, when Chino, from the Deftones, runs in and breaks it all up. I tell him to fuck off and run up on stage and do my show. It pissed him off bad that he didn't rattle me—he was trying to get me to run for help. Then he came up on stage and started lifting Stephanie off her drums and shutting off our monitors. So, right after the show, I went up to Kevin Lymon. 'You guys want some fuckin' gangster shit? Cool—I'm down with it. I see you walkin' around here every day. You aren't hard to get, motherfucker. Watch tommorrow, when I fly in some fuckin' hardnosed motherfuckers from Detroit who will blow this fucker up for the next three cities, straight up thugs who would like nothing more than to come and eat mohawk for breakfast. You want a problem? I'll give you a fucking problem.'

"After that, phone calls are being made, everythings

"So Can Kid Rock?," *Orbit,* October 1998. ▲ ▶

going on. Pretty soon there is apology made. The next day Fletcher pays me $120 for my chain. Everything worked out, I got a lot of respect for it. After that, nobody fucked with us at all."

All except for the Ladies Lounge, "stupid-ass thing with some girls that looked retarded trying to DJ, and everyone thought they were good 'cause they were girls, but they really sucked."

They kicked drummer Stefanie out because she was with Kid Rock and they didn't like his lyrics. His next time on stage, Rock told the crowd what was happening and dedicated his song, "Fuck Off," "to all the bitches in the Ladies Lounge." He also had a stripper come out on stage with him—"You never seen a mosh pit stop so fast in your life." For some reason, the Ladies Lounge let her back.

Rock has to get the RV back. He wants to rent it again, except he told the lady he rented it from it was for camping. He's got to take it to a place so far on the east side, they probably use chopsticks. My east side ignorance is obvious. "You've never partied on Lake St. Clair?" Rock asks dumbfounded. "If there is anything as a high class eastsider, that's where they party. And any low life like me who can talk his way onto a boat…" We decide to continue the interview next Saturday on Lake St. Clair.

Muscamoot Bay: The Indians Called it Tranquil

Muscamoot Bay is the destination of every eastsider with an outboard motor and a substance abuse problem. It's the shallow part of Lake St. Clair, where the water is the warmest—no doubt, from all the pee and gas fumes. On a Saturday afternoon, there are hundreds of boats crammed into a tiny corner of the giant lake. Apparently, we're too late and our cruiser is too large, so we have to anchor on the outskirts.

Why does everyone head for Muscamoot Bay? "It's easier to get girls to take their tops off in Muscamoot Bay than Wild Woody's. Water and whiskey brings out the best in women." Rock points out the beeper on a girl's bikini.

We are piloted by Captain Leon, who looks like a graduate of The Hazelwood School, except the Exxon Valdez couldn't hold as much booze as they've got on this cabin cruiser. DJ Bad Rockin' Brad has brought his booth and hooks up the six-foot speakers. Families flee in terror as 2 Live Crew roars across the bay. Rock knows every rhyme to every old school rap song and every Lynyrd Skynyrd song as well (as I'll find out later in the day). He tells me as they get drunker, girls will be taking off their bikinis. Instead, an old man, flabby belly bouncing to the beat, idiot-dances on his boat. Soon other boats are attracted by the DJ booth. They start parking around and lashing up to the sides and forming a sloppy island of vessels.

By the time Rock breaks into the PBR (having already finished his first 12 pack), the party is in full swing. Fifty yards away, girls are coaxed into reluctant flashing and grinning drunkards start mooning. Bad Rockin' Brad rips out with the Kid Rock. This attracts a contingent of Rock's sunburned Romeo homies, who wade over to the party from nearby boats.

While Rock is the biggest thing in Romeo since the cider mill, he is just starting to hit in other cities. In St. Louis, his song "Bullgod" is number one. It's surprising they play him at all with the drug lingo—I never knew there were so many rhymes for 'shrooms. Rock recalls a radio interview: "They put this caller on line, and this bitch starts screaming at me. 'All you sing about is smoking dope, screwing girls and money'…I'm like, 'so, what's your point?'" Rock's facial and verbal expression are equally dumbfounded.

Even if he wasn't Kid Rock, he would probably be the center of attention at a party. As Rock dances with two girls, an aggressive third girl pushes her large ass into the fray and humps his leg like a dog in heat. I quote him from his own song, "I don't care much for small cars or big women, but somehow I always find myself in them."

"No shit," he laughs. "Everything I write about is true."

The water cops drive by and Brad blares Ice Cube's "Cop Killer" at 200 decibels. The cop is looking for the captain and ends up in a discussion with Bad Rockin'

Brad. The party can continue as long as he plays the cop's request. The opening bars of "I Shot the Sheriff" blare across the white trash flotilla the Hot Damn! schnapps breaks out. I stare at the cigarette butt and beer can-strewn seas and realize it's going to be a long day.

Ain't No Party Like a Cleveland Party

The band looks truly surprised to see that I've shown up in Cleveland. Thursday night in the Flats and Peabodys is near capacity, about 300 people, mostly old school fans.

"My name is Kiiiiiiiiiiiiiiiiiiiiiiidddddddddddddddd! Kid Rock!" Just in case you didn't hear his name, it is emblazoned Viva Las Vegas-style in tracer lights behind the stage. The fist-waving crowd starts thrashing as the band goes into "Bawitdaba," probably unaware that Rock built the rock chant around old-school nonsense rhymes, like the Sugarhill Gang's "Rapper's Delight." The fans mouth the words to most of the songs, especially the vulgar ones like "Balls in Your Mouth."

Eventually, the show gets a little sloppy, and 3-foot-nine-inch-tall MC Joe C says something derogatory about Cleveland. This raises the ire of a group of Flats cruisers, obviously out of their element. They chant, "Ain't no party like a Cleveland Party 'cause a Cleveland Party…" over and over. The band never notices. When I head back for a beer 15 minutes into a 20-minute Lynyrd Skynyrd tribute, the Flats frats are still chanting. They haven't played or practiced since the Warped tour. Rock is pretty wasted, and the band is pulling songs out of their asses. By show's end, Rock is waving his hands at the band like a conductor in an experimental game of musical chairs. Rather than leading them, he's trying to screw them up. There's no encore, but a throng of kids wait for autographs.

Kid Rock has a lot of fans to win over. "Oklahoma City sucked. Four guys in cowboy hats and one guy yellin' 'PLAY YODELING IN THE VALLEY.'" To make matters worse, the band got nailed at a drug checkpoint coming out of Oklahoma City. "They set you up. They set up a sign that says DRUG CHECKPOINT NEXT EXIT. So anybody who has drugs gets off the exit before that. All the cops are sitting right there with dogs, buses, shit, like everything. Then they have a sign that says FAMILY REUNION and they've got an arrow. They ask, 'what are you guys doing?' 'My uncle Sam is having a reunion …' 'OK—EVERYBODY OFF THE BUS!' We had to give up our paraphernalia. Luckily, we didn't have anything in the RV. They let us go, but it was scary."

We take Joe C to the topless bar next door, but first we have to wait for Rock to talk to every fan in the State of Ohio. At the Circus Gentleman's Club, the doorman suspiciously eyes Joe C's ID and acts like we're trying to get a kid inside. Then the dancers come over and check out Joe C. Rock walks in with a big girl. She's dumped her date and is hanging all over the singer. He buys Joe C a table dance, and the diminutive MC is nearly buried in flesh. The dance ends and the dancer stays. It's sweet, kind of like Madonna and child. A bouncer from Peabody's tells us the Rock's latest fan's date is looking to kill him. We decide to not to join the band at the jacuzzi suite and head back to Detroit.

The State of Rock

It's two weeks later. Ticket sales to the White Trash On Dope Tour have been good with tonight's walk-ups, and there are over 2500 kids. The usaual State Theatre draw for Kid Rock has doubled. No doubt, a lot want to hear "yo-da-lin," but more are here because "Bullgod" is getting play on three radio stations. "I'm sick of it. It's four years old. We pulled it out of the closet and re-recorded it." But Rock is going to be singing "Bullgod" a lot longer—they're shooting the video for the breakout single tonight. Even though the band has already played the song, they still go nuts when it's played three times in a row for the video shoot.

So what is Rock's favorite cut from the album? The Segar/Skynyrdesque, "Only God Knows Why." "It's three chords. I wrote the first verse in jail, Cracker wrote the last verse in the studio."

After Rock was signed, he rented a limo and took the band out for a big night on the town—Mt. Clemens. "Some guy got jealous and socked me. My buddy hit him over the head with a beer bottle. Next thing you know, the cops are there, so we're fightin' all the cops and the bouncers. They carted us off to Mt Clemens PD. I told the cops I had a nine mil and I was going to bust a cap off at 'em. Told 'em they all sucked dick—basically yelled obscenities like all night." They hauled him off for an extended stay in the Macomb County Jail, "so I basically had a little time and I wrote songs."

In my best drill sergeant voice, I ask Rock if he's been rehabilitated? "Fuck no. A 12-step program couldn't keep me clean." ⊕

TWISTED BROWN TRUCKER

Kenny Olson
PAST: K.O.B., Scott's Pirates, Enemy Squad, Filth Eater, 4 Pimps in a Cadillac, a solo album; for years a L.A. studio guitarslinger-for-hire.
CREED: "It's been a long haul, but one day I might grow wings."
EXPERIENCE: Between sets at a high school house party, fell out of a second-story window and didn't spill his beer.
POST-DEAL ACQUISITION: Paid off the fingerbreakers.
DELIVERS: "Mood, loud-ass guitar, and tastefulness when needed."

Jason Krause
PAST: Death metal bands: Aftermath, Black Anthem.
CREED: "Keep it real."
EXPERIENCE: Playing in front of 20,000 kids a day for a month versus playing in front of a handful of kids.
POST-DEAL ACQUISITION: Guitar amp (our advances weren't as big as Bob's)
DELIVERS: "A Flying V, Marshall amps. All the metal, headbanging, idiot mosh pit stuff kids like to kill each other to."

Joe C.
PAST: Marine Corps Young Heroes Award — "for being sick and having a disease (celiac)." Also a high school diploma.
CREED: "Life sucks, but you have to deal with the hand you were dealt."
EXPERIENCE: Hanging with the Beastie Boys and playing the State Theatre.
POST-DEAL ACQUISITION: Four Wheeler-still paying on it.
DELIVERS: "Excitement, a shock to the crowd, and a 10-foot dick."

Jimmy Bones
PAST: Robert Bradley's Blackwater Surprise, New Barbiturates, Lovemasters, Karen Monster, Jimmy Bones and the Graverobbers. Studio whore.
CREED: "Live hard, play hard, stay hard."
EXPERIENCE: "For one night, I was, and possessed, the only male member in the Truncheons and everyone wanted it."
POST-DEAL ACQUISITION: Big bottle Crown Royal.
DELIVERS: Some greasy, funky B-3 organ and bass in "real time."

Cracker
PAST: Kid Rock's DJ since he was 16 - Another DJ quit and Kid Rock threw him behind the turntables and he faked it.
CREED: "Middle finger for all."
EXPERIENCE: Got totally socked and woke up in Blackfoot's dressing room, ate all their food and drank all their booze. Too bad I didn't smoke cause the singer only had one lung.
POST-DEAL ACQUISITION: A Rolex.
DELIVERS: "I don't add shit. I'm there for moral support and some back-up vocals."

Stefanie Eulinberg
PAST: Nation of Teflon Souls (Cleveland), Top 40 bands that stayed and played in Marriots, Just started Puppy Steak (Minneapolis) when DJ Swampp referred her to Kid Rock.
CREED: "It may not be easy, but just be your damn self."
EXPERIENCE: "In a traffic jam, our guitar player Dan tried peeing out the window. When it didn't work, he then filled up three coffee cups, splashing the band."
POST-DEAL ACQUISITION: "Told boss 'I quit' and bought two bottles of Bolo wine."
DELIVERS: "The blackness, titties and groove."

Kid Rock finger cartoon, *Orbit*, January 1999. ▲
Jimmy Doom and Kid Rock at Gusoline Alley, *Orbit*, April 1999. ▶

were just open-minded folks who were into art and cool shit, and they knew how to have a good time," said Ritchie.

The October 1997 issue of *Orbit* reported that Ritchie had inked a major deal with a new label, Atlantic Records. Less than a year later, in August 1998, Kid Rock would release the record that would put him over the top, the multi-platinum-selling *Devil Without a Cause*. Mixing elements of rock, specifically a southern rock sound, with hip-hop, the record would spin off six singles onto the *Billboard* charts with "Bawitdaba" peaking at number 10 in July 1999. The song was nominated for two Grammy awards, and since its release, the album has sold over eleven million copies. Based on sales numbers, *Devil without a Cause* is on the same tier as the Beatles' *Sgt. Pepper's Lonely Hearts Club Band* and Nirvana's *Nevermind*.

Kid Rock appeared in *Orbit* twenty-five times during the magazine's nine-year run. His attitude meshed well with the sensibilities of the magazine, but the staff was never above taking a shot at him. In the January 1999 issue, the *Orbit* crew poked fun of Ritchie's constant use of the middle finger in photos. A photo cartoon shows the finger speaking for itself and saying it's time to go solo. "Without me he's nothing!" the finger says. "Except for the swearing, I'm his whole damn stage show!"

In *Orbit*'s final issue, a two-page, full-color photo re-creation of *The Last Supper* featured Ritchie as a sort of rock and roll Jesus, soon the title of a Kid Rock album, thanked Detroit fans for their support. The photo was taken by Jerry Peterson and was later used by Ritchie during his tours.

"I just loved it, it was that kind of David Letterman/Beastie Boys humor that I was really into. I thought *Orbit* was cool, and I was trying to be cool, and I'm still trying to be cool. [Laughs] I've been working at it my whole life—some days it works out, some days it doesn't," said Ritchie.

"Under the Town," *Orbit* karaoke, *Orbit*, January 1997. ▶

Big Chief

Another band *Orbit* music writers loved was Big Chief. They loved them so much they were dubbed "the greatest band ever." Big Chief emerged from the ashes of several notable local hardcore bands. Singer Barry Henssler came from the Necros, drummer Mike Danner was with the Laughing Hyenas, and guitarist Mark Dancey played for Born Without a Face, three bands that were fixtures in the Michigan and northern Ohio hardcore scene in the 1980s. Bassist Matt O'Brien and guitarist Phil Durr rounded out of the lineup of mostly University of Michigan grads.

▼ Big Chief calendar listing, *Orbit*, August 23–September 20, 1990.

Photo: C. M. Linabury

Just back from a two day tour of Ohio, **BIG CHIEF**, the pride of Ann Arbor, bring their peculiar brand of low-brow, hair-shaking, funk-powered rock to the Motor City. With three singles under their belt (including one on the trendier-than-thou Sub Pop label) Big Chief have achieved near celebrity status in their home town. Success hasn't spoiled these hometown heroes. A typical day finds lead singer Barry Henssler recanting tales of his hardcore heyday to the local punks, while the rest of the band work numerous odd jobs to help support Barry's record collecting habit. Opening act: Sub Pop artists L-7, a no man's band from California. St. Andrew's Hall Sat Sept. 1st. **DM**

In the past two decades Big Chief is one of the few Detroit area rock groups to get a "major lable" deal, simultaneously inspiring awe and jealousy. With a big fat Sub Pop contract and a European tour under their belts, the world is Big Chief's oyster, and they are attacking it with lemons and extra-spicy cocktail sauce.

Formed out of the ashes of popular area hardcore combos, B.C. is assaulting the hearts and minds of a generation too young to remember when moshing was called slam dancing and the mohawk hair-doo was the riguer de' couture. They continue to defy the modern rock establishment; eschewing management, marketing analysts, rock dieticians and other pop parasites. Big Chief is hellbent on their own path – may it lead to stardom or destruction.

When Nirvana turned the podunk Sub Pop company, into a positive cash flow empire, the bands career kicked into gear. Their first full length LP, *Face* was both universally revered and reviled, a tenacious serving of slop delivered in a explosive fashion not heard since the Enola Gay dropped the big one on Tojo and his evil buck-toothed lackeys. But, the band originally resisted signing with Sub Pop who had been pursuing them virtually since their inception.

"We avoided Sub Pop because we're not from Seattle, we're not part of that scene. And they thought we were called Crack Whore," stated guitarist, Mark Dancey. He also confided that they didn't make friends or influence people on the coasts. Big Chief garnered a bad reputation, not only for the band, but possibly for the entire mid-west.

Singer Barry Henssler seems genuinely bereaved, "We always try to be on our best behavior, but our brand of rock is intentionally physical, so if we should happen to hurt someone's feelings while dispensing it, well... we do mean well, and that's important." While that kind of insincere banality may make sweet press releases, it doesn't sell records. Dancey exonerates a Big Chief credo, "When we make songs, riffs rule, chords suck."

The band learned a lot touring with the Beastie Boys, "People think backstage is some kind of a Nirvana (no pun). They are willing to do any kind of humiliating thing to get backstage. Unsolicited, they would bare their breasts..." and Dancey pummeled our ears with the sordid details of desparates, willing to risk eternal damnation for a few minutes in a typically empty dressing room.

STOOGES WAX MUSEUM

Most of our readers should already be familiar with the stories surrounding The Stooges Wax Museum. This Motorbooty Pop culture creation has been virtually elevated to legendary status in the modern rock community thanks to the unrelenting promotion of Big Chief members. Here are a few of the museum's VIP visitors:

- Just last month after seeing Big Chief members wearing Stooges Wax Museum T-shirts, the group Spiritualized was inspired to take their limo straight to Ann Arbor in search of the famed hall.

- Mudhoney's experiences were reported in SPIN magazine.

- Julian Cope was asking about it. It's uncertain whether he was able to pay homage.

- Matthew Sweet, to important to go in person, sent a runner.

- But, The Feelies reportedly returned from their museum visit dejected, apparently it didn't live up to their expectations.

- Always searching for a new angle, writers from across the country are sent to land the real story.

MIND OVER MOTOR THE BIG SHOW

The next adventure; "Detroit Muscle," November 25 at the State Theater. The show which features the '92 Big Chiefs in glorious Autorama, options include a nitro-charged stage show highlighting the fervor of horsepower. The band promises to introduce "quite a few new songs" for the benefit of fans "who may be getting sick of them." In keeping with an auto show atmosphere, muscle cars will be on display along with fire-breathing transvestites, body builders and belly dancers. High-performance artists Satori Circus and well-oiled supporting acts Rollinghead and Mouth round out the extravaganza.

THE MOTORBOOTY CONNECTION

Lots of kids think it's real cool how Big Chief uses the same artist as those Seattle superstar swingers, Soundgarden. Well that's because super-guitarist Mark Dancey is also super-artist and CEO of Motorbooty (The Eyes, Ears and Ovaries of the Bozo Underground) Magazine. The other band members contribute to the sporadically printed comic, satire and music 'zine. This should give Big Chief automatic cover stories, rave reviews and centerfolds, but honorably, there is a no mix/no propaganda rule at magazine central. It's unlikely the band could so much as a discount on a classified ad. But Big Chief does have access to a world class artist. Heck, they probably don't even have to pay him.

▲ Big Chief, *Orbit*, November 17–December 1, 1992.

BIG CHIEF SPEAK WITH FORKED TONGUE

Mark: "I gave this 14-year-old kid our CD. He said it was too mellow. So I gave him *Face* and told him that if he didn't like that one, we'd break up."

Mike: "*Mack Avenue Skullgame* is *My Fair Lady* for the '90s."

Barry: "Our fans tend to be really smart, good-looking females with lots of money to spend."

Matt: NOT PRESENT

Phil: "What comes around goes around."

It's been 5 years since Big Chief first began their perilous journey towards Rock Stardom (or indie anonymity, whichever comes last). In that time they've released three albums, something like nine singles, and have toured extensively, both at home and abroad. Their latest platter, *Mack Avenue Skullgame* has taken everyone from hardcore fans to longtime detractors by surprise. Where past releases have been Rock-heavy, with a decidedly Westbound beat lurking in the background, *Mack Ave* is a full-on funk assault. Featuring horns, keyboards, as well as guest vocals from local blues diva Thornetta Davis, *Mack Ave.* is leagues ahead of the bands previous releases. In an effort to understand why this drastic change in direction took place, and to find out where the band plans to go next, ORBIT spoke to Mark Dancey, Mike Danner, Phil Durr, and Barry Henssler (Matt O'Brien was at a Billiard "retreat" in New Haven). Unfortunately, we didn't really get the answers to any of our questions, but the result was an entertaining, if not exactly informative look into the private world of Big Chief.

ORBIT: I think it was Pete Townshend who called your new record derivative.

Phil: Derivative of who, Pete Townshend?

Barry: So we're exploring our feminine side, what's wrong with that?

Mark: Well, I'll admit it. It's sort of our version of *Tommy*. It's our rock opera.

Barry: *Mack Avenue* is our *Tommy*, and Thornetta is our Tina Turner.

ORBIT: But with CD technology, I guess this won't be coming out as a double LP.

Mike: Well it is coming out on vinyl, but it fits on one disc.

ORBIT: What's the bonus track?

Barry: The bonus track is a little acoustical number that Phil wrote and sings called "Mouth F!@#er."

Phil: It's in the key of D# minor. It's the saddest of all keys.

Barry: Matt got his song on our new single ("Another 20 Seconds", the b-side of "One Born Every Minute"), we had to give Phil something. So he said "I gotta put 'Mouth F!@#er' on the new album."

Phil: The lyrics are simply: "Mouth f!@#er, mouth f!@#er, that's what you are." Repeat. Repeat.

ORBIT: How many copies has *Mack Avenue* sold so far?

Barry: Six. All by hand… to our parents.

Mark: I gave this 14-year-old kid our CD. He said it was too mellow. So I gave him *Face* and told him that if he didn't like that one, we'd break up.

ORBIT: How many do you hope to sell?

Barry: Fifteen. I like to keep my horizons low. It's definitely gonna go aluminum.

ORBIT: What percentage of your audience is mall rats?

Phil: Right now? Not nearly enough.

Barry: Hopefully soon an ever-increasing amount.

Mike: A larger percentage of the band is

mall rats. We'll sell more records when we're mall rock. But that's not 'till next year. That'll be our schtick.

ORBIT: So is this album a permanent change in direction?

Barry: We'll wait and see how many people buy it. If a lot of people buy it, hey! that's our new direction.

Mike: Since that *Singles* soundtrack did so well, how could we not do a soundtrack?

ORBIT: How do you respond to people who say the new album is racist?

Phil: What's wrong with being racy?

Mark: In the true story that the album is based on, all the principal characters are white, but since it's a Detroit story, we thought the music should reflect all the good Detroit music that's influenced us over the years.

Mike: Thus the similarities to *Live Bullet*.

Barry: We just kind of went in there and did what we wanted. There were no specific reference points, just general ones like early Funkadelic, New Birth, and other soundtracks. A lot of the lyrical ideas were influenced by different slang terms in books by Iceberg Slim, Nathan Heard, and Robert Blake.

ORBIT: How did the idea for *Mack Ave* come about?

Barry: Well, we're all really into musicals, as many people know, and while it's hard for us to pick a favorite, we all really dig *My Fair Lady*.

Phil: It's hard to top Lerner & Leow.

Barry: So *Mack Avenue Skull Game* is our tribute to that genre in general, and *My Fair Lady* in particular.

Mike: It's *My Fair Lady* for the '90s.

ORBIT: Tell us about the movie.

Phil: We're not at liberty to discuss it.

ORBIT: Oh, come on.

Phil: Well, our people are talking to Harvey Keitel's people. Antonio Fargas,

Max Julian, and Yaphet Kotto want to be in it, and Shirley Hemphill has offered us money to be in it.

Mark: Michael Caine is going to play the doctor. Sandra Bernhart is going to play Sonica.

Barry: You won't print any of that stuff, will you? It's all off the record.

ORBIT: Sure, no problem.

Barry: Thanks.

ORBIT: What's the best stuff you've ever gotten in the mail?

Mike: Pot.

Phil: Pot was cool.

Barry: Free records, which we just take and trade in for *pot* down at the pot exchange.

Mike: Mark's the one who gets all the free stuff. He puts out a magazine so he'll get free stuff.

ORBIT: Ever get food in the mail?

Mike: We've gotten things that we've eaten.

Mark: Sometimes they send candy. One time, this guy we stayed with in Philly sent the hairball that was formed in the drain. A little momento of our stay.

Barry: And we promptly stir-fried it and chowed it right down.

ORBIT: How much more handsome or attractive has being in a band made you?

Phil: Lots. It gets us all laid by very high-profile women several times a day.

Mike: We don't appreciate p!#$y like we used to, being in Big Chief. It's so plentiful. So many women have had us.

ORBIT: Do people treat you differently because you're in Big Chief?

Barry: Yeah, people are nicer to our faces and meaner behind our backs.

Mike: We have more fans, and more enemies than we used to.

ORBIT: But I bet you don't appreciate your enemies like you used to.

Barry: No, I appreciate them more. Because I love to hate.

ORBIT: You mentioned rock *schtick* earlier, what's your *schtick*?

Barry: Looking good and kicking it out.

Phil: I don't think we have one. We should have people write in.

Barry: The schtick is a long-standing tradition in Detroit rock, so we should have one. We should have a contest. Your readers can write in and tell us what our *schtick* should be.

Phil: What does the winner get?

Barry: The winner gets a date with you. And they pay. And you pick the restaurant and the entertainment.

Mike: And you get to decide what they

have to wear.

ORBIT: Describe your typical fan.

Barry: Our fans tend to be really smart, good-looking females with lots of money to spend.

ORBIT: What's the future of Big Chief?

Mark: Our goal is to have a Big Chief Club. People will come from miles around to check us out.

Barry: We'll never have to tour. We'll just play at our club, and a busload of people will come to see us every night.

Mike: We'll play six nights a week, two shows a day.

Mark: We've been talking to Mike Illitch. We're hoping to get in on the whole Second City development.

ORBIT: Tell us about being on tour.

Barry: Mostly when I'm on tour, I just go to porno places.

Mike: You do. I just start eating hash from the day we leave till the day we get back, so I don't even remember. We're not going to Europe, though, unless everyone in Europe puts all their money together and sends it to us first.

ORBIT: Where do you go over best in Europe?

Phil: Germany's cool, Belgium's great. Mostly the places where people like to drink and get really f!@#ed up, we do amazingly well.

ORBIT: What does that say about you?

Mike: We're right there along side them.

Phil: What comes around goes around.

Barry: In Holland people just look at you like they're watching some huge T.V.

Mark: The English are just so hopelessly bored, they can't stand it.

Phil: And we can't stand them either.

Mark: The French just don't know what to do.

Barry: The French want to rock. As long as you say a couple words in French to the French, they love you.

ORBIT: Since this is the Octoberfest issue, what's your favorite beer?

Mark: I like Grolsch, because you get a free toke stone with each bottle.

Mike: Crazy Horse is pretty cool. It's what all the Indians drink.

Phil: I'd say Hacker Pschorr Wiess Beer.

Barry: I'll agree, just for the ritual of it and just 'cause I dig it.

ORBIT: What's Matt's favorite beer?

Barry: He's an Old Milwaukee Light man.

ORBIT: Any last words?

Barry: No.

Mark: No.

Mike: Nope.

Phil: (Belch!) Just that.

▲ Big Chief interview, *Orbit*, October 1993.

BIG CHIEF
Mack Avenue
Skullgame
-Sub Pop

Mack Avenue Skull-game is not only a great Detroit record, it's as honest and thorough a distillation of Motor City popular music history as has yet been committed to laser-guided grooves.

DISC-O-GRAPH

MOVIE TIE-IN   NICEST GUY IN ROCK

9

GOOD BEATS   EASY TO DANCE TO

The DISC-O-GRAPH proportionally represents criteria (as indicated) by which recording was judged. Score represents the overall view on a scale of 1 to 10, 10 being the highest.

Indeed, groove might be the operative word here. The album's seamless nearly-50 minutes are juiced with raunchy P-Funkadelica (*Mack Ave.* is dedicated to the memory of longtime George Clinton guitarman electrique, Eddie Hazel), Denis Tek/Ron Ashton-esque guitars aflame and powerhouse cameos from legendary locals Thornetta Davis, David McMurry and Rayce Biggs, among others.

Most gratifying is that for a concept record (it's the soundtrack to the "film" of the same name), *Mack Ave.* has songs. "My Name is Pimp" is a rolling, tumbling descent into the Mind of Darkness, and "One Born Every Minute" and "No Free Love," both featuring the vocal stylings of Thornetta Davis, are soul-funk-rock hybridizations that bring to mind the vocal contributions of Nona Hendryx to *Remain In Light*-era Talking Heads, but without the art school pretensions. *Nein.* Big Chief are compelling because behind all the additional dressings, *Mack Ave.* retains a primitive, masculine growl that freezes you with its naked intensity, a testosterone rush. A tough band from a tough town baring its raw soul right now. Get it while it's still hot. -W.W.

Combining hardcore roots with two legendary Detroit musical threads—the hard rock/proto-punk of the MC5 and the Stooges, and the hard funk of Parliament/Funkadelic—Big Chief created a potent sonic mixture. Dancey said the band was about claiming something uniquely Detroit that had influenced other bands worldwide: "We felt it was our birthright: the Stooges, the MC5 and Funkadelic—really aggressive but with a groove to it."

Iggy Pop promoted Big Chief on MTV in 1993, and local record stores took out ads in Orbit in May 1995 urging readers to call local radio stations to request Big Chief songs because "not since the MC5 and the Stooges has a Detroit band turned so many heads."

◀ Review of Big Chief's *Mack Avenue Skullgame, Orbit,* October 1993.
▼ "Barry Henssler, *Orbit*'s Man of the Year," *Orbit,* October 1994.

BARRY HENNSLER
ORBIT'S MAN OF THE YEAR

By Scott Sterling

As I recline on one of the many pillows that cover the priceless Persian rug of Barry Henssler's apartment, occasionally hitting the 8-person *hukkah* in the center of the room, it becomes apparent why the lead singer of Detroit-bred rock lords Big Chief was unanimously voted *Orbit* Magazine's first-ever Man of the Year.

As the collected group of models, reporters and various other pop culture dignitaries mill about the space (everyone just ignores MTV's Kennedy as she keeps peering through the window in hopes of getting in), marveling at Barry's vast art collection (he's got a series of signed Mark "Beyond Frank Kozik" Dancey originals that must be worth millions), I realize my tape recorder is missing. It's lost somewhere in the lavish spread of Thai food, countless bottles of vintage wines and a stack of vinyl LP's that Barry personal pulls from his incredible library to illustrate a point.

"Here's something I picked up a couple of weeks ago at this little sports card shop in Plymouth," he grins, handing over a sealed copy of the Beastie Boys' *Paul's Boutique* (with the original multi-gatefold cover) as tears well up in my eyes at the sight of something so precious. Nothing less extraordinary than locating the proverbial needle in the equally proverbial haystack, *c'est la vie pour* Barry Henssler. "Hey, here's your tape recorder," says Barry, uncovering the missing device under a stack of original Sun Ra albums.

Just a few days before Big Chief' jets off on a quick club tour, Henssler seems ready to deal with the worldwide adulation that's sure to follow once his band's latest album, the ingenious *Platinum Jive*, emerges as one of the finest pieces of wax in 1994.

"It's all part of the game," he opines. "We'll go out, rock some asses, do some record shopping, you know. If people wanna get in my face, so be it."

Containing some of the finest tracks Big Chief have recorded over the course of their long, illustrious career, this "greatest hits" package comes pretty damn close to defining the hard-to-define Big Chief. Songs like the skull-crushing Metal monster "Lot Lizard" (from their 1984 "Big Rock" classic *Power Hour),* sound right in sync with fuzzed-out Soul side "Takeover Baby" (the second single from 1969's *Titty Twist Whitey,* which was the first B.C. cut to feature Detroit diva Thornetta Davis). Currently, it's the big beat, end-of-the-world anti-junkie ode "John's Scared (from '77's *Midwest Rules,* and was covered by both Aerosmith and Ted Nugent back in the day) that rules my stereo.

"This whole thing isn't going to be about me, is it?" Barry calls from his reading room, where he's showing some people his collection of autographed Iceberg Slim tomes. "Talk about the other cats, too."

Given B.C.'s wealth of freshness, that's easy enough. Any band that boasts Mike ("John Bonham as sampled by Pete Rock doing a remix of '72 Sabbath") Danner on drums, Phil ("Eddie Hazel lives") Dürr and Mark ("Riffs Come First") Dancey both on guitar, and Matt ("I Let My Fingers Do The Talking" groove merchant) O' Brien on bass will be talked about.

But it's Barry ("the best hair in Rock") Henssler that personifies Big Chief. From his Robert Johnson ripping through the first Bad Brains record vocals to his college-educated and street smart brain power, the mere mention of his name strikes fear in the hearts of many, even Courtney Love. When she somehow got it in her head that he was going to write about her for a prominent fanzine (which he wasn't), she had her publicist calling around the world to stop it from happening. When asked about this incident, Henssler just shrugs and asks, "Courtney who?"

An avid connoisseur of fine food, Barry lists places like Steve's Soul Food in Detroit and Ann Arbor's famous Mr. Rib (legendary director Melvin Van Peebles asked for their number after sharing a "Soul on A Roll" with Henssler at a Big Chief record release party) as two current faves.

Having finally muscled my way through this decadent scene, reminiscent of "The Wolf's" party in *Pulp Fiction* crossed with a chapter from Led Zeppelin's *Hammer of The Gods,* to finally corner Barry (and brutally elbowing an irate Liv Tyler in the process), it's my turn to really get the lowdown on the ever-elusive Barry Henssler.

"So what do you wanna know? Necros tour stories? My top ten Jazz lists? My recipe for Pad Prik? I'm here, talk to me."

When the phone rings, the moment every writer dreams of is cut brutally short. "Sorry, but I gotta go," Henssler apologizes. "That was Car City Records. I guess somebody just brought in a stack of old Black Flag 7" singles, and I'm off to go check 'em out."

Rats, foiled again...

If there was one band that the music writers felt was on the verge of breaking big, it was Big Chief.

Said vocalist Barry Henssler: "I had never got to go to Europe with the Necros, and that was kind of a goal. . . . Mudhoney had stayed at my house, and they had just gotten back from Europe. They were playing in the Heidelberg in Ann Arbor to a hundred people. They were telling me about playing Europe, and I was like, 'oh, man. I've got to do that.' So, the main kernel of inspiration was maybe we could go to Europe with another band."

The group's first shows were outside of Detroit. The idea, according to Dancey, was to build national respect for the Detroit-area band and make them more than just a local draw. Dancey's music/comic magazine, *Motorbooty,* also featured contributions from members of Big Chief.

A year after Big Chief formed, Seattle-based Sub Pop released the band's first single as part of the label's legendary Singles Club, which featured early records from Nirvana, Mudhoney, Soundgarden, and other bands that helped create the Seattle sound of the 1990s.

Between 1990 and 1993, Big Chief released two records, *Drive Off* and *Face,* to a growing legion of fans and positive reviews. Big Chief sold out venues such as St. Andrew's Hall.

By 1993, Big Chief was at the height of its creative powers with the record *Mack Avenue Skullgame.* The concept album was conceived as the soundtrack to a non-existent exploitation/crime film about a love triangle gone wrong between a doctor, a young prostitute, and her pimp boyfriend. The story was based on a real Detroit crime story involving noted psychologist W. Alan Canty Jr. For several years in the early 1980s, the Grosse Pointe doctor carried on a double life as the sugar daddy to a young prostitute in Detroit's Cass Corridor until he was murdered and dismembered for refusing to continue to furnish the prostitute and her pimp boyfriend's lifestyle. *Mack Avenue Skullgame* garnered glowing reviews from *Orbit* and other music press nationally.

In 1994, Capitol Records signed the band. That same year, Big Chief released *Platinum Jive: Greatest Hits 1968–1999.*

By 1995, however, the band had started to slow down. Several factors—some personal, others creative—led to its demise a year later.

"[Big Chief was] grungy but they weren't grungy in a stereotypical way. . . . They were a band with a groove and they were grungy but you could dance to it. They were smart and also kind of devilish. One of those kinds of bands you don't want your sister to go out with . . . At a certain point in your life, you are at a place where something like the right music, done the right way with a right kind of presentation, attitude, can change your life or have an impact. Big Chief did that for people," said *Orbit* writer Walter Wasacz.

Orbit called Big Chief "the greatest band ever" in the September 1994 issue, and if that glowing praise wasn't enough, Big Chief's albums received enthusiastic reviews, and singer Barry Henssler was dubbed "Man of the Year" in November 1994—the first and only person to ever receive the honor.

By the time Big Chief called it quits in early 1996, Henssler said he was already living in Chicago. Looking back on that period, he said, "Detroit's changed a lot. There were always bands. You know when the White Stripes came up I remember friends telling me that bands were moving in from out of town to live in Detroit to say they were from Detroit. Nothing like that was happening when I was living there. It was like I left town and everyone felt free to be creative then or something, I don't know [laughs]."

SO WHAT'S WITH THE CLOWN SUITS?

What can we tell you about ICP that Esham can't tell you better?

"I know ICP because they're out there and they're making a move to get past Detroit. They're down, but they ain't making music for the hood, they're making music for the world."

History Lesson

VIOLENT J: We got started about three years ago, but before that I used to make basement tapes over other people's instrumental's. We made one and put a color copy cover on it and thought it was cool so we took it to a record store. My brother knew a guy at the store and we ended up selling some copies of it. The owner called us up and said "let's get together and try to do a real tape and put it out." So he put some money behind us, and we put out a real tape. I've been rappin on and off since I was real young since like the seventh grade. We sold something like 19 copies of it, which really ain't nothing, but the fact is that it was just a Maxell dub and somehow kids were buying it. So we went from there.

Detroit Sound

VIOLENT J: It's demented and strained, it's unlike anything else. It's not Gangster Rap. It's like Horror Rap. It's almost science fictional. It's something beyond. You can't imitate it. The sound here in Detroit is so bizarre. It doesn't have to be murderous or anything like that, but it's bizarre to me basically because it's new. I grew up loving it and now I do it.

Detroit Influences

It's being influenced by the other music in Detroit. Esham and Real Life productions laid the paths, and things spawned from that. if you listen to music coming from Detroit and you believe in that music as you're coming up, your music might have the same type of flavor. It's like everything coming out of Compton is Gangster Rap because those rappers who are coming out now they grew up listening to N.W.A. and all that other Gangster stuff. It influences them because they feel part of it.

What's up with Detroit?

VIOLENT J: There's a few people that I respect, people that accept the Detroit sound and work with the Detroit sound. If you look at the local rap scene, the people who really sell units are people who are sticking with the Detroit sound. Michigan has definitely caught on to the Detroit sound. You got groups coming out here selling just as many records as Ice Cube sells in Michigan because people in Michigan have caught onto it and it's like a phenomenon here, this strange sound that only Detroit has. Once the rest of the nation catches on to that as hard as Detroit it will become a mainstream thing that will be the new sound for everybody.

Formula For Success

VIOLENT J: The people who stick together are the people who come out with original work. It's like the whole G-Funk thing right now. That was started in L.A. and everybody is trying to do that. I think the reason why this Detroit thing is so hot is because kids here are exposed to it. Once the rest of the nation is exposed to it as hard as Michigan is, it'll take off. Soon you'll have people from Tennessee or Florida whatever trying to do the Detroit sound because it'll be hot and the cool thing to do. But like I said, I only respect a few artists from Detroit because the only artists that I respect are the ones doing original stuff. I don't want to hear somebody try to rap over a G-Funk beat when it's so obvious what they're trying to do.

New Projects

VIOLENT J: We got a new EP coming out called *The Terror Wheel* and that will be out on the 28th. Also 2 Dope has a single, "Psychopath." We've got 2 Dope's solo album, *Shag the Clown*, and that's going to be out in the late summer or the beginning of fall. And then we got the third Jumper Sky album coming later this winter. ICP has six joker cards. Each album is a different joker card and by the time the sixth joker card is dropped I don't think the world will be in any condition to release our record. It's kind of like a countdown to the destruction of everything. Look at the way the world's going now. It's getting crazy, not just here in Detroit but all over the world.

No Respect

2 DOPE: I think the rock bands in Detroit should accept what Rap is and stop dissing it because we don't use live instruments. When a rap act is selling 25 times more records than they are I don't think they have any room to say anything. Rap is a studio art. I make music in the studio and that's how rap originated. It's inner city music. It's easier to get a drum machine than buy drums, guitars and all the stuff you need to have a live band. Just get a drum machine and you can do it. Beatbox originated ten years ago and it was easy and everybody could do it.

VIOLENT J: The Detroit DJ's should support more Detroit Rap.

Interviews by Jim Stevenson

ICP

Homegrown artists like Big Chief and Kid Rock were staples in the magazine and a major component of its visual appeal. But no band was quite as striking as the infamously face-painted duo of Joseph "Shaggy 2 Dope" Ulster and Joseph "Violent J" Bruce—the Insane Clown Posse. ICP made their first appearance in the July 1994 issue of *Orbit* as part of a feature on local hip-hop that included respected Detroit underground rapper and ICP influence Esham.

"Most bands that were serious, including us, would find their name pop up in *Orbit* long before it would pop up anywhere else, whether it was a full story, a little column, or a comic. Your band didn't have to be huge to get a write up in *Orbit*. They just seemed to cover everything from the bottom up," said Bruce.

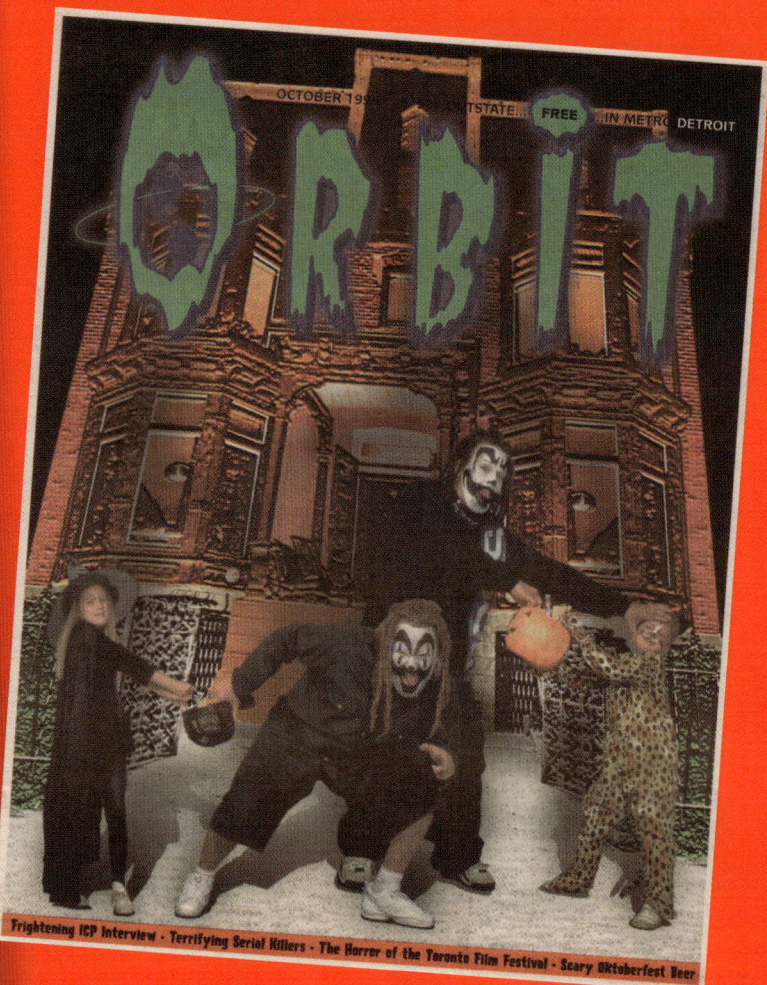

▲ ICP on the cover, *Orbit*, October 1996.

◄ Insane Clown Posse interview, *Orbit*, July 1994.

By October 1996, ICP was so well established in Detroit that *Orbit* put the group on the cover of its Halloween issue, a rare honor considering Peterson preferred covers to be eye-catching and artistic, not PR for bands. The cover shoot was fun but annoying, said the publisher's nephew, Ryan Peterson. The magazine's Anniversary Boy and his older sister, Chelsea, were featured as two kids trick-or-treating as ICP tries to snatch their candy bags. Ryan Peterson, seven at the time, had no idea who the band was: "I think I had the flu and I'm meeting these guys and my uncle is all excited, and they are like, 'Hey, what's up?' and I didn't quite know how to react to them. I remember that they were grabbing us and I was like, 'Get your hand off my head.'"

The group had become a major advertiser by the time *Orbit* ended, taking out full-color ads to promote upcoming records and shows.

"*Orbit* was the place to advertise. It was the place to be. They had the audience you wanted. Everybody cool read *Orbit* first. For us, it just felt like *Orbit*'s readers had more of an open mind toward a band like ICP," said Bruce.

ICP's wicked clown concept caught on, and within a few years the pair was signed to Hollywood Records, a division of the Walt Disney Company. Mickey Mouse's corporate parents soon decided the wicked clowns were not worth the heat they were receiving from right-wing moralists in the media. After agreeing to changes, including recording new lyrics and removing objectionable songs, *The Great Milenko* was released in June 1997. The album hit the Billboard top 100, but the complaints were too much, and the band was dropped from their label in the middle of a promotional tour a few days after the album was released.

Since ICP's brush with corporate control, the band has maintained its own affairs through its label, Psychopathic Records, and found great success in sales and merchandising. Since its formation, ICP has sold over six million records and earns several million dollars a year in merchandise sales. The group has starred in several self-produced independent films, appeared as characters on Cartoon Network's *Adult Swim*, and been parodied on *Saturday Night Live*. The group's annual Gathering of the Juggalos festival attracts thousands of fans and performers such as Parliament/Funkadelic founder George Clinton, rappers Vanilla Ice, Ice Cube, Ice-T, comedians like Jimmie Walker and Cheech and Chong, and professional wrestlers.

WHAT'S GOING ON HALLOWEEN

Violent J: Every year is a surprise. All I'll say is that we will never play the Royal Oak Music Theater again. I want to apologize to anybody who went there last year, cause that place sucks. We got a deal with the Paladium this year so that there won't be any barricades. The kids can act as wild as they want. They can jump on stage, jump off and no security's gonna choke your face. We've got surprise special guests and the full Dark Carnival and it's spirits will be there.

UNADULTERATED FAYGO LUST

2–Dope: When you're a kid you know there's like you and four boys sitting on porch sweating' your ass off in the sun, everybody busts out the quarters. You get two liter and just pass it around like that. You could come up with a Faygo recipe. You know what I'm saying? Plus, it's every fucking flavor you can think of, comes in every color of the rainbow, fucking clown colors. Fucking grape, lime, fucking bubblegum, ginger ale, Faygo water, peach, fucking moonshine.

Violent J: I'll tell you what flavor I don't like—Arctic Sun. That shit tastes like butt. Peach is nasty. People can like Peach but Arctic Sun is

IN THE BEGINNING

Violent J: I used to hang out with his brother. There used to be three of us in the group. We pretty much met behind Joe Louis Arena.

INSANE CLOWN POSSE

WHO ELSE CAN PLUNK A BOX OF CDS ON THE COUNTER OF RECORD TIME AND SELL OUT IN A DAY?

The speed their recordings fly out of record stores is legendary. Enough that their Soundscan numbers landed a contract with Jive.

They outdraw national acts. What other band can walk into a 2,000 plus capacity club, plop enough cash down for a Saturday Night's rent and walk away with the door on a SRO show?

They make more on merchandise than most local bands will make in their entire careers. What other bands can afford to paste their big ugly smiling faces in pricey full page ads in local publications liken Orbit and The Metro Times?

Despite the fact that have never been and probably never will be heard on the radio, ICP are the biggest group in Detroit.

Sure ICP is huge but they're even bigger one night of the year Halloween
See 'em live at the Paladium

2-Dope and Violent J

WHAT'S GOING ON HALLOWEEN

Violent J : Every year is a surprise. All I'll say is that we will never play the Royal Oak Music Theater again. I want to apologize to anybody who went there last year, cause that place sucks. We got a deal with the Paladium this year so that there won't be any barricades. The kids can act as wild as they want. They can jump on stage, jump off and no security's gonna choke your face. We've got surprise special guests and the full Dark Carnival and it's spirits will be there.

UNADULTERATED FAYGO LUST

Violent J: The deal with the Faygo is, when we were kids we-I mean when you're a little kid, hanging out in the summer, sweating to death, we'd gather up money by bottles to go and get a two liter. You could always afford Faygo. Faygo's like the poor man's

school when it'd be like a kid's birthday party and everybody'd be asking for snacks? Well at my school they used to laugh at the kid who brought you Faygo. Cause it was the cheapest, he was the cheap ass. That kid was me! I always had the Faygo, so I'm down with Faygo. We try to turn it around so that it's the shit. You go to an I.C.P. concert you see lots of kids carrying around two liters of Faygo and shit, like it's cool or something. But you step back and look at it-look how fucking stupid it is! But that's what's cool about Faygo-it's fucking lame. I don't know what the fuck we talk about Faygo for. But back in the day we used to do graffiti, and I used to go by the name, Faygo Joe cause we always had a two liter in my hand, you know.

Violent J: The guys in Faygo, they like us, but to the public, they don't want you to know that they like us. They don't want to endorse us, but they give us plenty of free Faygo.

2-Dope: They don't want to tarnish their image.

Violent J: They've got a family product and we're not exactly family-oriented music, you know. You won't here us on any *Snow White* soundtracks. But Faygo likes us though, because we hooked them up with a little extra fizz. So they give us a lot of free Faygo and ship us out boxes of Faygo shirts.

IN THE BEGINNING

Violent J: I used to hang out with his brother. There used to be three of us in the group. We pretty much met behind Joe Louis Arena.

2-Dope: We'd hang out in back wrestling and shit.

Violent J: We'd hang out getting autographs from wrestlers. I could never afford a ticket

2-Dope: When you're a kid you know, and there's like you and four boys sitting on the porch sweating' your ass off in the summer, everybody busts out the quarters. You get a two liter and just pass it around like a forty. You could come up with a Faygo real quick, you know what I'm saying? Plus, it comes in every fucking flavor you can think of! It comes in every color of the rainbow, like clown colors. Fucking grape, lime, lemon, fucking bubblegum, ginger ale, Faygo water, peach, fucking moonshine.

Violent J: I'll tell you what flavor I don't like-Arctic Sun. That shit tastes like butt. Peach is nasty. People can like Peach but Arctic Sun is butt.

2-Dope: And cream soda ain't no good either.

Violent J: Basically, we like Faygo because nobody else does. Remember in elementary

or nothing, you know.

2-Dope :There used to be three of us in the group. There were a couple third members, but there's just two of us now, and that's how it's going to stay-it's not going to change.

Violent J: We've made three albums and three EPs together. We may be gaining a new audience here and there, but we're nothing new. And a lot of bands, they always have friction in the studio, and shit but there are no signs of friction here. Maybe it's because there's only two of us.

2-Dope: There's no friction whatsoever because it's just us two in the studio.

Violent J: So we've been down since he was like 10 and I was like 12. And we'd just take a bus downtown and fucking be wrestlers. And I'd be glad to see him out there, you know. We'd be talking. And finally one weekend I was like "Yo! I've got all these wrestling magazines, come check 'em out! " And we just started hanging from there.

IS WRESTLING ON THE LEVEL?

Violent J: We've met every single wrestler there is. You name 'em.

2-Dope: We used to keep books of autographs and pictures.

Violent J: I like wrestling 'cause it's fake, it's not real. I mean, if you go to a wrestling show, this is what you'll see. You see 10,000 blue-collar, hard-working fathers with their sons, all cheering and having a good time. Everybody knows it's fake, but they're all just having a good time.

DOES ICP AUDIENCE = WRESTLING CROWD?

Violent J: These kids are all fucking having gang troubles, their parents are busting out on them about getting a job. We attract a lot of kids just like us. They're basically having a real fucked up time growing up. And when you come to our shows, we like it to be a time when it don't fucking matter. Nothing matters.

2-Dope: It don't matter who you are, where you come from, don't matter what the fuck you do, you're down with the clown when you're in that building. And you can do whatever the fuck you want. You don't gotta have no fucking job, it don't matter if you got dropped out of school when you were two. At our shows, everybody is down with everybody.

Violent J: It's a chance to be in your best clothes and put Faygo all over them motherfuckers. If you look at a clown, clowns are always fucking up. Getting high, stoned, slipping on his ass and getting laughed at. This is a chance for all the nerds to get together, all the outcasts, the losers, the freaks. All the freak shows, all the fucking class clowns to get together and just say "Fuck it! Cause all

ICP feature, *Orbit*, October 1996. ▲ ▶

this shit don't matter anyway!"

It's illusionary shit that everybody can relate to. We're not from the ghetto, we're not from a rich neighborhood. We're just straight up scrub. And everybody in our audience is the same way. We're all just like "Fuck it!" It don't have to make sense. It's like wrestling. Everybody knows it's fake, but everybody's like "Fuck it!" And we're not fake or anything. A lot of the topics we address are really, really real. It's some serious shit, but it's a chance to say "Fuck it!" Just insane shit that doesn't have to have a bottom line.

SAFE FOR THE WEE ONES?

Violent J: Well I don't think there's anything on that record that those kids aren't saying in junior high already. Anybody who's got a problem with stuff like that, I mean they got to wake up and smell the reality. Fucking, in junior high those kids are cussing worse than adults. Those kids are talking about the nastiest shit. Those kids know what sex is way before sex education. This ain't *Leave it to Beaver*. This is the real world now. These kids in junior high are getting high, having sex. And all I'm trying to say is that my music isn't anything they haven't already heard. I'm not trying to say, "Let's help endorse that shit," I'm just saying that my lyrics ain't nothing they haven't heard before. I'm not saying that's cool, I'm just saying we ain't nothing new.

2–Dope: And on top of that, it's kind of stupid because some junior high kid listens to our record they can't strap a fucking dead guy's arm to their neck and go bouncing with a fucking leg hanging out their ass or whatever. But they can listen to some other shit and go and get a gun and smoke a bowl and drink a forty and shoot somebody.

Violent J: Just like he's saying. You can't imitate what we do. This is some fourth, fifth dimension shit. You can't go bouncing with a bunch of dead bodies. You can't call upon the dark carnival. You can't do that shit. But other rap, you can do. You can go drink a forty at lunch and shoot somebody in the head. I mean, I'm up for all rap. But we have a really young audience, and I don't really know how that happened, but all I'm saying is that we ain't showing them nothing they don't know.

2–Dope: I think they started out young, and they're finally getting older.

Violent J: In Michigan, there's a really different audience than we have out of state. Out of state we have like an older, college audience. And that's really weird. But here we've got really young gangstas. Kid's that want to be gangstas, kid's that are gangstas. We have a big suburban audience. We dis rich suburbs a lot, and that's where most of our audience is from. And that's cool cause it's like they're rebelling against what their fathers are. We can go down South, and have 5 or 600 kids show up to a club, and we're shouting "Fuck your rebel flag!" and it's cool cause they're shouting it too. We got a young audience here in Michigan, but I'm down with whatever it is. It's all apart of our carnival. The young audience is obviously here at the best time cause when you're young, you learn. You can't teach an old dog new tricks, but you can teach his son many - shit like that.

MYSTERIES OF THE DARK CARNIVAL?

The words, Dark Carnival - there's a set up. The meaning behind it runs a lot deeper. It's real. It's something you can feel, it's something you're a part of. Some people don't feel it. Now when you come to a building and you see thousands of kids all throwin' Faygo all over each other, singing the words to songs that make no sense, that's part of the Dark Carnival. Either you get it or you don't.

What I hate is when people don't get it, they got to start dissing us and talk about how shitty we are. How we ain't got no talent and how we suck. You know, if you don't get it motherfucker, walk on. We don't shove nothing on your face, we don't trick you and tell you Barry fucking Manilow's going to be there. And when you show up, we jump out. Either you love it or you don't. Either you're part of it or you ain't. And if everybody in the State is part of it, then that's what they are. And if nobodies apart of it, then we'll still be doing a show for each other.

The Dark Carnival-it's real man. It's like the make-up, the clowns, the freak shows, the ringmaster, the riddles, the Great Milenko. It's all real and it's all happening. The clowns are coming, the freakshows are coming. You know, it's 1996-there's all types of shit coming. It's for the new millennium and so on.

THE FIRST SHOW

Violent J: The first show we ever did was opening at Ferris State University, Big Rapids, Michigan. We drove up there through a blizzard.

2–Dope: Fucking blown-up truck tires busting through the windows, fucking cops pulling us over cause he thought we were driving drunk.

Violent J: We got all the way up there, played one song and got booed off. We went all the way home in tears. The second show we did was paying a guy $500 to open up for him in front of 200 people-that was Esham. We paid him $500 to open in front of 200 people. That fucking sucked! And on top of that, they wouldn't let us wear make-up. We just had wigs and no make-up. Nobody knew what the fuck we were doing. That show fucking sucked. And the third show we ever did was at Todd's with a bunch of hard core punk bands. And their was a lot of racial tension just from the music we were doing. And after we played

Continued on page 39

Continued from page 29

INSANE CLOWN POSSE

we had to run out and jump in the car and leave.

The first show we sold out was the Magic Bag Theater, and every show we've played since in Metro Detroit has sold out. And that's the main thing. Anybody that comes to our shows, it ain't two dope performers performing for an audience. It's the audience performing for each other. It's like the *Rocky Horror Picture Show* in there. Everybody's having fun. No one's looking at the movie at *Rocky Horror Picture Show*; nobody's looking at the screen.

FIRST RECORD

2–Dope: The first one I actually bought was called Twilight 22 or something.

Violent J: Sir Mixalot. NWA, *Straight Outta Compton*, that's what really did it. But I think the first rap record I ever bought was *Jam On It* by Nucleus

DETROIT MUSIC

Violent J: Detroit's music scene is the atom bomb right now. This is how I feel. Three or for years ago, it sucked. All the bands sucked to me. But now-look at Charm Farm. They're local, but I can put their tape in and get the same rise and feeling that I get when I listen to my favorite artist. It's that good. It's not like,"Let's listen to this because it's local." I love that record. Sponge's record is really good too. And Detroit is blowing up. You've got Speedball. The Suicide Machines are completely in the house. Four years ago everything sucked! But now there's a lot of acts that have major potential.

2–Dope:My top five for right now would be Charm Farm, The Suicide Machines, Speedball, Verve Pipe and Sponge. And that's only five. Look at how many incredible acts there are that I'm leaving out. As for us, we're not like a radio act. We're not going to get any MTV or anything.

Violent J: As far as mainstream is concerned, Detroit is fresh. Charm Farm and the Suicide Machines are the bomb though. As far as the rap scene goes, there's a lot of stuff that's coming out that I'm really excited about. There's a band called Ruckus, their new stuff is really good. Esham's new stuff is really good. The ROC is really good. I'm geeked about it all. I feel really good saying I'm from Detroit. And I want to be a part of it. Whenever I see an article that talks about the good things coming out of Detroit, I want to be a part of that. And I hope other bands look at my music the same way I look at theirs.

STILL DOWN WITH ESHAM?

Violent J: Yeah, we're friends with Esham. I never got my $500 back, but we're definitely cool with him. I think he and his brother are geniuses. They started everything we do. What we do is what they started. But I don't feel bad doing what somebody else did because look at how many gangsta rappers there are out in L.A. Stuff like that though, is what Detroit is known for. If you go out of state, Detroit is known for what we do. For what Esham does. Acid rap, crazy, bizzare Steven King-type stuff.

THE END

His Name Is Alive

By the time another local musician—Livonia native Warren Defever—started releasing records as His Name Is Alive, he had already been part of the *Orbit* universe. During the 1980s, Defever and his brother John were members of the 1980s psychobilly outfit Elvis Hitler. The group's name, not to mention its music, grabbed the attention of *Fun* magazine writers in the late 1980s. While still performing with Elvis Hitler, Defever started working on a completely new approach. In the place of punk-infused rockabilly music was something more ethereal, spacey, and experimental. Since then, Defever has recorded and produced music with chamber music ensembles, avant-garde jazz legends, noted Detroit rockers, and Noise Camp—an annual event featuring all manner of musical ruckus. "Occasionally, people will describe the music as 'experimental,' and I think it's the opposite of experimental music. There's no theoretical plan behind it, and there are no ideas; it's really just about what's going on in my life. So, I think it's ultra-personal," said Defever in a 2011 interview with WDET.

Much like his music, Defever was often hard to pigeonhole. He made up stories during interviews about his past and his creative process, as he felt rock journalists didn't care about the truth anyhow. Defever soured on the rock press after reviewers took personal swipes at him when the first His Name Is Alive album was released, only to heap praise on his second album less than a year later.

Eventually, Defever's tall tales started to pile up, and *Orbit* magazine decided to separate fact from fiction. Music editor Liz Warner, under a pen name, fact-checked many of Defever's claims and statements for an article in the February 1999 issue: "[He was] on my radio show a few times for interviews. I would ask him a perfectly serious question, and he would come back with something that was completely off the wall, but it sounded like it could be true. But it was fun to kind of debunk that because that is his game. . . . He is a great storyteller. He's a fun storyteller. He's actually in line with that whole *Orbit* idea because he tells stories that are fun and interesting to read. But they're just totally manufactured."

Defever said he didn't mind the piece. In fact, he compliments *Orbit* for its place in the media soup of Detroit in the 1990s, saying he felt its lack of pretense made it a better cultural barometer of the city: "Because it was such an open process, it was very democratic and it did probably a better job representing what was happening in Detroit music-wise and art-wise because anybody could get in there. The *Metro Times* seemed like they [needed] to be a little editorial about it and say, 'This isn't really worth covering or this is below our level of standards' . . . or whatever. Like the *Metro Times* wouldn't mention the Gories—it was, like, under the radar. Whereas [with] *Orbit* or *Fun* magazine, it was like, it was a hot band. So, I felt like possibly the *Metro Times* was being a little more judgmental of what was considered valuable to the community, whereas *Orbit*, obviously their goal wasn't 'let's have this for the people,' but it ended up being a more of a universal. Not to say anything positive about it [Laughs]."

His Name Is Alive calendar listing, *Orbit*, September 27–October 11, 1990. ▶

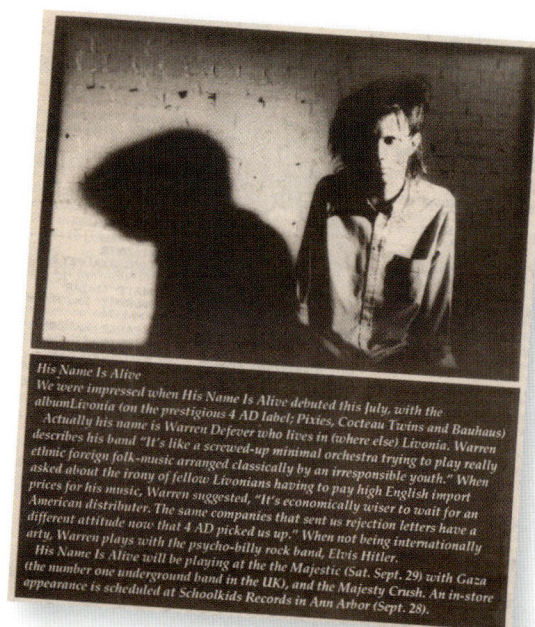

His Name Is Alive
We were impressed when His Name Is Alive debuted this July, with the album Livonia (on the prestigious 4 AD label; Pixies, Cocteau Twins and Bauhaus). Actually his name is Warren Defever who lives in (where else) Livonia. Warren describes his band "It's like a screwed-up minimal orchestra trying to play really ethnic foreign folk-music arranged classically by an irresponsible youth." When asked about the irony of fellow Livonians having to pay really high English import prices for his music, Warren suggested, "It's economically wiser to wait for an American distributor. The same companies that sent us rejection letters have a different attitude now that 4 AD picked us up." When not being internationally arty, Warren plays with the psycho-billy rock band, Elvis Hitler. His Name Is Alive will be playing at the the Majestic (Sat. Sept. 29) with Gaza (the number one underground band in the UK), and the Majesty Crush. An in-store appearance is scheduled at Schoolkids Records in Ann Arbor (Sept. 28).

Sonic Boom

TRACKS & HOT WAX

DJ Clark Warner's Top 10

Ten reasons to put on head-phones.

1. Sheila Chandra "ABoneConeDrone" (RealWorld)
2. As One "Light" (Likemind)
3. R. Hawtin "Revolution" (Plus 8)
4. Ken Ishii "Overlap" (R&S)
5. Bochum Welt "Module 2" (Rephlex)
6. Dark Comedy "Clavia's North" (Art of Dance)
7. Fusion "Block Out the World" (Planet E)
8. Gus Gus "Polyesterday" (DA:four)
9. Harold Budd/Hector Zazou "Pandas in Tandem (phume rmx)" (SSR)
10. Spacer "Contrazoom" (Pussyfoot)

Found Wax: *God Bless Tiny Tim*/Tiny Tim (Reprise) For all of his sallow-cheeked, ukelele-wielding, deviant eccentricities, Tiny Tim could teach all of us a thing or two about life. On this, his first release, he sings and cackles the praises of just being alive. He explores the meaning of it all in songs like "Livin' in the Sunlight, Lovin' in the Moonlight," "Daddy, Daddy, What is Heaven Like?" and "Strawberry Tea." His signature song "Tip-Toe Thru' Tulips" made its debut here and hearing it—so fresh, so new—pushes a tear or two to the surface. "The World Is Wide With Many Things Within, But Few So Rare As He. God Bless, Tiny Tim," was his message to the world. It's all too much. Humanity could learn a thing or two from this truly great man.

Band of the Year: His Name Is Alive

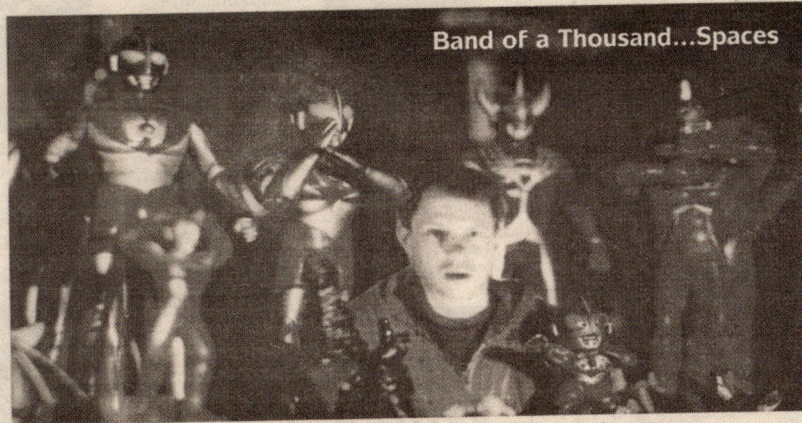

Band of a Thousand...Spaces

In the 1980s a teenager from Livonia, Michigan named Warren Defever began making homemade music under the nomer His Name Is Alive. The swirly, effects-laden enchantments of Scotland's Cocteau Twins and the 4AD studio project This Mortal Coil were a jumping-off point for Defever's own musical experiments, incorporating a modern psychedelia with a personal psychology of frag-mented lyrics and found sounds.

4AD, London's prestigious indie record label, also recognized a fresh and kindred spirit in the early tapes sent to them by Defever, and in 1990 released the groundbreaking His Name Is Alive debut *Livonia*. Seven years and five albums later, the high school project has become a multi-headed hydra of uncompromising artistic offshoots such as the audio-visual label *by Ralph Valdez* TimeStereo, and Detroit's premier noise/theatre outfit Princess Dragon Mom. Defever's fast, furious and prolific output stems from friendships re-combining, and the shuffling of key players in kaleidoscopic creations with like-minded mini-geniuses.

"Because we record at home, we have the luxury of doing things differently," Defever explained. "Each song has a long story behind it. The first songs were written and recorded when I was 16. It's hard to say exactly what I was trying to do (then), but the stuff came out pretty weird, and it's very different now. It's always changing, and there's no definite plan." Though, recent live shows exhibit an energy and cohesion less like their early ephemeral space-capades, and a music more akin to an MC5 or Butterfield Blues Band concert Defever shrugs, "A year ago it was probably something differ-ent, and two years ago...I don't know what it was. I don't really pay that much attention to the changes and that's probably part of the problem." Problem? More like an absent-minded solution to the paradox of "rock" and its ever-changing sameness.

His Name Is Alive's latest record, *Stars On ESP*, is a perfect avant/pop blend of the deeply exper-imental and the simple sing-along. With contributions from a twisted array of local and international talent including a gospel choir, Matt Smith of Outrageous Cherry and The Volebeats, former Pale Saint Ian Masters and Godzuki's Erika Hoffman, the album is held together by the group's primary vocal-ist Karen Oliver. *Stars On ESP* extends His Name Is Alive's serious yet playful disintegration of musi-cal labels.

After countless interviews and reviews from around the world and at home, what's the worst thing someone could say about HNIA? "That we sound like Brian Eno or Robert Fripp...it doesn't seem like they're having very much fun," Defever says. The art/rock dichotomy and mind/body struggles aside, true fans know the HNIA studio/home called Super Fun is just that. When asked if older fans ever denounce the band's increasingly friendly, rockier sound Defever responds, "People have criticized us for not being as 'spooky.' When we do some of the older songs they've yelled things like 'Play it right!' We've done shows where they've complained that we did all new material, when really it was all old songs!" Re-inventing themselves while revitalizing the local underground music scene seems like an afterthought for Defever and friends. Though the fortunes of more traditional local groups may be sources of pride, helping to re-direct the spotlight on Detroit and Michigan, HNIA stands out for standing out and making the rules fit their game.

Hollywood is knocking on Defever's door for more musical contributions including Cameron Crowe's latest, *Jerry Maguire*, but Defever says, "The movie business is all bonus." ...Or did he say, "all bogus?"

Beyond hard-earned local success, His Name Is Alive's impact has been felt world-wide with musi-cians and non-musicians alike drawing inspiration from Defever's nonconformity and home studio D.I.Y. wizardry. Popular response has finally started to catch up with the critical acclaim of this nearly decade-long career. How does it feel to be recognized as Orbit's "Band of the Year?" Defever answers, "I keep thinking that it's some kind of a joke."

Endomorphic Joy
36D
Small Stone Records

Do you want a rare treat? Pick up this quintuple-breasted rack of rock recorded back in '91—before grunge was the misguided law of the land. This lascivious powerfest joined members of Big Chief with hardcore outfit Born Without a Face to produce the finest booty-moving music heard around these parts in years. Groove intensive songs such as "Horse" & "Maybe I Was" pack more than enough wallop to make your ears bleed. Yet, that is what true rock is all about. Grab one quick and be cool, there are only 1000 in print. —*Bob Koval*

Telegram
Björk
Elektra

Björk's third is an animated feature-length film of all the re-mix ideas that were left on the cutting-room floor of her little head from her first two releases. These are a few of her favorite things, collaborated with a few of her favorite people. She dispels the notion of "re-mix" as a money-for-noth-ing record company term, ennobling it more to the likes of standard classics being reworked countless times by assorted talents, in the jazz tradition. Each partner-in-crime she chose took a track over where she left off and re-created it to be their own. Biggies like the Brodsky Quartet, Eumir Deodata, British techno stars Outcast and re-mixer Dillinja, Finnish techno band Metri, and longtime partner Graham Massey were all invited to Björk's tea party. There is one new track, "My Spine," which she wrote and recorded with amazing percussionist Evelyn Glennie. It took using exhaust pipes to get just the right sound. Björkies unite! Your elfin princess has done it again! Also: Keep your peepers peeled for the new video, animated by now-really-famous, still-local, Orbit fave Glenn Barr! —*BMS*

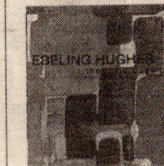

The Little Bugs Glow
Ebeling Hughes
Rust Belt

Exquisite vintage tones (circa Syd Barret's Pink Floyd), spheric melodies... a stunning, exploratory, boundary-smashing record. Charles Hughes breathes away his resonant and washy whispers like a lifeline, leading through the other side of Robert Ebeling's rhythmic hailstorm pulse-and-surge free spirited arrangements. Sound complex? It's as simple as gazing at the stars. Not music for the light-willed, for what thoughts do these gazes unfold upon us? —*Janelle McCall*

555
Mog Stunt Team
Small Stone Records

From the ashes of Loudhouse and the Cosmic Bandito rises...Mog Stunt Team. (No—not the cat—the band.) By now you've heard of them—sporting devil horns and dreadlocks and touting influences from Bob Marley to Tesla. (No—not the band—the scientist.) Mog Stunt Team is on a quest to infiltrate your mind with self-described fight anthems that would make Hussein smile. Ignore the rumors of the guitarist's possession by Jimi Hendrix's ghost or that the drummer is the *original* bionic man—these guys are for real! The moods on Mog Stunt Team's first full-length CD are like Michigan weather—intense and unpredictable—sonically flowing one moment, furious and unchained the next. All the tracks stand out but "Bug's" jazzy bassline, "Capt. Lee"—which will undoubtedly de-throne Sinatra's "My Way" as a karaoke standard—and a cover of Motorhead air-guitar classic, "Iron Fist" come highly recom-mended. All 10 songs do as much as they can to bring you close to Mog Stunt Team's heart and soul

---

▲ "Sonic Boom," "Band of the Year: His Name Is Alive," *Orbit*, January 1997.

His Name Is A Liar

We all know the facts about His Name Is Alive. They're from Livonia, they've released several albums now on 4AD and the visionary of the collective, Warren Defever, seems to have a strange aptitude for lying. It seems that whenever the opportunity knocks—and even when it doesn't—there's some type of misinformation flowing out of his mouth. We decided to corner Defever on a few specifics. In the end, we managed to wretch the truth out of him in some instances, while being told yet more lies at other times.

by Colin Webcott

Orbit: Alright, buster, I've been doing some research.

Warren Defever: Great! Then you already know all of the facts!

O: *Non-facts.* Like the title of your album, *Ft. Lake.* You claim it's named after an abandoned military fort, but where is it on the map? [Exhibit A: Supposed history, taken from CD release flyer.]

WD: Supposedly, it's in Goodrich, Michigan. There's an exit off I-75.

O: But have you seen it on a map?

WD: No.

O: Have you seen it on a map?

WD: No!

O: How did you find out about it?

WD: I don't remember. It's just something you're aware of if you grow up in Michigan. I'll have to assume that you haven't…

O: But I *have!*

WD: Oh. Well, it's just one of those things. Kids are born with it in their DNA now. It's just universal knowledge. What's the question?

O: It's about the legitimacy of Ft. Lake.

WD: O.K. I think the real question is, "Can you prove that there isn't one?"

O: O.K. Can you? Of course not, right? Because there *is* one, right?

WD: Of course. There's never been any question in my mind.

O: My records show that your grandfather made you play the violin, accordion, slide guitar and banjo. [Exhibit B: *Paper* 9/96.]

WD: Yeah. He'd always play in bands. He was in a band called the Westernaires. He had all these instruments. He would force me and my brothers to play them. This was really my first introduction to music. [I

was] four or five. I have really no recollection of music before sitting down at his house, and him saying, "O.K., this is a polka, this is a waltz, this is country-western music. We learned Hank Williams and every rotten old song that I now love again, but there was a long stretch where I hated that. As far as I knew, that was music. It was just no way to learn about music.

O: Well that's more of an introduction than most kids have.

WD: Yeah, but as soon as I was in the fourth or fifth grade, I realized that that's *not* what kids like! I figured out that it was *not* cool. Elvis was cool. Rockabilly was cool. Surf music was cool. After that, in the sixth grade, I started listening to punk, and that's when it really started coming together. That's all true. And there's a tape on Time Stereo called *3/4 Time*, which is recordings of my grandfather's bands that I've acquired and mixed. He recorded things, but nothing had ever been released. It's a good one, too.

O: Speaking of songs of the past, let's talk about your song "Beech Boys" on *Stars on E.S.P.* During a radio interview, you claimed that you had never heard the Beach Boys song, "Good Vibrations."

WD: O.K., I'm going to go on record here. That was incorrect. I think I just didn't really remember.

O: So you're going to tell me that you didn't lie?

WD: Oh boy…Is it possible to just remember incorrectly? Is that different than lying?

O: I don't know. Let's call Ronald Reagan…

WD: To me, early on, "Good Vibrations" was a psychedelic song. I don't think that now, but to me that's what it meant for a long time. Usually what happens is you go to a place like Los Angeles, and there's a really smug, super intelligent, super egotistical DJ or journalist who thinks that not only do they know everything about music, they themselves have helped notate it. You can't tell them the truth. You're doing the world a great disservice to tell them the truth.

O: What do you think would have happened if you told the truth?

WD: Someone who's in my situation shows up, and they're like, "This is the hillbilly kid from Michigan, the guy who just fell off the back of a turnip truck. This guy doesn't know anything about music." There's an element of that that makes you want to go with it. You want to say, "O.K. You're going to treat me that way, and now you're really going to get it. I'm going to sit here, you're going to ask me to play a song, and I'm

going to play three folk songs from a hundred years ago. I'm going to act like this is what people play in Michigan. I'm going to spend a half an hour talking about playing country-western and waltzes and polkas, and act like we don't even have electricity." Plus, especially if you're in Europe, you start to develop a southern accent.

O: It seems like Europe is more accepting of your music, but do people in the industry have a lot of preconceived notions?

WD: You really have to put up with people who assume they know more about what you're doing than you do, and all you can do is shoot them down.

O: In Europe or everywhere?

WD: Everywhere.

O: So that's like you're, uh…

WD: That's my policy.

O: Your defense mechanism? Maybe to help them to open up their eyes a little bit?

WD: It's really for their education.

O: I was reading in a *Livonia*-era bio that you "write words every day and music every other day and record one song per week." [Exhibit C: HNIA official bio sheet.]

WD: [A long pause.] That, of course, would amount to a lot of songs….Whether or not it's three songs a week, I don't know, but there's an extremely large quantity of music being recorded and produced here—and remixed.

O: Remixes! You recently did a remix for Thurston Moore on *Root.*

WD: Yeah, that was a good one. That was the first remix I ever did where I did the remix without listening to what they'd sent before I did it. It was the first remix I did that contained no elements of the original tape.

O: That's what I was going to ask you about!

WD: It was the first remix I ever sang on.

O: So not only did it contain no original elements, but you actually *sang* on it. What was it that you were supposed to remix?

WD: What he sent out was 30 different one-minute guitar pieces.

O: Guitar excerpts that you didn't use. So what did you do instead?

WD: I sang and played guitar. And there's my interpretation of what I think Thurston Moore should be doing in 1999.

O: Kind of like a tribute to him rather than a remix?

WD: It was more for his education. It was more like a subtle hint.

O: Did he realize that that's what you did?

WD: I don't know. I have not gotten a response.

O: Did the record label Lo realize that's what you did?

WD: No.

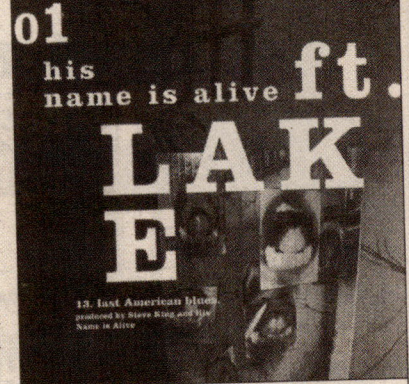

O: So they thought it was a remix.

WD: Where remixes are at in this point in time is so open to interpretation. Like me, I would consider that a remix, although technically nothing was ever remixed.

O: I wonder what Thurston would say about that one. I would seriously be interested in his response. I'm sure he listened to it. He probably thought, "He must have really strangely fit in something in a very subtle way."

WD: Right. It turned out real good, I think.

O: So would you jump off a cliff just because someone called you "mister?" [Exhibit D: *Mean Street* 9/96.]

WD: Yeah. Now this is something I've been

wondering about for a long time. That happened many years ago, probably 1988. But it's all true. We were on tour with Elvis Hitler in British Columbia. My brother and some other people were there….We were up on this cliff…checking out the scene, and some kid yells, "Hey mister, don't be afraid of your freedom!" And that doesn't happen every day.

O: Well, yeah, especially when you're on top of a cliff.

WD: It's part of a national park there, and we were probably two or three miles into the woods, and we came across this really scenic oasis with young boys with no shirts on, cliff-diving. It was really strange. So exciting….When the kid yelled at us, I took it to mean *me.* He's talking to *me.* That voice spoke to *me.* What do you do in that situation?

O: Jump off a cliff, of course!

WD: You take off your shirt and you jump off a cliff. Elvis jumped, too.

O: What was it like, jumping?

WD: It was very freeing. To me, it really opened up the possibilities. The whole scene was very idealic to begin with. It was like we were on another planet, or in a dream. I think it definitely altered my course. It wasn't long after that that I quit Elvis Hitler and decided to concentrate on His Name Is Alive full-time.

O: So next time I see you on a cliff, if I say, "Hey mister…" would you still jump?

WD: Sometimes you need a reminder.

O: What if there was cement at the bottom.

WD: Hey, you can't be afraid.

O: Sometimes when you're playing out of town, you'll tell an audience that you're thinking of moving to their city, which you've had no intention of ever doing.

WD: The fact of the matter is that I've lived in Livonia in the same house for 29 years, and I'm not going anywhere.

O: So you're saying that just to tease them.

WD: It's a combination of a couple of different things. Part of it is that it's always good to tease your audience. It's sort of like an ironic take on saying, "I love your sports team," or making lame references to tourist sites and things like that. It works on a cou-

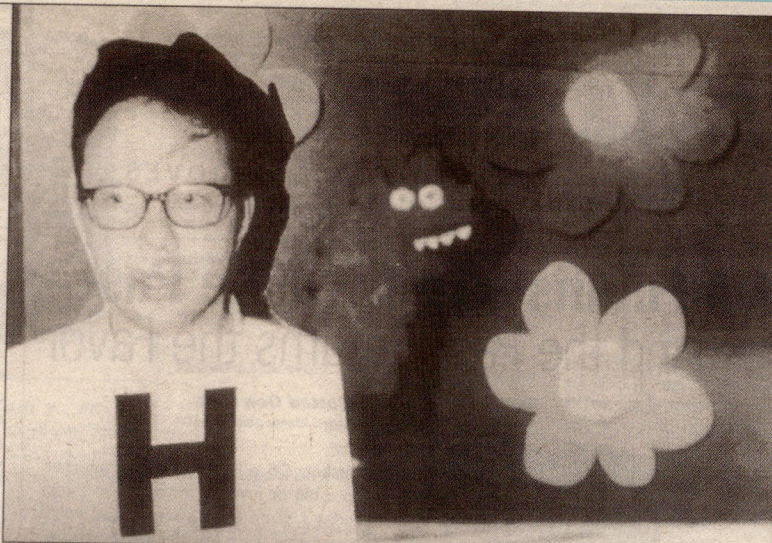

opportunity to enlighten, educate and entertain the people of Detroit. Our attempts to resuscitate the alien were unsuccessful.

O: This was done during a live show?

WD: At that point, there was no choice but to try and figure out how he died. Actually, it ended up being a she.

O: A she? How did you figure that out?

O: If they didn't?

WD: No, if I said that.

O: Nothing, but this is an investigative report here.

WD: Oh. Right. The way I look at it, when you buy a magazine, it's partially for education, but it's primarily for entertainment. I find that extremely boring. I like things that are more fantastic, more exciting. I would say that 90% of all interviews read exactly the same.

O: Even if they're not true?

WD: Yeah, because the quality of music journalism is so low, that even when you read the most basic facts, they're incorrect. If they're going to get it wrong, I would rather be the person that got it wrong and have it be at least remotely interesting. If that means digging an alien out of the Detroit River, then that's the way it's got to be. That's what I have to do every day, is look around for these things. It's part of my job.

O: Even if you have to say during an interview, "It's all lies, every word of it." [Exhibit G: *Albany Student Press*, October 9, 1990]

WD: Ultimately, it's all lies anyway. There are so many lies.…When I write my book—

O: Now you're going to write a *book*??

WD: Yeah—it's going to have it straight!

O: Wait, what's the book going to be about?

WD: I'm not sure.

O: It's going to be about you?

WD: I think it's just going to set the record straight, whether it's about me or just what I've seen in this world.

O: Is it actually going to set the record straight, or is it going to make it crooked?

WD: It's going to name names and point fingers.

O: So you've already started working on this book?

WD: No.

O: Oh. I thought you were going to say yes…

WD: See, that was a good opportunity… I've got notes, I've got a few chapters, outlines. I don't have a title yet. Actually, it's called *I Want You to Live a Hundred Years.*

O: Hey, I've heard that before.

WD: Oh boy.

O: Where have I heard that before?

WD: That's the name of my new solo album! Warren Defever: 1899-1999: *I Want You to Live a Hundred Years.*

O: Ahh, O.K. Well, where can you find this?

WD: Uh, it's not out yet. It's going to come out on Lo recordings, and in the US it'll be available on Time Stereo, probably closer to April.

O: Just you and nobody else?

WD: Just me. It was recorded in one day, and then mixed on a different day.

O: Two days?

WD: Yup. Um, [Volunteering!] I went to CMJ this year, and I was on a panel to discuss the relationship between the actual artists and college radio. The host opened up the panel, and said, "I'm going to start the questions off with something for those of you on the panel that weren't born or raised in this country. How has that affected your perception of college radio? This one will go out to Warren." All I could think was, "What country do they think I'm from? What story do I need to stick with, or do I tell them the truth?" I found myself in the middle of a great Seinfeldian dilemma.

O: So what did you do?

WD: I took the mic and said, "When I was growing up in Canada, we didn't have college radio. But sometimes we could hear some of the stations from Detroit."

O: Did anybody flinch?

WD: There were a couple of people from 4AD there, and the publicist was in the front. I could see them. They were just ready to die when they heard the question. They said that when they stuck my name to the question, my jaw just dropped—that I looked confused.

O: Should we believe that you are currently doing work with StunGun? (The rumor is that he's producing some songs.)

WD: Yes, but I wouldn't believe it until you've heard some. I think it's going to surprise a lot of people.

E

I don't know where Alvin's is, but from the looks of the little booklet thingie that comes with the Time Stereo "UFO Doctor" video, it looks like Alvin's is an important historical site, where an amazing alien autopsy took place. Look around for signs and keep your nose open for strange smells, ok? Traces of alien blood last a long time

ple of different levels because as a group, the audience isn't thinking that hard. It really puts them, as a group, into being the audience, and they cheer—they get excited. "His Name Is Alive is moving to our town. What great news is this?" But then, as a sociological experiment, you can see their faces as they realize, "They're not going to move here! That guy's never going to move!" And they look disappointed. And then it's sad, but what can you do?

O: Well, I could give you a suggestion—

WD: And then after the show, people say, "You're not really going to move here, are you? This town sucks! You really don't want to move here." That's the funny thing —they warn us. And then I'll say, "You know what? You're right! I'm not going to move here! Thanks for the tip!"

O: So you still tell people that today?

WD: Yeah.

O: Well, we'd better warn everybody then.

WD: To me, that's just the traditional part of being a traveling entertainer. There was something that Hank Williams would say in every city he visited. He'd say, "You know, I never been to St. Louis before, but if I come back, I'll have been here twice." And it cracked him up every night. It's a tradition. I'm just playing out my part.

O: It is claimed that you have sold at your shows a Time Stereo video called *UFO Doctor* that contains an actual alien autopsy. [Exhibit E: Fan e-mail.]

WD: Yeah. My friends and I had discovered the body of what was apparently a UFO driver.…In the Detroit River.

O: You were…swimming in the Detroit River???

WD: I can't remember what we were doing. But immediately we alerted the press and set-up a show. This was a great

WD: Well, you've just got to look!

O: So they're not much different?

WD: They're not much different. They're taller, though. A lot of people think they're shorter, but this one was very tall. We were very surprised by the things we found in it—her.

O: Like what?

WD: There was a license plate. Because it was in the Detroit River, it was the typical things you'd find in large fish or sharks.

O: So you think this alien was actually living in the River?

WD: I'm not sure how long this thing had actually been down there. It's possible that that's just the kind of thing you get from the River. I don't know. We'll never know!

F

they come out. After that, it varies. It's really well distributed in my home town, Livonia, Michigan. It's a really neat place. Even the ones in the area of Detroit and Ann Arbor seem to carry it, featuring stickers, "Yes, they're really from Livonia."
YF: You don't do any singing on Livonia, do you?
W: Yeah, I do. I sang the last song "I'll

O: So you're claiming that it's an actual alien. From where?

WD: I have no idea. But it was tall.

O: When *Livonia* first came out, you claimed that some of the shops in the area used stickers that said, "Yes, they're really from Livonia." [Exhibit F: *Your Flesh* Winter '90–'91]

WD: That's true!

O: That's *true*?

WD: I think so. I can't remember. That was ten years—

O: You can't *remember*??? We're back to that again?!?

WD: Um, let's say they didn't. What would be wrong with that?

G

answers with tongue planted firmly in cheek: "It's all lies, every word of it."
The music of His Name Is Alive

O: How?

WD: The sound. The combination of them and me is something that you wouldn't expect either one of us to do.

O: How did you get involved with that?

WD: That's a good question. Um, Davin [Brainard; fellow Time Stereo cohort] had met them at Kinko's. They were admiring the Electric Bear rubber stamp.

O: So you're saying it wasn't at a show or anything? It was at Kinko's?

WD: It was really the Electric Bear.

O: It would probably seem to a lot of people like a strange pairing, although it makes me very curious to hear the result.

WD: To me, that's what makes it exciting. You don't want to hear the obvious band doing the obvious thing. Where's the magic in that?

O: That's true. That's kind of like the premise of all these lies, too.

WD: It's all about quality entertainment. People want to have a good time, and I'm here to give it to them. 🌀

Be on the lookout for a new His Name Is Alive compilation, Always Stay Sweet *(4AD) at the end of this month, primarily focusing on material from the first three now unavailable albums. At least that's what we're told.*

Fun and *Orbit*, and who was featured occasionally in *Orbit*, was Jack White. He said that the magazines created by Peterson and his staffs seemed to have one ear closer to the ground than some other media in town, and that was great for musicians starting out and looking for attention:

I suppose it was all gravy to any musician. . . . Something about the printed word legitimizes what you've been struggling with in your attic or basement for so long. The big papers, [Detroit] *Free Press* and [Detroit] *News* were always good to local bands and the mobs I was in. The *Metro Times* I always found cynical and negative, and when they brought in a new editor from outside of Detroit around [2000], it became absolutely atrocious and not supportive of local art and music at all, which should be the point of a free weekly. While *Fun* magazine and *Orbit* felt a lot more supportive and positive to me and also full of satire as well—which is the positive side of that sort of "hip" culture, cynicism being the negative side.

U Said it

How do you want to die?

Irene O'Nickle
23, Crispin Glover's Girlfriend

With a smile on my face.

Mr. D. Miller
32 & 364/365, Master of Nothing

Stretched till pulled apart.

Nancy & Leslie
31, Evil Twins

We were born together, we want to die together.

Jack White
22, Upholsterer

High-powered rifle, three blocks away.

Kramer-Shaw
30, Beauty Operator

Pretty.

▲ Jack White in "U Said It," *Orbit*, March 1998.

U Said it

What's keeping you from being a professional model?

Toni Jedlowski
23, waitress/ writer student

I'm really short. Because I'm so stunning all other models would be jobless.

The Baroness
21, piano teacher

My looks, I'm a rock star.

Craig Posegay
28, 89X promotion director

Quarterpounders with cheese.

Eminem
20-something, rap super star

I'm such a little bastard.

Terry Bruns
54, retired

Too damn fat.

▲ Eminem in "U Said It," *Orbit*, April 1999.

Goober in "U Speak," *Orbit*, ▶
November 8–20, 1999.

Wanna Date?

Before the Internet, local newsweekly calendars helped to spread the word about when music shows and other events were happening. *Orbit* writers also found ways to inject humor into what could be a rather dull listing of names, places, and dates.

ORBIT SEPTEMBER 1998 29

CRITICAL DATES

SEPTEMBER 2 – SEPTEMBER 30

Wed, Sept 2

Blues Music Festival
Pine Knob, Clarkston
(248) 377-0100

...and the Neville

...Gallery,

...her love
...and
...integrating
...lives, embellish
...ives. Runs
...month.

...Birmingham
...680
...with new work by
...eff Rosi, Deform,
...Showing all

...pt 3

...etroit Jazz
...owntown Detroit
...za with The Sun
...d Diane Schuur.

...Mr. Freedom
...or Image
...873
...pop, or snap,

Knee Deep Shag w/
Baked Potato
Blind Pig, Ann Arbor
(734) 996-8555
Go early because we all know it
...potatoes to

JUST A GIGOLO

No, it's not **Sammy Hagar**, it's the guy who used to sing with **Valerie Bertinelli's** husband's band. Yes, the incomparable **DAVID LEE ROTH** will be bringing his brand of raucous rock to the **NEW PINE KNOB on JULY 15**. You better see him quick before he loses the rest of that luscious head of hair.

Kid Rock & Twisted Brown Trucker
Friday, September 25, State Theatre, Detroit (313) 961-5450

Musically, we are expecting the best show since that Bob Seger Live Bullet thing where Bob tells the crowd he was reading in *Rolling Stone* that Detroit audiences were the best rock 'n' roll audiences in the world. And then Bob goes on to say that, shit, he's known that for ten years! Well, expect that at least for "Only God Knows Why," Kid Rock's genuine trailer park rock ballad. The rest of the show is going to be the kind of thundering hip-hop-rock that is going to push Twisted Brown Trucker over the top. This is the first show in Kid Rock's White Trash On Dope Tour and the first since his major record label (Atlantic) deal CD, *Devil Without a Cause*, (great #%&*ing album, by the way) has hit the stores. So here's your chance to see the Bullgod, the illegitimate son of man, fresh off the Warped (where Rancid's twelve-step program trailer couldn't keep him clean) and sky rocketing towards stardom. We could sit here all day and tell you how great Mr. Olson, Mr. Bones and the rest of Twisted Brown Trucker is. Or tell a tale or two about Yodeling in The Valley with the rude, crude and lewd Kid Rock. But you're going to have to see it with your own bloodshot eyes. Of course don't forget there's Joe C., three-foot-nine with a ten-foot...well, you're just going and see that for yourself, too.

A STATE OF MIND

Hinduism teaches us **NIRVANA** is a perfect state of blissfulness and tranquility. So perfect in fact, your soul leaves your body and joins the great oversoul in the heavens above and you die. Pretty neat eh? Experience these some feelings and live to tell about it **OCT. 11, ST. ANDREWS HALL**.

...Phoenix

...val
...featuring
...s and

...Orby's
...forming:
...cle. The
...oy,
...Big
...ers. The
...more
...f

...zz

...etroit

...cked

...before the end of the month to:
Listings %o Orbit
919 S. Main, Royal Oak, MI 48067
or e-mail to orbit@mich.com

...Jenny

...heir to
...a GAP
...with that?

Six Finger Satellite
w/ A StoveBoat and White Stripes
Friday, September 11,
Gold Dollar, Detroit,
(313) 833-6873

It's new wave meets punk rock, and, dammit, you're not gonna forget it! (New wave = keyboards, in this case the all-time favorite Moog! Punk rock = harsh, crashing guitars.) Since 1992, Providence's 6FS have been known to frighten audience members that stand too close to the front. Oh no, this isn't your typical Devo—they were just too innocent to create such dark energy. Their newest album, *Law of Ruins*, is especially dark and especially spaced-out and mean at the same time! The drama is fully realized through the muffled, intense vocals. And don't miss StoveBoat (also from Providence), who, for lack of a better description, play incredibly strange-looking instruments.

Sat, Sept 5

DJ Top Kat
Motor Lounge, H
(313) 369-0080
Get your bad self h
get down, get fun
with the dance D,
You just never kn
throw Kraftwerk o
mix to totally *!(a
mind and body, I
6 and every Saturday

Some of...
today from...
Brooks, To...
Stars, Tasli...
McKinney, ...
Jazz Vangu...
His Red Hot ...
Franz Jacks...
Colectivo, Ka...
Leon y Orque...
Pistol Allen Q...
and New Wo...
'Thunder' Wa...
Allen Quartet...
lovers. Plus m...

Landstride...
Lantern Jac...
Gold Dollar, D...
(313) 833-68...
Also playing Unf...
Four Eyes and T...
noise, indie pop,

Wayne Newt...
The Palace, Aub...
(313) 377-0100
So Mr. Las Vegas...
turn and lands in D

Masters of N...
JD's Macomb Th...
Mt. Clemens
(810) 913-1921

Immortal Wino...
The New Way Bar,
(248) 541-9870

The Delta Child...
Band
Grand Cafe, Farmin
(248) 615-9181

Broadzilla w/ The...
Workhorse Move...
Paycheck's Lounge,
Hamtramck
(313) 874-0254
I somehow feel that it should read
Broadzilla vs. The Workhorse
Movement.

Poignant Plecostomus
w/ Spy Radio
Blind Pig, Ann Arbor
(734) 996-8555
That's a lot of syllables.

William Barnhart
(Square-type design
here)uzelac Gallery, Pontiac
(248) 332-5257
How do you find (Square-
design here) in the phone

Marie Baie Des Ar...
DFT, Detroit
(313) 833-2323
Wet, nekkid French kids
in all sorts of "teen-age
ntes." Take your parents
Sun.

Monaural w/ Visi...
Magic Stick, Detroit
(313) 833-9700

Louie Anderson
The Ark, Ann Arbor
(734) 761-1800
A rare club appearanc
guy for a really good
or the Homeless Emp
Relationship Organiz

...the House, Scully and Mob
Mentality.

Hatchet Job w/
Gutter Punx
Shelter, Detroit
(313) 961-MELT
Gotta love those bands that think
it's cool to substitute an "x" for a
"ks."

Arts Beats and Eats
Downtown Pontiac
Day Two of this really fun week-
end festival of art, food and music.

DANZIG (W/TYPE O NEGATIVE and GODFLESH)
Monday Dec. 5
State Theatre
One time, my little sister and her friends had a slumber party. Tired of downing Doritos, trying out new hair styles, and puffing away on their very first cigarettes, they decided to get really crazy. They turned on the tube, and low and behold, Headbanger's Ball was on MTV. And that was when the teenyboppers got their first glimpse of the muscle-bound Glenn Danzig himself. Being the witty kids that they are, those crazy grrrls made up their own lyrics to "Mother." And to this day, when I hear Danzig, I quietly sing "Mother...If you want, burn goats tonight..." (Not actually the real lyrics).

I know it may sound bizarre, but I just can't take Danzig that seriously when most of their fans are not drugged-out long hairs, but suburban kiddies who are fans due to shows like Headbanger's Ball and Beavis and Butthead. (Huhuhuh...Danzig ROCKS!) Since the show is all ages, the mosh pit should be a melange of peoples, from the true bangers to the clean cut kids who want to go to their first "All Ages Show." Godflesh, whose popularity has been on the upswing because of a newly released album, and Type O Negative will also be present adding to the overwhelming loudness of the show. Due to the fact that the show is at the State Theatre, I'm predicting that a large quantity of body-suited and tight jeans type girls will mistakenly end up at the show and seduce Glenn and the boys. Rock On, alterna-teens. *-E.E.B.*

Rush/Primus
Sunday, March 27
The Palace
Like the persistent date-seeker for prom, Rush just won't get lost. After their last abysmal album, *Roll The Bones* (in which bassist frontman Geddy Lee actually tried his hand at some wretched rapping), *Counterparts*. Give them character points, I guess, for sticking around and insisting on truly embarrassing themselves once and for all before disappearing. And why exactly does Primus feel the need to go on tour year after year, anyway? Their self-appointed "Primus Sucks" logo rings more and more true with time. *-N.R.H.*

▲ "Critical Dates," *Orbit*, September 1998.

MELISSA FERRICK
THURSDAY, MARCH 31
BRAZIL COFFEEHOUSE

Oooh, those haunting eyes that follow you around the room. Oooh, that expensively disheveled post-post mod look of a "Reality Bites" extra. Oooh, those "I heard Natalie Merchant and it changed my life" vocals. Oooh, that way over-produced, "where's the song?" sound. Oooh, she's doing the coffeehouse hipster tour. Appropriately enough, she's on the same label as Juliana Hatfield. Oooh…-S.T.S.

SHERYL CROW
Wednesday, August 10
St. Andrews

Is it me, or does Miss Crow play in Detroit more than White Zombie? But I'll cut her some slack, seeing how she tries to liven up the proceedings without resorting to that lame (but oh so popular) current trend of her contemporaries ripping off Stevie Nicks circa *Rumours*. And that song that goes "all I wanna do is have some fun" is my guilty pleasure of the month (hey, it's been a slow month). -S.T.S

THE EAGLES
Thursday, February 16
Palace of Auburn Hills

You would think with all the senseless violence in the world that somebody would get sensible and inflict some bodily hurt on these money-grubbing has-beens. Hell Freezes Over? I think it's time that Don, Glenn, Joe and whatever that other coke-head's name is went back to their mountain retreats in Aspen and let Hell get back to a comfortable temperature. -Brendan Rohan

CHEAP TRICK

Fri.–Sun., November 27–29, St. Andrew's Hall
(313) 961-MELT

Back in the '70s these guys were Pearl Jam huge. Remember the Dream Police? Playing "Surrender" as you tried to ball the chick you picked up hitchhiking in Hines Park in your customized van (with the "Ass, Grass or Cash, Nobody Rides for Free" bumpersticker)? We don't either, but it sounds like a screen play. The two cute guys have gotten old and creepy looking, but the two weird guys still look weird. It has been a long time since they've done Cobo, but thanks to the Smashing Pumpkins they are playing three nights in a row at St. Andrew's (versus one night at IROCK). Don't forget to keep shouting "I Want You To Want Me" while the band plays. The Nuge is rumored to bring his gun down and shoot 'em all.

Sun, Sept 13

Aerosmith w/ Monster Magnet
Pine Knob, Clarkston
(248) 377-0100
The guy who fixed my plumbing assures me that these guys "rock," and he's got the tattoos to prove it.

Mon, Feb 16

Ben Folds Five
Clutch Cargo's, Pontiac
(248) 333-2362
Ben Folds Five? With only three guys in the band? Is someone pullin' me leg? It doesn't even matter, 'cause the show's sold out.

Fri, Feb 20

Grace Jones
Clutch Cargo's, Pontiac
(248) 333-2362
If you need me, I'll be cowering in my closet.

Are You Gonna Laugh at That?

Fun's sense of humor and love of satire carried over into *Orbit*. Whether it was in an interview with a band, or in a restaurant or movie review, a joke was never far away. *Orbit* writers also created humor features. Easy humor pegs could always

Orby says: "He who laughs last is not the brightest."

be found around holidays, with ads for fake toys around Christmas, a listing of the best cheap motels to make your Valentine's Day extra special, or where to go on your summer vacation.

Some of the more notorious humor pieces came later in *Orbit*'s run and were penned by editor/writer Jeremy Harvey. "The best was the garage sale, it was really, really good," Harvey said. "That was this mock garage sale that we set up. That was before . . . Tom Green was on MTV [and before] *Jackass*. So, it was kind of this new thing to pull a prank and film it or write an article about it. It was just a garage sale, but it was just filled with the worst things that you could find, and me and Jerry were just completely crazy, running the show. We would be mock customers and start fights. It was just really hysterical, that was probably my favorite moment in *Orbit* history."

The humor that Harvey and other writers created played on expectations and put people in uncomfortable positions. Everyone, including Harvey, felt uncomfortable when he visited a nudist beach for an article. "I completely doctored up my genitalia so it looked like I was covered in STDs. I had fake warts and I put a bunch of glue around my testicles so that when it dried it would be all flaky and fall off as I talked to people, and I used makeup to put rashes everywhere," said Harvey.

Sometimes good ideas get out of hand. Such was the case with the "Win a Dream Date with Stun Gun," the popular all-female band in Detroit. The dream date turned into a nightmare, especially for members of the band. According to Harvey, who was friends with Stun Gun, "A huge fight took place in the limo between the guitarist and the singer—this huge fistfight. I was snapping photos. That was, like, a huge exposé in *Orbit*. That was really good," said Harvey.

Some of the humor came with a price. *Orbit* had already run into some trouble with their food column, and the "How to Be a Better Stalker" feature proved even more controversial. Writer Ron Wade said it was scary how people didn't get the joke and started to turn on the paper: "We caught so much for that. It was the first time I felt persecuted. A U of M feminist group thought we were making light of violence against women. Did it go to the line? Yes. Would I write that today? No. As the father of a daughter? No. I thought it was hysterical. It was at the time that stalking started to get attention. They [said they] would picket, boycott the advertisers. They started taking the issues on the U of M campus and [putting] them in the trash. That's the first time I got called in. Jerry was like, 'Any publicity is good publicity. If the advertisers start walking away, then we might have some issues.' Luckily none of them did."

In the 1980s, Little Caesars Pizza owner Mike Ilitch started buying up buildings near downtown Detroit. The area would later be dubbed Foxtown. Along with his purchase of the Detroit Red Wings hockey and Detroit Tigers baseball teams, Ilitch became a major player in the revitalization of the city. At the same time, he started to advocate for a new ballpark, moving the Tigers from the corner of Michigan and Trumbull for the first time in over a hundred years. This got the *Orbit* team thinking. Was Ilitch making a play to reshape Detroit?

This year, give them
something they really want.
Better than "Barney" or Barbie" or any
store bought cruddily-dud. Give them

Gifts From the Heart

Christmas is a time for families, caring and sharing, giving and living. This year you're going to get a little help from St. Orby. A gift you can build for your son or daughter, niece or nephew. A gift from your heart.

A gift they are sure to love that you can build yourself!

BLOCKY™

Imagine their surprise when they unwrap their gift on Christmas morning and discover BLOCKY!

There is nothing your loved ones, especially kids, will appreciate more than a gift you made with your own two hands. When you give a child a homemade gift, you are telling that child "You know I love you or I wouldn't have labored hours and hours for you. I could have gone to the store and plopped down a pile of cash on the latest overpriced toy they advertise on TV. But I didn't. I built this just for you, because I love you."

BLOCKY doesn't cost an arm and a leg!

BLOCKY is constructed from items you probably already have laying around the garage, just apply a little elbow grease and a dash of love.

BLOCKY is EZ to build

You don't have to be a rocket scientist to assemble BLOCKY. You can build BLOCKY in about half the time it would take to assemble any department store hunk o' junk. Simply follow the easy instructions below, and clear out a special spot under the tree.

BLOCKY is durable

With the proper care and handling, your BLOCKY will last forever.

BLOCKY is sturdy, made from American hardwood, unlike so many of the shoddy plastic and cheap electronic

toys you'll see on department store shelves or advertised on television.

Best of all, BLOCKY is lovable!

Everybody loves BLOCKY! BLOCKY is the most huggable, squeezable, lovable toy in the whole world. Imagine your child's pride when they show-off BLOCKY to their friends!

A gift from you. A prize you labored over. The gift of love...BLOCKY.

Accessorizing your BLOCKY

If your child is a little older, or a teenager, you may wish to customize your BLOCKY. Designer packages are available from *Orbit* at nominal cost.

Choose from any of our deluxe BLOCKY packages:

• Deluxe BLOCKY Goo Goo eyes – $4.00 per set of two

• MRS. BLOCKY™ "Paint & Glue Hair" – $2.95 a headful

• Vidal Sassoon Designer Hair Doo – $1.95

• BLOCKY Mobile Template (not pictured) – $2.95

• Deluxe BLOCKY Mobile Wheels & Headlamps $4.00

• BLOCKY Face Template – $2.00

• Ninja BLOCKY Action Figure Samurai sword – $2.75

Complete BLOCKY kits

• BLOCKY Kit (all parts, instructions) – $5.95

• Deluxe BLOCKY Kit – $7.95

• Pre-Assembled BLOCKY – $9.95

Continued on page 42

Instructions

You'll Need:
• 1 Board (2 x 6 x 6)
• 4 Nails
• 4 Pipe Cleaners
• A Marker
• Saw
• Hammer (or large wrench)

Step 1: Using saw cut a length of 2x 6 into six inch squares. Board should be square after cutting. (Hint: You'll save over 30¢ a foot by using rough grade lumber. Better yet, check behind factories for discarded shipping pallets.)

Step 2: Pound nails into right side of BLOCKY one quarter inch from top & bottom. Nails have a natural tendency to bend, so just keep pounding till they stick. Repeat on left side.

Step 3: Attach pipe cleaner to nail by twisting cleaner around nail. Repeat on all nails. You can use wire coat hangers if you can't afford pipe cleaners.

Step 4: Using template (see ordering instructions below) draw cute BLOCKY face with permanent black marker.

Gifts *Not* From The Heart

Gift Guide for Spoiled Rich Bastards (e.g. Pimps, Drug Dealers, Unscrupulous Lawyers, Shameless Celebrities, Decadent Rock Stars, Junk Bond Traders, U.S. Congressmen, etc.)

Wouldn't it be great if you had rich, powerful friends who actually bought you cool, expensive stuff for Christmas? Imagine what kind of gifts friends of Roseanne get, or how about your Congressman sharing some of his bribe money with his closest Mafia buddies. Kind of chokes you up with the Christmas spirit just thinking about it.

Orbit recently talked to a local retailer to the stars (who wished to remain anonymous) to find out what the other half was stuffing in their loved ones stockings with this Christmas. If you want to feel the pure, unadulterated yuletide cheer like Spoiled Rich Bastards, you might want to buy a few items of these for yourself.

The Shell – Manufactured by Earthian's Inc., the Shell is the fashion statement for the nineties; a stylish piece of clothing that doubles as a bullet proof vest. It comes in two parts, with the inner part being the armor which zips into the outer part to become hip urban nightware like a leather vest or jacket. A must for any aspiring hip-hop artist or those who want too look good when the bullets start to fly. ($800–$900 Earthian's Inc.)

NVX-15 – For just a few hundred small monthly payments, Sony can hook you up with their Global Positioning System. This high-tech gizmo replaces the primitive technology of a compass or esoteric knowledge of how to figure direction from the sun or stars. It will find your way out of the wilderness and onto the right highway, state or local road, hotels to sleep in, even restaraunts to eat at. If you can afford this, chances are you could just hire a chauffer. ($2,200 Sony)

Nikon 35TI – Nikon made this for those who like the convenience of point-and-shoot cameras but want to spend a lot more money. It combines Nikon's SLR image quality with a compact lightweight titanium body. ($800 Nikon)

Grundig YB-400 FM/AM/Shortwave Receiver/Clock Radio – Now that every radio station, from urban contemporary to album-oriented rock, has gone top 40 alternative, it's time to get your hands on the "world's best portable radio". The AM sound is the best of any portable, so you can tune into Golden oldies or Motown or pull in some shortwave transmission from way down the block. ($249.95 Grundig)

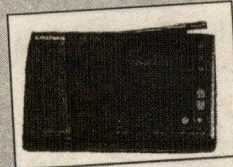

Yet More Gifts From the Heart

A treasure they'll never forget, because YOU made it yourself

Written by Kathy Wonderkraft

Photos by Brett Carson

The Kno-Knit Patchwork Sweater Vest

We'll bet you would love to knit a nice fuzzy warm patchwork sweater vest but don't have the time. Well what would you say if we told you could put together a patchwork sweater vest in under 45 minutes. Simply coat a 13 gallon (24"x28") kitchen trash bag with your favorite craft glue and apply your dryer lint in a festive patchwork pattern. Softer than cashmere with the durability of 2-ply polyethylene, this hand-crafted classic will be a fireside favorite for many X-mases to come.

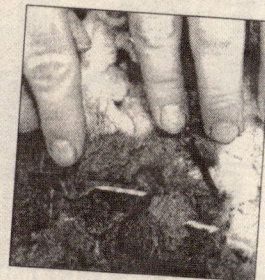

Glue the lint directly to the backing material, NEVER onto other pieces of lint.

The Ultimate Gift For Ketchup Lovers

Here's the perfect gift for the ketchup lover on your list. You won't find the Ketchup Lovers Tree in any department store or specialty shop. That's because it's made by you. Simply roll a piece of cardboard into a cone (a pizza box should work just fine but if you really have a huge ketchup lover on your hands you can build a life size tree from a refrigerator box). Attach several hundred fast-food ketchup packs side by side to a length of shiny silver duct-tape, and wrap in a clockwise direction around the cone. You'll have a striking centerpiece, and your ketchup lover will never be lacking when it comes to snacking. (No ketchup lover on your list? A festive holiday tree can be built using any fast-food condiment package).

Mad Mod Dorm-Room Decorator Pillow

Is your child away at college? Spruce up that dreary dorm room with a little personality. Have any old resort wear T-shirts destined for the rag bag? Good, you're on your way to a custom designer pillow, that is "hip" enough to make your child the envy of their dormitory. Simply sew or staple the neck and arm holes shut. Then stuff the "pillow" with wadded up newspaper balls (single sheets yield best results). A few quick stitches along the bottom and voila! you'll have a decorator doozy that will make the kids say "rock and roll"! Best of all, they'll appreciate a gift from the heart a lot more than the impersonal act of sending money. Hint —Write their name on the back in large permanent letters, dorm room brighteners have a funny habit of getting stolen.

Oodles Of Toys

If your neighbors are as wasteful as ours are, you'll notice they are always throwing these big plastic containers away. (Plus we often find a craft-makers bonanza inside; glass jars, magazines, newspapers, plastic jugs and tin cans). Here's an easy one that's a sure-fire X-mas hit guaranteed to please everyone, the Oodles Of Toys Toy Box. A gift that encourages kids to keep their room clean, too! Imagine the surprise when your children race to open the largest present under the tree, and find it was made by you!

Christmas Joy for Girls and Boys

America's TOP TEN TOYS!

"What's that weird sound under the bed?"

"Your parents were just eaten by giant sharks!"

Teddy Nightmare
Special hidden diode recognizes when bedroom light goes off, then little Teddy begins to chatter.
$4.49

"My parents sacrificed my twin sister"

"Will you be my vile, unspeakable acts play friend?"

"If you tell, your puppy dies"

Suzy Secret Satanic Ritual Abuse Doll
It can't cope, until you pull the hidden string and repressed memories start flowing like accusations at a witch trial. Great for show-and-tell day at the daycare center. $4.98

E-Z Bake Ant Farm
Right about the time Tommy starts to bond with the little vermin, a retractable cord allows parents to fry the entire colony alive.
$2.98

Junior Militia Man Shooting Gallery
Show Timmy or Debbie how to shoot straight and spot those who would deny our constitutional right to bear arms. Targets included: UN Blue Helmets, ATF Agents, international bankers, FBI sell-outs, and a bulls eye featuring Janet Reno.
$1.98

GI Vet
Can't readjust to life in the toy box. Has realistic flashbacks and sleepwalking fits during which he may actually harm child.
$3.49

"BLOCKY" the Toy Sensation that's sweeping the nation. $29.95

Reverend Wrathful Right-To-Life Enforcer Kit
The action toy of the '90s. Junior will be the toughest human-rights advocate on the block. Includes Bible, protest signs, surveillance camera, gruesome photo pamphlets, make-your-own firebomb kit and real working gun.

KILL ... ERS
HOLY BIBLE

Orbo Toys are truly inspirational - and there are none finer! Designed for maximum educational play value, an Orbo Toy is a toy with purpose.

Performance Art!
The art toy that doesn't require any talent. Kit includes fake liberal-arts degree, blank journal to record innermost ramblings, and toy syringe. Yams, urinal jar and crucifix sold separately.
$9.99

Performance ART KIT

Bucket O' Sharp Things
Suitable for preschoolers. Each piece is handcrafted to fit snugly into baby's windpipe.
$2.49

Bucket 'O Sharp Things

Deluxe Finger Pointer Set
lately   mom   dad   sis   bro   uncle   sister   grandma   neighbor   your best friend
Play the Blame Game

Deluxe Finger Point Set
A fun and educational kit that teaches your kids how to assign blame and scapegoat effectively. From the makers of BeLittle Nancy.
$1.98

You'll find ORBO Toys Wherever toys are sold!

Prices slightly higher west of the Mississippi and in Canada

▲ "America's Top Ten Toys," *Orbit*, December 1995.

SCOOBY DOO, THE UNANSWERED QUESTIONS

by Doug Dearth additional writing & research Dr. J.R. Vile & the Reverend Kingo

CAST OF CHARACTERS

FRED: Seemingly straightforward, yet wears his clothes with a curious "California" flair. Fred always drives the van, *the same type of vehicle used in the bombing of the World Trade Center!*

DAPHNE: (Gaelic: to be daft; to be foolish, giddy). Cute but trifling, or is the helpless female act a ploy? Is she a bi-sexual swinger looking for kinky kicks?

VELMA: Brainy, squat, "nice-personality," and manipulative. She peers through thick *horn*-rims and wears a cowl-neck outfit not unlike robes worn by satanic covens. Possibly controls the entire cult.

SHAGGY: Tall, lanky, unkempt, spineless and unshaven, Shaggy is an unseeming role model, yet why do so many of today's children emulate him by dressing in the "grunge" fashions he inspired.

SCOOBY DOO: This domesticated quadruped of the genus Canis Dane Greatus has the ability to travel on his hind legs for extended distances. Speaks in a humanoid yet decidedly demonic voice. Intelligent in spite of himself, perhaps *too intelligent!*

Scooby Doo, a harmless cartoon? Four curious teens and their lovable talking dog who solve strange occurrences around the country. Yet could there be another side to these "innocuous mysteries?" A dark side that may terrify you to the bottom of your soul?

Follow Orbit as we pick away at the friendly veneer of Scooby's cartoons to uncover the clandestine reality underneath. Be prepared: you'll delve into an evil underworld where murder, devil worship, terrorism, homosexuality, sado-masochism, bestiality, pornography, and rampant drug use may well reign supreme.

Basic Plot

Circa: 1972. Four young people on one long, extensive "freak out", complete with a psychedelic van. A care-free life on the American road, in search of answers, with a mystery around every corner. These "kids" investigate unexplained phenomenon, uncovering pointlessly convoluted plots perpetrated by bungling adults. Each enigma concerns the appearance of some ghostly entity or space creature, concocted by criminals to disguise a nefarious plot. Although such activity would usually bring on a media firestorm from "Sightings," The *Weekly World News*, or *Newsweek*, it seems only to attract these "kids," who by some unearthly power unravel these conundrums with uncanny ability. Never thought about that, did you?

More Questions Than Answers

Where did these jobless "kids" get the money for the souped up, psychedelic "Mystery Machine"? Who bankrolled their junkets across country? Why are they always surrounded by evil? Could they have just been elaborate cover-ups for drug deliveries and terrorism? Perhaps a child pornography ring? Or is the plot deeper; have we stumbled into Satan's insidious nationwide network?

Just Say No

One must remember this was an open, naive time where sexual and chemical experimentation was the accepted norm. Is everyone here as forthright and above reproach as we would believe? Let's examine Shaggy. Could he be a wanton drug abuser? Consider these facts:

• **Insatiable hunger.** "Munchies." Upon entering a haunted house would you raid the refrigerator? Yet Shaggy can only focus on his unappeasable craving for food. Remember Jeffrey Dahmer's refrigerator? Now what's your answer?

• **Unbridled Paranoia.** Sure, anyone would be scared, but most people would remain calm, rational and focused. Shag's distorted reactions to the smallest noises brings panic attacks bordering on dementia.

• **Lack of Personal Hygiene.** The drug addict often forsakes grooming and essential personal care.

• **Profoundly Delusional.** Typically confused and disoriented, as if in some state of chemical-induced stupor.

• **Bizarre Behavior.** Talks to Scooby Doo. A dog.

• **Scooby.** Rhymes with "doo-bie."

And what exactly is in a Scooby Snack? Why is the craving for these "snacks" so life-controlling? Those hooked on narcotics often exhibit the same behavior; every waking moment is spent enslaved to their habit. The drug addict is willing to do anything, no matter how degrading or life-threatening for that all-consuming next fix.

Sleeping Arrangements

Where do these kids, unsupervised by any adults, bed down at night and who with?

Let's examine Fred, sharply dressed, well-groomed, and in good physical shape. Heterosexual? You'll have to ask Shaggy. Which leaves us with the butchy intellectual Velma, who is constantly admonishing fellow traveler Shaggy for his insatiable hunger and cowardice. Sounds like a prototypical sadomasochist relationship to us.

Which leaves Daphne, an obvious beauty but weak and clingy. A preposterous supply of villains is on-hand to tie-up poor Daphne—how convenient. It is common for the "master" to have a number of slaves (submissive sexual partners) of both sexes which they willingly share with peers. Could Velma be the "dominant," a Manson-like ringleader who directs the sexual agenda this cult?

Even more perverse: the appearance of Scrappy Doo in later episodes. Just where did this Scrappy Doo come from? And how did he develop such a thorough command of the English language and why is Velma always smirking?

Still have doubts? Ask yourself, if you wore an ascot like Fred's and could still coax a chick into bed, would it be Velma? And what about that ever-present camera? Could it have been used for purposes other than catching crooks red-handed? Was it used to fuel the multi-billion dollar underground pornography industry?

To date, no photos of an orgiastic "anything goes" scenario, with each person switching from partner to partner without regard to virtue, monogamy, sex, or species, exists.

Dog or Demon?

Worshipers of the Devil meet in small groups called "covens" and perform unspeakable acts of sin and perversion. Could the Scooby bunch be a front for one of these Satanic covens?

In ancient times it is reported that animal "familiars" (typically ravens, goats or large dogs much like Scooby) were sent by Lucifer to communicate with his followers. It is widely accepted as fact that a chosen few can actually "talk" with this Scooby Doo, a dog.*

And as for Scrappy Doo, what depraved act did Splayfoot demand of his followers to create such an abomination?

"I Would Have Gotten Away With Everything If It Wasn't For Those Meddling Kids!"

So just how do these kids always turn up in such spooky places to solve unsolved mysteries? Could this be dismissed as mere coincidence? Or was the information provided in advance? Are the Scooby bunch Satan's foot soldiers, helping in his conquest for souls? Are these evildoers being brought to "justice," or is this Horny Head's way of calling in his forces and consolidating his troops? And what happens to television viewers after they've seen six hundred and sixty-six episodes?

Summary

It seems the story of Scooby Doo is a compilation of many stories. A frayed tapestry, a crumbling mosaic, a tangled and barbed thicket that when examined closely are all aligned and pointing in one direction—evil. An innocent children's cartoon or a cover-up involving drugs, terrorism, pornography, perversion, slothfulness, and the Number of the Beast? And while the easy answer may be Satan, so is four when the question is 2+2.

* This could easily be explained away through the process of evolution with a dog such as Astro (the Jetson's K-9), but with a present-day mutt like Scooby Doo the answer more likely lies in Hades.

Just What is a Scooby Snack?

▲ *Scooby Doo* humor feature, *Orbit*, April 1995.

Orby Calling

Orbit: Hello!

Keebler: Hi, is this Jerry Peterson.

O: Yes it is.

K: This is Peggy from the Keebler company. I've been told that you were concerned that we mislabeled our products.

O: Yes.

K: Do you have the package available?

O: Yes I do. It's right in front of me. I brought it in with me to work today.

K: Let me first say that I'm sorry to hear that your children have been through pain from having hot liquid spilled on them, because I have a son and it's not a pleasant experience. What do you see on your package?

O: [annoyingly slow] I see waffle bowls, 10 waffle bowls. I see an elf with a bowl of ice cream in the bowl. It's got chocolate syrup on it. Appears to have some nuts. That's either marshmallow or whipped cream—and there's a cherry

K: ......

O: The elf is wearing a red hat with a yellow band. And a green coat.

K: I'm familiar with the elf; that's the same mascot that we would show on any of them. But thank you.

O: Oh and it says Keebler. There's a tree, with a shield. On the other side, it says waf-

fle. Then, in huge letters "Bowls." Ten waffle bowls. Stay fresh inner a wrap.

K: It's similar to the front side.

O: Then on the other side it's got like what's on the front except this time the elf is standing up.

K: A lateral version.

O: The bowl on this side has what looks like vanilla ice cream, chocolate syrup, walnuts. And what looks like whipped cream and a cherry. Now on the back it has nutrition facts, serving size. One bowl in parentheses. Serving per container.

K: What's on the fourth side.

O: That's the first side I gave to you. We've been through this already.

K: I was a little surprised that you put hot liquid in a waffle bowl.

O: It's a bowl!

K: It's a waffle bowl.

O: Haven't you ever had a taco salad. They're hot.

K: Yeah, but it's not a liquid.

O: Go to Taco Bell.

K: Well, it's not the best kind of...

O: You put dressing on it— that's liquid.

K: It's not a hot, soluble liquid.

O: What about the taco meat; that's hot.

K: I'm very sorry that your kids got burnt. I'm a little amazed that a five-year-old got hot liquid served to him. But that's your personal choice.

O: What are you! Oh, you're trying to blame it on me! Look, I know how much the lady got from being scalded at

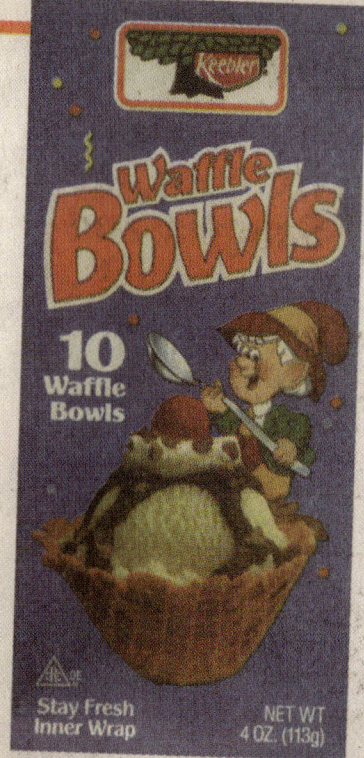

McDonald's! I could have called a lawyer! But instead I called nicely. I'm not the kind of guy who takes a big giant corporation to court. Even If I could make 10 million dollars; that's not the kind of person I am. But I don't think I should be yelled about the way we take care of our kids!

K: I haven't yelled. I'm just surprised.

O: Well, surprise!

K: I'm a parent first and an employee second.

O: [indignantly] Do you give your kids cold soup?

K: I don't give it to them in waffle products.

O: Well, the kids love this; they used to love this.

K: I'm sorry that you had hot liquid in these bowls. It was never Keebler's intention for anyone to get hurt...

O: I didn't say that it was your intention. I just think that it should have a warning on it.

K: I'm noting that. This is the first time that something like this has come up.

O: There's one other thing. The lady on the phone earlier said that she would send a coupon for more waffle bowls in the mail. But I think that you should send a coupon for the soup as well.

K: She wrote that it was Campbell's Chicken Soup. We don't own Campbell's Chicken. You'll have to contact them if you think that you need a replacement for their product.

O: I don't think it was their product's fault. They couldn't possibly list all the things that you couldn't pour their soup in.

K: Well, could we possibly list all things that you should put in our bowl? Like don't put hot oil or all the...

O: If you just said don't put hot things, that should cover 99% of it.

K: This in an ice cream serving product.

O: I kind of think that it's your fault that we lost the can of soup.

K: It's a waffle product. I wouldn't want to think that someone would take one of our waffle sugar cones and put soup in that. Just because something is a receptacle for something, it doesn't mean that...

O: Well, you wouldn't eat soup out of an ice cream cone—it's a cone. I didn't put soup in it because it was called waffle. I put soup in it because it was called bowl!

K: So, you're concerned that the word bowl is misleading?

O: "Bowl" is the biggest thing on the package.

It's Not Our Fault—Well Kinda

As you can see these pictures are indeed in focus. However on the Snap page they are blurry, along with a few others. It's a computer thing. We caught it on the proofs, we didn't have any time to fix it, but we did see it. So this is just to let you know, we aren't total buttheads.

Extra special thank you for **John Monaghan** and **Jimmy Doom** for their continuing contributions.

▲ "Orby Calling," *Orbit*, Fall 1999.

The World's Creepiest Garage Sale

OUR MEAGER OFFERINGS
There are some things money can't buy, and some things you can't give away.

Women's Wear
Hairbrush—clogged with cat hair • Neon green thong G string • Two really ugly mens wigs • Single nylon stocking with runs • Rusty clothes iron • Box of shoes (all singles/no matches)

Antiques & High Ticket Items
Dubiously-stained mattress • Antique-looking art nouveau picture frame (plastic) rigged to fall apart if touched • Oak-look toilet seat lid (cracked) • Crumbling to the touch Jesus picture • Moth-eaten felt X-mas stocking • Plastic X-mas ornaments • Single rusty metal coaster • Framed cardboard print of a old sea captain by fireplace ($300) • Spider web besotted radio with smashed case • Sad dog print and cat painting (set) • Plastic green wastebasket with a long strip fly paper inside (flies at no additional charge)

Collectibles
Star Wars: The Phantom Menace paper place mats that come with any Taco Bell purchase ($2) • Mouse-eaten National Enquirer—dying Rock Hudson cover • Kids Meal R2D2 (Right half) $1 • Kids Meal R2D2 (left Half) $1 • A empty snow globe ($2) • Beanie ghosts

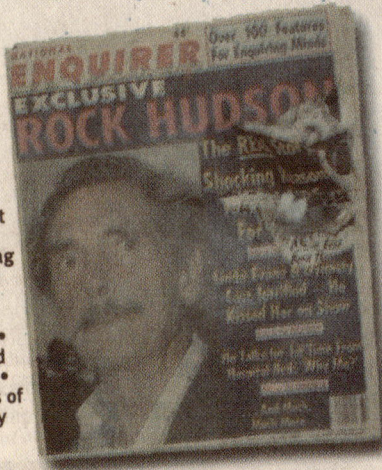

Kids toys
Grubby rubber baby doll • A dog chewed rubber brain monster • Chinese Checkers game without board • Broken Sweet Valley High cassette • A squirt gun in unopened package with $1 price tag and original 50 price sticker from store

Mens /tools
A rusty circle saw blade ($3) • A couple screws • Stiff paintbrush • Electric socket [non-grounded with several coats of paint] • Tiny wrench ($2) • Butter knife [marked as screwdriver] • Sections of cracked washing machine hose ($3) • Incredibly wrinkled pink shirt •

Assorted Items
Wire Hangers • Used scouring pads • Virtually empty tubes of acrylic paint • Lint covered furnace filter • Obviously used Water-Pik still in '70s box—marked 'NEW' • Dirty cracked and curling piece of linoleum (tile mat) • Empty shampoo bottles ($1) fancy ($2) • Box of Grand Mariner Century—empty ($20) • Severely damaged B&W television($10) • Severely damaged old headphones—NEW! still in its rotted box • Home Cheesery—cheese maker still in box • Assorted squares of formica samples (50¢ ea.) • Chrome stove burner protectors with burnt in stains [marked—protect your stove from fire] • 8-track tapes—labeled as cassettes • Current movies that would of sold except we wrote wrestling and soap operas on every tape ($5)

Food
A packet of microwave pork rinds • Can of soup-expired in 92 • Canned papaya, both ends bloated-out • Canned chicken paté • A packet of 'not for resale' powdered cheese • French fried onions (slightly open) • Tin filled with fast food condiments.

Adults Only section
Several porn magazines that had been sprayed with water and ammonia • Very old Vaseline jar (1/2 full) • A sticky bottle of massage oil (half empty) coated in dust, mold and cat hair • A latex sex device that was left in a garage for 20 years and is now covered in mold spores

ORBIT · June 1999

THE PLAN: It was determined we would throw the most horrible garage sale in the history of garage sales. We would have the worst stuff we could find—not obvious garbage, that would tip it off. We found horrible things no one would want—from the pee-stained motel mattress we had in a basement (long story, don't ask) to hot collectible Star Wars placemats that came with yesterday's super-value meal. All we needed was a lure for the suckers and a place to real them in.

THE SET UP: Fortunately, we had friends that live at the super busy intersection of Woodward and Lincoln in Royal Oak—garage sale heaven. To maximise our pathetic merchandise, we organised them in sections; kid's, women's, tools, etc. We wrote our price tags on masking tape and where applicable directly on the product. We made our prices redicu-lously high, except on scary stuff like food. If a product was nicer, we wrote the price in permanent felt pen—to further devalue the wares.

THE ENTICEMENT: Our Giant Estate Sale signs (advertising antiques, furniture, electronics, fine art, tools, etc.) were the perfect enticement for hooking the fish. We increased the attracting power using dayglow cards announcing, "Yes, we have Beanies!"

(continued next page)

23

▲ "The World's Creepiest Garage Sale," *Orbit*, June 1999.

THE RUB: We pulled the hidden-camera van parallel to the tables, supported by hidden mics and manned with digital video (by Kurt Massos of TVW productions.) Kurt had stuck another camera in the back of the yard and 12-year-old Colin and friend hid under the porch with a third camera. There was a sign stating: "WARNING SHOPLIFTERS! YOU ARE UNDER VIDEO SURVEILLANCE!" Brilliant, given that there was nothing remotely worth touching—much less stealing.

Doffing a dirty hand-written "How May I Help You" T-shirt and flood pants, editor Jeremy Harvey posed as the proprietor. Now all we had to do was sit back and let the entertainment come to us.

The rabble was showing up before we got back from hanging the first streetcorner sign. We could see them repulsed by our merchandise and storming off in angry fits. Even at a block away, we had to bite our hands to cover our howls of laughter. Jeremy was doing a good job: annoyingly informative, overly eager to please, willing to barter at the touch of an object and constantly maintaining a straight face.

Here are some highlights:

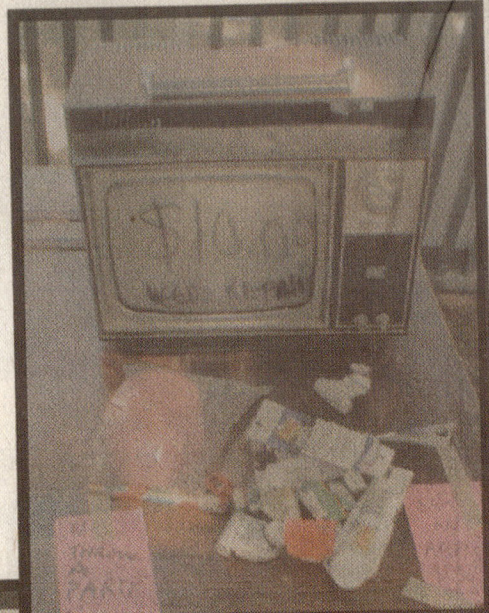

People seemed truly disappointed that our GIANT ESTATE SALE turned out to be a rinky-dinky yard sale. They still sifted through our crap hoping to get lucky— some asked how long we'd been open. They read our enticing sales pitches and, being too damn polite to complain, made excuses for not purchasing anything. Their constant smirks and occasional disgust was caught by our hidden cameras as they turned to make sure our proprietor wasn't looking.

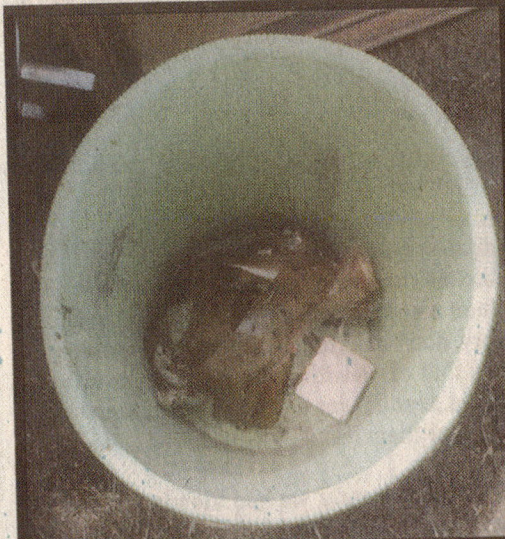

The last thing most people saw. Once they saw the well-used flypaper at the bottom of this basket, they made a bee line for the exit.

The suckers that pulled in by the "Yes, we have Beanies!" on our "Estate Sale" signs were quite disturbed to say the least.

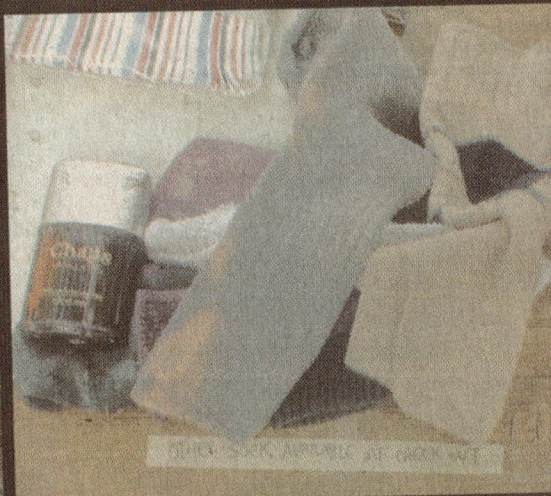

Nothing is sadder than peddling one's defiled underwear and socks at a garage sale. As a shoplifting deterent, we only displayed one sock—the mate being available upon purchase. Also pictured is a partially full bottle of Chaps cologne and package of '70s-era K-Mart "Challanger" brand bikini breifs.

Pointing at the sign, "Resuable and can be cut to any size.", a husband threatened to buy our scum-layered furnace filter for his wife.

"Would make a hilarious picture frame!" reads the sales pitch on this slightly cracked, oak-look "antique" toilet seat.

The second scariest item in the sale may have been the worn out, dubiously-stained motel mattress. Those bending closer to inspect the antiques were in danger of having their faces perilously close.

Our hot and spicy "Adult Section!" Issues of porn magazines were sprayed with an ammonia solution to make them wet, sticky and stinky. The close-ups details the mold spores on our sex aid.

This sap pulled out a quarter for our rickety, dog-turd encrusted shovel. When told it was $25, he became irate claiming he could buy a new shovel for $12. We didn't budge; our shovel was an antique family heirloom. Storming off he muttered, 'I don't need an antique, I need to dig a hole!'

A lady warned our bloated can of papaya could kill someone— we told her she could have it for half-price—7¢, but she still wasn't buying. The other cans were also expired by years. The condiment sign reads "Flavor your food. 5¢ a pack."

Our only sale of the day! Complaining the Unreal People mag was a little "moist," this client chiseled us down from $5 to $1.50 on the raunchy swinger's catalog.

Our estate sale sign promised fine art. We refused to break up this set and any customer who even looked in the direction was told so. We also told them that they were painted in prison by uncle Harry. These were the only things somebody might have purchased, had they not had the fine art price tag of $200.

Posing as a customer, our hidden camera captures our editor knocking over "the expensive stuff" table. Refusing to pay $80.00 in damages, we threatened to call the cops. "I'm going to call the cops, too!" He yelled back. "The garage sale cops! This is the crummiest garage sale I ever been to!" While we were packing up, a lady wheedled her way in. We frightened her daughter by offering her a cute dolly for free!

▲ "The World's Creepiest Garage Sale," *Orbit*, June 1999.

Orbit Gets Nude, Rude, Lewd, Crude, and Really Grossed-Out

Article and Illustrations by Jeremy Harvey

WHAT COULD BE COOLER THAN the concept of a nude resort? It sounds so perfect on paper. A lazy day lolling under the sun where the most strenuous activity is looking at naked bodies. Although haven't you ever been a little suspicious of the people who go there? These guys want everybody—I mean everybody, to take off their clothes. According to them all children from newborns to 100 years young, the Rubenesque, the physically challenged, and the extremely hairy should all happy-go-luckily interact with each other completely in the buff. To them there's no such thing as a physical oddity or an unpleasant body. We decided to see how true that really was: here's how. [See The Ruse.]

The nude resort chosen was Whispering Oaks in Auburn Hills. The entrance stipulations are couples and single women only so I brought my friend Jesse as my decoy girlfriend for the evening. On the phone a lady enticed me with a wide assortment of activities and amenities, even free food. She painted a picture of a serene and tranquil Fantasy Islandish experience, however what I got was more like Zug Island. We were promised thirty acres with a lake—what we got was a trailer park with a murky green swamp that literally had a half inch layer of tarp-like scum that made the water look like a giant diarrhea fondue.

I've been told in the past that nudism has nothing to do with eroticism. That's the biggest fucking understatement I've heard in my entire life. I knew that there was no way that a nude beach could legally live up to my imagination, but I

would have been more sexually stimulated getting castrated. Besides the obvious circus tent, there was one article of clothing that was desperately needed here—diapers. Everybody might have seen themselves as divine creations but all I saw was a bunch of pasty flab, fetid genitals, and greasy holes. And to think, I almost popped a few Mini-thins so I wouldn't get embarrassed by my hard on. It's been about four days later and I still can't get one.

I saw this whole nude resort experience for exactly what it

was—group therapy. Anyone who is truly comfortable with their body would not display it among these wrecks. These people come here to get the acceptance that they would never find in real life. They get some kind of confidence boost that comes from wallowing around bare-assed among a community that's more or less equally repulsive as they are. Every time I started to feel guilty for trying to defile this little dream world that they cooked up, I'd remember that I had to dish out $40 for me and

my friend to be there. If they really wanted to make some cash off this dump they should charge by the pound.

The last thing you want on your first time at a nude resort is for a bunch of doughy old hawkers and horn-dog grannies to come up and try to make you feel comfortable. I don't know how many times I heard "Is this your first time on a nude resort? Just relax and make yourself at home. I know it might seem a little bizarre at first being naked around a bunch of strangers. But you get used to it after awhile. It's natural, we were put on the Earth this way and...blah, blah." This didn't happen quite as often once I took my clothes off.

That's when I quickly discovered that flies, mosquitoes, chiggers, gnats, and ticks love the genital area. I'm a born nature hater to begin with but let me tell you nothing made me wish that they'd bulldoze this place for a condo harder then having a swarm of insects buzz around my dick. At one point during a ten minute rest, I found that a hornet had taken an interest in my shaft. While running for my life I saw that it's nest had been perched just above my head.

The first twenty minutes were a little awkward, so I went straight for the wood trails hoping to start small with some one-on-one interaction. A lot of people pretended that there was nothing unusually wrong with me. Some honestly wouldn't have cared if I came with a leek colostomy bag in my side and a giant squash hanging halfway out my ass. Although not everyone was that relaxed around me.

One hippie lady around forty

The Ruse

I smeared the entire base and shaft of my genitals with thin coating of Elmer's glue. Once this dried, I pulled and tugged until the hardened layer had cracked and torn into a flaky diseased like mess. Next I glued on a thick Witches Wart that was purchased from Gags and Games. I adhered the wart on the base of my testes, just under the shaft so it would be undetected until I did any type of quick erratic movement, then it would rear it's ugly head like a cancerous jack-in-the-box. For a final touch I applied red and black makeup to certain areas to give the impression of rashes, bruises, cancer, poor hygiene...whatever.

started yakking my ear off once I bummed a cigarette off her [I was a little hesitant to put it in my mouth when I realized that she had no purse or pockets.] The peace and love, brown rice, Krishna babble stopped as soon she glanced down at my midsection. However she didn't want to seem rude so she resumed her conversation like there wasn't anything out of the ordinary happening. I could tell she was leery of whatever it was that was festering on my cock so I put her to the test. Pretending like I tripped, I stumbled right into her, brushing my genitals across her thigh. She did a poor job of holding back the disgust, but kept on answering my questions until I let her go a few minutes later. I then saw her head straight for the showers.

Later on I was talking to an old man at the shuffleboard court. He didn't seem to pay any attention to me until a one inch flake fell off my testes. We both watched as my pseudo-scab gracefully fluttered down like a Autumn leaf to land right between his bare feet. He looked like he was going to puke but I made no attempt to pick it up and kept right on talking.

There was not one hot girl in sight except for my friend but she didn't count. I started checking in the camper windows for anything even remotely worth ogling—nothing. I figured this would be the last place that I'd be busted for being a peeping Tom and I was right. It wasn't too long before I walked past the hawker trailer. An overly eager troll hurriedly came outside to make my acquaintance and to enlighten and enrich me about the new and exciting world of nudism. He seemed like the happiest man in the world until he got an

78

eyeful of my sick sack. He let out a panicky sort of hiccup and then tried to excuse himself. I couldn't say anything to get this guy to stay, I even asked to check out his camper. After I was sure that he wasn't going to come back out I decided to head to the pool.

This was quite possibly the most criminal I ever felt. My sole intention was to go to the pop machine to get a Mountain Dew. After about a minute or so I noticed that there were five little girls in the water who were fixated on me with glassy eyed disbelief. I don't know how you handle a bunch of nude children gawking at your own nakedness but it freaked the hell out of me. Needless to say I was about as well received as one of those sickos who masturbates in their car when the local high school gets out. An elderly codger, maybe the grand mother swam over and put her arms up while reminding the kids that it's not nice to stare at strangers. Because

of her little lecture everyone started glaring at me like I was Pogo the clown—well excuse me, it was your dumb ass not me who dragged your kids to this pagan love-in. If they want to look at my doctored-up penis then it's probably because their sick of your withered and curdled tits. Anywhere else and I would of gotten the chair, but here it's all part of the nudist movement. That gave me very little comfort as I headed back to the wood trails.

There I met a old feral duffer who wanted to talk to me all about farm equipment. He made a quick break to go pee behind a tree, but kept on talking like I was still in front of him. I guess the nudism movement doesn't cover safety taps because little drops of urine would sporadically drip out of his urethra afterward. Naturally this is what happens if you don't have a underwear filter, I had to run and wash my hands—I shook his during our introduction.

While hanging out by the bathroom I spent the next ten minutes checking out various asses because I was curious if people don't wipe either. I was also dying to catch someone with toilette paper hanging

out their sphincter. I soon had to stop my examination when too much bile was spitting up my throat. The timing couldn't have been more perfect since it was dinner time.

This was the grand finale, sickest thing that I seen that day—the buffet. Normally I'm the biggest buffoon for an all-you-can-eat pig out. But just imagine 200 leathery private-parts wagging and flopping about your potato salad and see how hungry you feel. There's just too many things that drip, squirt, and spew out

of sexual organs for me to want to eat there that night. In fact I'd have to go about a month without eating before I'd even consider it. My boss later yelled at me because I didn't brush my own stuff against the food, but I'm sorry, I didn't come here to catch something that would make my dick to look sick for real. Everyone was trying their damnedest to hustle me over to the food coral so I could enjoy a hearty plate of hepatitis, but they might as well have been inviting me to lap up a toilet. My friend and I concluded that this would be a good time to leave. This was partially because we were bored and partially because the last thing we want to do is to be with these people in the dark.

▲ "Naked Truth" nudist colony feature, *Orbit*, Fall 1999.

SEX

How To Be A Better Stalker

Like anything in life, being a stalker is something that takes practice, perseverance, and above all, total disregard for the wishes of others. Some people here at Orbit have more experience than others in matters of the stalking (or stalked) heart, and we are passing our knowledge on to you.

by Ron Wade

Illustrations by Tristan Eaton

The Stalker's Party Pack
For the novice sociopath, we have a list of all of the tools needed to make her/his/its heart yours:

Telephone
For placing hundreds of unwanted phone calls to your beloved.

Reliable transportation
Car, bike, skateboard or scooter for driving by his or her home several times a day.

Infrared night vision binoculars
To get up close and personal.

An endless supply of bad poetry
To read in the middle of night through a bullhorn.

Caffeine
To stay awake during those marathon photo shredding sessions.

The Catcher In the Rye
For some reason, every stalker thinks that he is Holden Caulfield. If you're not motivated, feel free to substitute the Cliffs Notes.

Rats and mice
To send with dead flowers on the anniversary of your breakup.

Rohypnol (roofies)
To make "NO!" mean "Yes!"

Computer
For sending love notes, doctored photos of your beloved, and for looking up "unlisted" phone numbers.

Five hundred pictures of the object of your affection
Cut their head off in every one.

Knife
Not a butter one, but a large, O.J. Simpson—mercenary-disembowel-your-enemy knife.

One gun (unloaded)
For when you threaten to kill yourself.

Phony positive pregnancy test (girls only)
Self-explanatory.

A Day of Stalking
The key to being a good stalker is to FOCUS. The only way to win the heart of the person you're after is to spend every moment of every day trying to make that person love you. Quit your job, don't pay your bills, don't shower.

6:00 A.M. Call John/Joan Doe. Tell them you were thinking about them.
6:01 Call back and ask them why they hung up.
6:02 Stare at their bedroom window. Write love letter until he/she wakes up.
7:00 Call and ask why they aren't up for work yet.
7:01 Call back and ask why they hung up.
7:10 Stare at bathroom window through binoculars.
7:14 Call and tell them that they need to eat more fiber.
7:15 Call back and ask why they hung up.

7:45 Stand next to their car and ask him/her if you can marry them.
7:46 Call car phone and ask why he/she said no. Cry hysterically.
7:47 Call back and ask why they hung up.
8:00 Go through his/her garbage looking for underwear to sniff.
8:45 Break into his/her house. Steal underwear and photos. Leave behind your underwear, dead roses, dead rat and notebook of poetry. Put roofies in Tylenol bottle.
9:25 Visit him/her at work. Refuse to leave until he/she agrees to meet you for dinner. (Girls, this would be a good time to spring the pregnancy test.)
9:30 Ask where he/she wants to register for gifts.
9:31 Call back and ask why they hung up.
9:45–4:50 P.M. Write another notebook full of poetry while staring at stolen pictures and sniffing stolen underwear. Call his/her answering machine every 20 minutes. Leave different message each time until tape runs out. Masturbation is optional.
5:20 Beat him/her back to their place and steal their mail.
5:22 Call and let him/her know that you've got their mail. Offer to trade the bills for dinner date.
5:23 Call back and ask when hell is supposed to freeze over.
5:24 Call back and ask why they hung up.
6:00 Run from police.
7:32 Make bail. Immediately go back to his/her house.
8:00 Take dead roses and poetry book out of trash for use tomorrow.
8:10 Call and ask why the cops were called.
8:11 Call back and ask why they hung up.
8:30 Sing poetry through bullhorn. In Spanish.
9:27 Pay bail.
10:00–6:00 A.M. Stare at bedroom window. Call every 10 minutes to see if he/she is sleeping.

Who Should You Stalk?
Anyone (or anything) is fair game, but remember, if you get arrested and convicted, you will be forever associated with that person. So when you're in the market for a famous stalkee, *choose wisely!* Do you really want to be known forever as the Matt Pinfield stalker?? For those of you who are unmotivated to choose your own, we offer you a listing of who's good to stalk among the rich and famous, and who's bad:

Good	Bad
Madonna	Madonna's kid
Richard Ashcroft	Richard Simmons
Fanchon Stinger	Emery King
Orbit ad reps	Orbit writers
Marilyn Manson	Charles Manson
Leonardo DiCaprio	Danny DeVito
Luscious Jackson	Jesse Jackson
Beck Hansen	Hanson
Neve Campbell	Glenn Campbell
Courtney Cox	Courtney Love
Kelly Brown	James Brown
Chelsea Clinton	Hillary Clinton

Bonus Tips
Many celebrity addresses are published in a book called the Celebrity Address Book. Feel free to write your favorite several hundred times. Send poetry, cut toenails or DNA samples, if you like.

▲ "How to Be a Better Stalker," *Orbit*, February 1998.

The Orbit Guide to Suicide

by Z. Lenn

Are you sick and tired of being sick and tired? Does life treat you the way a dog treats a fire hydrant? Do your letters come addressed to "The Worthless Waste of Human Life"? Welcome to the real world, pal! Most of us just suck it up and go another 24, but if you want to take the cowardly way out because you can't take any more pain, then far be it from us to stop you. Most people think there's too much pee in the gene pool anyway. Besides, if you've got determination and drive, we probably couldn't stop you. On the other hand, if you had determination and drive then you would be a huge success and other people would be trying to kill you instead. If you're at the end of your rope, and don't have the money to go to Dr. Kevorkian, we'll teach you how to get off Darwin's Magic Bus Ride in the Orbit guide to suicide.

Pre-suicide planning

Should you commit suicide?

For some people, this answer is very clear, for others it's as murky as a Mexican restaurant's toilet. You should probably remove yourself from the gene pool if you meet any of the following criteria:

- You've seen an entire episode of *Hee-Haw*.
- You have a dream catcher hanging from your rear view mirror.
- Lifetime prison sentence combined with bad case of hemorrhoids.
- You're upset that The Presidents of The United States broke up.
- You've been seen in public with your boyfriend/girlfriend wearing identical clothing.
- You're a mouth-breathing, tobacco-chewin', rebel flag-sportin', monster-truck drivin' hick with a gun rack and a bumper sticker that reads "Bad Ass Boys Drive Bad Ass Toys".
- Ozzy Osbourne told you to.
- You're a 45 year-old virgin who lives with his parents.
- You're a Spice Girl.
- You've seen *Titanic* more than three times.

Personal Items

Once you're dead, you have little or no control over what happens to your personal belongings, so if you want to give that autographed copy of *Foreigner's Greatest Hits* to your best friend Marlene, you better do it before the big dirt nap.

Spend ALL of your money. It's yours! Why would you want to leave it for the money-grubbing good-for-nothings that drove you to suicide in the first place? You can't take it with you, so you might as well go out in one last consumer blaze of glory. Burn $100 bills, rent $1000-a-night escorts, run the Visa bill to the max. Make them bury you wearing nothing but a toe tag and stick them with the bill.

Location, Location, Location

The most important thing to do once you decide to die is to make sure *no one* finds you until you're dead! If someone stops you in the act, you could be paralyzed, maimed, or worse yet—sterilized! You don't want to end up blowing your gonads off because Aunt Alice opened the attic door. If you have a favorite enemy, do it at their place. Not only will they have the unenviable task of finding you, but they're also responsible for the cleanup, and for a few days, they're a suspect in your murder. If you're killing yourself to impress someone else, videotape it. Nothing says "I hate you!" like a pool of your own blood.

Take advantage of the situation

One of the strange things that happens when you commit to suicide is that once you accept your inevitable death, life becomes a lot more fun. Most of the rules of life don't apply to you, because you're already dead. Stop dieting, do drugs, rob a bank, have sex with many strange people. Every night is Saturday Night! Just remember, if you wuss out, you've got to deal with the consequences.

The Suicide

Once you commit to suicide, don't tell anyone unless you want attention. You don't want someone talking you out of it, or worse yet, killing themselves with you and stealing your moment of gory glory. Remember, your body will fight you every step of the way—if your life doesn't pass before your eyes, then you're not doing something right. If it does, and you liked what you saw, then you're probably doing something right.

Suicide Pacts

Avoid them at all costs! Suicide is your last selfish act! You don't want your final breath to be lumped in with someone else's. If you let some death mooch die with you, prepare for an eternity with him/her. Some religions believe that you'll spend the entire afterlife with the person that was physically closest to you when you bite the bullet.

*Bonus Tip: If you want to leave a good looking corpse, wear extra-heavy diapers because when you die, you crap your pants. You might want to consider an enema before-hand.

Suicide Notes

You have to leave a note! Tell everyone why you did it, unless you're a rock star. If you're a rock star, everyone will buy your records is search of clues that you were going to off yourself. Your record company will be very appreciative.

Trivial reasons to kill yourself

- No Pearl Jam show in Detroit.
- Your Beanie Babies told you to.
- Because Nancy Kerrigan won't forgive Tonya Harding.
- You've landed new job—Orbit writer.
- NBC cancelled *Jenny McCarthy's Show*.
- You bet all of your money on the Lions to win the Super Bowl.
- Couldn't get a table at Fifth Avenue Billiards.
- Because Leonardo DiCaprio dies in *Titanic*.
- Because they're tearing down the Hudson's building.
- Because you missed *Ally McBeal*.

The Stupidest Ways to Die

- Walking drunk on the Royal Oak train tracks.
- Ice fishing when it's 45 degrees.
- Attempting the first around-the-world balloon flight.
- Skiing into a tree.
- Drinking Pepsi and eating Pop Rocks.
- Hanging yourself nude with pictures of your girlfriend all around you. (Michael Hutchence only.)
- Complications from a penile enlargement.
- Dancing on a balcony at a Rolling Stones concert.
- Resisting arrest (Detroit only).
- Burned to death by hysterical zealots because you work at Orbit.

What to Do Once You're Dead

You're family's got a big choice to make once you're dead and bloated—spend a lot of money on your sorry ass, or let you rot in some field like you probably deserve. If you're one of those people who's so anal that you have to plan everything, here are some options:

Burial

Cost: $1,000 to $10,000
What it says about you: You want to be just like everyone else. You probably danced the Macarena, for which you deserve to die anyway.
What the funeral will be like: Long, slow and with more crying than a PTA screening of *Titanic*.
Decomposed by: Worms, bacteria and more worms.
Chances of resurrection: It's only happened once—not counting John Travolta's career.
Appropriate music: "Down In It" by NIN
Number of pallbearers: Four strong men, or twelve rice-cake eatin', macrobiotic, vegetarian animal rights activists.

Cremation

Cost: $495.00 at All County Cremation
What it says about you: You always wanted to be a bowling trophy.
What the funeral will be like: A Bill Clinton date—lots of insincere feelings, with you being blown in the end.
Decomposed by: El Niño
Chances of resurrection: It would take more work than God is willing to do.
Appropriate music: "Fire on Babylon" by Sinead O'Connor
Number of pallbearers: One old lady with a poodle.

Mummification

Cost: over $20,000
What it says about you: You crave eternal life, and desperately want to have a good-looking corpse.
What the funeral will be like: An art gallery opening.
Decomposed by: Embalming chemicals.
Chances of resurrection: In the movies, good. In reality, bad.
Appropriate music: "Walk like an Egyptian" by The Bangles
Number of pallbearers: Several hundred slaves or two paleontologists.

Cryogenics

Cost: Approx. $75,000+ storage fees
What it says about you: Filthy Rich
Funeral: Party like it's 1999, if you're an heir!
Decomposed by: Freezer burn
Chances of resurrection: Lookin' good!
Appropriate music: "Ice, Ice, Baby" by Vanilla Ice—Hey, you're dead anyway!
Number of pallbearers: Two guys in those Intel Devo suits.

E-Z Self-Storage

Cost: $38/month for a 5'x5' box
What it says about you: So cheap that you probably turned your underwear inside out to save on laundry soap.
What the funeral will be like: Straight out of *Pulp Fiction*.
Decomposed by: Hungry guard dogs.
Chances of resurrection: Only after the bill is paid.
Appropriate music: Muzak
Number of pallbearers: One forklift

▲ "The *Orbit* Guide to Suicide," *Orbit*, March 1998.

As a new employee in a new country there are many rules and regulations you will have to follow. One of the most important things to remember is we are in a Christian country. It is important from now on you tell everybody you are a Chaldean, who unlike other Middle Eastern peoples, is a God-fearing family person who believes in Jesus Christ our Lord, Amen. Now get to work.

Like Family

As an employee of my store I will treat you like one of my family. You will find a cot to sleep on in the corner of the basement. Please stay in the employee corner. The rest of the basement is rented to my brother-in-law and his family. Don't dishonor my family by sneaking over to my brother-in laws side and trying to seduce his daughters.

It is only fair to warn you not to even look at my daughters, lovely as they are. If you are caught looking at one of my lovely daughters you will be painfully castrated and sent back home, penniless, where you will be the shame and scourge of the entire village.

Stealing

I am aware of every penny that comes in to and leaves the store. I have eyes in the back of my head and my spies are everywhere. I will know if you are stealing. Do not eat any of the food in the store without paying for it. That too is stealing, and most of it is so old it will make you ill for days (unpaid I may add). Those caught stealing have their wiping hand chopped off. They become penniless social outcasts in a strange cruel country and die horrible deaths.

Payment

Only Achmed is allowed to touch the cash register or the combination safe. You will take the money from the customer and hand it to Achmed the register. Most Americans don't count their change. Achmed does.

Pricing

All pricing is rounded off to the highest dollar. Never put a price tag on beer or any item in the cooler, these are sold according to what you perceive the customer will pay without complaining too loudly. If the customer is wearing a suit and tie raise the price by 25%. If the customer appears to be uneducated, prices may be raised 30% to one dollar, whichever is higher. If the customer is drunk, prices can be raised 50%, unless it is close to 2:00 A.M., when it is "market price".

Achmed's OASIS PARTY STATION

Welcome to Achmed's
It is very important you read this, but please not on company time.

Food Stamps

Food stamps can be used to purchase anything in our store, from dog food to cigarettes. However, if food stamps are used to purchase non-food items such as a crack pipe or a bottle of gin they must be discounted by 50%

Return Policy

You didn't buy it here. We don't except returns. Get out of the store or I will kill you.

Deposit Bottles

Our policy is "We can not possibly accept this many bottles". If your customer becomes angry or belligerent, point out the sign.

Check Cashing

We act much like a bank or moneylender for many of our customers. People without transportation such as the poor and

---

Dealing with Americans

Americans love convenience and friendliness. What better place to be treated friendly, than their neighborhood convenience store.

Men
Call every male who comes in "buddy" and "my good friend". As you learn to recognize steady customers, memorize what brands they purchase. They are sure to be impressed, when you start using personal nicknames such as "Budweiser-man" and "Mr. Kool Cigarettes".

Females
American women love attention and affection. This is because unlike the women from our homeland, all American women are whores—please treat them as such. When possible, lean over for an open mouth kiss making sure to fondle their breasts. Female circumcision is not a tradition in this country, if you can touch the forbidden region you should be able to have quick sexual encounter in the cooler. Occasionally, some may spurn your advances. Please don't let that deter you. Eventually, the slut will give into your intentions. Any gifts you give them will be deducted from your pay.

Poor People
The poor are never to be trusted. They are untrustworthy and shoplift. They will cheat you every chance they get and yell loudly when shortchanged.

English
Always speak English except when arguing amongst ourselves or when making lewd comments about whorish American women with their slutty American ways.

Achmed's OASIS PARTY STATION

the elderly depend on us for their existence. The fair and equitable rate for cashing checks is:

Achmed's 1999 Check Cashing Rate

Paycheck, tax-return check with proper ID 25%

Social Security Check, Welfare Check 35%

Paycheck, tax-refund check without proper ID 60%

Obviously stolen check 85%

Credit cards (always run two slips.) 20-70%

Coupons

We do not except coupons from customers. Part of your job will be removing the manufacturer's coupons from the newspaper boxes in a five mile radius of the store. These coupons will be handed in directly to Achmed or his brother Amir.

Promotions

Often a supplier will ask us to participate in promotions. These include: buy one get one free, a gift packaged with the product, and special low prices. We participate in all of the promotions. However, our customers do not. It is important you destroy or hide any promotional posters or displays, lest the customer feels cheated.

Porno Mags

We are not a library, porno magazines are not to be previewed by customers. Do not sell porno magazines before Achmed has a chance to look at them. Always place them low, where they can be more easily seen by children. The youngsters may return when not in the company of parent and buy one.

Store Defense

Often a customer may come in for the purpose of stealing Achmed's money. These are not the customers we want in our store.

Shoplifters

Pleased to find an AK-47 bolted under the counter. In addition there are two handguns; a Magnum .45 and a Saturday-nite special. If you shoot a suspected shoplifter, place Saturday-nite

This book is not your property. It belongs to the Ishtar Convenience Store Cartel.

special in the hand before rigor mortis sets in.

Armed Robbery

There are five inches of Bullet-Proof Armor Plate Ghetto glass which surrounds our counter. It is impervious to all bullets. Unfortunately, there are times we must venture out. If you are subject to a robbery follow these procedures.

1) Your life must always act as a shield between any potential criminal and the cash register or Achmed.

2) Do not reveal the combination to the safe, a bullet in the head is a more pleasant way to die than what awaits you, if you should reveal the combination.

3) Should you live, do not report to the police or insurance company how much money was taken. Achmed will handle these matters personally.

Cleanliness

Although this is not a stall in the town market, it should be kept as clean as if it were. Part of your duties will be keeping the store's appearance up to Achmed's high standards.

Floors

Contrary to popular belief, our floors are not dirty, they are made out of natural dirt. Sweep or rake debris each season.

Shelf Items

Boxes, cans, jars, etc.—These items must be dusted off every three years. Cans that are starting to get round should be stepped on until they appear flat.

Cooler—There should be no more that four inches of sludge on the bottom of the cooler, the grey fuzz on shelves should cover less than 90% of space.

Non-Perishable Cooler Items (Cans, bottles, lunch meat)—Grime on can tops should be no higher than tops of pull-tab, aluminum should be visible in at least one place.

Semi-Perishable Cooler Items
Perishable Cooler Items (milk and non-coagulated dairy products)—Expiration dates should be removed from all cartons. When the square milk cartons turn round, you will be expected to pour them into the cottage cheese cartons.

Semi-Perishable Cooler Items

Lunch Meat/Cheese—If meat turns a funny color or gives off an unpleasant odor, it must be removed from the cooler immediately. It is to be taken to the back room where it can be turned into delicious deli sandwiches. Meat or cheese that is hard or crunchy should not be used in deli sandwiches! It should be soaked in the big sink and taken to the grinder where it can be ground up for counter sausage. Meat that refuses to soften with repeated soaking should be placed on the radiator for jerky preparation. *Caution:* If you are timid of insect swarms, it is advised you to thoroughly spray the grinder with the bug killer before turning it on (usually kept by the fresh vegetables).

Counter Sausages and other Homemade Meats—Keep counter sausage free of mold and insect larva, particularly in the summer when it sweats.

Freezer—All items in the freezer should be purchased at the beginning of winter when they are on sale. All items should have a sticky coating to keep them from falling over. Muck on the bottom should be free of lichen. Each spring this flavorful muck should be scooped up and loaded into the Soft-Serve Ice cream machine. Kindly remove all loose ice-cream bar wrappers before loading into the machine.

▲▲"Achmed's Oasis," *Orbit,* Fall 1999.

Detroit is going to have a new flavor... pepperoni!

ILITCHVILLE

Not since the glory days of Henry Ford has one man done so much for the people he loves! You've no doubt seen Ilitch's entertainment complex plans in the city's "lesser papers" and on TV. Now, this exclusive Orbit investigative report uncovers what could very possibly be Ilitch's "real plans" for the revitalization of the city of Detroit.

These plans were mysteriously delivered to the swank Orbit offices in a pizza box (the driver sped away too fast for us to read the license number or delivery sign), and while Orbit is not claiming that this is anything other than a ploy for public attention, there are those cynical enough to believe that these plans represent the Hidden Agenda of the Ilitch Empire.

THE DETROIT CAESAR PRESS BUILDING
Market research has proven that attempts to censor negative press only result in more negative press.

MACEDONIAN TOWN (Formerly Greektown)
Heralded as the center of Macedonian culture in Detroit, this area boasts an array of impressive ethnic restaurants, featuring exotic dishes like "OPA! OPA!" (a delicious flaming mozzarella cheese dish) as well as the many fine wines of Macedonia.

THE PIZZA DOME
Ilitch's revolutionary "Stadium! Stadium!" gives the public two sports games for the price of one: The Detroit Tigers and the resurrected Detroit Caesars professional softball team. Rumors have been flying that Ilitch's son Atanas has shown such great form in throwing the opening pitch, that he will be named the Tiger's starting pitcher.

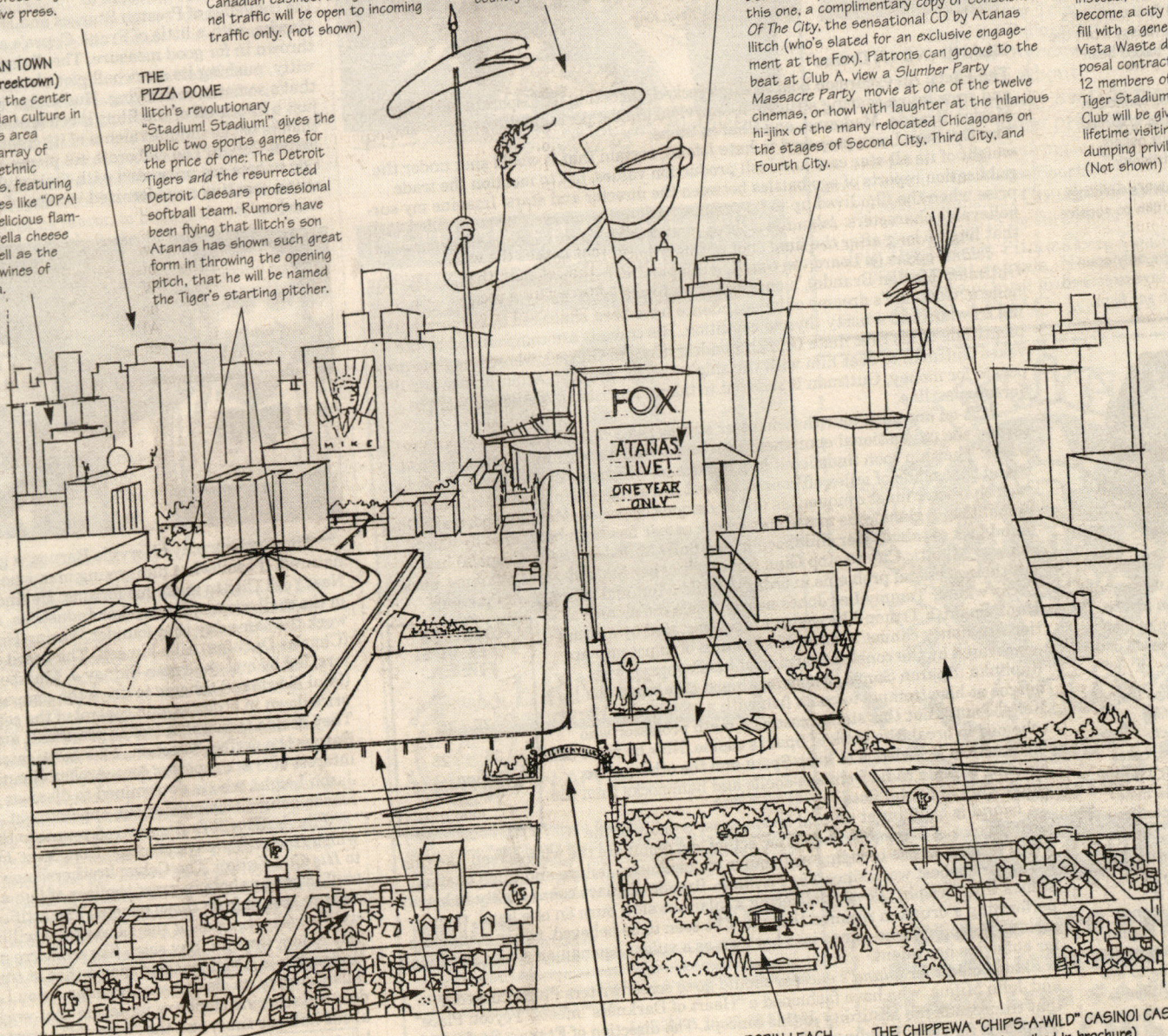

THE GREAT WALL OF CANADA
As Ilitchville expands towards the river, a great wall will be erected to ensure that visitors and natives aren't tempted to waste their highly disposable income in any Canadian casinos. Bridge and tunnel traffic will be open to incoming traffic only. (not shown)

COLOSSUS OF DETROIT
Billed as the eighth wonder of the world, the gigantic statue is purported to be a gift from the country of France.

JUMBOTRON
Boasting more neon than entire city of Las Vegas, the Jumbotron is a perfect vehicle for advertising anything from entertainment events to pizza. Heck, you could even show your home movies on it, if you owned it.

FOX THEATRE ATANAPLEX
Detroit taxpayers get a bonus included with this one, a complimentary copy of Conscience Of The City, the sensational CD by Atanas Ilitch (who's slated for an exclusive engagement at the Fox). Patrons can groove to the beat at Club A, view a Slumber Party Massacre Party movie at one of the twelve cinemas, or howl with laughter at the hilarious hi-jinx of the many relocated Chicagoans on the stages of Second City, Third City, and Fourth City.

FUTURE PLANS: Tiger Stadium
Ilitch has promised not to tear down Tiger Stadium. Instead, it will become a city landfill with a generous Vista Waste disposal contract. All 12 members of the Tiger Stadium Fan Club will be given lifetime visiting and dumping privileges. (Not shown)

FOX
ATANAS LIVE! ONE YEAR ONLY

MIKE

LCE EMPLOYEE SHANTY TOWN
Since LCE will employ approximately 90% of Detroit's population (all city workers and bureaucrats will be contracted to LCE), Mr. Ilitch has generously donated this land for affordable and compact employee housing. In keeping with the "Conscience of the City" theme, the entire project will be constructed using environmentally-friendly recycled pizza packaging and pizza by-products. The extremely affordable rent will be payable in LCE company script and coupons. Since Mayor Archer will not be living in the Manoogian Pizza Cafe, he may choose to reside in one of the deluxe executive hovels featuring double cheese insulation.

PIZZAMOVER
Archaic elevated transportation system retrofitted and routed through incinerator ovens to convey hot pizza snacks to the hungry masses.

GATES OF WRATH
Entrance to Ilitchville will include an exceptionally ornate wrought-iron entrance to give it that "high class" Ilitch touch. A state-of-the-art detection system, as well as a crack squad of "Troopers! Troopers!" will insure that no contraband weaponry, Orbit magazines, or Domino delivery vehicles will be

ROBIN LEACH GUEST HOUSE
Just in case a certain someone should drop by unexpectedly.

THE CHIPPEWA "CHIP"S-A-WILD" CASINO! CASINO! AND RESERVATION (as described in brochure)
To promote Native American culture, employees will dress in authentic-looking tribal uniforms. High rollers with plenty of "wampum" will get a friendly "How" from one of the many celebrity greeters, such as Chief Running Archer. Conventioneers won't have any "reservations" about holding their power pow-wows in this bigwig-wam.

VIEW: LOOKING SOUTH DOWN ILWOOD AVE. (formerly Woodward)

▲ "Ilitchville," Orbit, April 1994.

"Ilitchville"—home of "Stadium Stadium," a riff on Little Caesars "Pizza Pizza" promotion—was not only a prophetic joke, as Comerica Park and Ford Field would be built next to each other less than a decade later, but an unfunny one, at least to Ilitch. After years of ridiculing the singing career of his son, Atanas, in *Fun*, Ilitch decided this was the last straw and banned *Orbit* from placing their issues in Little Caesars Pizza locations.

Orbit writers found humor in the more peculiar aspects of life in Metro Detroit—from party stores owned by people of Middle Eastern background to the redevelopment of Royal Oak, Hamtramck's Euro style, and Detroit's long history of freak shows.

As seen, *Orbit*'s irreverence made the magazine the target of social critics. Following a November 1995 issue humorously highlighting sex, southeast Michigan's LGBTQ organization, the Triangle Foundation, called on advertisers to reconsider their sponsorship of *Orbit*. Sensing an opportunity to make a point, the *Orbit* writers deconstructed the campaign against them.

Orbit's anarchic sense of humor may have offended some, but it never disappointed editor/writer Jeremy Harvey: "It's the funniest thing that ever came out of Detroit. There were things in *Orbit* that made me laugh harder than anything."

Shameful History

In July 1995, about twenty-five hundred Newspaper Guild–represented employees at the *Detroit Free Press* and the *Detroit News* went on strike. In a town steeped in labor union history, "No Scab Papers" signs started to pop up on lawns around Metro Detroit like dandelions. By that fall, violent clashes between the union members picketing the papers and the police were reported. It was in this charged atmosphere that *Orbit*

had just begun a relationship with a man whose work as a reporter was well regarded. His name was Bill McGraw.

Working under the pen name Silas Farmer, a nod to the late-1890s Detroit historian and geographer, McGraw wrote a column for *Orbit* titled "Detroit's Shameful History," mostly while walking the picket line during the newspaper strike. Before coming to the *Detroit Free Press*, McGraw was already a veteran of two legendary underground papers, *The South End* and *The Fifth Estate*. As a reader, McGraw said he enjoyed *Orbit* because the paper had a more "off-the-wall and skeptical, question authority" philosophy than other papers in town. McGraw said he was brought in by then-editor Matt Beer, a former *Detroit News* columnist, to do the column at *Orbit*. "I think it was an outlet," McGraw said. "I figured I was a bit older, in my forties, than the average *Orbit* reader. I figured they were in their twenties.... I wanted to write [stories about Detroit history] so maybe someone like me chanced across them at an age when it was influential. It would get them to think about the alternative history of Detroit."

Detroit's Shameful History by Silas Farmer premiered in the May 1995 issue with an article on the Greektown raid of 1966. McGraw tells the tale of the uncovering of a police payoff and corruption scandal where pretty much no one was punished for crimes against the public trust. Over the next two years, McGraw wrote about black eyes in Detroit's past in his columns. From racist mayor Charles Bowles and the disappearance of interurban trains, to race riots, to the *Detroit Free Press*'s support of the South during the Civil War.

McGraw said he didn't really worry about people finding out he was the author. The way he looked at it, the people who would be upset about him writing for *Orbit* weren't hip enough to pick it up and read it anyhow. McGraw said writing the

▼ "Detroit's Shameful History," riots in Detroit, *Orbit*, July 1995.

DETROIT'S SHAMEFUL HISTORY

The Detroit Free Press

MARTIAL LAW AT 10 P.M.
U.S. TROOPS MOVE IN

—Silas Farmer

▼ "Detroit's Shameful History," anti-Semitism in Detroit, *Orbit*, December 1995.

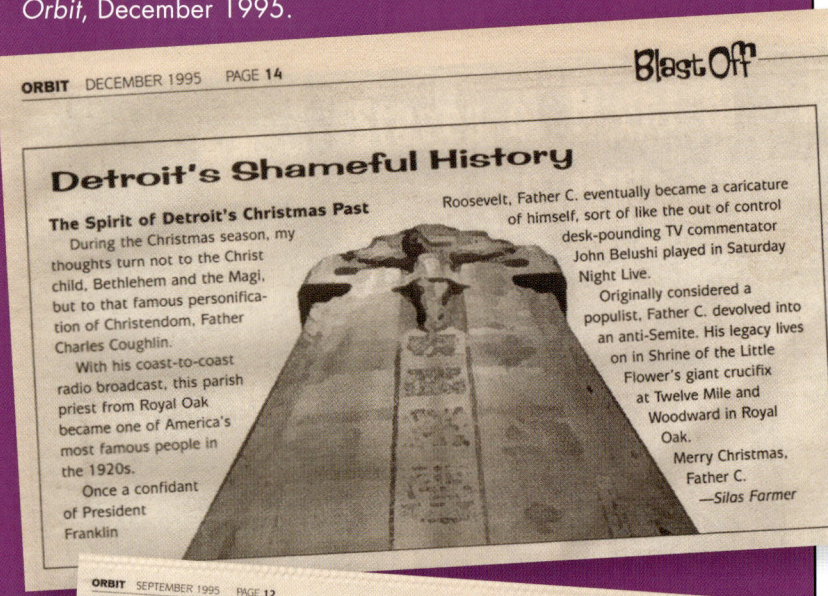

ORBIT DECEMBER 1995 PAGE 14

Detroit's Shameful History

The Spirit of Detroit's Christmas Past

During the Christmas season, my thoughts turn not to the Christ child, Bethlehem and the Magi, but to that famous personification of Christendom, Father Charles Coughlin.

With his coast-to-coast radio broadcast, this parish priest from Royal Oak became one of America's most famous people in the 1920s.

Once a confidant of President Franklin Roosevelt, Father C. eventually became a caricature of himself, sort of like the out of control desk-pounding TV commentator John Belushi played in Saturday Night Live.

Originally considered a populist, Father C. devolved into an anti-Semite. His legacy lives on in Shrine of the Little Flower's giant crucifix at Twelve Mile and Woodward in Royal Oak.

Merry Christmas,
Father C.
—Silas Farmer

ORBIT SEPTEMBER 1995 PAGE 12

Detroit's Shameful History

—Silas Farmer

▲ "Detroit's Shameful History," the *Detroit Free Press* and slavery, *Orbit*, September 1995.

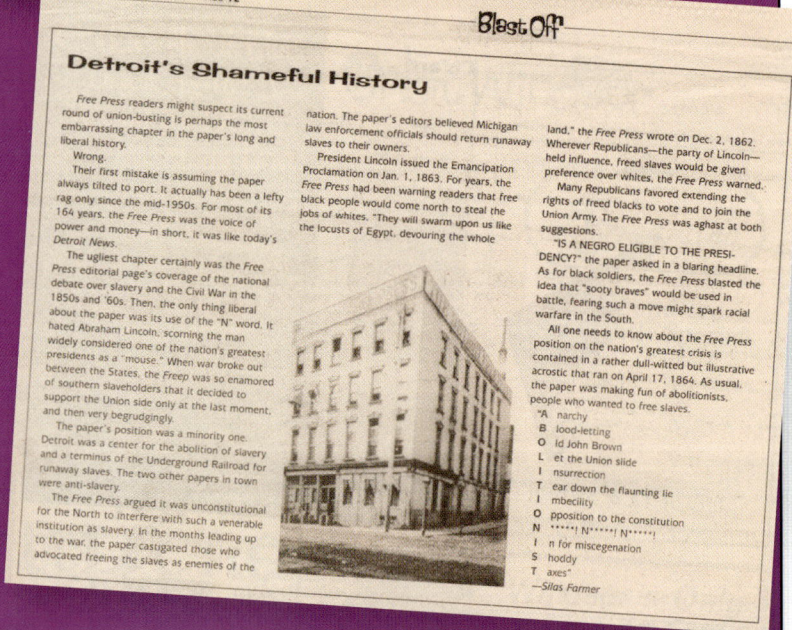

piece about the *Detroit Free Press*, his employer, made him feel like he was breaking the rules: "Some of my friends knew. Anyone who would care what I was doing and thought it was wrong wasn't reading *Orbit* or didn't even know that it existed. . . . The bosses [at the *Detroit Free Press*] wouldn't have liked it. Even for a forty year old, it was kind of naughty."

The final "Detroit's Shameful History" was in the August 1997 issue. It told of a battle between youth cruising Woodward Avenue and police in Royal Oak in 1970, a history lesson just in time for that year's annual classic car event—the Woodward Dream Cruise. The final column describes how several days of insurrection took place after cops in riot gear descended on a park where young cruisers often hung out drinking and doing drugs, staging anti-war protests, and making love.

As for the two dailies, the *Detroit Free Press* and *Detroit News* strike ended when the unions called it off in February 1997. Still, the unions would go to court and the strike wouldn't be settled until December 2000. McGraw returned to the paper in 1997 after the strike ended and contributed award-winning work. He also co-authored *The Detroit Almanac*—a history book on the city published just in time for the city's tricentennial in 2001. McGraw retired from the *Detroit Free Press* in 2009.

The Last Page

Following on a tradition started in *Fun*, *Orbit* always featured jokes and activities on the last page of the magazine. Titled, creatively enough, "The Last Page," the section mostly featured syndicated cartoons and humorous columns, like work from underground comics artist Charles Burns and columns from NPR's Dr. Science. The last page often included a humorous glossary and "Street Seen"—a photo featuring some lucky Detroiter discussing his or her outfit and how much it cost.

ATOMIC LIVING

INNER SPACES AND OUTER WEAR

IN*TERIORS*

STREET SEEN

"It's an annoyance." That's how trend-setting publisher Ronald Williams describes his attitude towards fashion. Ron's modest, yet dashing outfit combines traditional elements of the business world (corporate executive blazer and snazzy tie) with the radical *devil may care* nonchalance of the '60s bohemian (faded dungarees and sneakers). Perfect for the power lunch or protest march.

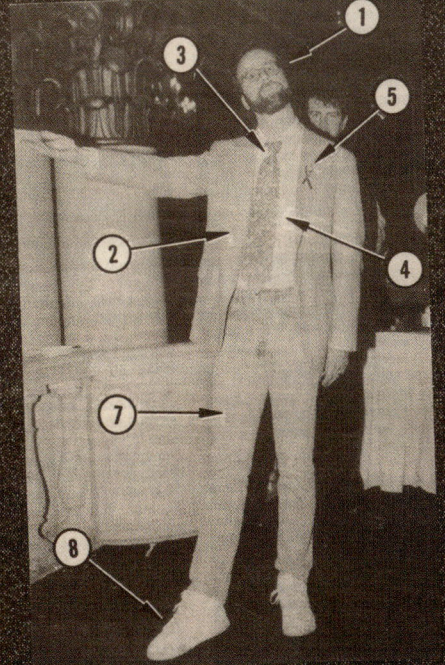

① Frames from Co-op Optical $200.00
② Suit coat from Norstrom (Seattle) $450.00
③ Tie with French sounding name $50.00
④ Button down shirt from The Gap.......$25.00
⑤ Political statement ribbon ....Free
⑥ Zenith watch (not pictured) $500.00
⑦ Self-faded jeans $35.00
⑧ White Reebok Sneakers $79.00
OUTFIT VALUED AT $1,339.00

IT'S PLEDGE TIME AGAIN

The calls are pouring in at the WDET studios. The pledge drive is on and they need your help. We know you love the Martin Bandyke Program, but are you willing to do your part to support Detroit's most popular radio personality? It costs WDET $1.8 million a year to bring you quality programming like Martin's, and 60% of that comes from generous listeners like you. It's essential that the WDET's studio's state-of-the-art equipment is properly maintained so that Martin can continue to play the grooviest sounds Monday through Friday, from 1 to 4 PM.

① This ain't no karaoke machine, that's a real microphone and it costs a lot of money, so call in your pledge today! ② Computers. This is the 90s, and computers are a necessary part of life. We don't have to tell you how expensive they are, so call in your pledge today! ③ Only a trained professional like Martin can even begin to understand the complexities of the mixing console. It's perhaps the most important piece of equipment in the studio, and it ain't free, so call in your pledge today! ④ Okay, so the CDs are free, but the players cost money, so call in that pledge now! No amount is too small! ⑤ CART tape machine. Regular radio stations usually use these to play commercials, but as you know, WDET is brought to you without commercial interruption. No ads means no *dinero*, so you'd better call in your pledge now! The number is 1-800-959-WDET. Operators are standing by to take your call.

▲ "Street Seen," *Orbit*, April 6–20, 1993.

ORBIT 195

The Last Page
FUN & GAMES

Street Seen

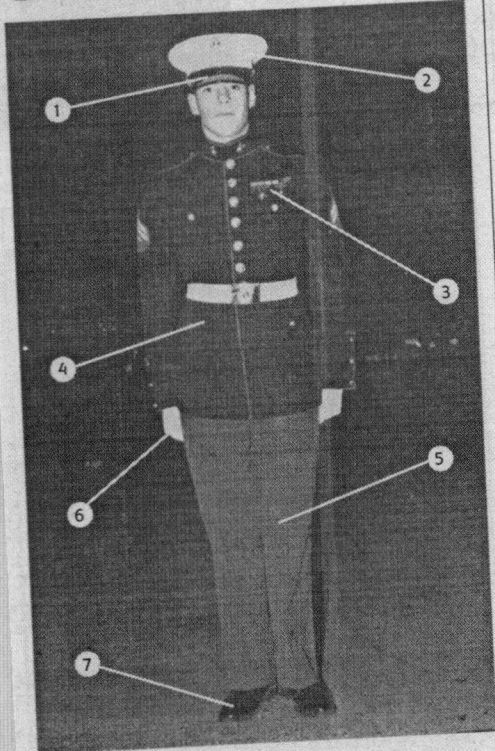

Loveable jarhead Dave Torok only has one thing to say about his fashion sense, "USMC rocks!" In fact, that was the only answer he gave to *any* questions we posed to him. (Items in outfit not sold separately. Total value of outfit does not include at least four years of indentured servitude to the U.S. Government.)

1. Hat . . . .
2. Hat cover . . . .
3. Awards . . . . .earned the hard way
4. Dress blue shirt . . . .
5. Pants . . . .
6. White gloves . . . .
7. Shiny shoes . . . .

Total value of outfit $350.00

Glossary of Terms

The Glossary of Terms is a less-than-comprehensive list of big words used in the magazine that you might not have known.

hum•ding•er *n. Slang.* Someone or something astounding, a marvel. And they know it.

an•thro•po•mor•phize *v.* To ascribe human characteristics to a non-human object or animal that inspires unease.

par•a•pher•na•lia *n.* The articles used in some activity. Like the one that is celebrated each spring at the top of the park in Ann Arbor.

dig•ge•ry doo *n.* When you get tired of your drum, you get one.

cou•tu•riere *n.* A chick dressmaker.

A DOG'S BREAKFAST BY t. COLON

An apple? You're trying to entice with an apple? A sports car or a beach house, maybe? But an apple?

THE AMAZING Cynicalman PLAYS THE LOTTERY ©Matt 91

LOOK! I FOUND A FOUR-LEAF CLOVER! WOW! THIS MUST BE YOUR LUCKY DAY!

YOU SHOULD BUY A LOTTERY TICKET TODAY! YEAH, RIGHT!

THE STATE LOTTERY IS JUST A STUPIDITY TAX!

I'VE GOT A BIGGER CHANCE OF GETTING HIT BY A METEOR THAN WINNING THE LOTTERY!

AND MY CHANCES ONLY INCREASE SLIGHTLY IF I BUY A TICKET! I'D RATHER HAVE A DOLLAR IN MY POCKET! OH, DON'T BE SO CYNICAL!

SCREEEE LOOK! A FALLING STAR! MAKE A WISH!

KABLAM!

ONE LOTTERY TICKET, PLEASE.

Ask Dr. Science

Dear Dr. Science:

When I was growing up, you could get stewed prunes at any pancake house in the country. Now, even with microwaves ovens, you can hardly find stewed prunes anywhere. What's going on? — Roger Harding, Rogue River, Oregon

Roger, yours is the kind of letter that lets me know that there are people out there whose minds work like mine does. Indeed, what has happened to the prunes of yore? When did pancakes supplant prunes? I think it had something to do with atomic testing on prune reserves in 1956, the subsequent great prune shortage of 1957. Or it might have to do with international pancake futures and insider trading in the maple syrup commodity market. These are complicated issues, ones better left to pruny old men, the kind you see on "Nightline."

Dear Dr. Science:

What does it mean when an appliance is labeled "Maintenance Free"? — Ben McArtle, Cedar Rapids, Iowa

It means it can't be fixed. That's good news for appliance salesmen and bad news for the rest of us. Seems nobody was buying those maintenance agreements, the ones they try to push on you after you've agreed to make a major purchase. So they got mad and sealed each appliance permanently. Sometimes you'll see a little warning sign with the caution: "No user serviceable parts inside." What they really mean is that there are little explosive devices attached to every removable part and any attempt to toy with the inner workings will prove fatal. All the people who used to service appliances are now working on the assembly line attaching these explosive devices. That's progress!

©1994 DUCK'S BREATH. Dr. Science's Book of Shocking Domestic Revelations *is available from* stores, or by mail ($17.50 postpaid) from Duck's Breath, P.O.B. 22513-SA, San Francisco, CA 94122, or call 1-800-989-DUCK

▲ "The Last Page," *Orbit*, April 1997.

▲ A Dog's Breakfast, *Orbit*, September 22–October 6, 1992, July 1994, January 1995.

A Dog's Breakfast

Terry Colon's comic *A Dog's Breakfast* launched in the pilot issue of *Orbit* in August 1990. The single-panel piece usually featured absurdist, surrealist humor and was the magazine's answer to Gary Larson's popular strip *The Far Side*. While he wasn't paid extra for the cartoon, Colon said the opportunity to use the last page to test out his ideas, design the magazine, and just be around Jerry Peterson had a great impact on his work: "[It was] a great learning experience, and it was a real creative environment being around Jerry. He was belly-laugh funny. I've worked with a lot of writers since then, really witty guys—the writers at *Suck*, Joel Stein from *Time*—and they are funny and witty, but they are not close to Jerry. He can make you fall down [laughing] . . . his stuff was just absurd, too, which was just so great about it."

Colon's work at *Orbit*, including *A Dog's Breakfast*, helped him to land illustration and cartoon work in national publications like *Entertainment Weekly*, *Cracked*, and *Time*. *A Dog's Breakfast* ran almost monthly between 1992 and 1995. It would appear occasionally thereafter until the last issue in the fall of 1999.

The Amazing Cynicalman

Much like Colon, Matt Feazell, a newspaper and graphic-design-industry veteran, was working in design at *Orbit* when he made his impact on "The Last Page." Feazell was working at the *Metro Times* when *Orbit* launched in 1990. He wound up at *Orbit* in 1994 through a temp agency, doing ads. In January 1996, Feazell's *The Amazing Cynicalman* appeared for the first time on "The Last Page" and remained a monthly feature until the final issue.

Who is *The Amazing Cynicalman*? According to Matt Feazell, who created the character in 1980, "He's America's laid-off superhero [who] struggles for truth, justice, and a second cup of coffee." Cynicalman had a history of being told no. Other local papers, including Feazell's former employer, the *Metro Times*, turned down the comic strip. Though

▼ A Dog's Breakfast, *Orbit*, February 1997.

▲ The Amazing Cynicalman, *Orbit*, October 1996.

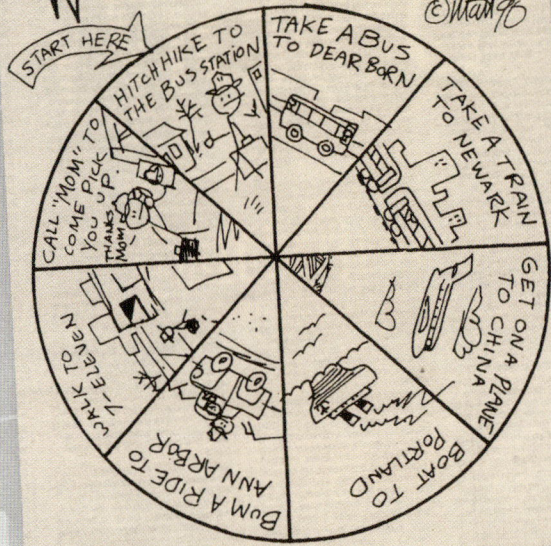

it may have contributed to the comic being rejected, Feazell's use of stick figures helped him to find his own unique voice and creative outlet as an illustrator: "The other types of illustration weren't working out. There is a way to get it wrong. It takes a little concentration to get it right. I suppose it is hard to draw Charlie Brown or Snoopy, it took Charles Schulz a time to do it, to get it right," said Feazell. By the time he got the opportunity to introduce Cynicalman to *Orbit* readers, Feazell had figured out how to make the strip work for a newspaper format instead of as a mini-comic book, which was what he'd drawn and self-published before coming to *Orbit*.

After *Orbit* was laid to rest in the fall of 1999, other newspapers, including Feazell's old employer, became interested in *The Amazing Cynicalman*. The strip ran weekly in the *Metro Times* for two-and-a-half years and was also self-syndicated to other newspapers around Michigan.

Since then, Feazell has continued to expand the Cynicalman universe. Several paperback collections of strips have been released. In 2012, he released *The Amazing Cynicalman* live-action independent film.

▲ The Amazing Cynicalman, *Orbit*, November 1996, November 1998, February 1999.

198 The *Orbit* Magazine Anthology

Reviewing his old strips, Feazell said his personal favorite doesn't revolve around his superhero at all. His favorite comic illustrates a local phenomenon the Hamtramck resident knows well.

As Feazell explained, "The cars change with the chair in the road, but the house and chair are the same. There's a habit of people putting out chairs to get their parking spaces. You had to leave a chair there to mark your space."

Orbit Covers

Throughout the run of *Orbit* magazine, only a handful of musicians graced the cover. Occasionally, a doctored promo photo for something like a film would end up on the front of the magazine. Jerry Peterson felt it was lazy to put a simple picture on the front of his magazine.

Orby the artist.

He was striving to differentiate *Orbit*'s covers from those of other alt weeklies and larger publications. Peterson pushed his design team and local artists to use the covers as a sort of experimental gallery space. Many Detroit creatives shared space on *Orbit*'s covers with internationally respected artists to make something eye-catching each month.

Glenn Barr

Of the Detroit-area artists who used their artistic skill to make *Orbit* covers something more than ad space, Glenn Barr set the standard for every artist to follow. The Livonia native and Center for Creative Studies alum found that life after graduation was not meeting his creative needs. So, along with two partners, he

▲ Glenn Barr covers, *Orbit*, June 1993 to January 1999.

created a design and illustration company called Studio X in the late 1980s. Around the same time, Barr met Chris Gore, *Fun* editor and *Film Threat* creator, at a local comic shop. That led to Barr creating covers for both Gore's magazine and *Fun*, as well as the ads for Dave's Comics that ran in Jerry Peterson's publication.

When Peterson decided to lay *Fun* to rest and take his newest publication to the next level, Barr was on the team. During *Orbit*'s nine-year run, Barr's artwork graced the cover of the magazine eleven times. The only art that was used twice was his Frank Sinatra cover from November 1990—it was re-colored for the memorial issue to the crooner in June 1998. Barr's style was fun, retro, and futuristic with a pop sensibility.

But when selecting a favorite, it's not the space-age stuff Barr liked the best. In fact, it's a more somber piece based on a well-known work by renaissance master Michelangelo that he created for the April 1995 issue, "The Death of Alternative": "I think Jerry might have come up with the concept. He didn't want to do Christ as an alternative guy, as the death of alternative, that's when coffee shops were popping up and everyone was getting tattoos and it wasn't hip or outsider to do that anymore. I don't know if he zeroed in on *The Pietà*. I think he wanted Christ on the cross. I was like, 'No, let's do something a little different here.' So, like I say, he was the sledgehammer and I was the finesser," said

During Barr's time creating covers for *Orbit*, he was exceptionally busy doing other work for print and television. Following a few visits to New York, Barr was hired to do work for Marvel and DC Comics. His best-known comic book art in that period was for *The Big Book Of* series and J. M. DeMatteis's autobiographical graphic novel *Brooklyn Dreams*, both published by DC Comics' underground/alternative flavored imprint, Paradox Press. Barr also continued to do covers for *Film Threat*. One such cover landed him a gig doing backgrounds for the second season of *Ren & Stimpy*—the hit animated show—after the creator of the program, John Kricfalusi, saw it. That's when Barr packed up and headed to L.A.—for a while.

"I was out there for about seven months. I moved out there while my wife lived here. I was married. Talk about a strain. That was the second season of the show. All the original guys were still there. At the same time, that's when Nickelodeon started to dictate what was funny and not funny, and they started to take the humor out of it, and John [Kricfalusi] was a basket case. I finished the season and moved back to Detroit. All I needed was a fax machine and FedEx. They would fax me the backgrounds, and I would paint them here and send them FedEx. It was magic. I got paid good for it too," said Barr.

Even though he came to *Ren & Stimpy* through a *Film Threat* cover, Barr said he believes the time at *Orbit* really helped him: "I wouldn't have gotten to do those [*Film Threat*] covers if I hadn't done those *Orbit* covers. You know, working with people. It's important to be able to visualize other people's ideas."

Barr became part of a group of artists connected to the magazine whose work was getting gallery space. Many of Barrs's covers, along with other work, were part of shows at ©POP Gallery. When Peterson started the Dirty Show, Barr curated the art and helped get what would become an annual exhibition off the ground.

Since 2001, Barr's work has traveled well outside of his Detroit studio. His work has been published in several art books, and has also been the basis for a series of art toys.

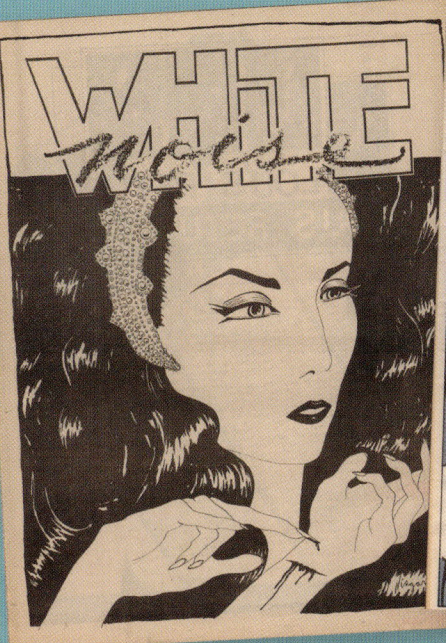

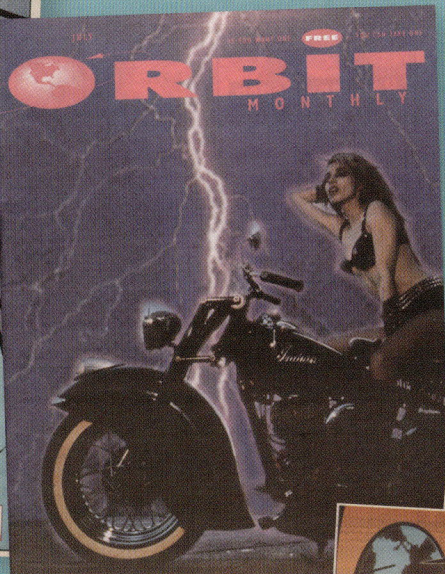

Barr. Since the end of *Orbit*, Barr's work has been featured in gallery shows across the nation.

Niagara

Of all the artists whose work has been featured on the cover of Jerry Peterson's publications, only one could claim a decades-old friendship forged in the glory days of punk rock—Niagara. Niagara met Jerry Vile in early 1978 during a show featuring her art-collective-turned-band Destroy All Monsters in Ann Arbor. Starting with the first issue of *White Noise*, which featured Niagara on the front cover and her line art gracing the back, Niagara would be a presence in Peterson's publications for the next twenty years.

As Niagara recalls: "Usually once or twice a year, he would say we wanted this for the cover and we want you to do it. Sometimes I would do a black-and-white ink drawing and then they would color it. I did a real painting for [one cover idea], and it's just this girl at a bar with the drink and it says, 'This band sucks,' and then it was our band in the background. Since I did that painting, the Colonel [Niagara's husband] has made prints of it and it is very popular. It fits for everyone's lifestyle. [Laughs]"

Niagara was featured on a 1993 cover of *Orbit* on a motorcycle and even wrote the horoscope, or as the feature was called,

▲Niagara back cover of *White Noise* #1, 1978, *Orbit*, February 7–21, 1991; July 1993; November 1996; November 1998.

During the *Orbit* years, Niagara was part of a stable of artists who showed their work at Detroit's now-defunct ©POP gallery. Niagara's art has also appeared in the Dirty Show. Since 2000, her art has been shown in England, France, and Australia. In 2011, *Return of the Repressed*, a retrospective showcasing her work as part of Destroy All Monsters, was held in Los Angeles to glowing reviews. In 2012, her longtime friend and DAM co-collaborator Mike Kelley died. That same year, the Museum of Modern Art in New York purchased a number of the works in the DAM retrospective for its permanent collection.

ARIES
Slumbering notions are awakened. "The desire of the moth for the star" (Shelley). The Sun has beamed into Aries heralding Spring and the advent of your enthusiasm. A coalition of promise is made when a fancy partner and thou team up. Brains + Energy = $. The world is your oyster…and you won't even get worms.

TAURUS
Venus goes Taurus April 2nd, gracing you with a charming countenance…and a rose colored monocle. Even if you've lived long with someone you have at times detested, you admit to their positive qualities. A beauty of a month for friendships, pacts, love. Secrets told late at night of lost comrades and the ones that got away. You can safely wear your heart on your sleeve.

GEMINI
Do you feel the electrical charge of Spring? Geminis never miss their kicks. You are Information Central this month, more than usual. Your network includes non-professional spies, professional hot-shots, party girls and semi-profound artists. You're IN THE KNOW and receive flowery karma only if you share it. Work for the good of your fellow citizens.

CANCER
You are searching for your Destiny. This month if you expand your mind and your horizons, you CAN find the key to your heart's desire. Hitch a ride on a slow boat down Moon River. We're after the same rainbow's end…my huckleberry friend. Be very perceptive: SEEK. You are offered the chance of a lifetime. Will you recognize it? P.S. It's not offered on TV.

LEO
Will you awake to humanitarianism? Justice? Kindness? Good deeds? In this stinking rotten world, we sometimes forget the ABCs of a worthwhile life. Do you have the courage? Your mind sees so clearly this month…long enough for you to see how to put it right. Do you have the courage? Your mind sees so clearly this month…long enough for you to see how to put it right. Do you have the character to pay your karmatic payments? Leos are best at giving. Is this you?

VIRGO
You don't want for better or for worse, for richer or poorer. You're like Goldilocks and you want it JUST RIGHT. This month, you're in business. The flair is there for a meeting of the minds with your beloved one. You give sex, lies and videotape a run for the money. Recognize yourself: Nothing is ever perfect enough. Try a martini.

LIBRA
Tis love that makes the world go round. But let's put that on the back burner for a second. If you play your cards right this month, you can get a heap o' dough. There's networking to be done. We're talking WORK but with a reward that equals the effort that you export. You can find the partner of your fantasies…for career moves.

SCORPIO
This April is national romance month for Scorpio. The possibilities are: 1)Past involvements are renewed 2) Your current love-life is intensified. 3) A romantic tête à tête with an older or mature person. Trying to explain how deeply and infinitely Scorpios get INVOLVED is like trying to tell a stranger 'bout Rock & Roll.

SAGITTARIUS
A very productive month only in the most avant-garde mode. Even *more* energy midmonth when Sun, Mercury, Mars, and New Moon bring power through your unique style. So you better think up one pronto. Home and family hijinks are resolved harmoniously. A split activity month that is outgoing yet homey. Two months in one.

CAPRICORN
Your manner of repartee is conducive to positive and expansive changes at work. A chance for you to show leadership qualities in group activities. Your community needs you, whether they know it or not. Stop the radio-active water. There's a task that'll keep you occupied. Capricorns are leaders in the New Phase. Work it.

AQUARIUS
Better than ever chances of career break-through. Bust a move in April. Take your reputation to the bank and cash it. Do your most ornate sales pitch. Aquarians know everybody. Your rep is looking good NOW so approach all guinea pigs and enlist them in the Aquarian Army. Stay on that phone long enough and you will soon rule the world.

PISCES
I swear, I know these Pisces people who seem elusive with gossamer idealism and outlandishly great expectations. Yet your weird wishes are actually materializing. You have strong backing from the stars now… and even the loftiest of aspirations are conceivable. I would advise to be practical but what for? Do it YOUR WAY…maybe IMpractical is best. And now you have SEX APPEAL on your side…case closed.

▲ "Your Monthly Orboscope," *Orbit*, April 1994.

"The Orboscope," for about a year, ending in June 1994: "I remember people coming up to me and saying it was accurate, but it was hard to be accurate because it was a monthly. I remember this one lady came up to me and said, 'My boyfriend says you hate Tauruses.' Yeah, that's true! [Laughs] It was fun."

After leaving the performance stage in the early 1990s to pursue art full time, Niagara found that support from Peterson and *Orbit* was important to her success: "When I went over to art in the early nineties, I was showing in the windows of shops— that was professional. [My work] sold. That was amazing because people don't buy unless they love it. Then I started to get galleries. Everyone was really nice in the press with the art. Not like the band—that's more competitive. Jerry was supportive and into it."

Tom Thewes

An artist who stumbled up the *Orbit* stairs to work right out of the Center for Creative Studies (now the College for Creative Studies) was Metro Detroit native Tom Thewes. Having grown up sheltered, Thewes admitted he wasn't very hip, even in his early twenties. "I was just this weird, secluded Catholic kid who went to art school and that opened my eyes a little bit. *Orbit* was really a big eye opener," he said. When he graduated in 1990, a lot of old ways of doing things were slipping away. Computers were taking over handmade, pasted-up graphics. The desktop publishing revolution was killing off art departments at advertising agencies. Jobs were hard to come by.

Just as *Orbit* was starting, Thewes went in for an interview with woefully out-of-date tactics: "It was the stupidest interview ever. I went to CCS, and they had a business class that was so horribly insufficient. They would tell us to get a suit for funerals and interviews. It's not going to be cool, it's going to be navy blue or gray. So, I wore my navy blue suit to meet Jerry, and Jerry comes stumbling in drunk with, like, sweatpants and a giant leather belt and his tie is askew like Andy Warhol and his hair is all a mess and he probably had a flask. He was like, 'This is great! Great portfolio! My God, what are you doing in Detroit? Alright, gotta get you in doing some art!' So ridiculous."

Peterson hired Thewes on a freelance basis, mostly small illustrations to decorate pages at the beginning. But less than a year after the magazine started, in April 1991, Thewes was given his first cover—a painting for a diet and exercise issue.

In total, Thewes would do about a half-dozen covers for *Orbit* in his hard-angled, futurism-inspired style. He said that Jerry "totally got what I was doing in the beginning and knew how to use it. I was young, and maybe I was experimenting a bit too much, but he was always trying to match the right artist with the right concept . . . I would have an idea, make some sketches, and we would talk about it, and then I would do a painting . . . And it was so fun doing stuff like that for him and for other newspapers."

In the final years of *Orbit*, Thewes would partner with the owners of Royal Oak's ©POP gallery—a place that championed many of the artists connected to the magazine. Thewes bought the gallery in 1999 and moved it to Midtown Detroit before that area was revitalized in later years. Thewes said the

late 1990s was a glorious time for his circle of Detroit artists and *Orbit* was a part of that:

> Glenn [Barr] and Niagara and Mark [Dancey] kept getting more and more successful, and now they are incredible world-famous artists, so I was just trying to step up and help that and get us into that national and international picture we were all a part of.
>
> [*Orbit*] was the perfect venue for ©POP. Those openings are legendary. *Orbit* was the local vehicle and *Juxtapoz* was the national/international vehicle. It gave us brand identity in a way. It brought people to the openings. Everyone looked in *Orbit* for what was going on, what was cool. It was key to get things off the ground and be considered legitimate in the street/underground culture.

Looking back on those early days and opportunities, Thewes said *Orbit* had a profound impact on him: "That was so important. . . . I could play and make mistakes, and it was something I just couldn't do in other places as an illustrator.

▼ Tom Thewes covers, *Orbit*, April 18–May 2, 1991, March 1997, July 1997.

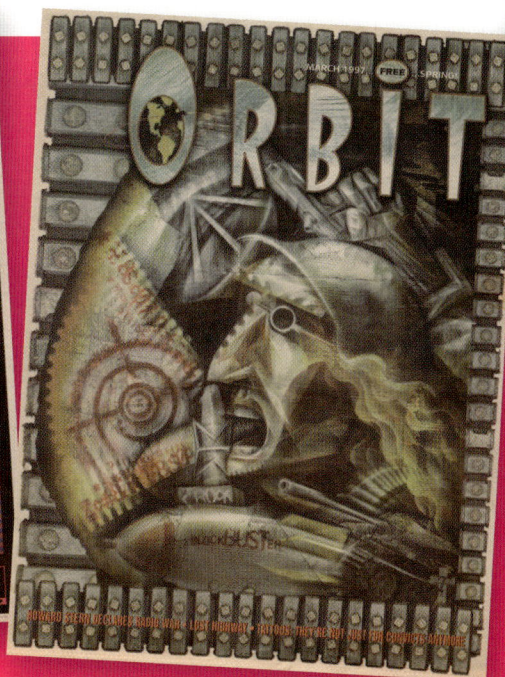

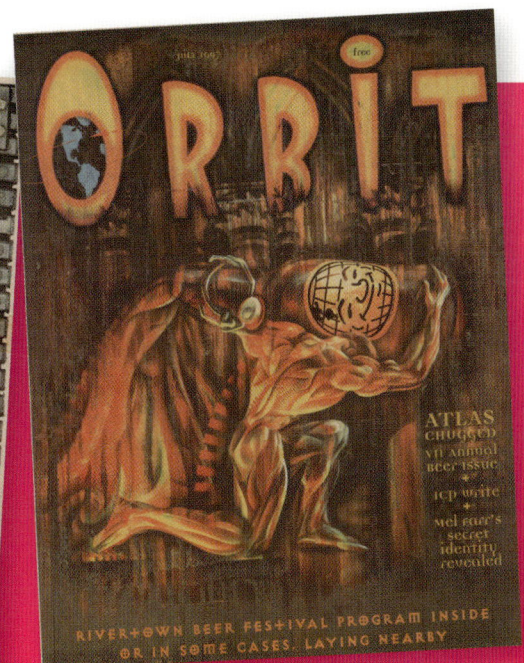

▲ Mark Dancey covers, *Orbit*, December 15–29, 1992, January 1997.

And everything in *Orbit* was so cool. It was so fun. So, it wasn't boring, trying to find something to make a boring article look fun, it was trying to find something that was going to be as good as the article. . . . It felt great to have a lot of confidence in myself as an artist and value where I was from. I used to teach a little bit and I would talk about it, that you need to understand yourself as an artist and where you are and location and time and place. *Orbit* gave me that context."

Mark Dancey

Before Mark Dancey ever did a cover for *Orbit*, he had already been featured inside as the guitarist for the Detroit-area band Big Chief. Dancey wasn't a stranger to print. In 1987, he and several friends, including future members of Big Chief and writers and artists he'd met while working at the University of Michigan's humor magazine, *The Gargoyle*, started an occasional magazine called *Motorbooty*. Mixing independent music criticism with an underground comics sensibility, *Motorbooty* pushed nine issues out nationally before folding in 1999.

Dancey designed two covers for *Orbit*: the 1992 Christmas issue and a 1997 issue on aliens. Dancey's work had also appeared in *Fun*. In July 1987, an early cartoon parodied an

old postcard inviting couples to visit romantic getaway Zug Island—a notorious industrial area located in the Detroit River.

Dancey said the people who gathered around *Orbit* were amazingly talented: "The main thing was just the people who went through there. [Peterson] had everybody in town. The list is great. Terry Colon is great. His brother [Craig] was a great designer. Gary Arnett—he does great stuff. Dave Merline was one of the *Motorbooty* guys who worked at *Orbit* as well."

But it wasn't always good times. In January 1998, *Spin* ran a cartoon drawn by Dancey and written by fellow *Motorbooty* scribe Mike Rubin about the Insane Clown Posse. The four-page feature showed the rappers in a less than flattering light, comparing them to minstrel performers. Following the *Spin* feature, ICP threatened Dancey in the press and online. Dancey said when he spoke to Peterson about the situation, he was told by the *Orbit* publisher, "Who do you want me to back? You or someone who takes a full-page ad every month?" ICP was a regular advertiser. Dancey said he never expected Peterson to "take sides," and he was taken aback by the state-

Jerry Peterson in *Motorbooty* #9 Spring 1999. (Art by Mark Dancey)
Mark Dancey cover, *Motorbooty* #9, Spring 1999. ▼

ment. Dancey did a follow-up cartoon on the controversy in the final issue of *Motorbooty* featuring a drawing of Peterson.

Following their conversation, Dancey said Peterson would call him from time to time to do covers, but Dancey decided not to work for him. Since *Orbit*'s demise, the two have moved on and are very supportive of each other's work.

Tristan Eaton

Of the artists who found *Orbit* to be a platform for growth and experimentation, Tristan Eaton was the youngest. "I think I was eighteen, and it was awesome," said Eaton. "It was all thanks to Rick Manore from ©POP Gallery. I was super-ambitious at the time and I already loved *Orbit*, so it was a huge opportunity for me! Rick brought me over to the *Orbit* office to meet Jerry Peterson so I could show him my portfolio. I remember being completely unimpressed by the office. I expected something glamorous, but instead found myself walking upstairs above a fucking car mechanic. But once I met the whole team, I knew it was somewhere I wanted to be."

▼ "Sonic Comics," Tristan Eaton and Ron Wade, April 1998, October 1998.

Dancey said working for *Orbit* led to other illustration work. He said the aliens cover led to a long-term freelance gig with the *OC Weekly* in Orange County, California, which included creating the logo for Gustavo Arellano's award-winning nationally syndicated "Ask a Mexican!" column.

Although Dancey continues to do freelance illustration work, he has transitioned from rock posters and album covers to oil painting. Since 1999, Dancey has had several series of oil paintings exhibited to great acclaim.

In early 1998, Eaton was just starting at the Center for Creative Studies in Detroit. Former ©POP owner Rick Manore said he was introduced to Eaton's work through the artist's mother, who showed him some of her son's art just days after the gallery opened in Royal Oak in 1996. Manore showed Eaton's work at ©POP and introduced him to Peterson and the *Orbit* staff. As Eaton recalled:

I met the whole team after four years of psychedelic experimentation, love of graffiti, comics, and selling hashish as a youngster. I left London, England, when I was fifteen and found Michigan to be pretty damn boring. I was thirsty for something more exciting, I missed city life, and I had no connection to any kind of art community or culture. *Orbit* was the gateway into the seedy [subculture] of Detroit. I needed that! One of my favorite memories was the first day I brought in my portfolio. I had all of my crappy art across the conference table in the middle of the room to show Jerry, and, all of a sudden, Glenn Barr shows up. Fuck! I'm a huge fan of his and was totally embarrassed. It was like being caught with my pants down. Then, Mark Dancey shows up! Fuck again. They were really nice to me, though. They're my heroes! I was really lucky to be around such great people as a teenager.

Eaton started at *Orbit* by doing small illustrations for features. His first was for the controversial "How to Be a Better Stalker" feature written by writer Ron Wade in the February 1998 issue. "There was a huge backlash to the article," Eaton said. "Some radio stations were calling on advertisers to boycott the magazine. So how did *Orbit* follow up such an offensive article? I illustrated the 'Orbit Guide to Suicide!' AMAZING! That's when I knew Jerry Peterson was a legend and *Orbit* was my home."

In May 1998, Eaton and Wade would begin working together to create a small comic strip for the music section. "Tristan Eaton and I would do these goofy little cartoons. I would write them with stick figures, and Tristan would come back with amazing art. I kept some of the originals. I knew he was way talented," said Wade.

"They came about because Ron was generous enough to ask me! Maybe they felt bad for me and were just throwing me a bone!? I don't know. But it was really fun. I love Ron for believing in me back then," said Eaton.

In just under a year, Eaton was given the title of illustrator, but his time at *Orbit* was short-lived. In the January 1999 issue, Eaton was given a send-off, leaving Detroit with one final show at ©POP. Since then, Eaton has become an internationally respected artist and designer, doing work for major brands and even the Obama presidential campaign, while creating murals in cities around the world.

Mark Niemenski

As one of the lead designers for *Orbit*, Mark Niemenski handled and formatted the original art provided by outside artists. He was also called on to create covers, sometimes at the last minute: "A lot of the covers I worked on we would have nothing, no references. We would just work, chop, masking stuff. I'd show [Jerry] some comps, we'd go over them. We had about a week."

Upon arriving in New York, Eaton started working as a muralist, creating public art. In 2004, an interactive concept called the "Dunny" was launched. Eaton, along with co-designer Paul Budnitz, developed a poseable white vinyl art toy. ("Dunny" is a mash-up of the words "devil" and "bunny.")

"I remember the community of it all [at *Orbit*]. There were so many great people involved. Some have passed away since then, but overall, I think many of us look back at that time as the good ol' days. Everyone was so nice and generous to me. I was just a kid and they didn't have to put up with me. But they did, and it gave me fuel to do more. I remember counting the pages that I had art on in every issue—it would make my day every time," said Eaton.

It's evident that Eaton's years in Detroit and at *Orbit* helped to shape his work. One needs only to look at the broad range of influences he listed in his CNN feature in December 2011. Pop artist Roy Lichtenstein, symbolist painter Gustav Klimt, and cartoonist Chris Ware are on the list, but the first artist Eaton named as an influence is none other than frequent *Orbit* cover artist Glenn Barr.

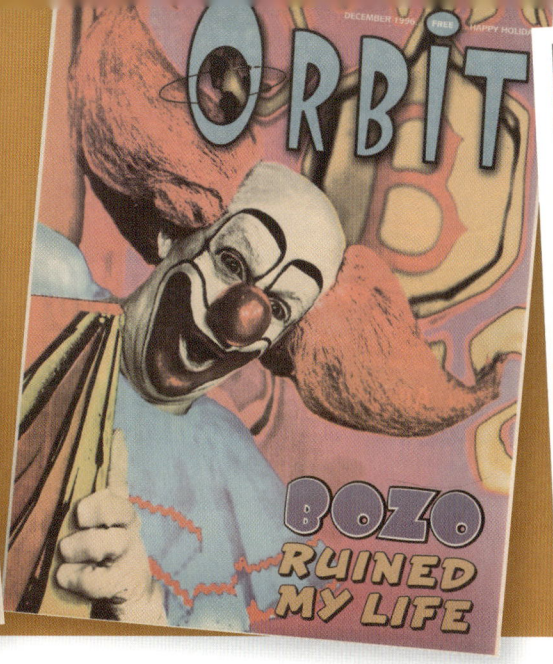

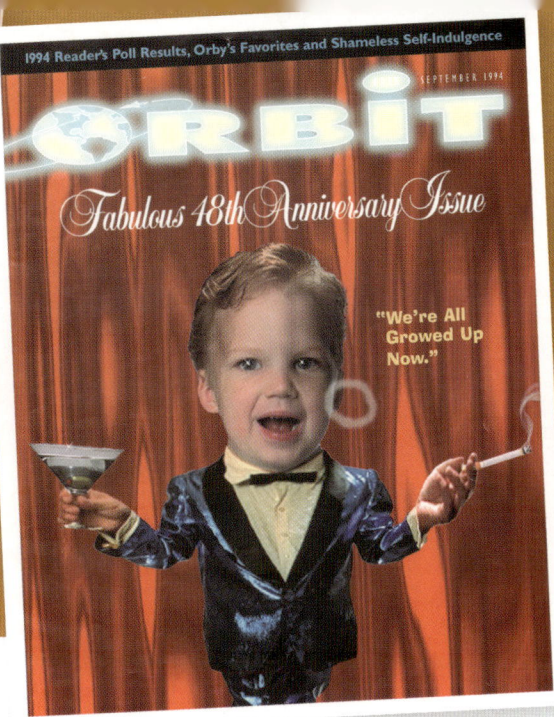

▲ Mark Niemenski covers, *Orbit*, June 1995, December 1996, September 1994.

When Niemenski contacted *Fun* about buying an ad for his band, the Hysteric Narcotics, in late 1986, Peterson saw Niemenski had a graphics background and asked him to work on the magazine. He would eventually work on *Orbit* as well, doing design, covers, and layouts.

Niemenski said one his favorite designs is the September 1994 cover, which took about two days to create. It led to an irate phone call from a woman who thought the magazine had actually given a young Ryan Peterson drinks and a cigar to celebrate *Orbit*'s fourth anniversary.

Niemenski closed out *Orbit*'s run by designing the cover of the final issue—a simple black cover.

After *Orbit*, Niemenski helped Peterson with his annual international erotic art exhibition, the Dirty Show.

Other Artists

Over the course of its nine-year run, *Orbit*'s striking and provocative covers became a staple for the magazine and forecasted many successful careers for local and national artists and designers.

Beyond helping create the magazine's original look and "Orby," designer Terry Colon also designed a number of covers for *Orbit*. Dearborn native Kevin "SLAW" Stanislawski's

In the rush to publish the last issue of *Orbit*, which would also mark the magazine's ninth anniversary, the cover had to come together quickly. Designer Mark Niemenski worked up an idea poking fun at end times and rapture paranoia—just perfect for the Y2K bug that was supposed to wreak havoc in just a few months.

The art features a giant Ryan Peterson—the anniversary boy—dressed in white, looking over a Detroit in flames. A road jags through the center of the image with a man holding his arms out to the God-like figure as an Orby-faced sun sets in the distance.

Niemenski said this cover idea was nixed because the magazine had to go to press and there wasn't time to finish it. The black cover with Orby's head was selected instead.

Unused cover version 2, Fall 1999. ▶

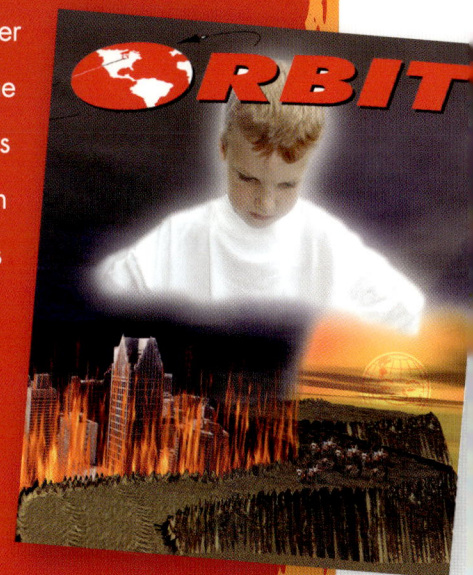

▲ Terry Colon cover, *Orbit*, August 1993 and May 1995.

Orbit also featured work by legendary underground comic artist, *Zap Comix* co-founder, and *Juxtapoz* magazine creator Robert Williams.

While as publisher Jerry Peterson had given many ideas and directed artists, he did create one cover under his moniker Jerry Vile in early 1992 to celebrate the year of the monkey.

The most infamous person to have art featured on the cover of *Orbit* was assisted-suicide activist Dr. Jack Kevorkian, whose painting "Fa, La, La, La, La," a send-up of Christmas-time commercialism, was featured on the December 1994 cover.

May 1999 mid-century modern cover welcomed in a new, sleeker era of *Orbit* in May 1999. Cleveland artist Derek Hess created artwork for *Orbit*'s 1995 "XMAS SUCKS" issue, and New York–based artist and filmmaker Steven Cerio designed August 1998's neo-psychedelic "Back to School" cover.

Now, a Word from Our Sponsors . . .

A free magazine is made possible by advertisers. What made being an advertiser with a Peterson publication attractive to some businesses was the ability to put their message out without censorship.

Formed in 1990, AWOL was an art collective founded by Greg Fadell, Matt Zacharias, and Pete Wardowski. The trio created photography, film, video, silkscreen, performance, collage, and installation work that was featured in galleries around Detroit and nationally. For the group's AWOL 99 solo show held at ©POP, the trio presented large-scale photos of dioramas that addressed race, class, and civil unrest. The June 1999 issue of *Orbit* features one of AWOL's pieces from the show—referencing the 1984 Detroit Tigers World Series riot—with the snarky headline "Summer Fun." Fadell said when they pulled out samples for the cover, Peterson knew instantly which one he wanted.

"I really saw him as somebody who was in the scene as well as promoting the scene instead of being a nine-to-fiver," said Fadell. Zacharias said the attention they received from being on the cover of *Orbit* was a great thing for the artists because creating and showing their work could be very isolating. He felt Peterson's background prior to starting the magazine helped the publisher value their work even more.

"He's a satirist, he's an artist, he's a musician. In a way, he's kind of a renaissance guy because he's had his hand in so many mediums, and moving beyond that he appreciates other people's art," said Zacharias. Since dissolving AWOL in 2002, Fadell and Zacharias have gone on to be respected artists in their own right, creating through paint and installations.

From top left (clockwise): SLAW cover, *Orbit*, May 1999. Derek Hess cover, *Orbit*, December 1995. Robert Williams cover, *Orbit*, May 1996. Steven Cerio cover, *Orbit*, December 1994. Jerry Vile cover, *Orbit*, Jan. 28–Feb. 11, 1992. Jack Kevorkian cover, *Orbit*, December 1994.

In issue #3 of *Fun* (December 1986), the magazine dedicated more than an entire page to ads the *Metro Times* had rejected from Royal Oak's Noir Leather. As the page read, "All ads appear in their entirety totally uncensored." Some featured BDSM, others featured scantily clad women. Store founder and owner Keith Howarth said a three-person review board at the *Metro Times* had to approve his designs before they went to press.

They put in one of my ads and they got a lot of complaints. So, after that, they would review my ads, and for some reason they would just earmark an ad and be like, "We're not running it, this is too over the edge." There wasn't really like a rhyme or a reason which ones they rejected, . . . which financially did hurt. So when *Fun* came on board I asked them, "How racy can I be with your paper? Because the *Metro Times* is giving me a lot of trouble with my ads." And they said, "Well, let's see those ads you're talking about. And I showed them to Jerry, and Jerry said this is what we are going to do. We're going to kick off the paper and run a center spread, a page, with all the ads they refused. So get us all the ads. So, I give him the collection. . . . And it was fantastic PR for me and maybe an eye-opener for *Metro Times* because now they had competition.

▲ Noir Leather ads, *Fun*, December 1986.

For over thirty years, Howarth has watched Royal Oak's downtown grow from empty to booming. Over the years of *Fun* and *Orbit*, Howarth said he liked the ease of doing business with the magazines, which were headquartered just down the street from his store: "*Orbit* was like a stepping stone for the creativeness in my ads. They used computers. [*Orbit*'s issues] were published on desktops and I think it was the first [to do that]. They were so close, I could go to their office and sit with a layout person, give them a photo, give them copy, and together [we] could create the ad in about an hour. That was really fantastic."

Through the *Fun* and *Orbit* years, Thomas Video, also in Royal Oak, was a consistent advertiser. Owners Gary Reichel and Jim Olenski said it's hard to tell what impact a single ad had, but the cumulative effect over time seemed to have val-

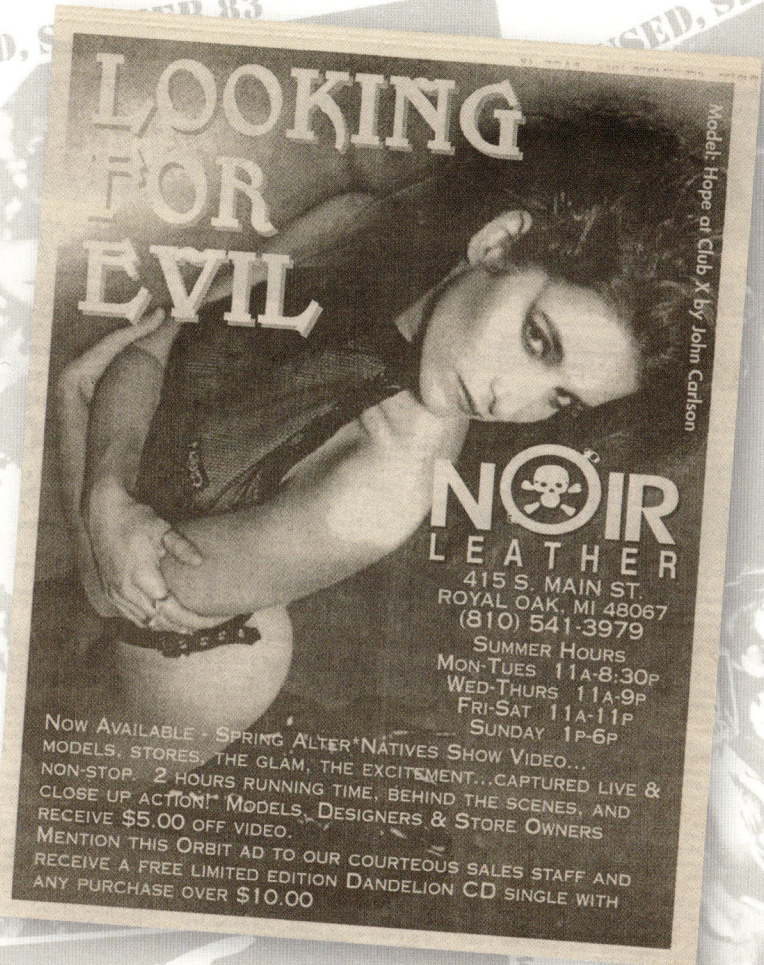

▲ Noir Leather ad, *Orbit*, September 1994.

ue. "Advertising is an intangible, it's hard to know. You pay a hundred dollars for an ad, you pay a thousand dollars for an ad, you don't know what you get back. You just never know. I recognized that if you do an ad, maybe nobody comes in off the ad or maybe a handful of people come in off the ad. But if you do a second, third, or fourth ad, then they go, subconsciously, 'Hey, I've seen some of these ads, maybe I'll come in,' and they do. For a small business, it's hard to keep shelling out the money when you don't know," said Reichel.

At the same time, Reichel said he saw a value to advertising in *Fun* and *Orbit* because both seemed to have a hipper, younger readership that might be more on-board with what Thomas Video was offering. "At that point, there was a lot of cult, weird movies coming out and we were trying to build up that reputation. We wouldn't put an ad in the *Daily Tribune*—'We have all these cult movies, come on down,' but *Fun*—that was our market," he said.

Thomas Video, which opened in 1974 and was touted by the owners as the first video store in America, went out of business in the summer of 2014.

In the late 1970s, VCRs were becoming popular. Originally founded as Thomas Film Classics in the early 1970s to sell film and home movie equipment, the Royal Oak store would help lead the charge in home video. Thomas Video's owners, Detroit punkers Gary Reichel and Jim Olenski of Cinecyde, claimed that Thomas Video was the first video store in America because it bought and rented the first tapes sold by Livonia-based Magnetic Video when Magnetic became the first company to license theatrical film on videotape in 1977.

Thomas Video ad, Orbit, November 27–December 14, 1991. ▶

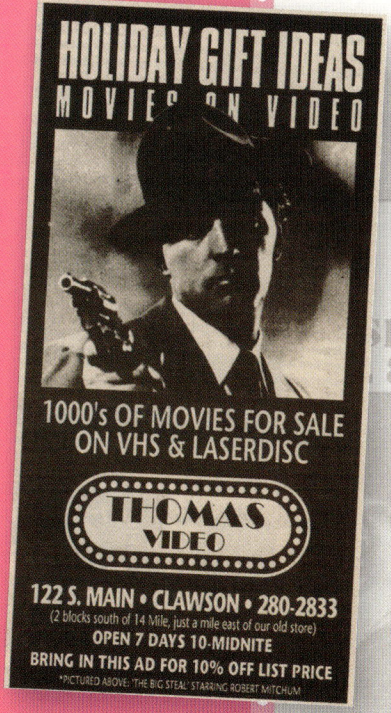

Delivering *Orbit*

From September 1990 to May 1993, *Orbit* was published twice a month. Then *Orbit* was monthly until the final issue in September 1999. It usually went out on a Wednesday night or early Thursday morning. A wooden pallet of magazines—fifty thousand in all, in neat, plastic-banded bundles—would be dropped off by truck in front of the *Orbit* offices on Main Street in Royal Oak. From there, they had to get to newsstands, bars, record stores, video stores, movie theatres, and college campuses around

Metro Detroit. Jerry Peterson offered creatives in Metro Detroit free ads in exchange for help with distribution.

Area musician Scott Campbell had worked to help get Peterson's magazines on racks as far back as *White Noise*; they also had a personal connection through Bookie's Club 870. By the time *Fun* and *Orbit* began, helping to distribute the magazine was less about doing a friend a favor and more about publicizing his shows; *Orbit*'s distribution could take its toll: "I would carry a thousand pounds of magazines in my minivan, and it would be stacked up to the windows. The suspension couldn't take it. I had to get my springs fixed because of the weight. The stuff I did, I will never do again," said Campbell.

Livonia natives Warren Defever and Davin Brainard, co-founders of Detroit's seminal Noise Camp festival, both spent time carting *Orbit* magazine around western Wayne County. Brainard met Peterson in the early 1990s while working at the Record Collector in Livonia. When he heard *Orbit* needed distributors, he signed up. "We would do it late because the stores didn't have to be open. It was really fun. A pickup truck, that's all you needed," said Brainard.

The guys said delivering *Orbit* was always a good time, but one place in Livonia, a bar featuring bikini-clad waitresses, brought out their competitive nature.

"We would fight over who got to bring them inside," said Warren Defever, laughing.

"We always gave them two bundles even though they were only supposed to get one. That way we could both carry them inside," said Brainard. For

▲ Unpublished cartoon by Davin Brainard.

Brainard, the work exchange was about being able to put something—anything—into a real newspaper.

"We were given a free advertisement in the magazine, which we used all the time, and it was super-fun to make ridiculous advertisements for things," said Brainard.

Beyond records, sundry items Brainard offered as part of his fledging Time Stereo label included "butter cake" incense that smelled of buttered popcorn and a whale-shaped table called, creatively enough, "The Whale Table."

Defever and Brainard said one of the best things about distributing *Orbit* was the networking opportunity it created, because they needed to make connections at bars, record stores, and other hip places for their other projects which helped their early ar-

▼ Time Stereo ad, *Orbit*, October 1997. (Art by Davin Brainard)

▲ Scott Campbell ad, October 1996.

tistic efforts in Metro Detroit immensely. Plus, "they acted like you were doing them a huge favor by delivering the magazine," said Defever.

Orbit Goes International

Windsor has a reputation in Detroit as the place to go to get things you can't in the States. When Michigan's legal drinking age became twenty-one, Ontario's was still nineteen, plus they had Cuban cigars and racier strip clubs. While there was plenty going on in Windsor, it was rarely covered in Detroit media at the time. However, starting with the April 20, 1993, issue of *Orbit*, the magazine branched out to cover the new casino coming to Windsor. From July 1993 until March 1999, *Orbit* featured a Windsor section—a small calendar, ads, and occasional write-ups on things to do on the other side of the border. It was the magazine's first attempt at broadening its appeal to other cities, but more ambitious international plans were just around the corner. The September 1994 issue announced that *Orbit UK* had just launched in Oxford, England, under the direction of John Dickerson—a former ad representative for the Detroit edition.

Dickerson had come to the states from Oxford in 1989. After settling in Livonia, Dickerson saw an ad in *Orbit* seeking sales help, so he called. "Jerry heard my accent and immediately, over the phone, he said, 'You're hired! You're going to come in and do sales!'" said Dickerson.

When he started in 1991, Dickerson's main mission was ad sales, but he would also help with deliveries and other odd jobs around the office. After a few years, Dickerson decided to go back to England for a while and thought, Why not take *Orbit* back home? "I mentioned to Jerry about starting up an *Orbit* magazine in Oxford, England. From what I remember, there really wasn't another magazine over there doing anything like it. There was a magazine that just did music, nothing else. But *Orbit* had so much fun stuff, cool features and things, and [Peterson] was like, 'Sure,'" said Dickerson.

About a year after returning to England, Dickerson was laid off from his day job at a construction company and decided it was time to start *Orbit UK*. Scanning the racks in Oxford, Dickerson said he realized there wasn't real any competition in the university town for a free magazine. The only other magazine of note was *Curfew* (which evolved into *Nightshift*), which covered the local

▼ *Orbit UK* Editions, December 1996, May 1997, November 1997.

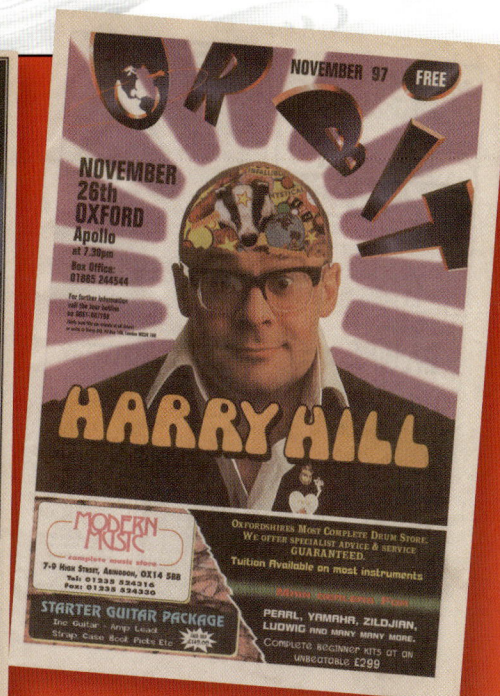

music scene and was notable for its early interviews and articles on local bands Radiohead and Supergrass. Dickerson said Peterson allowed him to take whatever he wanted from the Detroit editions, but it was up to him to put it together, sell the ads, and get it printed and distributed. The problem for Dickerson was that he didn't know anything about computers.

Orbit designer Mark Niemenski went to Oxford to help Dickerson set up the computers and design the first issue. The first edition of *Orbit UK* was put together over a weekend. "We had nothing set up. We had no proofreaders or anything. I didn't know what I was doing. And Mark came over and got me set up," said Dickerson.

A few thousand copies of the first issues were created in a small tabloid black-and-white format and featured reprints from previous issues of the Detroit edition. "I used to go to this Chinese takeout restaurant, and I was sitting here and all these college students came in. And they were like, 'What the heck is this?' They picked it up. I just sat there listening to them. They were like, 'Look at all these spelling [errors]!' and whatever. I thought, You know, the next one I'll have to improve," said Dickerson.

After the bumpy and rushed start, Dickerson found a good salesperson connected to the music scene in Oxford, which helped keep the publication afloat. Dickerson was also able to work out a barter arrangement with the Arena Nightclub in Oxford. In exchange for running ads, his team got office space. But problems quickly arose. Dickerson said club owners who didn't advertise didn't want the magazine in their establishment, and getting businesses to advertise was hard. Because it was a new magazine, he couldn't charge a lot for ads, but even a few pounds sterling seemed too much for some pub owners. "For the money it was nothing, really. Pub owners would say, 'Oh, that's too expensive.' But it would only be like

four pints of beer for the cost, but they were moaning about it. They wanted it cheap," said Dickerson.

About sixty to seventy percent of the magazine's material came from the Detroit edition. For all of *Orbit UK*'s struggles and deficiencies, Dickerson found that running record and movie reviews months before they were released in England gave him a jump on the latest in entertainment for his British readers. Meanwhile, Dickerson admits he sometimes repurposed Chris Kassel's food reviews of Detroit restaurants to fit Oxford-area restaurants.

While *Orbit UK* had a wellspring of humor and reviews to pull from back in the States, it was not just a cut-and-paste job. Dickerson would rewrite sections of the stories to make them sound more local, change some of the spellings, swap out obvious American English for the Queen's. For example, a humorous article about garage sales in Metro Detroit became a story about Oxford "boot sales," a sort of swap meet in parking lots or vacant fields where people sell odds and ends out of the trunk, or boot, of their cars. "People loved it. They thought it was great," he said.

As the Detroit edition of *Orbit* wound down, so did the UK version. Dickerson doesn't remember the exact date of the final issue, and there's no known archive of UK editions.

Orby Looks Westward

Quentin Tarantino's Orby T-shirt was the publication's first glimpse of L.A., but it wouldn't be the last. In the April 26, 1996, edition of the *Detroit Sunday Journal*—the weekly paper published by striking newspaper workers—Jerry Peterson said that he was planning to go to Los Angeles and launch a version of *Orbit* by the end of summer.

Diane Hofsess and Carol Teegardin wrote in their "Between the Lines" media column that "*Orbit* Mag king Jerry Peterson blasts off for L.A. in mid-May to get an *Orbit* rolling out there. He expects to commute back and forth for six months but eventually settle out there. Meanwhile, he sez, don't write the *Orbit*-uary for his cheeky Royal Oak-based mag; it'll do swell in the hands of managing editor Jayne Bowman Hallock. 'Now it's gonna be a chick magazine,' adds Mr. Decorum."

Jayne Bowman Hallock, former managing editor of *Orbit*, said, "[Peterson] really wanted to go out and open an *Orbit* in L.A. And he and I talked about that, and he was very nice to me. He said that I was the first person he trusted looking over his big ad accounts, like Absolut."

Peterson said the idea of taking *Orbit* to L.A. and beyond had been in the back of his mind for a while. "Had I done the L.A. thing earlier, it [would have been] to franchise it. I kick myself for starting *Orbit* in Detroit. *Film Threat* moved to L.A. Paul [Zimmerman] was like, 'These guys are getting jobs and offers.' I always knew it should be in a big city, but I never had the money to do it. So, *Orbit* was only a regional. A good magazine might work in any city. It was economics."

Peterson's line of thinking was not uncommon. *The Onion,* founded in Madison, Wisconsin, in 1988, started with a similar model. After publishing a local edition, the magazine expanded in the 1990s to other major cities near its headquarters, with Milwaukee and Chicago getting local editions.

As Peterson envisioned it, every edition of *Orbit* would carry the same content, with special content created for each city. The U.K. edition of *Orbit* was already modeling this concept. Similarly, the L.A. version would include many of the nationally focused and humor pieces written by the Detroit staff, but would also include L.A.-related features, a local events calendar, and market-specific advertising. Peterson thought this could be easily done, with only a handful of people in the L.A. office selling ads and writing pieces, as a majority of the magazine would come from headquarters back in Royal Oak. Beyond L.A., Peterson said he envisioned editions of *Orbit* in Chicago and several other cities.

By early 1998, *Orbit* was getting more attention nationally. In a *Detroit Free Press* article from January of that year, former *Details* magazine editor David Keeps said: "As a pop culture magazine, [*Orbit*] competes well with national magazines that cover the same subjects—movies, TV, music, art. In that arena, they are superior to most city magazines and papers I have seen. But it's difficult to do a local magazine in a market where there isn't a huge amount of advertising dollars." Another *Detroit Free Press* article from that month, "An Ever-Expanding Orbit: As His Detroit Underground Tabloid Gains National Attention, Jerry Peterson Launches New Ventures," highlighted Peterson new plans. Among them was a spin-off magazine to reach the over-thirty crowd. The new publication would be called *Vroom* and was planned as a "retro 'curve'—cars and girls—magazine." At the same time, Peterson told the daily that he was planning to step back in his role at *Orbit* and allow others—chiefly, managing editor Katy McNerney and new editor Scott Sterling—to run the show.

Despite ambitious plans and press coverage, Peterson's move to the West Coast never happened, nor did his new magazine concepts. Apart from the UK edition, *Orbit* remained a solely Detroit publication.

Orbit in Cyberspace

In 1994, *Orbit* designer Andrew Heaton started to tinker around with a newfangled contraption called the World Wide Web. The low-tech look of the early Internet took a while to get used to for someone coming from print, where interesting graphics and intelligent design were part of the process:

> [I remember] a student at Wayne State in the computer lab, and he was saying, "We should put *Orbit* online. That would be really cool." I was like, "What the hell are you talking about?" He said, "Come on down to the lab and I'll show you." So, I drove down to Wayne State, and he took me into the computer lab and he puts me in front of a computer and shows me the first browser and what the Internet looks like. "Does it have to be so ugly? What is this all about?" But he taught me how to code, this kid did, and I picked up a couple of books, and the very first features online were just like movie reviews and text from the articles.

Heaton's first web version of *Orbit* was a beta version of Netscape Navigator. The May 1995 issue of *Orbit* humorously and officially announced the *Orbit* website.

Orbit was the first Detroit publication to create an online presence, years before its main competitor, the *Metro Times*, and before any of the major dailies made the leap. The *Detroit Free Press* didn't start online operations until August 1996. But these early websites were "ugly," to use Heaton's word, and also not very intuitive for the programmer to create. It was mostly text, maybe a graphic or a photo—very primitive—what Heaton called "the caveman days of the Internet": "You couldn't even center an object. It was one of those things where Netscape came out and it would let you wrap text around a picture. Not in a good way, but it would start to mimic really basic layout of newspapers. There was nothing cool. No formatting. Not like today, where you can get away with anything."

Website announcement, ▶
Orbit, May 1995.

216

Like ORBIT Meets PONG!

Orbit Technology: *Bringing useless information to starving children around the world.*

Now on the World Wide Web!

Welcome to tomorrow— TODAY!

Now you can access the new, improved, vastly superior 21st-century Orbit compuzine from anywhere in the world—even Inkster! And unlike "old-fashioned" publications that use messy inks and environmentally-decimating paper, this "rad" new electronic version will run on your very own home computer (Fig. A).

Figure A: *Easily accessible from your personal computer.*

How did we do it? Well, remember we are light-years ahead of yesterday's "old-fashioned" publications. Insiders know Orbit was created by the same people who brought you FUN Magazine—perhaps the first desktop-published magazine in the Free World. And once more we did it again!

How's It Work? Glad you asked. Just hop on the information superhighway and get off at the Internet exit. From there you'll be able to access the Orbit Gigantitron XL-2000 Global Supercomputer (Fig. B) by typing in our secret World Wide Web address: **http://msen.com/~orby** And don't make a mistake, you could end up like Jeff Bridges in Tron! Although Orbit assumes no liability, rest assured. Web accidents are a thing of the past (Fig. C). But fear not, accessing Orbit via scary new computer technology will not harm you or your family.

What will you find? Yes, we have salacious and titillating stuff; record and movie reviews that just wouldn't fit in this issue. Things we were scared to print because it was too mean, too weird, or just plain smutty. You know— the good stuff.

Don't know how to get on the Internet? Too bad. You can always e-mail us at Orby@mail.msen.com.

Still reading "old-fashioned" outmoded print publications?

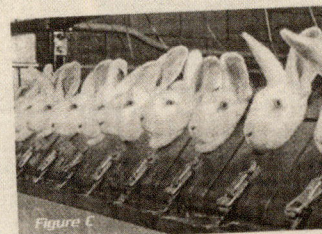

Figure C

Tested Safe

Years of rigorous product testing assure the Orbit Web is virtually safe for your entire family.

Have you ever spent hours downloading a magazine you could have picked up free at a bar or a record store? **You will.** And the company that will bring it to you will be Orbit Magazine.

The groovy Orbit World Wide Web page is accessible at **http://msen.com/~orby**

Figure B: *Orbit Gigantitron XL-2000 Global Supercomputer operators are standing by now for your data transmissions.*

Not that it really mattered. Those who were looking at the Internet in the early days were mostly computer geeks trying to figure out how to make it work. But despite the Internet's primitive nature, Heaton was able to figure out at least one way to make a few dollars online for *Orbit*: "I remember Keith [Howarth] from Noir Leather ran an ad online. It was before banner ads existed. But we're like, 'Hey, pay us a couple of extra bucks—basically, fund my time to sit behind a computer and do this—and we'll put an ad up there.' I think Keith got the best of it because there were all sorts of weird perverts online in those days."

Today, Orby.com is sadly no more.

Fun Returns—Kind Of

After *Fun*'s death, the publication continued to have a few post-mortem spasms. After *Orbit* got up and running in August 1990, *Fun* fell by the wayside until August 1994, when legendary Detroit TV anchor Bill Bonds was arrested for drunk driving.

"The Billy Wig" ad, *Orbit*, Fall 1994. ▶
Fun returned for a special issue in Fall 1994. ▼

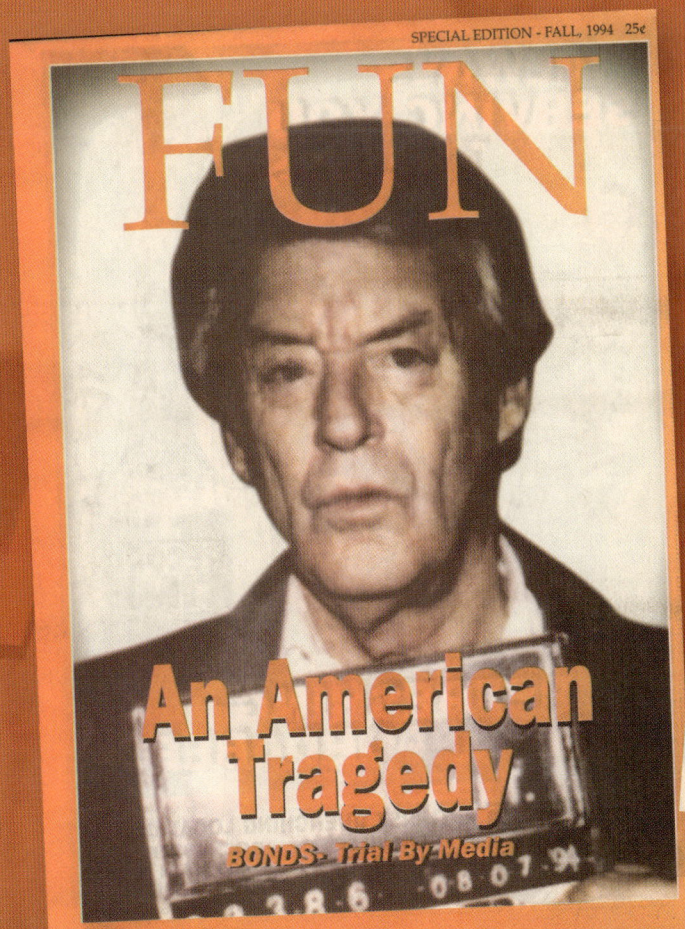

Bonds was a frequent target of jokes in *Fun*, so Peterson and the *Orbit* crew put together a special issue of *Fun* highlighting Bonds's arrest. "We heard about it in the morning, and by the afternoon, we had the videos/police transcripts. We had Matt Beer [*Orbit* editor and former *Detroit News* columnist] at the time, and he had newspaper experience and knew how to get that stuff," said Peterson. The staff used Bonds's mug shot to create a parody of the controversial June 1994 *Time* magazine cover featuring O. J. Simpson when he was arrested and charged with the murder of his ex-wife and her friend.

Inside the resurrected *Fun*, the editorial statement asks readers to enjoy the ride:

So sit back and watch us malign Billy the right way, with the usual mixture of fact and fiction, brilliance and vulgarity. Behold the unvarnished Bonds as only *Fun* can bring him to you: a booze-soaked, bewigged genius tottering on the edge of oblivion. How many cheap shots can you take on a guy with a drinking problem? Not to worry, this isn't a one-joke publication, we're also taking cheap shots at his toupee. . . . Remember folks, these are allegations. Mr. Bonds is innocent until proven guilty. No matter how much he slurs on the police video tape, he's entitled to a jury of his peers, in addition to this cruel trial by media.

The twelve-page mini-magazine focused on the arrest, Bonds's career, his drinking, and his hairpiece. The magazine opened with a three-page story showing stills of Bonds being arrested. The magazine also includes a parody ad for a hairpiece called "The Billy Wig." "Kids! Look just like your favorite anchorman!" the ad read. "Ladies! Turn your man into Bill Bonds and stop fantasizing!!" The piece also shows several anchors from other Detroit stations, like Channel 4's Mort Crim and Channel 2's Huel Perkins, as satisfied customers.

The special edition of *Fun* was hastily assembled. It should have been a triumphant tiny return for *Fun*, but it never reached newsstands because the printer didn't move fast enough. "We said fuck you to the printer—you're late. This is dated and we need it. A few days ago, it was funny. Now, it's not funny. So, we didn't distribute it. We didn't charge anyone. I think we only had like two stacks. It was never distributed," said Peterson.

Only about four hundred copies were printed. They were given to advertisers, friends, and staff members. At least one stack was still sitting, collecting dust, in one of Peterson's storage units in Metro Detroit as late as 2011.

Enter the "Fat Guy"

In October 1995, *Orbit* ran an ad for a Birmingham clothing store called Venus Flytrap. Local residents who'd received a ticket during recent police raids on various clubs and galleries could bring in their citation for a discount.

It featured a photo of a man dressed as a police officer walking down the street, with the caption "Cops Give Donuts a Bad Name." After the issue hit newsstands, it took almost a year before news of a libel and defamation of character suit reached the *Orbit* offices. The complaint stated that the man was not a model and, as Peterson and company soon learned, the photo had been used without his permission.

▲ Venus Flytrap "Fat Guy" ad, *Orbit*, October 1995.

The plaintiffs, Selden Moglovkin and his wife, Agnes, were seeking ten thousand dollars in damages. His attorney asserted in the complaint that the advertisement defamed Moglovkin and violated his privacy. The attorney also alleged that the wording of the ad was libelous due to its falsehood and had caused emotional distress, leading Moglovkin to transfer to another location for work and causing sexual problems in his marriage. From the legal brief filed by Moglovkin's attorney:

> The caption with the photo talks about cops, and donuts. These two facts are not truthful. Plaintiff is not a cop and plaintiff does not eat donuts.

> The implication is that Mr. Moglovkin, a short, overweight man, eats donuts. Mr. Moglovkin is not a cop. He was working as a security guard. Mr. Moglovkin is a diabetic. He has fought for weight control his whole life. It is difficult for a five-foot man not to be a little on the chubby side.

▲ Legal fund benefit ad, *Orbit*, January 1997.

> Plaintiff's photo in *Orbit* was unreasonable and highly offensive and an intrusion on the part of *Orbit* into Plaintiff's life. In American society, most persons do not like to have their weight drawn attention to. Plaintiff did not request that his stature and weight be drawn attention to in a magazine. Plaintiff did not even know that the

In response to the Moglovkin suit, *Orbit* planned a legal defense benefit. Dubbed "3 Floors of Freedom" and held at St. Andrew's Hall, the Glenn Barr–designed ad for the April 19, 1997, benefit included local acts ALD, Butterfly, Charm Farm, Hoarse, Jazzhead, Kid Rock, Larval, Mog Stunt Team, Speedball, Trash Brats, Volebeats, Walk on Water, and the Immortal Winos of Soul Orchestra. The event also featured DJ sets by Family Funktion, Plus 8, and Transmat, as well as an art show featuring work by Glenn Barr, Niagara, Mark Dancey, Derek Hess, Matt Feazell, and more.

Tickets for the benefit ranged from seven dollars for general admission to fifty dollars for VIP status.

Legal fund benefit ad, *Orbit*, January 1997. ▶

Law & Orbit

The Benefit

The Orbit benefit brought Detroit's best out from under their rocks. Venomous tongues and gossip mavens be damned—attendees were there solely for the support of Orbit. And because they knew it would be "The Best Party Ever."

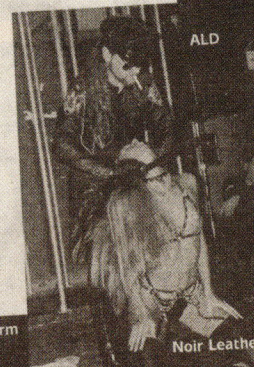

Here's What the fuss is about

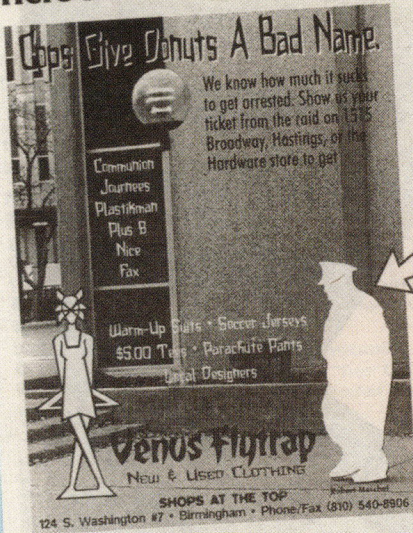

Cops Give Donuts A Bad Name.

We know how much it sucks to get arrested. Show us your ticket from the raid on 1515 Broadway, Hastings, or the Hardware store to get

Communion
Journeys
Plastikman
Plus 8
Nice
Fax

Warm-Up Suits • Soccer Jerseys
$5.00 Tees • Parachute Pants
Local Designers

Venus Flytrap

New & Used Clothing
124 S. Washington #7 • Birmingham • Phone/Fax (810) 540-8906
SHOPS AT THE TOP

The Fat Guy

*The subject is erased for obvious reasons. If this did cause the subject distress, we won't let it happen again. This time it's our responsibility and even though we are legally entitled to show it (it's part of public record), we won't.
Bottom Line: We're nice.

backless

ALD

Charm Farm

Noir Leather

Mog Stint Team

Kelly Brown

Walk on Water

Cheap glitz

Legal Technicali

So here's the deal. The above ad ran in Orbit* We were hit with a libel lawsuit claiming defamation, false light, negligence and even loss of consortium. Now the plantiff and his wife want over $100,000 to settle the case.

So why are we liable? We're not! Like every magazine we run ads. We printed an ad from Venus Flytrap, a now-defunct clothing store, in October of '95. They signed the same indemnity agreement (weasel words) as everyone else, saying they had permission to use the photo. We find out they may not have had permission from the subject, and are sued.

We don't know for sure if they had permission. We haven't found them or their photographer, Robert Merchel. (And if anybody has the whereabouts of the store's owners please contact Michael Morse at 810-350-9050.)

Our original lawyer files an answer and hits us with a $1,000 bill. This is looking really expensive, and we aren't feeling invincible. Orbit starts looking for a new lawyer—we're told that experts in the field can run up to $500 an hour.

Through a mutual friend we meet maverick attorney Michael Morse, an avid Orbit reader with a growing courtroom reputation. We like him. Before hiring him, Morse advises we call our insurance company who may pay the bill. We like him even more. Insurance company does cover libel, but weasel words in policy *specifically exclude publishers*. Damn!

We dump old lawyer and hire Morse. He's an accident/slip and fall guy, but he's smart. He already dug up different statutes and has caught the other side on technicalities. Best of all his rate is extremely reasonable. Informs us how much the case could cost if it goes all the way. Yikes. Morse doesn't think it will happen, but then again nothing is certain, this is a legal

continued on next page

THANK YOU

VIPS
BOB KOSAK, CHANGES
KENNETH GRAHAM MCNEIL
JOHN THOMPSON
KATH ARNDT, INO/UNO
ROBERT AMBRAMCZYK
KEVIN PACHLA
HOWLING DIABLOS
PERRY, DIANNA AND THE ENTIRE
STAFF AND MANAGEMENT OF ST.
ANDREW'S HALL AND RITUAL
2 STAR TABERNACLE
ALD
AWOL
GLENN BARR
BOOTSEY X AND THE
LOVEMASTERS
DJ BUBBLICIOUS
BUTTERFLY
C-POP GALLERY
CHARM FARM
MARK DANCEY
MATT FEAZELL
DEREK HESS
HOARSE
IMMORTAL WINOS OF SOUL
JAZZHEAD
KID ROCK
KYMM!
LARVAL
MOG STUNT TEAM
NOIR LEATHER
PLUS 8
PAPA RON/FAMILY FUNKTION
SPEEDBALL
SCOTT STERLING/TRANSMAT
TRASH BRATS
VOLEBEATS
CLARK WARNER/PLUS 8
WALK ON WATER
ATWATER BLOCK BREWERY
BARTON BEERS
BLUES BEER
DOUBLE DIAMOND
KING BREWING
MODEL NEGRA
MOTOR CITY
BREWING
PACIFICO
ST. PAULI GIRL
STONEY CREEK
JACOBY'S, DETROIT
HIGHWAY PRESS
TOM AT BIKESPORT, DEARBORN
COPPER CREEK, FARM. HILLS
DETROIT SCIENCE CENTER
CHRIS DAVIDSON, PJ JACOKES,
HEATHER B., RYAN DUPUIS, K.
YOUNG, LEAH FROM NASHVILLE
THE POST BAR, DETROIT•MARY
THOMPSON & THE DELTA
CHILDREN•THE WILD BUNCH•THE
WITCHES•JEFF THORPE•KURT
KOHL•NORM, ETCH MAGAZINE
CLINTON ST. GRILL,
DETROIT•SARAH SPURGEN, ST.
CLAIR COMM. COLLEGE•EDWARD
STROSS•2ND ST. SUB SHOP,
ROYAL OAK•ASCENCION UK,
DETROIT•WHITE LIGHT STUDIO
DAWN PHILLIPS, MICHIGAN PRESS
ASSOCIATION
AND MICHAEL MORSE FAMILY

Legal fund benefit recap, *Orbit*, May 1997. ▲ ▶

battle, not a horse race. We decide to throw a benefit.

Morse discovers there are no attorneys advertising in Orbit. We explain that's because our readers are good and never get in trouble. Morse offers to buy advertising anyway. Did we mention we really like this guy? He blasts out paperwork and starts the monster in motion.

St. Andrew's comes forward for the cause. Orbit swamped with volunteer bands and offers of help. Idiot publisher puts October date on ad instead of April. Ad also offers give-aways to VIP attendees—which causes Orbit to spend a ton on VIP hand-outs. Glenn Barr offers art and we silk-screen collectable posters. A few hundred readers are needed just to break even. Orbit needs to fill club to cover any legal expenses. Saturday April 19th, Orbit readers rally—St. Andrew's is packed.

Attorney Morse tells us don't worry, yet. He's going to win and if we run out of donations, he'll fight for us pro-bono (that's lawyer talk for free; free to lawyers doesn't include expenses; expert witnesses, video taping depositions or court costs, which ain't cheap).

He doesn't think we have a worry with libel. Basically, Orbit has the same protection afforded by the Supreme Court in the landmark Larry Flynt case. While Morse doubts a local Judge would care to overturn a Supreme Court ruling, anything is possible.

Morse remains unshaken. He vows he'd take it all the way to the Supreme Court if he has to—even though he believes the plaintiff's claim is frivolous. "This is a huge issue regarding the standard of care for a publisher. We've talked to the experts. Nobody in the publishing industry gets model releases. Look at the all ads in magazines and newspapers. Imagine the problem of getting model releases on everybody and storing them in the event of future litigation. What about super-star models whose pictures appear in thousands of magazines coast to coast? It's completely ridiculous."

If Orbit loses, it would be for doing what every magazine in America and every advertising agency already does—running ads using artwork provided by the advertiser, on the advertiser's word.

But in the meantime Morse is going to try to get the case thrown out. (Laws, technicalities and other strategies that we cannot reveal, just in case the fat guy's lawyer reads Orbit).

So thanks to the readers who came, and to those who couldn't come but sent money, and all those people, bands and organizations who put on the event. We'd also like to thank all the people who offered to help but we couldn't squeeze in.

Thanks to you, Orbit will be open for business for a long time.

We've built up a small war chest (and plenty of coffee mugs, hats, giant orby stickers and new T-shirts left over). Above all, we have the confidence that those who came to our aid when we really needed them. Thank you so much.

Feeling Guilty? Send your belated donation to: Orbit Defense Fund. (919 S. Main, suite #2001 Royal Oak, MI 48067.) Because it ain't over yet.

Orby and Swanky

photo was taken, that the photo was going to be sold, that the photo was being published.

Attorney Michael Morse had met Peterson a few years prior to the lawsuit and was a fan of the magazine, so he took the case for next to nothing. "[Peterson] had no money. I think I remember Jerry saying, 'Let him take the paper.' He didn't do this maliciously. I think he was shocked that this happened," said Morse.

To prove libel, a litigant has to assert that the facts presented in the publication are false, not adequately researched, and that they caused harm. Most libel and defamation cases hinge on proving that the author of the piece was seeking to cause deliberate harm to an individual. Morse believed that the fat guy's case was pretty weak because Peterson didn't know the man, so it would be impossible to prove malice. In a questionnaire sent by Morse to Moglovkin's attorney, the plaintiff was surveyed on his health, employment, marriage/sex life, and, befitting the nature of the case, his dietary habits. The survey sounded like something the *Orbit* writers could have cooked up in terms of absurdity: "Question #12 'Please state whether or not either plaintiff has ever eaten a donut in the last 10 years? If so, please state when, the type of donut, place of eating said donut, and the quantity consumed.'" Other portions of Morse's pleadings struck a more serious tone, touching on publishers' legal responsibilities.

Throughout most of 1997, *Orbit* updated readers on the progress of the case. In a May 1997 *Orbit* article, the paper states: "If *Orbit* loses, it would be for doing what every magazine in America and every advertising agency already does—running ads using artwork provided by the advertiser, on the advertiser's word."

An August 8, 1997, an affidavit of support from *Hour Detroit* magazine founder and publisher Thomas Hartle echoed the points made in the *Orbit* article: "To expect a publisher to call every single model in every single advertisement to see if that person gave permission to have his/her picture taken is nonsense and not reasonable." As Morse was building the case toward trial, he submitted a tentative witness list to the court. Included were a number of well-known figures in Detroit and the national media who would be called as expert witnesses in Peterson's defense.

After nine months of wrangling, the lawsuit was dismissed. Responding to the decision in the October 1997 issue, Peterson said, "I'm just glad we had Michael Morse. He not only cared about winning, he cared about how much it cost to win. Our original attorney had us fearing for our future—the fees were scarier than the lawsuit. From the day I met Morse, I knew we would win. He's a likable guy, but he's also a killer in the courtroom. And in the end, he did as good a job as any five-hundred-dollar-an-hour libel specialist would have."

Peterson also wrote that *Orbit* was planning to cash in with another benefit, but Morse was too quick with his legal skills in getting the case dismissed. The article featured an extensive thank-you list, which included nods to the Michigan Press Association and other local publications, as well as to all the people who came to benefit, donated, or otherwise helped the cause. One magazine that didn't get a thanks—in fact, it was singled out for scorn—was *Orbit*'s crosstown rival: "We would like to thank the *Metro Times*—but we can't. The *Metro Times* wouldn't help. In fact, virtually every publication in S.E. Michigan offered to help, except the *Metro Times*."

Are You for *Real*?

The year before *Orbit*'s death, Jerry Peterson decided to start something new—a free weekly.

In early 1998, Peterson and one of the top advertising sales executives at the *Metro Times*, John Badanjek, started to talk about a new alt weekly for Detroit. The pair had met at events

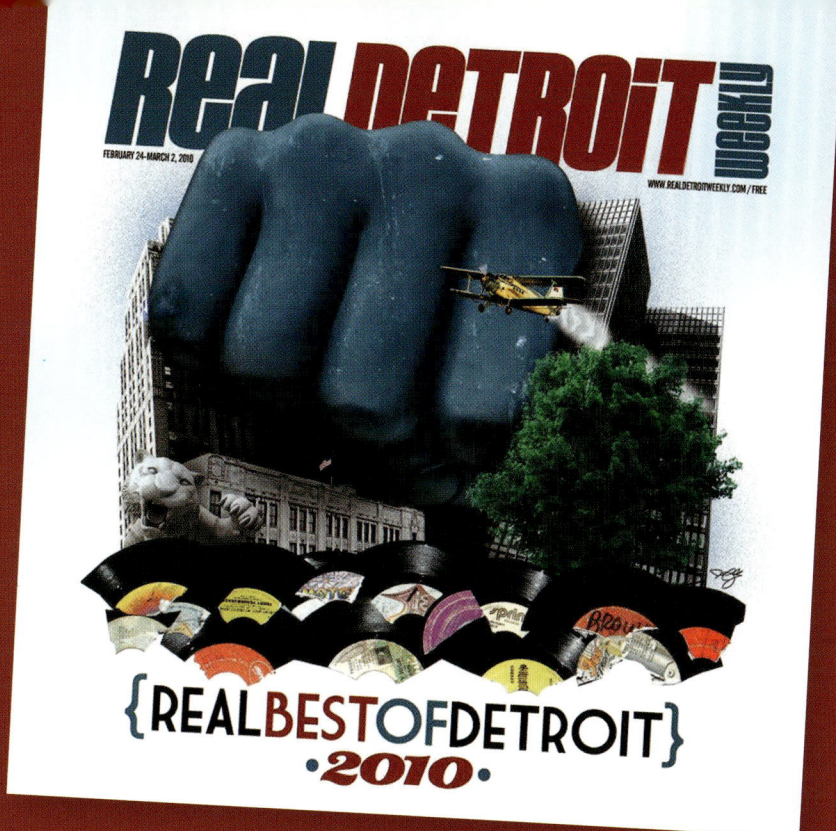

▲ *Real Detroit Weekly* cover, February 24–March 2, 2010.

around town. Both had a connection to the music business. Peterson had been in various bands, while Badanjek was the son of Johnny "Bee" Badanjek—the original drummer for Mitch Ryder and the Detroit Wheels. In time, the two realized they had something to offer each other. Badanjek understood how to make money with a free weekly. Peterson had the editorial ideas and content. Badanjek felt that with the man who made *Orbit* as his partner, they could bring something to the Metro Detroit market that was currently lacking in a free weekly.

Badanjek's original goal was to take *Orbit* weekly, but Peterson said that would have been impossible given how many enemies he'd made around town. He knew he had to start clean with a new magazine. "When *Real Detroit Weekly* was started, I figured out what Detroit needed, and I was more concerned about making a dollar. I had enough publishing legacy, and I didn't want to run *Orbit*. John Badanjek wanted to take *Orbit* weekly so bad. He had no idea how many enemies I had," said Peterson.

From a business angle, Badanjek said the creation of *Real Detroit Weekly* made sense to him: "I thought it was insane at

the time that Detroit, which was the seventh or eighth largest metro area in the US, only had one weekly. The clients had problems [at the *Metro Times*]. The clients were like, 'Why can't you write about a band coming through my venue instead of why the Detroit River is the wrong color or why Walmart's employees should be unionized?' I knew that the opportunity was there in Detroit to start another publication and work with advertisers that had been mistreated by the *Metro Times*. When you have a monopoly, you don't need to do shit like [work with the advertisers]."

Peterson said his ultimate motivation was to throw a monkey wrench into the gears of his competition. He'd learned through sources that a sale of the *Metro Times* was imminent. He expected that the establishment of *Real Detroit Weekly* would drive down the value and sales price of the *Metro Times* because there would no longer be a monopoly in Detroit's alt weekly market. Peterson figured someone, maybe even the buyers interested in the *Metro Times*, would buy his new alt weekly instead, at a cheaper price, in order to get into the Detroit market. According to Peterson, *Real Detroit Weekly* was never meant to last more than a year. "I did *Real Detroit* as a spoiler . . . just to fuck up their [*Metro Times*] sale. I figured maybe $250,000 for *Real Detroit*. [The *Metro Times*] would get six million at the most. The magazine wasn't worth that."

But Badanjek said he wasn't aware of Peterson's motives to sink the sales price of his old employer: "If *Real Detroit Weekly* launched a month earlier, the *Metro Times* would have probably sold for half of what it did to Times-Shamrock because also in that purchase [were papers in] Orlando and San Antonio, and neither of those markets were doing well. So, I think the only [people] who knew that the *Metro Times* was for sale [were founders and publishers] Ron Williams and Laura [Markham]. I don't think anyone else was aware of it."

Peterson's idea didn't go as planned. The *Metro Times* was sold, along with two other alt weeklies, to the Times-Shamrock newspaper chain in 1999. Although the sales price has never been disclosed, sources close to the deal claim it was near twenty million dollars. The *Metro Times* would be sold

again to Cleveland-based Euclid Media Group for an undisclosed price in December 2013.

The first issue of *Real Detroit Weekly* hit the streets in February 1999, but by then Peterson's personal interest in launching the magazine had flagged. The idea of the magazine was similar to *Orbit*—focused on pop culture and entertainment, but without the politics of other alt weeklies. Produc-

Having lived in Metro Detroit most of his life, and with a staff of writers who knew all the best places to wine, dine, and have a good time, Jerry Peterson decided to do something that would make the Chamber of Commerce proud.

When the second annual *Essential Detroit Guide* was released, the *Detroit Free Press* took notice. Bill McGraw wrote, "You never know who will turn up these days as a Detroit booster. But Jerry Peterson? The Jerry Peterson? The lead singer of the Boners, the 1980s punk-rock band? The guy who would dress in a nun's habit and swing suspended from the ceiling of Bookies while screaming the lyrics to "Dominique," a 1960s song by the Singing Nun? The abrasive editor of humorous tabloids that poked fun at Detroit and such icons as Bill Bonds and Mike Ilitch? That Jerry Peterson? Yup."

Peterson told the *Detroit Free Press*, "The food is better in Chicago. The people are prettier on the West Coast. There's more entertainment in New York. But I think overall this is a better place to live. Maybe because everything's not astronomically priced and you don't have to play some pretentious game." McGraw noted that the trademark sarcasm of a Peterson publication was mostly missing from the *Guide*. Peterson said he would have loved to put a few absurdist zingers in the relatively straightforward publication.

▲ *The Essential Detroit Guide*, 2008 edition.

"It really tortures me now doing the *Guide* because when we talk about Greenfield Village, I wanted to say that they even have the bus that Rosa Park used to drive. It would be so stupid and wrong, one of my favorite jokes that has never seen print. There's tons of the stuff like that," said Peterson.

Jerry "Vile" Peterson discussed his new approach in a 2006 conversation with the *Detroit Free Press*, noting that since the birth of his daughter, Kristalle, he'd toned down his style, both on and off the page. "I decided she would never see me drunk," he said.

tion started inside the cramped and cluttered *Orbit* offices. The two crews worked side by side for a few months, sharing space, computers, salespeople, and writers.

In order to help business, Peterson didn't put his name on the masthead of *Real Detroit Weekly*. He was amazed that people who advertised in *Real Detroit Weekly* but not *Orbit* because of bad blood didn't figure out he was part of the new publication. The publications shared an address: "We just used a different suite number, which I don't think anybody noticed. There would be *Orbit* advertisers that did know [about *Real Detroit*]. They thought I would be upset [about the new competition]. [*Real Detroit Weekly*] had good graphics and design. We bought a typeface that was cool and new and we wouldn't use that for *Orbit*. Ads would be changed."

By the time Badanjek moved *Real Detroit Weekly* into its own offices nearby, the partnership wasn't paying off as expected: "Jerry was a great, great writer, and that's what we were hoping for, and I would contend to this day that if Jerry had worked at *Real Detroit Weekly*, I could make the case that *Real Detroit Weekly* would have been light-years ahead. . . . The early years were rough, but having Jerry on board would have made my life a whole hell of a lot easier. He was to look over editorial and production and I was to head up sales, marketing, and events. I ended up having to do everything."

While smarting over his partner's lack of involvement in the editorial content of the magazine, Badanjek felt Peterson rubbed salt in the wound when he filed a lawsuit in the fall of 2000 seeking over $25,000 to buyout his end of the magazine.

"As much as Jerry was an owner of *Real Detroit Weekly*, he never wrote a story, was never the editor, never sold an ad," Badanjek said. "After we moved out of 919 South Main, we didn't see Jerry for a couple of years, and then lo and behold, 'Buy me out.' At the time, *Real Detroit Weekly* was young. We didn't have any money. He'd done nothing! I think there was a lot of anger and resentment on my part because when I partnered with Jerry, I wanted to partner with the genius that Jerry Peterson is and have the best, highest-quality editorial. There was a lot of resentment on my end, and that eventually led to us not being able to agree to a buyout. So, we let the lawyers figure it out," said Badanjek.

After about a year and a half of legal wrangling, and after questions were raised about back taxes related to the business, an undisclosed settlement was reached between Badanjek and Peterson in 2001. *Real Detroit Weekly* continued to roll forward, lasting longer than any other publication Peterson had ever been involved in. As for the former partners, they've mended fences.

Looking forward, Badanjek said if Peterson ever decided to retire from running the largest annual international erotic art exhibition, the Dirty Show, he would be more than willing to hire him: "If Jerry gets tired of hanging pictures of penises on the wall, maybe he'll come back and write. Hell, I'd hire him as an editor if he ever wanted a job."

Even though the offer was made, it doesn't seem likely Peterson will ever take it up. *Real Detroit Weekly* merged with its former rival, the *Metro Times*, in early 2014, and the final issue was published in the summer of that year.

Another one of Peterson's forays into publishing, the *Essential Detroit Guide*, "Your Essential Guide to Metro Detroit Attractions, Dining, Nightlife, Salons, Spas and Fashion," was quite a departure for him. The annual guide began its run in 2005 with the help of some former *Orbit* staffers. Peterson saw it as a way to reinvest part of his settlement money from *Real Detroit Weekly*.

▲ Jerry Vile at the Dirty Show, 2012. (Photo by Bruce Giffin)

PHOTO CENSORED

Carne D'Amour—Erotic At Show
Friday, Feb. 6 ,7:30 C-POP Gallery, Royal Oak 248-398-9999

Featuring: Glenn Barr, TM Caldwell, Brett Carson, Mark Dancey, Guy Davis, Tristan Eaton, Ewolf, Derek Hess, Kymm!, Vince Locke, Niagara, Bambi Paquette, Tom Thewes and Jerry Vile

It's an erotic show featuring the dirty side of underground Detroit circles. If our high school French serves us correctly, Carne D'Amour means Meat of Love, (However, it could be a canned Armour brand meat product en Español). Regardless, it's erotic. And isn't that all what we really hope for at art shows: The opportunity to openly stare at naked bodies, painted, sculpted or photographed. Juicy nude and sexily attired people, publically displaying what normally only happens behind closed doors. My nipples are getting hard just thinking about it.

▲ The Dirty Show's first incarnation, *Orbit*, February 1998.

The Dirty Show

For Valentine's Day 1999, Jerry Peterson decided to leave matters of the heart alone and aim a little lower—below the belt. And so, the Dirty Show was born.

The roots of the international erotic art exhibition can be traced to 1998 when ©POP Gallery needed a show for Valentine's Day. ©POP, a Detroit gallery known for pop surrealism, rock posters, and other contemporary art, was located near the *Orbit* offices in Royal Oak offices at the time. With input from Peterson, a show called *Carne d'Amour*, featuring erotic art mostly from Metro Detroit artists, was born. Owner Rick Manore said the ©POP show was a success, and that got Peterson thinking.

In early 1999, with *Orbit* still publishing and *Real Detroit Weekly* on the horizon, Peterson decided to add a third ring to his circus with the first official incarnation of the Dirty Show inside the *Orbit* offices. To help pull it off, Peterson recruited artist and friend Glenn Barr to curate the show, something he would do for the next several years. Barr said the idea was not to be pornographic, but funny, filthy, and irreverent. "It was supposed to be an artist take on the word 'dirty.' I'm thinking

satire, like *Mad* magazine," Barr said. "The first few years were great because we had some of the best and worst art, and we put it all on the wall, even if it's poorly executed. Some of the ideas were so out there that it was great."

Tom Thewes said the Dirty Show was always fun and a great way to make a sale in what was at times a struggling Detroit art market. Thewes also noticed the novelty of the audience Peterson's show was attracting. "These ladies who live in Birmingham and Bloomfield, that's like their one night a year to get crazy. They love it! That's excellent. That's the whole demo that Jerry never had, Birmingham women. The artists he has, it's incredible," said Thewes.

Because of the show's success, Peterson now makes his living off the annual exhibition, but the Dirty Show was not an overnight success. When he decided to move the exhibit out of the *Orbit* offices, some venues rejected it due to the nature of the show. The exhibition continues to be a gypsy, popping up at various hip places around Detroit. However, after more than a decade of running the Dirty Show, Peterson says, "It's way better than publishing, for the amount of hours

Glenn Barr said getting people into the spirit of the Dirty Show took a little bit of prodding in those early days: "One of the tables was a naked woman laying with food all over her . . . Everyone stood on the other side of the room, including all the artists in the show, and they wouldn't go near her, and I had to go over there and get a chip and dig into some cheese whiz that was on her breast. I was saying, "Come on you, chicken shits! This is the Dirty Show, damn it!"

"*Orbit* was definitely an influence on the Dirty Show because it still had that crazy manic satire," said Barr.

Since 1999, the Dirty Show has showcased broad range of artists including H. R. Giger, Clive Barker, Bunny Yeager, Eric Kroll, Annie Sprinkle, Mark Mothersbaugh, Gregory de la Haba, Lisa Petrucci, Jef Bourgeau, Camillo Pardo, S. Kay Young, Gilda Snowden, and many of the artists who created covers for *Fun* and *Orbit*.

"[Peterson] has the savvy and the know-how. Just working with all those sponsors at *Orbit*, he has the ability to do it. I would just have a heart attack or a breakdown," said Barr.

Orbit writer Jeremy Harvey added, "[The Dirty Show] seems to promote itself . . . There was nothing like it out there when [Peterson] did it. It's a lot harder now to start a group show and turn it into something that size. There just wasn't any competition . . . The show was a lot of fun and crazy . . . there was some amazing live entertainment and the art was great. It was just a very, very cool show."

Good friends, like former collaborator and former ©POP owner Rick Manore, trumpeted Peterson's success but saw it a bit differently.

"Jerry Vile has become the Sam Walton [Walmart founder] of Sex," Manore said. "I don't mean that as a putdown. He's made sex banal and boring. He's made it acceptable to even family publications that it's an event [to cover] . . . It's become a rite of passage for eighteen-year-olds—'I get to go to Dirty now.' It's like going to the bar or the strip club the first time. It's this huge organism—half clothed/half not—that kind of creates its own sociology. It's brilliant. . . . He's the single most important figure in Detroit subcultural history ever. [Activist and poet] John Sinclair might get some votes, but Jerry has remained here and he has changed the way people have looked at the world because of his visions."

invested and the amount of return. But [for] the first six or seven years of Dirty . . . it was a fun thing to do that lost money. It was a lark that happened to be something that was really good, at least for me. I pray it continues."

Former *Orbit* staffer Jeremy Harvey was a partner with Peterson on the Dirty Show for thirteen years before leaving to do other work. For him, it was hard to come up with new ideas every year in an effort to top what had been done before. Along with the work, he sometimes had to contend with gossip about just what went on at the show. But, Harvey said, a lot of the strangest stories were true: "[We had] a drag queen that had all the paint crammed up her ass and did the artwork with it and the paint did not want to come out. So, we had to put like a turkey baster [up there]. It took like ten turkey basters filled with paint, and this drag queen was just waiting and waiting. That was really funny."

The Detroit-made art show has toured to Miami, Chicago, and Los Angeles. Peterson has also franchised the name and con-

The Beginning of the End

It wasn't one thing but a patchwork of failures that started to take its toll on *Orbit*. Some blamed *Real Detroit Weekly*. The number of deadbeat advertisers, many owing *Orbit* tens of thousands of dollars, was a major contributor. Years of partying and drinking were also getting the best of Peterson, and he was starting to feel burned out from thirteen years of nonstop output. Since leaving his CADCAM software business in 1990, Peterson had been publishing full-time, was constantly busy, and had precious little to show for it financially.

Matters of the heart also played a role. Jerry Peterson and Katy McNerney had worked together on the magazine and had been together romantically for almost twenty years. Sometime in 1999, McNerney decided to leave the relationship as well as Detroit for a job with *Details* magazine in Los Angeles: "I think that Jerry kind of saw that as, 'Maybe I need to go out there, too,' because he had thought about going out there. I hate to say that it was because of me. [We were together] a long time, about twenty years, and I still love him and see him all the time," said McNerney.

As 1999 started, *Orbit* underwent some changes. The May issue was scaled down from tabloid size to a small, more colorful stapled magazine. *Fun* had been similarly downsized toward the end of its tenure ten years earlier, but *Orbit*'s editorials held out hope to readers that this would not be the end. May's "Orby Says" remarks, "We should be selling this damn rag!"

Explaining the new format to readers, *Orbit* joked that its realtor called the smaller size "cozier." A new logo and new icons inside were created for the food and entertainment features, and a "girls only" section—"High Style, You Know, for the Broads" —debuted. Some older features were done away with and "donated to Goodwill . . . for less fortunate publications."

The next issue, in June 1999, featured the first glossy cover. Titled "Summer Fun," the cover featured a photo diorama by Detroit art collective AWOL showing small figures trying to tip over a police car during a riot. Inside, the editorial warns readers that there will be no July issue because the staff was working hard on a big issue for August—a cool guide to the Motor City. The editorial also responded to readers and advertisers who would no doubt grouse about the new format: "This shiny skinned *Orbit* prefers to distance ourselves from our inferior competitors. Tabloids suck!"

Finally, the August 1999 editorial page revealed the truth to *Orbit* readers: the end was nigh. "This September 1999 marks the ninth anniversary issue and the LAST issue of *Orbit*!" the issue read. "We are tired. It would be great if we were getting rich. We make more money doing graphics for other people, and writing freelance. There aren't enough cool places in Detroit to support *Orbit* (in the manner of what we are accustomed to) so barring a miracle, we are pulling the plug."

The editorial went on to say that the plan to franchise to other cities once the Detroit operation was financially sound was flawed in terms of strategy. It said *Orbit* should have started in a bigger city, where there were cooler places with more money and more national advertising dollars to support a snarky arts/culture/humor rag, before being introduced to smaller markets like Detroit. It also gives fair warning to the dozens of deadbeat advertisers who owed *Orbit* money. Those who did not settle their accounts as soon as possible would be publicly shamed in a final issue: "You know who you are, but our readers don't."

The editorial finishes by saying *Orbit* should go out with a bang and invites everyone to take out ads to make it the biggest issue ever: "Buy an ad for yourself, a loved one, a favorite band or pet, a nasty one about somebody you hate (ask your lawyer about libel). We can't really succeed without your help."

The Final Issue

The final issue arrived a few weeks later. A simple black cover featured gray outlined numbers "1990–1999" under Orby's smiling face and, in the right corner, a "Parental Advisory: Explicit Content" seal.

Inside the issue, Orby says: "*Fuck it!*" as the mascot throws away issues of the magazine from his paperboy delivery bag.

From the first few lines of the editorial headlined "Don't Feel Sorry for Orbit . . . Feel Sorry for Detroit," it was obvious that Peterson and company were taking no prisoners.

▲ Final issue, *Orbit*, Fall 1999.

The really funny thing is, just one more ad—any size—and Orbit would have continued to publish. We had a secret goal, and we almost hit it. But it was one ad short (if you want to know the number you'll have to count). Any one of you readers could have save[d] it for a lousy 25 bucks. Don't think you'll be the city's big hero by send[ing] in the 25 bucks now—it doesn't work that way. It had to be an ad in this issue. . . . You have to carry a huge burden of guilt and feel absolutely horrible (or at least pretend like you do) for the rest of your life.

It's time for confessions. You remember all those homos, feminazis who have been calling us hate mongers. They were right. We were lying when we denied it. Jerry (OK—me) is such a homophobic [*sic*] that he hates every fag in the world. Even the ones who think he is their friend. Even his idol, Liberace . . .

Send all the hate you want. Me, I'm getting a part-time job delivering pizzas—just enough to keep me in weed. Oh, don't even think of telling my mom about this—she's dead. I keep her in my crawlspace with a few interns.

By the way, this issue represents the direction *Orbit* was taking. We call it our Fuck-You-We-Don't-Care-If-You-Don't-Advertise style —pretty much the same as usual, except there isn't [*sic*] any black bars over the nipples . . .

Everything I Ever Needed to Know...
I Learned at Orbit Magazine

Well, now that this is officially our last issue, I have the chance to vent my anger at my enemies (Local TV news) or praise my friends (Tristan Eaton, Ben Lefebvre) but instead I'd like to pass on to you the knowledge I've learned from being an Orbiteer for three years:

Movies, CDs, Concert Tickets, and Office Supplies should NEVER be paid for.
If you've got the balls to say you're a legitimate member of the press, have a PC and a fax machine, you can get tickets to just about anything. Once you're on their mailing list, they'll come to you begging to give you more stuff.

**BY RON WADE,
TYLER KENNEDY, Z. LENN
AND COUNTLESS OTHER
PEN NAMES THAT I'VE
FORGOTTEN.**

Never pay for what you can return after deadline.
Fax machines, digital cameras, computers, software, etc. Just save the receipt!

Don't do ANYTHING that an intern can do.
They're eager, naive, and full of boundless energy. Exploit this for as much as you can! Many interns have yet to fully grasp child labor or sexual harassment laws, so have fun! Make them floss your teeth for you! All you have to do in return is sign a glowing letter of recommendation that they wrote for you!

Never draw what you can trace; never trace what you can scan.

Ron Wade is an excellent employee with outstanding credentials and is willing to work for any magazine that might be hiring writers/editors! Email me at RonLWade@juno.com. SHAMELESS SELF-PROMOTION!

Blocky is both a boy and a girl.

Jackbooted-radical-brush-cut-wearin'-roll-their-own-tampon-man-hating-ovulating-bitchy-U of M women's study majors have no fucking sense of humor!
One clearly tongue-in-cheek story about "How To Be A Better Stalker" made these seething feminazis mail bomb our website, and caused me seconds of reflection and introspection. Try to piss off these women as much as possible. It will make your life better and theirs worse.

Porn stars are a lot of fun to talk to.
If you ever get the chance, I would highly recommend it.

Saying you work for a magazine will NOT get you laid!
I don't know this for sure, but looking around at Jeremy, Ben, Craig and Jerry, I have to believe it's true.

Never fry bacon naked.
TRUST ME!

Kid Rock and I.C.P. are very deserving of their success.
They were in the Orbit office and working the streets and doing all they could to make their rock 'n' roll fantasy come true, so give them their due!

The Metro Times knowingly sells ads to prostitutes, and they get away with it every day!!!
'Nuff said.

SOLD OUT concerts are never sold out.
Don't believe the hype. I'd tell you how to get into any sold-out concert, but I need a way to make a living after September 1st.

Most local music sucks.
That's why it's local, and that's why we supported the few good bands in this city!

If you get a chance to go to the MTV awards, do it!
Don't forget to take your girlfriend, though! Sorry, Holly!

Jerry Peterson has A.D.D.
The man can't focus on ANYTHING for more than 10 seconds.

Detroit has some kick-ass artists, and they deserve more press!
Tristan Eaton, Niagara, Glenn Barr, Jeremy Harvey, and Tom Thewes have become household names thanks to their exceptional talent, and support from people like Rick Manore, owner of C-Pop gallery. They deserve your support!

Well, that's about all I learned. I'd like to give thanks to some people who have made this job one of the most fun endeavors I've ever been a part of: Jerry, thanks for trusting a disaffected biology major when his confidence was low. Liz Copeland, I'd walk through hell with gasoline underwear for you! Ben Lefebvre, you are the best writer I've had the pleasure of working with (and the only cross-dresser). Katy McNerney is the axis on which Orbit spun—without you, no Orbit! Thanks for your patience. Craig Colon, thanks for putting up with my demanding computer needs! Al Behler, Sara Yousef, Heather Bozimowski, Chene Koppitz, Scott Ross, Scott Sterling, Jayne Bowman, Alyssa Miller, and everyone I've forgotten.
—Thank You! :)

We did our job. Now it's time to collect our rewards. (And our huge-ass pile of debts—if you thought we were nasty in print, just wait until you see us in court).

For now, *Orbit* is dead and already starting to stink. Put it in a Hefty Bag and turn out the lights.

I'm sorry God. I don't know why I said those horrible things. I guess I was just showing off for the readers. I don't want to be a wretch. And I don't wanna go to hell. Please forgive me. Jerry.

The idea was to put *everything* in the issue. To name names, push the humor to the edge, and leave nothing out, because it really didn't matter anymore. "We just didn't give a shit. What's the worst thing that could happen? They wouldn't advertise?" said Peterson. "They weren't already. The issue before, we started telling people off who weren't paying their bills. If everyone had paid their bills with *Orbit*, it would have been a national magazine. On paper, *Orbit* was perfect. It was really profitable. But collecting the money was harder than selling the ads. A lot of debt and a lot of people in this town that didn't pay their bills."

"The Highly Anticipated Weasel List and other people we wanted to make fun of" runs for three pages and starts with an explanation of what could have been:

Had we collected this money, we would have been putting out bigger, snazzier, high-profit issues—especially after reinvesting it in sales people and paying writers top dollar. We would have opened up branches on the coasts putting *Orbit* in the spotlight of national ad buys. Heck, if we just had part of the money some of these people spent on cocaine, we would be a national glossy. Instead, we struggled, putting out Detroit-sized issues to a huge cult following. But to write about "what could have been" is about the most pitiful thing we could do. Let's just say it's not worth the effort.

The following list comprises just a few of the deadbeats, skinflints and weasels who have screwed *Orbit* over the years. There are also a few people on it of whom we just wanted to make fun. Unfortunately, due to the limited number of pages, we can't possibly name everybody—it would be as big as the phone book. Entries were chosen for entertainment value rather than money owed. We did spare a few persons who owe us money but we still completely trust.

Looking at it today, Metro Detroiters will find most of the businesses listed have, like *Orbit*, long since folded. "The Weasel List" does provide "entertainment value," with its caustic, at times almost satanic, wit:

Merry Maids—Weren't so merry when they visited the *Orbit* offices. Screwed us out of their last ad, because one of readers called them and asked if they would come over and clean nude. (Believe us, you really wouldn't want that.)

Clubland—Steve Jarvis opened up the State Theatre. It was the hottest club until somebody got shot. It should have been him.

K-ROCK—You would think a big, rich millionaire like Howard Stern would fork over the measly 350 bucks it took to announce he was going

◀ Ron Wade Looks Back, *Orbit*, Fall 1999.

to be number one in the market. To make matters worse, the station is owned by CBS (which we think stands for Cheat, Bilk and Swindle).

Twingo's—Oui, oui, they are le cheapskates. Fork over the francs you faux frogs.

The Triangle Foundation—All watch dog groups suck. Just because they are gay, doesn't make them an exception. In fact, they probably suck more. Like all witch hunters, it's their job to find victims. Paranoid pussies like this take all the fun out of being gay. We're guessing most of them are old and ugly—the people that spent a life in the closet only to find sexual freedom with aging, wrinkling, flabby bodies. So rather than fuck, they become finger pointing knee-jerk reactionaries and see homophobia lurking behind every bush. Most everyone at *Orbit* has been physically or verbally assaulted at one time for looking like fags—but don't whine about being "victims." We've found our revenge in humor and we buy our ink by the barrel.

While *Orbit* directed its scorn at numerous businesses that had cheated it out of money and complained about its un-PC attitude over the years, the writers took the time to single out the store that had led to the magazine's major legal problems a few years before:

Venus Flytrap—Even though it's only $295, this might be the worst of all. Remember "The Fat Guy," the big legal benefit and all that razzmatazz? Well, this is the idiot that used "The Fat Guy's" picture in their ad, which ended up getting *Orbit*

"Ask Baby Jingo," *Orbit*, Fall 1999. ▶

sued. To make matters worse, Venus Flytrap never showed up for court. We didn't want to hire a private detective, so instead we had to hire a lawyer, Michael Morse (paid by you, well, some of you, lots of our readers are cheapskates, too). So if anybody knows how to track down Lauren, tell us, because we never got notice of bankruptcy and we would like to collect those legal fees."

In the midst of settling scores, the magazine also handed out a few thank-yous to people who'd supported it over the years:

Like islands in a sea of mediocrity. There are some people who do everything right—including the horrible stuff like paying bills.

Motor—Unlike many clubs, they pay the bills without pulling teeth. Looks like they do everything else right, too, as it is the best club in the city.

Record Time—Another small store that became an empire just by doing things right. Not only is it the best record store in the area, it's one of the best in the world. They are the coolest with local

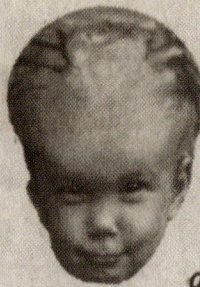

Ask Baby Jingo

Dear Baby Jingo,
Is this really the end of Orbit? Isn't there some solution you could find, after all you are the smartest baby in the world? —J. Vile

Dear Mr. V,
Unfortunately, this is indeed the demise of Orbit. I'm afraid that even my vast intellectual capacities cannot change this sorrowful circumstance. However, the only certitude in life is dubiety. Perhaps Orbit may sequester in an alternative sector of this mortal sphere.

fun

Our Favorite Jokes

Q: Did you hear about the fly on the toilet seat that got pissed off?
A: ha ha

Q: What does a lesbian bring on her second date?
A: Her luggage and her furniture

Q: How do you get a goth kid out of a tree?
A: Cut the rope.

Q: How do you make your boyfriend scream twice?
A: Screw him in the ass then wipe your wang on his curtains

Q: How do you keep a moron in suspense?

Dear God

What will happen to Detroit now that Orbit is gone?
—Bill Halford, age 12

Dear Bill,
I'd like to paint you a pretty picture but that's not what I do. A curse will be put upon this city. Tourism will come to a standstill. Many Detroiters in the entertainment industry will remain unsigned. The Downtown area will become riddled with abandoned buildings. Public transportation will become a mockery of other cities. Lack of exercise and poor eating habits will cause obesity among many locals. And worst of all gambling addiction will keep most of you living pathetically under the poverty level.
—THE ALMIGHTY

ORBIT · Final Issue · Fall 1999

▲ The Amazing Cynicalman seeks a new job post-*Orbit*, *Orbit*, Fall 1999.

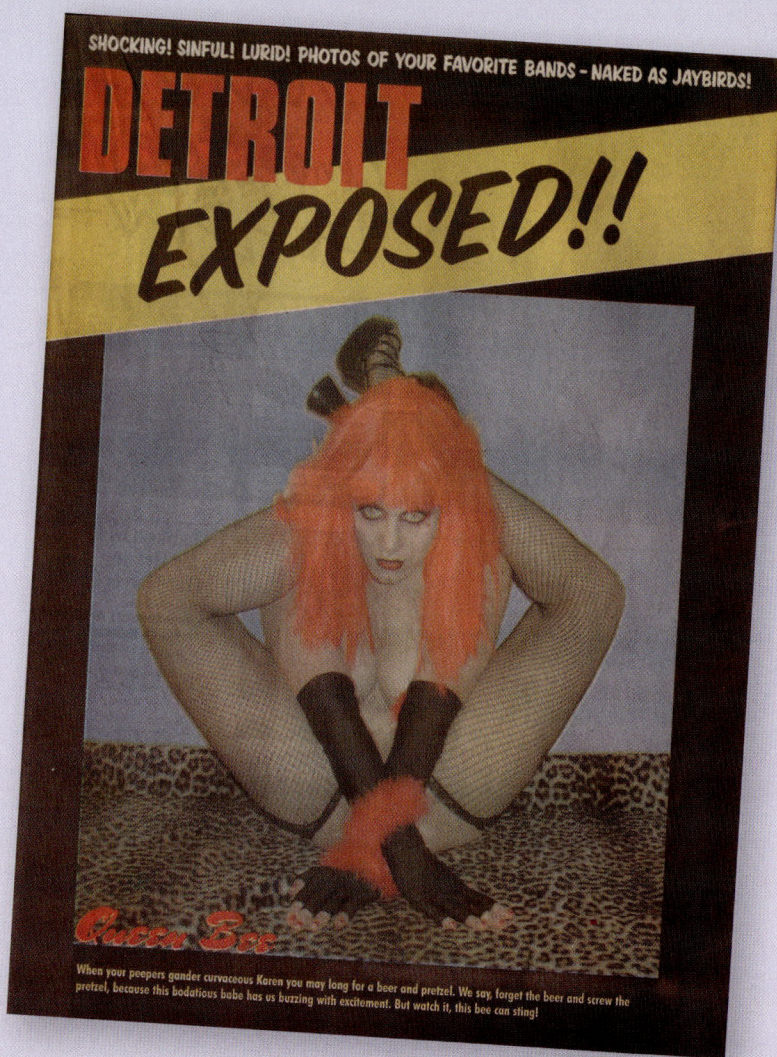

SHOCKING! SINFUL! LURID! PHOTOS OF YOUR FAVORITE BANDS - NAKED AS JAYBIRDS!

DETROIT EXPOSED!!

When your peepers gander curvaceous Karen you may long for a beer and pretzel. We say, forget the beer and screw the pretzel, because this bodacious babe has us buzzing with excitement. But watch it, this bee can sting!

▲ "Detroit Exposed!!," *Orbit*, Fall 1999.

music and not just the 1000 CD band kind—they have pushed the envelope of Detroit dance. In the entire history of *Orbit*, they only missed advertising in one issue (and it was our fault).

True to form, Record Time took out an ad in the final issue. The 1950s-style photo shows a woman holding a baby with the caption: "This child has his whole life ahead of him and will experience many wonders on the way. It's truly sad that he'll never see the humor, sarcasm, fun and spelling errors *Orbit* mag has given us for nine years. At least he'll have Record Time! (Good Luck, Jerry P.)" Record Time closed in 2011.

The 104-page final issue was bigger than any previous edition of *Orbit*. Beyond "The Weasel List," writers took aim at the magazine's usual targets, adding a few more politically incorrect features like "Achmed's Oasis"—a training manual for employees of a Detroit-area Middle Eastern–owned party store; and best and worst lists for restaurants, style, and toilets in Metro Detroit.

The writers also took sharp sticks to some well-known folks in the community with "You Talkin' to Me: The Cockiest Motherfuckers in Detroit." They even took aim at the founder and publisher himself.

Jerry Peterson:

Who he is: Publisher of shitty washed-up local rag and notorious booze hound [sic].

Who he thinks he is: Larry Flynt.

The *Orbit* crew also decided to give readers a feast for the eyes. Beyond Jeremy Harvey's piece of gonzo journalism in which he doctored his genitals and visited a nudist resort, the issue boasted a semi-nude musicians section. But what really caught readers' attention was the final line of the editorial: "there isn't any black bars over the nipples." A one-page photo spread of "Lady Pain"—an area dominatrix in a trench coat posing at various locales around Metro Detroit revealed that this was indeed true. But it's the "Detroit Exposed!!" section where the issue's humor and nudity harmonize.

In the heart of the final installment, *Orbit* readers were treated to nine different nude or semi-nude photos of Detroit artists and musicians: Queen Bee, Niagara, Joelle and Danielle of Stun Gun, the Demolition Doll Rods, Audra Kubat of Stunning Amazon, Lovetta from His Name Is Alive, and Tabitha of Radium.

Artist and Time Stereo owner Davin Brainard and His Name Is Alive's Warren Defever were also featured. The pair was nude except for a few expertly placed pieces of Noise

Camp gear. "That was really something," Defever said. "We brought a bunch of props to the *Orbit* offices, and we took our clothes off and Jerry took a picture. I don't remember why he was doing the all-nude issue. He just asked us because we came there to pick up the magazine to deliver."

"I was really happy to be in it," said Brainard.

"I still regret it. It was a like a big practical joke on anyone who picked it up and tried to read it," Defever said, chuckling.

The biggest laugh was saved for the centerfold. The two-page spread trumpets, "Va Va Voom—It's Jimmy Doom!" The photo shows the *Orbit* food writer and punk rock singer lounging on the bar of his favorite haunt wearing nothing but a smile. According to Doom:

[Jerry] didn't get the best-looking guy from a popular band. That wasn't the *Orbit* attitude. He got a fairly unattractive guy from a fairly popular band. "Sailor Rick" Metcalf took the photo on the bar of Gusoline Alley in Royal Oak.

Colleen at Gus's told the patrons that if they would be uncomfortable, they should leave. You have been warned. So, 2:00 p.m. Sunday afternoon rolls around. At first, they were going to hide my dick with a Bushmills bottle. Irish Catholic kid, kind of funny, but they could see my penis through the bottle. So, what do you want me to do? "Tuck it." I started laughing. And that's what I did.

▼ Noise Camp nude spread, *Orbit*, Fall 1999.

▲ Jimmy Doom centerfold, Fall 1999.

After the photo shoot, Doom said he was approached by an older patron, "an average, blue-collar guy drinking his Bud." "I go get dressed in the bathroom, pass him on the way back, and sit down to get a beer," Doom said. "He sits down next to me—'I like what you got. Would you like to come home with me?' I think that's flattering in a way, but I'm hung like a startled field mouse. The girl I was with, she was creeped out."

Although some people found the humor in Doom's full-frontal without the full monty, his mother, Detroit writer Molly Abraham, received an alarmed call from a friend.

"I've done some reckless things in life, but my mom has always been supportive," Doom said. "She calls me and relates a phone call she got from a friend the morning the nude spread came out:

"Oh, Molly, I'm so sorry."

"What are you talking about?"

"Jimmy."

"What about Jimmy? What the fuck happened to Jimmy?!?"

"That photo spread."

"You called me up like my son is dead. And what's horrible about that [photo]? I knew about that! Never call me again."

Orbit was finally laid to rest in grand fashion on Saturday November 20, 1999, at Saint Andrew's Hall with the Ninth Annual *Orbit* Magazine Anniversary Party (and Wake), featuring local bands, food, drink, and shared memories. The final issue's editorial page reminded people to mark their calendars, but Peterson and company knew their readers' attention spans might be a little short: "Heck, you probably will have forgotten what *Orbit* was by then."

Out of *Orbit*

Looking back on the magazine years later, some of the staff and creators feel mixed emotions about those times. "I feel bad, seriously, like I helped to bring the ship down," says Liz Warner "It's bigger than me, obviously, but it's not good to be there in the end because it makes you a little paranoid. But it never would have happened without the stubbornness of Jerry Vile. He left a mark. It was quite a ride."

"People ask me now what my favorite job was," said Jayne Bowman Hallock "It was hands down *Orbit*. I made shit pay. My boyfriend at the time completely supported me. I made what you would make at McDonald's or less, but it was unbelievably stimulating and super stressful. It wasn't *Orbit* if we weren't staying up all night until six in the morning. It's a monthly magazine, you would think we could get our shit together enough where we wouldn't be submitting stuff the day before. It was the broadcast news thing, people skidding underneath the desk, getting it to graphics, the guy outside is waiting to go to the printers. It was nuts, but it was easily, easily my favorite job."

"*Fun* and *Orbit* were magnets," Peterson said. "*Fun* attracted people and it was the labor of love. People got paid at *Orbit*. They might not have gotten as much as [at] a boring job, but it wasn't boring. People did well. Some didn't. But some got a career going."

Orbit's closure and the *Metro Times*'s sale to another paper are microcosms of a major trend in print media. Since 1999, print in all forms—from daily newspapers and monthly magazines to alt weeklies—have seen sharp declines in readership, sales, and profits as the main source of the American media diet has moved online. In the digital world, speed, search engines, and sharing have taken over.

Since the final issue of *Orbit* hit the racks, people have asked Jerry Peterson if there's a possibility to resurrect Orby from the grave and create a new Frankenstein's monster of fun and humor—maybe a print-online hybrid. But Peterson doesn't think it will happen with him in charge, because the way we consume media has changed radically since he left full time publishing in the late 1990s: "The Internet is way better for right now, but I haven't found a good local source on the Internet for anything. The Internet can tip you in directions you might not have gone, but it's a little harder to change your opinion or [get] enough info to do that. The Internet gives you a point. You don't know if it's a start or an end. The magazine controls your journey. Most people read magazines from the back to the front. I've studied people to see what they are doing in bars with magazines—if you are reading it, laughing and sharing with friends," said Peterson.

Ultimately, Peterson is jokingly hopeful about print: "I don't like to have a computer on my lap when I'm taking a dump. So, I think there's room for a magazine."

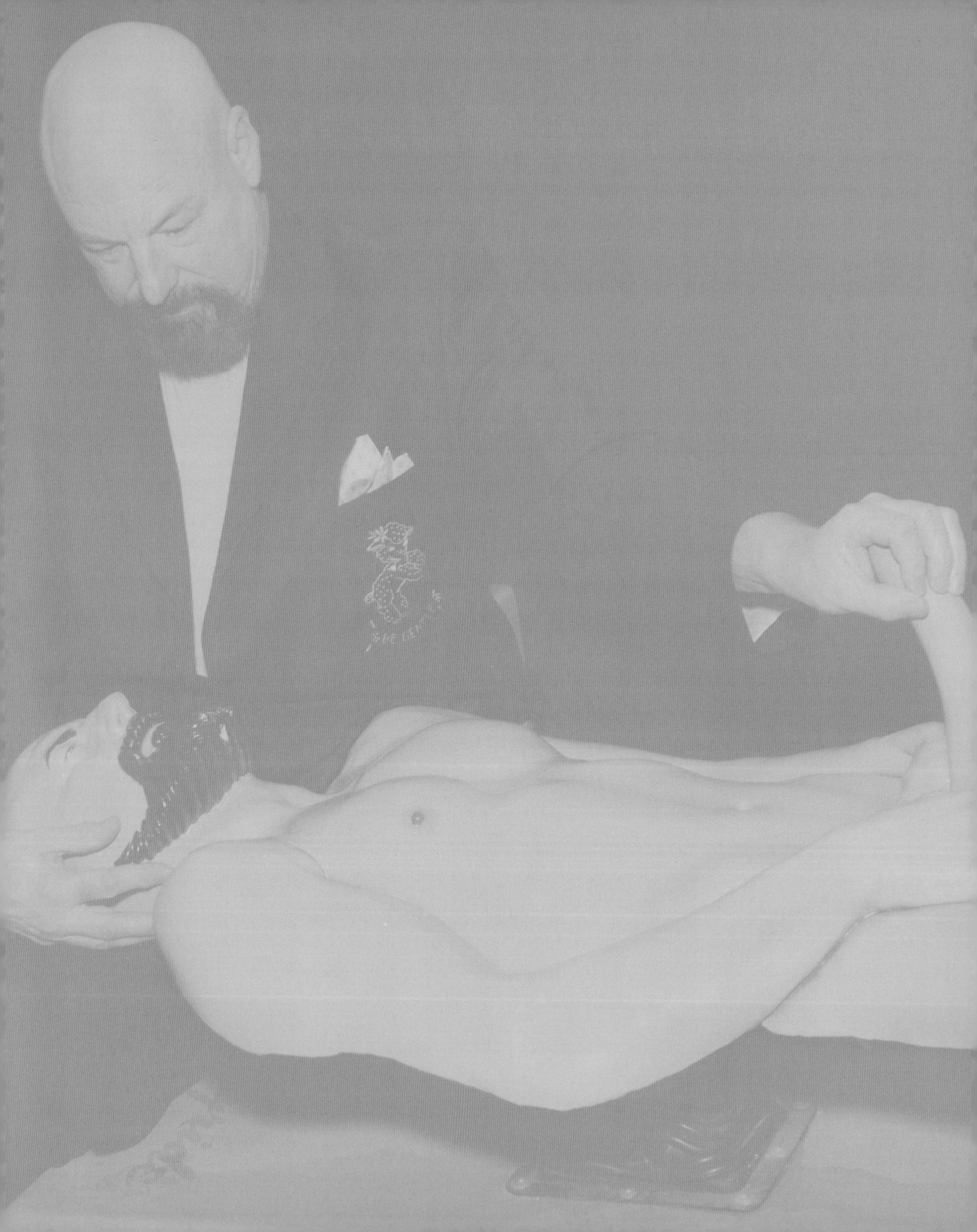

POSTSCRIPT

The Great and Powerful Vile

In May 2012, Peterson held a new solo art show at the Bankle Building on Woodward Avenue, just north of Foxtown. The space owned by artist and auto designer Camillo Pardo served as the backdrop for Peterson's psyche. His one-night-only show was titled Jerry Vile's "The Secret of Life."

Among the paintings, scale models, and two versions of his "Joyride"—a modified children's ride featuring a well-chiseled body with Vile's face and a large erect penis.

The night opened with a video projected into a round window at the far end of the gallery. Inside the glass, a green-tinted face, "The Great Vile," spoke to the crowd, taking his cue from the all-powerful Oz from the classic film *The Wizard of Oz*. "Silence! The great and powerful Vile knows why you are here."

Over the next five minutes, "The Great Vile" castigated art critics, intellectuals, hipsters—young and old—and buffet bingers who attend art shows only for the free food. Laughter and applause filled the room.

The most telling aspect of the evening was something that didn't make the final cut of the video, an exchange between "The Great Vile" and an audience member:

"You're a very bad man," says the audience member.

"No dear, I am a very good man, just a very bad artist. I am just an ordinary man trying to make it in this thing we call the Art Racket," says the Great Vile.

From punk rock to publishing to painting, Peterson's DIY ethic, knack for spectacle, and loyal friends have been central to his endeavors. Peterson has been able to offer opportunities to others like him who are hungry to create something, even if it's just a laugh or two.

Old friends from the early days came to the show that evening. There were hugs and supportive

handshakes. Some even helped Peterson hang his paintings and lay out the buffet—chocolate-dipped jalapenos and carrots next to real rattraps loaded with cubes of cheese. It's been over thirty-five years since the Bookie's Club 870 and *White Noise* days, and these friends have taken plenty of barbs from Jerry Vile—either in his magazines or in person. It's not something most people forget. Then again, maybe years have dulled the rough edges and the punker's past transgressions. At the bare minimum, old friends, and even Detroiters, seem to realize that Jerry Peterson may be prickly at times but that life with him is never dull. And that is the reason they are still glad to have him around.

Two years later, Jerry Vile brought "The Secret of Life . . . . Revealed, Again, For the First Time, Ever" to the Inner State Gallery in Detroit's Eastern Market. Because, well . . . it's hard to keep a Vile man down.

▼ *Secret of Life* exhibition promo materials, 2014.

WWW.JERRYVILE.COM
DETROIT, USA

JERRY Vile

You will end up selling your body on the streets for crack. You will suffer withdrawal often.

YES

- LUCKY NUMBERS -

7 12 14 23 36 53

The Great VILEDINI

OPENING RECEPTION
Saturday, April 26th 2014   7pm until 10pm

THE SECRET OF LIFE...
REVEALED, AGAIN,
FOR THE FIRST TIME, EVER.

Join Detroit's Most Cherished Artist,

Jerry Vile

ULTRA-SWANKY RECEPTION
CEREMONIOUS UNVEILING • IMPALPABLE BEAUTY
EXCEPTIONAL VALUE • UNTOLD QUALITY
UNPARALLELED INVESTMENT OPPORTUNITIES
MOUTH-WATERING SHRIMP COCKTAIL

Due to the significance of this momentous work,
a nominal $5.00 art viewing fee will be charged*
(blindfolds available for the frugal)

LATEST MASTERPIECE UNVEILED AT 8:23 SHARP
Don't miss it - ensure your place in art history with Mr. Vile!

INNER STATE GALLERY
1410 GRATIOT AVE. DETROIT MI 48207
313.744.6505 innerstategallery.com

*$5.00 viewing fee waived for Museum Curators, Institutional Buyers and Respected Critics
Public exhibition continues during gallery hours through May 3rd without viewing fee.

AFTERWORD

Ben Blackwell

Twenty years later, it's impossible to relay just how *difficult* it was as a teenager in the mid-nineties to access and truly connect with media. Without a car, kids were left grasping in the dark at any tiny counter-cultural crumb that might accidentally end up in the daily newspapers or on television. *Orbit* magazine, which never kowtowed to anyone, was an invaluable cornucopia of peculiarities. *Orbit* always gave the impression that it was doing *exactly what the fuck it wanted,* and that is decidedly difficult.

No sacred cows. No untouchables. Nothing off-limits. Everyone and everything is fair game for skewering. When your rule is no rules, you have a clean slate for something unique, fresh, important, and artful to happen. While in other hands such free rein would quickly descend into mindless jibber-jabber, Jerry Peterson and *Orbit* evolved it into a finely honed craft . . . never too childish yet never too serious. *Orbit* struck a wonderful balance between the absurd and the insightful without ever sacrificing a laugh.

Orbit operated as my own personal Internet—a concentrated hub of all that seemed interesting and odd and funny and subversive and informative—a full decade before the Internet truly became what it is today. It explicitly informed me of what was cool and what was lame. To accomplish what *Orbit* did in the terribly reactionary format of a monthly tabloid-sized newsprint is no easy feat. To be free on top of that? How did this thing exist for even one issue, let alone nine years' worth of issues?

I got my copies mainly from Hong Kong Chop Suey, a carry-out Chinese restaurant from a forgotten era a mere fifteen-second sprint from the house I grew up in. If the usually spot-on first-of-the-month delivery was late, I'd get testy. If the delivery came while the restaurant was closed, and I found the zip-tied pile of copies sitting in front of their door, I'd cut the tie myself and slip out a copy.

Every new issue was a gateway into a world of excitement. I never knew what to expect, and I can't say I was ever disappointed. It was the embodiment of cool culture wrapped with eye-catching graphics and whip-smart design.

In all my years, I have never encountered a more memorable specimen of journalism than the final issue of *Orbit*. While most folks' nature is to make good-bye an amiable, saccharine affair, there was no such sentiment from Jerry and *Orbit*. He used his bully pulpit to call out every deadbeat advertiser they'd ever dealt with and rip on them mercilessly. If that wasn't enough, they claimed that if they'd hit an unstated number of ads for that final issue, the magazine would have remained in print. The kicker was that they missed their supposed goal by one ad. Who did they lay the blame on? YOU! The lazy sod who didn't place an ad. Your favorite publication could have been saved. Too bad. You lose. We all lose.

As bummed as I was when it closed up shop, I'm glad it did. I don't think *Orbit* would have been able to compete or be as fresh as it was much longer. *Orbit* went out on its own terms.

I read this back to my wife, Malissa, a fellow *Orbit* devotee. Her initial comment was, "That's all great . . . but it sounds like adult Ben talking." True, I am now nearly twice the age I was when Orby ceased publication. It might be more genuine to begin this with something that'd likely come from fifteen-year-old me . . .

Holy shit! This book is hilarious! And it has facts!

I'm lucky, you're lucky, we're all lucky to have all these morsels here in one place for our reminiscence and enjoyment. Back in the nineties, I was ecstatic with one issue a month.

INTERVIEWS

The following interviews were conducted by the author
between January 2011 and December 2014.

John Badanjek	John Dickerson	Mark Kliem	Kid Rock (Bob Ritchie)
Glenn Barr	Jimmy Doom	Rick Manore	Sue Rynski
Randy Booden	Jim Dulzo	Derrick May	Brenna Sanchez
Jayne Bowman-Hallock	John Dunivant	Bill McGraw	Scott Sterling
Davin Brainard	Tristan Eaton	Katy McNerney	Dave Stimson
Violent J (Joseph Bruce)	Hobey Echlin	David Merline	Tom Thewes
Ben Burns	M.L. Elrick	Rick Metcalf	Ralph Valdez
Christy Burns	Greg Fadell	Michael Morse	Ron Wade
Tim Caldwell	Matt Feazell	Robert Mulrooney	Liz Warner
Scott Campbell	Chris Gore	Mike Murphy	Walter Wasacz
Craig Colon	Andrew Heaton	Niagara	Jack White
Terry Colon	Barry Henssler	Mark Niemenski	Ron Williams
Des Cooper	Keith Howarth	Jerry Peterson	Michelle Winstanley
Mark Dancey	Rob Jiranek	Ryan Peterson	Amy Yokin
Doug Dearth	Chris Kassel	Heather Pillot	Matt Zacharias
Warren Defever	S. Kay Young	Gary Reichel	Paul Zimmerman
Robert del Valle	Kevin King	Pogo Rey	

MAGAZINE STAFF LIST

The following names were taken from the mastheads of *White Noise, Fun,* and *Orbit* magazines. The author did his best to ascertain the correct spellings for each person responsible for the given magazines. Some are obvious pseudonyms— so, I guess you know who you are . . . maybe.

White Noise

Douglas Blair
Kim Browne
Scott Campbell
Christa
Mike Churchman
Rick Clevinger
Namkola Coppelle
Timmy Denizen
Jimmy Dogbrain
Johnny Garbagecan
Doug Garland
Geza Gideon

Gary Glenn
Paul Hodge
Kram Itt
Jean Jeannie
Leo Katz
BD Keeps
Sue Keifer
Steve King
Kevin Knapp
Joe Kuszai
Heidi Lichtenstein
Smelly McHippie
Katy McNerney aka

"Katy Hait"
Tom Mitchell
Bob Mulrooney aka
"Bootsey X"
Terry Murphy
Tom Murphy
Kent Myers
Mark Norton
Steve O'Leary
Sue Occott
Jerry Peterson aka
"Jerry Vile"
Scott Price

Sister Ray
George Romero
Joe Rulong
Mike Rushlow
Sue Rynski
Rick Schrader
Chrissy Slixx
Eric Smith
Christ Soyk
Joe Sposita
Gary Tenninch
Walter Wasacz
Douglas Weiner

Kirk Widdis
Sue Wild
Paul F. Zimmerman,
aka "Paul Stillborn,"
"Paul Ginsuknife,"
"Paul X"

Fun

Norman Anselment
Gary Arnett
Kim Austin
Glenn Barr
Matt Beer
Doug Blair
Mary Blair
Ralf Bonner
Al Brantner
Keith Brown
Christy Burns
Tim Caldwell
Suzanne Calimita
Scott Campbell
Dick Carter
Dave Chow
Terry Colon
Paul Corte
Carrie Cunningham
Mary DA
Amir Daiza
Doug Dearth
Jeff Demick
Bobby Doc
Debi Findlay
M. Fiscus
Bill Fold
Luis G.M.
Maria Giournas
Gary Glen
Chris Gore
Jim Gustafson
Dave Hanna
Linda Heydi
Dave Higgins
Kathy Hoffman
Mike Hunt
Todd Huskin
Daryl Hutchinson
Joe Hutchinson
Hymie
Hugh Jardon
Dan Jarvis
Chris Kassel
S. Kay Young

Kevin King
John Klein
Kevin Knapp
Julian Kraner
Jean Lannon
David Lee
Dave Linaberry
Dick Liquor
Angela Maiuri
Katy McNerney aka
"Katy Hait"
Ick Metca
Rick Metcalf
B. Mitchell
Rick Morris
Jim Morton
Bob Mulrooney
Mike Murphy
Tom Murphy
John Myer
Becky Myers
Mark Niemenski
Mark Norton
Gary Nowak
M. Otto
Chris Paycheck
Jerry Peterson
aka "Jerry Vile"
Len Puch
Judge I Rankin
Gary Reichel
Blip Rimbo
H. Rubinowitz
Rick Ruby
Diane Schroeder
Chris Scrocki
Steve Shaw
C. Sobcinski
Joe Sopkowitz
St. Souver
Tina Suchy
Ken Wagner
Jim Warner
Kirk Widdis
Tom Wiloch
Amy Yokin
Paul Zimmerman

Fun–1994

one-off

Gary Arnett
Matt Beer
Terry Colon
Doug Dearth
Andrew Heaton
Chris Kassel
Kevin King
Katy McNerney
Dave Merline
Rick Metcalf
Andrew Noseworthy
Mary O'Neil
Jerry Vile

Orbit

Dave Aikins
Joe Ajalony
Holly Allen
J.D. Allen
Josh Amberg
Rachel Angelini
Judy Ann Adams
John Anthony
April Archer
Gary Arnett
D. Arzner
Alana Askew
Dan Augustine
Sonya Avakian
Alisa Bambenek
Sandy Bandula
Phil Barash
Glenn Barr
Marcie Barry
Scott Beckerman
Matt Beer
Alan Behler
Mark Berger
Scott Berry
Caeri Bertrand
Jaime Bowling
Jayne L. Bowman
Heather Bozimowski
Bob Branstner
Monica Breen
Carol Brennan
Karl Briedrick
Molly Brodak
Christine Brooks
Robyn Brown
Timothy Brown
Denise Brylko
Maria Burak
Clint Burhans
Charles Burns
Carrie Byron
Dorion Cable
Clair Cainghug
Gus Calandrino
Tim Caldwell

Brett Carson
Elizabeth Carter
Jordan Catalano
Reina Cerros
Angela Chase
Mary Cherasaro
James Chesna
Dave Chow
Dan Christie
Tom Clynes
Craig Colon
Jeff Colon
Terry Colon
Harvey Coloni
Doug Coombe
Kim Coonce
Liz Copeland [Warner]
Daniel Costello
Stacy Craft
Brendan Curran
Brenton Curtis
Mike Daronco
Chris Davidson
Stephanie Davis
Pimpin' Leon de Luca
Brandon Dean
Doug Dearth
Sherry DeGeorge
Melanie Dellas
Evan Derian
Karen Deshais
Melissa Detiloff
John Dickerson
Kiran Divvela
Jimmy Doom
Michael Dougan
Duck's Breath Mystery
Theater
Bill Dunn
Ryan Dupuis
Erin E. Brown
Mark E. Gallo
Tristan Eaton
Hobey Echlin
Scott Eckerman
Claire Edwards
Mark Engbrecht

Ewolf
Matt Feazell
Krista Figacz
Elyse Fischer
Rudy Fischman
Krista Flame
R.F. "Russ" Forster
Tony Fusco
Linda G.
Luis G.
Chantal Gagnon
Marla Garfield
Curtrise Garner
Josh Garrett
Katy Gates
Vanessa Gaultieri
Tanya Gazdik
Roundtree Givhan
Josh Glazer
Mark Gowan
Derek Goyette
Mike Graye
Andy Grinbaum
Julie Hallbach
Chris Handyside
Dave Hanna
Marc Hansen
Jeremy Harvey
James Haynes
Andrew Heaton
Sidi Henderson
Buddy Hickerson
Dave Higgins
Mike Himes
Nima Hodaei
Tiffany Holtzkemper
Jennifer Hord
John Horn
Jeremy Hull
Chris Jackson
PJ Jacokes
Hillari James
Jane Jeddsen
Thom Jerk
Jofus
Luke Johnson
Tiffany Johnson

Alyssa Jones
Chris Kassel
Susan Kelly
Kenmore the Cat
Tyler Kennedy
Hanan Khaznehkatbi
Kevin King
Scott Kirkwood
Kevin Knapp
Chene Koppitz
Andrea Koran
Bill Kosidlo
Garret Koski-Budabin
Raj Kottamasu
Danielle Kozik
Aimee Kozlowski
Wally Krantz
Carson Kruger
Rachel Kucsulian
Pratema Kumayr
Ben Lafebvre
Laura Langa-Spencer
Stacy Lauwers
Susan Leigh
Douglas Levy
April Liberty
John Licardello
C.M. Linabury
Dave Linabury
Thad Lucken
Jennifer Luoto
Art Lyzak
Sue MacPhee
Angela Maiuri
Gary Malerba
John Mann
Gifford Maxim
Laura McCown
Maureen McCurdy
Colin McDonald
Katy McNerney
Dave Merline
Richard Metcalf
Wendy Metros
David Michael
Suzie Milenkovich
Adam Miller

Bridget Miller
Dan Miller
John Miller
Kelli Miller
Tracey Miller
Lori Molnar
John Monaghan
Sarah Monti
Chris Moritz
Michael Morse
Sadiq Muhammad
Kris Murphy
Mike Murphy
David Myatt
Kent Myers
Robert Myers
James N. Hoffman
Odell Nails
Alan Naldrett
Joel Neely
Chris Nicholson
Gary Niemenski
Mark Niemenski
Andrew Noseworthy
Tom Novacek
Jonnie O.
Mary O'Neil
Shannon O'Neill
Brian Oakes
Ron Obermeijer
Neil Ollivierra
Heidi Olmack
Rebecca Owens
Anthony Palacio
Connie Pampinella
Chris Papernik
Edwin Parungo
Jerry Peterson
David Pfister
Dayna Pink
Michelle Porter
Sidney Prescott
David Propson
David Ramirez
Todd Raven
Heidi Rehak
Tobias Roberts

Brendan Rohan
Elaine Roman
Katherine Ross
Scott Ross
Renee Rottner
Robyn Sadowski
Cynthia Sagamani
Brenna Sanchez
Ian-Michael Sanderson
Chris Walny
Christa Sarafa
Sandra Scamardella
Tom Schoenberg
Charles Sercombe
Robert Shankman
Theresa Shaw
Pamela Shecter
Jason Sherman
Doug Shimmin
Jeff Shovlin
Shuggy
Ton Shultie
Jennifer Simms
Jerry Sindicci
Kurt Sinnamon
Monica Sklar
Dirk Slammer
SmilEE
Alex Smith
Carolyn Smith
Janet L. Smith
Mark Smith
Lisa Sokolowski
Kim Sorise
Keith Soucy
Steven Sowers
Todd Sparks
Joe Sposita
Jill Stanley
Sean Stephens
Scott Sterling
Jim Stone
Alison Story
Peter Sucio
Micah Sullivan
Eric Swanger
Sarah Takenaga

Stephen Tamblin
Harold Taylor
Ken Taylor
Rob Taylor
Scott Telek
Ted Telvitie
Tom Thewes
Kristine Trever
Russell Trunk
Renee Tyndell
Lawrence Ulrich
John Unger
Daria Vaisman
Johnny Valentine
Gretchen Van Cleave
Scott W. Kirkwood
Ron Wade
Ginny Walker
Walter Wasacz
Marni Webb
Colin Webcott
David Weiss
Kirsten Weller
Dennis White
Herman Wiggly
Mike Williams
Richard Williams
Wendy Williams
WS Williams
Jennifer Wilson
Jeff Wong
Shepard Wong
Betsy Wood
James Worth
Josh Worth
Amy Yokin
Allison Yorktown
Allison Young
S. Kay Young
Dianne Yousif
Sara Yousuf
Tony Zaret
Paul Zimmerman

ACKNOWLEDGMENTS

Thank you to all the *White Noise, Fun, Orbit, Real Detroit Weekly,* and *Metro Times* staffers/freelancers who took the time to talk to me or help me find people and things for this book. It was an honor getting to know you and tell your story.

Glenn Barr—your cover art made me shout with excitement when I saw the sketch. Thank you for finishing the ride for us.

Kevin Knapp—without your punk rock archive, the complete set of *White Noise,* over one thousand flyers from the Bookie's era, and more, I would have been missing a huge chunk of history. Christy Burns—thank you for lending *Fungus Rodeo,* another part of this fascinating tale. Liz Warner—thank you for filling in the missing issues in the official *Orbit* archive; they will be lovingly cared for. Tim Retzloff—thank you for the information on Bookie's

and gay Detroit history.

Thank you to my extended family in southeast Michigan and beyond. I'm grateful to my mom, Anne McLeod, and dad, Tom St. Mary, as well as my departed grandparents who gave me the gift of curiosity, humor, and a work ethic growing up in Macomb County.

To my friends and co-workers in Michigan, Colorado, and worldwide for their support—it's hard to thank you all here by name. But special thanks to Chene Koppitz, Mike White, Chris Urbanski, Michael Pfaendtner, Bruce Griffin, Chris Council, and Erin Carr, my former colleagues at WDET, WOOD Radio, WSGW, WLEW, WJR, and KJAX. We'll laugh together soon, always.

Ben Blackwell—thank you for reaching out. As a fellow *Orbit* fan, you know why it matters. Your support, Third Man Records and beyond, means more than you know.

Thank you to Kathy Wildfong, Kristin Harpster, Bryce Schimanski, Gabe Gloden, Emily Nowak, Bonnie Russell, Sarah Murphy, Lindsey Alexander, and the whole team at Wayne State University Press for their support and guidance.

Jerry Peterson—thank you for the opportunity to tell your story.

Your support from day one has made it possible to learn more than I ever expected, and it's been amazing ride. It's been an honor getting to know you and laugh with you. I'm always looking forward to the next thing from Jerry Vile because . . . WE NEED IT!

Rick Manore—I thank you last because without your efforts to tie the connections together, this book never would have progressed beyond an idea rattling in my head for over a decade. Your support and counsel means more than you realize.

DONORS

The author and Wayne State University Press would like to thank those who supported the Patronicity crowdfunding campaign for *The Orbit Magazine Anthology: Re-Entry*.

Peter Anderson

Stephen Armstrong

Sonya Avakian

Jason Beaudoin

Scott Bridges

Chris Butzlaff

Brad and Mary Brynes

Dorion Cable

Diana Carroll

Dusan Cechvala

Rich Collins

Sarah Cook

Andy Curtis

Lee DeVito

Tim Dinan

George Eldred and
Laura Thielen

M. L. Elrick

Craig Fahle

Lori Foot

Mary Fortuna

Daniel Gillies

Joshua Glazer

Mark Thomas Gledhill

Stacy Glezman

Lisa Gnas

Matt Gold

Jayson Goodman

Christopher Hatty

Laura Herman

Susan Hillwig

Jessica Hopkins

P. J. and Lisa Jacokes

Greg James

Suzanne Janik

Andrew Jartz

Chip Kolbusz

Andrew Krieger

Nathan Labadie

Amanda Le Claire

Ben Lefabvre

Debbie Leggett

Kelly Lyczak

Joe Mahon

Dave Majkowski

Michael Malloy

Chuck Marshall

Bike Menson

Katie and Dan Merritt

Rick Metcalf

Wendy Metros Meyer

Saulius Mikalonis

Juana Moore

Jon Moshier

Susan Philips

Heather Pillot

Heidi Pio and Patrick Benton

Ivy Amanda Plesco

Joe Posch

Diane Reid

Bob Ritchie

Elaine Roman

Zak Rosen

Bonnie Russell

Cozette Russell

Tom Schoenberg

Brad Shanahan

Kris Shaw

Tracey Sims

Lara Slaughter

Marcia Smith

Kelly Sternberg

Greg Studley

Robert Teachman

Lea Thomas

Jim Tushinski

Michael Van De Mark

Ebrahim Varachia

Liz & Clark Warner

Ted Watts

Mike White

Michael Williams

The Frank R. and Faye M. Zimmerman Community Foundation for Southeastern Michigan

ABOUT THE COVER

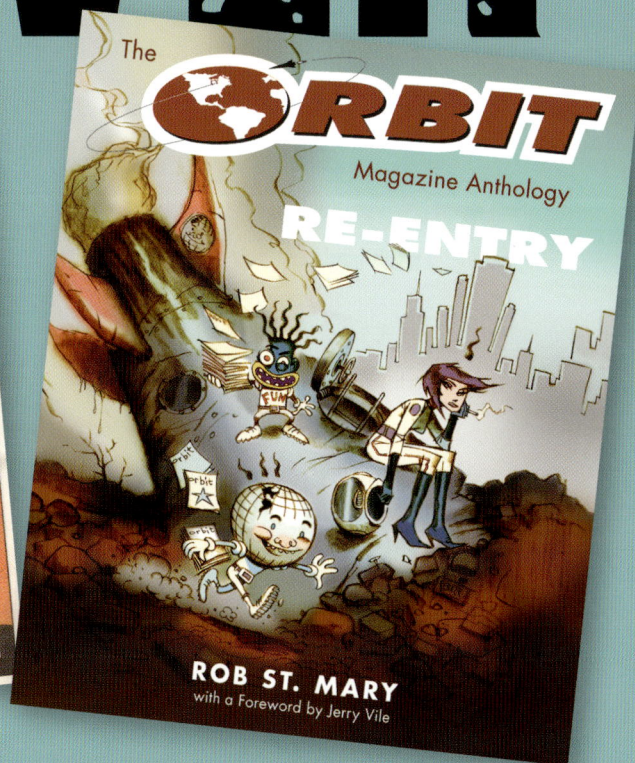

When Glenn Barr created the first *Orbit* cover, under the guidance of publisher Jerry Peterson, he was told that the first cover should look like a 1950s science textbook cover. With *Re-Entry,* his sensibilities shine "in the tradition of how I approached every cover," said Barr.

"Every cover was an experiment in technique and sometimes even abandoning my style to be in step with the subject of that issue. This cover was no different. In those days, I always thought I was teetering on the edge of success or disastrous defeat. I never knew how the art would translate to newsprint. I was very bold in that respect. I have all the confi-

dence in the world on this one. No newsprint here. We want folks to grab it from the shelf if only because it looks 'cool,' rather than have it get lost on the shelf," said Barr.

Barr's narrative showcases the rocket from the original cover, now crashed on the outskirts of Detroit, with Winky of *Fun* and Orby of *Orbit* excited to return to Earth with artifacts in hand to share. So, are they responsible for *Re-Entry?* Regardless, the rocket's helmswoman doesn't look too happy about having to deal with the crazed monkey and his globe-headed friend. Little does she know, the deviant duo is still hip to the coolest things around Detroit.

INDEX